LAW AND ORDER RECONSIDERED

"The Commission's staff has broken new ground. It has produced a literate government publication. Moreover, it is unafraid to be profound. Moreover, it may be one of the most important books of this fearful time, because it tries to go, as it says, 'as far as man's knowledge takes us' in searching for the causes of violence and the means of prevention . . .

"Milton Eisenhower's commission has written the kind of book that becomes a best seller because everybody is in it: the black militant, the lobbyist, the mayor, the senator, the rioter, the criminal, the victim, the policeman, the judge, the vigilantes, the student, the jailor, and the forgotten man."

—John Hart, CBS News, Washington

STATEMENT ON THE STAFF STUDIES

The Commission was directed to "go as far as man's knowledge takes" it in searching for the causes of violence and the means of prevention. These studies are reports to the Commission by independent scholars and lawyers who have served as directors of our staff task forces and study teams; they are not reports by the Commission itself. Publication of any of the reports should not be taken to imply endorsement of their contents by the Commission, or by any member of the Commission's staff, including the Executive Director and other staff officers, not directly responsible for the preparation of the particular report. Both the credit and the responsibility for the reports lie in each case with the directors of the task forces and study teams. The Commission is making the reports available at this time as works of scholarship to be judged on their merits, so that the Commission as well as the public may have the benefit of both the reports and informed criticism and comment on their contents.

Chairman

October, 1969

A NEW YORK TIMES BOOK

law and order reconsidered

Report of the Task Force on
Law and Law Enforcement
To
The National Commission
on the Causes and
Prevention of Violence

James S. Campbell
Joseph R. Sahid
David P. Stang

Special Introduction by David Burnham of
The New York Times

PRAEGER PUBLISHERS
NEW YORK • WASHINGTON • LONDON

PRAEGER PUBLISHERS
111 Fourth Avenue, New York, N.Y. 10003, U.S.A.
5, Cromwell Place, London, S.W.7, England

Published in the United States of America in 1970
by Praeger Publishers, Inc.

Library of Congress Catalog Card Number: 70–130527

Produced in cooperation with Bantam Books, Inc.

Printed in the United States of America

CONTENTS

SPECIAL INTRODUCTION

Every year, in cities all over America, a small number of policemen are presented medals for outstanding achievement, often for shooting it out with an armed and dangerous robber. To the police and most Americans, these medals and the indisputably brave deeds they stand for are the sum of law and order.

The strong belief that the narrowness of this definition is an obstacle to finding better ways of dealing with crime and other kinds of disorder is the inspiration for *Law and Order Reconsidered*, one of a series of important Reports prepared by the staff of the National Commission on the Causes and Prevention of Violence.

The extremely broad scope of the report, which tries to determine the extent to which the flaws in our institutions cause violence and how these flaws might be eliminated, is its great strength. The perception that law and order involve a great deal more than the police—a great deal more even than the police, courts and correctional agencies—is still a foreign vision to many Americans, including the political leaders they elect.

The perception that law and order also involve the preservation of the family, the prevention of unthinking cruelty by government edicts and the restructuring of nonresponsive institutions such as the public schools and the Presidential nominating conventions, is understood by even fewer.

One reason why the lesson has not been better learned may be its great cost. The lesson is costly because putting it into action would require the abandonment of many cherished myths and vast new outlays of tax dollars.

If the Report has a weakness, it is that the broad scope deliberately sought by the authors and editors has necessarily resulted in an overview of law and order, rather than a detailed description of its breakdown in particular cities. While most of the problems described in *Law and Order Reconsidered* infect every major city in the United States, the Report's description of the ugly reality of these diseases can be sharpened by attending to specific cases.

Consider one city. Consider America's largest city. Consider New York—eight million persons who each year call the police about 1,000 murders, 50,000 robberies and 150,000 burglaries. New York, where one out of ten of the shoppers walking into one department store steals something before leaving. New York, where 50,000 men, women and children each day inject into their bodies the false dream of heroin. New York, where reporters saw a large group of off-duty, out-of-uniform patrolmen beat up a small band of Black Panthers in a court house. New York, where slum dwellers during the last few years have ambushed at least four policemen and bombed precinct houses and patrol cars at least a dozen times. New York, where television cameras recorded Columbia University students being clubbed and beaten by detectives gone berserk, while two of the department's top commanders silently watched. New York, where more than 7,000 men are caged two and three to a cell, waiting months and sometimes years for a court to determine whether they are innocent or guilty. New York, where the problems confronting virtually all American cities are magnified to terrifying proportions.

Law and Order Reconsidered is divided into three unequal parts. First, there is a relatively brief section discussing the philosophical foundations of the rule of law, the basic requirements of social order, and the effects of deliberate disobedience to law as a political tactic.

The second section of the Report deals with many of the broad social problems facing America—such as the bitterness that now infects many whites and blacks about the question of race—and the failures and unwieldiness of our institutions of political and social order to deal with them. The effort here is to put "law and order" into a broader, institutional perspective.

The third and final section concentrates on the elements of what one of the Report's most important chapters calls "The Nonsystem of Criminal Justice"—the police, prosecutors, judges, probation officers, correctional officials and parole officers. It also discusses the laws that these agencies are asked to enforce and the constitutional rules they are supposed to obey while enforcing these laws.

The general findings of this section of the report come into sharper focus with a concrete example of how the criminal justice nonsystem of New York deals with the specific problem of robbery. Who is the victim? Who is the robber? Where, and under what conditions, does he attack? How many robberies result in arrest? What happens to the accused after arrest?

The victim can be anyone, a young junior high school student bullied into giving away his allowance, a gas station attendant held up at knife point, the branch bank invaded by a carefully rehearsed gang. But more likely than not, depending to some degree on the neighborhood, the victim will be old and weak. One recent study by *The New York Times* in a racially mixed, lower-middle-class section of New York found that three-quarters of the victims were white and almost two-thirds of the whites were 61 years or older.

The attacker, interviews with the robbery victims suggested, very likely will be young and black or young and Puerto Rican. In the racially mixed precinct mentioned above, for example, four out of five of the robbers were not white and virtually all were under 24 years old.

"This isn't a matter of race, it's a matter of economics," said the precinct commander. The Violence Commission, in its final Report, made much the same point. "Believing they have no stake in the system, the ghetto young men see little to gain by playing according to society's rules and little to lose by not. . . . The step to violence is not great; for in an effort to obtain material goods and services beyond those available by legitimate means, lower-class persons without work skills and education resort to crimes for which force or threat of force has a functional utility, especially robbery, the principal street crime."

Though the victims of robbery were not able to tell whether their attackers had previous arrest records, another study of robbers in Manhattan found that 82 percent of the sample had been arrested on at least one previous occasion and 46 percent had been arrested five or more times.

The attack, various studies show, is most likely to occur inside a building—in a bar, store or the lobby, elevator or hallway of an apartment building.

Partly because so few robberies occur on the street where patrolling policemen normally walk their beats, partly because a precinct with thousand upon thousands of residents may have only a few score policemen on duty at any one time, and partly because some uncaring policemen hide or sleep when they are supposed to be on duty, the police ability to prevent robberies appears to be seriously limited.

In a recent year in New York, for example, only one out of four of every reported robberies resulted in an arrest. And because studies show there may be 50 percent more robberies than are reported, the gap between actual robberies and arrests is much greater than is suggested by official statistics.

But arrest is just the first step in a long and uncertain journey. Of the 136 persons charged with assault and robbery in Manhattan during a single month, *not one* was found guilty of these charges. According to this study of the single crime that most disturbs the American people, the district attorney dismissed the cases against 31 percent of the defendants, he permitted 62 percent to plead guilty to lesser crime and he brought the balance—7 percent—to trial on lesser charges.

The average sentence for the defendants pleading guilty or convicted of lesser charges, according to this study, was slightly under a year. At the time the robbers were arrested, the mandatory sentence for those found guilty of first degree robbery was 10 to 30 years.

The explanation for the vast difference between the sentence required by the legislature and that set by the courts is the inability of the court system to handle the caseload and the subsequent pressure on all defendants to avoid time-consuming trials. A lesser charge and lighter sentence is the main carrot which the prosecutor and judge can offer to get defendants to plead guilty.

With parole, most of the small number of persons arrested for robbery who eventually end up in the city jail or in state prison return to the streets within nine months of being sentenced. And because of a critical lack of funds, very few of those going into these institutions will have received any schooling or training or other preparation to help them become constructive citizens by the time of discharge. In fact, there is evidence suggesting that the stay in most correctional facilities does the reverse: increases the probability that the inmate will commit another hurting crime.

Thus, the few available facts about the impact of the agencies of criminal justice on the crime of robbery in New York suggest a dismal picture: very few robbers are deterred from committing their crime by the presence of police. Very few individual instances of robbery result in arrest. Very few robbery suspects are provided swift justice in the courts. And rehabilitation, if it ever occurs, does so despite prisons rather than because of them. These findings, like those of the Violence Commission in its final Report, confirm the judgment of *Law and Order Reconsidered*, that we do, indeed, have a nonsystem of criminal justice.

Law and Order Reconsidered provides no easy answers for the concerned citizen. But among its two dozen chapters are many specific suggestions which, if honestly and exhaustively pursued, eventually might lead to significant improvement in the quality of service provided by the government and the system of criminal justice. Three proposals in particular warrant the attention of governmental policy-makers.

The first proposal, made in a chapter drafted by Lloyd N. Cutler, executive director of the Commission, is a plea for nothing less than the total restructuring of city government:

> It has become commonplace to speak of the urban crisis. Two-thirds of us now live in metropolitan areas. The major problems of our times are direct consequences of our need to live together in a crowded and highly mobile society. Rising crime, the process of slum formation, the decline in educational quality, the deterioration of the physical environment, the frustration of moving about, the lessening spirit of community —all these modern ills are at their worst in our large cities.
>
> Our response to the crisis had focused primarily on its physical and personal aspects. We add more police, more housing, more teachers and schools, more subways and roads. We sweep one set of rascals or incompetents out of city hall and install another. But we largely ignore an indispensible part of any solution—the restructuring of urban government itself.

Mr. Cutler notes that in the 227 urban areas designated as standard metropolitan statistical areas there are nearly 21,000 independent local government units: Chicago, for example, has 1,113, Philadelphia 876 and New York 551. He further notes that the populations served by these independent and often overlapping units range from less than 1,000 to several million people.

In an attempt to deal with the two problems suggested by the size and shape of these units—a widespread lack of participation by individual citizens and a lack of overall planning and taxing power for metropolitan areas—Mr. Cutler urges President Nixon to call an Urban Constitutional Convention.

This convention, he suggests, would devise a new form of unified urban government, perhaps along the model worked out in Great Britain with the Greater London Council—an overall planning agency based on local neighborhood governments, each having an average of 250,000 citizens. The convention would be advisory only, but would focus national attention on what the President has termed "the most conspicuous area of failure in American life today."

The second critically important direction suggested by the Report is related to the first: the creation of a Criminal Justice Agency in every city that would have broad powers to oversee the police, prosecutors, defense agencies and correctional units, and to develop new, intimate relationships with the traditionally independent courts.

The task of this agency, according to its proponent, Professor Daniel J. Freed of the Yale Law School, would be to develop a system of budgeting that would correct the various imbalances among the agencies trying to cope with crime; to begin to develop a criminal justice information system that would collect statistics of the number of crime reports, persons arrested, charges dropped, convictions and crime prevention steps, so the managers could know what they were doing to evaluate the effectiveness of the various agencies, and finally to develop minimum standards of performance for the police, courts and correctional personnel.

Such an agency could decide, for example, whether it would make more sense for a city to put its money into a new detention center or to hire more policemen, to increase the number of judges or to buy a large computer, to develop a sports program for potential juvenile delinquents or to construct halfway houses to ease the transition from incarceration to freedom.

A few cities, such as New York, Cleveland and San Francisco, have taken the first step in forming such agencies, but nowhere have they been given the power to have any real impact on the elements of the criminal justice process which they are supposed to coordinate.

A third critical area requiring complete rethinking, the Report suggests, is the use of criminal penalties to control what are called victimless crimes such as gambling, abortion, drunkenness and homosexuality between consenting adults. The potential benefits of abolishing many of these kinds of laws are significant because the hidden costs of enforcing them are incalculable.

About 600 of New York's 30,000 policemen, for instance, have been given the assignment of suppressing certain very popular kinds of gambling—playing the numbers and placing bets on sports events. Because so many New Yorkers want to engage in these proscribed activities, hugely profitable organizations have grown up which corrupt many policemen.

The laws on homosexuality are largely ineffective and, in

some cities at least, provide the police with a weapon for shaking down citizens.

The cost of making alcoholism a crime, in terms of the time that the police, courts and correctional agencies devote to taking care of derelict alcoholics is enormous. About one-third of all arrests in the United States are for public drunkenness.

These laws have a tremendous though frequently unnoticed impact on the taxpayer. First, every policeman who spends his time controlling gambling or picking up derelicts is usually not preventing muggings through regular uniformed patrol.

A second effect of the laws, at least those outlawing gambling, is to take the police out of the business of law enforcement and put them in the business of regulating illegal activities. In cities across the United States, the special police units assigned to gambling are over and over again found to be licensing it.

Third, and most important, the police corruption that grows from these laws has a corrosive effect on what the public thinks of the police—and by extension of law and order—and what the policemen think of themselves. For if the public at large sees policemen and judges bending the gambling laws, why should the black teen-ager respect the laws against burglary or the white businessman be concerned about the laws against price fixing?

Finally, many of the nonvictim acts defined as crimes by legislatures probably could be handled more effectively if approached differently. It appears likely that the clinic and voluntary infirmary now taking on most Bowery derelicts in New York is winning back a larger proportion of the men than the old method of arrest and lockup.

A number of the recommendations in this Report reflect similar proposals made previously by the National Commission on Law Enforcement and Administration of Justice and the National Advisory Commission on Civil Disorders. In addition to sharing many specific recommendations, the three Commissions shared one common assumption: if the best possible advice is "disseminated" to government managers around the country, it will be "implemented." It was this assumption that led each of the Commissions to seek the widest possible distribution of their Reports.

But in the face of the analysis by each of the Commissions that many levels of government are not responsive to the public will, was their assumption naïve, even foolish? Is the present crop of administrators—local or national—honestly trying to solve the choking problems that confront the United States, or have the size and complexity of these problems led civil servants to be concerned mostly with protecting themselves from public criticism? A few examples from New York suggest this is still an open question.

• A senior New York police commander recently decided to try to reduce the number of robberies in his jurisdiction by assigning a small number of uniformed patrolmen to a special anti-mugging team that would work in civilian clothes. Because this technique invaded the traditional prerogatives of the detectives, the chief of the New York detectives ordered that departmental charges be brought against the commander who had started the experiment. Although the charges eventually were dropped, the official who offended the detectives was told to end the test with no discussion of whether it was reducing robberies.

• An experimental project in the Bronx developed a new procedure greatly reducing the time it took policemen to process an arrested person and thus greatly increasing police patrol time. Because the technique also increased the number of cases presented the court, a top court official strongly resisted its expansion to other parts of the city.

• All three Presidential Commissions, including the one on which New York's Mayor John V. Lindsay served as vice chairman, strongly recommended a variety of concrete steps to improve the quality of the individual patrolman. Yet when Mayor Lindsay recently agreed to a new contract giving New York policemen a hefty raise, no provisions were added providing bonuses for policemen who went to collge on their own time. Nor was any attempt made to remove the old civil service regulation providing promotion points for men who give blood, but none for those with college degrees.

It can only be hoped that the weight and wisdom of *Law and Order Reconsidered,* when added to the previous Reports by the National Commission on the Causes and Prevention of Violence and the Reports of the Kerner and Crime Commissions, finally will convince us that we are failing and that radical improvements are required.

DAVID BURNHAM

ACKNOWLEDGMENTS

We are principally indebted to the dozens of scholars, practicing lawyers and other willing persons whose generous efforts, added on to already busy schedules, have made this Report possible. The names of those who have participated in the preparation of this Report are listed on pages 653 to 659 in three categories: contributors, consultants, and advisors.

Contributors are those whose papers appear as chapters (or as the principal source of a chapter) in the Report. Contributors are also credited at the beginning of the particular chapters for which they are responsible.

Consultants are those who submitted research papers which served as the building blocks for chapters or as important background pieces. Many of these are also credited at the beginning of the relevant chapters.

Advisors are those who provided assistance to us in evaluating and reviewing various chapters in draft form.

We are also in the debt of a research staff of devoted workers, led by Dale L. Smith, who spent long hours in libraries and on the phone conducting interviews, verifying source materials, and searching for hard-to-find facts. Their names appear on page 659.

We especially appreciate the contributions of Carol A. Honus and our other secretaries who typed, retyped and kept track of a tremendous volume of material of which this book is only the ultimate distillation. Their names also appear on page 659.

We wish to acknowledge the contribution of George L. Saunders, Jr., who led the Task Force during its early months and helped lay a foundation for its later work. Acknowledgment is also due to Leroy D. Clark for his assistance during this period.

Finally, we wish to thank all the Staff Officers of the Commission for their help, and especially to mention the invaluable assistance of Lloyd N. Cutler, the Commission's Executive Director, who took the time to review the several drafts of our Report, to offer many helpful suggestions, and to provide us with encouragement and support at all times.

As the planners and editors of this Report, we alone bear the responsibility for its final form, and all those who contributed to it are fully entitled to refer blame for its errors to our own wrong-headedness or oversight.

October, 1969

James S. Campbell
Joseph R. Sahid
David P. Stang

*   *   *   *   *

The publication of the Praeger edition of *Law and Order Reconsidered* has given us the opportunity—albeit a limited one—to revise, update and add to various sections of our Report.

For the added material in this edition, we are primarily indebted to two new contributors, Lloyd N. Cutler and Daniel Walker, and to Daniel Freed for a further contribution, this time on the subject of the Nixon Administration's preventive detention proposals. Richard Bonnie, Charles Whitebread and Dorsey D. Ellis, Jr. graciously agreed to update their chapters, as did Judith Toth, whose research and writing contributions to our Report in fact extend beyond the three chapters for which she is specifically and principally credited.

Other minor revisions and clarifications have been made in some of the other chapters, but most of the rest of the book has been left unchanged.

Our colleague, David Stang, due to other commitments, was unable to participate in any way in the preparation, editing, or review of the new material contained in this revised edition. Accordingly, we alone bear responsibility for this edition's added contents.

February, 1970

James S. Campbell
Joseph R. Sahid

PREFACE

From the earliest days of organization, the Chairman, Commissioners, and Executive Director of the National Commission on the Causes and Prevention of Violence recognized the importance of research in accomplishing the task of analyzing the many facets of violence in America. As a result of this recognition, the Commission has enjoyed the receptivity, encouragement, and cooperation of a large part of the scientific community in this country. Because of the assistance given in varying degrees by scores of scholars here and abroad, these Task Force reports represent some of the most elaborate work ever done on the major topics they cover.

The Commission was formed on June 10, 1968. By the end of the month, the Executive Director had gathered together a small cadre of capable young lawyers from various Federal agencies and law firms around the country. That group was later augmented by partners borrowed from some of the Nation's major law firms who served without compensation. Such a professional group can be assembled more quickly than university faculty because the latter are not accustomed to quick institutional shifts after making firm commitments of teaching or research at a particular locus. Moreover, the legal profession has long had a major and traditional role in Federal agencies and commissions.

In early July a group of 50 persons from the academic disciplines of sociology, psychology, psychiatry, political science, history, law, and biology were called together on short notice to discuss for two days how best the Commission and its staff might proceed to analyze violence. The enthusiastic response of these scientists came at a moment when our Nation was still suffering from the tragedy of Senator Kennedy's assassination.

It was clear from that meeting that the scholars were prepared to join research analysis and action, interpretation, and policy. They were eager to present to the American people the best available data, to bring reason to bear where myth had prevailed. They cautioned against simplistic solutions, but urged application of what is known in the service of sane policies for the benefit of the entire society.

xxii

Shortly thereafter the position of Director of Research was created. We assumed the role as a joint undertaking with common responsibilities. Our function was to enlist social and other scientists to join the staff, to write papers, act as advisers or consultants, and engage in new research. The decentralized structure of the staff, which at its peak numbered 100, required research coordination to reduce duplication and to fill in gaps among the original seven separate Task Forces. In general, the plan was for each Task Force to have a pair of directors: one a social scientist, one a lawyer. In a number of instances, this formal structure bent before the necessities of available personnel but in almost every case the Task Force work program relied on both social scientists and lawyers for its successful completion. In addition to our work with the seven original Task Forces, we provided consultation for the work of the eighth "Investigative" Task Force, formed originally to investigate the disorders at the Democratic and Republican National Conventions and the civil strife in Cleveland during the summer of 1968 and eventually expanded to study campus disorders at several colleges and universities.

Throughout September and October and in December of 1968 the Commission held about 30 days of public hearings related expressly to each of the Task Force areas. About 100 witnesses testified, including many scholars, Government officials, corporate executives as well as militants and activists of various persuasions. In addition to the hearings, the Commission and the staff met privately with scores of persons, including college presidents, religious and youth leaders, and experts in such areas as the media, victim compensation, and firearms. The staff participated actively in structuring and conducting those hearings and conferences and in the questioning of witnesses.

As Research Directors, we participated in structuring the strategy of design for each Task Force, but we listened more than directed. We have known the delicate details of some of the statistical problems and computer runs. We have argued over philosophy and syntax; we have offered bibliographical and other resource materials, we have written portions of reports and copy edited others. In short, we know the enormous energy and devotion, the long hours and accelerated study that members of each Task Force have invested in their labors. In retrospect we are amazed at the high caliber and quality of the material produced, much of which truly represents, the best in research and scholarship. About 150 separate papers and projects were involved in the work culminating in the Task Force reports. We feel less that we have orchestrated than that we have been members of the orchestra, and that together with the entire staff we have helped compose a repertoire of current knowledge about the enormously complex subject of this Commission.

That scholarly research is predominant in the work here presented is evident in the product. But we should like to emphasize that the roles which we occupied were not limited to scholarly inquiry. The Directors of Research were afforded an opportunity to participate in all Commission meetings. We engaged in discussions at the highest levels of decision-making and had great freedom in the selection of scholars, in the control of research budgets, and in the direction and design of research. If this was not unique, it is at least an uncommon degree of prominence accorded research by a national commission.

There were three major levels to our research pursuit: (1) summarizing the state of our present knowledge and clarifying the lacunae where more or new research should be encouraged; (2) accelerating known ongoing research so as to make it available to the Task Forces; (3) undertaking new research projects within the limits of time and funds available. Coming from a university setting where the pace of research is more conducive to reflection and quiet hours analyzing data, we at first thought that completing much meaningful new research within a matter of months was most unlikely. But the need was matched by the talent and enthusiasm of the staff, and the Task Forces very early had begun enough new projects to launch a small university with a score of doctoral theses. It is well to remember also that in each volume here presented, the research reported is on full public display and thereby makes the staff more than usually accountable for their products.

One of the very rewarding aspects of these research undertakings has been the experience of minds trained in the law mingling and meshing, sometimes fiercely arguing, with other minds trained in behavioral science. The organizational structure and the substantive issues of each Task Force required members from both groups. Intuitive judgment and the logic of argument and organization blended, not always smoothly, with the methodology of science and statistical reasoning. Critical and analytical faculties were sharpened as theories confronted facts. The arrogance neither of ignorance nor of certainty could long endure the doubts and questions of interdisciplinary debate. Any sign of approaching the priestly pontification of scientism was quickly dispelled in the matrix of mutual criticism. Years required for the normal accumulation of experience were compressed into months of sharing ideas with others who had equally valid but differing perspectives. Because of this process, these volumes are much richer than they otherwise might have been.

Partly because of the freedom which the Commission gave to the Directors of Research and the Directors of each Task Force, and partly to retain the full integrity of the research work in publication, these reports of the Task Forces are in the posture of being submitted to and received by the Commission. These are volumes published under the authority of the Commission, but they do not necessarily represent the views of the conclusions of the Commission. The Commission is presently at work producing its own report, based in part on the materials presented to it by the Task Forces. Commission members have, of course, commented on earlier drafts of each Task Force, and have caused alterations by reason of the cogency of their remarks and insights. But the final responsibility for what is contained in these volumes rests fully and properly on the research staffs who labored on them.

In this connection, we should like to acknowledge the special leadership of the Chairman, Dr. Milton S. Eisenhower, in formulating and supporting the principle of research freedom and autonomy under which this work has been conducted.

We note, finally, that these volumes are in many respects incomplete and tentative. The urgency with which papers were prepared and then integrated into Task Force Reports rendered impossible the successive siftings of data and argument to which the typical academic article or volume is subjected. The reports have benefited greatly from the counsel of our colleagues on the Advisory Panel, and from much debate and revision from within the staff. It is our hope, that the total work effort of the Commission staff will be the source and subject of continued research by scholars in the several disciplines, as well as a useful resource for policy-makers. We feel certain that public policy and the disciplines will benefit greatly from such further work.

❊   ❊   ❊   ❊   ❊

To the Commission, and especially to its Chairman, for the opportunity they provided for complete research freedom, and to the staff for its prodigious and prolific work, we who were intermediaries and servants to both, are most grateful.

James F. Short, Jr.   Marvin E. Wolfgang

Directors of Research

"Man's effort to control violence has been one part, a major part, of his learning to live in society. The phenomenon of violence cannot be understood or evaluated except in the context of that larger effort." —*From the Progress Report of the National Commission on the Causes and Prevention of Violence.*

TASK FORCE DIRECTORS

James S. Campbell
Joseph R. Sahid
David P. Stang

COMMISSION STAFF OFFICERS

Lloyd N. Cutler
Executive Director

Thomas D. Barr
Deputy Director

James F. Short, Jr.
Marvin E. Wolfgang
Co-Directors of Research

James S. Campbell
General Counsel

William G. McDonald
Administrative Officer

Joseph Laitin
Director of Information

Ronald Wolk
Special Assistant to the Chairman

NATIONAL COMMISSION ON THE CAUSES AND PREVENTION OF VIOLENCE

Milton S. Eisenhower
Chairman

INTRODUCTION

Violence is the breakdown of social order. Social order is maintained, and violence is prevented, by the effective functioning of society's primary legal, political and social institutions—including, among others, the agencies of law enforcement. As Benjamin Disraeli said, individuals may form communities, but only institutions can make a nation. By his institutions and the rules they make, man collectively solves his problems and civilizes his world. Today, however, the United States is afflicted by a kind of institutional paralysis, and we seem incapable of solving our manifold national problems.

• Despite great national wealth, millions of American children grow up in circumstances which effectively foreclose the opportunity for satisfying, productive lives.

• In a land dedicated to freedom and equality, many of our citizens still struggle for basic rights enjoyed by the majority.

• Our cities rot at the core, spreading a contagion of violence throughout the metropolitan area.

• The agencies of law enforcement falter, and individual safety is jeopardized.

Age-old conflicts flare with renewed intensity between order and justice, between the individual and the state, between private rights and public welfare, between rich and poor, black and white, young and old. Almost eagerly we embrace the "environmental crisis"—hoping it will prove easier to clean our air and water than it has been to establish justice and insure domestic tranquility.

But we must, somehow, learn to change our institutions so that they can more effectively solve the problems which press upon us from every side—not just economic and technological problems, but also, and most importantly, the human problems of men living together in society. More than 150 years ago, Thomas Jefferson observed that "laws and institutions must go hand in hand with the progress of the human mind . . . As new discoveries are made, new truths disclosed, and manners and opinions change with the change in circumstances, institutions must advance also, and keep pace with the times."

To what degree are the weaknesses, inequities and rigidities in our institutions responsible for the violence in today's America? In this Report we examine the institutions of law enforcement—police, courts, corrections—with particular care and concern. But we also treat political and social institutions such as urban government and the Congress, the family and the church, the school and the university: we forget at our peril that law and order depend upon the proper functioning of these institutions no less than upon the effectiveness of the law enforcement agencies.

Our theme, then, is the strengthening of America's institutions. The following excerpts indicate some of the ways in which this theme is developed in the ensuing pages of this Report.

* * * *

PART ONE—THE RULE OF LAW

Chapter 1. The Rule of Law

"Increasingly, our institutions are handled with a profound impatience over their shortcomings and, perhaps, an inadequate appreciation of their virtues. Change is valued over order, freedom over control. Legitimacy, the entitlement to rule, has to be earned, almost daily, and earned in the face of ever-increasing standards of performance.

"From this understanding . . . two important and obvious lessons can be learned for the maintenance of social order in America. First, social order in America requires that our social and political institutions be able to regenerate themselves and respond more effectively to the discontents of the groups within our society who are currently pressing their claims upon the larger public. Second, social order in America requires a modern system of criminal justice which will effectively control increasing levels of deviant behavior in a manner consistent with our ideas of fair and humane treatment."

Chapter 2. Disobedience to Law

"Out of the widening protest, one disturbing theme has repeatedly appeared. Increasingly those who protest speak of civil disobedience or even revolution as necessary instruments of effecting needed social change, charging that the processes of lawful change built into the system are inadequate to the task.

"The American response to this disobedience to law—to events which are contrary to our fundamental beliefs about the mode of social and political change—has been ambivalent. The reason lies in the fact that the American people are going through a crisis of conscience. The issues in whose name violence has been committed have deeply disturbed and divided the American people. The tactics of the demonstrators have encountered angry opposition, but many Americans continue to sympathize with some or all of the goals sought by the demonstrators."

PART TWO—INSTITUTIONS OF THE POLITICAL AND SOCIAL ORDER

Chapter 3. Law and the Grievances of the Poor

"The poor have, if anything, more legal problems than the rest of society. The recent surge of efforts on their behalf only emphasizes the terrible needs yet unmet in our civil justice system. They make only a long-delayed beginning; new ways and more lawyers are desperately needed. Long-range strategems to reform laws and institutions that work unfairly against the poor must be simultaneously pursued along with justice in individual cases. More counsel for the poor is basic, the *sine qua non.* Court costs should be abolished. The poor need legal redress for their legal grievances; to be poor is bad enough; to be poor and denied justice is intolerable."

Chapter 4.   Government and the "Forgotten Man"

"The Forgotten Man is the man in the middle, in the "silent majority," the ordinary guy for whom exceptions are not made. He is neither so poor that the government thinks it must try to rescue him, nor so rich that he can exercise independent power. He is unorganized, so that he is (and more important, *feels* he is) alone in his dealings with government. . . .

"Generalities about government being of, for, and by the people do not comfort the Forgotten Man when he sees the same government that socked him with a severe penalty for late payment of part of his $2,403.16 income tax, now forgive a million-dollar defaulter for 10¢ on the dollar (and issue a press release bragging about it), or when he sees his taxes apparently going to support minorities who rant and riot in protest over his more privileged way of life.

"As the receptive potential audience for racists, super-patriots, and ultra-vigilantes, the Forgotten Man can bolster or detract from the significance of their violence-supporting activities. With his massive numbers, the Forgotten Man is the key to their power."

Chapter 5.   American Society and the Radical Black Militant

"The radical black militant who attacks a policeman or bombs a college building is not simply a common criminal. He is indeed a criminal, but he is different from the burglar, the robber or the rapist. He is acting out of a profound alienation from society. He believes that the existing social and political order in America is not legitimate and that black people in America are being held in 'colonial bondage' by 'an organized imperialist force.' Thus he is able to interpret his act of violence not as a crime but as a revolutionary (or 'pre-revolutionary') act. As an isolated occurrence, this distorted interpretation would not be significant—but the interpretation is sustained by an articulated ideology that is today competing with traditional American values for the minds and hearts of the rising generation of black ghetto residents."

Chapter 6, Part 1. The Need for Urban Government Reform

"The demands for increased citizen participation in the government of large American cities are consistent not only with popular conceptions of democracy, but also with recent social science findings which strongly suggest that accession to these demands would reap large dividends to society as a whole, particularly at the local level. The key findings of current thinking from political and social sciences are that the perception of personal effectiveness in politics, or 'political efficacy,' is related to satisfaction with government and that a strong sense of political efficacy seems to be necessary to motivate persons to express their demands in conventional, nonviolent modes."

Chapter 6, Part 2. A Call for an Urban Constitutional Convention

"[S]urely we are capable of devising a means suitable to our own political system for addressing ourselves as a nation to the vital task of improving our own urban government structure. President Nixon has recently observed that 'the violent and decayed central cities are the most conspicuous area of failure in American life today.' Surely a national failure of this magnitude requires a national response. . . .

[T]o find such a means, we might profitably borrow a leaf from our past. The impotent and drifting Continental Congress was transformed into one of the most successful political structures in history by a constitutional convention made up of leading citizens from every part of the new nation. The crisis in urban government is equally grave, the need for a new step forward equally great."

Chapter 7. The Electoral Process and the Public Will

"The legitimacy of our system of government rests upon the people's belief that its institutions respond to their needs and represent their views. If the people lack confidence in the electoral system or if they feel excluded from decision-making processes and helplessly dependent on the discretion of governmental and quasi-governmental officials, the legitimacy of the system stands almost certainly in serious question, making for political alienation in America."

Chapter 8. Congress and the Public Will

"No feature of Congressional practices has drawn as much criticism as seniority. The seniority system has undoubtedly contributed to the unrepresentativeness of legislative leadership, because longevity in office tends to be associated with homogeneous, one-party districts. In the 90th Congress, for example, southerners comprised only about one-fifth of the membership of the Senate and a quarter of the membership of the House, yet they controlled the chairmanships of ten of the sixteen Senate standing committees and ten of the twenty-one House committees. Such men are frequently at loggerheads with the policies of the national party, a fact which can exacerbate conflict between Congress and the Executive branch."

Chapter 9. The Family and Violence

"The American family has clearly lost some of its solidarity. . . . Once it was the source of cohesion and security, the unit of economic activity, the means of recreation and education. Today it is increasingly disrupted. Divorce rates rise, but are outrun by the incidence of marital conflicts. Parents, especially working mothers, spend more time outside the home, and television changes the character of family recreation. A generation gap widens, as young people identify more with peer groups in colleges, dropout communities, and street cultures than with their own families.

"These changes do not necessarily signify a decline in the importance of the family. They do reflect the increasing pressures which the family is under—but these stresses frequently stem precisely from the fact that more is being demanded of family life than ever before."

Chapter 10. The Public School and the Children of Poverty

"When the school is a place where children find that they can be successful and can experience just treatment, they develop respect for law and for habits in harmony with the regulations of their society. But when the school is a place where children fail or where they experience unjust treatment, they become frustrated, they reject society's values, and they are more likely to resort to violence in an effort to solve their problems. In America we have both kinds of schools, and the children of poverty are to be found primarily in the second kind."

Chapter 11. The Church and the Urban Crisis

"Religious groups such as churches or parishes are probably the only institutions by which culturally different groups, or conflicting or alienated groups, may be brought to some sense of unity. Repeatedly in the past, the religious group has been able to bridge the gap between different social classes, different ethnic groups, different interest groups, by forging a common bond around common religious beliefs and practices. Thus, in the celebration of the liturgy, rich and poor, educated and uneducated, the powerful and the underprivileged, have frequently been able to celebrate the common beliefs in which they were one, despite the many differences which divided them."

Chapter 12. The Reform of the University

"Someone once said that no one should meddle with a university who does not understand it and love it. The comment was probably prompted by a realization that the university is a rather fragile institution, despite the fact that it has endured for a thousand years and has survived formidable threats to its integrity and freedom. The university is fragile because it is no more than people of good will committed to some very lofty principles: freedom, tolerance, mutual understanding, open communication, truth, and honesty. These are surely elusive principles—difficult to attain, easy to lose. They are, however, the only things that distinguish a university from any other cluster of buildings inhabited by humans with all their vested interests and venal shortcomings. By its own actions, the university has compromised some of these principles. Great social forces working on the university have also jeopardized them. Now, in a righteous frenzy to reform the university, its active critics imperil these principles. Freedom, especially, is in danger."

Preface to the Portfolio of Lithographs on Crime and
Violence

"[T]he combination of reason and law from the time of its
ancient origins has been unable to prevent jealous husbands
from taking to fits of passion which result in the murder of
their unfaithful wives. So too it has been unable to prevent
Cains from slaying Abels, parents from maliciously beating
their children. Nor has it been able to deter the emergence of
men like the Marquis de Sade, Jack the Ripper, or the
Boston Strangler. . . . In a sense, then, in our applying reason
and law to the subject of crime and violence, we are handicapped. Worse yet, our efforts are bounded not only by the
limits of the tool we utilize to treat the subject, but by
the pervasive, complex and irrepressible nature of the subject
itself. We are not dealing with a phenomenon which has had
its birth in America of the nineteen-sixties, but with a problem that has existed since mankind was born.

"We are here dealing with one small variation on the
ageless theme of good and evil, of right and wrong, of love
and hate. There is a mystery about this topic which tran-
scends reason—and which inescapably penetrates to the very
core of the human soul."

PART THREE—THE AGENCIES OF LAW ENFORCE-
MENT

Chapter 13.   The Nonsystem of Criminal Justice

"In the mosaic of discontent which pervades the criminal
process, public officials and institutions, bound together with
private persons in the cause of reducing crime, each sees his
own special mission being undercut by the cross-purposes,
frailties or malfunctions of others. As they find their places
along the spectrum between the intense concern with victims
at one end, and total preoccupation with reforming convicted
law-breakers at the other, so do they find their daily perceptions of justice varying or in conflict. The conflicts in turn are
intensified by the fact that each part of the criminal process
in most cities is overloaded and undermanned, and most of
its personnel underpaid and inadequately trained.

"Under such circumstance it is hardly surprising to find in
most cities not a smooth-functioning 'system' of criminal

justice but a fragmented and often hostile amalgamation of criminal justice agencies. To the extent they are concerned about other parts of the 'system,' police view courts as the enemy. Judges often find law enforcement officers themselves violating the law. Both see correctional programs as largely a failure. Many defendants perceive all three as paying only lip service to individual rights."

Chapter 14.   The Police and Their Problems

"A black policeman, asked why he decided to become a police officer, gave us this answer:
   'Man, when I was a little kid I thought cops were God, I lived in the ghetto and I saw drunks, addicts, cuttings, shootings, and husbands hitting wives and kids fighting on street corners and other bad scenes everyday.
   'Somebody always called the police. The police arrived in the middle of the hassle and were always cool and always got on top of the problem fast. If they could break it up by quiet mouthing it they would. If they had to bust somebody they did it quick and were gone. Whatever it was, they arrived on the scene, got with it fast, stopped the trouble and split—always with a cool head. I figured that was smooth and so I decided when I was a kid I wanted to be a policeman and do the same thing.'
"Understanding and coolheadedness—these qualities represent the very essence of a 'good cop.' "

Chapter 15.   Official Responses to Mass Disorder I:
Current Social Control

"The recent wave of urban disorders found law enforcement agencies ill-trained, ill-equipped and ill-prepared to deal with them. The Civil Disorders Commission noted these deficiencies and proposed measures to upgrade the levels of preparedness and response of these agencies. Since the Report of that Commission, significant but uneven steps have been taken to implement those recommendations.
   Army and National Guard units now stand better prepared to deal with domestic upheavals. This improvement has been due largely to effective staff organization, which proved capable of long-range detailed planning. The response of local

law enforcement agencies, however, has lagged. Two problems —adequate numbers of trained manpower and adequate communications—have yet to be solved."

Chapter 16. Official Responses to Mass Disorder II: The Circuit of Violence—A Tale of Two Cities

"The escalation of violence [at the Democratic Convention in Chicago] was . . . a response to unfolding events. Goaded by a few extremists who antagonized police by jeering them, the police responded by indiscriminately gassing and clubbing large numbers of protestors. More and more protestors, angered at this willful violence by policemen, struck back in the only ways they, as upper-middle class, college-educated youths, could—by swearing and throwing rocks. And so the escalation continued. Demonstrators provoked policemen. Policemen provoked demonstrators. The circuit of violence was closed. This cycle was never allowed to complete itself [in the Counter-Inaugural Demonstration] in Washington. Provocation by demonstrators was met with restraint. Provocation by policemen was terminated by police and city officials who intervened quickly to restore discipline. As a result, escalation never took place."

Chapter 17. Securing Police Compliance with Constitutional Limitations: The Exclusionary Rule and Other Devices

". . . [P]rimary responsibility for everyday police discipline must rest within the police department. Nevertheless, since internal review has been uniformly sluggish, some kind of outside pressure must be brought to bear to induce voluntary correction of illegal and otherwise abusive police conduct. . . . The civilian review boards are doomed to futility since they pit the aggrieved citizen against the police department in a formal adversary proceeding; in short, someone always wins and someone is always resentful. The ombudsman, on the other hand, shifts the focus from dispute resolution to evaluation of the department's grievance response mechanism. . . . What is needed is a hybrid of the ombudsman and the external review agency. . . ."

Chapter 18. Citizen Involvement in Law Enforcement

"When discussing the crime problem, people turn to the police, the government, and the courts and ask 'Why don't they do more?' Rarely do they ask 'What can I do?' Individual activity against crime usually reveals itself in sporadic bursts of indignant response to a specific act or a series of acts of crime, to the sensational, or to the crime that got a little too close to home this time. Nonetheless, the citizen can do a great deal to help not only the police and the community, but also himself."

Chapter 19. The Bail Problem: Release or Detention Before Trial

"Pretrial detention should not be permitted to serve as a substitute for an adequately staffed and efficient system of justice. A period should be set aside for genuine experimentation with effective means, short of detention, for protecting the community from the dangerous defendant, particularly greatly reduced pre-trial periods and increased supervision of released defendants. At the same time efforts should be intensified to develop techniques for more accurately identifying those few defendants who are so dangerous to the community that they may not be released before trial, even for a brief period. . . . The government should protect citizens from acts of violence, but the public is not protected when defendants are detained or released almost at random— according to either the amount of bail they can raise or the unsupported intuitions of the judiciary. The rights of defendants and the safety of the public deserve a better system."

Supplement to Chapter 19. The Administration's Preventive Detention Proposal

"On January 31, 1969, eleven days after taking office, President Nixon called for federal legislation to authorize pretrial preventive detention. Under the banner of law and order, he thus became the first President since the founding of the Republic to press for statutory curtailment of the right to bail pending trial in noncapital criminal cases."

Chapter 20. The Constitution and Rights of the Accused

"The charge that the Supreme Court's decisions 'cause

violence' is unwarranted, and insofar as it diverts our concern away from the real causes of violence, it is harmful to society. The charge that the Court's decisions materially hamper the ability of the agencies of the state to solve crimes and to convict those who commit them lacks sufficient empirical data upon which to base that conclusion. We do not as yet know, for example, the degree to which confessions are in fact crucial to convictions. Nor have we yet had sufficient experience with the rules laid down in the Court's decisions in this area to judge whether they will have any significant impact upon the rate of confessions, given the known propensity of many arrestees to confess even without interrogation.

"More importantly, even assuming that police may be less effective in securing convictions because of the Supreme Court rulings, the debate is not ended. As has been pointed out, each provision of the Bill of Rights was drafted expressly to make it more difficult to secure convictions. The more relevant question is whether the price we pay for our freedoms is too great to endure. Before we condemn a significant element of our heritage to obsolescence, we should ask whether there is a baby in the bath worth preserving. For it is clear that we could be of greater assistance to our police by appropriating the necessary funds to finance crime laboratories, adequate prosecutorial staffs, and proper correctional treatment. Few indeed are the criminals 'turned loose' on society by Supreme Court decisions, far fewer than those who are never caught in the first place."

Chapter 21. Court Management and the Administration
of Justice

"When courts are properly managed, the values of efficiency, economy and effectiveness are joined with the values of equality, due process, and justice for all. The joining of such values is what citizens seek from public institutions in a democratic society. For example, genuine thoughtfulness extended to witnesses and jurors may be a small thing, but it is important to obtain their cooperation. Public institutions quite often lack that decent grace which makes a person feel positively about his government. Sophisticated court management with a feeling for all people connected with the courts, for professional values, for constitutional and statutory standards can, in its own way, be a positive factor in preventing loss of respect for law and for courts."

Chapter 22.   The Administration of Justice Under
Emergency Conditions

"Criminal justice machinery in our cities during and in the wake of civil disorders and other emergency situations has failed to successfully deal with the physical and mechanical problems of handling the increased flow of arrestees and defendants. The standards of justice in the initial stages of criminal prosecutions, low in normal times, went still lower in emergencies, especially in the critical matters of bail and provision of counsel."

Chapter 23.   The Problem of "Overcriminalization"

"The criminal law is society's most drastic tool for regulating conduct. When it is used against conduct that a large segment of society considers normal, and which is not seriously harmful to the interests of others, contempt for the law is encouraged. When it is used against conduct that is involuntary and the result of illness, the law becomes inhumane. When it becomes a means for arbitrary or abusive police conduct, it can cause hostility, tension, and violence."

Chapter 24.   Problems of the Corrections System

"Almost the entire emphasis of correctional critics today is on the inadequacy of the resources committed to prison systems insofar as they relate to rehabilitation: the prison buildings are not suited for rehabilitation, the staffs are not large enough nor well enough trained to accomplish rehabilitation, the allocation of funds expended by correctional institutions is not designed primarily to achieve the objective of rehabilitation. All this is true, of course—but there is another point as well. *Inherent in most prisons is an environment in which vicious and brutal degradation of inmates regularly takes place.*"

PART ONE

THE RULE OF LAW

CHAPTER 1

THE RULE OF LAW*

THE EVOLUTION OF SOCIAL ORDER

A society, whether primitive tribe or modern nation, may be looked upon as a complex of human institutions whose purpose it is to secure some measure of social order. These institutions may have other purposes and fill other needs; but the achievement of order is a fundamental part of their function.

Why is social order so universally sought by groups of men? A number of answers might be offered. One important answer is that human welfare demands, at a minimum, sufficient order to insure that such basic needs as food production, shelter and child rearing, be satisfied, not in a state of constant chaos and conflict, but on a peaceful, orderly basis with a reasonable level of day-to-day security. Ancient Mesopotamia, perhaps the first society that we can call civilized, arose from disciplined cooperation among men in the task of irrigating the Tigris-Euphrates river valley.[1] Today, the infinitely complex social order of the United States and the agricultural abundance it has produced make it possible for us to ask impatiently, for the first time in man's history, why it is that *anyone* in this country of 200 million people should go hungry.

How is social order attained? It does not come naturally and without effort. Since man first moved into communities and attempted to cope with the exigencies of life through joint and collective effort, he has been faced with the fact that not all members can be relied on to follow the rules of the community. Even in the simplest, most homogeneous societies, problems of deviant actors within the community have appeared time and time again. Accordingly, social-control techniques have been developed by all societies, simple as

---

*This chapter was written by James S. Campbell based in part on the research contribution of Warwick R. Furr, Esq., Washington, D.C.

3

well as complex, to deal with the problem of disruptions of the community order and degradations of community values.

Social control techniques vary from society to society, depending upon the range of needs and stage of development of each society. In primitive societies, social order may result in large measure from a homogeneity of basic values, reinforced by strong kinship systems, tribal rites, taboos, and commonly accepted religious beliefs. A highly formalized legal structure thus may not be necessary or even possible.

In the nomadic Eskimo culture, for example, the demands of survival in a harsh environment may effectively foreclose the development of detailed, structured political systems with institutionalized legal machinery. The basic unit of government is the family, because the basic unit of economic activity is the family; and magic and religion, rather than formal legal institutions, regulate most behavior.[2] Similarly, other primitive societies, such as the Trobriander Islanders, achieve social order primarily through the dominant role of clan-kinship systems, reinforced by custom and by generally held religious beliefs. Although in such cases there would appear to exist the leisure time necessary to develop more formalized governmental structures with concomitant lawmaking and law-enforcing institutions, apparently such structures do not develop because the homogeneity of values allows the existing system to work fairly well with a minimum of friction and disorder.[3] Where deviant behavior occurs in primitive societies, simple techniques, such as ostracism of the offender from the tribe, may be adequate to maintain order.[4]

Even in societies which have evolved far beyond the primitive stage, the institutions of family and religion may predominate over strictly legal institutions in the process of attaining social order. In pre-Communist China, for example, the family clan retained a central role in social ordering because of its utility in stabilizing the neighborhood and in facilitating the work of local administrators.[5] In the international society of medieval Christendom, it was the Church that primarily determined the form of the social order.[6]

As societies grow more complex, however, methods of obtaining social order, settling disputes and reinforcing key social norms tend to become more complex, highly structured, and impersonal. Highly formalized legal institutions tend to supplant traditional institutions as the primary means of maintaining order.[7] There are many reasons for this change.

For one thing, consensus, the shared belief in basic norms, becomes more difficult to achieve as a society becomes more diverse. The loss of dialogue between citizens holding different jobs and living in different neighborhoods is a product of social evolution which leads to a decline of community consensus. Additionally, the modern phenomenon of extreme geographic mobility coupled with urbanization reduces the effectiveness of community consensus as an element of social order. The opprobrium of community disapproval to unacceptable and disruptive conduct, found in the small town, is no longer a realistic means of social control in the anonymity of the urban center, where people come and go with a minimum of long-term neighborhood contacts.

Many other desirable, or at least necessary, features of modern life operate to weaken (though by no means wholly to eliminate) the social-control function of traditional institutions. Thus, the existence of public schools and compulsory attendance laws, juvenile courts, the draft, and the impact of mass media, all contribute to and reflect a lessening of family discipline as an ordering influence. The notion of a "wall of separation" between Church and State represents for many a cherished political belief, but at the same time, it must be recognized, something of an implicit discounting of organized religion's importance in insuring stability of the social order.

The discussion could be prolonged but the basic point is clear enough: when a society becomes highly complex, mobile, and pluralistic; the beneficiary, yet also the victim, of extremely rapid technological change; and when at the same time, and partly as a result of these factors, the influence of traditional stabilizing institutions such as family, church, and community wanes, then that society of necessity becomes increasingly dependent on highly structured, formalistic systems of law and government to maintain social order.

In large measure, this is a picture of contemporary American society. We have moved, through a process of social evolution, to a stage where our formal legal institutions and procedures necessarily occupy a preeminent position in the preservation of social order. We have traveled too far, we are too diverse, too complex to rely as heavily as we have on traditional institutions to perform the functions of social control. For better or worse, we are by necessity increasingly committed to our formal legal institutions as the paramount agency of social control.

THE NATURE OF THE RULE OF LAW

Most of us are generally familiar with the operation of the major elements of the criminal justice process—police, courts, and corrections—and we are well aware of the roles played by at least the more visible legal institutions of Federal and State government—President and Congress, Governor and legislature. Less often, however, do we reflect upon a more fundamental kind of question: what is it about these institutions that enables them to perform the function of maintaining social order? What makes them able "to insure domestic tranquility" and, conversely, what makes them fail? This is a difficult, complicated question, but the violence and disorder in America today require us to reflect upon it.

One answer is that the institutions of law and government maintain order and control deviant behavior primarily through force, through the forcible apprehension and incarceration of offenders, and the deterrent effect on others produced by the omnipresent threat of such action. It has been said:

> The really fundamental *sine qua non* of law in any society
> —primitive or civilized—is the legitimate use of coercion by
> a socially authorized agent.[8]

It seems clear enough that the institutions of social control function in part in this way. Yet lately it has been fashionable to minimize the unpleasant truth that a society must often—indeed, routinely—resort to force to maintain the orderly process upon which the welfare of all its members depends. The need of a society for a police force and an army says something about human nature that many do not want to hear.

Even among social scientists, there has been much skepticism about the proposition that "negative sanctions" significantly affect conformity or deviance from society's norms, and some sociologists and psychologists have gone so far as to take the position that legal punishment for criminal behavior is at best irrelevant and at worst a barbaric anachronism.[9] This tendency has been attributed in part to the current disrepute of the "classical" school of criminology, which viewed human beings as selecting certain courses of conduct on the basis of a rational calculation of the pleasure or pain likely to result from the conduct—and in part to uncautious generalization from the research findings that *cap-*

6

ital punishment does not act as an effective deterrent to murder.[10] Also, it is well known that imprisonment often fails to prevent further criminal behavior, but this fact does not provide any evidence one way or the other on the question of whether the likelihood of punishment serves as a deterrent to potential offenders who have not yet been punished or caught in a criminal act.[11]

Recent studies indicate that the deterrent effect of swift, certain application of sanctions may be underestimated. An intensive study of parking violators at a midwestern university, before and after more stringent regulations and enforcement policies were imposed, found a significant reduction in violations after the severity and certainty of the penalties were increased.[12] In a recent research project, indexes of the certainty and severity of punishment for homicide in the United States were calculated, and strong evidence was found to suggest that higher probabilities of certain apprehension and long imprisonment are associated with lower homicide rates.[13] Another study related certainty and severity of punishment for crime to crime rates for the different states. A strong and consistent relationship was observed between greater *certainty* of punishment and lower offense rates in almost all cases (but no similar association for *severity,* except in the case of homicide), and the author concluded that "sociologists must take the idea of deterrence seriously."[14]

Deterrence has generally been taken seriously by political scientists and lawyers. James Q. Wilson, for example, has recently noted that in our humanitarian concern for the rehabilitation function of our criminal justice system, we have instituted reforms that may have reduced the system's deterrence of criminal behavior without offsetting gains in rehabilitation.[15] In testimony before the Violence Commission, James Vorenberg, the former Executive Director of the President's Commission on Law Enforcement and the Administration of Justice, stated:

> I do think we know, from the relatively few studies that have been made, that increasing the number of police does reduce crime without increasing the arrest rate . . . simply by serving as a deterrent. I think there are some other points in the [criminal justice] system where increased resources might have a deterrent effect . . . [such as] making the court system more efficient. . . .[16]

But if sociologists have frequently underestimated the utility of deterrence as a means of social control, lawyers and others have often overestimated it. And this brings us to a second major answer that must be given to the question of how legal institutions maintain social order.

Public order in a free society does not and cannot rest solely on applications or threats of force by the authorities. It must also rest on the people's sense of the legitimacy of the rule-making institutions of the political and social order and of the rules these institutions make. Persons obey the rules of society when the groups with which they identify approve those who abide by the rules and disapprove those who violate them. Such expressions of approval and disapproval are forthcoming only if the group believes that the rule-making institutions are in fact entitled to rule—that is, are "legitimate."

The income tax laws, for example, make this point clear. In a way, these laws represent consensual taxation. True, some potential violators are deterred by the strong probability of detection and punishment, but detection and punishment remain possible only because the great majority voluntarily obey the law. Unless the great majority of citizens voluntarily maintained accurate records and filed accurate returns, the tax structure would collapse. No amount of investigation or force could insure the success of our tax laws as presently written. Regardless of the popular folklore, however, most Americans are apparently more honest in reporting their incomes voluntarily than the citizens of many other nations with far less violent crime than we have.[17] They do so because they recognize, albeit grudgingly, the legitimacy of the rule-making institution itself. But if this kind of episode occurs too frequently or persists for too long without change— as in the case of prohibition or the decision to wage war in Vietnam—the institution itself will soon begin to suffer a loss of legitimacy.

This concept of acceptance of rules based upon legitimacy may be termed the "rule of law." The phrase is useful to describe the willingness of a people to accept and order their behavior according to the rules and procedures which are prescribed by political and social institutions—such as legislatures and universities—and enforced, where necessary, either by those bodies or by other institutions—such as governors, police, and courts. The "rule of law" expresses the idea that people recognize the legitimacy of the law as a means of ordering and controlling the behavior of *all* people in a

8

society, the governors and the governed, the rich and the poor, the contented and the discontented.

THE RULE OF LAW IN AMERICA TODAY

Abstractions like the "rule of law," or its popular accompaniment "respect for law," though useful, also have a way of obscuring hard facts. We have already referred to the fact that law operates in part by force, and this is an aspect of social order that sometimes gets overlooked in discussions about the rule of law. We must also not let such phrases keep us from recognizing the increasingly radical nature of the legitimacy of American institutions.

In our society, for well or for ill, legitimacy is becoming more and more fully equated with utility.[18] Despite the common man's reservoir of trust and deference toward his own elected government which has been a feature of our democracy,[19] there has always been in our history a competing attitude—now becoming stronger than ever before—of insistence on results as a precondition to consent by the governed. This attitude has been powerfully reinforced by the philosophy and accomplishments of the modern welfare state, and has been further nurtured among the young by contemporary higher education's skeptical probings of political and governmental power. For many Americans there is now no right to govern independent of what government does for their benefit or for the benefit of the groups in society with which they identify. In this view, institutions are accorded the right to make rules only to the extent that those rules clearly contribute in a positive way to the achievement of accepted goals.

In this matter of the legitimacy of institutions, there is good reason to think that Americans may be too practical, too skeptical, that we take at once too narrow and too demanding a view of the utility of our legislatures and universities, our President and our police. This is particularly true of young Americans, who often unrealistically demand that institutions achieve *now* (or at least before the term ends) full implementation of the society's professed values. If the institution fails to do what is right, quickly and honestly, its legitimacy is gone and action must be taken, almost regardless of what is reasonably possible for the institution to accomplish, and of what are the consequences of the action for the stability and welfare of the institution.

Some who are older or who have read more history are less

9

demanding and more concerned to preserve even imperfect institutions. Writing shortly after the Second World War, Christopher Dawson spoke for this point of view:

> [O]ur generation has been forced to realize how fragile and unsubstantial are the barriers that separate civilization from the forces of destruction. We have learnt that barbarism is not a picturesque myth or a half-forgotten memory of a long-passed stage of history, but an ugly underlying reality which may erupt with shattering force whenever the moral authority of civilization loses its control.[20]

For all its persuasiveness, however, this conservative point of view cannot be expected even to hold its own in America today. Increasingly, our institutions are handled with a profound impatience over their shortcomings and, perhaps, an inadequate appreciation of their virtues. Change is valued over order, freedom over control. Legitimacy, the entitlement to rule, has to be earned, almost daily, and earned in the face of ever-increasing standards of performance.

The tone of today's and tomorrow's America is to be heard, not in the concern for social order as a value in itself, but in remarks of the kind recently made by the Mayor of New York City:

> If you wonder why so many students seem to take the radicals seriously, why they seem to listen to clearly unacceptable proposals and tactics, ask yourself what other source in the past has won for itself the confidence of young people.
>
> Is it the government, telling us that victory in Vietnam was around the corner, or that we fight for a democratic ally that shuts down newspapers and jails the opposition?
>
> Is it the military, explaining at Ben Tre that "it became necessary to destroy the town in order to save it"?
>
> Is it the moralizer, warning of the illegality of marijuana smoking as he remembers fondly the good old days of illegal speakeasies and illegal bathtub gin?
>
> Is it the television commercial, promising an afternoon of erotic bliss in Eden if you only smoke a cigarette which is a known killer?
>
> Is it the university, which calls itself a special institution, divorced from worldly pursuits, while it engages in real estate speculation and helps plan and evaluate projects for the military in Vietnam?
>
> Where is the voice that in fact deserves the allegiance of concerned youth? The voice that can in fact draw lines to stop violent or disruptive protest and enforce those lines with the full support of these young men and women?[21]

Of course, the voice that draws the line between the acceptable and the unacceptable is nothing else but the law—and this is the almost impossibly realistic notion of "law," that we as a nation bring to the challenges of an increasingly pluralistic, rapidly changing society. This is the "law" in the "rule of law" and the "respect for law" which we all devoutly wish to promote.

From this understanding of the rule of law, two important and obvious lessons can be learned for the maintenance of social order in America.

First, social order in America reuires that our social and political institutions be able to regenerate themselves and respond more effectively to the discontents of the groups within our society who are currently pressing their claims upon the larger public.

Second, social order in America requires a modern system of criminal justice which will effectively control increasing levels of deviant behavior in a manner consistent with our ideas of fair and humane treatment.

The rest of this report is an examination of these two basic requirements.

REFERENCES

1. William H. McNeill, *A World History* (New York: Oxford University Press, 1967), at 11.

2. Edward A. Hoebel, *The Law of Primitive Man* (Cambridge: Harvard Press, 1954), at 67-99.

3. Bronislaw Malinowski, *Crime and Custom in Savage Society* (New York: Harcourt, Brace & Co., 1926), at 63-68.

4. Karl N. Llewellyn and Edward R. Hoebel, *The Cheyenne Way* (Norman: University of Oklahoma Press, 1941), at 12-13.

5. Inger Hellströmm, "The Chinese Family in the Communist Revolution," 6 *Acta Sociologica* 256-262 (1962).

6. Christopher H. Dawson, *Religion and the Rise of Western Culture* (London: Sheed & Ward, 1950); Roscoe Pound, *Social Control Through Law* (Hamden, Conn.: Archon Books, 1968), at 18.

7. Selznick, "Legal Institutions and Social Controls," 17 *Van L. Rev.* 79 (1963).

8. Hoebel, *supra* note 2, at 26.

9. See references in Tittle, "Crime Rates and Legal Sanctions," in *Social Problems*, forthcoming.

10. Chambliss, "The Deterrent Influence of Punishment," 12 *Crime & Delinquency* 70 (1966).

11. Tittle, *supra* note 9.

12. Chambliss, *supra* note 10.

13. Jack P. Gibbs, "Crime, Punishment and Deterrence," 48 *Southwestern Social Science Quarterly* 515 (1968).

14. Tittle, *supra* note 9.

15. James Q. Wilson, "Crime and Law Enforcement," in *Agenda For the Nation,* ed. by Kermit Gordon (Washington, D.C.: Brookings Institution, 1968), at 184-85.

16. Testimony of James Vorenberg before the National Commission on the Causes and Prevention of Violence, Sept. 25, 1968, tr. 452.

17. E.g., Italy, France, Switzerland. *New York Times,* April 15, 1969, at 4.

18 Testimony of James Q. Wilson before the National Commission on the Causes and Prevention of Violence, Sept. 18, 1969, tr. 185 *et seq.*

19. Robert E. Lane, *Political Ideology: Why the American Common Man Believes What He Does* (New York: The Free Press of Glencoe, 1962).

20. Dawson, *supra* note 6, at 18.

21. Address by John V. Lindsay before the Yale Law School Association in New Haven, Connecticut, April 26, 1969.

CHAPTER 2

DISOBEDIENCE TO LAW*

Over the past two decades increasing numbers of people seem to have embraced the idea that coercive and even violent acts of disobedience to valid law are justified for the purpose of achieving a desirable political goal. This idea found widespread support in the South as the white majority in that region resisted enforcement of the constitutionally defined rights of Negroes, and some such notion was probably not far from the minds of the Alabama State Troopers when they attacked Dr. King's peaceful demonstration at Selma in 1965. No doubt it was also prominent in the thinking of the Chicago policemen who administered punishment to the demonstrators in Chicago during the Democratic Convention of 1968.

The same idea—that coercive acts of disobedience to law are justified in a good cause which can be furthered in no other way—is also widely held by many students, black citizens and other groups pressing for social change in America today. It is the illegal and sometimes violent activities of these groups that have been most perplexing and disturbing to the great majority of Americans. Their actions have prompted the most intense interest in the ancient philosophical question of man's duty of obedience to the state. Business lunches and suburban cocktail parties have come to sound like freshman seminars in philosophy, as an older generation has argued back and forth over the rightness and the wrongness of "what the kids and the Negroes are doing."

When violent or coercive disobedience to duly enacted, constitutionally valid law is widely engaged in as a tactic to further a political goal or to force concessions, and when "civil disobedience" is a topic hotly debated on every side, it

---

* This chapter was prepared by the Directors of the Task Force, based in part on contributions by Francis A. Allen, Dean of the Law School, University of Michigan, Charles Monson, Associate Academic Vice President, University of Utah, and Eugene V. Rostow, Professor of Law, Yale University.

13

is impossible for a Task Force on Law and Law Enforcement to file a report that does not discuss this age-old subject, however briefly.

THE AMERICAN IDEAL

In a democratic society, dissent is the catalyst of progress. The ultimate viability of the system depends upon its ability to accommodate dissent; to provide an orderly process by which disagreements can be adjudicated, wrongs righted, and the structure of the system modified in the face of changing conditions. No society meets all these needs perfectly. Moreover, political and social organizations are, by their nature, resistant to change. This is as it should be, because stability—order—is a fundamental aim of social organization. Yet stability must not become atrophy, and the problem is to strike the proper balance between amenability to change and social stability.

Every society represents a style of living. The style is represented by the way in which people relate to the social structure, the way in which social decisions are made, the procedures which govern the ways people in the society relate to each other. In a democratic society such as ours, the governing ideals are government by the rule of law, equality before the law, and ultimate control of the law-making process by the people. We depend upon these principles both to accommodate and to limit change, and to insure the style of living we prefer.

As Tocqueville observed, America is peculiarly a society of law. The law has played a greater part among us than is the case in any other social system—in our restless and jealous insistence on the utmost range of freedom for the individual; in our zeal to confine the authority of the state within constitutional dikes; and in our use of law as a major instrument of social change. The practice of judicial review in the United States has had an extraordinary development, with no real parallels elsewhere. It has kept the law a powerful and persistent influence in every aspect of our public life.

We believe with Jefferson that the just powers of government are derived—and can only be derived—from the consent of the governed. We are an independent, stiff-necked people, suspicious of power, and hardly docile before authority. We never hesitate to challenge the justness and the constitutional propriety of the powers our governments and other social institutions assert. In the robust and sinewy

14

debates of our democracy, law is never taken for granted simply because it has been properly enacted.

Our public life is organized under the explicit social compact of the Constitution, ratified directly by the people, not the States, and designed to be enforced by the Courts and by the political process as an instrument to establish and at the same time to limit the powers of government. As Justice Brandeis once observed, "[t]he doctrine of the separation of powers was adopted by the Convention of 1787, not to promote efficiency but to preclude the exercise of arbitrary power. The purpose was, not to avoid friction, but, by means of the inevitable friction incident to the distribution of the governmental powers among three departments, to save the people from autocracy.... And protection of the individual ... from the arbitrary or capricious exercise of power ... was believed to be an essential of free government."

The social contract of our Constitution goes beyond the idea of the separation of powers, and of enforceable limits on the competence of government. The governments established by the national and state constitutions of the United States are not omnipotent. A basic feature of the Constitution, made explicit in the Ninth and Tenth Amendments, is that rights not delegated to governments are reserved to the people. The Amendments may not be directly enforceable in the Courts, but the idea they represent animates many judicial decisions, and influences the course of legislation and other public action.

In a multitude of ways, the Constitution assures the individual a wide zone of privacy and of freedom. It protects him when accused of crime. It asserts his political rights—his right to speak, to vote, and to assemble peaceably with his fellows to petition the Government for a redress of his grievances. Freedom of speech and of the press are guaranteed. Religious liberty is proclaimed, and an official establishment of religion proscribed. And the Constitution seeks assurance that society will remain open and diverse, hospitable to freedom, and organized around many centers of power and influence, by making the rules of federalism and of liberty enforceable in the Courts.

The unwritten constitution of our habits is dominated by the same concern for preserving individual freedom against encroachment by the State or by social groups. The anti-trust laws; the rights of labor; the growing modern use of state power to assure the equality of the Negro; the wide dispersal of power, authority, and opportunity in the hands of autonomous institutions of business, labor, and education—all bespeak a characteristic insistence that our social arrangement protect liberty, and rest on the legitimacy of consent, either through the Constitution itself, made by the people, and capable of change only by their will, or through legislation and other established methods of social action.

In broad outline, such is the pluralist social compact which has evolved out of our shared experience as a people. It has its roots in our history. And it grows and changes, in accordance with its own rules and aspirations, as every generation reassesses its meaning and its ideals.

OUR CONTEMPORARY DISCONTENTS

Today there are many who maintain that these ideals, and the institutions established to maintain them, no longer operate properly. In recent years, increasing numbers of Americans have taken to the streets to express their views on basic issues. Some come to exercise their right to dissent by parades and picketing. Some dramatize their causes by violating laws they feel to be wrong. Some use the issues being protested as drums to beat in a larger parade. For example, the Vietnam war has been used on one side as a dramatic moment in the ubiquitous, always evil Communist conspiracy; on the other as an exemplar of the fundamental diabolism of western capitalist nations. Some take to the streets in the belief that the public, if made aware of their grievances, will institute the necessary processes to correct them. Others come in anger; not hopeful, but insistent; serving notice, not seeking audience. Finally, there are even a few who take to the streets to tear at the fabric of society; to confront, to commit acts of violence, to create conditions under which the present system can be swept away.

Out of the widening protest, one disturbing theme has repeatedly appeared. Increasingly those who protest speak of civil disobedience or even revolution as necessary instruments of effecting needed social change, charging that the processes of lawful change built into the system are inadequate to the task.

The American response to this disobedience to law—to events which are contrary to our fundamental beliefs about the mode of social and political change—has been ambivalent. The reason lies in the fact that the American people are going through a crisis of conscience. The issues in whose name violence has been committed have deeply disturbed and

16

divided the American people. The tactics of the demonstrators have encountered angry opposition, but many Americans continue to sympathize with some or all of the goals sought by the demonstrators. After all, although one might argue that the Negro has advanced in the last ten years, few would maintain he has attained full first-class citizenship. And who would say the ghettos are not an agonizing disgrace? Similarly, Vietnam is hardly an open-and-shut case. The only point of view from which it is clearly praiseworthy is the self-interest of ourselves and our allies. The draft, another key issue, is at best a regrettable and clumsily administered system. Finally, when the young charge that our system—political and social—is shot through with hypocrisy, only the most fanatic feels no twinge.

We must, of course, realize that civil rights demonstrations arise from great suffering, disappointment and yearning. We must recognize the importance to the democratic process, and to the ultimate well-being of our nation, of young people combatting hypocrisy and indifference. But when these emotions become a basis for action and when that action creates social disorder, even the most sympathetic are forced to judge whether and to what extent the ends sought justify the means that are being used.

The difficult problem in this endeavor is to maintain perspective. The issues have reached a stage of polarization. Partisans on each side constantly escalate the rhetorical savagery of their positions, adding nothing but volume and abuse. There is a great temptation to take sides without thoughtful inquiry—if for no other reason than because it is simpler. What are some of the considerations which should guide us in this inquiry?

MORAL JUSTIFICATIONS FOR DISOBEDIENCE TO LAW: THE NEEDS OF THE INDIVIDUAL

The idea that men have the right to violate the law under certain circumstances is not new. The oldest justification for such action seems to have been through appeal to a higher "natural law" which is the only proper basis of human law. This theory, which dates at least as far back as Plato, and which is in our own Declaration of Independence,[1] has recently found expression in the thought of Martin Luther King:

A just law is a man-made law of God. An unjust law is a code that is out of harmony with the moral law. To put it in the terms of Saint Thomas Acquinas, an unjust law is a human law that is not rooted in eternal and natural law.[2]

For St. Thomas political authority was derived from God and hence binding in conscience, but where authority was defective in title or exercise, there was no obligation of conscience.[3] Such a condition arose in the case of a ruler who had either usurped power or who, though legitimate, was abusing his authority by ruling unjustly. Indeed, when the ruler contravened the very purpose of his authority by ordering a sinful action, the subject was under an obligation *not* to obey. In the case of abuse of authority, St. Thomas apparently endorsed nothing more than passive resistance by the citizen; but where the ruler illegitimately possessed himself of power through violence, and there was no other recourse for the citizen, then St. Thomas allowed active resistance and even tyrannicide.

Later Catholic thinkers, such as the Jesuit Francis Suarez denied the divine right of kings, holding that the ruler derives his authority immediately from the people and only ultimately from God. These doctrines led logically to the conclusion that in any circumstances in which a ruler turns into a tyrant, whether originally a legitimate ruler or not, he may be deposed by the people, by force if necessary. This conclusion became, of course, the generally accepted view in the secular world, with the theories of Locke and Jefferson and the American and French Revolutions in the eighteenth century and the rise of liberal democracy in the nineteenth.

The notion of a "social compact" was always closely bound up with the emerging ideas of popular sovereignty.[4] This theory, especially prominent in John Locke, expresses the view that governments evolve by the consent of the governed and that the constitution establishing a government is a contract or agreement which, once it is established, is binding upon all men, both those opposed to it and those who favor it. When government's laws are consistent with terms of the covenant, then the people must obey them. But the people "are absolved from obedience when illegal attempts are made upon their liberties or properties, and may oppose the unlawful violence of those who were their magistrates when they invade their properties contrary to the trust put in them. . . ."[5]

Most of the unlawful opposition today to the Vietnam war

18

is justified on the ground that the war is itself immoral and "unlawful" in various respects. Since it is immoral, the argument goes, there is no moral duty to obey those laws which are in the aid of the conduct of the war. Indeed, the argument continues, one's true moral duty is to resist the war and to take affirmative action to impede its prosecution. On theories of this kind, Americans have refused to be drafted; they have disrupted selective service facilities and destroyed selective service records; they have vilified the President, the Secretary of State and the Secretary of Defense and attempted to disrupt their public speeches; they have attempted to bar companies and governmental agencies participating in the war effort from university campuses and to disrupt the universities that refused to accede to that demand.

At the level of individual morality, the problem of disobedience to law is wholly intractable. One is tempted to suggest that even if the war is immoral, the general level of morality of the country is not much improved by the conduct described above. Moreover, if we allow individual conscience to guide obedience to the law, we must take all consciences. The law cannot distinguish between the consciences of saints and sinners. As Burke Marshall has said:

> If the decision to break the law really turned on individual conscience, it is hard to see in law how Dr. King is better off than Governor Ross Barnett of Mississippi, who also believed deeply in his cause and was willing to go to jail.[6]

Where issues are framed in purely moral terms, they are usually incapable of resolution by substantially unanimous agreement. Moral decisions are reached by "individual prudential application of principle, with the principles so general as to be only of minimal assistance and with almost the whole field thus left to prudence."[7] This fact is illustrated by the story of the exchange that occurred between Emerson and Thoreau, the latter of whom had in 1845 personally seceded from the United States in protest against slavery. As part of his anti-slavery campaign, Thoreau was spending a night in jail. Emerson paid him a visit, greeting him by saying, "What are you doing in there, Henry?" Thoreau looked at him through the bars and replied, "What are you doing out there, Ralph?"[8]

But the issue raised by conscientious disobedience to law also has some more tractable social dimensions. What is the effect upon our society of this kind of conduct? For instance,

19

how does it affect the people who engage in the disobedience? Does it have an effect upon other people? What does it
do to our system of laws?

THE PROBLEM OF CONTAGION: THE NEEDS OF SO-
CIETY

Although there are some who argue that tolerating any
form of law violation serves as an encouragement of other
forms of anti-social or criminal behavior by the violators,
some research in this area suggests precisely the opposite. A
series of studies of approximately 300 young black people
who engaged in a series of acts of civil disobedience were
undertaken in a western city. On the basis of their observations, the authors concluded: "[T]here have been virtually
no manifestations of delinquency or anti-social behavior, no
school drop-outs, and no known illegitimate pregnancies. This
is a remarkable record for any group of teen-age children of
any color in any community in 1964."[9]

In any event the evidence is insufficient to demonstrate
that acts of civil disobedience of the more limited kind
inevitably lead to an increased disrespect for law or propensity toward crime. In fact, some experts have argued that
engaging in disciplined civil disobedience allows people to
channel resentment into constructive paths, thereby reducing
the propensity for engaging in antisocial behavior.

But the fact that disobedience to law does not appear
adversely to affect the attitudes of the people who engage in
it is only one small part of the problem. For such conduct
does have a serious adverse effect both upon other people in
the society, and, most importantly of all, upon the system
of laws upon which society must inevitably depend.

The effect of civil disobedience upon others in the community is clear. Except in the case of those acts designed solely
to appeal to the conscience of the community, the purpose of
much contemporary disobedience to law is to influence community action by harassing or intimidating the members of
the community into making concessions to a particular point
of view. In the case of the opposition to the Vietnam war,
for example, those engaged in acts of disobedience are largely bent upon making miserable the lives of public officials
who support the war, upon bringing economic pressure to
bear on commercial enterprises participating in the war
effort, and upon generally inconveniencing the public to dramatize a disaffection for war and convince others that the

war is not worth the trouble it is causing. To the extent that these efforts succeed, others are obviously adversely affected.* But the most serious effect of all is suggested in the following question:

> [W]hat lesson is being taught to the wider community by the precept and example of civil disobedience? Is it tutelage in nonviolence or in defiance of authority, in rational confrontation of social ills or in undisciplined activism?[10]

There is every reason to believe that the lesson taught by much of the current disobedience to law is disastrous from the standpoint of the maintenance of a democratic society.

The experience of India in this regard is instructive because that country has had such a long and widespread familiarity with the practice of civil disobedience:

> The fact is that the effect of protest behavior on the functioning of the political system has been palpable. We have already seen that Indians compel official attention and constrain decision-making by deliberately engaging in activities that threaten public order. Violence or the threat of violence has become an important instrument in Indian politics. Public protests involving a threat to public order and nonviolent civil disobedience have become habitual responses to alleged failures by government to do what a group of people want. While it is true that political accommodation is real in India, it is achieved at a higher level of political disorder than in any other of the world's democracies.[11]

The experience of India seems to indicate that civil disobedience has a strong tendency to become a pattern of conduct which soon replaces normal legal processes as the usual way in which society functions. Put in American terms, this would mean, once the pattern is established, that the accepted method of getting a new traffic light might be to disrupt traffic by blocking intersections, that complaints against businessmen might result in massive sit-ins, that improper garbage service might result in a campaign of simply dumping garbage into the street, and so on. Of course, these kinds of actions are not unknown in America today, but in India they have become a necessary part of the political

---

* Even in the narrowly defined situation of acts designed solely to appeal to the conscience of the community, adverse effects frequently flow to others. Thus a refusal to accept induction into the armed services means that someone else must serve.

system. Without a massive demonstration to support it, a grievance simply is not taken seriously because everyone knows that if the grievance were serious, there would be a demonstration to support it.

The adverse effect upon normal democratic processes is obvious. Though not intended to destroy democratic processes, civil disobedience tends plainly to impair their operation. This is a fact to which those who engage in civil disobedience should give consideration lest, in seeking to improve society, they may well seriously injure it.

This observation, however, will not answer the arguments of those who believe that the urgency of their message is so strong that illegal tactics are weapons that must be used— whatever the risks that such use may entail. But even urgent messages too frequently repeated lose their appeal. Where once people at least listened patiently, now only deaf ears are turned. Moreover, as Martin Luther King recognized, violence against an oppressor only tends in the long run to justify the oppression. Repeatedly putting one's body "on the line" does not enhance, but diminishes, the worth of that body to the dominant society. Those militants who now advocate revolution as the only alternative have recognized this truth.

The belief that a violent revolution is necessary to achieve social justice depends on the assumption that certain injustices are intrinsic to our system and therefore not amenable to change within the system. For revolution is justified only as a last resort, when justice is achievable by no other means.

We agree with the overwhelming majority of the people in this country that our problems, serious as they are, are not of the kind that make revolution even thinkable, let alone justifiable. We believe that political and social mechanisms do exist and have produced significant change in recent years. The remedy for the discontented, we believe, is to seek change through lawful mechanisms, changes of the kind that other chapters of this report suggest.

But our beliefs and our worlds are really beside the point. What is important is rather the beliefs of those diverse, alienated groups in our society for whom the political and social mechanisms do not seem to work. We can only hope that the majority will respond convincingly to the needs of the discontented, and that the discontented will remain open to the possibility of achieving this response through peaceful means.

CONCLUSION

Official lawlessness—by some southern governors, by some policemen, by corrupt individuals in positions of public trust—is widely recognized as intolerable in a society of law, even if this recognition is too infrequently translated into effective action to do something about the problem. We believe that the time has also come for those participating today in the various protest movements, on and off the college campuses, to subject their disobedience to law to realistic appraisal. The question that needs to be put to young people of generous impulses all over the country is whether tactics relying on deliberate, symbolic, and sometimes violent lawbreaking are in fact contributing to the emergence of a society that will show enhanced regard for human values—for equality, decency, and individual volition.

For some in the protest movement, this is not a relevant inquiry: their motivations are essentially illiberal and destructive. But this is not descriptive of most of those engaged today in social protest, including most who have violated the law in the course of their protest: their intention is to recall America to the ideals upon which she is founded.

We believe, however, that candid examination of what is occurring in the United States today will lead to the conclusion that disobedience to valid law as a tactic of protest by discontented groups is *not* contributing to the emergence of a more liberal and humane society, but is, on the contrary, producing an opposite tendency. The fears and resentments created by symbolic law violation have strengthened the political power of some of the most destructive elements in American society. Only naive and willful blindness can obscure the strength of these dark forces, which, but for the loosening of the bonds of law, might otherwise lie quiescent beneath the surface of our national life. An almost Newtonian process of action and reaction is at work, and fanaticism even for laudable goals breeds fanaticism in opposition. Just as "extremism in defense of liberty" does not promote liberty, so extremism in the cause of justice will extinguish hopes for a just society.

REFERENCES

1. "We hold these truths to be self-evident, that all men are created equal, that they are endowed by their Creator with certain inalienable Rights, that among these are Life, Liberty and the pursuit of Happiness."

2. King, "Letter from the Birmingham Jail" (1963).

3. See generally the illuminating article by MacGuigan, "Civil Disobedience and Natural Law," 11 *Catholic Lawyer* 118 (1965).

4. See Copleston, *History of Philosophy*, vol. 3 (Westminster, Md., 1953), at 348-49.

5. Locke, *Second Treatise on Civil Government*, ch. 19, "Of the Dissolution of Government," sec. 228.

6. Marshall, "The Protest Movement and the Law," 51 *U. Va. L. Rev.* 785, 800 (1965).

7. MacGuigan, *supra* note 3, at 125.

8. *Id.*

9. Pierce and West, "Six Years of Sit-Ins: Psychodynamics, Causes and Effects," 12 *Int'l J. of Social Psychiatry* 30 (Winter 1966).

10. Allen, "Civil Disobedience and the Legal Order," Part 1, 36 *U. Cinn. L. Rev.* 1, 30 (1967).

11. Bayley, *Non-violent Civil Disobedience and the Police: Lesson to be Learned from India,* at 15.

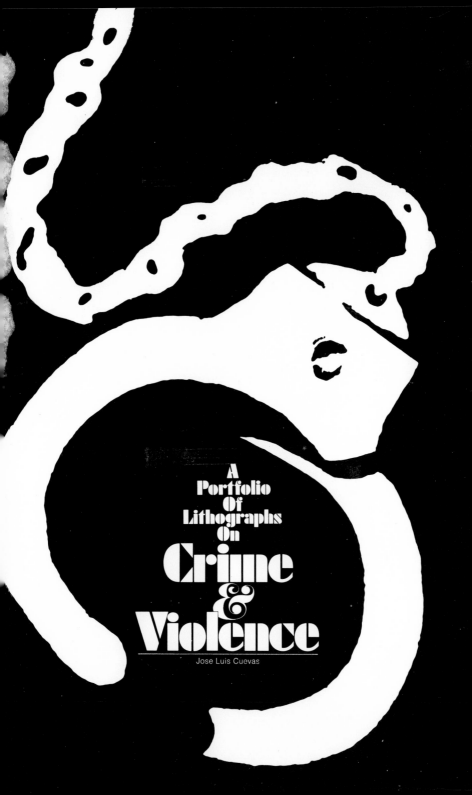

A
Portfolio
Of
Lithographs
On

Crime
&
Violence

Jose Luis Cuevas

Prefatory
Note

Throughout this report on violence and crime, we approach the subject matter armed only with the tool of reason. We attempt to analyze the problems of a violent society by standing at a distance, free from emotional involvement, employing dispassionate rationality.

In one regard, this is a good thing. It is good because, in a sense, it is all we are capable of doing. Yet in another sense, limited by our training, we attempt to evaluate a subject the very nature of which involves irrationality. Reason can only deal with that which is susceptible of being comprehended by reason.

Violence and crime, for the most part, are not phenomena which represent the product of man's rational achievements. On the contrary, violence and crime are more often the expression of what the ancient philosophers called passion.

The jealous husband, although capable of reason, abandons it by momentarily subordinating rationality to a fit of passion. He murders his unfaithful wife, or her lover, or both, and sometimes himself as well.

The law in its majesty makes allowances for this. Instead of convicting the killer of murder in the first degree — which by definition involves a cold blooded pre-meditation, supposedly free from compulsion—the law finds the killer guilty of murder in the second degree or of manslaughter. These latter offenses are meant to apply to persons whose principal motivation was not reason but passion.

Yet ironically the combination of reason and law from the time of its ancient origins has been unable to prevent jealous husbands from taking to fits of passion which result in the murder of their unfaithful wives. So too it has been unable to prevent Cains from slaying Abels, parents from maliciously beating their children. Nor has it been able to deter the emergence of men like the Marquis de Sade, Jack the Ripper, or the Boston Strangler. Neither law nor reason was able to prevent the Israelites from battling the Philistines or the East from waging war with the West. Nor was either reason or law able to prevent the violent clashes between labor and management which occurred in this country earlier in the century, the violence on the campuses and in the ghettos which has happened more recently, or the violence of high suicide rates in the modern, tranquil, law-abiding countries of Scandinavia.

In a sense, then, in our applying reason and law to the subject of crime and violence, we are handicapped. Worse yet, our efforts are bounded not only by the limits of the tool we utilize to treat the subject, but by the pervasive, complex and irrepressible nature of the subject itself. We are not dealing with a phenomenon which has had its birth in America of the nineteen-sixties, but with a problem that has existed since mankind was born.

We are here dealing with one small variation on the ageless theme of good and evil, of right and wrong, of love and hate. There

is a mystery about this topic which tran-
scends reason and which inescapably penetrates to the very core of the human soul.

Carl Jung, the distinguished analyst and
moral philosopher, once noted:

> Even on the highest peak we shall never
> be "beyond good and evil," and the
> more we experience of their inextricable
> entanglement the more uncertain and
> confused will our moral judgment be. In
> this conflict, it will not help us in the least
> to throw the moral criterion on the rub-
> bish heap and to set up new tablets after
> known patterns; for, as in the past, so in
> the future the wrong we have done,
> thought, or intended will wreak its ven-
> geance on our souls, no matter whether
> we turn the world upside down or not.

Our knowledge of good and evil has dwindled with our mounting knowledge and experience, and will dwindle still more in the future, without our being able to escape the demands of ethics.

But in each of us there is a desire to forget that we must constantly choose and be bound by our choices. The more difficult the moral decision the more we try to avoid it. As Dostoyevsky so dramatically noted in his *Brothers Karamazov:*

Man prefers peace, and even death, to freedom of choice in the knowledge of good and evil . . . Nothing is more seductive for man than his freedom of conscience, but nothing is a greater cause of suffering.

Indeed, as haunting as the conflict we often

face in trying to repress almost irrepressible impulses to do evil to our fellow man, or to ourselves, is the companion dilemma of being forced so often to make "free" moral choices without knowing with comfortable certainty that what we choose is right or wrong. Some of these "free" moral choices relate to ends, others to means. When we think we have found a good end, how tempted we are to use any means to achieve it.

It is the rhythm of good and evil which plays in the soul of each of us, beyond the limits of reason and law, that Cuevas so forcefully portrays in his series of lithographs on crime. It is the frightening—almost Sisyphean —constancy of the drama of good and evil, of victim and criminal, that is the theme of his art and the limitation of our Report.

"Title Page": Self-Portrait

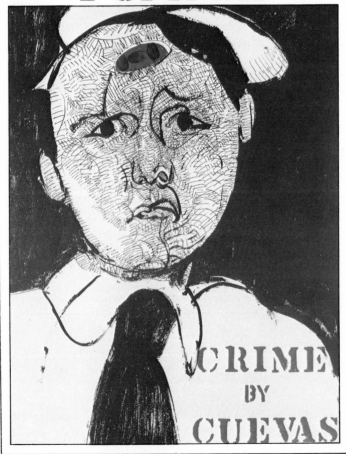

CRIME
BY
CUEVAS

The first lithograph in this Cuevas portfolio is a self-portrait in which the artist represents himself as a juvenile delinquent. Curiously, it is a self-portrait after death as evidenced by the bullet wounds on the forehead. All of the elements of the composition emphasize anguish and desperation: the complex lines curve down the face distorting the expression; the intense, fixed look seems to be a plea for help, demanding that we participate in the boy's drama; the bullet wounds remind us that it is too late. This is a poignant introduction to the series in which the artist has placed himself in the role of both criminal and victim. In the prints that follow Cuevas suggests that in every individual there are latent criminal tendencies as well as recurring fears of being victimized by crime. This perception of Cuevas has an almost oriental air about it, and is suggestive of the Asian poet Coomarasivamy's statement that, "In reality, slayer and dragon, sacrificer and victim, are of one mind behind the scene. . . ." ☐ ☐ ☐ ☐ ☐

"History Of Crime"

The horror film and the literature of the macabre have had a haunting and inescapable impact on Cuevas since his childhood. Here, the artist introduces us to his private gallery of sinister characters, existing in part in reality and in part in his imagination. His figures are not unlike those drawn by Grosz, who presented the decadent cafe society of the 1930's, or Hogarth, who depicted an 18th-century life style of depravity. In the lineup for identification are Raskalnikov, the murderer relentlessly pursued by his conscience; the Marquis de Sade, with his brilliant imagination given to sado-masochistic adventures; the Man and the Beast, the romantic representation of the eternal struggle between reason and control versus madness and violence. Here too is the representation of good and evil, the Good being the fat creature who indifferently holds a poster with the image of the Quasimodo-like figure, the Bad. At the bottom center of the print are two figures whose necks are attached by a single rope; the movement of each would necessarily effect the other. A steel ball representing fate is suspended between them. Should the ball drop the figures' heads would violently collide. ☐ ☐ ☐ ☐ ☐ ☐ ☐ ☐ ☐ ☐ ☐ ☐ ☐ ☐

"Rasputin"

Rasputin was the victim of one of the most sordid crimes in political history. Because of his influence over Empress Alexandra, whom he seduced by means of his personal magnetism, doubtful religious doctrines, and a supposed knowledge of medical remedies that would cure her son, he became one of the principal figures in the court of Czar Nicholas II, advising him on all matters of political importance. Outraged by his unscrupulous tactics as well as by the fact that their positions had been usurped by a peasant, a group of nobles invited Rasputin to a feast on Christmas Day, 1917, for the sole purpose of killing him. He was poisoned, stabbed, and shot and, incredibly, was still breathing when thrown into the Neva River. A year later his body was exhumed, exhibited publicly and burned. By his choosing to do a portrait of Rasputin, Cuevas is suggesting the calamity which necessarily follows when men cast aside the universal moral code of love, dignity and self-respect. That violence breeds violence is borne out by the fate of this infamous man. □ □ □ □ □ □

"Dreams Of Rasputin"

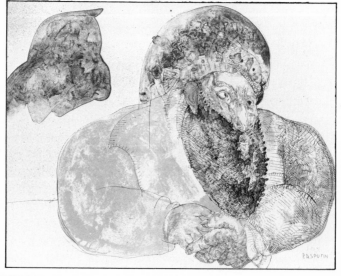

In this lithograph Rasputin seems to foresee his fate: his expression is brutal and hypnotic; his hands are clasped in a frozen position. Rasputin was the product of the oppressed Russian peasantry, and his ambitions developed in direct proportion to the social abuses he suffered. Once in the position of power, he, however, became the oppressor and the object of hatred for the group temporarily subdued. As the friction developed between the rulers and the ruled, the situation became increasingly unstable and resulted in violence. The violence escalated and Rasputin was cruelly put to death. The advice of Steinbeck in his *Grapes of Wrath* came too late to help Rasputin: "Repression works only to strengthen and knit the repressed." □ □ □ □ □ □ □ □

"Borgia"

Cesar and Lucretia Borgia's public appearances were subject to the most rigorous protocol, always highly elegant, but never lacking an element of surprise. One biographer notes that Cesar always received his ambassadors while in a reclining position or on horseback, never seated or standing. Lucretia was never seen by her subordinates without her jewels, and her formal audiences had the aura of theatrical productions common to Hollywood in the 1930's. Unfortunately, their moral standards were not subject to the same discipline. The Borgias' castle was a devil's arsenal — floors and walls had false openings that led to suffocating dungeons; folding screens and brocade curtains hid spears and darts. Unsuspecting victims were killed by lethal poisons contained in rings, flowers, gloves and handkerchiefs. Cuevas has drawn the Borgias with a light, mannerist accent. There is a touch of the medieval in the velvet costumes and jewelry; the Borgias' expressions are cold and penetrating. Ironically, Cesar with each hand makes the sign of the jettatori, which, in the ancient Italian culture, was thought to be capable of warding off evil. □ □

"Jack The Ripper"

Plutarch would not have objected to including in his *Parallel Lives* the biographies of Jack the Ripper and the Boston Strangler. The two had much in common: both carried out their murders systematically; their victims were women; and in the case of each victim there was evidence of sexual abuse. The Boston Strangler was much less discriminating in that his victims were both young and old and belonged to no particular class. Jack the Ripper limited his victims to a specific type—the prostitutes whom he encountered during the night in London's Whitechapel district. Scotland Yard never discovered the identity of Jack the Ripper, but because of his skillful dismemberment of the bodies, it was conjectured that he might be a medical student or perhaps a surgeon. What similarities can be found between the lives of the two men, who lived respectively in the London of the 1880's and the Boston of this era, that might have contributed to the development of such distorted and diseased minds? In both cases it could have been a nightmarish childhood accentuated by parental neglect and the tensions of the hostile center-city environment. □ □ □ □ □ □ □ □

"From My Sketchbook"

Whether in Mexico or elsewhere, Cuevas constantly makes sketches which he later develops into finished drawings. A critic has referred to his work as "a roving reporter's notations of visual images." Following the tragic assassination of Robert Kennedy, Cuevas commented he was fearfully reminded of the haunting similarity of his own sketchbooks and the notebook of Sirhan Sirhan. Two self-portraits of the artist are drawn on the upper part of the page. Here he again depicts himself as both the assassin and the victim. Although the theme of the political assassination is suggested, a new element is introduced. The murderer commits an act of vendetta; he believes his crime to be morally justified. On the lower half of the print, Cuevas has drawn a sadistic physician, who performs ghoulish experiments on his patients. ☐ ☐ ☐ ☐ ☐ ☐

"L'amour Fou"

Cuevas dispassionately depicts the scene moments following a murder. The character at the left appears tortured and at the same time aloof, almost melancholy. At his right, his victim lies in a slumped position, dead from bullet wounds. The title "L'Amour Fou" indicates that the murder was committed out of jealous rage, so typical of many homicides. Human emotions, Cuevas suggests, sometimes seem no longer capable of being restrained when one confronts a crisis situation. Whether it be the case of a child who experiences hunger and loneliness or an adult who feels humiliated or rejected, violence is often the result. The fear of punishment and the knowledge of the inherent wrongness of violent acts too often are incapable of deterring the expression of homicidal impulses. The tone of this print seems to convey a sense of hopelessness in dealing with this irrational aspect of man's nature. □ □ □ □ □ □ □ □ □ □ □ □ □ □

"Van Gogh's Criminal Obsessions"

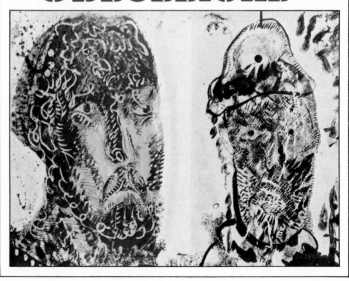

There has long been controversy over the inter-relation between the creative processes of the mind and the destructive or neurotic processes, which often seem to clash in the lives of artists. Freud provided a new insight into this problem with his interpretation of dreams and his study of Leonardo da Vinci, relating sickness with creativity. The life of Van Gogh (shown on the right) was an example of this struggle. It contained a series of manic-depressive cycles, in which he alternately experienced suicidal and homicidal impulses separated by periods of love and compassion for his fellow man. Shown here at the left is Gauguin, for whom he had an obsessive hatred and a recurring desire to kill. . . . Van Gogh's life and his work represent the existential conflict between a sense of futility which breeds self-destruction and hope from which can evolve freedom. ☐ ☐ ☐ ☐ ☐ ☐ ☐ ☐ ☐ ☐ ☐

"Man In Jail"

The modern-day prison is a flagrant anachronism in the midst of a so-called progressive society. The primary objective of the penitentiary system is supposedly the rehabilitation of the criminal with a view to his reintegration into society. But far from accomplishing its objective, the system tends rather to perpetuate and even reinforce the habits and attitudes of criminals which were originally responsible for their incarceration. With the assistance of his brother, who is a psychiatrist, Cuevas was permitted to visit Mexican prisons in 1954. His drawings at that time reflect the "black period" of Goya. In this lithograph it is evident that his memories of that experience are still vivid. The figure of the prisoner is distorted in cubist volumes to provoke a monstrous image. His arms and legs are useless stumps; his expression is one of strange passivity, lacking hope, expecting nothing. ☐ ☐

"Wanted"

Cuevas here portrays members of the family of organized crime who ruthlessly derive their livelihood by exploitation of human weaknesses. The group owes its subsistence to drug traffic, prostitution, gambling and extortion. There is a ghostlike quality to the figures shown in this lithograph and an impression of an era of decades past suggested by the spotted background and the characters' mode of dress. It is almost as if one were looking at a photograph of a lineup of members of a crime syndicate, perhaps taken in Chicago during the 1920's or 1930's. Cuevas' descriptive powers are strongly evident. On the right, there is a young man with open jacket and striped pants posing an attitude of arrogance, toughness and hostility. His is the role of the apprentice. The two "gentlemen" dressed in dark suits are the intermediaries or "strong men" of the organization. The "master mind" of the syndicate sits in a wheelchair; and to his left—indicated faintly with the number eight on his back—is the hired assassin. The artist ends his series of lithographs on crime with the seemingly indestructible element of organized crime which, like the phenomenon of crime itself, survives society's manifold attempts to stamp it out.

This portfolio of lithographs by Cuevas depicting crime was made available to the Task Force through the courtesy of Touchstone Publishers, Ltd., 134 East 70th St., New York, N.Y.

Cuevas' works are in the permanent collections of leading museums in the United States, France, Peru, Venezuela, and Colombia. He has illustrated a number of books, notably "The Works of Kafka and Cuevas" (1959) and his autobiographical "Recollections of Childhood" (1962). A portfolio of 12 lithographs, "Charenton," was published by the Tamarind Shop, Los Angeles, in 1966. His recent set of lithographs, "Crime by Cuevas," has been widely acclaimed here and abroad.

The notes for each lithograph were prepared by Mr. Luis Lastra, a close friend of the artist and editor of the *Art of Americas Bulletin.* Mr. Lastra was assisted by Miss Jane Harmon, of the Visual Arts Division of the Pan American Union, who provided the translation from the Spanish text. The prefatory note was prepared by David P. Stang.

PART TWO

INSTITUTIONS OF THE POLITICAL
AND SOCIAL ORDER

LAW AND THE GRIEVANCES OF THE POOR*

. . . to the poor man, 'legal' has become a synonym for technicalities and obstruction, not for that which is to be respected. The poor man looks upon the law as an enemy, not as a friend. For him the law is always taking something away.—*Robert F. Kennedy.*

If it is true that the poor are especially prone to violence, it is true in part because violence is a response to frustration—frustration from never being listened to, from always being bypassed, from continually being told to "come back later," and from having a series of petty officials talk down to you.[1] The poor get into legal trouble easier than anybody else. They seem to court exploitation. They seldom read the small print, and because they are poor, they want things more.

W. T. Grant Co., a department store chain, conducts a campaign to sell coupon books worth $200 in merchandise, payable in $10 monthly installments for 2 years ($240). The customer thus pays 20 percent interest on the money, regardless of when he uses the coupons or whether or not he ever uses them. The customer bears the risk of theft, loss, or nonuse of the coupons. Any default on a monthly payment allows the retailer to get a judgment for the whole $240 plus a $10 penalty.[2] The poor and the unsophisticated will accept the offer to "buy now and pay later."

In 1957, Walker-Thomas, an appliance store in Washington, D.C., sold a relief mother of seven $1,800 worth of merchandise on installment contracts. In 1962 when she was

---

* This chapter was prepared by Patricia M. Wald and Robert L. Wald of the District of Columbia Bar, in substantial part on the basis of research contributions by Jerome Carlin, Director, Neighborhood Legal Assistance Foundation, San Francisco, Calif.; Linda R. Singer, District of Columbia Bar; and Barbara Curran of the American Bar Foundation, Chicago, Ill.

within $170 of final payment, she was solicited to buy a $515 stereo set. Subsequent failure to make her payments on the new purchase resulted in an action to repossess not only the stereo but all the other items dating back to 1957. In obscure fine print the contracts had said that an unpaid balance on any one item would be distributed among all prior purchases. That meant everything could be taken back.[3] As an added flourish to this kind of exploitation, holders-in-due-course of such contracts purchased from the original seller take the contracts free from any responsibility for fraudulent inducement, mistake, unconscionability, or other legal doctrines that inhibit exploitation of the unwary.[4]

In 1966, eleven ghetto retailers in Washington, D.C., secured 2,690 repossession judgments, one for every $2,200 of their total sales. The judgments against such buyers are generally by default.[5] The Federal Trade Commission found in the same city that ghetto furniture and appliance merchants charged over 60% more for their goods than those who sold to the general public.[6] They used installment contracts three times as often.

Collection practices against poor debtors are often unscrupulous. Customers sign a "confession of judgment" along with the sales contract;[7] as soon as they miss a payment, the seller can sue for the total unpaid balance without notice. He can obtain a lien on the debtor's property for that judgment. He can garnishee his wages. Collection agencies specialize in *in terrorem* techniques against the nonpaying debtor by threatening phone calls, harassment of employers, and verbal abuse.[8] Employers frequently prefer to fire a casual employee rather than submit themselves to such tactics or undergo the administrative inconvenience of wage-withholding.[9]

The poor tenant fares no better with his landlord than with his creditors. His options are limited to a few square miles of slums in the inner city. He pays suburban prices for peeling plaster, unlighted hallways, defective furnaces, rubbish, and rats. Usually, he signs a 30-day lease, terminable without cause by the landlord and without notice for any rent default. He disclaims any warranty of habitability; and he agrees to make all repairs and to accept the premises "as is," even to waive any damages for the landlord's negligence. If he tries complaining to the authorities about housing code violations, he may be evicted in retaliation.[10] Half the time he is in violation himself for overcrowding.[11]

When the inevitable eviction notice comes—if indeed it does not go by default through "sewer service"—the tenant has few defenses.[12] Most courts do not see any relationship between the tenant's duty to pay rent and the landlord's duty to keep the premises in minimally decent condition. They are "independent covenants." Stays of eviction are not normally granted for the ordinary hardship of being thrown out on the streets.[13]

Within the confines of their peeling walls, the poor reap the whirlwind of poverty in their personal lives. A woman deserted by her jobless husband cannot afford a divorce. She drifts into casual relationships; both parties know there is no future marriage in the cards. The children born of such transient unions bear the stigma of illegitimacy. If the mother is on relief, the state may step in and try to take the children away under a "presumption of neglect" stemming from their illegitimacy. The couples who do stick it out suffer the corrosive effects on their life and love of ill health, ill housing, and hunger. There are seldom any marriage counsellors for the poor. As a condition of welfare, wives must sue the father for support of any children whether or not there was ever a marriage. Old people must clutch at any available relative for support, pulling their young down with them. Dignity is not for the poor.[14] Too often the poor make each other the whipping boys of their barren and desperate lives.

From birth to death the curse of poverty follows a man or woman and the law gives little succor. Its trappings are of an infinite variety. In one week the following situations found their way into a single poverty law office in one city:

A child presumed legitimate because "born in wedlock" must officially be pronounced illegitimate so that the mother can bring a paternity suit to reimburse the welfare department.

An abandoned mother with 7 children, three of whom have chronic bronchitis, is evicted by the U.S. Marshal. The landlord calls the police to take the children away to the local orphanage, but the mother threatens him with a kitchen knife. She is taken away for mental observation. Her children join 600 homeless offspring of the poor, hidden conveniently "across the river" in the local orphanage. (The marshals will not evict if there is 40% chance of rain. The poor pray for rain.)

A 10-year-old girl is slapped across the face by a teacher for getting out of line waiting for cafeteria. When her mother goes to the principal to complain, there are two policemen waiting to tell her she has no case.

A 12-year-old boy arrested for petty larceny is put into the detention home because he has no 'suitable home' in which to await trial. There he is homosexually attacked by gangs of older boys, to the point where he must ask for guards to go to the bathroom.

A tenant sued for eviction for nonpayment of rent in a tenement where he has had no heat all winter is told in court it is "irrelevant" that the landlord had 1200 Housing Code violations outstanding on the property. Across the street in the U.S. District Court the landlord is suing in "equity" to recover the rent money the tenant's council has deposited in escrow to pay for repairs. The landlord wants it with no strings attached to use to pay off the mortgage. He is planning to sell to a new owner against whom the old violations must be prosecuted anew.

The domestic relations court denies the petition to proceed as a pauper in a divorce action of a welfare mother with 7 children, deserted 8 years ago. The judge says she can "budget" her money to afford the filing fee, and her poverty lawyer is "stirring up" litigation by representing her free.

The public housing authority denies space to a couple with eight children living in desperate misery in two rooms. The children are all theirs; they have lived together for 10 years; he has supported the mother and children as best he could all that time. They have never married because she cannot afford a divorce from her first husband. The manager of the project says they would be an affront to the morals of the project; they are "living in sin."

A woman complains that she and her children are starving but they can afford food stamps "only in summer." There is a minimum purchase amount and in winter her utility bills cost so much she can't save up the minimum.

An old grandmother would like to adopt her daughter's abandoned epileptic son to prevent his being "put away," but she hasn't the fee for the adoption papers and the Welfare Department doesn't think she is a proper custodian.

The Welfare Department tells a grieving mother whose 8-year-old son has been run over by a truck while playing in the street that she must bury him in a strange funeral parlor across town because that is the only firm the Department has a burial contract with. The only coffin she can have is one made out of cardboard.

THE POOR AND THE BUREAUCRACY

There are special agencies to help the poor. Too often, however, they create a new set of legal problems and spawn new sources of frustration for the poor. The welfare system is the foremost example. Its most basic purpose is to provide the necessities of food, shelter, and clothing for the poor. Nearly one out of every 25 people in the United States is on welfare.

As it now exists, welfare intrudes into every aspect of the recipients' lives; it determines where they live; with whom they live; whether children get new clothes for school; what kind of food they buy and where; where they go when they get sick. It is like life-long probation.[15]

For every person admitted to the welfare ranks, one or more is denied.[16]

An applicant becomes eligible for assistance when he exhausts his money, gives a lien on his property to the Welfare Department, turns in the license plates of his car and takes legal action against his legally responsible relatives. When he is stripped of all material resources, when he "proves" his dependency, then and only then is he eligible.[17]

Denial is usually based on length of residence, existence of a "responsible relative" (regardless of how he feels about you); the age of your children, whether you are "employable" (whether or not you actually have a job); and, until recently, whether you had a boyfriend (regardless of whether he helped with money). Need alone is never enough.

Once on welfare, continuation is precarious. Regulations guide your every waking moment. In Los Angeles, the welfare regulations weigh 115 pounds.[18] Since recent legislation,[19] there must be a fair hearing on request before final withdrawal of federally financed welfare programs. The hearing need not, however, come before the benefits are actually withdrawn. The withdrawal can be based on information the recipient never confronts, or obtained in violation of her rights to privacy and to freedom from unreasonable search and seizure.[20] Welfare recipients have been prey to the inspector's knock on the door any time of day or night.[21] Overpayments, even when the agency is at fault, can be collected at any future date from the recipient. The Welfare Department has a lien on whatever meager resources the recipient may pass on to heirs.

And there are always the fluctuations of legislative mood and public feeling to contend with, over and beyond agency administration. "Welfare cuts," "crackdowns," new and more restrictive conditions come with political change. The "right" to any kind of welfare grant on any condition is always tied to the basic appropriation of money about which there is

31

never any certainty for the poor. Consider the ramifications of a recent New York 5 to 8 percent across-the-board budget cut in welfare allowances to one family.[22]

"My children will probably have to starve," said Mrs. Escobar, "because right now, I can't get along on what we're getting." Mrs. Escobar and her three children, ages 4–8, (an average welfare family) are presently living on $2536 a year in relief payments. That includes $100 every three months in a flat grant to pay for essentials not included in the $2,136 basic grant.

However, because of the Legislature's welfare cut in the budget, $40 of the basic grant will go. And because of a new welfare assistance bill, all of the flat grant will go.

"It is not enough. The food we've been having is not enough. I would like my children to eat. I would like them to have meat every day." Mrs. Escobar said she only eats meat "once in a while. Now I won't eat any."

Their troubles are many: she has asthma and stomach trouble. She will undergo surgery Monday to remove a tumor from her left side. She was deserted by her husband four years ago in Puerto Rico. Her oldest son, Raphael Zapata, has asthma. The flat grant elimination, which includes clothing, troubles her the most.

"My oldest son must have warm clothing in the winter," she said. "I just don't know what to do. I just won't be able to send him to school. As it is now I can't dress any of the children right."

* * *

And now what can Mrs. Escobar do? She doesn't know who her Assemblyman is. She doesn't even really know where Albany is. So she just shrugs and says: "I'll try."

Public housing is society's good will gesture toward the low income renter who cannot afford decent private quarters at today's market rates. There is, however, never enough public housing for all those who need it. Waiting lists are 3 and 4 years long. As a result, public housing administrators are driven to scrupulous scrutinization of applicants to eliminate all but the most worthy.[23] Unwed mothers, if not disqualified altogether, may be limited to one illegitimate child; couples must be married no matter what the circumstances. Thirty day leases, terminable at the landlord's will, were until recently the standard for public housing as well as private slumlords.[24] Ironically, public housing projects often hold themselves out as exempt from the municipal codes governing private landlords.[25] Although rent-controlled, public housing in most cities elevates its poor tenants very little above the slums from which it rescued them.

32

Education is the latchkey out of the prison house of poverty, the means by which the second generation of immigrants can traditionally step up on the economic and social ladder to middle class respectability. In actuality, the slum child today faces not only dilapidated buildings, outmoded equipment, inferior or undertrained teachers, but also an administrative bureaucracy determined to push out all nonconformists and troublemakers. An overwhelmed public school system has only time to teach those who learn easily. The slow learner, the emotionally mixed-up and acting-out adolescent is suspended and expelled when he proves "disruptive." Such suspensions are often accomplished with no prior notice to the parents; the child gets no hearing or opportunity to confront his accusers on questions of fact; there is no right to have counsel present to speak for the child. Yet the consequences to his future in an age of mass specialization are unthinkable. Most big city school systems have "special adjustment classes," "twilight schools" for some of the educationally or socially intolerable, but by every evaluation they are holding actions up to the dropout age. They label and isolate, and so destroy the urge to learn. In every city, hundreds or thousands of school-age children wander the streets, courting trouble with the law, because they have no legally enforceable right to stay in school.

Besides the agencies that offer direct help to the poor, there are those that are supposed to protect the poor from their potential exploiters: consumer fraud bureaus, human relations and antidiscrimination commissions, housing code authorities. Yet their record of achievement in championing the poor is generally an unprepossessing one, for several reasons.

These agencies have adopted too passive a stance; they tend to wait for complaints to come to them. The poor are traditionally apathetic, and their articulation before grievance bureaus is not formidable. Either they don't know the agency exists or where it is located, or they don't want to waste a day's pay going downtown. Or, more basically, they don't expect it will do much good.[26]

Housing code authorities are typical. If they rely on complaints by tenants, enforcement can only be sporadic, piecemeal, and even unfair.[27] Yet their resources are seldom adequate to allow systematic and periodic general inspection. When they do locate violators, they generally "negotiate" for compliance within a "reasonable time." Periods of grace and extension are liberally allowed; a tenant can live without heat

33

or under a leaky roof 18 months before the landlord finally must comply. Even then, most housing codes carry only criminal penalties which judges are reluctant to impose. Landlords are rarely sent to jail; the fines are miniscule.

Insufficient manpower, low salaries, high turnover characterize these "protector agencies" of the poor. They are the first to be cut from the budget and the last to be reinfused. Those that occasionally try "aggressive action" on the part of their clientele bring down the wrath of "harassed" merchants, "struggling" landlords, "red-taped" employers. As a result, they would rather "advise," "recommend," "mediate," and "refer." Few have real teeth to order businesses to cease and desist, to impose substantial and cumulative civil penalties, to initiate injunctive court proceedings.

The administrative process has proved of little help to the poor. Agencies like Welfare, designed solely for their benefit, acquire an antiwelfare bias: they become instead guardians of the public purse.[28] The administrators must—to survive—become highly sensitized to community and legislative attitudes about "chiseling." Caseworkers in turn are victims of a "paper-work explosion" to insure that no recipient gets an unauthorized nickel.[29] They have too little time left to help.[30] The bigger the bureaucracy, the less human the response. Responsibility for putting a poor person on or taking him off of welfare becomes fragmented; he never knows whom to blame, the caseworker, her supervisor, the hearing officer, the head of the agency, the legislature who fails to vote the funds.[31] In such a Kafka-like regime, he is denied even the luxury of hate.

As for the "do-gooder" agencies that claim to protect him from commercial exploitation and racial discrimination, he remains skeptical. Their strength and numbers do not vary with his need, but with the general good will and legislative largesse. Housing code inspectors rarely can compete with welfare inspectors in the blood bath of budget making.

THE COURTS AND THE POOR

The last resort of the poor as well as the rich is in the courts. They are there to do justice, whatever the cost. They must stand between the individual citizen and the carnivorous merchant, the profiteering landlord, the arbitrary administrator. If he cannot find justice there, the poor man is lost.[32]

The courts of the poor are the courts of "inferior" jurisdiction, the "people's courts." The judges in these lower courts

34

tend to be younger, less experienced, from less prestigious law schools.[33] The caseloads of these courts tend to be the greatest.[34] The deliberate pace of the superior courts is not for the poor; their tribunals more nearly resemble the racetrack on opening day.[35] Cases of enormous importance to the participants are handled in an assembly-line fashion, with less than five minutes to a case.[36]

Specialized "social" courts—family courts, drunk courts, juvenile courts—or specialized "legal" courts—landlord-tenant courts, small claims courts—handle the bulk of cases involving the urban poor. In the "social courts" the judges rely, too heavily if at all, on reports of probation officers, intake officers, social workers, and referees to dispose of the parties' complaints. The reports are often not available to the parties, they contain inadmissible and hearsay evidence, and their drafters cannot be cross-examined. In the "legal courts," no account at all is taken of the equities: the tenant owes rent, the debtor owes money; that is that.

In these courts, parties are most often not represented by counsel; the proceedings are not recorded; appeals are infrequent.[37] Dispositions are commonly arrived at in such courts without a full adversary hearing. In the Municipal Court of California, only 5 percent of all dispositions were after trial, compared to 10 percent in the Superior Courts.[38] Without a formal challenge to the other party's facts in open court, the poor person is usually at a disadvantage.

The small claims court stands as a prime example. Created to help the poor creditor collect his claims without fuss or fanfare, it has been perverted into a mass collection agency for stores and businesses against the poor. A study of the Oakland-Piedmont Small Claims Court showed that two out of every three users were either business firms (jewelry and department stores, mail order houses, finance companies) or local government agencies (principally the County of Alameda with claims for hospital services rendered and for unpaid taxes). Most (85 percent) of these organization plaintiffs filed several claims at a time, and were regular users of the court.[39] By dispensing with "legal technicalities" and emphasizing "settlement," small claims courts pit unskilled and inexperienced debtors against the paid agents of companies who handle such claims by the thousands.

The poor do not collect in small claims courts; they are only collected from. In Philadelphia, the dockets of the Magistrates Court do not even have a form in which to record a judgment for the defendant; court clerks there cannot recall such a happening in 20 years.[40] In Washington, defendants most often agree to a "settlement" with the collection agency attorney out of the judge's hearing, involving only a token reduction. When counsel on both sides are present, however, the claim is more likely to be reduced by 50 percent or dismissed altogether. The collection lawyer will frequently postpone the case if he suspects an unfriendly judge, and then will charge the costs to the debtor.

A judge in the Washington, D.C. Small Claims Court remarked about the predominantly Negro poor who are its defendants: "It's a miracle they don't burn down the courthouse. All they see is white people enforcing white laws designed to do them in."[41]

Another obstacle to justice for the poor in our courts is the high cost of litigation.[42] There are filing fees to initiate suit ($10 in the District Court in Washington, D.C.; $32 in the Superior Court in California); process serving fees ($3 in D.C.); jury fees of $8; witness fees of $20 a day in D.C. In some proceedings, special costs add up: $100 for appointed counsel for the defendant in an uncontested divorce case, $50 for a blood test in a paternity case. Security bonds are often required: in replevin, 10 percent of twice the value of the goods; in rent actions, twice the amount owed. Surety bonds cost the poor more because they are poorer risks. Then for pretrial preparation there may be interrogatories, subpoenas *duces tecum,* depositions, and discovery. Poor persons or their lawyers can seldom afford any of these. The transcript itself goes for about $1.00 a page. Investigators cost $10 an hour plus a retainer. Expert witnesses—to testify on quality of products in consumer cases and property evaluation in landlord-tenant cases—can cost up to $300 an appearance. Publication costs in nonresident actions may accumulate to $100 or more.

Many states have *forma pauperis* laws which will exempt some of these fees for poor persons. But typically the exemptions are limited to the fees of court officials, filing and clerk fees. They do not cover the area of charges to independent entrepreneurs who carry on their businesses in the courthouse corridors and courtrooms, and without whose cooperation litigants may not proceed. Thus *forma pauperis* laws will not usually cover the court reporters, medical or other experts, or surety companies. Moreover, the laws are permissive; it is up to the judge's discretion to decide who deserves this privilege. Often judges will decide that the poor do not need certain kinds of legal relief allowed others, such

36

as divorce or personal injury claims. The *forma pauperis* laws thus become a screening device for judges to prejudge who can enter the arena of justice. They also allow a measure of control over the legal traffic of the poor not obtainable over paying litigants.

There is no question that the costs of justice impede the efforts of counsel for the poor. OEO legal service programs have small litigation funds which can be exhausted by one or two major test cases. They must often tell the clients they cannot go to court unless they can raise the fees.

It is time for our courts to do away with this vestige of justice bought and sold in the courthouse.

> [W]hy have we put the administration of justice by one of the three great coordinate branches of Government on a basis of pay-as-you-go? No one would ask Executive Branch, or the Legislative Branch to justify itself as a self-liquidating institution. The people are perfectly content to pay for those services by way of taxes. Why should not the people be equally entitled to the service of the Judicial Branch of Government without being required to pay fees every time they turn around, or to take a pauper's oath in order to get into the courthouse. . . .[43]

Officials now occupying a quasi-official function like court reporters or process servers should be brought under the court umbrella and paid salaries so that their essential services need not be bought. A court-controlled bonding agency has been suggested to adjust security to need and means. A revolving fund for the necessary costs to outsiders like expert witnesses and investigators would aid the poor on the "extras." There should also be some mechanism similar to the Criminal Justice Act provision to allow litigants to pay what they can afford in such cases and be exempted from the rest.

THE RIGHT TO COUNSEL

Our system of justice is an adversary one. To make it work, there must be lawyers on both sides. The poor traditionally have the least access to private lawyers.[44] Those they have used have generally been the least competent and responsible. They lack the money to pay the lawyer and, sometimes, to sit out the course of extended litigation.[45] They don't know many lawyers.[46] A California survey found only 30% of the poor persons interviewed had any contact with lawyers; only 8% of persons with commercial grievances knew enough to seek legal help.[47] When a poor person does go to a lawyer, it is usually too late; his goods have been repossessed, the eviction notice served. Preventive legal services are an unknown commodity.

Legal Aid Societies have been in existence since the turn of the century.[48] But despite dedication, they could not make a dent in the needs of the poor. In 1949 there were 37 legal aid offices and 20 Bar Association offices in America where civil indigents could go for help. Less than 4 million dollars a year was expended in civil legal aid. They tended to shy away from causes that would engage them in controversy or antagonize private contributors.[49]

Not until the 1960's did more aggressive efforts for the poor emerge. *Gideon* v. *Wainwright* (392 U.S. 335) mandated counsel for serious criminal offenses; *In re Gault* (387 U.S. 1) did the same for juvenile offenders: the Legal Services Program became an intrinsic part of the war against poverty.[50]

The OEO program focused on accessible neighborhood law offices, participation of the poor themselves in the governing bodies of the program, aggressive action on behalf of the poor in trying to reform the substantive law and the institutions which affect their lives. By 1968, 250 such programs existed, handling almost 800,000 cases a year, and winning 70% of their court trials (40,000) and 60% of their appellate cases (400); and 1,800 staff lawyers labored for the poor in 85 neighborhood offices in 46 jurisdictions. One bar association president said:[51]

> The one institution with power to raise [the poor person's] sights beyond the invisible wall and the invincible system is the all too new Legal Service field office. For the very first time, he has at his disposal the one tool that he could never afford—a well trained professional whose sole and only interest is to assist him in his sorry plight. More important than the [legal] assistance he is receiving is the fact that this is his. This in itself gives him a new status and, even more, it gives him hope.

They have begun the long range task of changing the law of the poor. Through their efforts, in at least some jurisdictions, not only must there now be hearings prior to welfare cutoffs,[52] but welfare departments cannot set flat ceiling rates on payments to large families. Inspectors cannot invade recipients' privacy at any hour; grants cannot be cut off merely because the mother is living with or seeing another man. Children cannot be taken away solely because they are illegitimate and their mother is on welfare. Tenants cannot be evicted because they report code violations; public housing residents must have some kind of hearing before eviction. Leases executed when code violations exist may be declared illegal and unenforceable against the tenant. Grossly exorbitant interest charges and repossession rights may make a contract "unconscionable." Suits have been brought to declare housing authorities' location of projects in *de facto* segregated areas unlawful; to require counties to take advantage of food stamp programs and to administer them in a way that will benefit the very poor; to insist on apportionment of education funds so that disadvantaged children will get as much or more than the children in advantaged areas; to enjoin urban renewal projects where adequate provision is not made for relocating present area residents; to outlaw garnishment of poor debtors' wages; to require credit companies to keep accurate records and open their files to complaining victims;[53] to compel federal government agencies to insure adequate low income housing for employees before they move to the suburbs.

But the OEO lawyers are the first to admit they are just scratching the surface. Most of them are swamped in volume, constantly torn between the demand for individual service and the need for concentration on basic law reforms. They are mostly young; after a few years and because of economic demands, they move out into more lucrative private practice or government service.

In this program you get used to having everyone mad at you. You seldom get to help your client in any basic way out of the interminable mess he lives in. You stay the eviction for one more week; get him a few more dollars on welfare; maybe keep the disturbed kid in his home a few months longer on probation before he gets in real trouble and is put away in training school. But so what, big deal. We don't get jobs for people; or build them houses; or give them real hope. We just take the edge off of the "big lie." Like demarol while your leg is being slowly amputated.

The city agencies look upon you like a seven year plague: wait and suffer and it will go away. They tell the lawmakers and the budgetmakers plaintively how much money you cost them with your endless litigation over "hopeless cases" and small sums. The judges are worried about backlogs and court delay and cannot stifle their annoyance when you ask for jury trials in eviction cases, interpose eight defenses (none of them yet established at law) to a rent action; file 25 *forma pauperis* divorce petitions in one week. The appeals and test cases you hear so much about. They take so long. The test may be a success but the client has died, or been evicted, or moved away without his money. It takes over a year to get a case up to the Court of Appeals; our program has been going on for almost five years and we're just getting decided the cases the law professors were talking about back in 1964. The most basic kind of law reform will take decades in the courts; yet people think we should have gotten it done already. By the time you win the case, it's "old hat" in the law journals, and they tell you you should be thinking more innovatively. An antitrust suit may drag on in the courts for 5 years with teams of fulltime lawyers and millions poured into; but a landlord-tenant victory that takes that long leaves everyone mad at you.[54]

"The vast needs of the poor for legal services are not being met," an OEO-commissioned report says in 1969.[55]

Estimates of the number of poor persons needing subsidized legal services goes as high as 40 million and rarely as low as 10 million. The American Bar Association says up to 20 million cases need free legal counsel. That would cost $400-$600 million. We now spend in the vicinity of 30 million. Individual legal service lawyers are now handling hundreds of cases a year, well beyond the toleration level for high quality service. If 250 OEO services programs and the legal aid programs which operate in 600 of the nations 3,100 counties have not been able to even plumb the need, where do we turn? If there were to be one lawyer for every 6,000 poor, it would take 5,800 lawyers; if lawyers were to be available to the poor in the same ratio as the general population it would take 137,000. One urban law expert pessimistically summed it up: "If all the attorneys in the United States did only legal aid work, the resources would still be inadequate."[56]

Obviously, then, the OEO effort—and the similar VISTA and Smith Fellows programs—needs not only continued support but vast expansion if it is to make the desired impact. The legal services program will otherwise be another in a long line of broken promises to the poor. The expansion of the right of counsel into every aspect of our "law-ridden nation" means that there must be counsel to implement that right.

But even that is not enough. Radical experimentation must simultaneously pursue other lines to supplement the poverty

40

lawyers. One way is to reduce the need for fullscale lawyers by creating mechanisms in our society for problem solving. Thus effective complaint or grievance centers and consumer fraud bureaus put the burden on government to right its own wrongs and to police sales practices. An American adaptation of the Scandinavian ombudsman has been urged, independent of government yet a public servant;[57] the practice is already being experimented with in Buffalo by OEO. Washington, D.C., had an experimental citizens complaint center and concluded from the experience that a "special expediter" in the Mayor's office and a "public protector" accountable to the City Council were necessary concomitants to any such center.[58] Lay mediators, community courts to settle disputes short of official justice, are another avenue of relief. An OEO-sponsored arbitration project in Cleveland deals with land-lord-tenant differences; a mediation service in Los Angeles; a rabbinical court in Boston to bind fellow communicants. The American Arbitration Association is training indigenous community leaders as conflict resolvers in their own neighborhoods, and it also offers its own services to merchants, landlords, and governmental agencies such as schools and urban renewal agencies in settling disputes with poor citizens.

Self-help is being practiced by the poor themselves in banding together in tenant councils and welfare rights organizations to bargain collectively for their rights in the tradition of the early labor organizations. They negotiate, demonstrate, picket, boycott and even strike. In a few states they have received statutory recognition of their right to do so.[59]

There are, too, a burgeoning number of institutes financed by private foundations for research and litigation on urban problems. They specialize in the test case, the investigative report, and potentially in representing the interests of the poor before municipal bodies and before state and national legislatures and administrative agencies.[60]

Worthy of duplication also is the device of allowing counsel fees to be taxed against the losing party in certain kinds of suits. This is now done in Clayton Act and Civil Rights Act cases and might well be done in tenant suits and consumer fraud actions. Or the government itself might prosecute the claim by assignment as it now does in wage collection cases and reciprocal support actions. This technique might profitably be carried over into local support actions for poor wives. Several of the new welfare and health care laws include the right to a fair hearing and insist that counsel be provided, if necessary at agency expense. HEW has recently

41

announced its financial support of legal service programs by local welfare agencies that will provide across the board legal help to recipients.[61] The lawyers can come from the private sector, OEO, or public agencies (if no conflict results).

Finally, there is a resurgent interest in the development of legal paraprofessionals who can handle the tremendous volume of paperwork in the investigating, interviewing, and "social work" that consume so much of a lawyer's time. Such legal specialists could leave the lawyer free to focus on the development and implementation of the winning strategy for the client. Initial research and limited experimentation has shown, however, that development of these legal technicians is no easy task: the lawyer yields his prerogatives—no matter how cumbersome—reluctantly. But efforts along these lines reap a double harvest: less routine and more productivity for the lawyer, and meaningful jobs for others.

But the legal rights of the poor cannot be left only to OEO, Legal Aid, and public agency lawyers. The private bar must bear its share. In the past it has performed charity services through Bar Referral services, seldom taken advantage of by the poor. New directions are mandatory. One suggestion has been a mass program for assigning counsel to civil indigents in much the same fashion as is done for the criminally indigent. Some civil equivalent of the Criminal Justice Act would be necessary to compensate such counsel.[62] Several factors mitigate against success of any such scheme, however.

Experience with assigned counsel under the Criminal Justice Act has shown that experience is the key to quality representation.[63] And "compensating counsel does not itself guarantee better quality criminal defense."[64] Specialists in the field are preferred, whether the field be criminal or civil. Young lawyers in large firms do not need the money; in fact, many drift away if they think the need is being met by those who do need the pay. Despite good intentions, the occasional appointment must be given lower priority than the firm's retainer clients. Poverty law is, moreover, a specialized business: the *OEO Poverty Law Reporter* competes with the CCH Tax Service in the number of pages and the complexity of content. Representing a client at a welfare or social security hearing is just as demanding as representing a corporate client before the Federal Trade Commission.[65] Consumer and landlord-tenant law is probably developing faster than any other branch of law today; it requires constant updating as well as intense familiarity with procedural forms and rules to do an adequate job. Poverty law is no more a "one-shot deal" than antitrust law.

The poor need specialized, continual legal help. Their civil problems are multifaceted and require follow-up and time. And an assigned counsel system does not by itself provide the answer.

A variation on the assigned counsel system is Judicare, which introduces the element of free choice. The poor man can pick out his own lawyer, and payment will be at specified rates, paid from public funds. The private practitioner in turn can integrate his poor clients into his regular practice. It is particularly attractive to struggling young black lawyers who want to serve their own people. The system has been tried in Wisconsin and New Haven. The Wisconsin plan pays 80 percent of the state minimum fee schedule (about $16 an hour). Judicare costs more than legal services attorneys (an estimated $60—70 per case completed) but a mix of the two is probably the most desired system.[66]

Other proposals for private bar participation are cropping up. Private law firms might donate the services of young associates for periods up to 18 months to neighborhood offices, OEO or jointly run with other firms. Backup clerical, library, messenger and senior consultative help would accompany the donation.[67]

The downtown firm might establish its own branch office in the ghetto. Members and associates would be rotated to the office, and enjoy the same firm privileges and status for their time so spent as their associates serving the more traditional clientele. Such a setup is billed to attract top young talent which wants to serve the poor at the same time they build a personal future. It represents a long-term commitment of firm resources to public service in an organized, effective manner. Two major law firms in New York and Baltimore have already pioneered this effort.[68]

Finally, there are constructive proposals to bridge the gap between the increasing black majorities in the inner cities and the predominantly white legal communities. Only 1% of lawyers are black. Those black lawyers that do practice among the city's poor are usually underfinanced, overworked, and overwhelmed with charity cases. OEO lawyers increasingly recognize the desire of black people to be represented in proportion by their own people. One black lawyer put it this way:

One need not be a "black racist" to see that a succession of

43

young white knights on their legal chargers, over the long run, can have a negative effect. Disrupted self-image is as much a part of the ghetto syndrome as poverty. The black professional performing adequately and competently can provide role models that go a long way toward restoring the confidence that is a precondition for a people seeking nondestructive means of coping with their problems. He also can be the most potent recruiter of students for law schools. By example he can encourage young blacks to see the law as a profession relevant to the needs of their people. Irrational forces are intensifying in the ghetto; the lawyer is an excellent agent for rationalizing those forces and directing them into constructive channels. It is likely that only blacks dealing in good faith with other blacks can accomplish this.

He suggests that downtown white firms subsidize black lawyers to work with the poor in the ghettos. The financial backing would allow the black lawyer to concentrate on high quality service to his people without fear of economic ruin. The firm could send its young associates who want this kind of experience to work with him. He could call on the firm's expertise to incorporate black businesses, and he could be house counsel to poverty rights groups. Affiliations with law schools might provide additional manpower in the way of third year law students.[69]

Providing adequate legal services for the poor is a job just begun. The OEO effort of the past five years has served mainly to show how huge are the dimensions of the job; what the pitfalls of high volume caseloads are; how laborious the process is of reforming a body of substantive law in effect since 1776; how frustrating serving an indigent client can be and how time-consuming and specialized is the practice of urban poverty law. Even with substantial expansion such offices can only do part of the job. New ways have to be found to provide alternatives to legal action for solving the problems of the poor; more daring use must be made of nonprofessionals to perform subsidiary tasks now done by lawyers; and basic reorientation of institutions serving the poor is needed so that they are less often the poor's adversary. Concerted lobbying efforts are essential to block repressive laws, incorporate fair procedures, expedite modernization of statutory law governing merchant-consumer, landlord-tenant, government agency-citizen relations. The private practitioners can by no means relax with the idea that a corps of young, dedicated lawyers are "out there" doing their job. In no foreseeable future will there be enough lawyers to do justice. The firms must build into the fabric of their practice institutionalized and efficient ways to participate in civil justice. They must give of their time, money, and thought.

The cost of all this may seem astronomical. The alternative, however, is to build to the breaking point the accumulation of grievances that now have no effective means of redress in our political or legal system. We already know that this cost is too high for our society to bear.

CONCLUSION

The poor have, if anything, more legal problems than the rest of society. The recent surge of efforts on their behalf only emphasizes the terrible needs yet unmet in our civil justice system. They make only a long-delayed beginning; new ways and more lawyers are desperately needed. Long-range strategems to reform laws and institutions that work unfairly against the poor must be simultaneously pursued along with justice in individual cases. More counsel for the poor is basic, the *sine qua non*. Court costs should be abolished. The poor need legal redress for their legal grievances; to be poor is bad enough; to be poor and denied justice is intolerable.

REFERENCES

1. Among the most intense grievances underlying the riots of the summer of 1967 were those which derived from conflicts between ghetto residents and private parties, principally the white landlord and merchant. *Report of the National Advisory Commission on Civil Disorders* (hereinafter cited as Kerner Report) (Washington, D.C.: Government Printing Office, 1968), at 92.

2. *Law in Action*, June, 1968, at 3-4; See *W. T. Grant Co.* v. *Walsh*, 36 *Law Week* 2626 (N.Y. Dist. Ct. 1966).

3. Wright, "The Courts Have Failed the Poor," *New York Times Magazine*, Mar. 9, 1969, at 102.

4. See generally, Littlefield, "Good Faith Purchase of Consumer Paper: The Failure of the Subjective Test," 39 *So. Calif. Law Review* 46 (1966). Nine states have modified, to some degree, the absolute immunity of the holder-in-due-course.

Massachusetts, Oregon, Vermont, California, Delaware, Hawaii, New York, Pennsylvania and Texas. Most of these states however retain stipulations that the buyer notify the finance company of any defense within ten to fifteen days, after which all other defenses are waived.

See also, S. 2589, 90th Cong., 2d sess. 4.102 (1968); Report

Relating to Consumer Protection in the District of Columbia, at 5-9. The new Uniform Commercial Credit Code, proposed by a special committee financed primarily by the credit industry itself, recommends that the doctrine be abolished.

5. A recent study in the District of Columbia found that in almost 70% of the default cases, the seller had assured the debtor that he need not come to court. *Washington Post*, Sept. 21, 1968, at B1, B2. 90–95% of consumer cases in New York are default judgments. Caplovitz, Rubin, Sparer & Rothwax, *Default Judgments in Consumer Actions: The Survey of Defendants*, Sept. 1965, at 1 (mimeographed release).

6. Federal Trade Commission, *Economic Report on Installment Credit and Retail Sales Practices of District of Columbia Retailers* 10 (1968). FTC Chairman Paul Rand Dixon says that the agency would have found much the same situation "if we had studied Philadelphia, Louisville, or San Francisco." 2 *Law in Action* 1 (April 1968).

7. Thirty states allow confession of judgment with certain limitations. Five states and the District of Columbia have ended the practice. Senate Committee on the District of Columbia Report Relating to Consumer Protection in the District of Columbia, S. Rep. No. 1519, 90th Cong., 2d sess. 14 (1968).

8. *Garney Miller* v. *Retail Adjustment Bureau* U.S.D.C. #900-69.

9. The Consumer Credit Protection Act recently limited garnishment to 25% of a debtor's disposable income. Publ. L. No. 90–321, Tit. II, 202 (May 29, 1968). Although some states require that the judgment debtor be notified before garnishment is served, the requirement is generally ignored in practice. Note, "Consumer Legislation and the Poor," 76 *Yale L. J.* 745, 766 (1967). See Jordon & Warren, "The Uniform Consumer Credit Code," 68 *Colum. L. Rev.* 387, 438 (1968). Brunn, "Wage Garnishment in California: A Study and Recommendations," 53 *Calif. L. Rev.* 1214, 1245 (1965). Labor organizations have apparently been unable to bargain effectively on this issue. *Id.* See also Wald, "Law and Poverty" (prepared as a working paper for the National Conference of Law and Poverty, June 23, 1965). Note, "Project: Legislative Regulation of Retail Installment Financing," 7 *U.C.L.A. L. Rev.* 741-42 (1960).

10. See *Edwards* v. *Habib*, 397 F. 2d 687 (C.A.D.C. 1968): Wright, *supra* note 3, at 108.

11. *Id.* at 110. In 1964, Detroit redevelopment projects resulted in the uprooting of 5,530 families.

12. LeBlanc, "Landlord-Tenant Problems" in *The Extension of Legal Services to the Poor*" 52-53 (U.S. Dept. of HEW, 1964). Sewer service is just as pervasive in the debtor field. An estimated ⅔ to ¾ of consumer defendants in New York City are victims of sewer service. See Note, 2 *Colum. J.L. & Soc. Prob.* 1, 10 (1966); Caplovitz, Rubin, *supra* note 5, at 5; see generally Note, "Abuse of Process: Sewer Service," 3 *Colum. J.L. & Soc. Prob.*

46

17 (1967). A study of the Magistrate's Court in Philadelphia showed that:

". . . constables are required by law to file a return of service stating the precise manner in which service was made. This return is the only evidence available to the magistrate to enable him to decide whether he had jurisdiction over the person of the defendant. Nevertheless, in one court no returns of service are made. In other courts, where thousands of returns of service were examined by Justice Investigators, it was found that hundreds of returns were defective on their face, and in all those cases the magistrate had proceeded to give judgments by default.

"In some cases judgments were entered even though the constable's return stated affirmatively that he had been unable to make service at all."

Report of the Attorney General on the Investigation of the Magisterial System 30 (Department of Justice, Commonwealth of Pennsylvania, 1965).

13. A few jurisdictions have enacted laws allowing tenants to collectively deposit rent into court until the landlord makes the necessary repairs, or allowing the city to make the repairs and charge the landlord. Neither have been a great success, primarily because there has been insufficient funds to accomplish substantial renovations of badly deteriorated buildings. See, e.g., Multiple Residence Law 305-a (outside New York City); Multiple Dwelling Law 320-a (New York City). Michigan has gone the furthest to enact the "first substantial change in 1,000 years" in common law landlord-tenant relationships. In 1968 it passed a new law to:

Require that every lease contain a pledge by the landlord that the premises are habitable and that they will be kept in that condition.

The tenant thus has a cause of action if the landlord fails to comply with the covenant.

Prohibit evictions in retaliation for the exercise of lawful rights, such as reporting violations of housing codes to the city government. Make code enforcement a civil rather than a criminal matter, and enable tenants to take court action to obtain enforcement. Legal remedies available to the tenant include injunctions, repairs by the city with a lien put on the property for the cost, appointment of receivers to make repairs, and withholding of rent in an escrow fund for repairs.

See 3 *Law in Action* 5 (August 1968).

14. Until the Supreme Court decision in *King* v. *Smith*, 392 U.S. 309 (1968) many jurisdictions would deny relief altogether to any mother who had a "man in the house" regardless of whether he helped support the children. Most recently, the Court has invalidated the practice of most states to deny welfare to anyone not a resident of the state for at least one year, regardless of need. *Shapiro* v. *Thompson*, 89 S. Ct. 1322 (1969).

47

15. Wright, *supra* note 3, at 111-12. Contrast this with the attitude taken toward the numerous other subsidy holders in the American economy.

Now a new philosophy of social welfare is struggling for acceptance in this country. This modern school of thought considers dependency a condition ordinarily beyond the control of the individual and seeks to establish the status of welfare benefits as rights, based on the notion that everyone is entitled to a share of the common wealth. This conception of welfare seems justified in view of all the others in our society who receive government subsidies and largess, not as a matter of privilege or charity but as a matter of entitlement. For example, the transportation industry is dependent on public assistance; airlines are subsidized on short hauls; shipping is directly subsidized and indirectly aided by laws favoring American-flag vessels; trucking is aided by public roads. Second-class mail rates are essentially a subsidy to the magazine industry. Home-owners are given many types of financial guarantees and assistance, while farmers have been beneficiaries of public-assistance programs for many years. Other subsidies are less obvious. Docks and airports are supplied to the shipping and airline industries at public expense; channels of the radio and television spectrum are given without charge to the broadcast industry. Intellectual activity, especially scientific research, is also subsidized. Perhaps the biggest subsidies of all are some of our tax exemptions.

Despite the pervasiveness of public assistance throughout our economy, only the welfare recipient is singled out for special, degrading supervision and control. When a farmer receives Government subsidies, the payments are not presented as relief but as an attempt to restore an imaginary balance in the economy, thrown out of kilter by large anonymous forces depressing agricultural prices.

16. Professor Edward V. Sparer would base a right to public assistance on a "right to life" implicit in the Constitution. He views the refusal or withdrawal of welfare from a poor family as a "taking of life." Address to National Institute for Education in Law and Poverty, Washington, D.C., May 9-11, 1968, 3 *Law in Action* 7 (May 1968).

17. Report by Greenleigh Associates to the Moreland Commission on Welfare 78 (New York).

18. Selby, "Watts: Where Welfare Bred Violence," *Reader's Digest*, May 1966, at 69.

19. 42 U.S.C. Sections 302(a) (4), 1202(a) (4), 1352(a) (4), and 1382(a) (4).

Note, "Withdrawals of Public Welfare: The Right to a Prior Hearing," 76 *Yale L. Rev.* 1234 (1967). See generally, Reich, "Individual Rights and Social Welfare: The Emerging Legal Issues," 74 *Yale L.J.* 1245 (1965); Reich, "The New Property," 73 *Yale L.J.* 733 (1964).

20. The following examples are illustrative. The New York Department of Public Welfare discontinued benefits to one woman on the basis of an erroneous letter from the New York City Board of Education saying that the recipient was a fulltime employee. The Ohio Welfare Department terminated aid for the aged to one woman "at the request of the recipient," although notified that no such request had been made. In each case it took a court action to have aid reinstated. 3 *Law in Action* 8 (May 1968).

There are now lawsuits pending to require that withdrawal hearings conform to the following due process criteria.

Specific notice of the basis for the proposed action;
Confrontation and cross-examination of persons giving adverse information; and
A reasoned decision, based on the record, determining the issues raised at the hearing.

3 *Law in Action* 8, 9 (May 1968).

21. See, e.g., *Parrish* v. *Alemeda Civil Service* 57 Cal. Rep. 623, 425 P. 2d 223 (1967).

22. *New York Post*, Apr. 4, 1969, at 22.

23. Standards of undesirability may be extremely vague. In New York City they cover families deemed: (1) a detriment to the health, safety, or morals of its neighbors or the community; (2) an adverse influence on sound family and community life; (3) a source of danger to the peaceful occupancy of the other tenants; (4) a source of danger or cause of damage to the premises or property of the Authority; or (5) a nuisance. New York City Housing Authority, Resolution Relating to Termination of Tenancy, Res. No. 60-8-684, Art. II, Sec. 202(g) (1960), at 206. See Comment, "Title VI of the Civil Rights Act of 1964—Implementation and Impact," 36 *Geo. Wash. L. Rev.* 824, 997 (1968).

24. The Department of Housing and Urban Development recently ruled that no tenant be given notice to vacate "without being told by the Local Authority, in a private conference or other appropriate manner, the reasons for the eviction, and given an opportunity to make such reply or explanation as he may wish." Local authorities are to maintain written records of evictions from federally assisted projects, including the specific reason for each eviction. *Thorpe* v. *Housing Authority*, 89 S. Ct. 518, (1969).

25. See, e.g., *Knox Hill Tenants Council* v. *Washington* (U.S. D.C., D.C. #22781, 196) on appeal to the United States Court of Appeals for the District of Columbia, #22781.

26. A study of the New Jersey Civil Rights Division concluded that despite extensive statutory powers to initiate enforcement proceedings,

it narrowly construed its powers to act at all, devised a series of procedural steps which operated against vigorous enforcement, and compromised and settled cases at a rather high rate, with a relatively low level of relief.

Blumrosen, "Antidiscrimination Law in Action in New Jersey: A Law-Sociology Study," 19 *Rutgers L. Rev.* 187, 196 (1965); See also *Report of the Governor's Committee to Review New York Laws and Procedures in the Area of Human Rights*, March 1968, at 8.

27. Comment, "Enforcement of Municipal Housing Codes," 78 *Harv. L. Rev.* 801, 807 (1965).

28. "The simple fact is that the vast majority of us, in the comfortable prosperity of our affluent society, do not approve of the poor . . . [We] have set up every kind of barrier to exclude or discourage the desperately poor from even [a minimal] level of aid: arbitrary definitions of eligibility related to age, family relationship (such as the absurd requirement in many states that there be no man in the home), employability, duration of residence in the state, and every sort of procedural hurdle and humiliation," E. Wickenden, *Administration of Welfare Rights*, 2-3, 4, paper presented at the National Conference on Law and Poverty, Washington, D.C., June 1965.

29. *The Moreland Commission Report, supra* note 17, at 76, included the following:

"From my own experience and research," said one witness at our public hearing, "50–60 percent of a caseworker's time is spent on bookkeeping. I thought I would be able to help people, but I was a bookkeeper." He related an instance in which an elderly couple—each getting Old Age Assistance, and each treated as a separate case—moved to a new neighborhood and the rent went up. To revise the rent allowance upward, the witness said, he had to fill out and file 30 different pieces of paper. This paperwork explosion plagues welfare workers everywhere . . . The files bulge with records—in triplicate, quadruplicate and quintuplicate—all designed to set forth facts and to substantiate action and justify reimbursement. Accountability is necessary. But at what point does filling out froms pass the point of diminishing returns, and become record keeping for the sake of record keeping? At what point does desk work become so demanding that social workers have little time to serve the needy and the dependent?"

30. Unrealistically high caseloads intensify the problem. In 1964 there was one fully professionally-trained caseworker for every 23,000 relief recipients. May, *The Wasted Americans: Cost of Our Welfare Dilemma* 104 (1964). The turnover rate averaged 26% with 40% in many cities. *Id.* at 109.

31. See, e.g., Carrier L. Guest, C 29589 (D.C. Dept. of Public Welfare) in which the hearing examiner made the following finding, accepted by the Department Head: ". . . the Hearing Officer is of the opinion that the evidence has established that the public assistance budget standards for the District of Columbia are not adequate to meet the cost of living for Claimant's family and the families of others similarly situated."

32. "It seems to me that if one were disposed to blame courts for the present impasse in which we find ourselves, he could with

a good deal more reason direct his attack not to the Supreme Court of the United States but to the courts of original criminal jurisdiction in urban centers throughout the country. These are the courts which meet members of the disadvantaged and alienated communities, and I think it must be said that unfortunately these courts have done great damage to the reputation of the law with these groups." Testimony of Dean Francis Allen before the Commission.

33. J. Carlin, *Lawyers' Ethics* (1966), at 85-86.

There is indirect persuasive evidence of the relation between the lower the court in the judicial hierarchy: (1) the lower the jurisdictional amount of claims (which means the more likely it will be used by lower-class persons), (2) the less likely that parties will be represented by private counsel (reflecting in part the fewer economic resources of parties whose cases go through inferior tribunals), (3) the more likely that lawyers who deal with the court will have a low-status clientele (see Carlin, *supra*), and (4) the more likely that the court will be processing cases reflecting problems which occur more in the lower than the upper classes. Thus, it is among the poor that we find the highest rates of divorce, separation or desertion (See W. Goode, *Family Disorganization in Contemporary Social Problems*, R. Merton & R. Nisbet eds. (1961) at 416-28. Mental illness (See B. Berelson & G. Steiner, Human Behavior: *An Inventory of Scientific Findings* (1964), at 33. Juvenile delinquency (See A. Cohen & J. Short, Jr., *Juvenile Delinquency*, in R. Merton & R. Nisbet, 1961), and drunkenness. (See D. Pittman & C. W. Gordon, *Revolving Door,* 1958, Ch 2.) At any rate, these problems are most likely to come to the attention of public officials when they involve the poor. The term "low level" or "inferior" tribunal refers to local or state trial courts of limited or special jurisdiction (including the family, drunk, psychopathic, small claims and juvenile courts) as opposed to state trial courts of general jurisdiction and appellate courts. Court level is usually correlated with the salary and tenure of judges and their educational background and experience. (See Carlin, *supra*, Ch 5.). It is interesting to note that in California, which has a consolidated court system, assignments to those departments in the Superior Court that correspond to low-level courts in other states (such as juvenile or domestic relations) are generally designated as the least desirable by judges.

34. The largest increase in the number of filings between 1928 and 1954 was found in the small claims, domestic relations, juvenile traffic and psychopathic courts. The smallest increase took place with respect to other civil cases; in fact, there was a 36% decline in the number of these cases filed in the Superior Court. See J. Holbrook, *A Survey of Metropolitan Trial Courts, Los Angeles Area* (1956), at 10, 14.

35. ". . . [A] study of a magistrate's court in a large eastern city said that, in 13 minutes on the morning after a local newspaper ran an editorial under the title 'Get Bums Off Streets and

Into Prison Cells,' 60 persons were tried and convicted of vagrancy by a single magistrate. In several cases, a defendant was convicted after the magistrate simply called his name, looked at him and pronounced sentence—usually three months in the city jail." Wright, *supra* note 3, at 26.

36. Thus, in a study on mental health hearings conducted in Wisconsin it was noted:

> In one urban court (the court with the largest number of cases) the only contact between the judge and the patient was in a preliminary hearing. This hearing was held with such lightning rapidity (1.6 minutes average) and followed such a standard and unvarying format that it was obvious that the judge made no attempt to use the hearing results in arriving at a decision. He asked three questions uniformly:
>
> "How are you feeling?" "How are you being treated?" and "If the doctors recommend that you stay here a while, would you cooperate?"

No matter how the patient responded, the judge immediately signified that the hearing was over, cutting off some of the patients in the middle of the sentence. Scheff, "Social Conditions for Rationality," 7 *Am. Behav. Scien.* 22 (March 1964).

37. Handler, "The Juvenile Court and the Adversary System: Problems of Function and Form," 1965 *Wisc. L. Rev.* 32 (1965).

38. Judicial Council of California, *1962 Annual Report* 151 (1963).

39. C. Pragter, R. McCloskey, and M. Reinis, *The California Small Claims Court* 40, 45, 55, student paper, University of California, 1963, subsequently published in condensed form in 52 *Calif. L. Rev.* 876 (1964).

40. *Report of the Attorney General of Pa., supra* note 12, at 31. Court personnel there even had a direct pecuniary interest in the outcome of the proceedings.

> Many constables own and operate their own registered collection agencies. Other constables simply advertise themselves as being in the collection business, while a third group of constables function as collection agents without forming a separate agency or openly advertising as such . . . When money is obtained from a debtor, the constable collects not only a fee for serving process in the case, but also retains from 25 percent to 50 percent of the amount collected . . .
>
> As a result, constables are engaging in practices designed to terrify the average citizen and to make it clear to debtors that by reason of the constable's close association with the magistrate who will hear the case, any attempt to resist collection is futile. *Id.* at 27.

41. See Murphy, "D.C. Small Claims Court—The Forgotten Court," 34 *D.C. Bar J.* (Feb. 1967, pp. 14-15.) (Quote from interview with J. Murphy, Sept 18, 1968.)

42. See Willging, "Financial Barriers and the Access of In-

digents to the Courts," 57 *Georgetown L.J.* 253 (1968). 274 *et seq.* (1968).

43. Judge Miller, U.S. Court of Appeals, speech at 1941 A.B.A. Convention, cited in 3 *Law in Action* 10 (May 1968).

44. Koos, *The Family and the Law* 9 (1949); Brownell, *Legal Aid in the United States* (1951) (only 3 out of 5 poor families with legal problems recognized their need for legal help and only 2 out of 5 legal service).

45. See e.g., Carlin and Howard, "Legal Representation and Class Justice," 12 *UCLA L. Rev.* 381 (1965); H. O'Gorman, *Lawyers and Matrimonial Cases* 61 (1963).

46. According to a Texas survey, 35 percent of respondents of low socio-economic status did not know a lawyer in their community, compared to 18 percent of those of upper- and upper-middle socio-economic status. J. Belden, *The Court and the Community: A Study of Contracts, Communications and Opinions Regarding a Specialized Legal Institution* (1956). (Unpublished manuscript at the University of Chicago Law School.)

47. "Paraprofessionals in Legal Services Programs: A Feasibility Study," University Research Corporation for the Office of Economic Opportunity (1968), at 6.

48. In 1921, the American Bar Association established a Standing Committee on Legal Aid Work and in 1922 recommended that "every state and local bar association . . . be encouraged to appoint a [similar] Standing Committee . . ." Brownell, *Legal Aid in the United States* (1951), at 151-2.

49. There are now 600 Legal Aid programs in 3100 counties. Brownell claims that "the chief reason for the bankruptcy rule seems to be the desire not to lose the goodwill of merchants and other creditors from whom the societies must seek settlements for their clients." Others have perhaps been more candid by indicating that what is feared is not simply loss of goodwill but the loss of Legal Aid funds. Several participants at the 1948 conference of NALAO observed: "That they encountered objection to their handling [of] these [bankruptcy] cases from merchants, doctors, small loan companies and others who contribute generously to the Community Chest." Sudnow, "Normal Crimes: Sociological Features of the Penal Code in Public Defender Office," 12 *Social Problems* 415 (1965). In 1963 local Community Chests provided 53% of the funds for Legal Aid societies. 1963 Annual Report of National Legal Aid and Defender Association.

50. 78 Stat. 516 (1964). See *Guidelines for Legal Service Programs* (Washington, D.C.; Community Action Program, Office of Economic Opportunity). See also Cahn & Cahn, "The War on Poverty: A Civilian Perspective," 73 *Yale L.J.* 1317 (1964).

51. Ortique, "Too Little, Too Late," 14 *The Catholic Lawyer* 158 (Spring 1968).

52. A district court recently ruled the hearing must precede the cutoff. 3 *Law in Action* 6 (Dec. 1968).

53. All these cases are reported in 16 *Welfare Law Bulletin*

(March 1969) and 3 *Law in Action* 6 (Dec. 1968). See also, Toll and Allison, "Advocates for the Poor," 52 *Judicature, The Journal of the American Judicature Society* 321 (1969).

54. OEO Study, *supra* note 47, at 1.

55. *Id.* at 10.

56. Bellow, "The Extension of Legal Services to the Poor—New Approaches to the Bar's Responsibility," speech given to the Harvard Susquecentennial Celebration 6 (1967).

57. "In Scandinavia, that excellent institution called the Ombudsman assists the ordinary citizen in seeing that the law is not administered with an evil eye, or an uneven hand. He also assists the public official by clearing the air of unfound [sic] charges. In both ways, the Ombudsman helps safeguard the integrity of equal protection. The Ombudsman—or rather the idea it embodies—appropriately adapted to our governmental institutions, towns, cities, states, and even the Nation could help in the realization of our ideal of equal treatment of all citizens by government officials." Statement of Former Justice Goldberg, in Hearing on S. 1195 Before the Subcommittee on Administrative Practice and Procedure of the Senate Committee on the Judiciary, 90th Cong., 2d Sess., at 5 (1968). See generally, Davis, "Ombudsmen in America: Officers to Criticize Administrative Actions," 109 *U. Pa. L. Rev.* 1057 (1961); Cloward & Elman, "Poverty, Injustice and the Welfare State: An Ombudsman for the Poor?" *Nation*, Feb. 28, 1966, at 230.

58. OEO, *Training and Technical Assistance Grants* 7-8 (1967) (mimeographed release); interview with Hugh D. Duffy, Chief, Planning & Research, Legal Services Program, OEO, Washington, D.C., Sept. 30, 1968. Institute for Political Service to Society, *Red Tape* (1968). See *Washington Post*, Oct. 18, 1968, at B1.

59. See generally, Note, "Tenant Unions: Collective Bargaining and the Low-Income Tenant." 77 *Yale L.J.* 1368 (1968). N.Y. Real Prop. Actions Law, art. 7A (McKinney Supp. 1967). See Rich, "Civil Rights Progress Out of the Spotlight," 38 *Reporter* 25 Mar. 7, 1968.

60. See, e.g., Columbia University Project on Social Welfare Laws, the National Office for the Rights of Indigents.

61. Robb, "HEW Legal Services: Beauty or Beast," 55 *A.B.A. J.* 346 (1969).

62. Federal courts have always been able to appoint counsel in civil cases. 28 U.S.C. 1915. But they rarely do. In a District of Columbia study 4 out of 7 assigned counsel in civil cases "declined." The general view is that courts cannot insist on such services from lawyers. Willging, *supra* note 42, at 264.

63. Oaks, "Improving the Criminal Justice Act," 55 *A.B.A. J.* 217 (1969). Average compensation was $120 for trial court representation and $322 for appellate court.

64. *Id.* at 220.

65. Many OEO lawyers candidly admit they are reluctant to

54

call in volunteer lawyers on a one-case basis because "it is easier to do it yourself" than to answer all their questions.

66. Habermann, "Judicare," 117 *Pitt. Legal J.*, March 1969.

67. Kiigis, "Law Firms Could Better Service the Poor," 55 *A.B.A. J.* 232 (1969).

68. See "Elite Law Firm Opens Office in Ghetto," *Washington Post*, March 20, 1969, at A19.

69. Clark, "The Minority Lawyer: Link to the Ghetto," 55 *A.B.A. J.* 61, 64 (1969).

CHAPTER 4

GOVERNMENT AND THE "FORGOTTEN MAN"*

During the last months before each Presidential election, the attention of the movers and the shakers of U.S. affairs turns to the "Forgotten Man," that great mainstream American who by the force of his ballot elects the man who shall lead the Republic. At the climax of the process, the chosen leader goes on to try to fashion a "Return to Normalcy" or a "New Deal," a "New Frontier" or a "Great Society." The Forgotten Man goes back to work, not to be formally consulted again until the time comes to ratify the President's stewardship or to replace him with another.

The Forgotten Man often feels that even at election time he does not have a choice of whom *he* wants as President, but a selection of two or three candidates that the kingmakers of rival power groups have offered him. In part, this explains why the "Forgotten Man" often does not go to the polls. It also explains the woman next door who never votes "because it just encourages them": she is the Forgotten Man's wife.

Between elections, the Forgotten Man feels he has even less influence over what the President and the lesser leaders do or do not do. His voice is heard in the councils of the mighty only as translated by pundits who assert they speak for him, or by pollsters who claim to have consulted a controlled sample of him from which it is possible to generalize. In truth, politicians from the White House to the Courthouse do listen to the pundits and read the polls, and they do pay attention. When the message is writ large enough, they sometimes take direct and drastic action, as in the case of President Johnson's abrupt retirement.

But situations are seldom that clear-cut. That is the big

---

* This chapter is based largely on a paper contributed by Arthur B. Shostak, Associate Professor, Department of Social Sciences, Drexel Institute of Technology, with additional materials supplied by William Edward Callis.

56

problem in dealing with the Forgotten Man: there are so many of him, each with his own attitudes and anxieties, that the composite which contitutes him can be difficult to determine.

WHO IS THE FORGOTTEN MAN?

The Forgotten Man is the man in the middle, in the "silent majority," the ordinary guy for whom exceptions are not made. He is neither so poor that the government thinks it must try to rescue him, nor so rich that he can exercise independent power. He is unorganized, so that he is (and, more important, *feels* he is) alone in his dealings with government, which aside from his rather remote vote, generally consists of IBM cards and form letters and more-or-less indifferent clerks who cite regulations as to why this must be done in exactly that way or perhaps, for no good reason, cannot be done at all. The clerks, of course, get *theirs* when they have to deal with some other government agency.

Generalities about government being of, for, and by the people do not comfort the Forgotten Man when he sees the same government that socked him with a severe penalty for late payment of part of his $2,403.16 income tax, now forgive a million-dollar defaulter for 10¢ on the dollar (and issue a press release bragging about it), or when he sees his taxes apparently going to support minorities who rant and riot in protest over his more privileged way of life.

The Forgotten Man, patronized by his so-called friends as "the little guy" and sneered at by his so-called superiors as "the great mindless mass," is in fact the source of stability and continuity in American life. He does his job, pays his taxes, obeys most of the laws, loves his country, gets along with his neighbors, cares for his family, goes to war when he must, stores up such treasure as he can, usually goes to church, and takes what pleasure can be found in this land of plenty—which does not seem quite plentiful enough for him— in a world of want. Running hard to hold his place or maybe to get a little ahead, he is warned by prophets on every hand that his fragile world is in danger of destruction from the right by militarism, from the left by communism, and from the center by complacency—the sin so often and unthinkingly charged against those who lead "lives of quiet desperation."

It isn't that the Forgotten Man isn't worried; it's just that, according to exhaustive polls, if you talk to ten of him, you will find that three don't feel they have any say in what the government does, four don't think politicians care what they think, and seven often find they just don't understand what's going on.

The following tables are from the Violence Commission's survey of October, 1968.

Degree of Endorsement of Political Efficacy Items
[In percent]

Item	Overall	White	Nonwhite
People like me don't have any say about what the Government does	35	35	41
Voting is the only way that people like me can have any say about how the Government runs things	54	51	73
I don't think public officials care much what people like me think	43	43	51

Those with lower income and lower education feel even less politically effective than those who are better off in these respects.

Agreement on Political Efficacy Items for Income and Educational Levels
[In percent]

	Income			Education			
	5,000	5,000– 9,999	10,000 and over	8th grade	Some High school	High school graduate	College
People don't have any say	49	33	26	49	43	33	22
Voting is the only way	65	55	43	72	66	53	34
Public officials don't care	57	42	31	60	53	42	25

The Forgotten Man identifies as an American who simultaneously is certain and confused about the meaning of

58

current events. He has confidence in ("This is a great country")—and yet is quite concerned about—the quality of public servants and political affairs. He becomes, therefore, the natural prey of the political extremists, especially of the populists and the far right, who offer simple answers to mind-boggling questions.

These self-contradictory ways explain the Forgotten Man's volatile character and his erratic impact on the American scene. Confused, for example, about the justice in civil rights campaigns, he is almost certain that the social and racial status quo cannot or should not be changed quickly. Confident his government is worth the ultimate defense in a contemporary overseas war, he is still suspicious of that government.[1] Law-respecting, he is open nevertheless to the beliefs of extremists bent on rewriting the laws to their own purpose. Overall, the single most widespread concern of the Forgotten Man is over the "decay of values"—as evidenced by street crime, race militancy, college protestors, Mafia inroads, political scandals, bureaucratic ineptitude, and the like, but going beyond this decay to include everything that suggests people no longer act in accordance with decent values and right reason. The very virtues he holds to are, in his eyes, conspicuously absent from society as a whole—and herein is *the* source of his discontent.[2]

The Forgotten Man does not perceive himself as a racial bigot, a witch-hunting super-patriot, a subversive, or a vigilante. Rather, he thinks of himself as "very much open-minded." As the receptive potential audience for racists, super-patriots, and ultra-vigilantes, the Forgotten Man can bolster or detract from the significance of their violence-supporting activities. With his massive numbers, the Forgotten Man is the key of their power. His decision about their appeal is far more important than that of the scanty number of erratic "true believers" on the far left or far right who receive far more exposure in the mass media.

PROFILE OF THE FORGOTTEN MAN

Much of the confusion in public and academic discussion in this matter reflects mutually-contradictory identifications of the Forgotten Man as a backwoods or "white ghetto" Wallaceite, or as a reluctant "old liberal" Democratic backer of candidate Humphrey. Some represent the Forgotten Man as lacking confidence in all levels of government, or especially in federal levels of government, or in all forms of authority, extending beyond the state to include labor and business institutions.

The Forgotten Man is best understood as essentially four different types of men. All share certain attitudes in common, but differ in their actions in a clearly identifiable way. The Forgotten Man's hang-ups include *resentment, envy, disappointment,* and *uncertainty.*[3]

Resentment ties to a perception of a loss of status and power to less well-off men (especially black Americans). In his eyes certain out-groups (or "minorities") seem to be sharply closing the social distance that previously had them "castes away."

Envy, associated with resentment, ties to the notion that the "power-grabbing" out-groups have potency and actual success in climbing the social ladder.

Disappointment draws on the notion that elements of government are not only not neutral, but have "gone over" to support the outgroup power-grabbers, and that all large organizations, whether government, labor, or business, "have it in for the little guy"—the plain citizen who is voiceless, powerless, and friendless.

Uncertainty ties to a commonplace historic preoccupation with political eccentricity and violence, that ours is a political record of innumerable splinter parties, and of a bloody political history (e.g., Shay's Rebellion, the Civil War Draft Riots, the presidential assassinations, and the like). If anything worries the Forgotten Man more than where the government is heading, it is the possibility that it all may come crashing down.

The Forgotten Man may take his own beliefs quite seriously, yet while holding them, he may entertain considerable doubts about them. He may be willing, even anxious to act on them, or he may be unwilling, even quite reluctant to take any overt action to support them.

At one extreme, a very small number of "hard core" Americans unreservedly endorse the Forgotten Man's resentment, envy, disappointment, and uncertainty, and they seek ways to act on these beliefs. Many "prefer the primer to the history text, and the quick-action revolver to both." In contributing to what Richard Hofstadter has identified as the "paranoid style" in our politics, the hard core nativists and segregationists supply "heated exaggeration, suspiciousness, and conspiratorial fantasy."[4]

At the other extreme from the tiny minority of hard core types is the vast majority of "quiet" types. Drawn from lower-middle-class ranks of respectable Americans, they want a return to the simple life, the "good old days" of American mythology. They avoid taking much action. Typical here are many of the suburban supporters of President Nixon, especially those who left the Independent or Democratic ranks to vote Republican in 1968 for the first time.

The next largest category, that of "inactive," is the Forgotten Man who takes his own self-identifying attitudes quite seriously, but cannot bring himself to act on his beliefs. Typical here are the millions of blue-collar trade-unionists who only deserted the Wallace candidacy in the closing days and hours of the campaign finally to vote for Hubert Humphrey and the traditional straight-Democratic ticket.

The fourth category, on the other hand, involves the "unmotivated," men who behave more earnestly than they believe. Typical are men who feel themselves compelled by the attitudes or urging of workmates, neighbors, or relatives to engage in racial discrimination or protest voting in a way which leaves them vaguely convinced that someone else is making decisions for them.[5]

The four types—Hard Core, Quiet, Inactive, Unmotivated—can become volatile in the extreme. Large numbers of these people frequently shift among the four categories, making it difficult to do more than loosely rank the blocs from large to small (quiet, inactive, unmotivated, hard core) and to stress how major political developments (riots, assassinations, close election outcomes, etc.) can lead to major shifts in the size, rank, and character of the four constituencies.

All four types—but especially the Inactive category—include women. Zealous in defense of their children's head start over others, the use of secular schools to reinforce sacred pieties (as with Bible-reading), and the reduction of the spirit-breaking tax load, millions of women form a strong force in perpetuating the Forgotten Man's attitudes. Examples range from the shrieking demonstrators outside Little Rock High School in 1956 to the millions of fearful, repressive "Law and Order" admirers of candidates who espouse greater use of the death penalty.

All four types—but especially the unmotivated—draw on oldsters for membership. Often deliberate non-voters, and commonly nostalgic admirers of a better time long since passed, many old-timers experience all four Forgotten Man feelings of resentment, envy, disappointment, and uncertainty. Strong in defense of life-honored guidelines, like "folks should know their place," in defense of the justice of insisting

61

others should also "make it the hard way," and in defense of massive government economies (in all but old-age benefits), millions of oldsters support the attitudes held by the Forgotten Man as a way of protesting against the human costs of growing old in America.

Unlike the included women and oldsters, those excluded from the ranks of the Forgotten Man are the very well off and the very poor. The former are not especially concerned with losing status and power to others, while the latter are conscious in recent years of securing small increments of status and power. Neither qualifies as "forgotten." While individuals in both classes may share specific attitudes and goals with the Forgotten Man, the necessary four-part complex of attitudes is seldom embraced as a whole by the bulk of the class members.

By this process of definition by four attitude-behavior types, and of exclusion by two social classes, we have a provocative residual understanding of the "Forgotten Man." Capable of a wide range of attitude and behavior, the Forgotten Man proves on analysis to be at least four kinds of men. Commonly drawn from median-income earning ($6,- 000–$12,000) blue-collar and lower-echelon white-collar workers, with median educational achievement (high school or less), and both suburban and urban residence, the Forgotten Man begins to look like an American Everyman.

PORTRAITS OF THE FORGOTTEN MAN

With a breath of individuality to give life to the foursided Forgotten Man, here are some singular portraits of the Hard Core, the Quiet, the Inactive, and the Unmotivated:

1. *Hard Core*

Mrs. Cahoon is a thirtyish lady who would be very attractive were it not for the fact that her lips are nearly always compressed in a thin line. She was alerted to the communist conspiracy by the way the Virginia Highway Department acted when they paved the road in front of her home in Roanoke. Mrs. Cahoon was born and raised in Iowa and moved to Virginia with her husband, a Marine sergeant she met at a dance sponsored by the Grange to raise money for a memorial to the town's Vietnam dead. When they built their home it was on a dirt road, and they liked it that way. But more people built nearby, and finally they petitioned the State to pave it, over the objections of the Cahoons and one or two others, who also didn't want high-speed traffic endangering their children.

When the paving project neared her home, a man appeared at her door to inform her that the arbor vitae hedge along the front of their lawn would have to be dug up and moved because it was in the State's right-of-way. He asked her to show him where she would like to have the bushes replanted by his men. Now Mrs. Cahoon knew that their property line extended to the center of the road, and she was damned if anybody was going to touch her arbor vitae. There was much showing of plans and explanation of highway easement, but Mrs. Cahoon would not be moved. Some days passed and a morning came when the highway district superintendent told his foreman to have the bushes dug up, taking care to keep plenty of soil around the roots, and place them gently on the Cahoon property outside the right-of-way. Mrs. Cahoon was washing dishes when she looked out the window and saw what they were doing and came out the door wildcat fashion. She scratched the foreman. He called the police. They told her about the law and she told them to go to hell. They took her to jail. The judge scolded her and put her under a peace bond, "after they had locked me up and this big fat woman with dirty fingernails (the jail matron) made me take off all my clothes and she poked me all over and I mean all over, I can't tell you any more than that, and the deputy said some dirty things to me you wouldn't believe. They treated me like a criminal, like I was a nigger." And the arbor vitae died.

Some years have passed since then and Mrs. Cahoon, who had had no previous experience with politics, has become involved in the Wallace movement. She is basically a shy person, but her new zeal is such that she finds herself able to knock on doors in neighborhoods where she knows Wallace people are not openly acceptable and to pass out literature on the street. She is a little impatient with Wallace sometimes ("I wish he'd stop talking about running over one of those freaks and go ahead and do it") but she believes the movement will prevail. "We got 18 million votes, and we're going to win next time," she said. "The people are waking up. They're not going to stand for being pushed around by a lot of reds and fairies and niggers. We've seen what happens when the Federal Government sets up the niggers to run everything. In that riot in Washington the nigger police encouraging their 'soul brothers' [she says the word as though it had quotes around it] and the white police couldn't do nothing about it because the nigger mayor wouldn't let them. I know plenty of people who saw it, right out in the street."

She understands now why she was treated so badly in the squabble over the road. "If I was a police officer and had my hands tied so I couldn't arrest anybody even if I saw them rob a man and they get turned loose next day anyway, I'd feel mean too."

Mrs. Cahoon confidently expects to see the Russians take over this country if Wallace doesn't get in. "They have so many people paying niggers and college students to agitate and start riots it takes two whole floors of the U.N. building just to hold them," she said.

Against that day her husband has outfitted the house with semi-automatic surplus military arms and what appears to be about 10,000 rounds of ammunition. Her husband has taught her how to operate them, and she can field strip an M-1 carbine in the twinkling of an eye.

2. Quiet

Vitale is a 55-year-old mother of two children, one an attorney and the other a schoolteacher. Separated from her husband when the children were still infants, she went to work as a laborer in a New Jersey textile factory to support herself and her children. A second generation American of Italian descent, she had been forced to quit school at the age of 16 to help support her own parents and 7 brothers and sisters during the depression, earning more than her father was making.

Still working in the textile factory, she has long been a member of a textile workers union. She has never crossed a strike line even though she describes her union leaders as corrupt and lazy. "They drive around in cadillacs while I work my hands to the bone. They're in cahoots with the bosses anyway. They get their payoffs for not starting any trouble and then they raise our dues." But Jimmy Hoffa was all right. "At least he got the men good wages."

Corruption doesn't anger her too much, however, for she realizes it is just part of a broader conspiracy. "It's the politicians who cause all the trouble. They ought to throw them all in jail."

One day in 1960 she read in the newspaper about a sit-in at a segregated southern restaurant, and that stunned her. She hadn't realized that Negroes in the south were treated that way. She liked John F. Kennedy, as she had liked Franklin D. Roosevelt, because he was for the "little people. The Republicans are just for the rich people." After his election, she had listened attentively to each of his television addresses as she had listened to Roosevelt's fireside chats. The assassination shocked and grieved her. A strong woman who had not cried for years, she wept bitterly.

She did not like Lyndon Johnson. Things were beginning to happen in the country that she could not understand and she expected the President to explain them to her. She tried to listen to his televised speeches, but they made no sense. "Just a lot of bullshit, if you'll excuse my language."

64

The riots distressed her. "What they ought to do is shoot them all. That will keep them off the streets." On top of that, her factory was hiring blacks that "don't know their ass from a hole in the ground." One black man in particular infuriated her. "He's with the NAACP, so they can't fire him or else they would be accused of 'discrimination' even though he doesn't do a damn bit of work. If I did what he does I'd be out on the street. The damn nigger. And the union is behind it all. What do they care. They get more dues to feed their faces."

The war on poverty did not make any sense to her. She made $15 a week during the depression, worked hard all her life, put her children through college, and still managed to put some money aside for a rainy day. Now her children could take care of her in her old age and she could babysit for them. That was the way it was supposed to be. Her father never had to accept any welfare, even during the worst of the depression. "Nobody ever gave me anything. I worked for every penny I have. The problem is those damn niggers just don't want to work. They like being on welfare. All they do is spend it on liquor and color television anyway. They have babies just so they can get more welfare."

It was no surprise to her when the local newspaper uncovered a welfare scandal. "Those damn politicians are all crooks. They bring the colored people up from the south by promising them a lot of welfare. That's the way they get their votes and stay in office. I know. Everybody at the shop agrees."

She did not want to have anything to do with Goldwater because "if he got in, he'd get us into a war." War wasn't any good. "They just make rich people richer. Rich people *like* wars. More business for them." One of her brothers and many of her friends had been killed during World War II and she did not want her son to go to Vietnam. She thought about it a lot, then went to see her state Senator, whose family had known her family from the "old neighborhood," to see what he could do. "The rich kids don't go to Vietnam. Their parents get them out of it. It's not what you know, it's who you know. Connections—that's everything. Let them niggers fight. They want to fight so much, ship them all to Vietnam. And all those college students who want to fight, taking over buildings and things. *That* will get them off the streets."

She did not get to see the Senator. "He's a busy man. But his secretary was nice. She took down all the information and said 'footsie,' that's what we used to call him in the neighborhood, would see what he could do." Neighborhood ties were never tested, however. Her son enlisted soon thereafter. "I guess it's better this way. The men have to fight. That's the way it always was, always will be."

She liked Robert Kennedy, though not as much as John. She would have voted for him had he not been assassinated.

65

After the conventions, she turned to Wallace. "Humphrey's just a tool for Johnson. Nixon is still a Republican." She voiced her choice to her friends and relatives loudly. In the end, she voted for Nixon. "Wallace didn't have a chance. If I voted for him I would just be throwing my vote away. Nixon was the next best thing, even though he is a Republican."

She argues politics a lot with her children. Her son is a liberal, and although she can't understand how a bright boy like himself can be so stupid sometimes, he does raise points she hadn't thought about before.

But she cannot understand what he sees in the youth movement. "They ought to beat them over the head with their clubs. That's the way they did it when I was young. You never caught us talking filthy to policemen. Daley knew what he was doing."

But she has no great love for policemen either. "They're just like the rest of them. They're in on all the deals with the politicians. I see them, sitting and drinking coffee all day in diners. My house was robbed and they didn't know enough to take fingerprints. I showed them a greasy fingerprint and, you know, they never took it. The stupids!" She thinks they are mostly bullies, anyway. "John Valone is a cop. We went to grammar school together. He used to push the little kids around then, and he still does the same thing now. He hasn't changed a bit. Give them a badge and a club and all of a sudden they're big deals."

She liked Ted Kennedy, and Julian Bond is a "pretty nice young man," but somebody had better "damn well listen to Wallace. He's the only one who makes any sense."

3. *Inactive*

Wilson is a 48-year-old white native of West Virginia who except for service in Europe in World War II (Bronze Star and Purple Heart) has lived all his life within 20 miles of Charleston, W. Va. He is of Anglo-Saxon (early mountain pioneer) stock, and is a former coal miner and son and grandson of coal miners. Since the war he has worked as a carpenter because when he was discharged he discovered that the mine where he used to work had been bought and closed down by a large steel corporation (as part of a program to acquire reserves of coking coal for future needs). "The Government promised we'd get our old jobs back when we came home," he said. "I know for a fact they tried to keep veterans out of jobs so we'd have to go on the welfare. That way we'd have to do what the Government said or starve, because they'd cut a man off like that if he didn't do what he's told."

Wilson does not distinguish among local, State and Federal Government agencies and officials, feeling that they all "set their hand against the little man." The only difference among them, he said, "is they start off with a County office, and they learn how to steal. When they get pretty good they get a State job; and the ones that steal the best, they go to Washington." He says they steal better than half of what he makes every year—Wilson is a very good carpenter and gets steady work that brings in between $8000 and $10,000 a year—in indirect and direct taxes and "the way they keep prices high to soak up any loose money they might have missed."

"They" are not just Government officials but big business as well. Possessed of but a seventh-grade education, Wilson doesn't use terms such as "the military-industrial complex," but he talks of the Goverment "taking all our tax money and giving it to the big companies to spend on crazy things like rockets to the moon. They land one on the moon and find out it's made of dirt. So now they got to send a man up there with a shovel so he can bring a pail of it back. If they want dirt, I got a whole mountain of it in the back part of my place, and I wouldn't charge them nothing like what they pay them rocket boys. I got to work all my life so they can take my money and throw it at the moon."

Wilson is a "lay minister" of an unaffiliated fundamentalist Protestant church (the "chief preacher" is self-ordained) and an effective public speaker. He has for some years been active in the Federal anti-poverty program, principally as a recruiter of young men who are unemployed or underemployed for the Job Corps or the local community action program. While he's at it, he manages "to slip in a word or two about the love of God," and has significantly increased the number of young men attending his church. He has no difficulty reconciling his enthusiasm for the poverty program with his distrust of all Government: "They just making suckers out of us, trying to keep the people quiet. But while the money's floating around we try to get a piece of it. It helps the youngsters some."

Wilson is pessimistic and cynical about the future of his country, believing that the Government is not of, for, or by the people and not likely to become so. His solution? "Revolution," he says, in a shockingly quiet and offhand way. "Them boys is dug in deep, and they ain't going to let go. We gonna have to drag a lot of them out and shoot them." It should be emphasized here that Wilson is a quiet, courteous, peaceful man, deeply religious, a more than ordinarily-devoted husband (his wife is a chronic invalid) and father of three children in their late teens who are all married and have moved to Chicago. He lives in a rambling, much-added-to cabin that he keeps in good repair. It is surrounded on all sides by lovingly-tended flowers which he has planted "because they are nice for the old woman to look out upon."

He believes his attitude towards Government is shared by

most of his peers and thinks that the recent emphasis on firearms control is the Government's response to the revolutionary threat. "They're scared and they're trying to get our guns away." His attitude does not seem to have any tint of racism; his populism is pure and embraces those he calls without embarrassment—or overemphasis—"our black brothers." He believes the FBI killed King and both Kennedys "because they were stirring people up."

4. *Unmotivated*

Cummings is a cop—that's the word he uses—and has been one for 30 years, first in Hampton, Va., and now in Norfolk. Although he is clearly of average or better intelligence, he has remained a patrolman because he cannot pass the written test upon which promotion partly depends. He has an unblemished service record and has been cited several times for outstanding performance, but put him at a desk with a pencil in his hand and he freezes up—sweats up, rather—and forgets "every damn thing I ever knew." Once they gave him the test orally and he gave every answer correctly, but the requirement that he write an essay on some aspect of police work could not be waived. "I like working the street anyway," he says.

He can't work the street any more. The department had to pull him off because he cannot cope with the investigation and arrest procedures required by Supreme Court rulings over the past several years. "I've spent all my life learning how to be a cop," he says. "If they'd told me I was going to have to be a judge and lawyer too, I'd have been a mechanic like my ol' Daddy." The guidelines set down in Escobedo, Miranda, etc., may not seem very complicated. But Cummings, like many law enforcement officers, finds them strange and intimidating. "You know," his sergeant said, "it's a funny thing, but he didn't have any trouble until we had a seminar to explain some of the new rules. They aren't very different from old department policies anyway, but Cummings went right out and blew one of our biggest vice busts (arrests) in years. We told him to take one of the guys in and book him and he takes the guy to his (the defendant's) girl friend's house and keeps him there for half the night, trying to squeeze information out of him and looking for narcotics."

"The Supreme Court says once we take a suspect in we can't talk to him, so I figured I'd take him somewhere else and talk to him first," Cummings said. He wasn't officially reprimanded, but after ruining or complicating several succeeding cases, he was assigned to station duty. Which means paperwork. Which he says he can't do. He's going to retire, and he's bitter.

"Police work used to be something a man could be proud to do," he says. "Now cop is a dirty name. You give a nigro (he seems to be halfway between "nigra" and "Negro," pronunciation-wise) a parking ticket and he falls down on the sidewalk and starts hollerin' police brutality, and they have a riot. You see a guy snatch a purse and you got to recite the Declaration of Independence at him while you're chasing him. You can't shoot him so you got to hope he'll start laughing and lose his wind. And then if you catch him he'll, jump and down and say, 'I'm guilty! I'm guilty!' and that means you got to let him go if he confesses before you can get a gag on him. You pull a guy in for stealing a quarter and the City buys him a hundred dollar lawyer to convince the judge to let him go. Pretty soon it'll be a Federal offense to arrest a murderer."

Cummings can and will go on in this vein for hours, but somehow it isn't convincing. It seems likely that Cummings has not been able to adjust to other facets of his work that have changed in recent years. The department has a substantial race relations program going, and conducts workshops designed to alert the men to their delicate role in society. It is a far cry from the "run 'em off or run 'em in" days, and Cummings does not seem to be a man who is given to introspection and situation ethics. He's not interested in trying to see himself through a black man's eyes the better to understand how to avoid a confrontation. Cummings thinks people who go around confronting cops ought to go to jail for disturbing his peace.

ATTITUDES OF THE FORGOTTEN MAN:
HISTORICAL SOURCES

Why does the Forgotten Man believe as he does? What combination of common elements from the nation's recent history especially explain the prevalence of resentment, envy, disappointment and uncertainty? Part of the answer lies in the recent history of this joint blue-and-white collar bloc. Even after making allowances for the wide age span involved, the largest number were born in the late 1920's or early 1930's. Their life histories ever since have encouraged the volatile political uneasiness that is their trademark.

The 1920's, for example, did not see blue-collar and lower-echelon white-collar workers sharing in the nation's paper-prosperity. Instead, the "Roaring Twenties" meant regional poverty, long-term unemployment, and inadequate relief for millions. Protective labor legislation was minimal. Women and children commonly substituted for working men. And employers used force or company unions to defeat the near-beaten trade unions. This interplay between the illusion of gay prosperity for all and the grim reality for many remains a critical key to understanding the entire decade. Millions of Forgotten Men began life at a time when resentment, envy, disappointment, and political uncertainty were warranted. What followed has been characterized as having packed a "bigger wallop than anything else that happened to America between the Civil War and the Atomic Bomb."[7] The Great Depression of the 1930's left 34 million Americans scarred by unemployment; one in five workers was unemployed or underemployed, and lived with a "dull misery in the bones." The present day Forgotten Man (or his father) entered the 1930's confident that his uneven luck in the previous decades would change for the better, and the social order would soon provide jobs. But the 1930's were worse. With dreams shattered, skills gone rusty, and children undereducated and unlikely therefore to achieve much more than their fathers, the little man suffered much.

Many Americans left the decade of the Great Depression impressed as never before with the built-in deficiencies of society (including the intricate connections that explained how a collapse in Wall Street speculation on paper margin could close real factories in 48 states and sponsor the human starvation of millions). Many left the decade shaken by the new heights reached in class consciousness and class warfare (". . . there were no neutrals . . . [it was] a landscape blighted more than anything else by the absence of pity and mercy").[8] Millions of men learned at the time to doubt their once characteristic faith in the Natural Order and in the Horatio Alger myth of individual success.

In an unprecedented way the victims of the Depression slowly and steadily came to place their reliance on the mechanism of government, as they enthusiastically came to place their trust in the modified welfare capitalism of the New Deal. Many also turned to the new giant countervailing power represented by the AFL and CIO labor organizations. By the decade's end, however, recessions in the late 1930's and a stalemate in mass organizing union campaigns made plain a serious loss of influence and momentum by both Big Government and Big Labor. The little man of the period understandably prolonged his new flirtation with political demagogues (Long, Bilbo, Talmadge, and others), arch-conservatives (Father Coughlin, Gerold K. Smith), vigilante groups (Detroit's Purple Shirts, the Knights of the White

Camilia, the Klan), and political illegalities (such as factory sit-ins).

Clearly the Forgotten Man of today was especially influenced by the Great Depression: "probably nobody can understand America, or hence himself, if he does not understand the Great Depression."[9]

The 1940's, much like the Thirties, saw the Forgotten Man oscillate between hope and fear, self-confidence and bitter envy, and early respect for, but later suspicion of government. The economic bonanza that war work and wartime prosperity represented stirred new hopes that the economy was finally back in hand. The extraordinary production records stirred new pride and confidence in self, even as recognition of the contribution of government control mechanisms (price ceilings, the directed location of war plants in depressed areas, and the "encouragement" of union efforts) led many to a new regard for Government's positive potential.

In a very special way the Forgotten Man had never had it so good, and remains even today nostalgic and envious of World War II days. Cost-plus contracts enabled employers to pay handsomely, and accumulated War Bond savings gave millions of Depression alumni their first real taste of economic security and prosperity. The terrible plight of poor Black Americans was temporarily relieved by unprecedented defense work, thus relieving the conscience of White America even as the abundance of available jobs limited any sense of racial job competition. Above all, work took on the ethos of a crusade: no personal sacrifice was denied if it might serve "our boys over there." The Forgotten Man drew together with others in a way that many even now remember longingly.[10]

With the War's end in 1945, however, new fears spread concerning a resumption of the Great Depression. While employment and consumption initially stayed high, earnings fell as employers reduced overtime. The Federal Government, despite warnings and controversy, lifted price and rent controls. The economy faltered, consumer demand sagged, and production contracted. By 1949, much as in 1939, unemployment was at its highest level for the decade.

Throughout the late 1940s the Forgotten Man reacted with the violence characteristic of many: labor strife peaked in the 1948–50 period, and industrial strikes set lasting records for duration and bitterness. Also, labor union "civil war" saw the CIO in 1949 and 1950 expel eleven international unions on grounds of communist domination. Fathers and sons fought and much violence accompanied new internecine "dual union" struggles.

In a fashion never since forgotten by the Forgotten Man, the Federal Government exacerbated problems by responding to the times with a weak program. A Full-Employment Act was passed in 1946, but it had limited effect. The same held true of widely-heralded federal home-building legislation. As if a display of false promise and impotence were not enough, the Government's Taft Hartley Act in 1947 revived much of the class warfare rhetoric of the 1930's.

Again, as in the early 1940's, things were set right in the early 1950's by the new wartime efforts. The Korean War initiated an economic boom that has continued with little interruption to date. Unemployment, however, remained high throughout the 1950's and early 1960's, rarely dipping below 5 percent. Furthermore, recovery from both of the recessions in 1958 and 1961 left the country with a higher rate of unemployment than had each preceeding recovery. While the employment picture has improved considerably, it remains nevertheless both uneven and unreliable (anxieties run high over the million jobs directly linked to the Vietnam War effort).

Inflation also proceeds in its own merciless, and seemingly uncontrollable way. In 1967, for example, the Consumer Price Index recorded its second largest climb since 1951, and spendable earnings of workers reached their lowest level since 1964. Throughout 1968 and on into 1969 the Index continued the consecutive monthly increases begun back in 1966. Overall paycheck purchasing power has shrunk regularly since 1965, the erosion of purchasing power becoming almost a fixed part of the American scene—or so the Forgotten Man feels.

This, of course, stresses only the important economic component of majority man's recent history.[11] Two other factors, also important sources of beliefs and memories, warrant mention: political developments and social changes.

Over the past 40 years the Forgotten Man appears to have been deeply influenced by four particular political developments, two that were appreciated, and two that were not. Especially well thought of are the Eisenhower years and to a lesser extent, the Goldwater candidacy, the first for its tone of calm and moderation, the second for its stand in favor of established ways and official pieties. He cherishes both political developments for their suggestion that law and order *can* be secured in the land, that many of the old ways remain best, and that America's moral health *is* redeemable.

Relatively unpopular with the Forgotten Man are two political developments related to the Under-Class. The first encompasses the last fifteen years of civil rights legislation, while the second focuses on the past five years of anti-poverty programs. He feels that the anti-poverty aid goes for the most part to those who do not deserve it; that it demoralizes and harms; that it discriminates unfairly and imposes an almost unbearable tax on those who work; and that it obviously does not succeed. Not even the recent sidetracking of the race integration effort and the substitution of "hunger" for "poverty" as a prime governmental concern relieves the resentment, envy, and disappointment generated.

The past 40 years have also witnessed a relevant set of social developments. Most important among these are an erosion in the authoritarian and partriarchal position of the male family head, a growing dissatisfaction by educated or "enlightened" females with their prime confinement to housewifery and child-rearing, and a rebelliousness and rootlessness among both young males and females that seem to the Forgotten Man to go beyond anything he can remember or understand. It is as if, having lost his self-esteem and authority with his indirect failure as bread-winner in the 1930's, the male household head has never recouped. Never-ending social change swirls around his head, leaving him dizzy, frightened, and not a little furious.

Looking back over forty years of history since the 1920's, then, one can understand more easily what shapes the beliefs and attitudes of this group of people: *resentment*—against the betrayal of aspirations by the economy, the State Department, the Supreme Court, and the like; *envy*—aimed at the Under-Class, with its allegedly disproportionate gains; *disappointment*—over the Government's failure to take hold and give direction and worth to American life (e.g., to curb inflation, root out dissidents, restore respect for the man of the family, etc.); and *uncertainty*—thereby leaving the Forgotten Man the political maneuverability he craves (more in rhetoric than reality) to make a political impact on the nation that will finally have others sit up and take notice.

ATTITUDES OF THE FORGOTTEN MAN: PERSONAL SOURCES

Four aspects of his personal life are important for the

73

Forgotten Man in his relationship with the institutions of government: rural origins, blue collar background, education level, and job satisfaction.

With 90 percent of the population now residing in urban areas, and the mass media lamenting over the exodus from the land, we lose sight of the fact that a vast number of adult Americans either grew up in the countryside or are only one generation removed from it (whether as immigrants or as "native" Americans). The Forgotten Man gives evidence of particular fidelity to his agrarian roots: men of the land are "more traditional in religious beliefs, ascetic, work-oriented, puritanical, ethnocentric, isolationist, uninformed, unlikely to read books or newspapers, distrustful of people, intolerant of deviance, opposed to civil liberties, opposed to birth control, and favorable to early marriage and high fertility than all or most classes or urban workers."[12] Raised against such a parental and community backdrop, the Forgotten Man, however long he may have been an urban or suburban dweller, may honor a backwoods fundamentalism all his life.

With the shift of the labor force from blue-collar to service and white-collar occupations, a vast bloc of adult Americans either grew up in the homes of blue-collar workers or were raised by parents who had. Whether the Forgotten Man today is employed at white-collar or blue-collar pursuits, he may live under the influence of three legacies from his background. First, many Forgotten Men have no particular confidence in their ability to influence public policy. They downgrade their event- and law-shaping potential, and are inclined to a political apathy that oscillates between occasional extremist adventures. Second, Forgotten Men remain intensely suspicious of "outsiders"; advice is respected most when it comes from other members of the same ethnic stock, religion, and "old neighborhood." Thus the Forgotten Man screens out a host of modernizing influences and insulates himself from change. Finally, the Forgotten Man is distrustful of the public rhetoric of authority. Whether it be the TV press conferences of officeholders or the stump speeches of office-seekers, the Forgotten Man declines to trust or believe; like workers everywhere, he fears being fooled as well as Forgotten.

In a nation taking pride in its steady increase in average education levels, a great many adult Americans nevertheless are either only high school graduates or dropouts. Given the importance of education in conditioning mental abilities, in shaping personality, and in helping to determine life chances, the Forgotten Man suffers frustrations over this complex and fast-paced life. Uncertain reasoning, depressed self-esteem, and poor career achievement take on new meaning in the face of his weak educational history. A preference for simple solutions to intricate problems, an impatience with exacting explanations, and a propensity to rely more on word of mouth than the printed word extend this bleak view of reality.

Unable to follow the refinements of current events, the undereducated often adopt black/white or self-serving explanations to political dilemmas:

> The less sophisticated and stable an individual, the more likely he is to favor a simplified and demonological view of politics, to fail to understand the rationale underlying the tolerance of those with whom he disagrees, and to find difficulty in grasping or tolerating a gradualist image of political change.[13]

Acceptance of the norms of democracy requires a high level of educational sophistication and ego security—both qualities which the Forgotten Man lacks.

Finally, despite the advances in work made by labor unions, by enlightened industrialists, and by industrial social scientists, a vast bloc of adult Americans enjoy few rewards from their work—and have even fewer illusions about soon getting much from it. It dehumanizes anyone to work in an auto assembly plant putting the same four screws in the same four holes in one car after another every seventeen and a half seconds with two twelve-minute restroom breaks and a forty-five minute lunch break day after day after day.

Most men at this occupational level have little intrinsic satisfaction; whether blue-collar or white-collar the workers are taxed by skill-dissolving specialization, by frequent speedups, and by job-eroding automation. In response, many workers adopt elaborate defenses, including withdrawal (daydreams, fantasies of leaving to start a small business), rationalization ("work has no meaning for anyone"), projection ("the work force includes others still poorer off"), and aggression (hostility toward the work process, the work, and the supervisors).

The dreary quality of the work of many men and women employed in highly-automated industries follows from the latest phase of the Industrial Revolution where men have become servers of the machines rather than the classic first-phase situation when machines multiplied the power and speed of the operator. To a large extent, the worker has become a troublesome auxiliary valued to the extent that he does not use initiative or ingenuity in his job—the machine isn't programmed for bright ideas—and to the degree that he does not, by exhibiting human foibles such as boredom and a sense of his own importance, interfere with the processes of a system designed around the machines rather than around the men. This development extends to a lesser degree to the crafts, where prefabrication makes high skills less useful, and the service industries, where the man who used to ferret out defects like a detective, now often simply pulls and replaces modular components. While the lower-echelon white-collar worker may be considerably better off, much clerical work still amounts to so much pencil-pushing and paper-shuffling.

Also, at the occupational level at which many of the group are found, jobs are often unionized. On the one hand, this offers a form of security and protection that many rightfully seek; but on the other hand, the trade union experience of many Forgotten Men proves a very negative one. They complain that union bureaucracies have grown inhuman, rigid, and unresponsive; that the rank-and-file no longer shape union policies or have a real chance of gaining important union posts; and that labor leaders overly-respond to industry demands which they find incomprehensible or indefensible, or to demands that minority group members get privileged consideration in jobs and apprenticeships.[14]

Feeling this way, many workers relate to their union locals much as to various levels of government. They casually dismiss any sense of personal responsibility or involvement. They rarely attend meetings, grudgingly pay dues, and resist dues increases or the creation of new taxes. They go to the election polls if the issues on the ballot are dramatized and if there is little personal inconvenience. Cynicism rationalizes the resultant state of affairs. They shrug off the absence in their unions of a legitimate opposition party, the conversion of elective posts into sinecures, or even occasional intimidation, as all part of the natural order of things. Can this attitude, asks Neil W. Chamberlain, extend to the broader society of which it is a part?[15]

Feeling this way as a trade unionist, the Forgotten Man also gets little satisfaction from Organized Labor's political activities. Rather than sense renewed personal power through his membership in Labor's 16-million-member lobby, he dismisses the AFL-CIO's political efforts as foreign and overly-complex. Sympathetic with the rigid anti-Communist stand of

AFL-CIO head George Meany, these men suspect the "ultra-liberal" stand the Labor Federation takes on domestic matters. Indifferent to Labor's efforts to reward and punish lawmaking "friends" and "enemies," the union Forgotten Man resents suggestions that Labor controls his vote. On occasion these men emphasize their independence by openly ignoring or defying Labor's political recommendations, and nurture instead their characteristic feeling of political aloofness, aloneness, and alienation.

THE FORGOTTEN MAN'S CASE AGAINST GOVERNMENT

In his "resentment," the Forgotten Man believes that his plight has been overlooked and that his detractors in public affairs outnumber and overwhelm his friends. He bitterly resents that his losses seem to go either unnoticed or are even accepted or applauded.

What merits do these complaints have? On the one hand, every presidential candidate since Herbert Hoover recognized, valued, and sought the distinct support of this particular group of people. While the campaign styles of George Wallace, FDR, Adlai Stevenson, and Thomas Dewey may represent a broad spectrum, all four realized the concerns of the Forgotten Man. On the other hand, in the long stretch between campaigns the undereducated, unorganized, and untrusting Forgotten Man might think himself both out of mind and out of favor with decision-makers. Even as a "squeaky wheel gets the most grease," and as the mass media concentrate on the violent and the sensational, so does concern shift away from the inarticulate, unseen, and little understood mass of people. The Forgotten Man may be right: his rather vague concerns do get lost between the ballot box, where he is supreme, and the decision-making process, where the action is. This nation little manages to care for many of its dying, much less its walking wounded.

Less convincing is the grievance that finds a conspiracy behind every government move that disappoints. With the episodes of McCarthy, Lattimore, MacArthur, Coplon, Forrestal, Rosenberg, and others in his mind, the Forgotten Man likes to explain governmental neglect in conspiratorial terms; he also thinks he is being victimized by the intellectuals, by the liberal "cosmopolitans," and by others who disapprove of his rigidity in sexual, religious, moral, patriotic, military, and political matters. Examples of this kind of conspiracy range

77

from unpopular OEO subsidization of birth-control clinics to the imposition by distant bureaucrats of race integration guidelines for local schools and the encouragement the Office of Education allegedly gives to the development of sex education curricula. These hardly qualify as conspiracy. Yet while it may help his ego to think such actions are taken with a conscious concern to hurt him, a bitter truth holds that they rather are taken with unconscious indifference to him.

Regarding "envy," the Forgotten Man believes both that he has lost power, and that he can specify who has stolen it away from him; but the relevant "evidence" on this issue is exceedingly mixed.

On the one hand, government funds, manpower, and creative effort have recently helped the poor catch up and cross the fundamental divide that separates the Underclass from the Working-Class. Nevertheless, this aid would never have gone to the Forgotten Man in any event, but would have remained undeployed or have been redirected to more powerful interests. Furthermore, no clear evidence supports success in the effort to catch up: regrettably, ghetto conditions in our cities remain an ugly reality. The Forgotten Man widely assumes that the bold promises made to the Underclass (which excluded any consideration of his needs) were fulfilled. So we have the farcical situation of the Underclass which is angry because the pie is still in the sky, and the Working-Class which is envious because of the pie the Underclass isn't eating.

The grievance over who has stolen his power generally reduces either to a vague indictment of the blacks and their white liberal allies, or to a specific castigation of "spokesmen" like Carmichael, Brown, Cleaver, and Newton. To argue that American history shows this nation's ability to sustain considerable overall advancement by a number of competitive class, ethnic, or racial groups is dismissed as irrelevant by the Forgotten Man. Contemporary turmoil is incorrectly seen as unique.

Regarding "disappointment," the grievance holds that the institutions of government have abandoned the American Way and are luring the bulk of the American population away from fundamental Americanism. Examples include the Supreme Court ban on religious observances in public school, the Federal Government's imposition of semi-socialized medicine on the structure of health care (via Medicare and Medicaid legislation), the Federal Government's pressure on citizens to alter personal habits (such as smoking), some

78

State governments' abandonment of the death penalty, and local government's employment of deficit-spending policies. Of course, all these examples also yield to a different interpretation.

Finally, regarding "uncertainty," the Forgotten Man grieves because there is no room for him inside, and little interest paid to him by, the two major political parties. Where the Goldwater capture of the Republican Party in 1964 and the surprising inroads made into Democratic Party affairs in 1968 by McCarthy and Kennedy point up the considerable latitude for major change in the two dominant parties, the record of the parties in getting the Forgotten Man involved hardly inspires confidence. The attitude of indifference dominates; ward leaders and block captains conspicuously appear before elections, only to go into hibernation afterwards.

As for the nature of current political thought and trends, the Forgotten Man may very well think he is not taken seriously enough. After all, he can point out, pollsters find one-third of all Americans agree that the cities are unmanageable, and that money spent in them is wasted. Forty percent agree that air pollution is just about impossible to control. Fifty percent agree that the courts have been too lenient on criminals and thus have encouraged disorder. Fifty-five percent agree that something is deeply wrong with our society. And eighty-one percent agree that law and order has broken down in this country, and that it is time for a crackdown on civil rights protestors.[16]

Impressed with such local-level moves as the increasingly stern use made of police and National Guardsmen to curb rioters, the Forgotten American is aggrieved that others make too little of such matters. He strongly thinks that it remains exceedingly possible to return this country to his brand of fundamentalism: one need only to employ such conventional means as the ballot (defeat of open housing laws, school bond issues, fluoridation acts), legislation (enactment of harsh penalties for college demonstrators, draft resisters, and war protestors), and party politics.

CONCLUSION

What governmental actions might help ease the Forgotten Man's alienation from the institutions of government and reduce the potential for extremism and violence which that alienation often represents? The Forgotten Man does not necessarily know himself what will help, at least not with clarity, for research demonstrates the considerable confusion and self-deception that characterizes emotion-laden matters.[17]

One important step at the national level is the successful control of inflation. In 1970, it is the most immediate threat to the Forgotten Man. He spends at least forty hours a week earning money for himself and his family, not counting the hours he may spend getting to and from his job. That money is usually spent in a diligently budgeted and frugal manner. Luxuries are few, added comforts are often expensive. The typical Forgotten Man is continually in debt with a home mortgage, and most of his durable goods are purchased on long-term credit. He is, because of his economic dependence, the outstanding victim of the price-wage spiral. He feels the pinch as he makes little or no headway out of the tightly oppressive cycle of work-spend-work-spend just to keep his family fed, housed, clothed, and healthy. A small variation in income or prices can make the difference between financial hardship or relative comfort.

Another matter on which the Forgotten Man could be better satisfied is taxes, which become even more painful under the pressures of inflation. According to outgoing Treasury Secretary Joseph W. Barr in his parting statement to Congress, "We face now the possibility of a taxpayer revolt if we do not soon make major reforms in our income taxes. The revolt will come not from the poor, but from the tens of millions of middle-class families and individuals with incomes of "$7,000 to $20,000 . . . who pay over half of our individual income taxes." He continued: "The middle classes are likely to revolt against income taxes, not because of the level or amount of the taxes they must pay but because certain provisions of the tax laws unfairly lighten the burdens of others who can afford to pay. People are concerned and indeed angered about the high-income recipients who pay little or no federal income taxes."[18] The term "revolt" may as yet be too strong, but embittered taxpayers are registering increasing protests over inequities such as the fact that in 1967 there were 155 individuals and couples who reported incomes of more than $200,000 each and paid no federal income tax at all.

But the federal income tax, even with the surtax, looms not as the worst villain in the eyes of the Forgotten Man. Rather, it is state and local taxes which are growing at unprecedented rates as the cost of goods and services shoots upward. State and local expenditures have been rising much more rapidly than Federal expenditures for domestic purposes, although the Federal government collects two-thirds of all the taxes whereas state and local governments collect only one-third. Thirty-five states have adopted an income tax, and many this year are raising their sales taxes at least one more percentage point. Property taxes have gone up most dramatically since they serve as the tax foundation for most communities. It is not unusual to see a ten to fifteen percent hike each year in the property assessment tax.

Even with these increased taxes, however, the Forgotten Man can see few benefits. The cities, the schools, and the streets continue to deteriorate. He sees no visible improvement in the quality of his living environment, and the rise in crime continues, as does the growth of minority discontent and the "staggering" welfare rolls[19]—all this combined with headline reports of tax loopholes for the rich and corruption and personal greed in high places.

The public services upon which the Forgotten Man increasingly depends cannot be allowed to falter. Law enforcement must more effectively keep the Forgotten Man's neighborhood safe from the fear of crime in the streets and in the home, especially as that neighborhood opens up to Negro residents escaping from the racial ghetto. The public schools must more capably teach the Forgotten Man's children the skills they need to ascend a step or two up the socio-economic ladder. Health care, legal aid, and other welfare services must be provided not only to the very poor but also to families with marginal incomes who cannot pay full rates without real financial hardship. As the National Commission on Urban Problems has urged, the services requirements of our metropolitan areas (where two-thirds of our population lives) must be met through the increase in federal tax receipts coming from the gains in national productivity, through a more humane reordering of national expenditures, and through reforms in our system of taxation.

But if the government is to take the necessary steps to meet the needs of the Forgotten Man for public services, the confidence of the Forgotten Man in those who run his government at all levels must increase. Otherwise, public support for these steps will not come. The degree of communication between officials and constituents must improve, so that government will not seem unconcerned about problems like crime in the streets which most trouble the Forgotten Man. Means must be developed for redressing the grievances of individuals against petty outrages by government bureaucracies, so that government will not seem to be permanently indifferent in its dealings with the Forgotten Man. Perhaps most importantly, dishonesty and greed among public servants must be prevented to the extent possible by formalized requirements of financial disclosure and ethical conduct, with appropriate enforcement mechanisms, so that government and its activities will not seem to serve private rather than public interest.

Only if the Forgotten Man's alienation and disaffection from his government are reduced, if not eliminated, will it be possible for America's leaders to initiate the increased commitment of needed resources to the public sector. Increasingly, the quality of life for each of us depends upon its quality for all of us.

REFERENCES

1. ". . . the brooding and uncomplicated mind, with proper encouragement, might detect subversion not only behind the UN and the TVA, but also the French and Indian War, the Pure Food and Drug Act, compulsory vaccination for smallpox, the abolition of entail and primogeniture, the bank holiday of 1933, the British Reform Act, Red Cross blood banks, the Congress of Vienna, the election of Grover Cleveland, Teapot Dome, and public venereal clinics." Willie Morris, "Cell 772, or Life Among the Extremists," *Commentary,* October 1964, at 38. See also Seymour Martin Lipset, "An Anatomy of the Klan," *Commentary,* October 1965, at 74-84.

2. For discussion, see James Q. Wilson, "A Guide to Reagan Country, The Political Culture of Southern California," *Commentary,* May 1967, at 37-45. See also Pete Hamill, "The Revolt of the White Lower Middle Class," *New York,* Apr. 14, 1967 at 24-29; Edward Schnerer, "The Scar of Wallace," *Nation,* Nov. 4, 1968, at 454-457. Hamill's essay is one of the finest on the subject available anywhere.

3. For relevant conceptual refinement, see Marvin E. Olsen, "Two Categories of Political Alienation," *Social Forces,* March 1969, at 288-298. For historical background, see Irene Taviss, "Changes in the Form of Alienation: The 1900's vs. The 1950's," *American Sociological Review,* February 1969, at 46-57; John H. Bunzel, *Anti-Politics in America* (New York: Knopf, 1967).

4. Quotations are from Morris, *supra* note 1 at 38. Harry Jones, Jr., *The Minutemen* (New York: Doubleday, 1968); C. Wright Mills, *White Collar: The American Middle Classes* (New York: Oxford University Press, 1951); Richard H. Rovere, "The Conservative Mindlessness," *Commentary,* March 1965, at 38-42.

5. In connection with both the Under-actors and the Under-

believers, see Arthur B. Shostak, "Chapter Fourteen: Blue Collar Politics" in *Blue-Collar Life* (New York: Random House, 1969). See also Herbert Gans, *The Urban Villagers: Group and Class in the Life of Italian-Americans* (New York: Free Press of Glencoe, 1962).

6. See, for example, Irving Bernstein, *The Lean Years: A History of the American Worker, 1920-1933* (Boston: Houghton-Mifflin, 1960).

7. Caroline Bird, *The Invisible Scar* (New York: McKay, 1966), at 17. See also David A. Shannon, ed., *The Great Depression* (Englewood Cliffs, N.J.: Prentice-Hall, 1960); Malcomb Cowley, *Think Back On Us* (Carbondale, Ill.: Southern Illinois University Press, 1967).

8. Murray Kempton, *Part of Our Time: Some Monuments and Ruins of the Thirties* (New York: Dell, 1967) at 1, 10.

9. David Cort, *New York Times Book Review*, March 24, 1968, at 38. See also Milton Derber and Edwin Young, eds., *Labor and the New Deal* (Madison, Wis.: University of Wisconsin Press, 1961).

10. See Adolph A. Hoehling, *Home Front, USA: The Story of World War II Over Here* (New York: Crowell, 1966); Milton Derber, "Labor Management in World War II," *Current History Magazine* June, 1965, at 340-341; "Fitter's Night" in Arthur Miller's *I Don't Need You Any More* (New York: Viking, 1967).

11. This section draws heavily on Shostak, "Chapter Two: Blue Collar Odyssey," *supra* note 5. See also David Danzig, "Conservatism After Goldwater," *Commentary, March,* 1965, at 31-37.

12. Norval D. Glenn and Jon P. Alston, "Rural-Urban Differences in Reported Attitudes and Behavior," *The Southwestern Social Science Quarterly,* March, 1967, at 381-400.

13. Seymour Martin Lipset, "Democracy and Workingclass Authoritarianism," *American Sociological Review,* August 1959, at 492.

14. See, for example, Sidney M. Peck, *The Rank-and-File Leader* (New Haven: College and University Press, 1963); Paul Sultan, *The Disenchanted Unionist* (New York: Harper & Row, 1963).

15. Neil W. Chamberlin, *The Labor Sector* (New York: McGraw-Hill, 1967), at 207.

16. From 1968 and 1969 polls provided by the Harris polling organization, as published in major city newspapers.

17. For the clearest and most compelling statement of the case, see Snell and Gail J. Putney, *Normal Neurosis: The Adjusted American* (New York: Harper & Row, 1964). See especially their discussion of "misdirection," or "behavior motivated by a need, but inappropriate to the satisfaction of that need," at 14-15. Also useful is Robert Endleman, "Moral Perspectives of Blue-Collar Workers," in Arthur Shostak and William Gomberg, eds., *Blue-Collar World: Studies of the Ameri-*

can Worker (Englewood Cliffs, N.J.: Prentice-Hall, 1964), at 308-315.

18. U.S., Congress, Joint Economics Committee, *1969 Economic Report of the President, Hearings,* prepared statement of Secretary of the Treasury, Joseph W. Barr, 91st Cong., 1st sess., Jan. 17, 1969, at 46.

19. The Forgotten Man has not been told that of the 8.4 million people on welfare in the United States, less than 80,000 are employable adult men. See National Commission on Urban Problems, *Building the American City* (Washington, D.C.: Government Printing Office, 1968), at 3.

CHAPTER 5

AMERICAN SOCIETY AND THE RADICAL BLACK MILITANT*

The Report of the Kerner Commission, published in March of 1968, concerned itself primarily with the phenomenon of urban rioting and with the appropriate responses of society to that phenomenon. Recent developments in our racially troubled nation make it necessary to consider how our political and social institutions should respond to a different but related phenomenon: the small but increasing number of "radical black militants" who actively espouse and sometimes practice illegal retaliatory violence and even guerrilla warfare tactics against existing social institutions, particularly the police and the schools.

This new kind of purposeful violence is potentially even more destructive than the urban riots have been. We as a nation must take effective steps to stop the spread of radical black militancy, and we shall be effective only if we as a nation understand what it is we are dealing with. This chapter is intended to contribute to public understanding by tracing the multiple causes of radical black militancy and by outlining the principles which should govern the response of our nation's institutions to this threat.

THE NATURE OF RADICAL BLACK MILITANCY

In the effort to achieve freedom, equality and dignity, Negroes in America have repeatedly engaged in militant action and have continuously experimented with a wide variety of tactics, ideologies, and goals: insurrection and riot, passive resistance and non-violence, legal action and political

---

* This chapter was prepared by James S. Campbell largely as a synthesis of material contained in the Reports of this Commission's Task Forces on Historical and Comparative Perspectives on Violence and on Violent Aspects of Protest and Confrontation, as well as on the basis of the Report of the National Advisory Commission on Civil Disorders. For a fuller description of sources, see the Note following this chapter.

organization, separatism and integration—all these and many others have been tried by black people in every period of our history. Black protest in America today is a similarly complex phenomenon. Many black leaders are working quietly but effectively "within the system" toward the same basic goals—black well-being and dignity—as those who have adopted more militant tactics. Even that part of the larger black protest movement which is now called "black militancy" is a complex, many-dimensioned phenomenon, and violence is only one part of it.

Three major themes stand out in contemporary black militancy:

(1) Cultural autonomy and the rejection of white cultural values;
(2) Political autonomy and community control; and
(3) "Self-defense" and the rejection of non-violence.

Each of these three themes is a cluster of ideas, values and activities which are shared in widely varying degrees and combinations by different groups and individuals. Those whom we call "radical black militants," and who are the main focus of this chapter, are Negroes who embrace notions of "self-defense" which include illegal retaliatory violence and guerrilla warfare tactics.

(1) *Cultural autonomy.*—The movement toward black cultural autonomy and rejection of white cultural values mixes both indigenous and international influences. Looking backward at the long history of white domination in this country, and outward at what is seen as contemporary American "neocolonialism," black militants increasingly question the traditional values of American culture. From the Negro perspective, the performance of this country under the dominance of Western cultural values must seem far less impressive than it looks in white perspective, and militant blacks are now looking to their own cultural heritage as a source of affirmation of a different set of values.

Supported by the revival of awareness of African history and culture, militant blacks have grown more and more impatient with what is seen as the attempt of American institutions such as the universities, the schools and the mass media to impose white cultural standards which ignore or deprecate the independent cultural heritage of Afro-Americans. A SNCC position paper proclaims:

The systematic destruction of our links to Africa, the cul-

86

tural cut-off of blacks in this country from blacks in Africa are not situations that conscious black people in this country are willing to accept. Nor are conscious black people in this country willing to accept an educational system that teaches all aspects of Western Civilization and dismisses our Afro-American contribution . . . and deals with Africa not at all. Black people are not willing to align themselves with a Western culture that daily emasculates our beauty, our pride and manhood.

(2) *Political autonomy.*—Contemporary black militancy is oriented strongly to the idea of black community control and the development of independent black political bases. The effort of the militants to overcome black powerlessness, while at the same time largely rejecting participation in traditional political avenues and party organizations, is a result of several influences.

Perhaps most important has been the failure of traditional politics to afford an effective means by which black leaders can exercise power on behalf of their constituencies. A recent study of Chicago politics, for example, showed that of a total of 1,088 policy-making positions in federal, state and local government in Cook County, only 58, or 5 percent, were held by Negroes in 1965, although blacks comprised at least 20 percent of the county's population. Nationwide, the number of black elected officials is estimated at less than 0.02 percent of the total of 520,000 elected officials—despite the fact that blacks are just under 12 percent of the population. ("Traditional politics" may yet prove responsive to black leadership aspirations, however: in 1965 when the Voting Rights Act went into effect there were but 72 black elected officials in the 11 Southern states; after the 1968 elections that number had increased more than fivefold to 388.)

Another major factor influencing the militants' thrust for black political autonomy is the fact that residential segregation has created the conditions for effective black political organization. Residential segregation has meant that, in the black belt of the South as well as in the urban North and West, blacks occupy whole districts *en bloc*. With the growing concentration of blacks in the central cities and of whites in the suburbs, more and more cities are developing black majorities: in the next 15 years the number of major cities with Negro majorities will rise from 3 to 13.

A third factor in the drive toward black community control is the sharpened political perception that control over the centers of decision-making means control over the things about which decisions are made, such as housing, employment, and education, as well as other focal points of black protest like the police and the welfare apparatus. Black power theorists like Stokely Carmichael and Charles Hamilton believe that such control can be achieved only through independent black political organizations:

> Before a group can enter the open society, it must first close ranks. By this we mean that group solidarity is necessary before a group can operate effectively from a bargaining position of strength in a pluralistic society. Traditionally, each new ethnic group in this society has found the route to social and political viability through the organization of its own institutions with which to represent its needs within the larger society.

(3) *"Self-defense."*—The civil rights movement of the 1950's and early 1960's stressed non-violence and what some called "passive resistance." But civil rights workers in the South sometimes found that they could not depend upon local or even federal officials for protection against violent attacks by the Ku Klux Klan and other white terrorist groups. Local police and sheriffs were often only half-heartedly concerned with the welfare of rights workers, and in a few instances at least were even active participants in terrorist groups. As a result, in the mid-1960's a number of civil rights activists and their local allies began to arm themselves, and local defense groups sprang up in several black communities in the South.

At this time the focus of black protest began to shift to the ghettoes of the North, and expanded notions of self-defense soon arose. After the Watts riot of 1965, local Negroes formed a Community Action Patrol to monitor police conduct during arrests. (A UCLA survey showed that three fourths of the Negro males in the Watts area believed that the police used unnecessary force in making arrests.) In 1966, a small group of Oakland blacks carried the process a step further by instituting armed patrols. From a small group organized on an ad hoc basis and oriented to the single issue of police control, the Black Panther Party for Self-Defense has since grown into a national organization with a ten-point program for achieving political, social and economic goals—and with an evident willingness to resort to violence when it appears that only force and coercion will be successful in attaining the Party's goals.

The confrontation between radical black militants and

some elements of the police has escalated far beyond self-defense and has in some cases become a bloody feud verging on open warfare. Aggressive attacks by black radicals on the police obviously far exceed any lawful right of self-defense (just as some of the instances of police aggression against black radicals are clearly unlawful), but the radicals nonetheless believe their attacks to be legitimate and to fall within "self-defense" when that concept is properly understood. As a militant leader argues, "We have been assaulted by our environment." This "assault" is considered to neutralize moral restraints against the use of counter-violence, which is thus seen by the radicals not as aggression but still as "defensive" retaliation.

How easily violence against police and other symbols of authority can be perceived as legitimate by radical black militants was demonstrated in the thoughts expressed before the Violence Commission by a moderate Negro leader:

> For you see, Mr. Chairman, what most people refer to as violence in the ghetto, I refer to as self defense against the violence perpetrated on the ghetto. Dr. King's widow has put it well: "In this society," she said on Solidarity Day, "violence against poor people and minority groups is routine."
>
> I must remind you that starving a child is violence. Suppressing a culture is violence. Neglecting school children is violence. Punishing a mother and her child is violence. Discriminating against a working man is violence. Contempt for poverty is violence. Even the lack of will power to help humanity is a sick and sinister form of violence.
>
> The people of the ghetto, Mr. Chairman, react to this violence in self defense. Their self defense is becoming more violent because the aggressor is becoming more violent.

How has it come about that substantial numbers of black people in this country, especially among the black youth, see the government and the white majority as an "aggressor"?

UNDERLYING CAUSES OF RADICAL
BLACK MILITANCY

In March of 1968 the Kerner Commission filed its historic Report at the end of a comprehensive investigation into the causes and prevention of the urban riots which have plagued this country in the 1960's. The Commission found that the causes of the rioting were "imbedded in a massive tangle of issues and circumstances—social, economic, political, and

89

psychological—which arise out of the historical pattern of Negro-white relations in America." The most fundamental strand in that tangle, said the Commission, is "the racial attitude and behavior of white Americans toward black Americans."

White racial attitudes, the Commission found, are essentially responsible for the "explosive mixture" in our cities that has recently erupted into large-scale rioting. Three main ingredients of the mixture were identified:

(1) Great numbers of Negroes have been excluded from the benefits of economic progress through discrimination in employment and education and their enforced confinement in segregated housing and schools.

(2) The massive and growing concentration of impoverished Negroes in our major urban areas has greatly increased the burden on the already depleted resources of the cities and created a growing crisis of deteriorating facilities and services and unmet human needs.

(3) In the teeming racial ghettos, segregation and poverty have intersected to destroy opportunity and hope, to enforce failure, and to create bitterness and resentment against society in general and white society in particular.

The Commission found that other factors catalyzed the mixture, factors such as the frustrated hopes aroused by the successes of the civil rights movement; the climate of encouragement of violence arising out of white terrorism and violent black protest and rhetoric; and the frustrations of black political powerlessness and alienation from institutions of government and law. Thus catalyzed, relatively minor racial incidents—frequently involving the police—are sufficient to spark the mixture into an explosion of violence.

The Kerner Commission's analysis of the causes of urban riots in largely applicable to the phenomenon of radical black militancy. Radical black militancy, like the urban riots, is ultimately a response to conditions created by racial attitudes and behavior that have widely prevailed among the white majority since the days of slavery.

The reaction of many white Americans to the Kerner Commission Report, however, was to deny angrily that they were "racists," to point to friendships with individual Negroes, and ask if the Commission thought that it was "white racists" who were doing all the rioting. This response misconceives both the basic thrust of the Kerner Commission Report and the true nature of "white racism." That rather incendiary phrase should be understood as no more than a short-hand designation for a complex social condition, an enduring institutional and ideological legacy of white supremacy and Negro subordination, whose source is to be found only in the whole tragic history of race relations in this country. If we are to understand "white racism," we must understand this history in its three major phases—slavery, segregation and the ghetto.

(1) *The institution of slavery.*—Slavery was established in the New World almost immediately after its discovery by the nations of Europe. For the blacks who were subjected to slavery, the existing social systems of West Africa were interrupted, and new, traumatic ones were imposed. Tribal institutions and customs which prepared blacks to meet their needs and cope as adults in African societies were no longer useful or possible. A new kind of socialization was necessary in order to develop—not an adequate, competent participant in adult society—but rather a subhuman, dependent creature fully subservient to the master's needs.

Children born into the slave system were prepared from birth for a life of subservience. Nurture and physical care came from an adult—not in the interest of a family, kinship group or tribe—but in the interest of the master. Children were not destined to become elders, chiefs, warriors, or traders and to hold positions of respect and status within the tribe. Instead they were to become slaves, and the processes of their individual development were distorted by this unnatural end. Probably this is the reason why so many adult slaves cared so little for children—a fact which confounded slave owners and observers.

The adult slave was without power and without security. His legal status was that of a piece of property, without rights in court and without the protection of any institution. Completely subject to their masters' control, dispersed throughout a larger white culture, and unable to maintain the institutions of their previous societies (kinship ties, family organization, religion, government, courts, etc.), slaves were generally unable to run away en masse, to organize effective large-scale attacks against their oppressors, or even to turn inward on their own culture for psychological support.

Some slaves were able to run away to the Indians, to Canada or to "freedom" in the North. Most could not, however, but had instead to find ways of adjusting to the slavery environment. Some led a passive-aggressive existence in relationship to the white master—working as little as they could without being punished, feigning illness, sabotaging property and generally provoking the master. Some participated in the small, relatively unorganized insurrections that occurred occasionally during the slavery years. Others internalized their aggressions and engaged in self-destructive behavior and in violent acts against other blacks. Some found in Christianity a relationship to God and a place in a spiritual kingdom that enabled them to endure the sufferings of their life in this world. Still others adopted a life style which tried to copy, to the extent possible, the style of the white master. Common to all these adaptations, and shaping the form they took, was the overriding fact of the slave system.

The impact of slavery on white society was no less profound. Because of their profound belief that "all men are created equal" and that life, liberty and the pursuit of happiness are among man's "inalienable rights," whites could not rationalize the slave system simply on the basis of the economic need for manpower. If slavery was to be justified, it was necessary to believe that the Negro was inherently inferior, that he belonged to a lower order of man, that slavery was right on scientific and social, as well as economic, grounds. A large body of literature came into existence to prove these beliefs and the corollary belief in the natural superiority and supremacy of the white race. The ideology of white superiority and black inferiority was reinforced both by the destructive impact of slavery upon Negroes generally and by the institutional and cultural denial of individual Negro accomplishments in the face of overwhelming obstacles. For more than two centuries the institution of slavery studiously wove the strand of racism deep into the fabric of American life.

It is thus not surprising that the conditions of life in the United States were hardly better for free Negroes than for slaves. Some free Negroes achieved material success, a few even owned slaves themselves or had white indentured servants, but the vast majority knew only poverty and rejection by white society. Forbidden to settle in some areas, segregated in others, they were targets of prejudice and discrimination. In the South, they were denied freedom of movement, severely restricted in their choice of occupation, forbidden to associate with whites or with slaves, and in constant fear of being enslaved. In both North and South they were regularly the victims of mobs. In 1829, for example, white residents invaded Cincinnati's "Little Africa," killed Negroes, burned their property, and ultimately drove half the black population from the city.

(2) *Segregation in the aftermath of slavery.*—The violence of the Civil War tore the nation apart and succeeded in destroying the institution of slavery—long after France (1794) and England (1833) had abolished it in their overseas possessions in the New World. But the War proved incapable of rooting out the deeper structure of racism upon which slavery rested: that had been built up over too long a time and was too firmly embedded in American society, North as well as South. Indeed, as we have said, racism had become an integral part of the black man's experience in America: the large number of Negroes who could not or would not leave the plantation after slavery indicates the degree to which blacks had been absorbed into the master-slave relationship.

After the war, blacks were quickly, and often violently, closed out of the economic, political, and educational mainstream of American life. The program of Radical Congressional Reconstruction failed, for a variety of reasons, to provide blacks with a solid economic, political or social base and consequently failed as an adjustment tool. None of the organizational structures of the African culture remained to provide a basis for group stability and direction. Only remnants of previous African life-styles remained, greatly modified by the American experience and of little value in promoting adjustment in the post-slavery period. As a result of factors such as these, Negroes remained economically, socially and psychologically dependent on whites who retained almost complete control.

In some respects the condition of the Negro worsened after the war. Under the segregation system which rapidly developed (and which was ratified by a series of Supreme Court decisions culminating in the "separate but equal" doctrine embraced by the Court in 1896), control and authority over blacks were extended to all whites, most of whom were economically vulnerable and more in need of a psychological scapegoat than the wealthier slave-owning class. Whites outside the planter caste were more likely to act in an unjust, violent fashion toward blacks.

The first Ku Klux Klan, arising in 1865 and lasting until 1876, was a principal means of keeping the Negro in his place in the early postwar period. The Klan helped overthrow the Reconstruction governments of North Carolina, Tennessee, and Georgia, and was responsible, according to the findings of a Congressional investigation in 1871, for hangings, shootings, whippings, and mutilations numbering in the thousands. The commanding general of federal troops in Texas reported: "Murders of Negroes are so common as to render it impossible to keep accurate accounts of them." By 1877, when white governments had returned to power in all the Southern states, and Reconstruction had been abandoned, the Klan and its allies in the South had been so successful that the Negro was effectively eliminated from the political life of the South.

Still denied the opportunity for personal achievement and the resultant sense of adequacy and security which achievement brings, blacks made various adaptations to meet adequacy and security needs in a society in which they were now "free" but still rejected and abused. Religion was embraced more firmly. Many informal and formal Afro-American mutual support organizations developed after slavery, reflecting the need for black sharing and mutual support in a hostile society. Some blacks continued as employees of their former masters and in many cases identified strongly with whites. Some wandered about, disorganized and hopeless.

Under the segregation system's omnipresent threat of violence, black parents had to teach their children to avoid aggressive life-styles which might lead to disastrous conflicts with whites. Such socialization, similar to that under slavery, naturally led to the diminution or destruction of the capacity for exploration, learning and work in many Negroes. Inadequately socialized, many blacks were largely pleasure-oriented, responding to inadequately controlled sexual and aggressive drives by behavior that often resulted in violence and in conflict with the larger society. Such behavior was not viewed by whites as the natural product of a society which had failed to create the conditions for adequate social and psychological development among many blacks—instead it was viewed simply as "the way niggers are."

(3) *The rise of the urban ghetto.*—In 1910, 91 percent of the country's 9.8 million Negroes still lived in the South. During World War I large-scale movement of Negroes out of the rural South was stimulated when the industrial demands of the war created new jobs for unskilled workers in the North, while floods and boll weevils hurt farming in the South. The Depression temporarily slowed this migratory flow, but World War II set it in motion again. The migration proceeded along three major routes: north along the Atlantic Seaboard toward Washington, Baltimore, Philadelphia, New

94

York, Boston; north from the Mississippi to St. Louis, Chicago, Detroit, Milwaukee; west from Texas and Louisiana toward Los Angeles and San Francisco. While the total Negro population more than doubled from 1910 to 1966 (from 9.8 million to 21.5 million), the number living outside the South rose elevenfold (from 0.9 million to 9.7 million) and the number living in cities rose more than fivefold (from 2.7 million to 14.8 million).

The early pattern of Negro settlement within the Northern cities followed that of other immigrants; they converged on the older sections of the central-city because the lowest-cost housing was located there, because friends and relatives were likely to be living there, and because the older neighborhoods then often had good public transportation. Unlike other immigrants, however, the Negro remained—and remains today—largely confined in the original ghetto—still the prisoner of the American racial heritage.

In the light of our whole racial history, should we be surprised that, for the Negro, the great cities of the North have not been ports of entry into the mainstream of American life? Can we fail to see that the black ghetto is ultimately the product of slavery and segregation, that it is but the third great phase of the black man's bondage in America? The Report of the Kerner Commission has exhaustively described the conditions of the black ghetto and the manner of its formation. For our purposes we need only to illustrate a few of the many continuities which exist between life in the ghetto and the black experience under slavery-segregation.

● Race riots and violent racial conflict were a hallmark of the early-20th century Negro experience in northern cities, the Negroes invariably suffering most of the violence. In East St. Louis, Ill., a riot which claimed the lives of 39 Negroes and 9 whites erupted in 1917 against a background of fear by white workingmen that Negro labor was threatening their jobs. Other major riots by whites against blacks took place in 1917 in Chester, Pa., and Philadelphia. In 1919 there were riots in Washington (D.C.), Omaha, Charleston, Longview (Tex.), Knoxville, and Chicago. In Chicago between July 1917 and March 1921, 58 Negro houses were bombed, and recreational and residential areas were frequent sites of violent racial conflict. Negro soldiers returning home from service in World War I in segregated combat units were mobbed for attempting to use facilities open to white soldiers.

● Many Negro families in the ghettos attained incomes,

living standards and cultural levels matching those of whites who upgraded themselves out of ethnic neighborhoods, but they still remained in predominantly black neighborhoods because they were effectively excluded from white residential areas. Able to escape poverty, they were unable to escape the ghetto—and their confinement rendered their accomplishments less visible to the larger society which continued to embrace the old myth of innate Negro inferiority. More often, however, the pervasive discrimination in employment, education and housing rendered the escape from poverty even within the ghetto all but impossible.

● Many ghetto blacks responded to their condition of oppression with self-hatred and low self-esteem. These traits in turn gave rise to passive, self-destructive modes of behavior such as excessive use of alcohol and narcotics, violent assault on a friend over a dime or a bottle of wine, poor impulse control generally, low aspiration levels, and high rates of family conflict. Such patterns of behavior are reflected in the far higher Negro arrest rates for violent crime: urban arrest rates of Negroes for robbery are 16 times higher than white rates and for homicide they are 17 times higher.

● Another highly destructive pattern begun under slavery continued under conditions of unemployment in the urban ghetto: the Negro male often played only a marginal role in his family and found few cultural or psychological rewards in family life. Often the Negro father abandoned his home because he felt useless to his family, the absence of the father then condemning the sons to repeat the pattern. Today only three-fifths of all Negro children in central cities live with both parents, and in families with incomes under $4000 only one quarter of the Negro children live with both parents.

DIRECT CAUSES OF RADICAL BLACK MILITANCY

To say that an enduring structure of white racial attitudes and behavior is ultimately responsible for the phenomenon of radical black militancy is only to identify a first cause, an underlying matrix. We must also look to more direct causes in order to understand why radical black militancy has emerged at this particular point in our history. Four different kinds of direct causes can be identified, each inextricably interwoven with all the others and with the underlying social matrix created by slavery, segregation and the ghetto:

(1) the political cause: the frustrations of the civil rights movement;
(2) the ideological cause: the rise of an "anti-colonial" dogma;

(3) the economic cause: the widening gap between white and black material advancement;

(4) the psychological cause: the breaking of the Negro-white "dependency bond."

(1) *The political cause.*—From the decline of Marcus Garvey's separatist philosophy in the 1920's until quite recently, the dominant thrust of black protest was toward political, social, economic and cultural inclusion into American institutions on a basis of full equality. Always a powerful theme in American black militancy, these aims found their maximum expression in the civil rights movement of the 1950's and early 1960's.

For the civil rights movement, the years before 1955 were filled largely with efforts at legal reform, with the NAACP, especially, carrying case after case to successful litigation in the federal courts. There was a considerable gap, however, between the belief of the NAACP and other groups that major political changes were in sight and the reality of the slow pace of change even in the more advanced areas of the South. The gap was even greater between the conservative tactics and middle-class orientation of the established civil-rights organizations and the situation of the black ghetto masses in the North.

Since the NAACP, the Urban League, and other established groups continued to operate as before, new tactics and new leaders arose to fill these gaps. In 1955, Mrs. Rosa Parks of Montgomery, Ala., refused to give up her bus seat to a white man, and a successful boycott of the bus system materialized, led by a local minister, the Reverend Martin Luther King, Jr. Around the same time, with less publicity, another kind of organization with another kind of leadership was swiftly coming into its own in the northern ghettos: Elijah Muhammed and the Nation of Islam represented those segments of the black community that no one else, at the moment, seemed to be representing—the northern, urban, lower classes. It was this strange sect which would produce the man who was destined to rise from a petty criminal to a "black shining prince" and who would far overshadow Dr. King in influence among the new generation of black militants: Malcolm X.

Neither the direct-action, assimilationist approach of King nor the separatist, nationalist approach of the Black Muslims were new. Rather, they were both traditional strategies of black protest which had been adopted in the past in response

to specific situations. Direct action was used by the abolition-
ists prior to the Civil War, by left-wing organizers in the
ghetto in the 1930's, and by CORE in the early 1940's. It had
been threatened by A. Phillip Randolph in his march on
Washington in 1941, but called off when President Roosevelt
agreed to establish a Federal Fair Employment Practices
Commission. The roots of black separatism are equally deep,
reaching back beyond Marcus Garvey in the 1920's to Martin Delaney, a Harvard-educated Negro physician and novel-
ist who in the 1850's promoted the migration of American
Negroes to Africa, as philanthropist and ship-owner Paul
Cuffee had some forty years earlier.

The move to direct action in the south brought civil rights
protest out of the courts and into the streets, bus terminals,
restaurants, and voting booths. Nevertheless, it remained
deeply linked to the American political process and represented an abiding faith in the power of the federal government and in the moral capacity of white Americans, both
northern and southern. It operated, for the most part, on the
implicit premise that racism was a localized, essentially southern malignancy within a relatively healthy political and social
order; it was a move to force American morality and American institutions to cure the last symptoms of the diseased
member of the body politic.

Activists in SNCC, CORE and other civil rights organizations met with greater and more violent resistance as direct-
action continued during the sixties. Freedom Riders were
beaten by mobs in Montgomery; demonstrators were hosed,
clubbed and cattle-prodded in Birmingham and Selma. In
many parts of the South, civil right workers, black and white,
were victimized by local officials as well as by night-riders
and angry crowds. At the same time, the problems of white
violence were compounded by the intransigence of some
southern courts and juries, and by political constraints on the
federal government that prevented it from moving decisively
toward a radical alteration of the situation faced by the civil
rights activists. Deeply affecting the whole struggle were the
continuing unlawful resistance to integration by some southern governors such as Faubus, Barnett and Wallace, and the
relentless political pressure applied by powerful segregationists such as Senator Eastland.

The Mississippi Freedom Summer of 1964 was a hybrid
phenomenon, less of a moral confrontation than Birmingham the year before, and more of a new kind of power play.
Its sponsor was "COFO," the Council of Federated Organiza-

tions, a loose ad hoc consortium funded by established groups such as the NAACP, CORE, SCLC, and the National Council of Churches, but given its cutting edge by the leaders of SNCC. Masterminded by a SNCC staff disillusioned by white reprisals and violence against earlier voter registration drives, the COFO Project was presented as a massive effort to get voter registration off the ground with the aid of large numbers of vacationing white college students. But COFO's voter registration goal turned out to be a cover for a more ambitious and aggressive SNCC strategy: to provoke massive federal intervention in Mississippi amounting to an occupation and a "second effort at Reconstruction."

The Mississippi summer was an extraordinary one for many of the more than 2,000 participants from all over the United States. Three young men were murdered by a white conspiracy, and many others saw at firsthand the ugly face of racial repression. The project culminated, not with a second Reconstruction, but with the Mississippi Freedom Democratic Party's failure to get its delegation seated at the 1964 Democratic national convention (although two at-large seats were offered and special efforts were promised to open state parties to Negroes during the next four years). This symbolic, highly emotional defeat climaxed a growing disillusionment with "white liberals" among young blacks, and perhaps more than any other single event destroyed the faith of civil rights activists in the ability of "the system" to purge itself of racism.

By the middle of the decade, then, many militant Negro members of SNCC and CORE began to turn away from American society and the "middle-class way of life." Despite the passage of the Civil Rights Act of 1964 and the Voting Rights Act of 1965, they became deeply cynical about the tradition of American liberal reform. They talked more and more of "revolutionary" changes in the social structure, and of retaliatory violence, and they increasingly rejected white assistance. The new militants insisted that Negro power alone could compel the white "ruling class" to make concessions. Yet, at this time, they also spoke of an alliance of Negroes and unorganized lower-class whites to overthrow the "power structure" of capitalists, politicians and bureaucratic labor leaders whom they accused of exploiting the poor of both races while dividing them through an appeal to race prejudice.

The increased criticism of liberals, white intellectuals, and federal bureaucracies was part of a broader turn to a renewed critique of the situation of blacks in the North. To a

99

large extent, and despite such evidence as the Harlem uprisings of 1935 and 1943, most white northerners had congratulated themselves on the quality of their "treatment" of the Negro vis-a-vis that of the South. But direct action by civil rights leaders in Northern cities, largely in the form of street demonstrations, had failed to make any substantial impact on the problems of separate and inferior schools, slum housing, and police hostility, although it had succeeded in lowering some barriers to Negro employment.

With the explosion of Harlem and several other northern cities in 1964, attention among black activist leaders was drawn sharply to the problem of institutional racism in the North, and this shift of focus was accelerated by the Watts riot the following year. In a real sense, the outbreak of riots not only surprised liberal whites, but most established black civil rights leaders as well. While undermining the moral credibility of liberal northerners as to the nature of the racial situation in the North, the riots also left most civil rights leaders without a vocabulary with which to express the deeper emotions of the northern ghettos. There was a sense among many young Negroes that established civil rights leaders could not get results from the white majority, that they could not speak to the kinds of issues raised by the riots, and that a wide gulf separated those leaders—mostly of middle-class background—from the black urban masses.

In this setting the rhetoric of "Black Power" developed, and was brought dramatically to the nation's attention on the Meredith march from Memphis to Jackson in June 1966. SNCC replaced its non-violent leader John Lewis with Stokely Carmichael, and CORE elected Floyd McKissick, who refused to denounce the Watts riot of the previous year. Under Carmichael SNCC formally and deliberately disassociated itself from the civil rights movement's traditional commitment to nonviolence and took up a position on the leftward militant fringe. In 1967, while Rap Brown made incendiary speeches around the country, Carmichael traveled to Havana, Hanoi, and Moscow, popularizing a new black revolutionary ideology. The extravagant speeches and behavior of Carmichael and Brown amplified the psychological effect of the 1967 riots on both blacks and whites, while the riots themselves—and especially the then exaggerated reports of organized urban welfare—lent credibility to their rhetoric.

Thus, with the frustration of the civil rights movement and the outbreak of the riots, younger and more militant black leaders and organizations emerged to represent the interests of the Northern urban lower classes, and the older representatives of the civil rights movement were required to redefine their programs and techniques to accommodate these new forms of militancy. The impact of the riots on young Negroes and on established black leaders was graphically depicted in the testimony before the Violence Commission of Sterling Tucker, Director of Field Services of the National Urban League:

> I was standing with some young, angry men not far from some blazing buildings. They were talking to me about their feelings. They talked out of anger, but they talked with respect.
> "Mr. Tucker," one of them said to me, "you're a big and important man in this town. You're always in the newspaper and we know that you're fighting hard to bring about some changes in the conditions the brother faces. But who listens, Mr. Tucker, who listens? Why, with one match I can bring about more change tonight than with all the talking you can ever do."
> Now I know that isn't true and you know that isn't true. It just isn't that simple. But the fact that we know that doesn't really count for much. The brother on the street believes what he says, and there are some who are not afraid to die, believing what they say.

When black activists came to interpret the urban riots as purposeful rebellions, and to advocate violence as one technique for achieving black dignity and well being, the phenomenon of radical black militancy had become a part of the troubled American racial scene.

(2) *The ideological cause.*—By the mid-1960's, then, many militant black leaders had become convinced that the aims and methods of the civil rights movement were no longer viable. The failures of the white majority to meet black expectations, the fact of the urban riots, and the increasing American involvement in Vietnam all served to catalyze a fundamental transformation in militant black perceptions of the place of the Negro in American society. This transformation resulted in what can be called an "anti-colonial ideology," which is aptly expressed by a spokesman of the Black Panther Party as follows:

> We start with the basic definition: that black people in America are a colonized people in every sense of the term and that white America is an organized imperialist force holding black people in colonial bondage.

101

Unique when expressed by Malcolm X in 1964, the anti-colonial perspective now provides many miltant blacks with a structured world view—and, in the case of the radicals, with a rationalization for violence. Many articulate black militant spokesmen now see the final hope of black Americans in identification with the revolutionary struggles of the Third World. Even moderate leaders focus attention on the discrepancy between the massive commitment of American resources abroad and the lack of a decisive commitment to cure the social ills stemming from racism at home. Martin Luther King wondered, for example, why "we were taking the black young men who had been crippled by our poverty and sending them 8,000 miles away to guarantee liberties in Southeast Asia which they had not found in Southwest Georgia or East Harlem."

Black militants in America have in the past looked to Africa for recognition of common origins and culture, and the influence has been reciprocal. W.E.B. DuBois, one of the founders of the NAACP in 1909–10, saw that the "problem of the color line" was international in scope, and was a guiding force behind the movement for Pan-African unity. Marcus Garvey, founder in 1914 of the Universal Negro Improvement Association, and other American and West Indian black nationalists have stimulated the development of African nationalism and informed the intellectual development of some of its leaders.

Today the successful revolt against colonialism in Africa and other non-white regions has created a heightened sense of the international character of racial conflict and has provided the impetus for the growth of an anti-colonial ideology among American black militants. The revolt against colonialism has altered the structure of political power in the world, demonstrating to black militants in America that peoples supposed to be culturally and technologically "backward" can emerge victorious in struggles with ostensibly superior powers. "Two-thirds of the human population today," wrote Malcom X, "is telling the one-third minority white men, 'Get out.' And the white man is leaving." With the disintegration of white rule in Africa and the rise of autonomous black nations, political autonomy for Negroes in America—ranging from traditional democratic concepts of community control to notions of geographic separatism—has received a new impetus—and a new ideological component.

The success of the movements for political independence in the colonial countries required a recognition that the plight of the "native" was a political problem, and that political action was the most effective vehicle of major social change. Early nationalist movements in Africa, therefore, sought ideologically to turn nearly every aspect of life into a political issue. This was true, for example, of the area of culture, whose political importance lay in the fact that "natives," as people without history or culture, were also seen as people without political claims of their own, and therefore as people to be dealt with from above—benevolently or otherwise.

Political ideology also worked its transforming magic on violence. Through the same process of "politicization," instances of black resistance in history were ideologically redefined as precursors of contemporary political struggles. Native crime was redefined as "pre-revolutionary" activity. Instances of rebellion were sought in the past and their significance amplified.

This process extended to the creation of a whole new world view. History was viewed as an arena of struggle between colonial power and native population, with heavy emphasis on the intrinsically violent character of colonial domination and its supposedly irrevocable hostility to the interests of non-whites. Colonialism was seen as dependent on the routinization of violence, both physical and psychological, against the native. Consequently, revolutionary violence against the colonial regime was not only necessary, but justifiable, on both political and psychological grounds. Colonialism, wrote Franz Fanon, "is violence in its natural state, and it will only yield when confronted with greater violence." Further, he said, "at the level of individuals, violence is a cleansing force. It frees the native from his inferiority complex, and from his despair and inaction; it makes him fearless and restores self-respect."

Under the influence of radical militant propagandists such as Stokely Carmichael, similar ideological developments have taken place among some blacks in America. The anti-colonial ideology has enabled black radicals to see urban riots as the harbingers of revolution and to see in urban violence the means of destroying white domination and achieving black dignity. If, as the Panthers would have it, "White America is an organized imperialist force holding black people in colonial bondage" then it follows that violence against the police and other agents or symbols of authority is not crime but heroism, not merely an unlawful act but a revolutionary gesture against an illegitimate government.

This poisonous ideology has found fertile soil in the black

ghettoes of America. Its roots do not yet, perhaps, go very deep, and the commitment to organized violence is found only among a relatively small group of black radicals. Most Negro leaders continue to believe that change can come in this country through legitimate, orderly political processes, and, indeed, that this is the only way it will come. But the anti-colonial ideology has the potential for further growth, and it will grow to the extent that the white majority can successfully be cast by radical propagandists in the role of oppressors of the black majority.

(3) *The economic cause.*—History teaches us that men's frustration over the material circumstances of their lives is a frequent cause of collective violence. The more intense and widespread the discontent is, the more intense and widespread the violence is likely to be. Of course, the occurrence, extent and form of economically motivated violence are strongly influenced by other factors: the degree of legitimacy which the discontented group accords to the existing social and political order; the effectiveness of agencies of direct social control such as the police; the extent to which political institutions afford peaceful alternatives to violence; and many other factors. But the economic motive, the frustrated desire for improved living conditions, has undeniably been one important cause of violence in many periods of man's history.

Has this cause been operative in the rise of radical black militancy? The answer is clearly yes. A dominant theme of black protest in the United States has always been the improvement of the material circumstances of the Negro, and this goal has proved most frustratingly unobtainable precisely in the cradle of radical black militancy: the northern urban ghettoes.

The conditions of life in the racial ghetto have been exhaustively examined elsewhere, particularly by the Kerner Commission. It is unnecessary for our purposes to repeat these findings again in detail, since even a few of the facts of life in the ghetto are enough to suggest the level of frustration that prevails there:

● Unemployment rates for Negroes are double those for whites. In the ghettoes in 1966 the unemployment rate was 9.3 percent overall and even higher for blacks. Moreover, in these urban poverty areas two and one-half times the number unemployed were *under*employed: part-time workers looking for full-time jobs, full-time workers earning less than $3,000 per year, or dropouts from the labor force. Among nonwhite teenagers—a group well represented both in riots and in radical black militant activities—the unemployment rate in 1967 in poverty neighborhoods was approximately 30 percent.

● Blacks own and operate less than one percent of the nearly 5 million private businesses in the country—typically small, marginal retail and service firms. Twenty-odd banks out of a national total of 14,000 are black-owned; 7 automobile dealerships out of 30,000; fewer than 8,000 construction contractors out of a total of 500,000. In Washington, D.C., blacks comprise two-thirds of the population but own less than 7 percent of the business. Ninety-eight percent of all black income is spent outside the black community.

● In the metropolitan northeast, Negro students start school with slightly lower scores than whites on standard achievement tests, by sixth grade they are 1.6 grades behind the white students, and by 12th grade, they are 3.3 grades behind. Many Negroes—between one-third and one-half among male students—fail to finish high school, the Negro drop-out rate being more than three times the white rate.

● In 1965 a black woman was four times as likely to die in childbirth as a white woman; the black child was three times as likely to die in infancy as the white child. White people on the average lived 7 years longer than black people.

● In 1966 the national illegitimacy rate among non-white women was 26 percent; in many large city ghettoes it is over 50 percent: in Harlem 80 percent of the firstborn are illegitimate. In 1966 over 50 percent of the known narcotics addicts were Negroes. Rates of juvenile delinquency, violent crime, venereal disease, and dependency on public assistance are many times higher in disadvantaged Negro areas than in other parts of large cities.

In the face of undisputed evidence of the disadvantaged condition of blacks in the urban ghettoes, some persons tend to minimize the importance of deprivation as a cause of riots and of radical black militancy. Two observations are commonly offered in support of this point of view. First, it is pointed out that Negroes have long suffered from frustratingly inferior living conditions, yet they have never before resorted to collective violence of the magnitude that has occurred in the last five years. Secondly, it is urged that while the lot of the Negro may be an unsatisfactory one, nonetheless it has been continually improving, particularly during the precise period when the greatest violence has occurred. In support of this second point, the following facts can be offered.

105

• The non-white unemployment rates in 1966 and 1967 was the lowest since the Korean War, and in 1968 the black unemployment rate in poverty neighborhoods had dramatically declined by more than 50 percent in comparison with the 1966 figure.

• The seven black-owned automobile dealerships (out of a total of 30,000) are seven times as many as there were 2 years ago. New black-owned banks are in formation in seven cities, and one recent study showed that in certain areas of Harlem, black business ownership has risen to 58 percent. Between 1960 and 1967 there was a 47 percent increase in the number of blacks in white-collar positions, craftsmen and operatives—the better jobs—compared to a 16 percent increase in the number of whites in such jobs.

• The percentage of non-white persons enrolled in school is higher in each age group than it was in 1960. In central cities, the median years of school completed by Negroes 25 to 29 years of age has increased by about one year, and the proportion of this group completing high school has risen from 43 percent in 1960 to 61 percent in 1968.

• The non-white maternity mortality rate in 1965 was 20 percent less than what it was in 1960 and less than one-ninth of what it was in 1940. The proportion of non-white households situated in housing that either is dilapidated or lacks basic plumbing has decreased sharply since 1960 in all areas, especially in large cities. Although the *number* of non-white families living in poverty areas in large cities has been fairly constant between 1960 and 1966, of the total number of non-white families the *percentage* living in such areas has declined sharply since 1960.

One fatal difficulty, however, undermines most of this seemingly plausible case against the proposition that the disadvantaged condition of the Negro has been a significant cause of ghetto violence. That is the failure to pay adequate attention to the *comparative* economic condition of whites and Negroes, and to make this comparison over a longer period of time than the last few years. The lesson of history is not that poverty as such causes violence, but rather that frustrations arising out of poverty can cause violence. There may often be poverty but no frustration: the frustration is present only when the disadvantaged person expects, or feels entitled to, better material circumstances than those he is living under. Increasingly, the black man in America has come to expect living conditions on a par with those of the white man and has come to believe that he is entitled to such equality.

These expectations that the economic gap between black

and white will be closed have stemmed in part from the Negro's experience of economic progress, and the frustration has occurred because in the late 1950's and the early 1960's the gap between black and white stopped narrowing and in some respects began to widen.

One basic measure of the gap between black and white is median family income. Figure 1 plots median family income (total, white, and Negro) for the years 1950 to 1967. Examination of this Figure reveals that while median Negro family income has risen steadily since 1950, the dollar gap between white and Negro family income has also steadily increased in nearly every year.

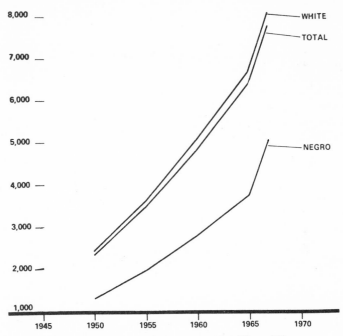

Figure 1.—Median family income—total, white and Negro.

Figure 2 expresses median Negro family income as a percentage of median white family income. It indicates no significant Negro progress in closing the gap between the years 1950 and 1965—but it does show a heartening upsurge between 1965 and 1967.

In Figure 3 a further refinement of this analysis is introduced. In that Figure the average family income for the total population and for the non-white population has been divided

107

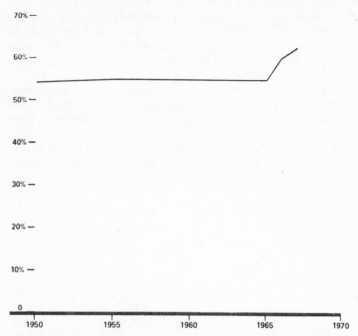

Figure 2.—Median Negro family income as a percentage of white family income, 1950–1967.

by the average years of schooling for each group, and the resulting figure for the non-white population has then been expressed as a percentage of the resulting figure for the total population. This percentage can be considered an "index of non-white economic satisfaction": if blacks and whites with the same amount of education were earning the same amount of income, the index would be 100 percent and blacks would be as satisfied economically as whites. Figure 3 shows that this is not the case, that the progress toward closing the gap between white and black stopped in the early 1950's, and that the relative economic position of the Negro worsened over the next 10 years. Only in the last few years has the gap begun to close again, and still the index of non-white economic satisfaction is below its high point in the early 1950's.

The analysis in these three figures is confirmed by other economic and social indicators. Thus, for example, although the non-white unemployment rate in 1966 and 1967 was the lowest since the Korean War, the ratio of non-white to white unemployment remained roughly the same: two to one. Al-

108

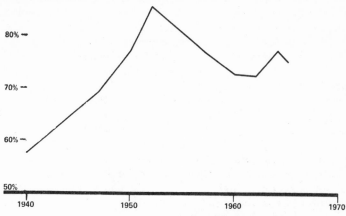

Figure 3.—Index of non-white economic satisfaction, 1940–1967.

though the school enrollment gap has narrowed for kinder-
garteners and 16- and 17-year-olds, it has widened for persons in their late teens and early 20's, and proportionately
more whites are going on to higher education. (Obviously, if
proportionately higher percentages of non-white students do
not continue on to college and graduate school, the relative
gains of Negroes in professional and skilled jobs of the past
decade may soon level off.) In 1940 the illegitimacy rate
among non-white women was 17 percent; in 1966 it had
risen to 26 percent. Between 1950 and 1966 the percentage
of fatherless families among Negroes rose by one-third while
the percentage of fatherless families among whites remained
substantially constant.

What these facts all add up to is that after a period of
black progress and rising expectations following the Second
World War, a slackening of progress occurred and, by many
indicators, the relative economic position of the Negro deteriorated over the next 10 years. From defeated expectations of progress, and an unsatisfactory condition to start
with, frustration arises. It was this frustration which has been
one important cause both of the recent ghetto riots and of
the rising violence of radical black militancy.

(4) *The psychological cause.*—All men are born with
drives and needs which conflict with those of other human
beings. In all societies, parents, caretakers and authority
figures of one kind or another are charged with the responsi-

109

bility of meeting the child's basic needs and helping the young convert their drive energy into skills and patterns of behavior which will help them cope with the demands of an adult society. This is the process of "socialization." Without satisfactory socialization, these energies may result in a variety of troublesome forms of personal behavior, including self-destructive action and unwarranted conflict and violence against people and property.

When, however, the young are adequately developed and socialized and are able to cope as adults, they enjoy a sense of adequacy and security. Being able to cope and as a result receiving the respect and acceptance of significant peers is the primary way an individual meets basic and man-made needs. When members of a society experience satisfactory patterns of socialization, a high level of peace and stability can exist in families and the society without the use of physical force to control individuals or groups.

The basic pattern of socialization running through the black man's history in America has been the destructive, unsatisfactory relationship of dependency and subordination vis-a-vis the white man. In slavery the master functioned as a father, ruler and god. The condition of total power in the master and total powerlessness in the slave, with the master providing and regulating the slave's most basic needs, resulted in an intense emotional bond between the black slave and the white master. Over time the values of the white master and of the slavery system were often internalized by the slaves and transmitted from generation to generation under the continuing influence of the slavery system. The myth of Negro inferiority and white supremacy was widely and deeply ingrained into black man and white man alike.

Under segregation and in the ghetto the same pattern prevailed, although in a constantly weakening form. The clear implication of segregation was still that whites were superior and Negroes inferior, that the white man was the father and the Negro, the "boy." But other social forces were now unleashed: even under the segregation system black dependency on white power was sharply decreased in comparison with slavery, and in the teeming racial ghettoes of the Northern cities the old relationship of dependency became attenuated in the extreme.

The widening "crack" in the pattern of forced dependency was the beginning of the development of a positive black group identity. Many blacks, as preachers, teachers, physicians, lawyers and other professional service people, began to develop skills which gave them a sense of adequacy and the capacity to cope. In the South in particular, successful business communities developed. Black youngsters were able to identify with people like themselves in positions of leadership and respect. Obviously the level of self-respect was limited by the implications of a segregated system, but nonetheless it was of tremendous value in enhancing black self-esteem. More among the black masses were better able to earn enough money to take care of their families and as a result were able to develop a sense of personal adequacy. Involvement in two world wars and achievement in entertainment, athletics and other areas, together with the myriad effects of migration to Northern cities, began to change the black American's image of himself. A more positive sense of self began to replace the previous negative self-contempt.

Black adequacy and competence is now built on more than white approval. A significant number of black parents no longer teach their children to accept white authority right or wrong. On the other hand, many whites, now economically more secure and better educated, no longer need or approve of the scapegoating of blacks. The white majority is increasingly transcending the limits of the old racial myths of America. In short, the tie that bound—the old socialization pattern of black social, economic and psychological dependence on a dominating, often oppressive white community—is now breaking decisively for the first time in American history.

With the destruction of the old socialization pattern and the breaking of the dependency bond have come expected responses, some constructive, some destructive. The painful social process is in some ways analogous to the difficult period of adolescence in the individual when the achievement of adult independence often seems to the youth to require a destructive rejection, not merely a quiet putting away, of childish things. Many militant blacks who are now seeking a positive cultural identity and a new pattern of black socialization also experience a "black rage" against whites who seem to block this development by their unwillingness to "get off the back" of the striving black man. In the case of the black radicals, this rage is expressed in aggressive violence against the newly vulnerable symbols of white authority such as the police.

The breaking of the dependency bond, acceptance of blackness as a positive value, and a sense of outrage is an energizing, explosive set of psychological developments for

111

the rising generation of militant blacks. The black American often experiences intense and ambivalent feelings as a result and is confronted with numerous questions and conflicts. Should he attempt to become a part of the mainstream of his society—now changing but once so abusive and rejecting—or is he obliged to retaliate or reject it? Does manhood require retaliation, rejection or even violence? Can he trust what he sees as a white America which has never before demonstrated itself trustworthy with regard to recognizing and protecting the human rights of black Americans?

The new feeling among blacks sometimes results in a loss of self-control after "trigger incidents" (reflecting the old pattern of white superiority and black helplessness) with attendant burning of property and other acts of violence. With a temporary breakdown in personal control, some blacks loot and plunder the "symbolic enemy." This reaction is not one that is found only among a small "riff-raff" who are sometimes thought to be responsible for urban riots. Studies of participation in the 1967 riots have found that (1) a substantial minority, ranging from 10 to 20 percent, participated in the riots; (2) one-half to three-quarters of the arrestees were employed in semi-skilled or skilled occupations, three-fourths were employed, and three-tenths to six-tenths were born outside the South; and (3) individuals between the ages of 15 and 34 and especially those between the ages of 15 and 24 are most likely to participate in riots.

In the one-to-one black-and-white relationship where mutual respect exists and where interaction occurs on a personal rather than symbolic level, constructive interaction between the races is less difficult, perhaps more so than ever before. It is in his abstract role as the symbolic enemy that the white man is anathema to some radical black militants. Disturbingly, this symbolic perception of whites has filtered down to youngsters, sometimes as young as three or four years of age. Just as young members of the Klan and other children of the "white ghetto" are taught that it is permissible to abuse blacks, some young blacks are now being taught that it is permissible to abuse whites—in particular, white policemen (or "pigs" in radical argot).

The energy released by America's rejection of the old racial pattern and the development of a positive group concept among blacks is profound. If channeled, it can be a powerful force for black community development, pride and constructive change within the present social system. But if it is to be channeled and if new, healthy patterns of socializa-

112

tion among blacks are to replace the old pattern of white superiority and black subordination, then it must be clear to blacks that support of the society's institutions and peaceful participation in them is in the interest of justice for the black masses.

Constructive attitudinal and economic changes have been made. In many places, members of the white majority have shown an unprecedented interest in facilitating black entrance into the mainstream of American life. The interaction is establishing new and more healthy ground rules for black-and-white relations. But often the complex factors related to emergence from a dependent, despised position to full participation in the society are often neither well understood nor subject to control in the short run. Thus the black man's passage to full dignity and well-being in America has been, and will continue to be, marred by violence and destruction as well as by constructive action and positive social change.

RESPONSES TO RADICAL BLACK MILITANCY

What are the principles which should guide the nation in dealing with the problem of radical black militancy? What are the policy implications of our analysis of the nature and causes of this phenomenon?

First: because radical black militancy is a highly complex phenomenon, with many different causes, no unbalanced, one-dimensional solution is possible—whether it be a program of intensified law enforcement or a program of expanded social reform.

Our analysis of radical black militancy has been an effort both to see this phenomenon in the perspective of the larger militant movement and to uncover the different kinds of factors which have operated to produce a commitment to illegal violence on the part of a small but significant element in the black community. We have seen that the radicals' destructive notions of "self-defense" or guerrilla warfare are often interwoven with constructive ideas in the areas of politics and culture. We have seen that in the rise of radical black militancy there has been a strong political factor—the new black radical leaders who have emerged following the failure of the society to respond adequately to the civil rights movement in the mid-1960's; there has been an ideological factor—the spread of revolutionary "anticolonial" propaganda; there has been an economic factor—the frustration bred

113

by living conditions in the racial ghettoes; there has been a psychological factor—the violent emotions unleashed as blacks break out of their dependent position. Moreover, underlying all these elements has been the historic institutional legacy of white supremacy and black subordination which has decisively shaped the Negro experience in America, including the recent emergence of a virulent radical black militancy.

In the face of complexities of this magnitude, it is impossible to believe that any one-dimensional package of solutions can effectively meet the problem of radical black violence. Improved law enforcement can undoubtedly deter and apprehend some radicals who engage in illegal violence—but the policeman and the judge have little power to check the spread of an ideology, to improve economic conditions or to alleviate psychological pressures. Vigorous efforts to secure the political rights of Negroes and accelerated social reforms in employment, education and housing can undoubtedly open the doors of opportunity and constructive citizenship for increasing numbers of blacks who might otherwise be tempted to violence—but in the short run incendiary leaders, violent ideologies and black rage can prove dismayingly unresponsive to well-meaning programs of social and political reform. Radical black militancy is not a one-sided problem—and it does not admit of one-sided solutions.

Second: because radical black militancy is, like urban rioting, a phenomenon deeply rooted in the enduring legacy of white supremacy and Negro subordination, we must continue and intensify our national commitment to secure the full and equal inclusion of black citizens into all aspects of American life.

In order for there to be a remission in the cancerous growth of black violence, we must have unprecedented national action in support of the goal of black dignity and equality. Today's violent racial outbursts and race hatred are the outgrowth of fundamental attitudes, customs and institutions—both white and black—that have worked their way into our society for centuries. Today we reap what we have sown. We need action—in the words of the Kerner Commission, "compassionate, massive and sustained, backed by the will and resources of the most powerful and richest nation on this earth"—to create quickly, as a nation, what we as a nation have destroyed through centuries of slavery and segre-

114

gation: the necessary preconditions for equal black participation in American life.

The movement to secure the inclusion of black citizens in all aspects of American life must be continued and intensified. In particular, obstacles must be removed which block the opportunities for duly elected—rather than self-appointed —black leaders to enter into the political process and to seek to advance the interests of their constituencies. The demand of local black communities for greater control over decisions that affect them and for "self-determination" is not inconsistent with the fundamental goal of inclusion. Rather, this demand is consistent with the historic commitment of the United States to democratic, local decision-making, as well as with the realities of the process by which other minority groups have made their way into the mainstream of American life. Unless the political rights of the "inner city" are respected and new local government structures are found under which these rights can be exercised, then radical black militancy will continue to attract more and more Negroes at the expense of the goal of peaceful inclusion of black and white in a single society functioning according to universally accepted political processes.

Third: because radical black militancy is a powerful ideological force among Negroes in the lower socio-economic brackets, the efforts which must be made to control the violence of black radicals must also involve attention to the effect of such efforts on the legitimacy of the existing social order.

The radical black militant who attacks a policeman or bombs a college building is not simply a common criminal. He is indeed a criminal, but he is different from the burglar, the robber or the rapist. He is acting out of a profound alienation from society. He believes that the existing social and political order in America is not legitimate and that black people in America are being held in "colonial bondage" by "an organized imperialist force." Thus he is able to interpret his act of violence not as a crime but as a revolutionary (or "pre-revolutionary") act. As an isolated occurrence, this distorted interpretation would not be significant— but the interpretation is sustained by an articulated ideology that is today competing with traditional American values for the minds and hearts of the rising generation of black ghetto residents.

115

Whenever the police illegally harass a radical black militant leader, whenever the courts fail to accord such a person equal justice under law, whenever political leaders advocate indiscriminate suppression of all expressions of discontent, then the anti-colonial ideology gains new adherents: new proof appears to have been given that the social order in the United States is inherently and unalterably oppressive of the black race. On the other hand, when leaders of undoubted goodwill and decency vacillate in the condemnation and control of unlawful black violence because of the grievances underlying it, or when responsible authorities minimize or conceal the seriousness of the violent crime problem among ghetto Negroes so as not to be "racists," then such leaders seem to admit that the social order is so burdened with an ineradicable "guilt" as to be almost unworthy of preservation: this too feeds revolutionary violence. To deal effectively with the developing ideology of radical black militancy, we shall have to have able and effective leaders, skilled in the practice of statecraft, who will energetically strengthen, and not impair, the legitimacy of the institutions for whose preservation and improvement they are responsible.

Fourth: because radical black militancy is but one highly visible aspect of our total racial problem, uncommon courage and compassion will be required of the American people if the necessary steps toward solution are to be taken.

America's racial problem, of which radical black militancy is but one highly visible aspect, is grave and deep. It may be, however, that today we as a nation understand for the first time the full, terrible dimensions of this problem and what it has done to our people, both black and white. Perhaps we realize that its solution will require far more of us than merely to recover old values or to improve on old techniques. Perhaps we now see that racial peace and justice will require us, white and black alike, in fact to transcend our whole history—to create, often painfully, new institutions, new customs, new attitudes, in which the old self-validating judgment of white supremacy and black inferiority will be finally superseded.

Uncommon courage and compassion will be required from all our people if this challenge is to be met. We must all do what is right because it is right—not in the vain hope that it will quickly put an end to violence. A nation does not easily find its way out of a problem of this magnitude: we shall

116

have to have the courage and the compassion to try and fail and try again, to see it through, to hold together, until we finally become, for the first time, one society, black and white, together and equal.

SOURCE NOTE

This chapter is an effort at synthesis and evaluation of materials on contemporary racial violence contained in the reports of other Task Forces of this Commission and in the Report of the Kerner Commission; it is not based to any significant degree on original research by the Task Force on Law and Law Enforcement. The principal sources are: Graham and Gurr, *Violence in America, Historical and Comparative Perspectives,* Report of Task Force on Historical and Comparative Perspectives on Violence in America, Ch. 11—"The Dynamics of Black and White Violence" (Comer), Ch. 9—"Black Violence in the 20th Century; A Study in Rhetoric and Retaliation" (Meier and Rudwick), and Ch. 19—"The J-Curve of Rising and Declining Satisfactions as a Cause of Some Great Revolutions and a Contained Rebellion" (Davies); Skolnick, *The Politics of Protest,* Report of Task Force on Violent Aspects of Protest and Confrontation, Ch. IV—"Black Militancy"; *Report of the National Advisory Commission on Civil Disorders,* Mar. 1, 1968, particularly Part II ("Why Did It Happen?"); also, *One Year Later: An Assessment of the Nation's Response to the Crisis Described by the National Advisory Commission on Civil Disorders,* Mar. 1, 1969, prepared by Urban America Inc. and The Urban Coalition.

117

THE NEED FOR URBAN
GOVERNMENT REFORM*

The growing discontent with American urban government goes beyond an occasional desire to "vote the rascals out" and is increasingly focused on the basic structure and procedures of local government. This disaffection takes two forms stressing one or the other of the two basic sets of expectations toward government: that government will be (1) effective and (2) accountable. The former expectation is being emphasized by those groups, predominantly middle and upper class, whose fundamental concern is the cost-effectiveness of local government. The latter desire for accountability of local government officials reflects the widespread feeling among the young, the old, the poor, and especially the black and Spanish-speaking minorities, that local government not only fails to produce what they want, but also, and more importantly, even to listen.

Out of these two categories of disaffection from urban government, two agendas for reform are being articulated. One, much in the tradition of the earlier muncipal reform movement, stresses the need for metropolitan government, with clear powers to coordinate efforts to overcome problems such as environmental pollution, land use and transportation planning. The other agenda for local government reform calls for inner city decentralization to give a greater opportunity for citizen participation in those affairs most closely affecting ghetto residents: law enforcement, education, housing, and municipal services of various types.

Although these two agendas for reform appear to be in conflict with each other—insofar as one calls for greater centralization and the other for greater decentralization—more careful comparison of the two reveals complementarity. The difference is rather one of emphasis, stemming from the different attitudes and environments peculiar to each set of

---

* This chapter was prepared by Jon Ellertson, Department of Political Science, Massachusetts Institute of Technology.

reformers. Moreover, past experience with municipal reform indicates the practicality of the two groups working in common to effect a coalition to accomplish their respective goals. Both categories of disaffection are being expressed in demonstrations, typified by the taxpayers' revolt on the one hand, and welfare sit-ins on the other. The demands for greater participation, if frustrated, are more likely to lead to violence than frustration of the demands for greater effectiveness. The frustration of the metropolitan reformers may intensify, to be sure, but this set of reformers has a much stronger sense of personal effectiveness, a sense that the political system is open to their influence in general, although perhaps not to their particular reform measures. As a result, they can continue to channel their frustrations and dissatisfactions through the conventional means of influence.

The other set of dissidents, on the contrary, represents a constituency which has a low sense of political efficacy. This sense of futility promotes withdrawal from the conventional channels of political influence (for them largely non-existent in any meaningful sense) only to erupt sporadically in violence. Recent research confirms that riot-prone citizens have a lower sense of political efficacy than do demonstration-prone individuals.[1]

The search for responsive local government by these two groups is of critical concern since "some sort of claim to ultimate responsiveness has come to replace custom or religious belief as the legitimating grounds for popular support and obedience."[2] A rapid and dramatic effort to satisfy the demands for increased responsiveness of local government seems necessary for the effective maintenance of public order in our cities.

THE SHORTCOMINGS OF THE MUNICIPAL
REFORM MOVEMENT

When it was initiated in the last century, agitation for reform sought to improve local government's responsiveness both in terms of efficiency and accountability. Basically the goal was to make government more consistent with the predominantly middle-class White Anglo-Saxon Protestant values of the reformers, which included a frankly patronizing attitude toward the problems of the lower classes. The agendas for reform, therefore, included an elimination of the graft and incompetence of the "spoils system" in general, and the urban political machine in particular, as well as various

119

benefits for the poor. Two principal goals were to make the "business of local government" more competent, and to "reduce the impact of partisan, socio-economic cleavages on governmental decision making, to immunize city governments from 'artificial' social cleavages—race, religion, ethnicity, and so on."[3]

One of the reformers' guiding assumptions was that it was possible to identify a general interest, the so-called "public interest," which applied to the city as a whole and which should prevail over competing "partial interests." Toward this end, the ward basis of representation to city councils gave way, in many cities and towns, to an "at large" system. Political parties at the municipal level were believed to be unnecessary and actually pernicious. Instead, the municipal reform ideal placed its faith in a *bureaucratic,* rather than political, process for the identification of the "public interest." As Edward Banfield and J. Q. Wilson have described this ideal, the solution "was to put affairs entirely in the hands of the few who were 'best qualified,' persons whose training, experience, natural ability, and devotion to public service equipped them best to manage the public business."[4]

By denigrating partisan politics and weakening the party machine, the reformers inadvertently reduced the responsive capability of local governments vis-a-vis important minorities. Moreover, according to Theodore Lowi, this decline of the political machines was matched by the development of "New Machines," professionally organized autonomous career agencies.[5] Urban bureaucracies, writes Lowi, "are relatively irresponsible structures of power. That is, each agency shapes important public policies, yet the leadership of each is relatively self-perpetuating and not readily subject to the controls of any higher authority." As a consequence, the modern city is efficiently run, but poorly governed due to the existence of—

islands of functional power before which the modern mayor stands impoverished. No mayor of a modern city has predictable means of determining whether the bosses of the New Machines—the bureau chiefs and the career commissioners —will be loyal to anything but their agency, its work, and related professional norms. . . . The New Machines are Machines in that the power of each, while resting ultimately upon services rendered to the community, depends upon its cohesiveness as a small minority in the vast dispersion of the multitude.[6]

Many among this powerless "multitude" are the poorly educated lower-class minorities who are excluded from participation in these "New Machines" because of the establishment of "merit" criteria for job selection. The "New Machines" are therefore insulated both from authority above and from penetration below.

Thus the urban bureaucracies have not lived up to the reformers' expectations of responsiveness. The inability of mayors to coordinate the relatively autonomous functional subcenters of power contributes to the feeling of many that urban priorities are jumbled and often inconsistent. The functional decentralization of authority has increased the efficiency of government in dealing with the specific activities around which each bureaucracy is organized, to the neglect of "those activities around which bureaucracies are not organized or those which fall between or among agencies' jurisdictions." In the latter cases, "the cities are suffering either stalemate or elephantitis—an affliction whereby a particular activity, say urban renewal or parkways, gets pushed to its ultimate success totally without regard to its balance against the missions of other agencies. In these as well as in other senses, the cities are ungoverned."[7]

Nor do many citizens have easy access to these new sources of autonomous power, either indirectly via the mayor or councilmen, or directly for the redress of grievances. Indeed, attempted access by groups of urban residents constitutes "political interference" in the terminology of the municipal reform movement. Dissatisfactions are generated which remain unresolved in the absence of channels for the expression of needs and demands.

In sum, the municipal reform movement, which sought to make local government more responsive, inadvertently promoted structural changes which in fact reduced responsiveness to the interests of certain groups. Nonpartisanship eliminated some articulation channels. By divorcing technical competence from political accountability, the reformers overlooked the necessity to mediate and balance demands for the application of that technical competence. The assumption that "there is no Democratic or Republican way to pave a street" neglects the need to decide which streets will be paved and which not, given the inevitability of scarce municipal resources.

Of course, allocation of scarce resources is not a problem if everyone agrees that, in the public interest, there is only one optimum solution. Where reformed local governments do serve relatively homogeneous communities, they retain their quality of responsiveness and legitimacy:

> Winnetka [is] a suburb of Chicago the residents of which are almost all upper-middle-class Anglo-Saxon Protestants. Winnetkans are in fundamental agreement on the kind of local government they want: it must provide excellent schools, parks, libraries and other community services and it must provide them with businesslike efficiency and perfect honesty. Politics, in the sense of a competitive struggle for office or for private advantage, does not exist. . . . [T]he civic associations agree upon a slate of those 'best qualified to serve' which the voters ratify as a matter of course. Members of the city council leave 'administration' entirely in the hands of the city manager.[8]

The greatest shortcomings of the reform movement are in the large cities which wholly lack such homogeneity of interests—and which contain a number of quite different lower-class constituencies.

Although considerable scholarly debate exists as to the relative advantages and disadvantages of the machines and the reform movement, a recent analysis by Greenstone and Peterson concludes that—

> both the machine and the reform movement had conservative consequences. For businessmen 'on the make,' machine politics provided franchises and special privileges. For their better established successors good governmnent seemed both efficient and morally praiseworthy. The machine *controlled* the lower-class vote, while somewhat later the reformers' structures *reduced* it. By drastically reducing party competition each protected vital business interests from significant political interference.

Greenstone and Peterson also note that following World War I, the social conscience of the reform movement was conspicuously absent, and reform focused more on corruption than on social ills and the needs of the lower classes.[10]

THE MOVEMENT FOR CITIZEN PARTICIPATION AND COMMUNITY CONTROL

As this neglect of their interests has been perceived by members of the inner city lower classes, some have been motivated to join the middle classes in the move to the suburbs to escape from their dissatisfaction with irresponsive big city government. But those minorities prevented by poverty and discrimination from exercising that option have been developing their own distinct municipal reform agendas.

These new agendas for reform stress the growing desire of inner city residents to have a form of local government which is as responsive to their expectations about the education of their children, the protection of their values, and the provision of services as they perceive a typical suburbanite's government is. The experience of many residents, in the black community in particular, with the large service bureaucracies has taught them that the desired degree of responsiveness, particularly accountability, can only be acquired through some sort of decentralization and increased citizen participation in local government. More and more, the consensus is, "We'd rather do it ourselves."

This desire for more citizen participation grows out of a combination of increased positive self-awareness and dignity on the one hand, and increased frustration in attempting to deal with local officials on the other. The underlying motivation is the quest for equality. Having been denied equal geographic mobility because of poverty and "suburban separatism,"[11] many black Americans have turned toward a ghetto control and transformation strategy. The demand for citizen participation has also received impetus from the various federal urban renewal programs specifying that local planning agencies are to provide for citizen participation. Under the anti-poverty legislation, moreover, the symbol of participation was elevated by the clause providing for "maximum feasible participation" of the poor. Since its appearance, some self-assertive individuals have given the clause a "radically transformed construction which drops the 'feasible' and reads 'participation' to mean 'control.' "[12]

Just as "maximum feasible participation" provided sufficient ambiguity to cover divergent opinions, the term "community control"[13] gives rise to different understandings. For some, it is an enhanced advisory role in certain city agencies. For others, it means complete separation from City Hall. The distribution and strength of these interpretations of the demand for greater participation undoubtedly differs from city to city. There seems to be no single model for implementation of these ideals, although the evidence of lack of consensus in the ghetto is probably strongest in the minds of "outsiders" who are neither privy to neighborhood meetings nor take advantage of reading the black community press. The unmistakable thrust of the demands for citizen participation and community control is a decentralization of authority.[14]

THE MOVEMENT FOR MODERNIZATION AND CONSOLIDATION

This emphasis provokes a predictably negative reaction from many Americans, including some heirs of the municipal reform movement (many of whom enjoy suburban residence). Their concern about local government has recently focused on the excessive fragmentation of local jurisdictions, both functional and geographic. Their agendas seek to make local government more responsive through coordination and consolidation. Much of the sentiment behind these reforms reflects middle- and upper-class reluctance to pay taxes which cannot be efficiently used. Cost effectiveness is the emphasized criterion.

These reformers likewise see the need to "modernize" the business of government, which has become outmoded because populations and problems have spilled beyond old jurisdictional boundaries. Urban problems, in this view, are metropolitan problems: environmental pollution, transportation and land-use planning. Some who see the necessity of creating larger, metropolitan jurisdiction also envision solutions to the inequities of municipal finance with the accompanying problems of equity in housing, education and related services which strain inner city coffers and lead to civil unrest.

An important example of this category of local reform sentiment is the 1966 statement by the Committee for Economic Development, which made the following assessment:

(1) Most local government units are too small to provide effective and economical solutions to their problems;
(2) Extensive overlapping layers of government cause confusion and waste the taxpayers' money;
(3) Popular control over local government is ineffective because of the excessively long ballots and the confusions caused by the many-layered system of government;
(4) Policy leadership is typically weak, if not nonexistent;
(5) Archaic administrative organizations are totally inadequate to the functional demands made upon them; and
(6) The professional services of highly qualified personnel are typically not attracted to local government.[15]

124

The CED report concluded that the most pressing problem of local government in metropolitan areas is the "bewildering multiplicity of small, piecemeal, duplicative, overlapping local jurisdictions" which are unable to cope with the difficulties of managing modern urban affairs. "The fiscal effects of duplicative suburban separatism create great difficulty in provision of costly central city services benefiting the whole urbanized area. If local governments are to function effectively in metropolitan areas, they must have sufficient size and authority to plan, administer, and provide significant financial support for solutions to area-wide problems."[16]

The CED assessment has been echoed and expanded by the more recent Report of the National Commission on Urban Problems, popularly known as the Douglas Commission. Although much more comprehensive, the Douglas Commission's recommendations for "Modernizing Urban Government Structure"[17] seem to emphasize the same interpretation of responsiveness. At the same time, the Douglas Commission recommendations stress more clearly than the CED that a reduction of fragmented authorities would enable responsibility to be fixed at a focal point from which coordination and balance in priorities can be made and efficiently executed. Moreover, the Douglas Report is more realistic about the obstacles to reform and cognizant that different kinds of improvements could result from "changes that fall short of the comprehensive amalgamation of all local governments in each metropolitan area."[18]

Like the CED statement, the Douglas Report places less emphasis on the need to meet the widespread demand for greater citizen participation although both do recognize these demands in a number of their proposals. Both tend to stress, however, the deconcentration of authority from city hall, rather than the devolution of authority—an important distinction obscured by use of the word "decentralization." *Deconcentration* is "the delegation of authority adequate for the discharge of specified functions to staff of a central department who are situated outside the headquarters,"[19] a notion which is inherent in the Commission's proposal for neighborhood city halls. *Devolution,* on the other hand, is "the legal conferring of powers to discharge specified residual functions upon formally constituted local authorities,"[20] an idea recognized in the CED proposal for neighborhod councils and in the Majority report of the Douglas Commission[21] but more strongly emphasized in the Douglas Commission Minority Report. *Decentralization* embraces both of these

125

processes of structural adaptation, though the latter is significantly different in promising greater potential subunit autonomy.

Designed to serve 25,000 to 50,000 residents, the neighborhood city halls envisioned by the Douglas Commission are expected to help fulfill what the Commission called "the great need for a feeling of participation in decisions by the neighborhood residents whom the decisions will affect."[22] But the Majority Report conveys considerable ambiguity about what types of citizen participation ought to be allowed. On the one hand, there is a concern for "reaching the more disaffected, inactive members of a community,"[23] for providing, through the neighborhood city hall, "an office to entertain citizen complaints and problems."[24] On the other hand, the Majority Report makes it clear that these new offices are intended primarily to provide service assistance to the "unsophisticated" welfare recipient, not a podium for "angry, organized citizens protesting the location of a new school, the demolition for an urban renewal project, the rerouting of a sewer line, or the laying down of a freeway."[25] Citing the experience of the OEO Community Action Program, the Majority adds the warning that "trying to institutionalize protest under the very auspices of city government will not succeed."[26]

The Majority Report consequently responds rather cautiously to the demands for greater citizen participation. It does advise that some devolution of power to the neighborhood level may be permitted, such as—

the power to make or direct the making, of small neighborhood improvements. Examples are addition of more trash receptacles, minor repairs to public property, and tree and flower planting. Still more popular would be better lighting of streets and alleys, more frequent trash pickup, stop signs at certain intersections and so on. . . . This is the kind of small improvement that is easily made, but which unsophisticated residents simply do not know how to obtain.[27]

The Majority Report suggests, optimistically, that this minor concession to demands for greater resident involvement "would cost the city little but would enlist the immediate enthusiasm of the residents. . . . Slight as it seems, the knowledge of area residents that they have an accessible means of affecting their own immediate environment can have a multiplier effect on citizen self-confidence and involvement."[28]

This discussion by the Douglas Commission majority is a recognition of the idea, familiar to political science, that

126

successful influence attempts increase the individual's sense of political efficacy. It remains to be demonstrated, however, that such small successes could indeed reverse the strong feelings of futility conditioned by ghetto life. Although small victories may win wars, many who are restless and dissatisfied with the current non-responsiveness of local government would not consider the suggested "participation" of sufficient salience to warrent involvement. Instead, such suggestions are likely to be spurned as merely "token", as of no importance in comparison with other concerns, such as education, police-community relations, employment, or housing.

The overriding issue, which is noted by the Minority Report, is the issue of equality of political expression:

> Even with a thorough-going metropolitan area plan of government, there are many functions that will still reside with the small communities in the suburban areas. It seems logical, then, that certain similar functions should reside with inner city communities. This then, would mean that the taxpayer and voter in the inner city of a metropolitan area would have the same kind of leverage on the policies that affect his neighborhood growth, redevelopment, or maintenance, as his fringe area counterpart.[29]

In this sense, the demands for greater citizen participation are really demands to eliminate a double-standard in American local politics—a paternalistic bias which is sometimes perceived as an attempt by the dominant majority to relegate low-status minorities to a subject role in society.

POLITICAL EFFICACY AND TRUST

The demands for increased citizen participation in the government of large American cities are consistent not only with popular conceptions of democracy, but also with recent social science findings which strongly suggest that accession to these demands would reap large dividends to society as a whole, particularly at the local level. The key findings of current thinking from political and social sciences are that the perception of personal effectiveness in politics, or "political efficacy," is related to satisfaction with government and that a strong sense of political efficacy seems to be necessary to motivate persons to express their demands in conventional, nonviolent modes.

Individuals who feel ineffective in using the conventional modes of political action are likely to seek alternative channels for the expression of needs. Lacking the opportunity to enjoy occasional success in the conventional channels of influence, they seek success through more militant channels. These channels may in turn contribute to a sense of revolutionary effectiveness. Utlimately, the sense of effectiveness in using any mode of political expression depends on the degree of success which an individual experiences.

Since society denies the legitimacy of violent channels of influence, it must at the same time strengthen the conventional channels so as to promote the feeling that the system is being responsive to every conscious group of interests in the political system. The blockage of demands will not obliterate them, but rather "transform what might have been a pacific continuous flow of demands into a spasmodically violent, eruptive one." The tendency for demonstrations, mass rallies, and riots to be important channels for expressing and communicating demands will be strengthened if such blockage persists.[30]

"Channel blockage," or the perception of such obstacles to political expression, hinders the development of a sense of political efficacy—the "belief that political and social change can be effected or retarded and that [one's] efforts, alone or in concert with others, can produce desired behavior on the part of political authorities."[31] The elderly, the poorly educated, and the depressed minorities, notably Negroes, are more likely to lack this important sense of political effectiveness.

The feeling of political inefficacy particularly describes perceived isolation from the "input" channels to the political system. The related component of political alienation is *cynicism,* or lack of trust, the sense that the "outputs" or policies of government neglect the individual. The distinction becomes important because a recent study suggests that those who "participate" in unconventional fashions—demonstrating and rioting—share a strong cynicism, but that demonstration-prone individuals are more likely to have higher feelings of political efficacy than riot-prone individuals.[32]

These two aspects of the alienation syndrome are, of course, related to each other. In general, persons who have a high sense of political efficacy are less likely to be cynical about politicians and the political process. This relationship, however, does not hold where local politics are dominated by a political machine. In Litt's study of Boston,[33] where the legacy of past machine control is still sensed, no matter how efficacious persons felt about political action, they still did not trust politicians. On the other hand, Litt found the expected direct relationship between political trust and efficacy in surrounding Boston suburbs. Litt's findings thus suggest that a restoration of the urban political machine would not reduce this sense of alienation.

The citizen-bureaucrat interface is often a locus of critical political learning, or socialization, which can either promote or reduce feeings of alienation. Ronald Lippitt provides an everyday example of the unfortunate informal negation of a formal civics lesson:

> *Socialization decision:* The city council has before it a proposal from two of the council members to establish a city youth council which would have on it representatives from all youth-serving programs including agencies, school systems, churches, etc. It was also proposed that the chairman of the youth council should sit ex officio on the city council as a linkage or liaison between "youth affairs" and "city affairs." After much wrangling and hassling, the idea was changed considerably to an invitation to all student councils and other youth groups to send representatives as observers to city council meetings to "learn how the city does its work" so that they could help the young people understand city affairs.
>
> *Socialization consequences:* The discussions in most of the groups were quite desultory, and the members seemed uninterested. In a few groups there were active discussions which usually focused on the theme "Who wants to sit and be an observer? Why don't they trust us to meet and think about what ought to be done to improve things like delinquency and drinking in town and to make recommendations to the city council for things that ought to be done?" Very few representatives turned up as observers at the council meetings. A few council members noted this circumstance and felt it confirmed their belief that "the young people aren't interested in this kind of thing." Others didn't even remember the invitation.[34]

That political attitudes are re-inforced or weakened by the quality of informal contacts with officials suggests that the selection, training, and promotion of local civil servants who deal with the public should give recognition to qualities of rapport and personableness. "Merit" is not just technical competence.

The critical need to promote feelings of trust and self-confidence in approaching political institutions and personnel is tragically manifested in outbreaks of violence. Survey data on the sense of political efficacy collected by the Survey Research Center since 1952 show a disturbing trend since 1960.[35]

Political Efficacy
[In percent]

1. People like me don't have any say about what the government does.

	1952	1956	1960	1964	1966	1968
Agree	31	28	27	29	34	35
Disagree	68	71	72	70	60	63
DK (depends)	1	1	1	1	6	2
	100	100	100	100	100	100

2. Voting is the only way that people like me can have a say about how the government runs things.

	1952	1956	1960	1964	1966	1968
Agree	81	73	73	73	69	55
Disagree	17	25	25	26	26	43
DK (depends)	2	2	2	1	5	2
	100	100	100	100	100	100

3. Sometimes politics and government seem so complicated that a person like me can't really understand what's going on.

	1952	1956	1960	1964	1966	1968
Agree	71	64	59	67	70	67
Disagree	28	36	41	32	26	30
DK (depends)	1	*	*	1	4	3
	100	100	100	100	100	100

4. I don't think public officials care much what people like me think.

	1952	1956	1960	1964	1966	1968
Agree	35	27	25	37	35	43
Disagree	63	71	73	61	56	50
DK (depends)	2	2	2	2	9	7
	100	100	100	100	100	100

Source: Survey Research Center; 1968 data from the Harris poll prepared for the Violence Commission.

Particularly distressing is the trend of responses to the question, "I don't think public officials care much what people like me think" (item 4). Since about 1960, an increasing number of respondents have agreed with that statement, indicating a particular source of the feeling of isolation from government. A perhaps encouraging countertrend is the growing feeling that there are alternatives to voting for the expression of individual sentiments (question two). The data do not allow a determination, however, of which alternative channels of communication the respondents had in mind

130

—conventional letter writing, or non-conventional protest such as demonstrations, even violence. Robinson, Rusk, and Head at SRC concluded on the basis of these and related data that "common conditions or events could be said to be causing people to be less trustful of the government (or how it is run) and also less sure of their own effectiveness in influencing the course of governmental actions."[36] They add that the manifestations of these feelings of political cynicism and inefficacy on the part of large segments could be either withdrawal from the political system entirely or revolt against it. In either case, democracy would be the loser.[37]

EFFICACY, TRUST AND CITIZEN PARTICIPATION

The feelings of political efficacy and trust which contribute to political allegiance can be fostered by increasing the responsiveness of local government. The alienation syndrome need not suggest a personal pathology, but rather a malfunctioning of the political system. It is important that the system institutionalize responsiveness by assuring free and open access to those political channels deemed legitimate and "proper" by the political culture.[38]

The "capillary" structure of democracy, to borrow an analogy from Almond and Verba, is a useful one if we do not press it too far. The great secondary components of the democratic infrastructure—political parties, interest groups, and the media of communication—are analogous to the veins and arteries of a circulatory system. Unless they are connected effectively with the primary structure of community— family, friendship, neighborhood, religious groups, work groups, and the like—there can be no effective flow of individual impulses, needs, demands, and preferences from the individual and his primary groups into the political system.

The overwhelming majority of the members of all political systems live out their lives, discover, develop, and express their feelings and aspirations in the intimate groups of the community. Where the primary structures remain outside the polity or are passive objects of the polity rather than active participants within it, then the individual has only three choices: to fully involve himself in politics, withdraw from it, or become a passive object of it.[39] When there is an adequate development of secondary structures for the articulation and aggregation of political sentiments and needs, complaints and aspirations, the alternatives for the citizen are not so stark. Most people have other activities which keep them busy most of the time. But everyone, at one time or another, feels the need to express his feelings and to communicate his needs to the political system, whereby the society as a whole makes binding allocations of values.[40]

Needless to say, expanded opportunity for participation will not by itself quell the sense of dissatisfaction which distresses our society. As Sidney Verba wrote in a recent analysis pertinent to the current crisis of participation, "Participation is not necessarily successful participation . . . [but] only [at least] occasionally successful participation is conductive to a feeling of satisfaction with one's political role as a citizen."[41] Additionally, opportunities for participation must be salient to elicit a response, particularly among the young and self-aware minority group members, whose growing, but often untested, sense of self-assertion and competence tend to spill over into politics, giving rise to the sentiment of "We'd rather do it ourselves." These sentiments seek a positive response from the system for sustenance and encouragement.

As the American psychologist M. Brewster Smith has aptly put it:

> . . . the strategic factors of the social structure that gear into these . . . attitudes of hope and of self-respect are . . . *opportunity, respect,* and *power.* Opportunity corresponds to hope and provides its warrant. Respect by others—more important in this regard than love or approval—provides the social ground for respect of self. And power is the kingpin of the system. Power receives respect and guarantees access to opportunity.

Smith adds a warning: "When opportunities are offered without a sharing of power, we have paternalism, which undercuts respect, accentuates dependence, and breeds a lurking resentment that the powerful are likely to condemn in righteousness as ingratitude."[42] In the place of conventional paternalism Smith recommends "good 'parentalism,' . . . [which] sees to it that the child has real problems and challenges to face, and that his solutions are his own."[43] This comment makes explicit the desirability, if not the necessity, of adaptation of leadership styles as well as channels of influence.

Recalling the unintended consequences of municipal reform for the quality of governmental responsiveness to the lower classes, one is well advised to seek a balance between competence and accountability in government, a distinction which corresponds to that made by Almond and Verba: "On the one hand, a democratic government must govern; it must have power and leadership and make decisions. On the other hand, it must be responsible to citizens."[44]

CONCLUSION

In spite of the points of explicit and implicit conflict between the two main movements for local government reform—the inner city demands for greater citizen participation and devolution of authority, and the metropolitan reform sentiments for greater consolidation and efficiency—there is reason to believe in the possibility of balance between these goals.

The urgent need is for experimentation in the spirit of a common search for structural arrangements which will provide the context for increasing the citizen's sense of efficacy and satisfaction with his government, as well as a modified output of policies. Many such experiments are under way in the various Federally-assisted local programs such as Model Cities, Neighborhood Development Program, and the Community Action Program. The novelty of these and other adaptations of more familiar ways of running local governments has led to considerable debate and speculation about their utility, and it is still too early for a balanced assessment.[45] The search for new forms to increase both the competence and accountability of local governments is in the tradition of a nation which has adapted to considerable strains in the past and which will have to continue to do so in the future if local governments are to retain their legitimacy. Jack Dennis and David Easton have written:

> The racial crisis of the 1960's has vividly revealed that even though the prevalent white and Anglo-Saxon ideology has been built around melting-pot aspirations and even though this has mitigated against alternative ways of conceptualizing the American social context, the United States has been unable to escape the strife and turbulence of many other multi-ethnic societies. American ideology has failed to constrain American reality. This may ultimately force the United States to alter its political self-image radically so that it may begin to reinterpret itself for what it really is, a society composed of several large and residentially concentrated ethnic groups—black, Puerto Rican, Mexican American, American Indian, and

133

others—in tense juxtaposition to the dominant white, English-speaking population.[46]

Now that demands have been made for recognition of the legitimacy of some degree of community control in these minority communities, the responsibility lies with the dominant white group, itself composed of many separate but related identities, to respond. Our citizens expect a dynamic balance between the twin goals of governmental competence and political accountability, and such a balance is thus essential to the strengthening of that legitimacy of government by which law enforcement can be primarily voluntary rather than coercive.

REFERENCES

1. See text accompanying note 31, *infra*.

2. Gabriel Almond and G. Bingham Powell, Jr., *Comparative Politics: A Development Approach* (Boston, Mass.: Little, Brown, 1966), at 201. And see the discussion in Chapter 1 of this Report.

3. Robert L. Lineberry and Edmund P. Fowler, "Reformers and Public Politics in American Cities," in *City Politics and Public Policy,* ed. by James Q. Wilson (New York: John Wiley & Sons, 1968), at 109.

4. Edward C. Banfield and James Q. Wilson, *City Politics* (New York: Vintage Books, 1963), at 139-140.

5. "Foreward to the Second Edition: Gosnell's Chicago Revisited via Lindsay's New York," in *Machine Politics: Chicago Model,* 2d edition, ed. by Harold F. Gosnell (Chicago: University of Chicago Press, 1968), at x.

6. *Id.* at x-xi.

7. *Id.* at xiii.

8. Banfield & Wilson, *supra* note 4, at 140.

9. J. David Greenstone and Paul E. Peterson, "Reformers, Machines, and the War on Poverty," in Wilson, *supra* note 3, at 270.

10. *Id.*

11. Robert C. Wood, *Suburbia: Its People and Their Politics* (Boston: Houghton Mifflin, 1959).

12. Sumner M. Rosen, "Better Mousetraps: Reflections on Economic Development in the Ghetto," *Social Policy Papers,* No. 1, July 1968, at 2.

13. Adam Yarmolinsky in *On Fighting Poverty: Perspectives from Experiences,* Vol. II, Perspectives in Poverty Series, ed. by James L. Sunquist (New York: Basic Books, 1969), at 34-51.

14. Among the many specific articulations of this demand by blacks for greater participation, see in particular Charles Hamilton, in *Harvard Educational Review,* Fall 1968, at 669-685, which

treats the necessity of school decentralization as a prerequisite for restoring the legitimacy of educational authority.

15. Modernizing Local Government, A Statement on National Policy by the Research and Policy Committee for Economic Development, (July 1966), at 11-13, as paraphrased in the National Commission on Urban Problems (hereinafter cited as *Douglas Commission Report*), *Building the American City* (Washington, D.C.: Government Printing Office, 1969), at 326.

16. *Id.*

17. *Id.* at 323.

18. *Id.* at 330.

19. Henry Maddick, *Democracy, Decentralization and Development* (London: Asia Publishing House, 1963), at 23.

20. *Id.*

21. *Douglas Commission Report, supra* note 14. This includes a Majority Report and Minority Report, the latter expressing the Chairman's views and that of four other Commissioners as stated in the "Supplementary Views on Community Advisory Boards," Part IV, Chapter 2, of the main report. This majority/minority distinction pertains only to this chapter and is used here for clarification of views.

22. *Id.* at 351.

23. *Id.* at 352.

24. *Id.* at 351.

25. *Id.*

26. *Id.*

27. *Id.* at 352.

28. *Id.* at 352-353.

29. *Id.* at 354.

30. David Easton, *A Systems Analysis of Political Life* (New York: John Wiley & Sons, 1965), at 122.

31. Kenneth Prewitt, "Political Efficacy," 9 *International Encyclopedia of Social Sciences* 225 (1966-67).

32. Everett F. Cataldo, Richard M. Johnson, and Lyman A. Kellstedt, "The Urban Poor and Community Action in Buffalo," paper prepared for delivery at the annual meeting of the Midwest Political Science Association, Chicago, Ill., May 2-3, 1968, which reported preliminary research findings. Final report to OEO entitled "Change Processes and Political Behavior in the Urban Community" is forthcoming.

33. Edgar Litt, "Political Cynicism and Political Futility," 25 *The Journal of Politics* 312-323 (1963).

34. Ronald Lippitt, "Improving the Socialization Process," in *Socialization and Society,* ed. by John Clausen (Boston: Little, Brown, 1968), at 332-333.

35. John P. Robinson, Jerrold G. Rusk, and Kendra B. Head, *Measures of Political Attitudes* (Ann Arbor, Michigan: Survey Research Center, Institute for Social Research, University of Michigan, 1968). Tables and graph are adapted from the SRC

data plus data from the National Violence Commission Survey, Nov. 1968).

36. *Id.* at 633.
37. *Id.* at 334.
38. For an elaboration of the concept of political culture, see Gabriel Almond and Sidney Verba, *The Civic Culture* (Princeton, N.J.: Princeton University Press, 1963).
39. *Id.* at 143-144.
40. Easton, *supra* note 30, at 122.
41. Sidney Verba, "Democratic Participation," 373 *Annals* 53 (1967).
42. M. Brewster Smith, "Competence and Socialization" in Clausen, *supra* note 34, at 313.
43. *Id.* at 315.
44. Almond and Verba, *supra* note 38, at 476.
45. The Urban Institute is sponsoring a series of studies on the topic of citizen participation, under the direction of Alan Altschuler of MIT and David Cohen of Harvard School of Education.
46. Jack Dennis and David Easton, *Children in the Political System: Origins of Political Legitimacy* (New York: McGraw-Hill, 1969) at 407.

A CALL FOR AN URBAN CONSTITUTIONAL CONVENTION*

It has become commonplace to speak of the urban crisis. Two-thirds of us now live in metropolitan areas. The major problems of our time are direct consequences of our need to live together in a crowded and highly mobile society. Rising crime, the process of slum formation, the decline of educational quality, the deterioration of the physical environment, the frustrations of moving about, the lessening spirit of community—all of these modern social ills are at their worst in our large cities.

Our response to the crisis has focused primarily on its physical and personal aspects. We add more police, more housing, more teachers and schools, more subways and roads. We sweep one set of rascals or incompetents out of city hall and install another. But we largely ignore an indispensable part of any solution—the restructuring of urban government itself.

Today this immense but vital task can no longer be postponed. Effective action in the urban crisis requires nothing less than basic structural change in urban government. As will be urged herein, an "Urban Constitutional Convention" could contribute greatly to the process of change by focusing the attention and the creative political energy of the nation upon the grave structural defects in most of our existing local government structures.

AMERICAN TRADITIONS OF GOVERNMENT

By tradition, we have a suspicion of being overgoverned in this country, and we enjoy criticizing our political institutions. Most of this suspicion and criticism, however, is directed toward the federal government. Yet compared to local government, the federal government functions with the efficiency

---

*This chapter was prepared by Lloyd N. Cutler of Washington, D.C.

and reliability of a seventeen-jewel watch. It is far more responsive to public demands and frustrations. It has authority over the conduct of all who live or work within its territory. It has ample power to tax. It has a Chief Executive who can select and dismiss all executive subordinates, over whose decisions he can exercise full responsibility and control. It is largely free of graft and corruption.

Most urban governments lack all of these attributes. As a result, they lack the power to govern effectively. Mayor John Lindsay of New York City is perhaps the most accomplished and articulate practitioner of the art of urban government on the scene today. Yet he would be the first to admit that his office—indeed the entire administrative structure of the city of New York—lacks the power to govern the New York urban area effectively. Indeed, it is no exaggeration to say that if one had the power to draft the 100 best qualified people in the country to fill the 100 highest posts in the government of New York City, the internal weaknesses of the city's state-legislated structure, together with is impotence in dealing with the suburbs, with the state governments of New York, New Jersey and Connecticut, and with the federal government, would still make effective government of the New York urban area an impossible task.

Our state and federal governments are deliberately structured units, similar in their essential elements, which are embodied in written constitutions adopted by large majorities of those governed. Within their respective spheres, their power to govern—to tax, to legislate and to execute—is complete. The structures of urban area governments are much more haphazard and varied; most of them were neither devised nor approved by the urban area's inhabitants; their power to govern even in their assigned field is often limited and shared with a wide variety of state, county or suburban units and special-function boards or commissions.

Our city governments were originally built on an English model of the eighteenth century—a model the English, as we shall see, have long since abandoned. That model is the municipal corporation—a charter granted originally by the Crown in England or by the Governor-General in each of the American Colonies to the members of a municipal council to exercise specified functions. The council members were a self-perpetuating group, and the municipal corporation relied for its revenues more on fees than on the power to tax. After the Revolution, the charter came to be issued by the state legislature, and in time the right of city residents to vote for council members and limited powers to tax were added. Popular election of mayors, instead of election by the council, became the vogue in the 1820's.

In the first half of the 19th century the structure of city governments had come to resemble that of the states—a bicameral legislature, an elected mayor with veto power, and a limited power to tax. City governments soon came under the control of the national political parties and greatly extended the range of their activities. The city of New York built the Croton Aqueduct, established a police force, sewered and paved the streets, and started a park system. City governments accounted for a much greater share of all public expenditures than is true today.

About 1850, a trend toward a board system developed. State legislatures amended city charters to provide independent executive departments for particular major functions, with the head of each department elected by the people or appointed by the state. The Boards or Departments became independent both of the City Council and of the Mayor: in some cases, the state legislature required them to be bipartisan. As a result, much of the effective power to govern passed from the Mayor and the Council to the state and the boards.

By 1880, the weaknesses of the board system had become obvious, and a return to the mayor system set in. In 1882, the charter of Brooklyn was amended to empower the Mayor to appoint the department heads, a power that many city mayors hold today. In other cities, the council is the appointing power, and the other executive functions usually vested in the mayor are assigned to an appointed city manager. In still others, independent boards or departments remain the vogue. Some cities retain vestiges of all three systems.

A more recent feature of some local governments is the metropolitan district, charged with responsibility for a single function, and for performing it throughout all the cities and towns within the metropolitan area. Such districts are usually independent of the city governments and frequently of the city's voters as well. With single-minded intensity, they often work at cross purposes with the city governments and with one another. Only in a handful of urban areas such as Miami, Nashville and, most recently, Indianapolis* is a broad spectrum of functions vested in a single area-wide metropoli-

---

* Toronto has also had such a system since 1954.

tan district whose officers are elected directly or indirectly by all the residents of the area.

Hardly any American city governments are organized in what might be called a "modular" form, in which a lower tier of neighborhood government is responsible for particular functions within a particular neighborhood, while an upper tier in which the neighborhood governments are represented manages other functions on an area-wide basis and exercises supervisory responsibility over the lower tier units.

Apart from these wide differences in internal structure, city governments have other common limitations. First, they are creatures of the states. Their powers and their substantive decisions can be changed by a simple majority of the state legislature, even though the majority of the city's residents and its own representatives in the legislature disagree. Second, they exercise power within limited geographical boundaries, usually narrower than the actual boundaries of the urban area itself. Third, they have limited powers of taxation, restricted both by law and by the practical competition of neighboring municipalities and counties within the same urban area.

As a result of these structural weaknesses, city governments have become impotent instruments for solving urban area problems. At the same time, the problems that city governments must solve have become enormously more acute. The migration of poor blacks and Spanish-speaking Americans to the great metropolitan areas, where the impact of discrimination concentrates them in the city core, has accelerated the process of slum formation, the deterioration and inadequacy of the housing stock, the strain on the school system and the spread of street crime. An incidental result has been to speed the flight of more prosperous residents to the suburbs, thereby hastening the deterioration of the city core, burdening the transportation system, creating de facto racial segregation and polarizing neighborhoods within the urban area against one another. At a time when urban area governments need to be stronger than ever before, they are drifting in the opposite direction. Urban area residents have largely lost faith and interest in the city government; they are turning more and more to the state and federal governments to solve urban problems.

THE BRITISH EXAMPLE

Effective urban government is not impossible, even in an

industrialized democracy. Great Britain's urban areas approach this country's in size and complexity. Britain's economy and social structure are changing rapidly, if not so fast as our own. Its problems of pollution, disadvantaged racial minorities, slum formation, housing, education and law enforcement are substantial, if not so acute as America's. Yet Britain's local governments function far more effectively than ours.

There are more homicides on Manhattan Island every year than in all of England and Wales. Street robbery in Britain is virtually unknown. Almost one-fourth of British urban residents live in new public housing—built by urban government units. Older neighborhoods do not degenerate into slums. The educational system has not broken down. The subways and buses run. The police are efficient and respected. Graft and corruption are virtually unknown.

It would be naive to attribute the superior performance of British local government entirely to the superiority of British local government structure. Many other factors, of course, are at work, not least the homogeneity of the British population and the absence of a large, mobile and disadvantaged racial minority. But governmental structure is far from irrelevant to British success in managing urban areas.

Great Britain, unencumbered by an intervening layer of states, regards the government of urban areas as a matter of national concern. The ancient City of London, as a technical matter, is a toy-sized entity that exercises a limited number of functions in a tiny portion of the London metropolitan area. But the jurisdiction of the Greater London Council has been extended ten miles beyond London airport. Organized on a modular basis—out of individual units averaging perhaps 250,000 people per unit—it encompasses dozens of boroughs, towns and open spaces. Throughout this area, it exercises all municipal functions save those which the national government has reserved either for the boroughs and towns (sanitation, the local constabulary and public housing) or for the national government itself (such as the health service and the Greater London police).

A few years ago the British Government appointed a Royal Commission to study urban government throughout the nation, and to recommend further changes for better management of the rapidly shifting and expanding urban environment. Chaired by Lord Redcliffe-Maud, the Commission filed its report in June 1969. Only eight months later, the

Government issued a White Paper accepting most of the Red-cliffe-Maud recommendations, and going beyond them in some respects.

The Government's proposals are to be presented to Parliament in 1971. Fifty-one unitary metropolitan areas will be formed throughout Great Britain. Below them will be a network of smaller councils for each town and village. In addition, there will be six metropolitan area councils or "conurbations" for the largest and most concentrated areas with populations approximating a million or more—London, Birmingham, Manchester, Liverpool, West Yorkshire (Leeds) and the Southampton Region. The six conurbations will have a two-tier system based on the present London model (in which some services are performed by the towns and boroughs and others by the area-wide council), while the fifty-one unitary areas will have a single tier responsible for all essential services within its territory, including both town and country. A single tax system and a single zoning policy will apply in each area. In at least ten of the largest areas, "ombudsmen" agencies would be created to investigate citizen grievances.

Whether the latest British proposals are suitable for American cities is not the important point. (It is significant, however, that just across our borders the Toronto metropolitan area has been successful with a similar plan.) What is important is that Britain as a nation is addressing itself to the critical problem of improving urban area government, and that even though the existing system works much better than our own, the British are already busy perfecting it to manage the exploding problems of urbanization that increasingly affect us all.

The British process of Royal Commission followed by government White Paper works much better in a parliamentary central government than in our own federalized system with its explicit separation of national powers and its reservation of local powers to fifty separate states. But surely we are capable of devising a means suitable to our own political system for addressing ourselves as a nation to the vital task of improving our own urban government structure. President Nixon has recently observed that "the violent and decayed central cities of our great metropolitan complexes are the most conspicuous area of failure in American life today." Surely a national failure of this magnitude requires a national response.

To find such a means, we might profitably borrow a leaf from our past. The impotent and drifting Continental Congress was transformed into one of the most successful political structures in history by a constitutional convention made up of leading citizens from every part of the new nation. The crisis in urban government is equally grave, the need for a new step forward equally great.

Under our system, the initiative for this new step can best be supplied by the President. The President could announce his intention to convene a year from now an informal Urban Constitutional Convention, to be composed of the Governors of the fifty States, the mayors of the fifty largest cities, ten representatives of the Executive Branch and ten from each House of the Congress. The Convention itself would be preceded by a smaller preparatory commission which the President would appoint immediately. The preparatory commission would draw up the convention rules and would draft a set of proposals for urban governmental reorganization, to be debated and revised by the Convention itself. With modern transport and communications, the Convention would not have to meet for an entire summer in Philadelphia; it might instead meet one long weekend each month for a year, with each meeting held in a different urban area.

Any decisions taken by such a Convention would, of course, be advisory only. Effective action would depend on subsequent proceedings in state legislatures and the Congress, and on any necessary revisions of state and federal constitutions. But great public interest and enlightenment would flow from the Convention proceedings, as would a number of creative and practicable proposals for legislative or constitutional change. With extensive television and newspaper coverage, such a Convention would start in motion the process of forming a consensus for structural reform upon which all hope for effective action must rest.

The Preparatory Commission and the Convention would have ample sources of material to draw upon. In addition to the British experience and the Redcliffe-Maud proposals, American cities offer a wide variety of alternative structures and empirical experience, and American political scientists have put forth any number of promising new ideas. The Committee for Economic Development has recently issued a thoughtful and provocative series of proposals for American cities that resemble the Redcliffe-Maud plan in many respects. Three major areas of reform would presumably attract the Convention's principal attention.

MODULAR NEIGHBORHOOD UNITS

Neighborhood "city halls" and multiservice centers have been recommended by both the Commission on Urban Problems (the Douglas Commission) and by the Commission on Civil Disorders (the Kerner Commission). As proposed, such city halls would largely be service agencies and listening posts. Services needed by the inner city poor, such as job placement, health care, legal and welfare services, would be made more accessible by concentrating the responsible offices in a neighborhood "city hall" rather than requiring the applicant to seek out obscure offices scattered about the city. A deputy mayor or city councilman and his staff would be located at the neighborhood center, to whom the citizens of the community could communicate their grievances and needs. Under the Urban Problems Commission's proposal, the neighborhood city hall would also control the making of small neighborhood improvements and might include an advisory council, made up of residents, to express neighborhood views on local problems and city policies and programs.

Some students of urban government have suggested that the neighborhood city halls, instead of being mere outposts of the central city government, should be transformed into a lower tier of modular neighborhood political units, with the authority to determine some of the policies and to operate some of the services presently performed by city-wide agencies. In order to restore the lost sense of community, and to make urban government more closely accountable to the people, their jurisdiction might be limited to neighborhoods not exceeding perhaps 250,000 people—the average size of the London borough. Members of the neighborhood council could be elected by residents of the neighborhood. Executive and administrative functions could be performed under the supervision of either an elected official or a professional manager. Such community governments could have a direct vote in the city-wide government or, in larger cities, in some intermediate tier which would in turn make up the membership of the city-wide government.

Experiment and experience in the operation of community governments over a substantial period of time are needed to determine the extent to which particular municipal services can be decentralized in this manner without producing unacceptable conflicts and inefficiencies. Results and local preferences may vary widely from city to city. The minor civil and criminal courts suggest themselves as logical candidates for attachment to these modular political units, as do some forms of police work, licensing and building code enforcement, some sanitation and health services, and some aspects of the neighborhood schools. How to draw the lines of demarcation between neighborhood and centralized responsibilities would have to be worked out over time, much as we have done in the fields of federal-state and state-city relationships.

Such a proposal should not be viewed as novel or radical. It exists in London today, and it may soon be extended to all British urban areas with a population of 1 million. It has recently been endorsed by the CED.

A century and a half ago, Thomas Jefferson, writing with some forty years' experience of self-government in our nation's infancy, proposed the adoption of a similar system. He suggested that, in order to make the government of Virginia more responsive to the people, the State should:

". . . divide the counties into wards of such size as that every citizen can attend, when called on, and act in person. Ascribe to them the government of their wards in all things relating to themselves exclusively. A justice, chosen by themselves, in each, a constable, a military company, a patrol, a school, the care of their own poor, their own portion of the public roads, the choice of one or more jurors to serve in some court, and the delivery, within their own wards, of their own votes for all elective officers of higher sphere, will relieve the county administration of nearly all its business, will have it better done, and by making every citizen an acting member of the government, and in the offices nearest and most interesting to him, will attach him by his strongest feelings to the independence of his country, and its republican constitution."

METROPOLITAN-WIDE GOVERNMENTS

While there is much to be said for adding a lower tier to the political structure of our larger cities, there is an equally strong case for the proposition that most city governments are too small, and that they lack sufficient territorial jurisdiction to govern effectively the metropolitan area in which they are located.

In the 227 urban enclaves designated as Standard Metropolitan Statistical Areas there are nearly 21,000 independent local governmental units. While twenty of these areas have fewer than ten independent governmental bodies, some have hundreds, as for example Chicago with 1,113, Philadelphia with 876, Pittsburgh with 704, and New York with 551. The populations served by these independent local units range from less than 1,000 to several million.

As might be expected, the proliferation of mutually independent governmental bodies within urban areas produces inefficiency, overlapping geographic and functional jurisdictions, competition for scarce financial resources and lack of accountability. These results in turn contribute to the inability of local governments to supply essential governmental services.

The consolidation of local bodies into metropolitan governments has long been urged by students of municipal government and has recently received strong support from the Commission on Urban Problems. The Crime Commission has also emphasized the need for metropolitan-wide coordination or consolidation of law enforcement functions. But, with the notable exceptions of Dade County, Florida, and Nashville, Tennessee, efforts to create metropolitan governments have been unavailing. However, the recent electoral success of proposed area-wide governments for Jacksonville in 1968 and for Indianapolis in 1969 suggests that past voter prejudices against such proposals may be largely behind us.

There are at least three areas of government responsibility in which effective action depends upon creating a tier of governmental units coterminous with metropolitan areas. One is law enforcement and the administration of criminal justice. As the Crime Commission has shown, the discharge of these responsibilities is hampered by municipal fragmentation with its attendant inefficiencies and geographic limitations upon the operations of local law enforcement agencies.

A second is housing and zoning. With very few exceptions, divided control over metropolitan land use among city, suburban and county authorities has had the effect of restricting the urban poor to the central city, while those who can afford to (and are not racially excluded) move to the safer and cleaner suburbs with their superior schools; and many industries do likewise. The compacting of the recently urbanized, unacclimated poor into the city core, where job opportunities are declining, accelerates the process of slum formation and its contagion of violence and lawlessness.

These problems could be alleviated in part by providing subsidized low rent housing for the poor dispersed throughout the entire metropolitan area. But suburban municipalities have largely resisted the construction of such housing, principally through land use restrictions. The creation of a metropolitan government with responsibility for area-wide planning, with the critical power to override local opposition when judged necessary, for the best interests of the entire area, is the *sine qua non* for achieving rationality of metropolitan land use.

The creation of metropolitan governments would also broaden the urban tax base, thereby providing more of the necessary financial resources for providing local governmental services to a comparable and equitable degree throughout the area, instead of unevenly as at present. The central cities, whose residents probably require more governmental services than their suburban neighbors, usually receive less. The need of central city governments to tax residents and business firms at substantial levels to meet the greater central city needs has plainly contributed to the flight of industry and middle and upper class residents to the suburbs where taxes are lower.

A metropolitan government with the power to tax all who live within the metropolitan area for all municipal services provided within the area would reverse this process. By having the capacity to impose uniform tax rates throughout the area, the metropolitan government could increase the revenues available without straining further the taxing abilities of the central city. It would create stability by producing a more equitable sharing of the burdens of local government and by diminishing the effect of varying tax policies in luring business and the stable middle-class citizen from the city to the suburb. At least as far as taxes are concerned, there would be no place to hide.

FINANCIAL RESOURCES FOR CITIES

The creation of metropolitan area-wide governments with area-wide taxing authority will go part way toward alleviating the need for increased funds and eliminating some of the inequities in our present local tax structures. But urban areas will need greater revenues than they can hope to collect from their present tax sources—revenues that can only be obtained from an income tax that rises along with increases in the area's income, and that cannot be evaded by shifting residence or plant location to neighboring areas with lower taxes.

The President's federal tax sharing program is a modest

147

step in this direction. But it depends on complicated formulas and on annual revisions by the Congress. It also runs the risk that the shared revenue will be retained by state governments, and will not flow to the cities that need it. Consideration might therefore be given to an alternate or supplemental means of tax sharing, one which would be simpler to execute, would channel more funds directly to cities, and would eliminate the existing competition among neighboring states and communities to lower their tax rates as a means of attracting businesses and upper income residents.

The alternative would be to allow a 100% credit against federal income taxes (instead of the present deduction) for all state and municipal income tax payments up to some maximum percentage of a taxpayer's net income. To prevent encroachment by state governments upon the municipal tax base, separate ceilings could be fixed for state tax credits and for municipal tax credits. Under such a system, both states and cities would face the practical necessity of levying local income taxes at least up to the level of permitted federal credits, and they could do so without concern about losing business and residents to neighboring areas. To simplify collection, states and cities could require residents to state the amounts declared on their federal returns (as many states now do), and levy their taxes upon this same base.

CONCLUSION

An Urban Constitutional Convention may not by itself produce a better structure for urban government. Many of the problems are intractable; many involve deep political and radical cleavages, or clashes between the general interest and the vested interests of public employees and other social groups that we are not yet able to resolve. But a Convention would at least move us off dead center. It would focus public attention on the "most conspicuous area of failure in American life today." And it would test whether we have inherited the political genius of our forefathers, and their remarkable ability to devise governmental structures that do not succumb to a changing environment like dinosaurs—structures that can manage a crowded society, and make life better, not worse, for the people who live under them.

SOURCE NOTE

The following works were consulted in the preparation of this Chapter:

Edward C. Banfield, *Urban Government and Regional Planning* (New York: Free Press, 1969); Edward C. Banfield and James Q. Wilson, *City Politics* (Cambridge: Harvard University Press, 1963); Daniel Patrick Moynihan, *Maximum Feasible Misunderstanding* (New York: Free Press, 1969); Jane Jacobs, *The Economics of the Cities* (Englewood Cliffs, N. J.: Prentice Hall, 1969); Jane Jacobs, *The Death and Life of Great American Cities* (New York: Vintage Books, 1961); *Report of the National Advisory Commission on Civil Disorders* (Washington, D. C.: U. S. Government Printing Office, 1968); Advisory Commission on Intergovernmental Relations, *Urban America and the Federal System* (Washington, D. C.: U. S. Government Printing Office, 1969); National Commission on Urban Problems, *Building the American City* (Washington, D.C.: U. S. Government Printing Office, 1968); President's Committee on Urban Housing, *A Decent Home* (Washington, D. C.: U. S. Government Printing Office, 1968); Great Britain, Royal Commission on Local Government in England, *Local Government Reform* (London: Her Majesty's Stationery Office, 1969); U. S., President, *Economic Report of the President together with the Annual Report of the Council of Economic Advisors* (Washington, D. C.: U. S. Government Printing Office, 1970).

CHAPTER 7

THE ELECTORAL PROCESS AND THE PUBLIC WILL*

The legitimacy of our system of government rests upon the people's belief that its institutions respond to their needs and represent their views. If the people lack confidence in the electoral system or if they feel excluded from decision-making processes and helplessly dependent on the discretion of governmental and quasi-governmental officials, the legitimacy of the system stands almost certainly in serious question, making for political alienation in America. It is not the purpose of this chapter to describe the phenomenon of political alienation, but to identify and understand the extent to which there are remediable defects in the national electoral process—convention, campaign and election—which may give rise to disaffection from the political system.

THE NATIONAL NOMINATING CONVENTION

Although there have been a multiplicity of "third" party movements which have frequently nominated candidates for the Presidency, only the Democratic and Republican parties have continued to compete for the control of the American Presidency and the Congress since the Civil War. The national nominating convention has endured as the formal method of these two parties to air the issues and select their candidates for the top office of the land.

For more than 130 years the convention system has furnished an orderly method for screening candidates for the Presidency. By comparison with its predecessor, the congressional caucus, the convention has broadened the avenues of

* This chapter was prepared by Judith Toth of Cabin John, Md., based in part on research papers on campaign finances contributed by Dr. Herbert E. Alexander, Director, Citizens Research Foundation, Princeton, N.J., and on nominating conventions contributed by Prof. Marvin G. Weinbaum, Department of Political Science, University of Illinois.

recruitment to the Presidency. More often than not, the convention has helped to build confidence in our electoral system. By offering a vivid illustration of the kind of integration that operated on a pluralistic nation, conventions, at the best, symbolize our political processes. The compromises of the convention underline the limited objectives and the moderate character of our electoral politics.

Despite these substantial virtues of conventions, critics continually call for reform of the presidential nominating process. As V.O. Key has stated: "Through the history of American nominating practices runs a persistent attempt to make feasible popular participation in nominations and thereby to limit or to destroy the power of party oligarchs."[1]

For 42 years of our nation's early history, years which witnessed eleven major Presidential elections, the members of the Senate and House meeting in party caucus selected candidates for the Presidency. Throughout those years, the caucus was consistently attacked as an aristocratic barrier to popular participation in the choice of the party's candidates.[2] *The Daily National Intelligencer* on December 5, 1823, colorfully described the caucus:

> A caucus! A nocturnal assembly convoked at short notice, after long preparation, bound by no rule, acting without authority, without the obligation of an oath, within the immediate reach of every sort of influence, calculated, if exerted, to mislead, to deceive, or to corrupt, guarding the people of these United States from the mischief threatened by their own Constitution![3]

The nominating convention, modeled after state constitutional conventions, answered to democratic demands for opening up the nominating process. In 1832, a national convention met to select Martin Van Buren as the running mate of President Andrew Jackson. By the time of the Civil War, the convention system had assumed substantially its present form.

The expanding democratic instinct did not seem entirely satisfied with the convention system, however, since party elites demonstrated quite early a remarkable capacity to adapt their ways to the new forms.[4] Consequently, in the 1840's, an alternate method of nomination appeared in some states—the choice of candidates for office through direct primary elections. By the end of the century, this new method had superseded the convention system in many localities.

The shift from conventions toward primary elections on

the state level, and toward the election of delegates to Presidential nominating conventions, represented an effort on the part of Progressive and Populist reformers to circumvent the concentrated political power of party machines. The concentration of political authority predominated, especially in the nation's rapidly expanding urban areas, swelled by immigrants from the farms and from Europe seeking to take advantage of America's industralization.[5] As city budgets grew and the patronage system matured, enormous resources became concentrated in the hands of the urban political machines. Although the machine could exercise considerable influence at the election stage, it also had to have control of the nomination stage: as Boss Tweed put it, "I don't care who does the electing, just so I can do the nominating."[6]

For the reformers, the direct primary became the instrument by which to pull down the old party apparatus. The direct primary, when accompanied by such other practices of "direct democracy" as the initiative, referendum and recall, would invest the popular will with the power to distribute national wealth more equitably, to regulate public utilities and to attack the trusts. The ultimate faith of the Populists and Progressives lay in their belief in an essentially rational and virtuous electorate. The electorate, they believed, was deceived by the political parties. Through decentralization of the party's apparatus, they hoped to reacquaint the common man with his political responsibilities. A local and simpler politics would allow citizens to reestablish control over the party, ending the party hierarchy's vital hold over the selection of delegates to attend party conventions[7]

During the first fifteen years of this century, the Progressives attempted to bring the national nominating conventions under popular control. Out of Robert La Follette's unsuccessful attempt to seat his Progressive Republican delegates at the 1904 convention, there developed Wisconsin's primary law providing for the direct election of convention delegates.[8] Further impetus to the primary drive came in 1912 when Theodore Roosevelt charged that the Republican Convention had been "stolen" by the Taft forces. But World War I and the subsequent conservative reaction brought pressures for election reforms to a virtual halt: from 1920 to 1949 only one state, Alabama, enacted presidential primary legislation, while 8 out of the original 26 presidential primary states repealed their statutes. Low voter participation, high cost of administration, and the ignoring of primaries by any leading national candidates, often contributed to the decline of the presidential primary.[9]

Not until 1944, when Wendell Wilkie attempted to demonstrate in the Wisconsin primary that he stood as the popular if not the professional party choice, did public attention again focus on the presidential primary.[10] Wilkie's crushing defeat in Wisconsin eliminated him from contention, but his entry pointed up the usefulness of the primary for testing public appeal. Harold Stassen similarly challenged the old guard of the Republican Party in primary states in 1948, and Minnesota, Indiana, and Montana subsequently enacted new primary laws. But disaffection among party leaders, regulars and liberals resulted in the repeal for a second time of the primary laws in both Minnesota and Montana. When Minnesota Democrats found themselves, because of Estes Kefauver's capture of the state's primary, unable to send either Senator Hubert Humphrey or Governor Orville Freeman as delegates to the 1956 convention, the state legislature quickly repealed the law.[11]

Although presidential primaries have not occurred in recent years in more than one-third of the states, they have had on certain occasions a very profound impact on the committed and uncommitted delegates. As John Kennedy's successes in Wisconsin and West Virginia demonstrated, the primaries have enabled candidates to gain national exposure and to demonstrate voter appeal—appeal without which they would have little standing at the convention. All the same, the candidacy of Estes Kefauver, as well as those of Taft and Stassen, demonstrated that primary victories do not necessarily secure a nomination. Nor, on the other hand, has a record of primary defeats always eliminated a contender.

* * * * *

In recent years, changing public attitudes have brought national nominating convention procedures into question and have even damaged the legitimacy of nominations. Two developments in particular have disenchanted the public with recent conventions. First, much of the electorate has the exaggerated notion that decisions regarding nominees and issues result from their expressed preconvention public preferences. Second, through television the public can intimately witness, in a fashion never before possible, the actual machinery and the full trappings of the national convention, revealing to the voter his own impotence.

More and more the convention appears merely to register the previously expressed wishes of select constituencies, as the increasing incidence of first ballot nominations plainly suggests. Whether or not that constituency composes the masses of party adherents, or merely the professional party cadre, however, stands challenged. No one can say with certainty that Richard Nixon, rather than Nelson Rockefeller, represented the choice of the relevant body of voters who in 1968 constituted—or would have constituted—the Republican Party, or that Hubert Humphrey rather than Eugene McCarthy represented the Democratic choice.[12]

In the past, party leaders, acting with only a casual eye to the electorate, could bargain among themselves in selecting a presidential nominee. Although they seldom chose a man wholly unknown to the public, they had little reason to fear grassroots dissent. By contrast, today's conventions attend to mass appeal; a candidate who fails to demonstrate at least potential popular strength probably will not receive serious consideration. Party professionals cannot easily dismiss aspirants with proven ability to mobilize voters when only few regular organizations today can deliver large blocs of voters in primaries or general elections.

Contenders for the nomination have little choice but to carry their cases to the people, especially if their ability to win at the convention hangs in doubt. In their appeals to the electorate, contenders work hard to convey the impression that each expression of public sentiment helps decide their candidacy. Throughout the preconvention campaign, the voter believes that the professionals are watching and that his preferences will not be ignored.

The polling industry shares responsibility for the public's belief in its own preconvention role. Surveys of opinion that add to the credibility or embarrassment of contenders also serve to cultivate the public's consciousness of its own voice. They also lead logically to the conclusion of the electorate that it has responsible, worthwhile opinions on candidates and issues.

In its televised proceedings, paradoxically, the convention seems both overly conscious and strangely oblivious of its national audience. It projects much that is either florid showmanship or tedious party ritual. More significantly, the proceedings of the convention may strike the viewing audience as largely irrelevant—the convention has not assembled to

154

ratify decisions made in the electorate, nor has it come to weigh the qualifications of the contenders or deliberate on the issues that divide the party. Too often the public feels itself an intruder, an unwelcome witness to the party's private business and family quarrels.

The rhetoric of conventions can readily augment public disillusionment. Convention managers speak the praises of "open conventions," yet few delegates seem free. Only a handful of delegates stand bound to the instructions of primary electorates; far more have committed themselves to follow their party superiors. Although convention procedures seem democratic in form, to many in the television audience, presiding officers appear to make arbitrary rulings, and speakers appear to be shouted down or denied access to microphones. Platform draftsmen pledge racial equality, while the convention seemingly condones racial biases in the selection of its own delegations.

Doubt, therefore, naturally surfaces about the convention's positive contribution to the national parties. Even when the large majority of the delegates display the solidarity of the party, the mass media more often identify the sources of disunity. Contenders' attacks on the qualifications of rivals and their doubts over the sincerity of their party's platforms clearly register on an already skeptical public. Moreover, contenders find it difficult to negotiate and compromise when everything is being aired publicly by the news media. Finally, the convention goal to publicize its national nominees sometimes backfires when floor demonstrations for the candidates readily prove counterfeit. It should, therefore, not surprise anyone that various polls in recent years suggest that from 60 to 70 percent of the American people want to scuttle the convention system as it now stands.

This poll does not mean, however, that conventions have outworn their function in the national parties and in the political system, nor that the mass media will in time destroy the convention system. Indeed, television can be an effective ally of the convention, particularly in its capacity to project new faces and ideas, and to activate party loyalties across the nation. Still, a discrepancy prevails between what the public has been encouraged to expect of conventions and what it is likely to perceive.

Accordingly, critics ask: "Is this cumbersome production really necessary to nominate a national slate?" A partial answer lies in the test of time: the convention has produced a very respectable line of Presidents and has helped hold together two stable and competitive national parties. National conventions have endured, moreover, while similar nominating machinery has largely disappeared in most, if not all, of the states. National conventions have also functionally contributed to political parties at three levels: state or local party organizations; the national organization; and the wider party system.

State and local organizations have a distinctive stake in the convention's survival, and the needs of individual delegations have been placed ahead of the national party's objectives. Next to the central purpose of agreeing on a Presidential nominee, the demands that state parties have on the convention system, such as granting recognition to loyal party workers, may seem peripheral, even trivial. But without the sustenance and satisfaction of its constituent units, the national party's existence wavers precariously.

The national parties have considerable stakes in the two-convention system. As V.O. Key, a respected student of American parties, wrote: "The national convention is at the heart of the national party system. Without it, or some equivalent institution, party government for the nation as a whole could scarcely exist."[13] The convention allows a feudal party to pull together and assert its national status. It assembles the party's barons and gives them a few short days to fall behind a single candidate and platform for the Presidential campaign. Factions and interests must put aside their very real differences and—an impressive achievement—reach common and binding decisions. The modern successful convention also allows the party to carry its standards effectively to a mass electorate, to rally the party's workers, and to stimulate its financial contributors. Never again in the course of the campaign will the party be able to monopolize the public's attention to the same extent.

Although the key to the longevity of the convention system may be its willingness to accept without challenge the autonomy of the party's units, the convention's power to set its own rules and, in particular, to judge the credentials of its delegations can have far-reaching effects on the practices and distribution of power in the state and local parties. That conventions may increasingly exercise this influence is suggested by decisions made at the 1964 and 1968 Democratic conventions such as those dealing with racial bias, party disloyalty, and the unit rule. These decisions go beyond the traditionally expedient functions of conventions. Only a party in its corporate capacity, as at its national convention, may force such change.

* * * * *

Of the various suggestions that have been made for outright elimination of the convention, the national primary has tended to dominate every recent discussion of possible change. The late Senator William Langer (R-N.Dak.) proposed that each party should hold a nationwide primary on a given day. The choice would be among all those who filed a petition signed by one percent of the party's national membership. The candidate with the highest number of votes would become the nominee. A less drastic proposal put forward by Senator George Smathers (D-Fla.) also provides for a national primary but each candidate would receive "nominating votes"—each state having the same number of nominating votes as electoral college votes—and nomination would require a majority of the national total of such nominating votes. If no one received a majority, a runoff primary would decide.

Before and since these two proposals, others have variously suggested doing away with the nominating convention— ostensibly to assure that the party nominee become the direct choice of the people. The most common proposal today suggests a direct national presidential primary with a run-off in the event no candidate receives a majority of the party's votes.

The major arguments in favor of a single national presidential primary summarize this way:[14] In the first place, such a primary, where the candidates and their ideas display themselves and contend openly for their party's nomination, would remove widespread public doubts as to the legitimacy of the present nominating system and would pave the way for broadening participation in—and strengthening—the democratic process. A national primary would inhibit or eliminate aspects of the system which lend themselves to political manipulation, and it would do away with the strategies which would confuse the party's rank and file. Moreover, because it would lessen the influence of party leaders, the national primary would make it possible for more well-qualified and highly respected men to seek their party's nomination, leading to selection of better candidates for the nation's highest office.

Secondly, a national primary would extend the two-party

system by encouraging the development of truly national parties with substantial strength in all sections of the nation. It would probably deemphasize the importance of selecting nominees from the more populous states with their large blocs of electoral votes, and it would inhibit the tendency toward appeals to particular segments of the population which have had an adverse affect on party unity. Thirdly, a national primary would reduce the physical and emotional burden on candidates for the nominations. As presently conducted, the state primaries devour the time, money, and energy of the candidates.

A number of arguments prevail against the national presidential primary. One, because the structure of the parties reflects the fundamental political conditions of the country as a whole, the existing system serves not only as a technical device for choosing the candidate, but also as a forum which best accommodates all varieties of local opinion in a particular election year. The present combination of state primaries and party conventions, separated in time, along with balloting in the national conventions, provides the flexibility required to sort out choices among multiple candidacies and come up with the most-favored candidate; it also brings forth candidates whose views concur with party principles, traditions and political needs. Moreover, campaigning nationwide for the primary, the run-off when required, and subsequently the general election would cost too much. Under the present system, a man of more modest means can enter a state primary and, if he wins, he can develop the necessary organizational and financial support as he moves toward the national party convention.

* * * * *

So much for a national primary. But what about the existing convention system and the reforms recently proposed and, to some degree, implemented in convention procedures?

Although the Constitution has been held to require that voting in the primary of a political party is a right which cannot be denied on the grounds of racial discrimination, it remains true that in some parts of the country, principally but not exclusively in the states of the Deep South, Negroes still do not have a chance to participate equally in party affairs. The exclusion, or underrepresentation, of Negroes in state delegations to national conventions of recent years still shocks the democratic conscience.

The Democratic Party, profoundly affected by this problem, has taken steps to deal with it. In 1964, the Convention, although it agreed to seat the regular delegation from Mississippi despite that state's systematic exclusion of significant segments of the population from full participation in choosing delegates to the Convention, nevertheless instructed the Democratic National Committee to include in its Call to the 1968 Convention the following provision:

> It is the understanding that a State Democratic Party, in selecting and certifying delegates to the Democratic National Convention, thereby undertakes to assure that voters in the states, regardless of race, color, creed or national origin, will have the opportunity to participate fully in party affairs. . . .[15]

In addition, the 1964 Convention directed the establishment of a Special Equal Rights Committee to make sure that state parties complied with the new requirement. Subsequently, the 1968 Democratic Convention rejected the Mississippi delegation on the grounds that it excluded Negroes from participation and thus reaffirmed its 1964 mandate of achieving voter participation in party affairs "without regard to race, color, creed, or national origin."[16]

Also the 1968 Convention dealt with the problem of a delegation from Georgia picked by the two top state party officials, by confining the handpicked delegation to half the convention seats, and by allocating the remaining seats to the group led by Julian Bond. As to the future, the Convention took steps to insure a far greater representation in selecting Convention delegates, by establishing a Special Committee to study the delegate selection processes in effect in the various states and to recommend improvements in order to promote broader citizen participation. The Special Committee will make its report to the 1972 Convention. Also, the Call for the 1972 Convention will contain the following language:

> It is understood that a state Democratic Party, in selecting and certifying delegates to the National Convention, thereby undertakes to assure that such delegates have been selected through a process in which all Democratic voters have had full and timely opportunity to participate.[17]

The election of delegates by direct primary offers an excellent way to open up the nominating process to greater public participation. The Florida primary law, for example, provides that delegates may run only as a slate, but that the statewide vote controls the election of delegates at large, and that the

159

district vote controls delegates running in the districts. Each slate may run either unpledged or under the name of its preferred Presidential candidate, which then also appears on the ballot. It does not require the formal consent of the candidate. If more than one slate files, preferring the same candidate, the candidate may choose which slate he wishes to represent him. This arrangement produces a valid mandate, and yet leaves open the possibility of drafts. One disadvantage obtains, however: those who vote for slates pledged to losing candidates may feel unrepresented at the convention itself.

The New York primary, on the other hand, directly elects individual district candidates, who run unpledged, although they may advertise their preferences as they choose. Candidates do not run on statewide slates, so that any prospective Presidential nominee can find some support within the selected delegation. The party organization chooses delegates at large. Under this system, the voter has approximately the same opportunity for seeing his preference expressed at the national convention as he enjoys in electing members of the state legislature.

Some proposals have suggested combining the present convention system with a national system of state primaries. Senator Estes Kefauver proposed direct primary elections in each state, at which time a slate of pledged electors would be chosen. Subsequently, at the national convention, each delegation would continue voting for the pledged candidate so long as he received at least 10 percent of the total vote. If no candidate received a majority on the first ballot, and no candidate could gather enough additional votes from those not committed by the 10-percent provision, then the convention would choose among the three highest ranking contenders. In Senator Paul Douglas' variation, federal grants-in-aid would finance primaries in states which choose to hold them. Delegates so chosen would have to vote for the winner of their state's preferential poll unless, or until, he received fewer than 10 percent of the total votes.

Criticism has also centered on internal convention procedures or rules which tend to prevent delegate voting patterns from reflecting the views of their constituencies. The most offensive prescription has been the so-called, "unit rule," by which the national convention honors the requirement, adopted by the state delegation, that the entire vote of the state be cast for one candidate. Thus, a majority in a unit-rule state could exercise more weight than a comparable

160

majority in a state operating without the unit rule. The Republican Party has specifically banned the binding of any delegation to its Convention by unit rule. However, the rule continued to be applied at the 1968 Democratic Convention. Nine delegations went to the Chicago Convention bound by the unit rule, with several others free to invoke the rule if they so chose. Debate over the future of the unit rule occupied much of the time of the Democratic Committee on Credentials, the Committee on Rules and the Convention itself. On the recommendation of the Committee on Credentials, the Convention approved a report stating:

> While it is indispensable to democratic processes that there come a time when a final decision must be reached by majority vote, a necessary consequence of the Unit Rule is the submergence of minority views and representation. The new [so-called "Special"] Committee should examine this question.[18]

The Convention also specifically provided that in selecting delegates to the 1972 Convention "the unit rule [shall] not be used in any stage of the delegate selection process."

Even if the unit rule goes, however, the spirit of the unit rule may linger on in some quarters. Observers at the 1968 Democratic Convention noted that even in some delegations *not* bound by any unit rule, the leader of the delegation would frequently vote all of the state's votes according to his own preferences unless the dissenting delegates specifically asked that their votes be cast a different way. Those who remained silent saw their votes announced without their ever having been consulted.

Internal convention practices might be considerably improved in other ways. Some have described the atmosphere of most national conventions as "confusion, childish horseplay, and irrationality not conducive to calm deliberation on party principles, programs and men."[19] On occasion, convention chairmen have misused parliamentary procedure to prevent the counting of dissenting votes or the expression of dissenting opinions. Galleries, packed to create a false impression of popularity for a particular candidate or for the head of the host state delegation, create greatly false impressions.

The parties themselves must improve the internal procedures of the conventions. Presumably, party leaders have become sensitive to the increasing disfavor with which the public greets arbitrary chairmanship and the stifling of debate. Lengthy parades and irrelevant speeches have no adequate justification today, when millions watch convention proceedings on television. No one can justify or excuse attempts by party "leaders" to exclude representatives of certain segments of the party from access to microphones, or to shout them down during speeches.

Awareness of the public presence has become a giant first step toward reform. Hopefully, the reforms of the 1960's will be dwarfed by those which will be adopted in the 1970's in order to make the parties more responsive to the will of their membership and the public as a whole.

THE POLITICAL CAMPAIGN

Americans are now more numerous, younger, more suburban, better educated and wealthier than ever before. They are also more mobile and less parochial. Over this kind of constituency, political organization can not hope for unquestioning loyalty. As it is, the number of voters who register as "independents" increases. These people will have to be wooed by the candidates with the help of polls, computers, mass mailings, television, and other means from modern technology. One observer has written:

> New campaign techniques as practiced by professional managers win elections. The traditional party organizations can no longer win elections when opposed by these new managers and techniques. Some have been slower to learn this than others and have paid in defeat at the polls.[20]

The new techniques require large sums of money, and a growing belief exists in this country that a small group of people, by reason of money, position and power, control the present government and have the ability to maintain that control in the future, regardless of the wishes or needs of the people. That this kind of notion could gain such widespread currency in a nation dedicated to the principle of a "government of the people, by the people, and for the people" has serious implications.

How much does it cost to elect a candidate and where, in fact, does the money come from? Is there, as some claim, an industrial-political complex?

Money, of course, is only one important factor among many affecting the outcome of elections. A certain amount spent in any competitive situation gives the candidate's name prominence and ensures visibility, even to remind voters of the names of well-known incumbents. Beyond such minimal

162

spending, however, ignorance prevails about the marginal increment per dollar or of the differential effectiveness of various campaign techniques. Moreover, spending represents only one aspect of the broader issue of access to the electorate through the communications media. Sympathy on the part of those controlling the mass media, or those possessing the skills for reaching the electorate, can play a significant part in the battle for men's votes.

In politics, as with most other enterprises, there is no guarantee against waste and inefficiency. The amount spent does not necessarily have any relationship to the caliber of the campaign or to the discussion of crucial issues. Campaign spending varies according to the availability of money, the nature of the contest, and the constituency to be reached. For example, a candidate may win because he could spend more money, or he may have attracted more money because he looked like a winner. The more popular candidate attracts not only more votes but also more money. Observers agree, however, that money has greater impact in the prenomination period than in the general election period.

Students of behavioral psychology and of advertising techniques say that the decision-making process betrays no more rationality in the arena of politics than in other areas of human activity. Indeed, the outcome of democratic political contests, whether elections or legislative struggles, can be substantially influenced by the quantity and character of the appeals for public support, as well as by their inherent rationality. Thus, while people, not dollars, vote, dollars help to influence voter behavior.

In 1952, about $140 million was spent on American politics at all levels. By 1964, the figure had risen to at least $200 million; by 1968, to about $300 million. National party organizations heavily depend upon large contributions—defined as those of $500 or more—to finance campaigns. Table 1 indicates the percentage of individual contributions of $500 or more received by the national level committees of the two major parties in recent years.

Table 1
(In Percent)

National level committees	1948	1952	1956	1960	1964
Democratic	69	63	44	59	69
Republican	74	69	74	58	28

The Republican achievement of 72 percent of income in 1964 received in contributions of *less* than $500 represents the highest percentage either party has attained in modern times, thanks largely to the Republican National Sustaining Fund, a tremendously successful $10-a-year membership program started in 1962. The drop to 53 percent in 1968 does not represent a drop in the amount collected under this program, but rather a marked increase in contributions above $500. The Democratic National Committee has likewise had a sustaining fund for more than a decade, but its success has been limited.

In 1964, approximately 12 million Americans gave money to some party or candidate, showing an increase of 9 million since 1952. The 12 million donors in 1964 represent about 17 percent of the number of citizens who voted in the 1964 Presidential election. These data suggest that while a relatively large proportion of the resources available to national organizations generally stem from donors of more than $500, small contributors—especially Republicans—have started to bear a greater share of the overall cost.

The investment of the "financial elite" in politics has been extremely difficult to document. By contributing to different campaign committees supporting the same candidate, for example, effective tracing of an individual's contributions becomes frustrated. Difficult to determine even with reasonable accuracy is the amount of the political contributions made by any person, group, association, or corporation.

In 1968, about 15,000 persons made reported contributions in sums of $500 or more, for a total of about $30 million. Over 400 of these made reported gifts aggregating $10,000 or more. In 1964, about 10,000 persons made reported contributions in sums of $500 or more, for a total of $13.5 million. One hundred and thirty of these made reported gifts of $10,000 or more for a total of $2,161,905, or 7 percent of the total. Of the 130 very large donors, 52 gave to the Republican cause and 65 to the Democratic, while 13 contributed to both.[21]

With the increasing complexity of government, combined with the affluence of the private sector of the American economy, the instances of wealthy contributors winning appointive office have become fewer. Of the first 27 noncareer Chiefs of Foreign Missions appointed by President Kennedy, only 7 had made recorded contributions of $500 or more. Of some 35 similar appointments by President Johnson during 1964–65, only 10 went to large contributors. Under President Nixon, 14 of 34 noncareer appointments have gone to heavy campaign contributors so far.

Nor have major contributors accounted for a large percentage of the other, nondiplomatic, major appointments in recent years. Of 253 major appointments made by President Kennedy through mid-1961, only 35, or 14 percent were found to have contributed $500 or more in the 1960 campaign. Four of those 14 had actually given to the Republicans. Under President Johnson, only 24 of 187 major appointees through September 1965 had given $500 or more in the 1964 campaign. Under President Nixon, only 27 of the 333 major appointments during his first year in office were of contributors of $500 or more in 1968.

In 1956, the Gore Committee analyzed reported large gifts ($500 or more) to candidates and campaign committees from the lists of officers and directors of 13 trade associations and special interest groups.[22] A continuation of the analysis through the 1960 and 1964 elections shows a decrease in giving by such individuals.[23] In none of these Presidential election years did more than 15 percent of the officers and directors of these combined groups contribute—not a much higher percentage than for the population as a whole. Admittedly, the percentages among the selected 13 groups become reduced considerably by the large number of noncontributors among the top leadership or such groups as the National Association of Real Estate Boards and the American Bar Association. (The ABA figures boggle, for members of a profession that consistently provides so many candidates for major public office; in 1964, among 267 members of the ABA House of Delegates, only 5 contributed an aggregate of $5,000.)

The highest percentages of recorded contributors represent the membership of the Business Council, which has been called the elite of business and finance, the essence of the so-called "establishment." Of the Business Council's membership of 119, 68 contributed an aggregate of $344,225 in 1968 ($257,925 to the Republicans and $83,000 to the Democrats). Fifty-three percent of the Business Council's members were listed among large contributors in 1964, almost 60 percent in 1960, 45 percent in 1956; the aggregate amounts of contributions from these men decreased between 1956 and 1964, but rose again in 1968. The special circumstances of the 1964 campaign brought a much higher percentage of Business Council membership giving to the Democrats, whereas before and since the overwhelming bulk of the member's gifts had gone to Republican causes.

If any group would seem to have special reasons for making significant contributions to the party in power, it would be persons associated with defense industries and receiving a large share of federal contracts. In part, the record of 1964 of those giving sums of $500 or more would seem to bear out the assumption. Twenty-four percent of the directors and executives of the 10 top defense contractors in fiscal year 1964 contributed, as opposed to 13 percent for the entire group of trade associations and special interest groups referred to above. But the amount of the contributions was not high. Also, in a year when the Democrats had been expected to retain the White House with ease, the officials of these defense contracting firms still gave more money to the Republicans.[24]

Another indication that men of wealth do not seek unduly to influence politicians is the absence on reporting rolls of persons hedging their bets by buying stakes in the campaigns of opposing candidates. On the national level, the number of individuals giving both to Republican and Democratic causes over the past several years has not been great. The list of those who gave to candidates competing for the same office or to committees operating at the same level is still smaller. The most common instance of split ticket giving occurs when one gives to the Presidential candidate of one party and to a Senate or House candidate of another party. These "split contributors" simply do the financial equivalent of splitting their tickets; they do not necessarily seek to maximize political influence by purchasing the favor of both sides.

* * * * *

What about wealthy candidates? Only a wealthy person, it is said, can run for high political office. Recent experience in Presidential elections does not support that view. Franklin D. Roosevelt, Dwight D. Eisenhower, John F. Kennedy, and Lyndon B. Johnson had wealth, yet only in Kennedy's case did it seem demonstrably decisive. Two losers, Adlai E. Stevenson and Barry Goldwater, both considered wealthy, do not demonstrate that their wealth had anything to do with their getting the nomination or losing the subsequent election. Their wealth may have had more to do with their entering politics in the first place. Harry Truman, Thomas Dewey, and Richard Nixon (in 1960) were not even moderately wealthy when they ran for President. Yet money can create sudden availability, as it did, of course, for John F. Kennedy in 1960, for Nelson Rockefeller in 1964 and 1968, and for Robert F. Kennedy in 1968.

Political managers often complain that it takes more money to publicize an unknown. They may be tempted to give nominations to men able to finance their own campaigns, in order to free party funds for other campaigns at other levels. Men less well endowed ordinarily start at lower elective levels and earn their way upward more slowly—except perhaps for certain other highly visible individuals, such as movie actors. Once in office, the wealthy incumbent has a freedom of action that others less wealthy do not have if they depend on political contributions for their funds.

Big money seems to exercise its greatest influence at the prenomination stage of the electoral process, when access to large numbers of small contributors becomes ordinarily less available than in the general election. The best estimates of costs of the preconvention Republican campaigns in 1964, for example, are as follows:[25]

Goldwater	At least $5.5 million
Rockefeller	Between $3.5 and $5 million
Scranton	$827,000
Lodge	Over $100,000
Nixon	Over $71,800

Conversely, the McCarthy movement in 1968 represents a major candidacy that basically did not depend upon large contributions. Starting as a "policy campaign," it turned into a full-fledged nomination campaign, managing from primary to primary to find the financial means to carry on. The financing came from a relatively large number of small contributors, a smaller number than in the Goldwater prenomination campaign of 1964;[26] it demonstrated that a left-of-center candidacy could also be financed from a broad base. Although the McCarthy campaign had several very large contributors, it nevertheless stands as a remarkable phenomenon in the nature of its financial constituency.

Personal wealth or access to the financial resources of others also acts as a screening device at other levels in the electoral process. Sometimes these screens are legally established. For example, in recent years, the Democratic Party of South Carolina has assessed up to $2,000 as a qualifying fee for candidates for Governor and U.S. Senator in the primary elections. In Indiana in 1964, before a candidate's name could be placed before the Democratic State Convention, he had to pay a filing fee to the party, ranging from $2,500 to $750 for statewide offices, $2,000 to $750 for certain judicial offices, and down to $250 for delegates and 100 for alternates to the Democratic National Convention. High filing fees are not uncommon in other states.

Moreover, a study conducted by the Citizens' Research Foundation of 1964 Democratic and Republican national convention delegates indicates that money can determine who may participate in this phase of the presidential nomination process. The median family income for Democratic delegates was $18,223, compared with the national median family income of $5,742 for 1964; for Republican delegates the median was slightly higher, $20,192.[27]

Existing federal and state laws relating to political finance are essentially negative in character, containing numerous prohibitions, limitations, and restrictions. Existing statutes seek to restrict both the sources of campaign contributions and the expenditures by candidates. The federal government and about 30 states forbid corporations to make contributions in connection with any election to a national office (U.S. Code, Title 18, S. 610). Similarly, statutes prohibit labor unions from making contributions or expenditures in connection with elections (or nominations) for federal office (Taft-Hartley Labor Management Relations Act of 1947), though these prohibitions do not apply to voluntary contributions of union members to be spent by the unions' political committees. A federal statute making it illegal for "whoever" enters a contract with the U.S. government to make a political contribution (U.S. Code, Title 18, S. 611) has not deterred officials of contracting corporations from making gifts. The Hatch Act makes it illegal for anyone to contribute in excess of $5,000 to a candidate for federal office; but, though this twists the statute, one can contribute to as many national or state committees as are active, and some states do not require reporting of contributions. More significantly, the federal gift tax probably limits political contributions more than the Hatch Act or any related state statutes.

Statutory limitation of expenditures has also been attempted. The Federal Corrupt Practices Act of 1925 limits the spending of candidates for the U.S. Senate to $10,000 and of candidates for the House to $2,500. The effect of these limits can easily be avoided by using multiple campaign committees, and the statute is a dead letter.

These laws represent unsuccessful piecemeal efforts to deal with problems as they arose. No comprehensive attempt to deal legislatively with the problems brought about by the role and influence of money in politics has ever taken place, yet a number of proposals have been offered in the areas of disclosure and publicity, governmental assistance and political broadcasting.

Proposals for mandatory disclosure of financial contributions vary considerably as to the scope of activities and contributions to be disclosed, the coverage as to types of candidates and committees, the content as to itemizing and totaling of receipts and disbursements, and the timing of reports, both pre- and post-nomination and election.[28] Securing disclosure is only a first step, however; the larger purpose is to inform the public about sources of funds and categories of expenditures.

To insure wide publicity, the President's Commission on Campaign Costs[29] recommended the establishment of a Registry of Election Finance in the General Accounting Office, supplanting the present practice of reporting to the Clerk of the House of Representatives or the Secretary of the Senate, who as political appointees are under more constraints than the GAO. The Registry would have the responsibility to receive, examine, tabulate, summarize, publish, and preserve the reported data, and to refer apparent infractions of law to appropriate enforcement agencies. In addition, President Kennedy proposed a registration system, under terms of which committees undertaking activities affecting candidacies reportable under the law would have to file official notice of intention to operate. Once registered, they would have to report periodically. The Registry would make reports available to the public, list and draw together relevant data regarding specific candidates, and undertake wide dissemination of the field data.

As for governmental assistance to candidates, public policy could follow one of two main paths: encouraging a vast expansion in the number of small voluntary contributors, or providing public subsidies to assist the parties and candidates in financing campaigns. With some exceptions, the Commission on Campaign Costs generally advocated the course of expanding the financial base of support for the parties. In recommendations made to the Congress in 1966, President Johnson followed much the same course.

One way of encouraging contributions is a system of limited tax credits and deductions for political contributions to give the potential contributor incentive to contribute by providing a financial benefit through the tax structure. Tax incentives have an advantage over direct subsidies in that the amount and direction of the assistance are determined by citizens in their contribution patterns, not by inflexible formulas. Five states have adopted deductions but because state income tax rates are low, their efficacy remains unproved. Their importance rests in dignifying political contributing, in giving government encouragement to giving, and in providing solicitors with an additional sales tool.

One form of help to candidates, both in pre- and post-nomination periods, is the Minnesota enactment permitting specified candidates (and certain party officials) to deduct from their gross state income tax liability a limited amount of campaign expenditures or political costs which they had personally paid.[30] The rationale is that politics should be considered a business for some persons and accorded similar, though limited, benefits, as compared to those granted to a business man incurring certain expenses in the course of business-connected activities.

A form of partial governmental subsidy compatible with expanding of financial constituencies was suggested, though not recommended, by the President's Commission, if the tax incentive system was first tried and failed. Under the "matching incentive" plan, the party organization would be given incentive to seek out large numbers of contributors; contributions in amounts of $10 or less per contributor raised by designated political committees would be deposited by the committees with the United States Treasury where the money would be matched by a like sum from public appropriations. The combined total would be available to the committee to meet authorized types of costs, payments being made by Government check to sellers of goods and services. Payment by Government check, as well as post-audit and public reports, would give assurance that appropriated and contributed funds were being properly used.

The 1966 Presidential Election Campaign Fund Act, authored by Senator Russell Long (D.-La.), provided a tax checkoff system under which each taxpayer (husband and wife could each check off on a joint return) could designate that $1 of his tax payments be diverted to a special fund for distribution to national political parties for use in Presidential general elections. This subsidy plan received an unfavorable reaction in the media, partly because of the way it passed (as an amendment to an unrelated bill, without consideration by

170

elections or appropriations committees), and partly because it was not accompanied by a revision of other laws affecting political finance, but merely added money without achieving reform. Also, the act raised serious constitutional questions, including the question of fair treatment of minor parties, and guidelines indicated expenses that could be reimbursed. As enacted, the subsidy would have gone to the national committee of a qualifying party, and thus could have changed the balance of power within the major parties by infusing large sums of money at the top of the party structure, previously dependent to some extent upon state and local funds filtering up to the top. Before the subsidy plan had a chance to operate, however, strong pressures developed for congressional repeal or modification of the law, and it was in fact rendered statutorily inoperative after having been on the books only seven months.

The Senate Committee on Finance later reported out a new bill (Rep. No. 714, Committee on Finance, U.S. Senate, 90th Cong., 1st sess.) which provided for both tax credits for political contributions and a subsidy formula for Presidential and Senatorial candidates. Under this bill, the subsidy would not have gone to the parties, as in the earlier formulation, but directly to the candidates, and thus might have had a splintering effect upon the parties by decreasing financial dependence of candidates upon their parties. This bill, however, was not enacted.

Another way to reduce campaign costs is to guarantee greater access of candidates to radio and television time. Broadcasters generally favor abolition of section 315a of the Federal Communications Act, the equal opportunity provision, which provides that when a qualified candidate for any public office is permitted to use broadcasting time, equal opportunity must be afforded all other candidates for the same office, even candidates of minor parties. This provision restrains braodcasters from affording free time as a public service to major candidates. (The equal opportunity provision was suspended with respect to the Presidential and Vice Presidential campaigns of 1960, thus permitting the "Great Debates" without requiring stations to provide equal time to the minor party candidates also running for President.)

One possibility short of repeal of the provision would be to revise the equal opportunity standards to permit "differential equality of access" for major and minor parties and candidates, so that major candidates could be alloted more time than minor candidates. Another proposal which has been made is to amend the Internal Revenue Code so as to give an incentive to broadcasters to program free time by permitting them to deduct from their taxable income a portion of the lost revenue for normal time charges in addition to out-of-pocket expenses of free broadcasts, now deductible anyway. Still another possibility could require broadcasting stations to give limited free time to political candidates as a condition of licensing. Alternatively, a free time requirement could be limited to public, or educational stations.

THE ELECTION

Basic to American political thought is the ideal that each man, white or black, rich or poor, should be heard through his representative. The broadening of the franchise to include the poor, the Negroes, women; the reapportionment decisions of the Supreme Court to bring about fair ratios of people to their representatives; the discontents of the electorate over the existing convention system and the electoral college—all have placed all Americans one step closer to the promise of democracy in this country.

Nevertheless, not more than 60-65% of the total voting age population goes to the polls during a Presidential election. Some stay away voluntarily, from either apathy or protest. The apathetic will always be with us; their role in society is limited to what contribution they make in pursuit of their own interests. But those who stay away from the polls in genuine protest against the proffered choice of candidates number very few; the fallacy of their method of protest is that it cannot be measured. The protestors blend with the apathetic and make no impact on the system.

Those who do not refrain from voting voluntarily—the disenfranchised—are another matter. Several features of state law still operate to restrict the franchise in the United States, some of them universally recognized as necessary prohibitions—like those against voting by mentally incompetent persons or children—and some of a more disputable nature, such as the variety of residence requirements that exist in the various states.

Today, all states have residence requirements of some nature. The most common requirement is one year, imposed by 33 states. Mississippi has the most stringent—2 years. The mildest requirement is West Virginia's, only 60 days. Most states also require a specified term of residency in the country, precinct or ward; in every case less than the requirement for residency in the state itself.

Exact figures are not available on the number of Americans actually disenfranchised by residency requirements. Population mobility has always been a prominent feature of American life, and each year about one of every five Americans moves. A large proportion of these moves are only on a local basis, however, so that many citizens can maintain their vote if they will go to the trouble of registering again at their new addresses. Some localities encourage registration by setting up evening registration in local schoolhouses, fire stations and the like; but many require the voter to appear at an inconvenient city hall or courthouse registration office during regular business hours, when he would normally be at his job.

In recent years, increasing opposition has mounted against the disfranchisement of voters in Presidential elections because of changes in residence. Even if a residency requirement can be justified for local elections, the argument goes, can it legitimately—and constitutionally—be used to prevent citizens from participating in Presidential elections? The mere fact of change of residence does not make a person any less a citizen of the United States, with any less stake in the Presidential election.

A longstanding problem of the gravest sort has been denial to Negroes of the right to vote. In the relatively short period since the passage of the Voting Rights Act of 1965, however, it has significantly advanced voter registration and political activity, especially among Negro citizens in the South. In 1960, the total number of Negroes registered to vote in our southern states was 1,410,148. By 1966, the number had increased dramatically to 2,469,837 or by 75 percent.[31] This progress has occurred thanks to the implementation of the Act by the Department of Justice and the Civil Rights Commission, by the efforts of private civil rights organizations, and by the acceptance throughout the country, but especially in the South, of the administrative enforcement of voting rights.[32] According to the Voter Education Project of the Southern Regional Council, in 1965 when the Voting Rights Act went into effect, 72 black officials were elected in the eleven Southern states. Since the elections in 1968, the number stands at 388. (This report only included those persons elected to public office, while gains have also been made in the number of appointive offices held by blacks.)

In the country now, the total number of black elected officials is estimated by the Democratic and Republican National Committees at well over 800. However, the total number of elected officials in the Nation is 520,000. Thus, with the black population just under 12 percent of the total, they are still only holding 0.015 percent of the elected offices.

Moreover, not one Negro Senator or Congressman has represented the South since the turn of the century, although 10 represent other parts of the country in the 91st Congress—the largest number since Reconstruction.[33]

Supreme Court decisions in recent years have also helped to extend the franchise. The "one man, one vote" reapportionment ruling has made political districts more reflective of the population distribution within the states. This ruling is presently being challenged, however, by the call to convene a constitutional convention which was led by the late Senator Everett Dirksen (R.-Ill.). In the event the states decide to answer the call, the convention could overturn the Supreme Court's ruling.

One clear defect in our political system that contributes to the loss of a feeling of legitimacy about the actions of government is the exclusion of young people from voting. Most 18-year-olds feel very strongly that they have every necessary qualification for voting, including particularly the qualification of exposure to compulsory military service; objectively, it is impossible to disagree with them. Yet only Georgia and Kentucky permit 18-year-olds to vote, Alaska, 19-year-olds, and Hawaii, 20-year-olds. The result is that in the rest of the country, millions of young people, interested in public issues and wanting to make their views on these issues felt, have little outlet for this feeling other than through participation as a worker in political campaigns. That thousands of young people have chosen this latter course of political action recommends them highly. But it does not alter the fact that our system of laws, by denying young people the right to vote, tends to force the expression of their views outside the legal system, in demonstrations on our campuses and in our streets, and other assaults upon our system.

Another feature of our election process that has come under increasing criticism is the electoral college. Under the Constitution, the November election is not for Presidential candidates themselves but for the electors who subsequently choose a President. All that the Constitution says of this stage of the election process is: "Each state shall appoint in such manner as the legislature thereof may direct, a number

174

of electors, equal to the whole number of Senators and Representatives to which the state may be entitled in Congress." In 1968, there were 50 states with a total of 100 senators and 435 representatives, plus three electors from the District of Columbia (added in 1961 as a result of the enactment of the 23d amendment). Hence, the total number of presidential electors in 1968 was 538. In practice, in every state, the political party obtaining a plurality of votes, no matter how small, names the entire slate of electors. This practice, however, is not required by the Constitution, and each state is thus free to change it at will.

The electors chosen on election day convene as "colleges" in their own states on the first Monday after the second Wednesday in December and cast their votes for a President and Vice President of the United States. If no Presidential candidate receives a majority of the electoral votes when these are formally counted in Congress on January 16, the task of choosing a new Chief Executive is constitutionally given to the House. (This phenomenon has occurred twice in history: first, following the elections of 1800, when Jefferson and Burr had tied in the electoral voting; and second, in 1824, during the Adams-Jackson election in which neither garnered a majority of the electoral votes.) The Constitution gives each state a single vote in choosing a President in the House, and a majority of the states is required to elect. The House must choose from one of the three top electoral vote recipients. The rules of the House provide for continuous balloting on President until a winner is declared. (It took 36 ballots to select Jefferson over Burr.) Under existing law, the balloting would start January 6, leaving 14 days until the scheduled inauguration. If no President were chosen by January 20, under the 20th amendment, the Vice President-elect would become President. But he would only be Acting President, subject to removal at any time that a majority of the delegations in the House agreed on a new President.

If no candidate for Vice President receives an electoral college majority, the Senate elects a new Vice President, with each *member* having a single vote and an absolute majority of the Senate membership required for election. Here the choice must be from the top two electoral vote recipients for Vice President. (Only once in history has the Senate been called on to choose a Vice President—in 1837, when Martin Van Buren's Vice Presidential running mate, Col. Richard M. Johnson of Kentucky, won only 147 electoral votes, one

175

less than a majority, but was elected by the Senate over the runner-up in the electoral vote for President.)

From the start, the method of electing the President has been a subject of debate and discussion. At the Constitutional Convention, a few key members, including Madison, Franklin and Gouverneur Morris, favored direct popular election. Others would have preferred to see the President elected by Congress or by State Governors. One of the main arguments for the electoral college system was that through the provision for at least three electors regardless of population, it gave the small states some protection against domination by large states. If we were to preserve our Federal System of government, it was felt, this was an important consideration, and this argument may have gone far in swaying the Convention.

Since January 6, 1797, when Rep. William L. Smith of South Carolina offered in Congress the first Constitutional Amendment proposing reform of our procedure for electing a President, hardly a session of Congress has passed without the introduction of one or more resolutions of this character. In the 57-year period between 1889 and 1946, 109 amendments were proposed and 172 in the period from 1947 to 1965. Most interestingly, probably more amendments have been proposed concerning the presidential election than concerning any other single provision of the Constitution.

Those who favor retaining our present electoral system argue that it has stood the test of time and that it has produced only three Presidents who failed to win a plurality of the popular vote (Adams in 1824, Hayes in 1876, and Benjamin Harrison in 1888). Only on two occasions since 1789 has the election of the President fallen into the House of Representatives (in 1800 and again in 1824), and only in one of these instances did the election by the House result in the selection of a "minority" President (Adams). Moreover, the existing system, with its requirement of an absolute majority of electoral votes and the general state-unit system which tends to produce the necessary electoral vote majority for one or other of the major parties, operates to freeze out third parties. The existing system's exaggeration of the winner's electoral vote helps assure stability, it is argued, in giving the appearance of nationwide backing in a particularly close and hard-fought campaign. Thus it may help the newly elected President to win general acceptance. The existing system "forces" a candidate to campaign in most of the states, whereas in a direct election, he would concentrate most of his efforts in densely populated states, and particularly in urban areas. Blocks of primarily rural states (e.g., the South) could be practically ignored or left to third party candidates altogether. Finally, it is said, too much uncertainty persists as to what is a better method.

Those who oppose the present electoral college system make several points. First, they criticize the office of presidential elector, including its "independent" nature and the authority of the states at any time to change the method of "appointing" or selecting the electors (i.e., to manipulate the system from election to election). Second, they argue that under the so-called "winner-take-all," unit-rule, or general-ticket method (which credits a state's entire electoral vote to the candidate receiving the most popular votes), great numbers of voters become disfranchised and, in effect, have their votes cast in favor of the candidate they opposed. Third, the present system in placing exaggerated importance on the large swing states with great blocs of electoral votes, inflates the bargaining power of minorities and pressure groups in such states where the popular vote closely divides and invites fraud in the large, crucial states where the vote may be close.

The proposed amendments to the Constitution of the United States which would provide new methods for the election of the President fall into five general classes: direct election plans, district plans, proportional plans, the automatic electoral vote or "non-elector" plans, and, lastly, a combination of these four.

The direct election plan, recently passed by the House of Representatives,[34] would abolish the electoral college and electoral vote altogether and would provide for the election of the President and the Vice President by a majority of the total popular vote in the country. In the event no candidate received at least 40 percent of the vote, a run-off election would decide between the two parts of candidates who received the greatest number of popular votes. The House-passed proposal would thus eliminate electors, the electoral college and the unit rule, and the throwing of the election into Congress.

The district plan, formerly known as the Mundt-Coudert Plan, would preserve the Electoral College but would eliminate the present procedure of giving a state's entire electoral vote to one candidate. Electors would be chosen by the voters, one for each district in every state, and in addition, two for each state at large. Before election the electors would have to pledge to support their party's candidates, a binding pledge. These electors would vote and the candidate who received the highest number of such electoral votes would be President, providing he had a majority; failing a majority, the Senate and the House, meeting jointly, would elect a President from the top three candidates.

The proportional plan, formerly referred to as the Lodge-Gossett Plan,[35] would abolish the Electoral College, but would retain the electoral vote. The electoral vote in each state would be apportioned among the Presidential candidates in accordance with the number of popular votes they receive, so that the candidate who received a plurality of the popular votes would not receive the state's entire electoral vote as he would under the present system.

The "automatic" electoral vote plan would also abolish the office of elector but retain the electoral vote of each state. Under this plan, however, the entire electoral vote of each state would be automatically awarded to the candidate receiving the greatest number of votes for President in that state (as it is at present).

The "mixed" or MacGregor plan, devised in 1969 by Representative Clark MacGregor (R.-Minn.), would have electoral votes counted for all presidential candidates as under the proportional scheme. However, if the high man did not receive 50 percent or more of the electoral vote, the decision would shift to the *popular* vote. If the high man did not get at least 40 percent of that, the President would be chosen by the Senate and House in joint session, with each member casting one vote for one of the two top candidates.

CONCLUSION

The procedures of our nominating conventions are currently undergoing substantial reforms. Other problems like campaign financing and the electoral college system lack effective solutions at this time (though the recent action by the House may signal the beginning of the end for the electoral college).

The events of 1968 perhaps exaggerated the degree of disenchantment of the American people with their political institutions, but some changes in the electoral process clearly are necessary to retain the confidence of the people in the system. The situation could be labeled "urgent". Many groups, especially the young and the blacks, want a more effective voice in the political process. The process of reform must

178

continue if the promise of democracy, equality, and participation is to be kept.

REFERENCES

1. Vladimir O. Key, *Politics, Parties, and Pressure Groups* (New York: Thomas Y. Crowell, 1964), at 431.
2. See Denis Brogan, *Politics in America* (New York: Harper, 1954), at 194; and J. S. Chase, "The Emergence of National Nominating Convention," (unpublished Ph.D. thesis, University of Chicago, 1962), at 11; and Theodore J. Lowi, "Party, Policy and Constitution in America," in William Chambers and Walter D. Burnham, eds., *The American Party System— Stages of Political Development* (New York: Oxford University Press, 1967).
3. Chase, *id.* at 100.
4. Brogan, *supra* note 2, at 66.
5. Charles E. Merriam and Louise Overacker, *Primary Elections, A Study of the History and Tendencies of Primary Election Legislation* (Chicago: University of Chicago, 1928), at 4.
6. J. W. Davis, *Presidential Primaries: Road to the White House* (New York: Crowell, 1967), at 15.
7. Merriam, *supra* note 5, at 29.
8. Ernst C. Meyer, *Nominating Systems: Direct Primaries Versus Conventions in the United States* (Madison, Wis.: published by the author, 1902), at 97.
9. Davis, *supra* note 6, at 27.
10. *Id.* at 28.
11. *Id.* at 30.
12. Alexander M. Bickel, *The New Age of Political Reform—The Electoral College, the Convention, and the Party System* (New York: Harper & Row, 1968), at 21.
13. Key, *supra* note 1, at 431.
14. Donald G. Tacheron & Jill Spier, *A National Presidential Primary? Presidential Primary Legislation in Congress: 1945– 1968* (Washington, D. C.: The Library of Congress, Legislative Reference Service, Nov. 20, 1968), at 49–57.
15. 1964 Proceedings, at 30–31.
16. Report of Committee on Credentials Adopted by 1968 Democratic National Convention.
17. Resolution 12 adopted by the Democratic National Convention, 1968.
18. Report of Committee on Credentials, *supra* note 16.
19. Quoted in Austin Ranney and Willmore Kendall, *Democracy and the American Party System* (New York: Harcourt, Brace & Co., 1956), at 315.
20. James M. Perry, *The New Politics* (New York: Potter, 1968), at 7.
21. All 1968 figures are still approximates. Substantial increases in

figures may in part be due to improved data collecting.
22. These are: American Bar Association, American Medical Asscciation, American Petroleum Institute, American Iron and Steel Institute, Association of American Railroads, Business Advisory Council, Chiefs of Foreign Missions and Special Missions, Manufacturing Chemists Association, National Association of Electric Companies, National Association of Manufacturers. National Association of Real Estate Boards, National Coal Association, and Chamber of Commerce of the United States.
23. Reported contributions:

Year	Republicans	Democrats	Miscellaneous	Total
1956	$741,189	$8,000	$2,725	$751,914
1960	425,710	63,255	2,500	491,465
1964	200,310	225,790	4,618	429,718

24. When it came to spending tax-deductible corporate funds to benefit the party in power, the top defense contractors were more generous. In 1965, eleven of the top 25 defense contractors of fiscal year 1965 bought full page advertisements, at $15,000 per page, in the Democrats' political advertising book, *Toward an Age of Greatness*. Not long afterwards, the Congress forbade corporations from claiming tax deductions for the expense of ads in political program books. Herbert E. Alexander, *Financing the 1964 Election* (Princeton, N.J.: Citizens' Research Foundation, 1966), at 99–104.
25. Because the Democratic incumbent was available for reelection, Democratic candidates spent very little at this stage of the campaign, though reportedly more than $600,000 was expended in the primary campaigns by and against George Wallace.
26. Estimated at 300,000 persons prior to 1964 Republican Convention; McCarthy estimates are perhaps half that number for 1968.
27. K. McKeough and J. Bibby, *The Costs of Political Participation: A Study of National Convention Delegates* (Princeton: N.J.: Citizens' Research Foundation, 1968). Table 4, at 85.
28. Existing federal requirements concerning disclosure of campaign *funds* are essentially the same as those enacted by the passage in 1925 of the Corrupt Practices Act. Reports of receipts and expenditures must be made not only by candidates for the House or Senate, but also by any interstate committee which seeks to influence federal elections and by any person who spends more than $50 a year to influence federal elections in two or more states. These reports are open for public inspection.
29. U.S. President's Commission on Campaign Costs, *Financing Presidential Office Campaigns* (Washington, D.C.: Government Printing Office, April, 1962), at 17–20.

30. Minn. Sess. Laws 1955, c. 775, amending Minn. Stat. Sec. 290.09, 290.21, 1953.
31. John Hope Franklin and Isidore Starr, *The Negro in Twentieth Century America* (New York: Vintage Books, 1967), at 373.
32. United States Commission on Civil Rights, *Political Participation* (Washington, D.C.: Government Printing Office, 1968).
33. Brooke, Mass.; Clay, Mo.; Chisholm, N.Y.; Conyers, Mich., Dawson, Ill.; Diggs, Mich.; Hawkins, Calif.; Nix, Pa.; Powell, N.Y.; and Stokes, Ohio.
34. See Cong. Rec. H8142–43 (daily ed. Sept. 18, 1969).
35. After the then Senator H. C. Lodge (R.-Mass.) and Representative Ed Gossett (D.-Tex.).

CHAPTER 8

CONGRESS AND THE PUBLIC WILL*

In 1790, when the United States was trying out its new form of government, the average U.S. Senator represented 220,000 people, the average U.S. Representative only 37,000 people. A third of a century later, in the Jackson-Adams presidential contest of 1824, only 356,000 votes were cast, less than half the present day population of the District of Columbia. As late as 1900, the average Congressman represented less than 200,000 people. The citizen, of course, also voted for state and town or city legislators representing even fewer numbers. Today, however, the average Congressman represents twelve times as many constituents as he did in 1790. Yet the American Congress is still supposed to be uniquely responsive to the will of the people.

Our form of government requires that the national legislature maintain a direct and intimate working relationship with the people and that Congress remain open and accessible. As the Joint Committee on the Organization of the Congress asserted in 1966,

> The Congress . . . is the only branch of the federal government regularly and entirely accountable to the American people. Indeed, it is the people's branch. Our constitutional system is based on the principle that Congress must effectively bring to bear the will of the people on all phases of the formation and execution of public policy.[1]

The two houses of Congress are designed to embody the will of the majority of citizens, insofar as that will is known or expressed. In providing that Members of the House of Representatives should be chosen "by the people of the several states," the framers of the Constitution left no doubt

---

*This chapter was prepared by Judith Toth of Cabin John, Md., based in part on a research contribution by Prof. Roger H. Davidson, Department of Political Science, University of California at Santa Barbara.

that they considered that branch a popular body.[2] And while the Founding Fathers had other ideas concerning the Senate, the history of the 17th amendment (ratified in 1913) demonstrates that the Senate has also come to be viewed as essentially a popular institution. Strong public pressure— expressed through the House of Representatives, state governments, pressure groups, petitions, and referenda— succeeded in amending the Constitution to provide for the popular election of Senators. Only in a secondary sense, perhaps, do members of that body represent political jurisdiction.[3]

Opinion polls of the past few years indicate, however, that large segments of the American people do not see Congress as responsive to the public will. In the past five years, public support of Congress has fluctuated widely. During the legislative stalemate of President Kennedy's administration, only 35 percent of a national sample of adults gave Congress a favorable rating. For those expressing a negative judgment (51 percent of the sample), the chief irritant was the dilatory handling of lawmaking. Three major unpassed proposals— civil rights, medicare, and aid to education—were frequently cited as examples.[4]

After President Kennedy's assassination, the long "honeymoon" between President Johnson and Congress unblocked major legislation in many fields. Public support for Congress soared, and late in 1965 it stood even higher than support for the President. Congressional action on legislation drew most of the favorable judgments: "passed a lot of bills," "passed civil rights bill," "made progress," and "supported President" were comments volunteered by citizens.[5] As crisis again gripped the nation, however, public support fell. According to a survey late in 1967, 41 percent gave Congress a favorable rating and 59 percent a negative rating.[6] This time, however, there was a close parallel between public ratings of the President and Congress, indicating that the dissatisfaction, unlike the situation in 1963, may have been part of a generalized alienation from the political process.

Periodic exposés of wrongdoing by individual members of Congress (or congressional employees, as in the case of Bobby Baker) also produce public dissatisfaction and encourage general cynicism about Congress. Reactions to the Dodd and Powell cases were extremely negative, many citizens professing at the time to believe that many Senators and Representatives were guilty of similar activities.[7] Disturbingly, cynicism prevails especially among better educated

183

citizens. Such attitudes are not confined to the intellectual community, however, where it has long been fashionable to view the foibles of Congress with considerable condescension —an attitude which may perhaps decline as the universities themselves enter upon a period of institutional suffering and new self-examination. The findings of the opinion surveys represent the judgments of millions of citizens of all walks of life.

How, then, does Congress respond to the public will and how does that response work in practice by means of seniority and the committee system, by the filibuster, and by the lobbies? And does the majority of Congress respond to external public demands, or to its own majorities?[8]

SENIORITY AND THE COMMITTEE SYSTEM

Congressional government, Woodrow Wilson declared long ago, is committee government. "Congress in session is Congress on public exhibition, while Congress in its committee rooms is Congress at work."[9] Standing committees enable Congress to divide labor on substantive issues and encourage individual legislators to develop expertise concerning matters handled by their committees. Most committees further divide into subcommittees to permit even more specialized consideration of problems—with the attendant benefits of expertise and the publicly visible association of members with particular issues. Since congressional government to a large extent means government by standing committee, the selection of committee chairmen and members, and the procedures followed by committees, are matters of fundamental importance.

Committee assignments are made by the party organizations. House and Senate Republicans and Democrats employ slightly different procedures in making assignments. In the Senate, the Democratic Steering Committee and the Republican Committee on Committees handle assignments. House Democrats rely on their members on the Ways and Means Committee, who are chosen to reflect balance among regions and factions. The House Republican Committee on Committees includes one member from every state having a Republican representation; but because each member casts votes equivalent to the number of Republican Representatives from his state, pivotal decisions are in the hands of members from states such as New York, Ohio, Illinois, and California, that have large Republican delegations.

Initial committee assignments are made in accord with a variety of considerations—e.g., the wishes of the committee chairman, the need for political or geographic balance on a committee, the relevance of the assignment to the member's background or constituency—but especially on the basis of seniority.[10] Even more delicate is the task of apportioning vacant committee posts among incumbents who want to trade their initial assignments for more desirable ones.[11] Elected party leaders exercise considerable influence in drawing up the assignments, though in no sense is their role controlling. While every assignment must be ratified by the entire party caucus (or "conference," in the case of Republicans), the original recommendations are seldom challenged.

Some committees deviate in significant respects from the membership of the parent bodies. Agricultural committees overrepresent rural areas and interior committees overrepresent the West because legislators from those constituencies tend to volunteer to serve on them. These committees are thus weighted in favor of producer interests, for example, and against those, such as consumers, whose interests are less direct or intense—or at least are regarded to be so. Seats are especially coveted on the most prestigious and important committees (like House Rules, the two Appropriations Committees, Senate Finance, House Ways and Means, and Senate Judiciary), and membership accordingly gravitates to legislators of some seniority. Once given an assignment, the individual legislator is considered to have a right to his assignment for the duration of his tenure in Congress, provided that it is uninterrupted by defeat at the polls. (Infrequently, a junior member may be "bumped" from a committee if his party loses enough seats in the House in order to justify changing the ratio of party members on the committee.)

Committee members advance by seniority (defined by continuous terms of committee service), with the most senior majority-party member being named chairman. This is the essence of the much-debated "seniority system."

While the "rule" of seniority is almost never circumvented, it is not a formal requirement, and the appointment of committee chairmen must be approved by the party's entire caucus.[12] Several recent precedents exist for caucus modification of seniority privileges. In 1965 House Democrats removed the seniority of two southerners who had supported the Republican Presidential nominee, Barry Goldwater, in the 1964 election. The two men, John Bell Williams of Mississippi[13] and Albert B. Watson of South Carolina, were placed

185

at the bottom of their committees' seniority lists. Williams was second-ranking Democrat on the Interstate and Foreign Commerce Committee, and the resignation of the Committee's chairman within the year meant that the caucus action had effectively denied him the chairmanship. (A relatively junior member, Watson later changed his party affiliation to Republican and has been reelected as such ever since.) Two years later, House Democrats voted to rescind the seniority of Representative Adam Clayton Powell, chairman of the Education and Labor Committee; Powell had been investigated and found by a House Committee to have misused House funds. The most recent case arose in 1969, when House Democrats voted to strip Representative John Rarick of Mississippi of his seniority for having supported third-party candidate George C. Wallace in the 1968 Presidential campaign. Rarick, a second-term Congressman, was lowest ranking Democrat on the Committee during the 90th Congress but would have moved ahead once a new crop of freshman Democrats were appointed to the Committee.

Tampering with seniority is not, however, an everyday occurrence. In Powell's case, action was taken against a man who not only was personally unpopular in the House and who had engendered strong pressures for some form of disciplinary action, but who had clearly embarrassed the body in the public eye. In the remaining cases, the men had failed to support the party's Presidential nominee.

No feature of congressional practices has drawn as much criticism as seniority. The seniority system has undoubtedly contributed to the unrepresentativeness of legislative leadership, because longevity in office tends to be associated with homogeneous, one-party districts.[14] In the 90th Congress, for example, southerners comprised only about one-fifth of the membership of the Senate and a quarter of the membership of the House, yet they controlled the chairmanships of ten of the sixteen Senate standing committees and ten of the twenty-one House committees. Such men are frequently at loggerheads with the policies of the national party, a fact which can exacerbate conflict between Congress and the Executive branch.

Middle-seniority legislators in particular often express impatience at the seniority system's inability to make adequate use of their talents and experience. Some reformers have proposed a frontal attack upon seniority. Former Representative Thomas G. Curtis (R.-Mo.), for example, long advocated rotation in office—a six-term limit in the tenure of all members. Representative Morris K. Udall (D.-Ariz.), an outspoken advocate of reform, has repeatedly suggested that each committee select its chairman from among the three top-ranking majority members. Such proposals seem to have little chance for adoption, however, in part because the very seniority leaders most threatened by the proposals have the most power—formal and informal—to prevent their passage.[15]

Other reformers, including long-time Representative Richard Bolling (D.-Mo.), therefore express hope that party caucuses could and would exercise their undoubted authority by refusing to appoint chairmen who repeatedly deviate from stated party policies. Bolling suggests that a Democratic Speaker (or Minority Leader) appoint the Committee on Committees and its chairman, all the party's members on the Rules Committee (including the chairman or ranking minority member) and the chairman of all other standing committees. Such choices would then be ratified by the party caucus. Though seniority would probably remain the most important criterion, Bolling believes, "the implied threat of party discipline . . . would give pause to the member who would bolt his party's program."[16]

Yet, troublesome as the seniority system is, it is generally conceded that no viable substitutes are at hand. However unrepresentative and inefficient, the use of the seniority system to appoint committee chairmen serves to isolate and reduce a potentially divisive set of decisions. Its very rigidity is no small virtue in a conflict-laden institution such as a national legislature.[17] Defenders of the practice also point to the advantage of ensuring that experienced members, and those who are relatively impervious to electoral pressure, are responsible for upholding congressional prerogatives in dealing with the increasingly powerful Executive branch.

Moreover, some of the criticism of the seniority system is misdirected. As the Joint Committee on the Organization of the Congress noted in 1966, "the power of the chairman is a more fundamental issue in sound committee operations than is his method of selection.[18] Though chairmen range from the ineffectual to the dictatorial, they possess impressive formal and informal powers. Most committee chairmen assume responsibility for assigning bills to subcommittees, for selecting subcommittee chairmen, for scheduling consideration of bills, for supervising preparation of reports on bills, and finally for transmitting reports to the Rules Committee. Most chairmen also assume full responsibility for setting subcommittee jurisdictions, for distributing travel and other expense budgets, and for hiring committee staff members. "The committee member who has served twenty years is not just five percent more powerful than the member who has served 19 years," Republican Morris Udall (D.-Ariz.) has observed. "If he is chairman he is 1,000 percent more powerful."[19]

The legislative process has enough detours so that the chairman of a standing committee can tie up important items of legislation for extended periods of time. The chairman may, or may not, take junior committee members into his confidence as he proceeds; he may, or may not, consult minority members. Many measures—in education, welfare, urban affairs, and civil rights—have been delayed or killed by unsympathetic committee chairmen. And while majorities on the Senate or House floor may in theory remove a measure from an intransigent chairman, the procedural devices for accomplishing this remain clumsy and difficult.

In reacting to abuses of the chairman's powers, a number of committees have adopted rules of procedure which guarantee committee members a part in making decisions. In recommending that such safeguards extend to all committees, the Joint Committee on the Organization of the Congress proposed a "committee bill of rights" designed to insure that committee majorities have an opportunity to work their will. As the Joint Committee explained:

> The chairman is charged with a heavy responsibility and should have authority commensurate with that responsibility. It is unrealistic to suppose that a committee could operate efficiently without allowing the chairman to propose the committee's agenda, to participate in the selection of staff, to assign members to subcommittees, and, in general, to manage committee business. Nevertheless, the chairman is the agent of the committee. The ultimate power does and should rest with a majority of the committee itself.[20]

The most feasible avenue of reform, the Joint Committee concluded, probably lies in strengthening the majority rule in committees. At minimum, committee rules should guarantee majority participation in calling meetings, transacting business, hiring staff, and planning the agenda. Minority party members, by the same token, should be assured adequate staff assistance (now left to the discretion of the chairman) and at least some meaningful role in framing the committee's agenda. The "committee bill of rights" included in the 1967 legislative re-organization bill would be a modest step in this direction. Passed by the Senate in 1967, the bill met objections from the House Democratic leadership, which kept the measure bottled up in the Rules Committee.

But reformers in the 91st Congress may be wearing down the resistance of Congressional elders to a general reform bill—the first since 1946. This bill aims particularly at curbing arbitrary actions by the powerful committee chairmen. Besides requiring written procedural rules for all committees, thus opening more avenues for a committee majority to override a chairman, the changes would: (1) restrict proxy voting by absent committee members, a device that now allows some chairmen and other senior members to control absentees' proxies to use as they wish; (2) give members of the minority party the right to hire some committee staff assistants of their own; (3) open committee meetings to the public, with a few exceptions, and allow radio and TV coverage of open hearings (the House now generally forbids broadcasting, and its Appropriations Committee, for one, holds almost all meetings behind closed doors); and (4) require public disclosure of all committee votes.[21]

THE SENATE FILIBUSTER

Perhaps the most celebrated facet of "minority rule" is the Senate's practice of tolerating "extended debate," or filibuster, to talk a measure to death. In contrast to the House, where debate is rigorously controlled, Senate Rule 22 makes it exceedingly difficult to close off debate if a few Senators wish to forestall a vote. A petition must be signed by 16 members, and then the issue of cloture is brought up two days later. Two thirds of the Senators present and voting must agree to cloture, after which each Senator still has up to one hour to speak on the issue at hand.

Every two years opponents of the filibuster regularly seek to strengthen the cloture provision—usually proposing to reduce the required votes from two thirds to a simple majority. Several times the Senate has come close to revising Rule 22, but the issue remains procedurally clouded by the question over whether or not the Senate is a "continuing body" and thus has *continuing* rules. The notion of continuity attracts more support than the substance of Rule 22 itself and has, thus far, prevented change.[22]

In 1957, however, the President of the Senate, Vice President Richard M. Nixon, suggested a rationale whereby a

189

majority of Senators could act upon rules changes without doing violence to the notion of the Senate as a "continuing body." In an informal advisory opinion rendered as President of the Senate, Mr. Nixon pointed out that, under the Constitution, each house has the right to "determine the rules of its own proceedings."[23] Because this right derives from the Constitution itself, it should not be restricted or limited by rules adopted in a previous Congress. Thus, he concluded, in each new Congress a current majority has the right to adopt its own rules.[24] Though Mr. Nixon's ruling was only advisory, retiring Vice President Hubert Humphrey actually made such a ruling in 1969, in the early days of the 91st Congress. But his ruling was explicitly rejected by a Senate vote—again demonstrating the appeal of the "continuing body" concept, quite apart from the filibuster issue itself.

One factor that bears upon the Senate's failure to eliminate the filibuster is the infrequency of its use. (Normally, Senate debate is closed by unanimous consent agreements.) Yet these few occasions have been deeply significant, since the major use of the filibuster in modern times has been to defeat civil rights legislation. For decades a southern minority, standing behind Rule 22, prevented effective and moderate action on civil rights. Only mass freedom marches, police dogs, and fire hoses, and the murder of civil rights workers, made possible the invocation of cloture to pass the Civil Rights Act of 1964 and the Voting Rights Act of 1965. The Civil Rights Act of 1968, which contained prohibitions against discrimination in the sale or rental of housing, was enacted when, after three unsuccessful attempts, the Senate finally voted cloture by the two-thirds vote required.

Defenders of the present cloture arrangement—one that has been successfully invoked less than 10 times in the four decades of its existence—argue that it promotes freedom of debate, which is a cherished Senate principle. Allowing a majority of Senators to close off debate would, they maintain, impair the deliberative function and render the Senate a mere copy of the House of Representatives, where legislation can be "gaveled" through briskly with only limited debate. Free, unhurried deliberation also permits small numbers of Senators who feel deeply on issues to make last-resort appeals to the court of public opinion. "It takes a good many weeks to inform the electorate in a country of 195 million," the late Senator Everett M. Dirksen observed in defending the filibuster in 1967.[25] If a few more votes are needed and a realistic chance exists of obtaining them—by persuasion, compromise, or public pressure—the filibuster can, it is argued, serve as a useful parliamentary tool.

The filibuster has been used in the past to obstruct legislation which, in retrospect, would have been destructive to individual freedom. An outstanding example is the filibuster during World War II against the Forced Labor Bill which would have frozen people in their jobs for the duration of the war. There have been many other cases where a filibuster, or the threat of one, was a tactic in a "liberal" rather than a "reactionary" cause. And just the threat of a filibuster can be enough to keep legislative action off the floor of the Senate (as in the case of the nomination of Abe Fortas as Chief Justice in 1968).

On the other hand, the present provisions of Rule 22 are at odds not only with the practice in the House of Representatives, but also with general principles of parliamentary law, early Senate procedures, and (almost without exception) parliamentary practice in legislatures throughout the English-speaking (and even most of the non-English-speaking world. Only in the Senate of the United States, observes Senator Clifford P. Case (R.-N.J.), must an opposition be beaten down by "physical exhaustion" and "the medieval practice of trial by ordeal still survives."[26]

Even if the cloture rule were strengthened to allow a simple majority to end debate, the right of the minority—indeed, of all Senators—to state their case would not necessarily be curtailed. The present cloture rule, once invoked, permits each Senator as much as one hour to speak on the substantive issue at hand. Thus, as many as a hundred hours of debate remain, even after cloture has been invoked. The vote required for cloture could be changed without changing the amount of time for debate between the voting of cloture and the vote on the substantive issue.

Proponents of the filibuster argue that no simple majority should prevail over a substantial minority that feels deeply enough about an issue to engage in "extended debate." Whatever may be the abstract merits of this argument, it is increasingly difficult to maintain it in view of the uses to which the filibuster has been put. "In the specific case of legislation for racial equality," Robert Bendiner has noted, "involving the most fundamental rights of a large minority of the nation's citizens, a plea for filibustering in the name of minority rights tumbles into absurdity altogether. . . ."[27]

191

THE LOBBY

For as long as our government has existed, people have banded together to give strength to their special interests by participating in pressure groups, or "lobbies." Pressure groups act out their special role in the democratic process at all levels of government, but most notably, perhaps, in relation to the Congress. Some groups are based on grass roots issues like "gun control" or "tax reform." Some are employment-oriented groups like labor unions. Some are purely economic— big businesses and small businesses, each looking out for their own particular interests. There are veterans' lobbies, church lobbies, lobbies for humanitarian causes. There are even lobbies for foreign governments or firms.

Lobbying is protected by the First Amendment to the Constitution—the right to petition the government for redress of grievances. No one is disposed to tamper with or restrict this right. Like the other First Amendment rights of free speech and free assembly, there can be abuse of the freedom guaranteed to petitioners to Congress, but this potential for abuse does not, in any case, demonstrate that the right does not or should not exist.

Nonetheless, a growing sentiment insists that lobbies are corrupt or corrupting. Time and again front page stories break on attempted bribes of government officials by lobbies, or of campaign contributions by persons interested in influencing the legislative policies of elected officials. Although these cases are the sensational and exceptional, they deeply disturb the faith of the electorate in their government. All too often, it seems to many people, only monied interests are effectively heard in the halls of government. Despite examples of victories of an aroused citizenry over big business, as in the case of the passage of the antitrust laws, or big labor, as with the Taft-Hartley Act, many feel that government is too big to listen to the "little" man.

The Congress is not unaware of the problems of lobbies. The Federal Regulation of Lobbying Act of 1946 requires lobbyists to make periodic public disclosure of the sources and purposes of their employment and the amount of their compensation. Thus it seeks to guard against those who would influence legislation clandestinely or from hidden motives, while not hindering those who wish openly and frankly to advocate their views to the Congress. Further strengthening of full disclosure laws of this type is much to be desired.

Perhaps the most fundamental problem of the lobby is that

192

minority groups (such as poor whites, Indians, blacks, etc.) are unorganized groups which have no lobby. Often they are outside the political process. If and when they try to enter, it requires monumental effort. Until the civil rights movement, many of these people—but especially Negroes—had little or no influence in the legislative chambers of this country. Even now, it takes the combined interest and money of the "enlightened" middle- and upper-classes, plus the tremendous outpouring of time and energy by black leaders, to sustain the movement toward black dignity and equality.

When the poor do get organized, as was ostensibly done in the summer of 1968 with the Poor People's March to Washington and the building of Resurrection City on the Mall near the Washington Monument, they constitute a powerful voice. That demonstration focused attention on their plight: the crusade against hunger in the United States now going on in Congress probably has come about as a direct result of the activities of this particular "lobby." Nonetheless, those segments of our population most alienated from the system have in general the least likelihood of organizing and effectively influencing government through their lobbies.

Our legislative process works when enough people want something badly enough to try to influence the legislators directly or through their groups; then *something* is usually done. If there is an effective and equally potent counterforce, then at least a compromise is obtained.

The gun control movement of 1968 offers a good example. After the assassinations of Martin Luther King, Jr., and Robert F. Kennedy, a tremendous outpouring of support thundered for strong gun control legislation in this country. Influence was exerted upon Congress by large numbers of individuals writing directly to their Representatives and Senators, by organizations, both small and large, and through ad hoc groups like the Emergency Committee for Gun Control and the Committee for More Effective Firearms Control. This movement was countered by letters from individuals against strict gun control, from local gun clubs and organizations unsympathetic to gun control, and from the massive effort of the National Rifle Association. The result was a compromise bill which sought to satisfy both pressure groups.

Similarly, there has recently been an accelerating grass roots movement for comprehensive tax reform. Letters on tax reform have been flowing into Washington. Largely due to the 10% surcharge, the cost of the Vietnam war, and extensive publicity given to national priorities and inequities

193

in the tax laws, change in the present tax structure was sought by all sides. The 91st Congress predictably reacted with tax reform legislation.

In cases such as these, lobbying clearly makes a positive contribution to the American political process. A great deal of our legislation gets initiated because some group has drawn attention to the need for it. Lobbyists provide information and other services which are welcomed by governmental decision-makers. If information from lobbyists and lobby groups was, for some reason, unavailable to officials, they would depend largely on their own staff for information and ideas. The clash of viewpoints between contesting groups is not only informative; it is also creative. Lobby groups and lobbyists define opinion with a sense of reality and specificity which political parties, the mass media, opinion polls, and staff assistants seldom, if ever, can achieve.

Lobbies, therefore, are necessary and useful, as well as inevitable. But just as some groups, such as the poor, do not have effective lobbies: so also do some issues not have effective lobbies,—issues such as the reform of Congressional procedures.

CONGRESSIONAL REFORMS

Several reasons can be given on why Congressional reform does not stimulate the formation of lobbies. For one thing, the average citizen—especially the average youthful reformer—has only an imperfect notion of what is wrong with the procedures of Congress and only a marginal attachment to specific, realistic reform proposals. Opinion surveys show that the public wants proposals for change,[28] but citizens lack basic information and understanding about Congressional personnel or procedures. Every opinion survey ever taken on the subject indicates that the internal workings of Congress are a mystery to most Americans.

Nor are the issues of procedure likely to catch the public's imagination in the foreseeable future. There is no instance within recent memory of strong public demands for reform of the structure or procedures on Congress. Legislators may receive mountains of mail asking for the censure of one Congressman (Adam Clayton Powell or Thomas J. Dodd); they may perceive strong public demand for breaking a specific filibuster (as in 1964 and 1965); but they hear relatively little from citizens concerning the enactment of a congressional "code of ethics" or the revision of the Senate cloture rule.

By the same token, opinion leaders have made little effort to create a public issue out of congressional reform. Mass media coverage of the problem is sketchy; and when newsmen deign to pay attention to the issue, their approach is often narrowly issue oriented or misdirected. Party platforms ritually pledge action to "modernize" Congress (although the Democrats neglected to mention the subject in 1968), but few politicians have found the issue fruitful enough to warrant much emphasis. Thus, there have been few efforts to raise public interest in reform. Indeed, as former Representative Donald Rumsfeld (R.-Ill.) has remarked: "Congressional reform is an issue without a constituency."

This leaves reform of Congressional procedures—for the short run, at least—to the Congressmen themselves. And so long as there is little public clamor for change in Congress, it is unlikely that sufficient numbers of Senators and Representatives will be interested in "preventive maintenance" of the role of the national legislature in our democracy.

A glance at the tangled history of the 1967 legislative reorganization bill will serve to illustrate the point.[29] The Joint Committee on the Organization of Congress was created in 1965 and devoted the better part of two years to hearing witnesses and drafting its report. In 1967, the committee's omnibus reorganization bill passed the Senate after 6 weeks of debates and 39 amendments (114 were proposed). The Senate-passed bill (S. 355) offered useful, but certainly not revolutionary, changes to tighten regulations on lobbying, to eliminate some patronage appointments, and to improve the hold of Congress on appropriations measures. The heart of the bill was its "committee bill of rights," already referred to.

Members of the Joint Committee were pleased with the Senate vote, but they had failed to reckon with the objections of the House leadership. Rather than referring the bill (S. 355) directly to the Committee of the Whole House for deliberation, the Speaker sent it to the Rules Committee, where it languished. Rules Chairman Colmer (D.-Miss.) held hearings for part of one day in April 1967, but held none after that. Rather than bringing the bill to a committee vote, a process of private negotiations ensued in which the bill was stripped of key provisions. A number of House members, including Representatives Bolling and Udall, tried to rescue

195

the measure, but the ultimate leadership-sponsored version was described by Representative Madden, co-chairman of the Joint Committee, as being "worse than nothing and would postpone the reform movement for the next 15 or 20 years." The leadership's version would have exempted House committees from major elements of the "committee bill of rights" and weakened the provision for minority staffing. It was partially this latter issue that prompted a group of younger Republicans to charge publicly that the House leadership was smothering the bill. A group led by Congressman Rumsfeld staged a semi-filibuster on the House floor in the closing days of the 90th Congress to protest the bill's fate after the Rules Committee had voted in July 1968 to defer action on the bill indefinitely.

Advocates of the reorganization bill are increasingly confident that during the 91st Congress the Senate will again pass such legislation, if, as now seems possible, the House finally acts. The Legislative Reorganization Act of 1969 (H.R. 2185) notably avoids the issue of seniority, but it does call for a substantial modification in the procedures of the standing committees. This bill is a compromise which, although piecemeal, will do much to update the internal operations of the Congress. Younger members of Congress in both parties are also pushing hard for reform of the seniority system and challenging the leadership of septuagenarian House Speaker John McCormack. As the second session of the 91st Congress was getting underway, the likelihood of substantial change in even the seniority system seemed closer than at any previous time in recent history.

Whatever the outcome of this struggle, and whatever the merits of the positions of the various participants, neither lobbies nor direct public pressure of any kind, it seems, will play a significant role. One may wonder what might be accomplished in our nation if some of the enthusiasm and energy now being poured into issues like ROTC on the campus and separate facilities for black students were redirected toward less dramatic, less emotionally satisfying problems like the congressional committee system.

CONCLUSION

The first maxim of democratic parliamentary procedure, in the words of the late Speaker of the House, Sam Rayburn, who served in the post longer than any other, is that "a determined majority can always work its will," whether in committee or floor deliberation.[30] Even such an elitist as Alexander Hamilton referred to "the fundamental maxim of republican government, which requires that the sense of the majority should prevail."[31] Minorities must be accorded reasonable opportunities to present their case to colleagues and to the general public; but to allow minority rights to become the equivalent of minority rule is to frustrate one of the principles of government which gives our system its legitimacy.

Like other important institutions of the political order, Congress seriously needs procedural reforms to make it more responsive to the will of its own members and, hence, to the public will. The present crisis of confidence in our political institutions lends added urgency to these needs. Ultimately, the future role of Congress rests upon its ability "to stimulate continuous and critical thinking about change—before change is forced upon it."[32] Clearly, Congress must act to realize the substance as well as the theory of majority rule, lest wide-spread public disaffection and cynicism produce an irreversible attrition of public support for Congress and the laws it enacts.

REFERENCES

1. U.S., Congress, Joint Committee on the Organization of the Congress, *Organization of Congress, Final Report,* Joint Res. 2, 89th Cong., 2d sess., 1966, at 1.

2. Art. 1, Sec 2. See *Wesberry* v. *Sanders,* 376 U.S. 1 (1964); *Welles v. Rockefeller,* 394 U.S. 542 (1969).

3. The movement for direct election of Senators is chronicled in detail in George Havnes, *The Senate of the United States, Its History and Practices* (Boston: Houghton Mifflin, 1938).

4. Louis Harris and Associates, *Washington Post,* Jan. 6, 1964, at A-1.

5. Louis Harris and Associates, *Washington Post,* Jan. 4, 1965, at A-1.

6. Louis Harris and Associates, *Washington Post,* Jan. 22, 1968, at A-2.

7. Louis Harris and Associates, *Washington Post,* May 8, 1967, at A-2.

8. J. Sundquist, *Politics and Policy—The Eisenhower; Kennedy, and Johnson Years* (1968), at 513.

9. Woodrow Wilson, *Congressional Government* (New York: Meridian Books, 1956), at 69.

10. *I.e.,* a member's wishes are normally granted in direct relation to the seniority he has amassed.

11. See Nicholas A. Masters, "Committee Assignments in the House of Representatives," *American Political Science Review* 345-357 (June 1961).

12. See, for example, John F. Bibby and Roger H. Davidson, *On Capitol Hill: Studies in Legislative Politics* (New York: Holt, Rinehart & Winston, 1967), at 153–169.

13. He was elected governor of his state in November 1968.

14. George Goodwin, "The Seniority System in Congress," *American Political Science Review* 412–436 (June 1959); Raymond E. Wolfinger and Joan Heifetz, "Safe Seats, Seniority, and Power in Congress," *American Political Science Review* 337-339 (June 1965).

15. Roger H. Davidson, Davie M. Kovenock, and Michael K. O'Leary, *Congress in Crisis: Politics and Congressional Reform* (New York: Hawthorn Books, 1967), at 100–103.

16. Richard Bolling, *House Out of Order* (New York: E. P. Dutton, 1964), at 241.

17. Nelson W. Polsby, " 'Seniority System' Isn't All Bad," *Los Angeles Times*, Sept. 20, 1968, at II, 5.

18. U.S. Congress, Joint Committee on the Organization of the Congress, *Organization of the Congress, Final Report*, Joint Res. 2, 89th Cong., 2d sess., 1966, at 9.

19. Quoted in Larry L. King, "Inside Capitol Hill: How the House Really Works," *Harper's*, Oct. 1968, at 67.

20. *Id.*

21. Norman C. Miller, "Updating Congress," *Wall Street Journal*, Mar. 27, 1969, at 1.

22. As long as the Senate considers itself a "continuing body" (unlike the House, which must organize anew every two years), then rules which are previously in force govern consideration of new rules changes. Hence, the biennial proposals for weakening the filibuster are themselves subject to filibuster.

23. Art. I, Sec. 5.

24. *Congressional Quarterly Weekly Report*, Jan. 13, 1967 at 41.

25. Quoted in Lindsay Rogers, "Filibuster Debate," *Reporter*, Jan. 8, 1959, at 21. Pros and cons of unlimited debate are discussed in George B. Galloway, *The Legislative Process in Congress* (New York: Thomas Y. Crowell, 1953), at 564–570.

26. Robert Bendiner, *Obstacle Course on Capitol Hill* (New York: McGraw-Hill, 1964), at 113–114.

27. *Id.*

28. American Institute of Public Opinion, surveys in 1964, 1966, 1967, and 1968.

29. Progress of the bill is summarized in *Congressional Quarterly Weekly Report*, June 9, 1967, at 975–978.

30. Quoted in *Congressional Quarterly Weekly Report*, June 7, 1963. at 87.

31. Benjamin Fletcher, ed., *The Federalist* (Cambridge: Belknap Press, 1961).

32. Davidson, Kovenock, and O'Leary, *supra* note 15, at 170.

CHAPTER 9

THE FAMILY AND VIOLENCE*

The family is the oldest human institution, the basic unit of society. During our lifetime, we ordinarily belong to two families—the first when we are children, the second when we are parents. One we are born into; the other we establish ourselves. These two experiences represent life's major activity from birth to death.

The American family has clearly lost some of its solidarity, however. Once it was the source of cohesion and security, the unit of economic activity, the means of recreation and education. Today it is increasingly disrupted. Divorce rates rise, but are outrun by the incidence of marital conflicts. Parents, especially working mothers, spend more time outside the home, and television changes the character of family recreation. A generation gap widens, as young people identify more with peer groups in colleges, dropout communities, and street cultures than with their own families.

These changes do not necessarily signify a decline in the importance of the family. They do reflect the increasing pressures which the family is under—but these stresses frequently stem precisely from the fact that more is being demanded of family life than ever before. Thus, as urbanization depersonalizes human relationships, husbands and wives become more dependent upon each other for the satisfaction of emotional needs that were previously met outside of the family. And, despite the impact of television, the family manifestly retains its central role in the upbringing of children.

The family is, after all, the primary channel through which human culture is transmitted to the young of the species. The

---

*This chapter was prepared by James S. Campbell on the basis of a paper submitted by Shlomo Shoham, Director of the Institute of Criminal Law and Criminology, Tel-Aviv University, Israel, and on materials made available to the Task Force by Commissioner W. Walter Menninger, M.D.

family and the home are the first molding cast for a child's behavior and the basic unit for the child's "socialization." Values are inculcated by example, teaching and interaction.[1] It is the function of the family to transmit to the children what the values of the society are, as well as to indicate what are acceptable and unacceptable means of achievement. In a culture, for instance, where violence in a commendable pattern of masculine behavior, the education of children in the family will include a permissive attitude toward violence. Conversely, if a society or distinct class within it prohibits over-aggression, the family experience will direct the children toward the solution of conflicts by other than violent means.

The crucial role of the family in disposing a child to violence or non-violence is generally accepted. Whatever be the hereditary predisposition and the biological factors contributing to a child's development, the patterns of behavior of the child are largely established by his early life experiences. Any observation of young children reveals the potential for aggressive behavior, destructive behavior, temper tantrums, and the like. It is the challenge to the family to orient or socialize these creatures to a principle of operation whereby their impulses of a socially unacceptable nature are controlled.

Of course, the ultimate development of any individual and his ultimate violence-proneness are the result of many factors. Crime and violence are the result of a complex interaction of individuals' biologies and life experiences. Criminologists have identified specific characteristics often associated with crime and violence, including social disorganization, cultural conflict resulting from migration, highly packed urban living, poverty, and other important elements. Nevertheless, despite the importance of these other factors, the family remains the first socializing agency to which the human being is exposed in the crucial formative years of his life. What, then is the ability of the family unit to instill a restraining, normative barrier against violence within the personality framework of the child?

FORMATION OF THE CHILD'S MORAL PERSONALITY

Personality growth and development is a complex process. The infant in the beginning does not have any conception of the values as expressed by society. The infant after birth is motivated by some basic drives to survive and to achieve satisfaction and relief of tension through the satisfaction of bodily needs. In addition, there are some basic psychological needs which include mothering, without which the infant will waste away. But the infant has no real conception or understanding, or capacity to understand in adult logic what is happening about him, or what the consequences are of his behavior.

The early years of life are occupied with the maturation and growth of all the organ systems and the beginning mastery of body skills; i.e., learning to grasp, sit, walk, talk, control body processes. The discipline and control of children as they first develop these skills of body control and locomotion depend entirely upon the parents. The child of two or three has no specific moral controls, no sense of right or wrong except in terms of a self-related reference. Something is right if it provides for his satisfaction and pleasure or relief of tension; something is wrong if it hurts him or causes pain. His response to something wrong is to attempt to retaliate or protest mightily. The basic moral law of the young child might be expressed in terms of the *lex talionis,* or an eye for an eye: "When I hurt, I want you to know I hurt, and I want you to hurt like I hurt. Therefore, if you hit me, I'll hit you back."

Self-centered behavior of this character makes for anarchy, and increasingly, as the child grows, parental discipline sets certain limits. Gradually, the child learns that he cannot always have what he wants when he wants it, and that there must be respect for other people—if only for the reality that he is going to be hurt when he transgresses acceptable limits. The child tends to absorb within his personality the standards of those about him, with their "norms" (rules) for violence as well as other kinds of behavior. This process of socialization, incorporating the parental and social values, is a process that evolves in varying degrees over the period of childhood. The initial absorption is in a concrete and mechanical sense; the child complies with parental rules because the parents have the authority to back up those rules. In due course the child achieves an autonomous ethical system, tested through a process of trial and error, by which he weighs his conduct according to his own inner standards.[2]

Sigmund Freud, from his clinical observations, noted a crucial period in the incorporation of an inner value system in the child around the age of 5 or 6. This he related to the process of the child's forming a more specific sense of identity as a boy or a girl, a process which also involves the child's developing a sense of his role in the family. Freud also related this development to his observation of a process he characterized as the oedipal complex. Simply stated, the boy who has up to this point selfishly wanted to have the mother all to himself, is forced to recognize that father has the inside track. Father is too big to be conquered in this competition, and therefore the young boy in effect operates on the principle that "if he can't beat 'em, join 'em." In other words, he gives up competing with the father for mother, and instead identifies with father *and makes father's values a part of himself.* A comparable process takes place in the young girl. Essentially, it is at this period of time that the child does develop an inner sense of rules, a conscience, a sense of right and wrong, and will then manifest some inner control which is not just related to parental correction.

This is a continuing process that is refined as the child grows older, and it reoccurs significantly during adolescence as the young person retests society's rights and wrongs, and through social-role experimentation works toward establishing an identity as an adult.

In adolescence, sometimes, the adult values have to be challenged and tested in order for the individual to prove that he has separate identity and is capable of independent action. This challenge to adult values may be done by an individual adolescent, but it is more commonly experienced as adolescents join together in groups or gangs. The gang membership provides a sense of security and strength in numbers which permits a youth to act in a way that he could not act on his own.[3] The gang in this sense, or the "street culture" as it has been called, provides a challenge to the family unit, but does so while replacing the family security with gang security and in establishing simple and consistent norms where values are sharply defined in black and white, without ambiguities.

Adolescence, then, is a period of development crises, which if not overcome may result in a predisposition to crime, violence, or deviance. This is not unlike the childhood diseases which everyone has to pass through but from which serious complications can arise. If the socialization in the family prior to or within this critical period has been faulty, there will not be any strong and clear normative barriers against delinquent solutions to life problems.

Jean Genet, the thief, playwright and philosopher, depicts with devastating sincerity the development of a criminal. Genet was born out of wedlock. His mother abandoned him in his cradle, and he was cared for in his formative years by an orphanage, which in due course entrusted him to a foster home, a peasant family in Le Morvan. He soon realized that he was not like the other village youngsters. He was a foundling, with no mother, no father, and therefore no clear identity to internalize. The village was a close community, and he soon found out that in the peasant family he was "Jean, the little bastard," the receptacle for all the residuary, unwanted and despised attributes of the family and the small peasant community.

When Genet commits a crime, he complies with the expectations of his immediate environment. This in itself is satisfying. He is no more Jean the nameless bastard, he is Jean the thief. Moreover, the newly found criminal self-image is a course of strength and achievement: compliance with the image of a criminal gives Jean an individual identity. Further, it makes him eligible for the group of other thieves and homosexuals, affording thus the opportunity for identification with a group and a sense of belonging.

SOCIALIZATION IN THE FAMILY

The general scheme of socialization in the family may be presented as a "norm-sending" process by which the father, for example, transmits the rules of behavior to the family members. This process may be divided for clarity's sake into three phases:

(1) *Statement of rules*: the father in our case states the desired behavior, verbally, by gestures, by some other mode of communication, or by his own behavior as a model for imitation.

(2) *Surveillance*: by the father (or other members of the family) to ensure compliance to the rules.

(3) *Sanctions*: applied for the infringement of the rules or for noncompliance to them.

The sanctions may be either negative in the form of punishment for noncompliance with the rules, or positive in the form of rewards for conformity to the rules. The child on the receiving end may conform to the norm for fear of punishment (sanction orientation); he may be induced to conform by the rewarding sanction (identification); or he may absorb the norm very deeply within his personality structure so that conformity becomes "the right thing to do" (moral orientation). At this deep level of internalization, where the norm becomes a personality element, surveillance and sanctions are essentially superfluous.[4]

The efficacy of the family norm-sending process and the depth to which the child absorbs these controls can be the crucial factor which tips the scale for or against violent behavior by the child. It determines the degree to which the child has internalized the restraining norm as a personality element and hence the force of the pressures which would be necessary to overcome or "neutralize" the restraining force of the norm in order to commit an act of violence. Without taking into account the factor of socialization within the family (or family surrogate), any explanation of violence (or any criminal, deviant or rebellious behavior) is bound to remain incomplete.

The starving Hindu has all the reasons (and all the pressures) in the world to slay one of the holy cows that roam the streets and fry himself a steak, but he would not dream of doing it because of the deeply internalized religious norm forbidding it.[5] The same idea is even more apparent in the actions of religious dissenters, "freedom fighters," and rebels throughout the ages who have undergone extreme torture and death but have not acted contrary to their deeply internalized sets of norms. Research carried out in Israel on delinquent and violent gangs sought to discover why some boys, not distinguishable from the rest by socio-economic background, did not participate in the gang's delinquent and violent activities but only in its nondelinquent ones. The most significant differences between the two groups of boys was the degree to which the norms concerning the sanctity of private property and the nonuse of aggression were internalized to form an initial barrier against criminal and violent behavior. Similar differences arising from different family socialization patterns help explain why even in the worst of slums plagued by poverty, bad living conditions, criminal gangs, prostitutes, and dope peddlers, only some boys become delinquent, whereas a far greater number remain law abiding.

Conflict situations, however, may make the whole process of norm-sending ineffective, so that the norm is internalized by the individual at a very shallow level or even not at all. Continuing conflicts in the norm-sending process may also injure a set of norms that has already been previously internalized by the individual. The greater the intensity and extent of conflict situations in the socialization process, the greater will be the shift away from moral orientation toward sanction orientation, and from fully internalized rules to rules which are followed only out of fear of being caught. At this state the normative barrier against a given crime or violent behavior is completely shattered, and the crime then is only in being caught and not in committing the offense.

Adolescence—the crucial stage in the norm-receiving process—is characterized by, among other things, a yen for absolute values and a desire for sharply defined roles. As described by countless works of literature, youth is not only a seething cauldron of idealism, but also passionately in favor of unequivocal statements of facts and rules—otherwise known, by the young themselves, as plain honesty.

> Gobesque, Balzac's stingy old scoundrel, sits before the fireplace with his teen-aged friend and promises him a loan without guarantees, because up to twenty a person's best guarantee is his age and 'because you, my young friend, are idealistic, you visualize great ideas, basic truths and beautiful Utopias while staring at the dancing flames. At my age, however, we see in the fireplace plain burning coal.'

Those youths whose socialization is most riddled with conflict situations are most liable to reject the offered adjustment to contradictory, hypocritical, and confused sets of norms. If this is adulthood, he prefers the more direct behavior and clearly defined normative system of the delinquent subculture. Because of his inability to internalize the contradictory norms of the adult world, he may be branded as "infantile" "rigid," "a permanent adolescent," "a troublemaker," and thereby be pushed further toward the values of his delinquent peers.

CONFLICTS IN THE SOCIALIZATION PROCESS

What are the kinds of conflict situations in the socialization process within the family which can have harmful effects on the creation of a normative barrier against violence?

The family "broken" by divorce, death, or prolonged or permanent incapacitation of one or both parents was once considered a major cause of delinquency, but research has revealed that the broken home as such may not have the crucial significance that was attributed to it.

Instead, continuous family tension and discord is a far more important factor in delinquency than the actual divorce of the parents. The rates of delinquency are significantly higher in unbroken but unhappy and conflict-ridden homes than in broken ones.[6] Divorce may even lessen the chances of children in a tension-laden family from becoming delinquent or violent.[7] A recent study published in Israel reveals that the most significant factor linked with delinquency was *lack of value consensus among family members.*[8]

Lidz observes that a child properly requires two parents: a parent of the same sex with whom to identify and who provides a model to follow into adulthood, and a parent of the opposite sex who becomes a love object and whose love and approval the child seeks in return by identifying with the parent of the same sex. But, he notes, a parent can fill neither of his roles effectively if he is despised or treated contemptuously by the other parent. The child internalizes directives from both parents and identifies to a greater or lesser extent with both; if the parent's personalities cannot be reconciled, a split may occur in the child's personality as he attempts to relate to both parents but finds that efforts to satisfy one may elicit rebuff and rejection from the other.[9]

Another kind of conflict that impairs socialization in the family is that which arises from an external source and which injures the prestige of the norm-sender. Families in communities that undergo rapid or sudden social change, especially immigrant families whose cultural tradition in their countries of origin is markedly divergent from the culture of the absorbing community, may suffer socio-economic injuries which harm or even shatter the status of the head of the family. These types of conflict stem basically from "external" sources such as industrialization, urbanization, mass immigration, and social change, and they create conflict situations within the family between parents and the offspring, with a high probability of injuring the prestige of the norm-source and thus hampering and injuring the norm-sending process. In Israel, for instance, this type of conflict has been proved a factor in weakening the cohesion of the family unit and thus shattering family control over the young.

In the United States, the impact of slavery and segregation on the Negro family has often had a similarly debilitating effect on its ability to socialize its children. The shattering of family control typically results in the "street-culture" replacing the family as the primary norm-sender. The Kerner Commission Report has described the process well:

> The high rates of unemployment and underemployment in racial ghettos are evidence, in part, that many men living in

207

these areas are seeking, but cannot obtain, jobs which will support a family. Perhaps equally important, most jobs they can get are at the low end of the occupational scale, and often lack the necessary status to sustain a worker's self-respect, or the respect of his family and friends.

* * * * *

Wives of these men are forced to work and usually produce more money. If the men stay at home without working, their inadequacies constantly confront them and tensions arise between them and their wives and children. Under these pressures, it is not surprising that many of these men flee their responsibilities as husbands and fathers, leaving home, and drifting from city to city, or adopting the style of 'street corner men.'

* * * * *

With the father absent and the mother working, many ghetto children spend the bulk of their time on the streets—the streets of a crime-ridden, violence-prone, and poverty-stricken world. The image of success in this world is not that of the 'solid citizen,' the responsible husband and father, but rather that of the 'hustler' who promotes his own interests by exploiting others. The dope sellers and the numbers runners are the 'successful' men because their earnings far outstrip those men who try to climb the economic ladder in honest ways.

* * * * *

. . . Under these circumstances, many adopt exploitation and the 'hustle' as a way of life, disclaiming both work and marriage in favor of casual and temporary liaisons. This pattern reinforces itself from one generation to the next, creating a 'culture of poverty' and an ingrained cynicism about society and its institutions.

A third kind of conflict situation is conflict between verbally transmitted rules and the actual behavior of parents. When parents pay lip-service to legitimate behavior but act contrary to these same norms, conflict situations are created. This phenomenon may help to explain some middle- and upper-class juvenile delinquency—the so-called "good home delinquents." On deeper analysis these homes may not be all that good, for conflict of this kind may have entirely destroyed the legitimate norm-sending capacity of the family.

Thus the parents may preach idealistic achievement, Christian love and spiritual values, but their actual behavior may be directed solely toward material achievement. Parents may *preach* law observance, but children may *see* their parents push their way up in the "rat race" or in the cutthroat competition for upward social mobility without being particularly scrupulous about the means used to achieve their coveted goals. The verbal rule may state that one's interests should be sacrificed to help others, but the way the parents behave reveals that their actual belief is "everyone for himself." Even if the children do not identify themselves with their parents' *acts* instead of with their verbally phrased norms, the norm-sending process is still hampered by the conflict situations created by the parents' preaching and teaching one set of norms and behaving according to another.

Another and deeper kind of conflict between verbally transmitted rules and actual behavior of parents stems from the fact that adults, as grown children, still have within them some of the unresolved struggle of growing up which gets played up in relationships to others in ways of which they may be unaware. Thus there can be unconscious communications by adults which are perhaps in absolute contrast to their conscious intent. Some dramatic work by investigators Johnson and Szurek demonstrated the degree to which children can present problems in behavior and be extremely difficult to manage due to a vicarious psychological participation on the part of the parent who consciously decries the behavior of the child. It is this kind of conflict between the consciously stated standards of the parents and their unresolved, underlying feelings about behavior such as violence and aggression that may prompt the youngster to act out the behavior as part of his relationship to the parent.

A fourth kind of conflict which impairs socialization is inconsistent or crudely punitive disciplining of children. Where sanctions are sporadic, erratic, and inconsistent, social conditioning does not take place and consequently the normative barrier against violent behavior is not formed. Too severe punitive sanctions are also detrimental to norm internalization. Some findings have indicated that unusually severe or harsh child-rearing practices are linked with poor and fragmentary norm internalization.[10] In like manner, too intense punishment is ineffective in suppressing undesired behavior.[11] A research finding which is directly related to violence indicates that children who have experienced rejection or extreme punitiveness from their parents are likely to show weak internalization of a sense of duty and responsibility and have bad control over their tendencies for aggressive behavior.[12]

A survey of delinquent group members revealed consistently that their parents were usually punitive and rejecting.[13] Professor Kohlberg also finds that parents of delinquents tend to be more punitive than parents of nondelinquents, although they do not differ in extent of "firmness" of socialization and home demands. They are less warm and affectionate and more inconsistent and neglectful than parents of nondelinquents.[14] Conversely, the parents', and especially the mothers', warm and affectionate treatment of the infant enhance greatly the efficacy of socialization. Consequently, withdrawal of affection or the threat of it is the most durable and effective sanction.[15] Delay of reward is also found to be effective in suppressing undesirable behavior.[16]

Middle class families resort more to withdrawal of affection as sanctions in socializing their children, whereas the lower classes inflict more repressive punishment.[17] This difference may help explain the lower incidence of violence among middle-class youth whose socialization is presumably more effective. As a rule-of-thumb conclusion, then, aggressive parents breed aggressive children, whereas the subtle manipulation of rewards may help create an effective barrier against violence.

WHAT CAN BE DONE?

In theory, we have many methods to prevent or to correct the effects of faulty, conflict-ridden socialization on delinquent and violent children. In practice, the effectiveness of most of these methods is limited by a number of factors.

Child-guidance clinics and family counseling bureaus may advise parents on desirable methods of child rearing and socialization, but those who most need help are not the ones who seek out such services even where they are available and of high quality. Sometimes an influential aunt or grandmother, or even a teacher or priest, may succeed in socializing children with whom parents have failed. But the "extended family," with a large network of relatives surrounding the nuclear family and participating in the raising of its children, is increasingly disrupted by social and geographic mobility, and teachers and clergymen have less and less personal contact with families in today's society.

It is a sad fact, but a fact nonetheless, that today for the most

210

part we are taught how to be parents by our first-born children (and by occasional desperate forays into Dr. Spock). We go through a process of trial and error, and we don't really have much in the way of social institutions that help parents effectively learn how to be parents. This vital skill is not generally taught in the course of formal schooling, and this is one area where there could be a major step—by building some effective training for parents into the formal educational process.

Many institutions report some success in efforts to correct the faulty socialization of delinquents and criminals. The Highfield Institution for Delinquents and the Boys Industrial School of Kansas, which has an association with the Menninger Clinic in Topeka, Kans., exemplify such intensive treatment programs. Professor Ernst Popanek, who directed the Wiltwyck School in New York, tried to counter aggression by friendship, permissiveness, and understanding which permeated the violence-prone boys' "total environment." Similar attempts have been carried out by Prof. Fritz Redl to ease the aggressivity of "children who hate"[18] at Pioneer House in Detroit, and by Professor Bruno Bettleheim at the Orthogenic School of the University of Chicago. In all these cases, aggressive and guiltless psychopathic children gained a fair measure of internalized guilt and their aggressivity declined.

The crucial question, however, is whether society is prepared to foot the immense bill for this kind of psychiatric treatment of every violent child. Intensive psychotherapy is expensive and, when successful, may take years to achieve positive results. How many children may be accepted in the select and experimental institutions which offer this complex, elaborate, and costly "milieu therapy"? Shouldn't the focus be on preventive strategies aimed at problem groups, rather than on corrective programs of this type?

A bewildering multiplicity of factors are involved in any preventive strategies, however. The ghetto Negro family, for instance, has tended to become matriarchal because of social influences that can be traced all the way back to the practice of slave owners to break up families by selling their individual members.[19] Prevention of the deleterious effects that this family structure has on socialization entails nothing less than a virtual revolution in American attitudes, mores, and race relations. This revolution is probably taking place right now, but before it is carried through many more cohorts of violence-prone Negro children will be born into the slums of our cities.

At the level of preventive individual treatment, the most severe difficulties are encountered. How can outside agencies detect violence-breeding socialization processes? Conflict-ridden socialization leaves its scars on the personality of the child at a very early age, and it often manifests itself only in quite subtle modes of familial interaction. The aggressivity or violence may not erupt until years later. Moreover, assuming detection were possible, how would we intervene? In America, even the rudest home is a castle, and even the most miserable family is a shrine. What agency would we dare let to trespass into this sanctuary when no law has been broken?

Neither government nor any other institution of society can make a husband and wife create a relationship of love among themselves and their children; they must do that on their own, as individuals. But government can at least try to create the conditions under which stable families can thrive.[20] It can make it possible for fathers to have jobs, and hence to have the self-respect that comes from being able to support a family. Government can act against hunger, disease, poor housing, and urban decay, thereby creating a humane environment in which humane personal relationships can develop. Schools can give hope to the young, and to the parents whose hope is in their children. Churches can awaken men and women to the moral and spiritual dimensions of family life.

Given the velocity of change in our society, it is inevitable that family structures will come under increasing pressures. These pressures are likely to underscore the family's importance even more than at present; for the stability of man, and his ability to respond nonviolently to his life experiences, depend on the stability of the family in which he is raised. The family, the central institution of human society, whose failure undermines all, can and must be strengthened by the operations of the other institutions of society.

REFERENCES

1. Lyman C. Wynne, Irvin M. Ryckoff, Juliana Day and Stanley I. Hirsch, "Pseudo-Mutuality in the Family Relations of Schizophrenics," in *The Family,* ed. by Norman W. Bell and Ezra F. Vogel (Glencoe, Ill.: The Free Press, 1960), at 573.

2. Lawrence Kohlberg, *Stage and Sequence: The Developmental Approach to Moralization* (New York: Holt, Rinehart & Winston, 1969).

3. Sophia M. Robison, *Juvenile Delinquency* (New York: Holt, Rinehart & Winston, 1960), at 81.
4. John W. Thibaut and Harold M. Kelley, *The Social Psychology of Groups* (New York: John Wiley & Sons, Inc., 1959).
5. Edwin H. Sutherland and Donald R. Cressey, *Principles of Criminology*, 6th ed. (Philadelphia: Lippincott, 1960), at 195.
6. Francis I. Nve, *Family Relationships and Delinquent Behavior* (New York: John Wiley & Sons, Inc., 1958), at 47.
7. C. R. Shaw and H. D. McKay, "Social Factors of Juvenile Delinquency," National Commission on Law Observance and Enforcement, *Report on the Causes of Crime, II* (Washington, D.C.: Government Printing Office, 1931), at 276 *et seq.*
8. L. D. Jaffe, "Delinquency Proneness and Family Anomie," *Megamot,* March 1962.
9. Theodore Lidz, *The Person: His Development Throughout the Life Cycle* (New York: Basic Books, 1968).
10. Justin Aronfreed, *Conduct and Conscience; the Socialization of Internalized Control over Behavior* (New York: Academic Press, 1968), at 305.
11. *Id.,* at 203.
12. W. McCord et al., "Familial Correlates of Aggression in Nondelinquent Male Children," 62 *Journal of Abnormal and Social Psychology* 79–83 (1961).
13. Albert Bandura and Richard Walters, *Adolescent Aggression* (New York: Ronald Press Co., 1959).
14. Lawrence Kohlberg, "Development of Moral Character and Moral Ideology," in *Review of Child Development Research,* Vol. 1, ed. by Lois W. Hoffman and Martin L. Hoffman (New York: Russell Sage Foundation, 1964), at 383–433.
15. Aronfreed, *supra* note 10, at 316.
16. C. B. Ferster and J. B. Appel, "Punishment of S Responding in Matching-to-Sample by Time-Out from Positive Reinforcement," 4 *Journal of the Experimental Analysis of Behavior* 45–56 (1961).
17. Aronfreed, *supra note* 10, at 318.
18. Fritz Fedl and David Wineman, *Controls from Within: Techniques for the Treatment of the Aggressive Child* (New York: The Free Press, 1954.
19. *Report of the National Advisory Commission on Civil Disorders* (Washington, D.C.: Government Printing Office, 1968), at 144–45.
20. See discussion and recommendations concerning the family in *The Challenge of Crime In a Free Society,* at 63-66 (Washington, D.C.: Government Printing Office, 1967); see generally the comprehensive review and bibliography in Rodman & Grams, "Juvenile Delinquency and the Family: A Review and Discussion", Appendix L of the *Task Force Report on Juvenile Delinquency* (President's Commission on Law Enforcement and Administration of Justice) (Washington, D.C.: Government Printing Office, 1967).

CHAPTER 10

THE PUBLIC SCHOOL AND THE
CHILDREN OF POVERTY*

Most children grow up to become constructive members of society, respecting law and settling their difficulties in peaceful and commonly accepted ways. Since violence and disrespect for law are evidently increasing, however, more and more attention is being given to the process by which children develop into responsible adults. Intensified efforts are being made to identify the experiences of children that assist, and those that hinder, their development as law-abiding citizens. Clearly, one of the most important institutions in this process is the school.

The school furnishes children with a major introduction to the larger society beyond the immediate family, and it bears the responsibility for equipping children with the skills necessary to the achievement of a satisfying role in that society. Often it is, as the President's Commission on Law Enforcement and Administration of Justice observed, "one of the last social institutions with an opportunity to rescue the child from other forces, in himself and in his environment, which are pushing him toward delinquency."[1]

When the school is a place where children find that they can be successful and can experience just treatment, they develop respect for law and for habits in harmony with the regulations of their society. But when the school is a place where children fail or where they experience unjust treatment, they become frustrated, they reject society's values, and they are more likely to resort to violence in an effort to solve their problems. In America we have both kinds of schools, and the children of poverty are to be found primarily in the second kind.

---

* This chapter is based primarily on materials submitted by Ralph W. Tyler, Director *Emeritus*, Center for Advanced Study in the Behavioral Sciences, Stanford University, and in part on research contributions submitted by Jean D. Grambs, Professor of Education, University of Maryland, and George Jones, Director, Task Force on Urban Education, National Educational Foundation.

PUBLIC EDUCATION TODAY

Public education in the United States today enrolls more students, employs more teachers, and receives more financial support than ever before.[2] In 1966-67, American elementary schools enrolled 36 million children and employed more than 1 million teachers; our high schools enrolled 13 million youth and employed over 850,000 teachers; and expenditures for that school year were $31.9 billion. These figures indicate genuine national accomplishment.

The average American has spent much more time in school than his parents did: now 75% of our teenagers finish high school—about the same proportion that finished eighth grade in 1929. In 1870 one-fifth of the white population and four-fifths of the Negro population were illiterate. Now only 2.4 percent are illiterate—mostly older people and Negroes, Mexican-Americans, Puerto Ricans, or Cubans concentrated mainly in the South and in large cities. The gap in median years of schooling between whites and Negroes has fallen from 3.4 years for those born in 1901 or before to one-half year for those born between 1942 and 1946, and it appears to be narrowing still further.

The resources used to educate each pupil have also been increasing. In 1956 there were 27 pupils per teacher, now there are 24. Now 93% of our teachers have college degrees, compared to 78% in 1956. Expenditures per pupil in elementary and secondary public schools increased from $2.25 to $3.43 per day (in constant dollars) between 1954 and 1964. Comparative test results support the tentative judgment that this increased investment is paying off: American children in the sixties seem to be learning more than their older brothers and sisters learned in the fifties.

Despite the clear accomplishments of our national educational effort, however, two groups in our society continue to suffer acutely from poor quality in education: the children of the inner city and the children of rural America.

Approximately one-fifth of the children in the United States do not attain the level of literacy required for available employment. These educationally deprived children are heavily concentrated among the urban and rural poor. In urban and rural slum areas, for example, 40 to 60% of the children in the *sixth* grade perform at the *second* grade level or below on achievement tests. A majority of the young men failing the Armed Forces Qualification Test, white and black

215

alike, are brought up in poverty and half come from families with five or more children.

Those young people from poor families who nonetheless do score well on achievement tests are much less likely to enter college than those who come from a higher socio-economic level. Only one-third of our more talented high school graduates (in the upper 60% in academic aptitude) will go on to college if their parents are in the bottom socioeconomic quarter of society. By contrast, 85% of the more talented children of parents in the top socioeconomic quartile will go on to college after graduating from high school.[3]

Rural adults and youth are the product of an educational system that has historically shortchanged rural people.[4] While rural youth may be getting a better education today than their parents got, their level of educational achievement is still lower than for urban youth. In 1960 the average schooling for the urban population over 25 was 11.1 years, compared with 9.5 years for rural nonfarm and 8.8 years for rural farm people. Rural students drop out of school sooner, and the percentage of those who go on to college after completing high school is much lower than for urban youth.

Because of low teacher salaries, rural schools are not able to attract and hold the better teachers. Small communities have fewer high school teachers with five or more years of college and more elementary teachers without a college diploma. The percentage of rural teachers not properly certified is about twice as high as for urban teachers.

The facilities in many rural schools are equally depressing. In spite of considerable consolidation of school units, rural schools in general are smaller and less well equipped than urban schools. There are still about 10,000 one-room schools in this country—mostly in rural America. Vast improvements have been made, but some of these small schools still have outdoor privies and are without running water. It is the products of these inadequate rural schools who inevitably migrate to the cities, propelled by economic necessity. They then become a potent force for disaffection and irrational violence.

Inner-city schools are over-crowded, poorly equipped, un-der-staffed, and underfinanced.[5] Between 1951 and 1963 Chicago built 266 new schools or additions mainly in all-Negro areas. Yet in 1964 5 of the 8 all-Negro high schools and 4 of the 10 integrated high schools had enrollments over 50% above designed capacity—compared with similar overcrowding in only 4 of the 26 predominantly white high schools. In Detroit, 30 of the school buildings still in use in inner-city areas were dedicated during the administration of President Grant. Negro pupils have less access to physics, chemistry, and language laboratories, and fewer books per pupil in their libraries.

The schools attended by inner-city children are commonly staffed by teachers with less experience and lower qualifications than those attended by middle-class pupils. A 1963 study ranking Chicago's public high schools by the socioeconomic status of the surrounding neighborhood found that in the 10 lowest-ranking schools only 63% of all teachers were fully certified and the median level of teaching experience was slightly under 4 years. By contrast, in the 10 highest ranking schools, 90% of the teachers were fully certified and the median level of teaching experience was over 12 years.

Despite the special problems presented by children entering the school system from disadvantaged backgrounds, our society spends less money educating ghetto children than children of suburban families. Twenty-five school boards in communities surrounding Detroit spent up to $500 more per pupil per year to educate their children than the city spent. Merely to bring the teacher/pupil ratio in the city in line with the state average would require an additional 16,650 teachers. In a study of 12 metropolitan areas, the Civil Rights Commission found that in 1950, in 10 areas the central cities spent more per pupil than the surrounding suburbs; by 1964, however, in only five areas did the central city spend more per pupil than the average suburb. The major reasons for this reversal are the declining tax base in the cities, and the increasing competition from non-school needs for a share of the municipal tax dollar.[6]

In addition to these inequalities, the schools to which well-to-do parents send their children, and the schools which are attended by the children of the poor in the inner city or in rural America are unequal for the apparently paradoxical reason that they offer essentially similar educational programs. The curriculum for the fearful, malnourished, linguistically different child is little different from that provided for the well-adjusted middle-class child from a supportive home environment. The result is effective educational inequality.

Most middle-class students are supported by parents who reinforce the rules, methods, and goals of the schools. These parents provide quiet rooms for study, encyclopedias, expensive equipment for science fair projects, instruments for music, trips to libraries, and the like. Their youngsters are strongly encouraged to do well. If kindergartens are not provided by the school system—as they generally are not in the South, for example, where low income rural families are concentrated—conscientious middle-class parents pay for such preschool education. The parents themselves are a hidden subsidy of the whole process of education worth many thousands of dollars per student.

The situation of children in the inner-city school or the schools in rural poverty is different. They have not had parents read to them, nor have they seen family or friends devote much time to reading. What they read in school is foreign to their home experience and their parents can take little interest in it.

Thus, where the middle-class mother will ask her child what he learned in school that day and encourage him to learn more, the ghetto mother may express more concern over his becoming a "troublemaker" in the eyes of his teacher. She chides her child: "Don't get into trouble! Don't do anything to make the teacher mad!" By taking this "antidelinquency" approach, she encourages her child to avoid active involvement in learning and simply to become passive. Similarly, the poor rural parent may want his child to get a good education so that he can get a good job—but the parent often places little value on the substantive content of the learning as such.

THE CHALLENGE TO AMERICAN EDUCATION

Children from homes of poverty belie our boast that we have universal education and equal opportunity for all. The greatest challenge to American education today is to find effective ways of helping the children of poverty learn the basic intellectual skills so that they can be more successful in school and compete more successfully for jobs and rewarding positions in the community when they become adults.[7] More than ever before, citizenship in our society requires education for adequate understanding of government and public problems, and for constructive family life and individual development.

The uneducated child and the poorly educated youth are not promising assets in a modern technological society. At the turn of the century farm labor constituted 38% of the labor force; now it is less than 7 percent. Unskilled labor represents less than 6 percent of the labor force and, as with

218

farm labor, the proportion continues to decrease. Meanwhile, the demand for educated people in the professions, the service occupations, management, engineering, and science exceeds the supply.

How can we meet the educational challenge which the children of poverty represent?[8]

Congress has recognized the imperative need for educating disadvantaged children by boldly and responsibly offering categorical aid to schools having a concentration of children from homes of poverty. Title I of the Elementary and Secondary Education Act of 1965 authorizes approximately $1 billion of federal funds for this purpose. Unfortunately, however, the majority of the efforts by schools receiving these funds have so far not been effective. Several reasons can be given for these failures.

In the first place, the added resources are wholly inadequate. For the child of poverty to overcome the disadvantages of his home and acquire the language habits needed to cope with a sophisticated, urban environment and a positive attitude toward his own potential as a learner requires major changes in school programs and practices that cannot be effected by expenditures of only 10 or 15 percent more than the ordinary school expenditures.

The inadequacy of federal financial support is critical. The local school or even the state cannot effectively secure the necessary financial resources. The property tax, which has been the traditional source of local support for education, can no longer be increased in most localities. Furthermore, when it is used as a local revenue base for supporting education, it guarantees inequality in educational opportunity, since the poor are most likely to be found in districts where the assessed valuation of property is the lowest. The current efforts to increase the proportion of school funds provided from state revenues have helped improve the financial situation in some states, but there are also great inequalities among the states in the available revenue-resources per pupil. For example, in 1967-68 the state and school districts of Mississippi levied a greater proportion of the total state income to raise the $413 per child spent on education than did New York State to obtain the $1,125 which was its average cost per child. Any large-scale reduction of inequalities throughout the nation can be achieved only through greatly increased federal contributions to the financial support of education within the states.

A second reason why federally-supported efforts have

largely failed to improve the education of the poor is that most of these efforts have focused on children from 6 to 17 years of age—yet the children who are disadvantaged in the first 3 or 4 years of life fall farther and farther behind as they go through school. In the metropolitan Northeast, for example, Negro students on the average begin the first grade with somewhat lower scores than whites on standard achievement tests, are 1.6 grades behind by the sixth grade and have fallen 3.3 grades behind white students by the 12th grade. As we have noted, the influence of the home, especially in the first years of life, can be decisive for the child's success or failure in school.

What is required is the *early* provision of a supplementary, educationally supportive environment for the children of poverty—people to read to them, converse with them, stimulate their curiosity, assist with their health and nutrition needs: in short, preschool programs like Head Start, only on a much expanded scale and better integrated into the total school system. Last year only about 220,000 children were enrolled in the full-year Head Start program; yet there are about 2¼ million children in the 3 to 5 age group from homes with extremely low incomes. Moreover, when the children leave the progressive learning environment of programs like Head Start, they often go into a traditional, restricted elementary school system that does not provide for continued development.

A third reason why we are not succeeding in our modestly larger efforts to educate the children of poverty is that we have failed to arrange for the necessary major modifications of the school setting, the school program, and the kinds of personnel employed. Our traditional pattern of education is simply not effective with disadvantaged children and youth for whom the school bears essentially the entire educational responsibility. Yet most of our programs and projects have made only minor modifications in the traditional pattern.

At the high school level, for example, adolescents from affluent homes as well as poor ones too often perceive little or no connection between the educational content of the school and their own concerns. Because they do not see the relevance of the high school to their present and future lives, they often ignore the learning tasks assigned. They turn their attention to other things such as athletics, social activities, artificial stimulants, or they may become quiescent, enduring the school routine until they can drop out. This problem has been recognized by many secondary schools over the years, but the steps taken have not been adequate to solve it.

In an effort to provide a meaningful and relevant program for the student, some schools have broadened the offerings of the curriculum, but within the same framework, so that the new courses were also outside the real concerns of the student. The history of Africa can be as lifeless as the history of Colonial America if both are seen as little more than a series of remote events to memorize. Other efforts to attack the problem have often been based on the assumption that the root of the difficulty was in the boy or girl, not in the school and its program. Hence, the focus has been on such strategies as counseling, without making any basic shift in school attitudes and practices.

What is required is basically the development of a close and active relationship, not simply a formal one, between the school and the responsible adult community, so that the student will be confronted by questions and problems outside the school that can be attacked only by what he learns in school. The school must be brought out of isolation. The emphasis must be upon learning what is relevant to the student's life, not upon grades, credits, and other artificial symbols. We must make a major effort to furnish high school students with significant adult activities—job programs, community service corps experience, work in health centers, apprentice experience in research and development, and in staff studies conducted by public agencies. We must redesign the high school to open it to the community and to utilize many different kinds of persons in education. The school will need to serve a wider range of ages and allow students to vary the amount of time devoted to studies. In this new interaction of school and community, "learning on the job" will not substitute for learning in school; rather, the job will present the youth with the challenges which he must meet by learning in school.

The kind of education described here has been shown to arouse greater interest and effort in many students than classroom study alone, to increase student understanding of the subjects studied, and to develop maturity of responsibility and judgment. Community service corps experience such as that developed by the Friends Service Committee has been found to arouse in many students greater motivation to learn and to develop social skills, social responsibility, and maturity of judgment. Communities have constructed the Neighborhood Youth Corps program to serve a similar purpose with young people from backgrounds of poverty and limited opportunity. The involvement of a broad range of people in the educational activities of youth has proved helpful, as has the provision of a variety of patterns to include, in addition to full-time enrollment, part-time school attendance while holding full-time or part-time jobs, and enrollment in high school, full time or part time, after a period of work, military service, or other activity. This varied pattern or experience and competence can be utilized constructively in an institution open to the community, whereas it is likely to be a handicap to a school operating in isolation, with study confined to textbooks and related materials.

An educational strategy of this kind obviously requires more than money—though it will require that in greater amounts than our society has heretofore provided. New institutional arrangements and new personnel will be needed: job coordinators, a community service corps, new means of certifying educational achievement. Changes will have to be made in child labor laws and in practices of employers and labor organizations. Teachers will have to be recruited differently, trained differently, and utilized differently. New curricula will be needed, with new instructional materials. Governors and legislatures will have to be furnished with more adequate staff to help them carry out their educational policy-making responsibilities. None of these manifold requirements will be easily met.

In sum, the educational problems of disadvantaged students—and increasingly of advantaged students as well—cannot be solved successfully merely by doing more of what has been done in the past or simply by concentrating greater effort on the same activities. New approaches must be found.

CONCLUSION

The failures of the children of poverty in our schools are not inevitable. Schools serving poor families can contribute to the development of adults who respect law and find a constructive role in society.

Today the schools of the inner city and of rural America are not accomplishing this task—and in the ghetto, rates of violent crime are 10 to 20 times what they are in the suburbs, while poor rural areas, especially in the South, are the *locus classicus* of the "forgotten man" with his often violent hostility toward Negroes and his alienation from government.

222

Our nation stands, as it were, in the schoolhouse door: either we will stay where we are, preventing the children of poverty from entering into the educational process, or we will go forward, taking these children inside new and better schools to true educational opportunity.

REFERENCES

1. *The Challenge of Crime In a Free Society* (Washington, D.C.: Government Printing Office, 1967), at 69. See generally *id.* at 69–74 and Appendices M and N of the Crime Commission's *Task Force on Juvenile Delinquency* (Washington, D.C.: Government Printing Office, 1967).

2. *Toward a Social Report* (Washington, D.C.: Department of Health, Education, and Welfare, 1969), at 65–72.

3. *Id.*, Table 3, at 21.

4. *Report of the President's National Advisory Commission on Rural Poverty* (Washington, D.C.: Government Printing Office, 1967), at 41 *et seq.*

6. *Id.* at 435.

7. *Toward a Social Report, supra* note 2, at 70.

8. Tyler, "Investing in Better Schools," *Agenda For the Nation,* Washington, D.C., Brookings Institution, 1968.

CHAPTER 11

THE CHURCH AND THE URBAN CRISIS*

The relation of the Church (or Churches) to violence is no less complex than the relation of organized society in general to the problem of violence. A common impression holds that the Church, standing for what is good and holy, must be opposed to violence and must uphold public order, and this view leads in turn to the judgment that the contemporary increase of violence indicates a failure of religion, a failure of the Churches. Consequently, it is argued, if the Churches could be made more "relevant" to contemporary life, order would be increased and violence diminished.

These common-sense impressions oversimplify the issues of order and violence and run the risk of obscuring the function of religion and the Churches. As Samuel Klausner has pointed out in great detail in a paper submitted to the Commission's Task Force on Individual Acts of Violence, religion often provokes and supports violent behavior. It is often disruptive; prophets are generally disturbing people.

Furthermore, as Klausner has vividly described, religion can become associated with the interests of a dominant group in society and be used to reinforce these interests to the detriment of the poor, the underprivileged, or the oppressed. Marx could marshal considerable historical evidence to support his charge that religion is the opiate of the people. By contrast, religion can also be the rugged basis for survival against oppression, as in the case of Irish resistance to England. Any discussion of the relationship of religion or the Churches to the maintenance of order or the curtailment of violence must be thus kept carefully within the perspective of the total function of religion in society.

---

*This chapter was prepared by Joseph P. Fitzpatrick, S.J., Professor of Sociology, Fordham University, based in part on research contributions by the Rev. Donald W. Seaton, Jr., Director, Center City Hospitality House, San Francisco, and Prof. J. Archie Hargraves of the Chicago Theological Seminary.

224

The problem which the Church faces is not whether it will induce or maintain order, but rather what order will it maintain and to whose advantage? In relation to the urban crisis specifically, it is clear that the Church has supported a public order which favors the affluent rather than the poor; in this sense, it has appeared to be "not relevant" to the urban crisis. On the other hand, the Churches are probably the only institutions in American society which will be heard with some confidence if they seek to clarify the common values which can bind the people of the nation together and form the basis on which a general harmony and order might be built.

The Churches in the past have been the institutions which provided a sense of security and solidarity which contributed to the adjustment of immigrant people to the United States. Perhaps they can still fulfill this function and at the same time help their people transcend ethnic isolation and develop a sense of higher unity in the nation. Especially in recent years, the Churches have developed the ability to achieve cooperation and understanding on common values despite the particular values on which they differ, and they may be able to project this skill to the nation at large.

LACK OF "RELEVANCE"—TO WHOM?

In the 19th century, stable urban neighborhoods had formed in American cities around churches, parishes and congregations. The Church grew with immigrant people as a central focus of their social life, a symbol of their identity, and the basis for that ethnic solidarity which enabled the immigrants to move with strength into the mainstream of American life. Indeed, an imaginative historian could write the history of American people by writing the history of their relationship to their churches. The Church not only integrated the lives of its members, it also served as an intermediary institution to link the lives of the congregation to the larger institutions of the entire society. Religious identity became an important factor in political life: it identified the loyalty and reliability of candidates; it was a sign of common interests; it suggested the support of common values.

This position of the Churches was not always achieved or maintained without conflict and violence. As the symbol of different and conflicting interests, religion often became the point around which hostility crystallized and which justified the defense of particular interests in the name of God. The

225

violence which the Catholics have suffered at the hands of Protestants is a sad feature of American history. But there was also serious conflict between German and Irish Catholics, between French Canadian and Irish in New England, as there is now between older Catholic immigrant groups and Puerto Ricans in New York or Mexicans in the Southwest. Tension and conflict between Christian and Jew have likewise been a troublesome feature of American urban life. The positive social function which religion played as the basis for group identity and solidarity thus became quite disfunctional as the basis for the defense of conflicting interests. Nevertheless, continuing efforts at peaceful co-existence tended to reduce the hostility, and neighborhoods continued in relative peace around the churches or parishes or congregations which identified the ethnic groups of the nation.

But conflicts continued to occur when newcomers moved into the areas of these parishes or congregations, threatening the older residents' stability, social solidarity and the sense of managing their own lives. This movement is never a simple "invasion," but rather a complicated process of neighborhood change. But it reaches a point when the older residents feel invaded and either set up hostile resistance or flee from the area to the suburbs. As part of this process, established churches or parishes are pressed by financial needs and traditional loyalties to seek to maintain contact with and relevance to the more affluent people who have fled, rather than to turn imaginatively to the service of the newcomers. As a consequence, they often give the impression at a particular point in time of pursuing their own vested interest in survival rather than becoming relevant to the needs of the poor.

This displacing and replacing takes many different forms. Most of the fashionable Protestant congregations in New York City have a suburban membership. In some Italian Catholic parishes, half the burials are of people who had left the area, but who have kept their ties to it until their deaths. This phenomenon can happen to Negro as well as white congregations. The Capitol Hill residential area was long a squalid Negro ghetto. Negroes who succeeded professionally or economically left the area, but returned regularly to worship in the Church in the neighborhood from which they themselves had moved.

Should violence occur in such areas as these, the Church will be helpless to intervene, having no links with the new population, or it may become itself the target of attack as an institution of a social group alien to the residents of the area.

In relation to situations of urban tension, conflict or violence, therefore, there are two distinct populations to which the effort of the Church must be directed: to the newcomers, and to the older members of the congregation, both those who have moved to the suburbs and those who have remained in the inner city. How does the Church become "relevant" to both in such a way that order with justice and dignity may be promoted, and violence contained?

THE CHURCH AS BRIDGE-BUILDER

The Churches can become relevant to the new populations in the inner city by doing for them what they did for the former residents, by becoming the focus around which a sense of identity and social solidarity can develop. Many of the black Churches already fulfill this role; the white Churches, and particularly many white priests or ministers, who have become relevant to inner-city people and issues, have to some extent achieved it also. Father Groppi in Milwaukee; Father John Powis in the Ocean Hill-Brownsville section of Brooklyn; the work that Father Harold Rahm started among the Mexicans at Our Lady's Center in El Paso; the East Harlem Protestant Parish; the work of Monsignor Robert Fox among the Puerto Ricans in New York—these are all examples of situations in which white clergymen have won the confidence of black, Mexican, or Puerto Rican people, and have become the basis for a sense of community, of social solidarity, of personal worth.

In situations like these, however, when conflict arises, the churches or the clergymen identify with the position of the underprivileged and frequently find themselves in conflict with older residents or parishioners. Thus Father John Powis became a very controversial figure during the turmoil about the Ocean Hill-Brownsville experimental school district, and Father Groppi is a fighting word in middle class conversations. It is forgotten that in these conflicts men like Powis and Groppi are simply doing what the Church regularly did in relation to its immigrant parishioners when they were poor and underprivileged. It became the basis for loyalty and solidarity, and provided deep religious motivation for a struggle which immigrants defined as a struggle to preserve their own values or promote their legitimate interests.

Moreover, in fulfilling this function, the churches and the clergymen are not simply centers of rebellion or protest. They provide an extraordinary link between the struggling newcomers and the larger society; they are an effective channel of communication; they are a source of confidence to the newcomers as they approach the larger society, and to the larger society as they seek to approach the newcomers. Troublesome and turbulent as they may sometimes be, these active clergy serve as bridge-builders between the old and new.

If the Church really succeeds in becoming the basis for a strong, stable, self-confident community, it is effectively preparing the way for a more orderly society. "One integrates from a position of strength, not from a position of weakness" is a well-established sociological principle. If the newcomers succeed in creating strong communities, the process of integration should move forward much more strongly. This is a long-range goal, and there are no simple, immediate evidences of its achievement. But community building represents one of the most important ways in which churches have been relevant in the past, and are likely to be relevant at the present.

Of course, the achievement of a strong sense of community in and around the Church creates problems for the Church's relationship with former residents, or members of the congregation. Part of the resistance of former established residents to the newcomers is due precisely to the fact that a strong sense of community solidarity and identity had been developed among them. They do not wish to lose this; yet the approach of newcomers is generally perceived as a threat to the sense of identity which the older residents had always been taught to consider a strong social value. For example, many Italians in New York City who have forged a strong community around their Church raise the question: "Why is it wrong for us to seek to retain the community solidarity which the in-coming blacks and Puerto Ricans are striving to achieve?" Will the churches, by identifying themselves with the newcomers, inevitably alienate all others?

This question raises the challenge of a genuine pluralism, in which the newcomers could have their own identity and sense of community, but in such a way that it does not prevent their achieving a unity and cooperation on a higher level with other groups which also have a sense of identity and community solidarity. Religious groups such as churches or parishes are probably the only institutions by which culturally different groups, or conflicting or alienated groups may be brought to some sense of unity. Repeatedly in the past, the religious group has been able to bridge the gap

228

between different social classes, different ethnic groups, different interest groups, by forging a common bond around common religious beliefs and practices. Thus, in the celebration of the liturgy, rich and poor, educated and uneducated, the powerful and the underprivileged, have frequently been able to celebrate the common beliefs in which they were one, despite the many differences which divided them. These different groups may have interpreted the common beliefs in different ways, and perhaps found different meanings in the celebration of the liturgy, but the deep and convincing common bonds were there. All accepted the belief that men are the children of God and this belief provided a fulcrum toward unity which would have been much more difficult to achieve if no such common belief existed.

Furthermore, despite the alienation of former established parishioners, the churches and parishes are more likely than any other groups to enjoy the confidence of the former parishioners. Traditionally, these parishioners depend on the churches to defend the ultimate values of their lives. If their religious teachers assure them that these new neighborhood or community developments are not a destruction of their basic values, their confidence in their religious leaders may bring them to some understanding of the social changes they see around them. The simple fact that the Church teaches this understanding does not mean that members of parishes or congregations will thereby accept it. They often resist strongly. But the Church can lay claim to a confidence that probably no other institution has.

For example, in the matter of black power, it is important for members of religious groups to perceive the fundamental religious inspiration beneath the black striving toward dignity and justice. The alienation of the black people from white religious groups is part of the total black effort toward identity, self-reliance, self-respect, and community strength. Unity of black and white in its traditional form will not be possible on a large scale in the near future. Whatever unity of black and white does emerge, or whatever involvement there may be of white churches or white religious ministers in black movements, it will develop along terms which the black people will set. It is important for the churches to interpret the religious basis of much of the black power movement for their white parishioners. The presence of so many black religious leaders in the movements of the black people for justice cannot fail to impress religiously minded people.

The presence of black religious leaders such as Martin Luther King has been important in preventing or moderating violence. The impressive and widespread non-violence of the black Americans should be an inspiration for a similar non-violence among white people in the presence of the struggle of black people for justice. And the Churches and congregations are the institutions best suited to emphasize this. The danger of violence in the white reaction to black non-violence is a constant threat to peace. Violent reactions may be contained among white Americans if the Churches will continually call attention to the religious character of the black movement, and emphasize that religious values which blacks and whites share together are the motivating force beneath much of what the blacks are doing.

Another example of the importance of common religious values and their role in building understanding and cooperation can be seen in the widespread support of the strike and boycott of the grape pickers in California. Cesar Chavez, the Mexican-American who is organizing these Mexican farm workers, has given a decidedly religious tone to his organizational efforts. The workers and pickets march under the banner of Our Lady of Guadelupe, and although Chavez has no hesitation about being involved in conflict, he uses the great religious symbol of the Mexican people to strengthen the solidarity of his own men and to provide a motivation for nonviolence. Many of the Churches and religious leaders around the nation have called attention to these significant features of Chavez' campaign with the result that it has enjoyed extraordinary sympathy among large segments of the middle-class community who sense a bond of unity in the religious values evident in the struggle of the Mexican workers.

It is precisely this role as a bridge-builder, as intermediary between the poor and the affluent, between white and black, between the newcomers in inner city neighborhoods and the older residents who have fled, that the churches are eminently suited to fulfill. Unless the resolution of these urban conflicts is going to be left to sheer pragmatic accommodation, it is essential that some common values be emphasized as the basis for understanding and cooperation between the many levels of people in American cities. And the Churches bear the greatest responsibility for asserting and emphasizing these common values.

NATIONAL CONSENSUS: PLURALISM
AND ECUMENISM

The assertion of common values between newcomers and older parishioners is the local dimension of the much larger problem of national values in relation to violence. Just as the churches can play an important role in asserting the common values which are the basis of understanding and cooperation in neighborhood or city, so also can they play a significant role in seeking to assert the basic values on which the unity and solidarity of the nation can be based. This latter role is obviously much more complicated and difficult, but unless there is a sense of common values among the citizens of the nation, and a confidence that these values are secure, it is doubtful that violence can be avoided. In essence, this is the problem of national consensus, and national consensus feeds back into local consensus. If there is a sense of confidence in the acceptance of common national values, it will be easier for the churches to assert these values among people in suburbs, cities, and neighborhoods.

In the effort to promote the common acceptance of values and goals, two significant features of the religious experience of the United States support the hope of favorable activity by religious groups in this role. In the first place, the experience of religious pluralism in the Nation has developed a tradition of understanding and accommodation among religious groups. Differences have been serious, and hostility often present, but there has also been a strong and growing tendency to examine religious differences and differences of values with a high degree of intelligent objectivity. Religious groups, probably more than any others, have been schooled in the art of accommodation. They have learned to pursue their own particular values in the presence of conflicting values. Through controversy and conflict they have learned the skill of recognizing areas of agreement and common values which would enable them to live together despite the differences. This American religious style has developed attitudes and skills which can flow over into other areas of life and influence the development of a similar style in the wide range of national events in which the danger of conflict is present.

A second promising feature of religious experience is the spirit of ecumenism which has developed remarkably in the past few years. This spirit has emerged from a large number of sources, but one especially significant source has been the recognition by all the churches that their common values are far more important at this moment in history than their differences. In other words, in the presence of a general challenge to the fundamental beliefs of all religious groups, the importance of differences between the religious groups diminishes in perspective. Religious groups which face a rapidly increasing number of men who deny that God exists are not as likely to pursue conflicts about differences in doctrines about sacraments or sacrifice as they would if there were not such a large number of non-believers. This increasing effort of religious groups to clarify and assert the .fundamental religious beliefs around which there is agreement, and to accommodate their differences in the context of agreement, has brought the religious groups to a point where they can be a major influence for unity in American life. This same spirit of dealing with differences of values and interests in a context of striving for agreement is directly related to many of the value differences which have troubled American life. Ecumenism is one significant sign that we have reached a new level of maturity and mutual respect in managing them.

If the experience with pluralism and ecumenism can be properly exploited, it should enable the churches to convert a sense of identity and solidarity into a strong basis for a generous and open attitude toward others. Emphasis on common beliefs and common rituals should lead to more vigorous efforts at mutual respect and understanding.

Particularly important in this regard is the value of repentance. Repentance is a fundamental religious value in all churches and one which is frequently ritualized on particular days and periods of penance. The need for penance for the long years of injustice and discrimination against black Americans should be strongly pressed—but in such a way that it leads to a desire for more extensive community of the faithful in justice and love.

CONCLUSION

In summary, therefore:

(1) Religious groups should seek to become the focus of identity and community solidarity for newcomers in a neighborhood, as they so effectively have been for previous immigrant and ethnic groups. In doing so, they must recognize the need to make common cause with the poor of these communities in their struggle to participate as equals in American society. This entails a greater reaching out of the church toward the community.

(2) Religious groups should take advantage of the confidence

they frequently enjoy among poor and affluent alike, and especially among ethnic and racial groups which have a deep sense of unity around a common religious identity, to build bridges of confidence and understanding between hostile groups. Religious groups should particularly work toward understanding and cooperation between formerly established residents and newcomers in a neighborhood by asserting the common values which should be the basis for unity.

(3) In these efforts religious groups should always be sensitive to the fact that the very sense of identity of people around religious values can reinforce group isolation, and leave religion in a situation where it is the basis for division and hostility.

(4) Religious groups must also be sensitive to the widespread alienation from national values and religious values which is prevalent, and recognize that this alienation is partially due to the identification of religion with interests which are no longer seen as deeply human or even deeply religious. If a genuine religious spirit can be made more evident in religious groups, in parishes and churches, they may serve once again as the basis for a renewal and a sense of identity around meaningful values and goals.

(5) The dramatic and public manifestations of non-violence inspired by religious motivation evident in the Black protest movement and among Mexican-Americans and Puerto Ricans provide a suitable basis on which religious groups should mount a much stronger and determined effort to cultivate a spirit of nonviolence throughout the entire American community.

(6) The increasingly cooperative and ecumenical efforts of religious groups, churches, and parishes in this Nation can be directed more vigorously toward: (a) identifying more clearly the central values of the Nation; (b) clarifying the manner in which these values should express themselves in social institutions and individual behavior; and (c) working toward an increasing national consensus around these values.

The effectiveness of religion as a peacemaker should not be overemphasized, however. It is not like a machine which works automatically, nor is it a blueprint for people to follow simply, step by step.

Religion is a call to the spirit, often muffled by the din of men's preoccupation with the world. Sometimes religion is most effective when it appears to be most helpless. The cry of the prophet is often a lonely one which may provoke violence against the prophet himself. He may speak more eloquently in death than he ever did during his life.

Nevertheless, the past gives promise that the Churches can be a genuine force for the containment of violence and for order with justice and dignity.

CHAPTER 12

THE REFORM OF THE UNIVERSITY*

Individuals may form communities, Benjamin Disraeli once observed, but only institutions can make a nation.

The observation is particularly relevant to this nation in these troubled times. Institutions are the inventions by which man has collectively solved his problems and civilized his world. When they become ineffective, a nation is in serious trouble.

The malaise which presently afflicts the United States results in large measure from a kind of "institutional paralysis." Our political, economic, religious, social, and educational institutions are in disarray; they are not sufficiently responsive to the demands of the present or the needs of the people; they seem unwilling or unable to reform. Americans, as a result, have begun to lose faith in their institutions and in the social system which they comprise.

This is somewhat unusual. We Americans have always been supremely confident of our ability to solve problems, to accomplish any goal. Now we are no longer so sure.

The Republic is plagued with problems that defy solution. Despite great national wealth, millions of Americans are poor. In a land dedicated to the idea of freedom and equality, many of our fellow citizens still struggle for basic human rights. Our cities are decaying and appear to be ungovernable. Our countryside is blighted and reveals a callous disregard for natural beauty and natural resources. Our air and water are polluted. A war in Asia has sapped our strength and divided our people; violence and mounting crime at home mock our laws and erode our unity. Age-old conflicts flare with renewed intensity—between order and justice, between the individual and the state, between private rights and public welfare, between the older and younger generations.

---

* This chapter was prepared by Ronald A. Wolk, Vice President of Brown University.

234

The context of modern life is change—bewildering, buffeting, incessant change. Problems multiply far faster than solutions. Events transpire so swiftly and so inexorably that they seem to have a force and a direction unto themselves. Our institutions, like sluggish ships, creak and strain in these winds of change. And our people grow weary.

Sociologist Wilbert E. Moore has written:

> Concerted action to meet crises, to extend power, or to resist tyranny is very old in human history. Concerted action to create crises, to institute change as a regular feature of social life, is rather new. In most societies through most of human history, the predominant effort has been directed toward holding things steady or restoring a steady state if it is disrupted by some natural or man-made crisis. The phenomenal thing about modern industrial states, and others attempting to follow the same path, is the great energy devoted to deliberate disruption of existing conditions and the creation of new ones.

In the face of this situation, many Americans despair and feel that they can do nothing to influence the decisions and developments that shape their lives. Others, perhaps equally desperate, struggle to regain control of their destiny through a massive restructuring of society's institutions.

It should not be surprising that the greatest effort to reform society and its institutions is being made by the young. They are by nature idealistic and impatient.

Nor should it be surprising that the greatest effort to reform is being directed at or through our institutions of higher learning. The campus is the subculture of the young. The university is their institution as well as their doorway to and lever on the greater society.

"It is in the universities that the soul of the people mirrors itself," Lord Haldane said half a century ago. Our colleges and universities in their present turmoil surely reflect to a significant degree the malaise of the larger society—just as they have in other nations in other times. What happens on the campuses, therefore, will be very important not only for higher education, but for the nation.

CAMPUS UNREST AND ITS CAUSES

Americans have never been so aware of their colleges and universities as they are today. Since World War II, higher education has made enormous progress and has accomplished marvelous things. But turmoil and violence have greater news value than teaching and research.

The first dramatic assault on a university came in 1964, at the University of California, when Mario Savio, a student, did battle with Clark Kerr, the president. The "revolution" which began then continues today. Mr. Kerr eventually became the first celebrated victim of the new era of campus unrest. There is some irony in that, for he so aptly described the hazards of the new "multiversity" that he presided over. Describing the president as "Mediator,"—and thus seriously underestimating his role—Mr. Kerr wrote in *The Uses of the University*:

> . . . peace and progress are more frequently enemies than friends; and since, in the long run, progress is more important than peace to a university, the effective mediator must, at times sacrifice peace to progress. . . . Power is not necessary to the task of mediation, though there must be a consciousness of power. The president must police its use by the constituent groups, so that none will have too much or too little or use it too unwisely. To make the multiversity work really effectively, the moderates need to be in control of each power center and there needs to be an attitude of tolerance between and among power centers with few territorial ambitions. When extremists get in control of the students, the faculty, or the trustees with class war concepts, then the "delicate balance of interests" becomes an actual war.

The idiom of war used by Mr. Kerr has become increasingly more appropriate. After Berkeley, a number of campuses erupted into turbulence of varying degrees. Students became more militant, and their tactics more disruptive. Recruiters for Dow Chemical and the military services were first picketed, then obstructed, and finally driven from the campus. Protests outside of buildings escalated to lockouts, then sit-ins, then seizures. Here and there the turbulence became violent and the police were called in. Then in the spring of 1968, fierce and bloody riots broke out at Columbia University.

The riots at Columbia in 1968 made the Berkeley revolt of 1964 seem quite tame. Savio fired at the university and bagged a president; Mark Rudd not only brought down the president, but wounded the university as well. Since then, the pace has quickened. San Francisco State College set a new pattern of disruption and violence: the first prolonged student strike, bombings, sabotage, and a campus kept open only by daily patrols of police.

Last spring, when it almost seemed that matters could

236

hardly become worse, Harvard University—cool, sophisticated Harvard which seemed always to do everything right—became the scene of a bloody "bust." Some 400 club-swinging policemen emptied University Hall of several hundred student protesters in a matter of minutes. It was quick, efficient, and very violent.

Almost before the television crews could find lodgings in Cambridge, a group of black students at Cornell seized a building and smuggled in arms and ammunition to defend themselves. The photographs showing them leaving the building, rifles in hand, and bandoliers across their chests, shocked a nation that by now had thought itself unable to be shocked.

A CBS television report later indicated that a substantial number of white students had armed themselves, thus prompting blacks to do likewise.

The wake of this campus turbulence is littered with casualties: Presidents by the dozens have quit or been fired; faculty have resigned; students have been expelled or have dropped out to make a profession of protest. Alumni and donors, on whom institutions depend for financial support, have reacted with anger. Legislators at the state and federal level have introduced scores of bills to curb the student demonstrations and punish the demonstrators.

Said one professor:

> The problems are similar to a city struck by sudden and protracted disaster: confusion, disorganization, self-interest rampant, a general malaise in which the cardinal principle of conduct is "every man for himself."

This account of campus unrest since 1964 is so brief and over-simplified that it is at best impressionistic. That is what it is meant to be. The purpose of this chapter is not to trace the evolution of campus protest and violence, but rather to offer some thoughts about the reasons for campus turmoil, various responses to it, and some of the possible consequences it may have for higher education as a whole.

First, however, some distinctions must be made regarding students and the nature of much campus protest.

To speak of "the students" as though they are a monolithic force rampaging on the Nation's campuses is, of course, inaccurate and misleading. More than seven million young people are enrolled in colleges and universities in the United States, and they are as varied in their social and cultural backgrounds, their attitudes, manners, and morals as the

237

society at large. The great majority of these students are not radical, or militant, or even activist. Most of them, in fact, attend the 1,600-or-so institutions of higher learning in the country which have not been disrupted by mass protest or violence. They represent what has been called "the silent majority," and like most students of previous generations they are concerned with preparing for and ultimately succeeding in a career. These students are not significantly involved in politics whether on or off the campus, and their basic values are not substantially changed by the college experience.

It is also misleading and inaccurate, however, to conclude from this that the turbulence on the campuses is being caused by a tiny minority of students and that order will be restored if this small, willful group is dealt with firmly. Although a majority of America's students are not part of the protest that has wracked campuses in recent years, a substantial minority is in general sympathy with it. A recent survey by Daniel Yankelovich, Inc., a major attitude-research firm, revealed that about 40 percent of America's college students (about 2.5 million) differ significantly from the majority. They tend to be somewhat disdainful of career preparation and financial success after college; they are likely to be majoring in the humanities and to be concerned with intellectual matters and social problems; they are interested in public issues and politics, and their attitudes are likely to be dissident.

The Yankelovich survey showed, for example, that about two-thirds of this "involved minority" think it appropriate to engage in civil disobedience in support of a cause. Two-thirds approve disruptive tactics in resistance to the draft. Fewer than half of these students feel that it is worth going to war to protect our national interest, or contain communism, or protect allies, or maintain our position of power in the world. Only 20 percent feel it is worth fighting to protect the nation's honor, and only 14 percent would fight to keep a commitment. Half of the "involved minority" indicated that they have less faith in democratic processes than their parents have, and about half feel that the United States is a sick society.

Attitudes are one thing, however, and action is another. Although the "involved minority" may hold dissident views and generally sympathize with much of the campus protest, most of them have not been active in their dissent. Harris and Gallup polls indicate that only about 20 percent of the

238

Nation's college students have participated in political or civil rights activities, and this includes traditional political activities like the 1968 campaigns of Senators McCarthy and Kennedy. An even smaller number have participated in campus protests.

Within the "involved minority" are the radicals, the militants, the active sympathizers, and the potential sympathizers.

The *radical students*—those who have given up on society and its institutions and would use violence to destroy them—are very few in number. Even on the larger and more active campuses like Berkeley, where radical students tend to congregate, they represent a mere handful. Nonetheless, radical students exert an influence out of proportion to their number, and they may express their extremism in acts of violence which trigger larger disruptions.

The *militant students*—essentially the New Left—number fewer than 100,000, less than 2 percent of the total student population. They are now convinced that society and its institutions have become corrupted mainly by a military-industrial complex, but they are still largely committed to change rather than destruction. Students for a Democratic Society (SDS) has been the most widely publicized and the most influential organization of militant new left students. Formed in the early 1960's to develop a new movement to affect American politics, SDS claimed about 7,000 dues-paying members last year, and a total of 35,000 members in its several hundred local chapters. Data collected by the Educational Testing Service reveals that in 1965 there were "student left organizations" on 25 percent of college and university campuses; by 1968, the number had grown to 46 percent. Now, however, SDS and the new left, like the old left before it, is tearing itself apart in factional disputes.

Among the militant students are the militant black students whose special interests and activities justify treating them as a separate category. Organized mainly into black student unions and Afro-American societies on scores of campuses, the black students have confronted administrators and faculty with several specific demands, and they have been militant in their objectives and their tactics. Distinctions must be made with regard to black students also, for not all of them are militants or even activists.

Between 4 and 5 percent of the student population might be described as *active sympathizers*. Though they may not consider themselves members of the new left, they are concerned with reform. Their dissident views make them receptive to the arguments and demands of the militants. The active sympathizers are not committed to demonstration and disruption, and most of them would probably find violent tactics distasteful. But they respond to issues and could conceivably be "radicalized" in a particular situation.

The remainder of the "involved minority" are *potential sympathizers*. They tend to identify more with their fellow students than with administrators or faculty. Though they may not devote much of their time or energy to reform efforts they are more likely to concur with these efforts than to oppose them. A given issue or a particular incident (like the appearance of police on the campus) might turn potential sympathizers into active sympathizers very quickly. Surveys show that nearly 20 percent of the "involved minority" feels a sense of "solidarity and identification" with the new left.

In addition to differentiating among students it is important to recognize that a substantial amount of the protest against colleges and universities—particularly until recently—was in reality protest against the larger society. In the early 1960's students used their colleges and universities as bases from which to launch attacks against a system which had for three centuries persecuted black Americans. In the mid-1960's, the Vietnam war became the target of student protest, along with war-related activities like military recruiting and defense research. In other words, the young began to question the legitimacy of the society, and it was inevitable that they should also come to question the legitimacy of society's institutions. As the protest movement evolved, the student attacks came to be directed at the colleges and universities themselves, first as members or agents of the "evil establishment," then as "reactionary" institutions in their own right.

Viewing universities as a surrogate of the society was not productive; they simply couldn't bear all the sins of society in scapegoat fashion. Focusing on the universities for their own sins, however, was another matter. There were enough things wrong on the campus to sustain a vigorous protest movement, and students soon learned that their confrontation tactics exert an effective influence for reform.

THE NEED FOR REFORM

The students were not the first to conclude that higher

education needs reforming. The more perceptive of the faculty and administration knew that. But students, unlike their elders, were unwilling simply to point to problems and wait patiently for change: they were determined that the university should move promptly to mend its ways. They focused on three main areas:

1. Undergraduate Teaching

What Sidney Hook once described as "subtle discounting of the teaching process" had become so unsubtle that it was now obvious to everyone, most especially to the undergraduates. In universities many of the teachers don't teach undergraduates, they conduct research and work with graduate students. Those who do teach carry heavier teaching loads and are as likely as not to be graduate student instructors or junior faculty. Many are highly specialized professionals who are strongly oriented to their disciplines, and thus more inclined to teach their specialty than their students.

William Arrowsmith, professor of classics at the University of Texas, spoke out sharply and eloquently in a popular magazine (an act that surely makes him an academic muckraker):

> What matters, then, is the kind of context that we can create for teaching and the largeness of the demands made upon the teacher. Certainly he will have no function or honor worthy of the name until we are prepared to make the purpose of education what it always was—the molding of men rather than the production of knowledge. It is my hope that education in this sense will not be driven from the university by the knowledge technicians. We will not transform the university milieu or create teachers by the meretricious device of offering prizes or bribes or teaching sabbaticals or building a favorable "image." At present the universities are as uncongenial to teaching as the Mojave Desert to a clutch of Druid priests. If you want to restore a Druid priesthood, you cannot do it by offering prizes for Druid-of-the-year. If you want Druids, you must grow forests. There is no other way of setting about it.

Former President of the University of Iowa, Howard R. Bowen, said recently:

> There is one aspect of academic life that has not changed very much. That is the liberal education of undergraduates. While much lip services is given to innovation, new technology, and the like, most teaching still centers around the professor,

241

the textbook, didactic lectures, close supervision of the student, credits and grades. Whatever gain has been made in effectiveness of instruction has occurred through improved motivation of students, better secondary preparation, and improved qualifications of faculty—not through improvement in the mode of instruction in colleges and universities.

It is a safe bet that the majority of students who earn the baccalaureate degree manage to leave the university without having had "the light turned on." The promises in the admissions brochures notwithstanding, the "whole man" is often not the concern of the university. A number of studies have failed to find that the college has any significant effect in liberalizing or liberating the undergraduate or in altering his structure of values. The emphasis in most curricula has been professional and preprofessional. Howard Bowen says:

> The curriculum has little impact on the life, values, goals, feelings, and deeds of the student. It fails to come to grips with the universal problems of human life and with the great issues of our times which do not fall neatly into the disciplines. It often seems to the student sterile and irrelevant, and fails to motivate him or even repels him. . . . Also, the curriculum, built up of randomly selected smatterings, lacks integration.

2. Student Life

Until very recently, the student drew little water in the academic sea. Leslie Stephen expressed a widespread attitude when he said: "What a blessed place this would be if there were no undergraduates! . . . No waste of good brains in cramming bad ones."

A university president, meeting with the Commission to discuss campus disorders, unwittingly declared: "I keep telling my faculty that *these days (added)* we must listen to the students."

For many years, the concept of *in loco parentis* prevailed, and the student faced on the campus the close supervision he would face at home. Presently, the young are kicking the final breath of life from this notion. They are demanding the right to be treated as adults. The chafing rules—smoking, drinking, sex, parietals, dormitory hours, etc.—are crumbling at a rapid pace. Last year, campus protests against dormitory regulations were second in number only to the protests against the Vietnam War.

Also, until recently, students had little or no say in the

management of extracurricular affairs or in matters of student discipline. Certainly they had no voice in the curriculum or the formulation of university policy generally.

The massive growth of higher education has also led to conditions which students find depressing. As campuses have tripled and quadrupled in size—some of them exceeding enrollments of 30,000—the student has felt himself relegated to the status of computer card. Faced with a problem, he is shuffled from one administrator to another in the growing bureaucracies made necessary by expansion.

Clark Kerr observed:

> The multiversity is a confusing place for the student. He has problems of establishing his identity and sense of security within it. But it offers him a vast range of choices, enough literally to stagger the mind. In this range of choices he encounters the opportunities and the dilemmas of freedom. The casualty rate is high. The walking wounded are many. *Lernfreiheit*—the freedom of the student to pick and choose, to stay or to move on —is triumphant.

The pressure of numbers is exacerbated by the pressure to achieve. Joseph Katz and Nevitt Sanford wrote in the "Causes of the Student Revolution":

> As is well known, the conditions of the post-Sputnick era have led to a tightening of standards of academic performance and an increased demand upon quantity of work by students. The resulting pressure is felt by good students as well as poor ones. In the more selective schools, all the students are able and well prepared, yet they still feel an enormous amount of pressure, because of the grading curve and the inclination of the faculty to assign more reading than anyone can do. People usually ascribe these pressures to the intellectual competition of the Cold War, but another factor is the higher birth rate, which has considerably increased the number of students applying to colleges and has thus provided both an economic and a moral base for increased selectivity.

Secondary school teachers report that junior high school students worry about qualifying for admission to a good college or university.

3. The University's Role in Society

For the most part, colleges and universities have gone about their business asking nobody's "by your leave." Faculties reserved the right (which they frequently did not exercise) to set academic policy; everything else was generally left to the administration and the trustees. If higher institutions deplored the plight of the Negro in America, they did so without stretching themselves to do anything about it. Colleges and universities came nowhere near reflecting in their student bodies, faculties, or administrations the proportion of blacks in the society at large. If a university needed room to grow, it took steps to acquire land with little more than passing thought to the disruptions that might ensue in the neighboring community. Many universities cheerfully accepted funds for programs of special interest to one or another special interest group—be it business, a foundation, or the Department of Defense. They aided in the recruitment of military officers with Reserve Officer Training Programs and complied with a law that specified credit for substandard courses and professorial status for unqualified military officers. Some institutions found nothing contrary to the spirit of free and open inquiry in conducting classified research on the campus.

For today's students, such a posture deeply implicates the university in what they view to be the worst shortcomings of society. The *Report of the Select Committee on Education* at Berkeley eloquently describes how the militant student views society and suggests why students have become disenchanted with the institution they know best and believe to be a molder of society.

As these students see it, while the dominant group claims to champion freedom, religion, patriotism, and morality, it produces and condones slums, racial segregation, migrant farm laborers, false advertising, American economic imperialism, and the bomb. In private life, moreover, the students find as much immorality and injustice as in public life. They commonly explain it as the product of an all-pervasive hypocrisy.

These examples, though not all-inclusive, at least indicate the need for reform. They should help to explain the frustration of students and their new militancy on the campus. But if the students have a right to press for reform—and they obviously do—they also have an obligation to try to understand the university, to learn how it has reached its present state, and to ponder the methods and goals of reform and their impact on the university.

Someone once said that no one should meddle with a university who does not understand it and love it. The comment was probably prompted by a realization that the university is a rather fragile institution, despite the fact that it has endured for a thousand years and has survived formidable threats to its integrity and freedom. The university is fragile because it is no more than people of good will committed to some very lofty principles: freedom, tolerance, mutual understanding, open communication, truth, and honesty. These are surely elusive principles—difficult to attain, easy to lose. They are, however, the only things that distinguish a university from any other cluster of buildings inhabited by humans with all their vested interests and venal shortcomings.

By its own actions, the university has compromised some of these principles. Great social forces working on the university have also jeopardized them. Now, in a righteous frenzy to reform the university, its active critics imperil these principles. Freedom, especially, is in danger.

THE UNIVERSITY TRADITION IN AMERICA

Freedom—what Harvard's Nathan Pusey has called "the freedom of the mind on which all other freedoms depend"— is both the gift *to* and the gift *from* the University. Only if they are independent and autonomous can universities perform the unique tasks which tradition and society demand of them. And only if these tasks are performed can society itself hope to remain free.

Universities perform many functions—some by choice, some by demand—but their central and unique missions are to seek and disseminate truth, to transmit the intellectual and cultural heritage from generation to generation, and to evaluate society and, when necessary, to serve as its critic.

"To fulfill these functions in the service of the community," writes Cambridge University's Sir Eric Ashby, universities "need the freedom to choose their own mode of action as well as continuous and critical awareness of the real needs of the communities they serve—which may not always be those that the community urges upon them so clamorously at any given moment of time."

These are dangerous duties, and, because they perform them, universities occupy a privileged position. Society grants them the material support they need, but permits them the independence and autonomy to govern themselves. Universities are fed partly so that they can bite the hand that feeds them. No other institution is so favored: but then no other institution fulfills this role.

245

The tradition on which this unique freedom is based began with the medieval university. It held that universities must be free to determine their own goals and to select the means to accomplish them—and to do both without interference from outside authority.

The tradition has survived because it is in society's own best interest, because scientific and social progress depend upon a search for truth unimpaired by arbitrary limitations, because an open society requires liberally educated and thinking citizens, and because "without fearless criticism, the nation would lose its power of self-renewal."

Whenever the freedom of universities is in jeopardy so is the freedom of the nation, for a society can only be as free as its universities. Or as Samuel Gould, president of the State University of New York, told his State legislature: "A society that can no longer trust its universities can no longer trust itself."

It is this freedom, this unique character of the institution that is at stake in the present struggle for control of the university. Unfortunately, many of those who would reform universities neither understand them nor love them. Their intent may be noble, but their actions often are not. Their zeal may not be questionable, but their goals often are.

Jacques Barzun, former provost of Columbia, said in his book, *The American University:*

> The fact remains that the university as an institution has become the object of an endless guerrilla [war], part organized, part fortuitous. It is perhaps time that this institution, which is still loved and respected, even by its impatient clients, should be better understood. The subject is complex and variable, but not beyond comprehension.
>
> The present crisis in the American university is a crisis of purpose, organization, and governance. The university is confused about its mission, inadequately structured to do what is demanded of it, and, as the present campus turmoil indicates, virtually unable to govern itself.

It is true, as critics charge, that universities are in trouble today because they have not changed to keep up with the conditions of a modern post-industrial state. But it is equally true—though the critics seldom realize it—that universities face this awesome crisis just because they have changed profoundly over the past several decades. This is not doubletalk. It is an acknowledgment that powerful external forces have greatly changed the American university and made it what it is today.

The American university was born nearly a hundred years ago as a new species of institution, and it contained the seeds of the crisis that now plagues it. It was conceived in the period of the land-grant movement during and after the Civil War, came of age during World War II along with the scientific revolution, and matured into a powerful and affluent institution worth fighting over during the past decade.

The colonists brought with them the English undergraduate college with its emphasis on religion and its mission of teaching the classics to the upper classes. Onto this stalk, late in the 19th century with the founding of Johns Hopkins as the "first true university," was grafted the German university concept of austere devotion to scientific research and scholarship and graduate education.

This in itself was an unlikely blend, but the new hybrid was then nourished in the soil of American utilitarianism and egalitarianism, from which came the land-grant movement with its dedication to mass higher education and service to society.

The land-grant movement introduced three revolutionary ideas into American higher education and launched three major trends which, in the past century, have fundamentally shaped higher education in this country. First, the land-grant movement created the precedent of direct federal financial support to higher education. Second, the movement established the concept of enlisting the resources of colleges and universities to meet pressing national needs. And third, the land-grant movement began the trend toward mass higher education.

The land-grant movement was marked by three major acts: (1) the Morrill Act of 1862 which awarded federal lands to the states to aid higher education and to endow state colleges to promote the "liberal and practical education of the industrial classes in the several pursuits and professions of life"; (2) the Hatch Act of 1887 which provided, for the first time, federal funds to states for "practical research"; and (3) the Second Morrill Act of 1890 which provided direct federal money grants to land-grant colleges for instruction in the specific subjects of agriculture, engineering, and the natural sciences. (Significantly, the second Morrill Act provided that Negroes would benefit from its provision, although it allowed for "separate but equal" treatment.)

These acts were enormously significant. They were both pragmatic and democratic. In the latter half of the 19th century, the United States desperately needed the skilled manpower, the knowledge, and the technology to advance industrial and agricultural expansion. The land grant acts met this need; they established "democracy's colleges" to give practical training to the sons and daughters of the working classes and to improve research and instruction in practical subjects. The land-grant movement laid the basis for the greatest system of public higher education in history—a system that has flourished with a growing commitment to a firm national policy that every American child is entitled to all of the education he is capable of.

The hybrid university of the late nineteenth century fared well in those less sophisticated and less frenetic times. In fact, if ever the term "community of scholars" had meaning, it was then. Untroubled as yet by the pressures of mammoth enrollments and the scientific revolution, universities conducted their affairs in relative harmony.

World War II changed all that. The war brought an end to the innocence of the university and ushered in a new era which has seen more changes in higher education than in all of the previous years combined.

When the war broke out, the government's own research laboratories proved inadequate to provide the research and technology necessary for a full-scale war effort. Washington, therefore, turned to the universities, and they responded with an enthusiasm to match that of the millions of men who were rushing to the colors. If this was the beginning of today's infamous "military-industrial complex," it was at least conceived with the best of intentions: the survival of the free world.

Before World War II, scientific research was somewhat limited in the universities. Few dollars were spent on it, and the giants of the scientific community fashioned their equipment from bits of metal and glass, left over machine parts, and ample measures of genius. Some $15 million in federal funds went to higher education for research in 1940—most of it to land-grant institutions for agricultural research. In 1944, a single agency (the Office of Scientific Research and Development) spent $90 million on contract research with universities.

The research effort in universities did not end with the War. Millions of veterans returned from the battlefields and flocked to the campuses. The tensions of the cold war prompted a massive and continued defense effort. Federal dollars flowed in greater amounts, mostly to the top 50 universities. The trends toward scientific research, academic specialization, and scholarly publication that began to be visible in the 1930's accelerated in the 1940's and have continued to grow in scope and intensity through the past two decades.

The decade of the 1960's has represented an unprecedented period of affluence and influence for the American university. The land-grant movement planted the seeds of mass education, research, and service to society. These seminal ideas blossomed during and just after World War II. The fruits have ripened during the past 10 years. Some statistics suggest the scope of the changes that have occurred in just 30 years.

(1) In 1949, there were 1,700 colleges and universities in the United States and they enrolled 1.5 million students. In 1969, there are more than 2,300 higher institutions with more than 7 million students.

(2) The federal government spent about $15 million on the campuses in 1940, nearly all of it for agricultural research. In 1968, the federal government's support to higher education approached $5 billion, of which about $1.4 billion was expended for on-campus research. As recently as 1958, the great bulk of federal support to higher education went for research; now some 70 percent of it goes toward such things as new buildings, student aid, and general grants to institutions.

(3) The states spent less than $154 million on higher education in 1940; today they spend about $5 billion on the campuses.

(4) In 1940, higher education's property and endowment was valued at $4.5 billion; last year the amount was nearly $30 billion.

No one who knew the universities of 1940 can say they have not changed. They have changed greatly and grown enormously, and tremendous strains have resulted. The pace has been incredibly swift and it proceeds ever faster. The hybrid university of the late nineteenth century is now full grown and so are the problems that were built in at its birth. Looking back, one can easily see that the potential for conflict was built in. The American university embodied three great missions—teaching, research, and service. Each now pulls it in a different direction. In fact, in the context of universal higher education and American egalitarianism these three missions may well be inherently incompatible in a single institution.

AMERICAN HIGHER EDUCATION

It is also necessary, if the present crisis is to be understood, to realize the meaninglessness of the term "American higher education." This suggests a system, an orderly and rational typology of institutions which does not, in fact, exist. Most people use the terms "college" and "university" generically to mean an institution of higher learning. This is understandable, but it leads to serious misunderstandings. The 2,300-plus institutions of higher learning in the United States are a diverse collection of institutions—private and public, secular and religious, large and small, old and new, urban and rural. There are senior "universities" which spend millions of dollars on research, train graduate students and operate institutes and professional schools. There are "universities" which do none of these things. There are 4-year colleges which concentrate on undergraduate education (some call themselves universities) and there are four-year colleges which offer advanced degrees and have professional schools (and do not call themselves universities). There are an increasing number of "junior colleges" which are 2-year institutions and which offer vocational training or academic preparatory work. There are technical institutes, arts schools, music schools, military schools, etc.—and they are all institutions of higher learning.

This confusion in terminology and definition is symptomatic of the more harmful confusion of purpose. By lumping all of these institutions together, we fail to differentiate on such important questions as what they should do and how they should do it. Higher education in the United States would be in a much more felicitious condition if society and higher education itself had long ago realized and acknowledged that there are many different types of institutions and that their functions, structures, and methods of governance should reflect these differences. What is "right" for Harvard is not likely to be "right" for Catonsville Community College and vice versa, though sometimes it seems that neither Harvard nor Catonsville (nor society, for that matter) knows it.

In the best of all worlds, perhaps, a system of higher education would lead to some logical division of labor. The universities—some 150 graduate and research institutions—would truly be intellectual communities devoted to scholarly inquiry and training at the highest levels. The colleges—both public and private—would devote themselves to undergraduate teaching primarily. And the junior colleges would offer training programs suited primarily to the needs of the communities in which they exist.

Each type of institution would serve society in ways most compatible with this clearly perceived primary mission and with its resources. Each would operate at its optimum size and efficiency. Faculty and students would choose the college or university best suited to their needs and abilities. Each institution would receive from a variety of sources the financial support required to fulfill its stated goals, and society would wisely value and reward each type of institution for its own distinctive contribution.

This is not the best of all worlds. Universities are expected to teach undergraduates and graduates in large numbers, to conduct research, and to provide unlimited services to society—and to do each exceedingly well. Society does not value each function equally, but prizes research and service above teaching, and spends its money accordingly. Most students and faculty follow the money and the prestige it buys, regardless of their needs and abilities. As a consequence, some universities are monstrously large and cannot build fast enough to house their students or their programs. Some colleges are small and have great difficulty finding money, faculty, and students. In the large universities, students complain about being computer cards, about bureaucracy, about poor undergraduate teaching. In the small colleges, faculty complain about lack of money, research, and prestige. Junior colleges want to be four-year colleges, which in turn want to be universities. All want more support, better faculty, brighter students, and—the coin of the academic realm— prestige. Nobody, it seems, is happy in higher education any more.

Because the universities set the pattern for all of American higher education, what happens to them is extremely relevant to all institutions. If academic freedom and institutional autonomy are to be preserved or lost, it will be in the university that the die is cast. The crisis in function, structure, and governance in the university wilts the ivy across the whole spectrum of higher institutions. It is in the universities that reform or revolution must begin.

Consider some of the developments which have led to the crisis:

The demand for knowledge and technology has put a

premium on research and has created a single track system for individual rewards. To a young academician, research and publication are the only sure path to promotion and scholarly prestige.

A graduate student in a Southern state university surely spoke for many of his colleagues when he said:

> I don't really care much for research; I'd rather teach. But that would immediately put a lid on my career and doom me to second class citizenship in the academic world. So I'll play the game; dig deeper and deeper into my speciality, scratch for government grants, and publish as much as possible.

Research has also fostered a parallel single track for institutional advancement. Research attracts money and the best faculty, and a college that wants its share of both is under considerable pressure to develop graduate education and research programs. This was one of the problems that led to the faculty disaffection at San Francisco State College. Faculty there resented the fact that Berkeley across the Bay had cornered the market on research and the money and prestige that follows it. The same situation exists in many state systems, where public colleges are pressing for the authority to offer the Ph.D. and thus to become competitive with their sister universities in the search for faculty, students, and federal funds. Even small private liberal arts colleges are flirting with the notion of adding graduate programs for the same reason.

The trend makes the lip service to the value of diversity in higher education ring ever more hollow. If the colleges feel compelled to emulate the senior universities, they will not only lose their own distinctions, but they will simply add to the number of mediocre universities.

Research and the scientific revolution (of which research is both cause and effect) have led to the increased specialization and professionalization which have caused painful problems for both faculty and students. Faced with a curriculum constantly expanding to embrace ever more academic specialties, the student despairs of what to learn and the faculty of what to teach. While the subject matter fragments and fragments again, the faculty struggles vainly to bridge the gaps of communication and intellect by building interdisciplinary bridges.

Editor, writer, and professor Irving Kristol has written:

Only on a few small campuses does "the professor" still survive. The "professionalization of American life" has radically emptied that category. A professor of sociology is now, by profession, a sociologist. He is not a member of any particular campus community, but of a nationwide—nay, international—corporate body of learned men. He is not even likely to reside on any one campus long enough to be a familiar figure there; and, while in residence, he is taken to be—and regards himself as—a representative of his discipline within the academic congregation. His standing and his prestige derive exclusively from his reputation among the 11,000 members of the American Sociological Association. The fact that he happens to teach is incidental. Unfortunately, however, the overwhelming majority of the members of these acedemic professions are fated to spend their lives doing what is incidental—merely teaching. This fate becomes, for most of them, a confession of professional failure.

The growing emphasis on service to society has many of the same consequences as the emphasis on research. Service, like research attracts money—most of it from the federal government, but significant amounts from business, foundations, and state governments.

As far as the student is concerned, service—like research—takes the professor from the classroom. And though the professor may earn extra income or gain in prestige, service represents for him another major commitment of his time. A prominent professor of biology says: "Considering my research, my teaching, my commitments to university committees and administration, my membership on government panels, and my various consulting jobs. I have committed 150 percent of my time."

The university is expected to help solve society's many problems—from rescuing ghetto children to purifying the air, from advising government officials to developing new weapons systems.

The University's response during the past few decades to society's needs for science and technology has been nothing short of miraculous. Today, however, there is a growing demand for answers to social and political problems. Society is concerned about law and order, urban blight, overpopulation, regional government, racial discrimination, poverty, education, and a myriad of other "nonscientific" problems. Having witnessed the miracles in the march of science, Americans now look for miracles in the social and behavioral sciences to help solve problems which in many cases have been caused by scientific developments. Neither the institutions nor the scholars are equipped to provide these answers. Their response, nonetheless, is to call for more research (almost a conditioned response now) in the social sciences, to think in terms of institutes, centers, even the creation of a National Social Sciences Foundation parallel to the National Science Foundation.

Useful as such increased emphasis on social science research may ultimately be, it is a somewhat sterile answer to society's desperate need for solutions to staggering social problems. A more effective response—*the one which activist students seem instinctively to feel and express in their demands for curricular and academic reform*—is to reemphasize teaching. The great and unique contribution higher education could make to the social revolution which confronts us in the second half of the twentieth century is to produce a new breed of American—young men and women who are "turned on," who will reassert a dying concept of individual worth, who are committed to closing the gap between the promise and performance of the American democracy. Research on the phenomenon of racism will not accomplish as much as enlightened curricula and teaching designed to liberate men from their prejudice and ignorance.

The debate over higher education's obligations to perform services for society has been raging for many years, and it will rage for many more. Some urge the academy to resist the pressure for more and varied services, arguing that universities have become "supermarkets" or "service stations." Others strongly disagree and argue that colleges and universities fulfill their noblest goal when they serve society—even to the point of attending to the moral and spiritual health of society. Students take both sides of the debate—condemning institutions on the one hand for serving society by conducting military research, and condemning them on the other hand for not serving society by failing to lead the battle for civil rights.

This raises the difficult issue of when a college or university should take a stand—as an institution—on political, moral, or social issues. Much of the disenchantment of today's youth seems to turn on this point. They cannot reconcile the existence of an affluent and aloof institution in the midst of evil and injustice. They call upon their universities to do battle.

This is a hazardous course the students urge. A university's function is to universalize. All action is highly specific, and when an institution acts in moral or political issues, it jeop-

254

ardizes its basic mission of providing an atmosphere for the objective and dispassionate search for truth. Sociologist Nathan Glazer puts it this way:

> There may be times when a university should hurl all of its resources into the battle against some great evil—but there always have been and always will be grave problems, and there will always be those who would propel the university into conflict.

Some issues impinge upon the functions of the university and demand that the university take a stand. Assaults on academic freedom, compulsory loyalty oaths, legislative interference in campus governance are such issues. But to extend this involvement—as some students and faculty demand—into contemporary political and social issues would seriously impair the university's obligation to transcend the times through which it passes and its freedom to reflect without bearing the responsibility to reform. Moreover, institutional neutrality does not prevent individuals within the university community from taking stands on moral and political issues—indeed, institutional neutrality does not prevent individuals within the university community from taking stands on moral and political issues—indeed, institutional neutrality makes such individual action possible without fear of retribution from society.

The dilemma for higher education is a painful one, dependent as it is upon society for support. The tough questions remain unanswered: Which services are legitimately the business of the university, and which would be better performed by some other institution? How can the university remain sufficiently detached from the problems and politics of contemporary society to preserve their objectivity? How can the university remain detached without losing touch with the needs of society?

Society's needs are so urgent that it may not wait for higher education to answer these questions. It may decide. Sir Eric Ashby notes:

> . . . Forces from outside the university which formerly had only a marginal effect upon its evolution are, in the next generation, likely to exert a powerful influence on its evolution. Governments which heretofore had been content to abide by a convention to leave the universities alone are now tempted to exert more and more dirigism upon them. Querulous protestation about this would be useless. Universities are enormously

expensive to run. None of them can hope to survive without patrons. Between universities and their patrons there have always been buffers of convention. Their patron is now the man in the street; universities must negotiate with him and establish new conventions which safeguard their heredity.

UNIVERSITY GOVERNANCE

This confusion of purpose, then, has led to many of the most serious problems on the campus. They and the present disarray in higher education have raised questions about the ability of the university to govern itself.

The power to govern in higher education has been traditionally shared by three groups: Trustees, administrators (mainly presidents), and faculty. Alumni, donors, students, and others have sometimes exerted an influence, but they rarely shared in governance.

The trustees, in most cases, are granted by law full authority over the institution. But custom is stronger than law in this area, and the trustees delegate most of their power most of the time to the president.

In theory, the president's powers are wide ranging; in fact, he relies more on persuasion than power to accomplish anything. If he is to lead at all, it must be by consensus.

Tradition gives to the university faculty the power to determine the academic and intellectual style and substance of the institution. Their actual power, says Ford Foundation President McGeorge Bundy, is far greater: "It is the faculty which is the necessary center of gravity of the policies of the university, for teaching, for learning, for internal discipline, for the educational quality and the character of the institution as a whole." But Mr. Bundy goes on to argue that the faculty has usually used its power in a negative way, and, in its preoccupation with personal professional matters, has left the task of governance to others. (In many instances, the faculty has not acted because it has not really perceived its potential power or its rightful responsibilities. In part, this is a legacy of an era of strong authoritarian presidents.)

The net effect of this has been a power vacuum—one which activist students have begun to fill with astonishing political sophistication.

It must be kept in mind, as one regards with contempt this management consultant's nightmare, that we have deliberately built over the past century an institution of shared power. When one or another group has become so powerful as to

256

upset this delicate balance, the results, as revealed by history, have been sad for the university. Such a scheme of shared power seems to be in keeping with the university's style of operating, with its dedication to thorough discussion and deliberation of every issue before taking a decision. The difficulty today is that the issues proliferate and the demand for immediate action is compelling. Universities are being pressured into making decisions which they are incapable of making (without creating ill-will and dissention) in a matter of hours or days.

The result of this awkward situation is either a kind of institutional paralysis—which is likely to lead to a student revolt—or arbitrary action by one group on the campus—which is likely to lead to the kind of campus war which Clark Kerr described and fell victim to.

Once again, the situation tends to make everyone unhappy. The trustees feel their legal authority is being eroded and their ability to act constrained. The President is caught between opposing forces, none of whom he is likely to please. The faculty, with other fish to fry, resents the endless meetings and diversions. And the students think that all the others are really only delaying and pettifogging in an effort to avoid doing anything meaningful. Meanwhile, legislators, alumni, parents and others on the outside looking in grow increasingly certain that nobody is in charge and that everybody is irresponsible.

If the university indeed appears to be irresponsible, if society does lose confidence in the university's ability to determine its own goals and manage its own affairs, then the danger to freedom is indeed great, for the ultimate fate of the university rests with society.

"The abstention of government from major intervention in the affairs of the academy," writes a political scientist, "is not the result of a recognition of an absolute right of the academies to do with their hallowed halls anything whatsoever, no matter what the subsequent impact on society may be. Rather it is conditioned upon academies meeting their obligations and responsibilities both as members of a self-regulating profession and as citizens of a free society. And if this is not done even the most liberal minded of governments might well be forced into a position of exercising its residual power of regulation in the interest of order."

What most people—especially students—fail to see is that governance is not the university's strong suit. Unlike the state, the academy's primary function is not to govern or

257

rule. By forcing the university to emphasize governance, militant students and faculty threaten to destroy the essential nature of the institution which has made it worth trying to control.

Robert Brustein makes another important point. The young, he says:

> Are creating conditions in which it is becoming virtually impossible to do intellectual work. In turning their political wrath from the social world, which is in serious need of reform . . . to the academic world, which still has considerable value as a learning institution, they have determined, on the one hand, that society will remain as venal, as corrupt, as retrogressive as ever, and, on the other hand, that the university will no longer be able to proceed with the work of free inquiry for which it was founded. As an added irony, students, despite their professed distaste for bureaucratic administration of the university, are now helping to construct—through the insane proliferation of student-faculty committees—a far vaster network of bureaucracy than ever before existed. This, added to their continued meetings, confrontations, and demonstrations—not to mention occupations and sit-ins—is leaving precious little time or energy either for their intellectual development or for that of the faculty.

Nonetheless, the university must fulfill what has been called its "order-teaching and order-maintenance" function. Unless the university community upholds a code of behavior which protects the rights of all to think, study, and speak, it will cease to exist as a university. Violence and disruption are simply incompatible with the concept of rational discourse which must characterize the academy. Moreover, one must wonder with some apprehension what the effect will be on students who spend their college years in an atmosphere of confrontation, disorder, and disruption. Students learn dangerous lessons when they learn that change can be accomplished by threat and violence, that there are no penalties for the violation of communities rules, that the right of others can be disregarded in the name of a cause.

CONCLUSION

The university, then, has changed too fast but not fast enough. It has undergone revolution but not reform. It is in danger of losing its traditions of the past and of failing to keep pace with the future. It is a center of power in the post-industrial society, but seems powerless in its present crisis.

Sir Eric Ashby says:

> Universities . . . are mechanisms for the inheritance of culture. Like other genetic systems they have great inertia. They are living through one of the classical dilemas in evolution. They must adapt themselves to the consequences of their success or they will be discarded by society, they must do so without shattering their own integrity or they will fail in their duty to society.

It is an awesome challenge, a hazardous blindfolded walk on the high wire, made infinitely more difficult and dangerous by those who push and pull it and hasten it onward.

Sir Eric has a somber warning for the impatient reformers:

> . . . Academic evolution like organic evolution is accomplished in small continuous changes. Major mutations are generally lethal. And changes must be based on what is already inherited.

PART THREE

THE AGENCIES OF LAW ENFORCEMENT

CHAPTER 13

THE NONSYSTEM OF CRIMINAL JUSTICE*

Despite broad agreement that crime is increasing faster than the ability of most cities to cope with it, deep division prevails among those who prescribe anticrime remedies. Energy that ought to be devoted to action programs to reduce crime is being poured instead into words—into an escalating conflict between proponents of the hard line and of the soft line. Political campaigns, legislative hearings and court arguments find intelligent citizens taking all-or-nothing positions on such questions as: Are law enforcement officers handcuffed or brutal? Should we support or reform the local police? Should prosecution policy be tough or selective? Should prison sentences be long or flexible?

While to an informed observer the answers to such questions are complex, a multitude of persons holding positions of authority or power behave as if they were simple. Instead of seeking the very large common ground on which the hard line and the soft line converge, law enforcement "experts" have shown an increasing tendency to focus on symbolic issues, such as Supreme Court decisions, civilian review boards, capital punishment and preventive detention, as if they held the keys to the crime problem.

The anger with which such issues have been debated in recent years has contributed little to public confidence, to the safety of streets or to the effectiveness of criminal procedures. It has, however, caused actual reform in the institutions of public order and justice to lag far behind the excellent recommendations of three presidential crime commissions (National, D.C., and Civil Disorders) which have reported since the end of 1966.

The chapters which follow contain discussions of some of

---

*This chapter was prepared by Daniel J. Freed, Professor of Law and Its Administration at Yale Law School and formerly Director of the Office of Criminal Justice in the U.S. Department of Justice.

the reforms which need to be addressed promptly if the sad record of the 1960's is to be bettered as law enforcement and criminal justice face the challenge of the 1970's. As a backdrop for those discussions, this chapter considers three questions:

1. What does a typical criminal justice system look like today?
2. How well is that system integrated into the program of cities for meeting the problems of urban inadequacy?
3. What new directions should comprehensive reform of the criminal justice system take?

The responses set forth below sketch a profile of today's criminal justice process and suggest some of the ingredients for its improvement.

THE SYSTEM: THEORY VS. PRACTICE

Our society has commissioned its police to patrol the streets, prevent crime, arrest suspected criminals, and "enforce the law." It has established courts to conduct trials of accused offenders, sentence those who are found guilty and "do justice." It has created a correctional process consisting of prisons to punish convicted persons and programs to rehabilitate and supervise them so that they might become useful citizens.

It is commonly assumed that these three components—law enforcement (police, sheriffs, marshals), the judicial process (judges, prosecutors, defense lawyers) and corrections (prison officials, probation and parole officers)—add up to a "system" of criminal justice. The system, however, is a myth.

A system implies some unity of purpose and organized interrelationship among component parts. In the typical American city and state, and under federal jurisdiction as well, no such relationship exists. There is, instead, a reasonably well-defined criminal process, a continuum through which each accused offender may pass: from the hands of the police, to the jurisdiction of the courts, behind the walls of a prison, then back onto the street. The inefficiency, fallout, and failure of purpose during this process is notorious.

The dismal crime control record to date is well known. According to the 1967 report of the President's Commission on Law Enforcement and Administration of Justice, well over half of all crimes are never reported to the police. Of those which are, fewer than one-quarter are cleared by arrest. Nearly half of all arrests result in the dismissal of charges. Of the balance, well over 90 percent are resolved by a plea of guilty. The proportion of cases which actually go to trial is tiny, representing less than 1 percent of all crimes committed. A large portion of those convicted are sentenced to jails or penal institutions; the balance are released under probation supervision.

Nearly everyone who goes to prison is eventually released, often under parole supervision. Between two-fifths and two-thirds of all releasees are sooner or later arrested and convicted again, thereby joining the population of repeater criminals we call recidivists.

Nearly every official and agency participating in the criminal process is frustrated by some aspect of its ineffectiveness, its unfairness or both. At the same time, nearly every participant group itself is the target of criticism by others in the process.

Upon reflection, this turmoil is not surprising. Each participant sees the commission of crime and the procedures of justice from a different perspective. His daily experience and his set of values as to what effectiveness requires and what fairness requires are therefore likely to be different. As a result, the mission and priorities of a system of criminal justice will in all likelihood be defined differently by a policeman, a trial judge, a prosecutor, a defense attorney, a correctional administrator, an appellate tribunal, a slum dweller and a resident of the suburbs.

For example: The police see crime in the raw. They are exposed firsthand to the agony of victims, the danger of streets, the violence of lawbreakers. A major task of the police officer is to track down and arrest persons who have committed serious crimes. It is often discouraging for such an officer to see courts promptly release defendants on bail, or prosecutors reduce charges in order to induce pleas of guilty to lesser offenses, or judges exclude incriminating evidence, or parole officers accept supervision of released prisoners but check on them only a few minutes each month.

Yet the police themselves are often seen by others as contributing to the failure of the system. They are the target of charges of ineptness, discourtesy, brutality, sleeping on duty, illegal searches. They are increasingly attacked by large segments of the community as being insensitive to the feelings and needs of the citizens they are employed to serve.

Trial judges tend to see crime from a more remote and

neutral position. They see facts in dispute and two sides to each issue. They may sit long hours on the bench in an effort to adjudicate cases with dignity and dispatch, only to find counsel unprepared, or weak cases presented, or witnesses missing, or warrants unserved, or bail restrictions unenforced. They find sentencing to be the most difficult of their tasks, yet presentence information is scanty and dispositional alternatives are all too often thwarted by the unavailability of adequate facilities.

Yet criminal courts themselves are often poorly managed and severely criticized. They are seriously backlogged. All too many judges are perceived as being inconsiderate of waiting parties, police officers and citizen witnesses. Throughout the country, lower criminal courts tend to be operated more like turnstiles than tribunals.

Corrections officials enter the crime picture long after the offense and deal only with defendants. Their job is to maintain secure custody and design programs which prepare individual prisoners for a successful return to society. They are discouraged when they encounter convicted persons whose sentences are either inadequate or excessive. They are frustrated by legislatures which curtail the flexibility of sentences and which fail to appropriate necessary funds. They are dismayed at police officers who harass parolees, or at a community which fails to provide jobs or refuses to build halfway houses for ex-offenders.

Yet jails are notoriously ill-managed. Sadistic guards are not uncommon. Homosexual assaults among inmates are widely tolerated. Prison work usually bears little relationship to employment opportunities outside. Persons jailed to await trial are typically treated worse than sentenced offenders. Correctional administrators are often said to be presiding over schools in crime.

In the mosaic of discontent which pervades the criminal process, public officials and institutions, bound together with private persons in the cause of reducing crime, each sees his own special mission being undercut by the cross-purpose, frailties or malfunctions of others. As they find their places along the spectrum between the intense concern with victims at one end, and total preoccupation with reforming convicted lawbreakers at the other, so do they find their daily perceptions of justice varying or in conflict. The conflicts in turn are intensified by the fact that each part of the criminal process in most cities is overloaded and undermanned, and most of its personnel underpaid and inadequately trained.

266

Under such circumstances it is hardly surprising to find in most cities not a smooth functioning "system" of criminal justice but a fragmented and often hostile amalgamation of criminal justice agencie. To the extent they are concerned about other parts of the "system," police view courts as the enemy. Judges often find law enforcement officers themselves violating the law. Both see correctional programs as largely a failure. Many defendants perceive all three as paying only lip service to individual rights.

Mechanisms for introducing some sense of harmony into the system are seldom utilized. Judges, police administrators and prison officials hardly ever confer on common problems. Sentencing institutes and familiarization prison visits for judges are the exception rather than the rule. Neither prosecuting nor defense attorneys receive training in corrections upon which to base intelligent sentencing recommendations.

Nearly every part of the criminal process is run with public funds by persons employed as officers of justice to serve the same community. Yet every agency in the criminal process in a sense competes with every other in the quest for tax dollars. Isolation or antagonism rather than mutual support tends to characterize their interwined operations. And even when cooperative efforts develop, the press usually features the friction, and often aggravates it.

One might expect the field to be flooded with systems analysts, management consultants and publicly-imposed measures of organization and administration in order to introduce order and coordination into this criminal justice chaos. It is not.

A recognized profession of criminal justice system administrators does not exist today. In fact, most of the subsystems are poorly run. For example, court administrators are rare, and court management by trained professionals is a concept that is taking hold very slowly.

The bail "system," which should involve coordination among at least a half dozen agencies, is presided over by no one. Few cities have neutral bail agencies to furnish bail-setting magistrates with reliable background data on defendants. Prosecutors usually ignore community ties and factors other than the criminal charge and the accused's criminal record in recommending bail. Defense lawyers rarely explore nonmonetary release conditions in cases involving impecunious clients. Detention reports on persons held long periods in jail prior to trial are rarely acted on by courts, and bail review for detainees is rarely requested. Enforcement of bail

restrictions and forfeitures of bond for bailjumpers are unusual. Bail bondsmen go unregulated.

Effective police administration is hard to find. The great
majority of police agencies are headed by chiefs who started
as patrolmen and rose through the ranks, whose higher education is scanty, whose training in modern management techniques, finance, personnel, communications and community
relations is limited, and whose isolation is profound. Lateral
entry of police administrators from other departments or
outside sources is usually prohibited by antiquated Civil Service concepts.

Apart from lack of leadership, the process of crime control in most cities has no central collection and analysis of
criminal justice information. It has no focal point for formulating a cohesive crime budget based on system needs rather
than individual agency requests. It has no mechanism for
planning, initiating or evaluating systemwide programs, or for
setting priorities. It has no specialized staff to keep the mayor
or other head of government regularly informed of the problems and progress of public safety and justice. Crime receives
high-level attention only as a short-term reaction to crisis. An
effective system does not exist.

This bleak picture should not obscure occasional bright
spots. Within recent years, scattered about the country, some
promising developments have appeared: innovations have
been introduced, new leadership has emerged, modern facilities have been built, a systems approach has been tried. While
the impact has been small, hopes have been raised. States
here and cities there have shown that crime control and
justice can be improved. The question is whether isolated
reforms can grow into a pattern.

CRIMINAL SANCTIONS AS A SOLUTION TO
URBAN PROBLEMS

The internal disorganization of the criminal justice system
is not its only handicap. Even if it functioned like a well-oiled
machine, it would—without other changes—probably fail to
achieve either a substantial reduction in most categories of
conduct now labelled as crime, or a material increase in
public respect for law.

The likelihood of failure is promoted by two traditional
features of criminal law administration: (1) the criminal
sanction applies by statute to much more human behavior
than it can realistically control, and (2) the criminal process

operates too largely in isolation from other programs aimed at the breeding grounds of antisocial behavior. Until the target conduct of criminal penalties can be narrowed and the myth of full enforcement dispelled, and until crime reduction is perceived as requiring better education, housing, health and employment opportunities for would-be offenders, the criminal process will continue to suffer from demands that it accomplish more than is possible with less help than is indispensable to success.

SCOPE OF SANCTIONS

The case for limiting the use of the criminal sanction has been advanced most effectively by Professor Sanford Kadish in his *Annals* article on *The Crisis of Overcriminalization* (1967) and by Professor Herbert L. Packer in *The Limits of The Criminal Sanction* (1968). For present purposes, their relevant point is that the demands made upon the police, the courts and the penal process, far exceed the capacity of these organizations collectively to investigate, apprehend, prosecute, adjudicate and correct individual behavior.

The overload means that full enforcement, speedy trial, fair procedure and effective sentencing have become slogans rather than facts. The crimes of violence society fears most— murder, forcible rape, robbery, assault—are currently processed through many of the same channels as conduct which injures third parties least, e.g., prostitution, homosexuality, intoxication, gambling, marijuana use, vagrancy, and other minor offenses. The disabling impact on law enforcement is suggested by the fact that the police are overloaded with minor cases at a time when their clearance rate for serious crimes in virtually every city is less than 25 percent.

Without condoning conduct which offends prevailing moral standards, a community could undoubtedly act more expeditiously and effectively against violent invasions of person and property if fewer of its law enforcement resources were detoured into crime objectives of low priority. Finding alternative ways of handling low priority offenses would make particular sense in the case of conduct which is extremely difficult to detect (because it occurs voluntarily and often inside private homes), produces no injury to another person, and offers little likelihood of deterrence or cure even if criminal penalties are imposed. The sporadic and discriminatory enforcement, the charges of abuse of police discretion, the assembly-line justice and the ineffective sanctions which characterize most of the present effort to deal with these lesser offenses tends to perpetuate cynicism and disrespect for law.

The search for nonpenal techniques to control behavior involving consenting parties should be viewed not as a soft approach to lesser offenses, but as a realistic route to meaningful sanctions against crimes that injure society the most. Some forms of conduct should probably be eliminated entirely from regulation by statue. Some, like intoxication, should be dealt with through voluntary health reforms, such as those being pioneered by the Manhattan Bowery Project. Others, like traffic infractions, might be transferred to an administrative or regulatory process, as California and New York have done. But until the wide range of behavior now subject to arrest, trial and sentencing is materially reduced, the police, courts and prisons are likely to remain overwhelmed and underachieving.

RELATIONSHIP TO CIVIL PROGRAMS

Just as the conduct amenable to criminal sanctions needs to be narrowed, so should the range of community-based programs tied to the criminal process be broadened. Education, job training, medical care and shelter are needed at least as much by juveniles and adults charged with crime as by their counterparts in the deprived community who have not been so charged. The criminal justice process cannot continue to function in isolation from the more affirmative social programs for improving individual lives. The objective of integrating criminal and noncriminal programs is easy to advocate but difficult to achieve.

For example, a major goal of an offender's contact with the criminal process is said to be corrective—rehabilitation followed by reintegration into the community, with enhanced respect for law. Yet the opposite is often true: the typical prison experience is degrading, conviction records create a lasting stigma, decent job opportunities upon release are rare, voting rights are abridged, military service options are curtailed, family life disruptions are likely to be serious, and the outlook of most ex-convicts is bleak. The expectation of the community that released offenders will be "corrected" is matched by outdated laws and community responses which tend strongly to defeat those expectations.

This unfortunate pattern is not confined to the handling of convicted offenders. The odds are high that unconvicted

270

persons will encounter similar, and sometimes greater, constraints. Cities are full of people who have been arrested but not convicted, and who nevertheless served time in jail and were stigmatized in other seriously disabling ways.

Thus, local facilities in which arrested persons are detained prior to conviction are typically worse, in terms of overcrowding and deterioration, than the prisons to which convicted offenders are sentenced. Accused first offenders are mixed indiscriminately with hardened recidivists. The opportunities for recreation, job training or treatment of a nonpunitive character are almost nil.

If released, a person's arrest record alone becomes a substantial liability. In many segments of a community, the difference between arrest status and that of conviction is indiscriminately regarded as a technicality.

In its present state of disrepair, the criminal process—when it operates alone—at best performs a holding function. This function may provide society respite when a serious offender with a long record and minimal prospect of improvement is identified. In such cases, denial of release for as long as the law allows may seem reasonable, even though almost all convicts are eventually released.

In nearly every case, however, a city candid about its own criminal justice deficiencies needs to ask whether full enforcement aimed at detention, prosecution and imprisonment, will in the long run reduce or reinforce criminality.

The traditional assumption has been that punishment will reduce crime. In attempting to separate myth from reality, however, it is worth noting that experienced judges have resorted increasingly in recent years to various forms of postconviction probation. They have done so after weighing the possibilities for rehabilitation if the offender is so released against the usually disastrous prognosis which would accompany his incarceration. It is a painful choice, little understood by the public. But the decision to seek correction of an offender in the community reflects less a compassionate attitude toward law-breakers, more a hardheaded recognition, based on data, that long-term public safety has a better chance of being protected.

The alternatives are no longer simply prison or outright release. Integrating the criminal process with community programs requires closely supervised forms of release: daytime work release, release in the custody of reliable counselors, pre-release guidance centers, alcoholism and narcotic treatment centers, halfway houses.

Community-based programs will, of course, fail equally with prisons if the resources and attitudes which accompany them are no better. Identifying the offender's needs in terms of education, job training, employment, family aid, hospitalization and shelter, and providing for them, must be seen as inuring to society's benefit as well as his own.

The stage at which these services are furnished should whenever possible be advanced from after conviction to after arrest. Voluntary correctional programs should be offered without a prior finding of guilt. As urged by the National Crime Commission, accused offenders should be routed away from the criminal process at the earliest stage that vindication of the community's interest permits.

Most such efforts will tend to reduce the cost of criminal prosecution by eliminating it when it is not needed, and to increase the speed and firmness of prosecution for hardened offenders for whom no meaningful alternative exists. Public funds thus diverted from the revolving door functions of imprisonment, warehousing, degradation and contamination can be invested instead in community programs where the crime reduction payoff is higher.

GUIDELINES FOR CRIMINAL JUSTICE REFORM

Against this background of the criminal justice nonsystem, and unrealistic expectations as to what its sanctions can achieve, emerged the 1967 Report of the President's Commission on Law Enforcement and Administration of Justice and the 1968 Omnibus Crime Control and Safe Streets Act. In theory, the 1968 legislation provided the framework and the funds for massive federal grants to the states with which the comprehensive and detailed recommendations of the President's Commission could be implemented. In fact, early performance has been handicapped by unrealistic deadlines, inadequate funds and a shortage of experienced manpower to convey a criminal justice system approach to the states.

During the first year since its launching, the federal program to assist states and cities in dealing with crime has come under attack from several sources, e.g., the Conference of Mayors, the National League of Cities, the National Urban Coalition. Instead of emphasizing federal leadership to guide the development of sound criminal justice systems at the local level, as originally proposed by the President's Commission, the Act has assigned the leadership role in distributing block grants and guiding their application to the states. State planning groups have failed in many instances to represent the full range of citizen as well as official interests in crime control. Friction has erupted between cities and their state governments over the question whether funds should be allocated on the basis of population or crime rate. Agencies of the criminal process have tended to plan their own individual programs by themselves. Crime control has continued to remain isolated from social programs aimed at employment, education, housing and health. Outside expertise to augment local planners has remained scarce. The consequence, in many instances, has been pedestrian state plans.

Unless some new ingredients are added, deficiencies such as these foreshadow the channeling of massive federal funds into old programs, and into higher salaries for old-line personnel. They will thereby tend to reinforce rather than reform the inadequate criminal justice institutions and to perpetuate the polarized attitudes which exist today.

There are, of course, no short cuts to the reduction of crime. More money and personnel, new equipment and revised procedures will all be essential to the goal. Yet without new organizations and relationships to help spend money wisely and use personnel well, history suggests that significant changes are unlikely.

Reform in the criminal field has a long record of excellent recommendations never carried out. A substantial portion of the National Crime Commission's proposals in 1967 are, for example, remarkably similar to those urged by the Wickersham Commission established by President Hoover 37 years earlier. Despite that Commission's equally impressive documentation, conservatism and presidential prestige, little follow-through was mounted. Experience with commissions at the state and local levels shows similar results. Library shelves are crowded with reports on police inadequacy, court chaos and prison disgrace, and reform proposals which never produced effective action.

Moreover, money poured into the crime problem does not by itself buy crime reduction. Wealthy states and localities which have spent vast sums for crime control have become no more noticeably crime-free than jurisdictions which haven't. The District of Columbia, with a superb crime commission report, constant oversight by Congress and federal money close by has failed to achieve anything resembling what two Presidents have called a model system of criminal justice.

This pattern suggests the existence of substantial built-in

obstacles to change. It suggests that unless much more attention is spotlighted on the inability and unwillingness of present crime control systems to effectuate reform, new money may go down old drains. Vexing problems of politics, organization and leadership underlie the maintenance of the status quo and need to be faced up to directly.

In the search for new approaches to the implementation of crime commission recommendations, two promising but comparatively untried strategies have been suggested by recent experience on the frontiers of criminal justice in several cities: (1) a program to coordinate public criminal justice agencies more effectively, and to link them to companion social programs, by placing them under the supervision of a new high-level criminal justice staff or agency; and (2) a program to develop private citizen participation as an integral operating component, rather than a conversational adjunct, of criminal reform. The success of citizen participation will in many ways be dependent on the establishment of a central criminal justice office.

THE CRIMINAL JUSTICE AGENCY

The pervasive fragmentation of police, court and correctional agencies suggests that some catalyst is needed to bring them together. An assumption that public agencies will operate consistently can no longer suffice as a substitute for deliberate action to make it happen in real life. Arrested offenders—the common target or client of criminal justice agencies—afford their only continuous link today.

Periodic crime commissions—which study these agencies, file reports and then disappear—are valuable, but they are too transient for the catalyst role. A law enforcement council—consisting of chief judges and agency heads who meet periodically—will likely constitute little more than another committee of overcommitted officials.

A full-time criminal justice office should be considered basic to the formation of a criminal justice system. Its optimum form and its location in the bureaucracy need to be developed through experimentation.

The function could be vested in a criminal justice assistant to the mayor or county executive, with staff relationships to executive agencies, and liaison with the courts, the bar and the community. Or it could be established as a new agency, a ministry of justice, possessing authority under the direction of a high ranking official of local government (e.g., Director of

274

Public Safety or Criminal Justice Administrator) to oversee and coordinate the police, prosecutorial and correctional functions. Special kinds of administrative ties to the courts and the public defender office would have to be evolved to avoid undermining the essential independence of the judiciary and the adversary role of the defense.

The establishment of a new office or agency should not be permitted to disparage or overwhelm the diversity of values and perspectives which are essential to preserve in the separate agencies of a criminal justice system. Otherwise, a single official—oriented too heavily toward law enforcement or toward individual rights—might seriously disturb the balance of an entire system. The appointment of a carefully representative criminal justice advisory council, composed of key public officials and knowledgeable private citizens can help guard against this danger as well as promote the broad interests of reform.

Whatever the form of the new agency, its basic purposes would be to allocate resources, to introduce innovation within as well as among the constituent agencies so as to improve the fair and effective processing of cases and to develop understanding and respect among the component parts of the system. For example:

It would develop a system of budgeting for crime which takes account of the interrelated needs and imbalances among individual agencies and jurisdictions;

It would initiate a criminal justice information system which, as an adjunct to personnel, budgeting and legislative decisions, would embrace not simply crime reports (as is typical today), but arrests, reduction of charges, convictions, sentences, recidivism, court backlogs, detention populations, crime prevention measures, and other data essential to an informed process;

It would perform a mediating and liaison role in respect to the many overlap functions of the criminal process, e.g., development of programs to reduce police waiting time in court, to improve pretrial release information and control, to enlist prosecutors and defense attorneys in cooperative efforts to expedite trials, to bring correctional inputs to bear on initial decisions whether to prosecute, to improve relations between criminal justice agencies and the community;

It would perform or sponsor systems analyses and periodic evaluations of agency programs, and encourage innovations and pilot projects which might not otherwise have a chance in a tradition-oriented system:

It would develop minimum standards of performance, new

incentives and exchange programs for police, court and correctional personnel.

Most of all, the comprehensive grasp of the system by an experienced criminal justice staff would facilitate informed executive, judicial and legislative judgments on priorities. It would enable wise planning and action by the city with funds received from the Law Enforcement Assistance Administration and the state. It would help decide, for example, whether the new budget should cover:

A modern diagnostic and detention center to replace the jail, or 1000 policemen;

Additional judges and prosecutors, or a prior management survey of the courts;

A computerized information system or a roving leader program for juveniles;

New courtrooms or a half-dozen halfway houses.

For a full-time well-staffed criminal justice office to be successful, it must achieve a balanced perspective within its own ranks on the problems of public safety and justice. Practical experience in law enforcement, in the assertion of individual rights, and in the efficiency and effectiveness of programs must be represented in the staff as well as in the advisory council.

The transition from today's chaotic process to a well-run system will not be easy. Most troublesome is the fact that the criminal process does not operate within neat political boundaries. Police departments are often funded at the city level; county and state police and sheriffs must also be taken into account. Judges are sometimes appointed, sometimes elected, and different courts are answerable to local, county and state constituencies. Correctional functions are a conglomerate of local and county jails, and county and state prisons. Probation systems are sometimes administered by the courts, sometimes by an executive agency. Prosecutors may be appointed or elected, from all three levels of government. Defense lawyers usually come from the private sector but are increasingly being augmented by public defender agencies.

Reform will be difficult even within a single jurisdiction, where political control of criminal justice agencies is traditionally loose. Many mayors have difficulty with the concept of the police department as a subordinate agency. "Keep the politics out of policing" has become a watchword often used by inbred police departments to resist the recruitment of new leadership from outside police civil service rosters. By deferring more to police chiefs than to the heads of other critical city agencies, mayors avoid making crime their own problem. At the same time, the police themselves have avoided responsibility for crime control, especially in recent years, by attributing the increase in crime to Supreme Court decisions.

If this confusing pattern makes the creation, location, staffing and political viability of a criminal justice office difficult, it also symbolizes why little semblance of a system exists today. Fragmentation is in many ways inherent in the antiquated structure of local government. The challenge of crime poses a high priority inducement to reallocate political power and make government more effective.

An adequately staffed criminal justice office will be more than most cities can currently afford. Its need is not presently seen as high on their priority lists. To encourage the development of such offices, the Violence Commission should recommend the enactment of federal legislation to provide direct financial aid to cities or counties submitting suitable plans for structuring and staffing them. Caution will have to be exercised to avoid funding new operations which are systemwide in appearance but prosecutorial in purpose. Some commitment should be required to assure the recruitment of a balanced staff. The applicant's plan should also spell out in detail the contemplated relationship between the proposed office and the relevant governmental structure of the city, county and state.

Helpful insights in establishing such offices may be derived from the experience of state law enforcement planning agencies established under the Omnibus Crime Control and Safe Streets Act. Useful precedents may also be found in the criminal justice coordinating role developed by Mayor Lindsay's office in New York over the past 2 years and now being explored by several other cities, and in the experience of the Office of Criminal Justice established in the Department of Justice in 1964 by Attorney General Kennedy, and initially directed by Professor James Vorenberg of Harvard.

PRIVATE CITIZEN INVOLVEMENT

Government programs for the control of crime are unlikely to succeed all alone. Informed private citizens, playing a variety of roles, can make a decisive difference in the prevention, detection and prosecution of crime, the fair administration of justice, and the restoration of offenders to the community.

Each function is being grossly underplayed today. New citizen-based mechanisms are needed at the national and local levels to spearhead greater participation by individuals and in groups.

NATIONAL CRIMINAL JUSTICE
CONSULTING CENTER

Enlisting all segments of business and citizen life in constructive crime programs is no easy task. The Federal government has not done it. No existing private organization appears to combine enough prestige, knowledge and experience. To serve as a catalyst, a national citizen group must know the crime problem intimately and broadly, have practical insights into its complex solutions and possess a stake in the outcome.

At least four groups in recent years have developed such a background and achieved the desired visibility: the Miller Commission (President's Commission on Crime in the District of Columbia), the Katzenbach Commission (President's Commission on Law Enforcement and Administration of Justice), the Kerner Commission (National Advisory Commission on Civil Disorders), and the Eisenhower Commission (National Commission on the Causes and Prevention of Violence). Each had a distinguished, bipartisan and largely non-federal membership, containing liberals and conservatives.

Each of the three which have completed their tasks has seen a diverse membership combine to produce a compelling report and sweeping recommendations. To a remarkable degree, their findings and directions for the future are the same, or fall into a consistent pattern. At the same time, most of their proposals have gone unimplemented.

To capitalize on the work of its predecessors, and profit from the lessons of inadequate follow-through, the Violence Commission has a notable opportunity to go beyond the writing of its final report and the closing of its doors. It can, if it will, take the initiative in creating an ongoing mechanism to promote nationwide the kinds of criminal justice systems toward which it and its staff have been writing.

Specifically, the Violence Commission should convene a session to which its predecessor commissions and their executive staffs are invited. The Brown Commission (National Commission on Reform of Federal Criminal Laws), whose important work on overhauling criminal statutes is still in process, should also be invited. The Violence Commission should lay before this expert group a proposal to establish a new national organization, perhaps known as the National Criminal Justice Consulting Center. The proposal should include the following ingredients:

A Board of Directors composed of three representatives from each of the Presidential Commissions, including their executive directors;

A full-time staff, with generous allowance for consultants, recruited from among staff members of each commission, staff leaders of state and local law enforcement planning agencies established pursuant to the Omnibus Crime Control and Safe Streets Act of 1968, persons with experience in the Law Enforcement Assistance Administration (LEAA) and related federal agencies, and persons with backgrounds in the work of criminal justice institutes such as those pioneered in recent years by the Ford Foundation;

Financial assistance sought from a combination of private and public sources, e.g., business, foundations, LEAA and other federal agencies;

Close working arrangements with national organizations which specialize in important parts of criminal justice systems reform, e.g., International Association of Chiefs of Police, American Bar Association, American Correctional Association, National Council on Crime and Delinquency, National District Attorneys Association, National Legal Aid and Defender Association, American Civil Liberties Union.

The proposed NCJCC would assist localities in working out the details of specific reforms which cut across the operating lines of criminal justice agencies. It would be a how-to-do-it consultant, helping cities implement reforms rather than confining itself to drafting plans. It would serve as a catalyst and clearinghouse, bringing innovations developed in one city to the attention of persons working on the same problem in another. It would furnish proven budgets, job descriptions, court rules, legislation, and operating know-how. It would cross-fertilize new approaches, aid public education where antiquated notions prevail, and offer workable answers to the persistent citizen question—what can I do to help?

Such an organization could fill the national leadership void created whenever a prestigious and educated commission, which over time has developed consensus out of diversity, dissolves and disperses.

By being private in composition, the NCJCC would avoid the strictures against Federal control of state programs by which Congress narrowed the LEAA leadership role when it enacted the Omnibus Crime Control Act of 1968. While NCJCC's guidance would be unofficial, the collective experience it represented would substantially assist those in Federal, state and local government who vitally need expert support in their difficult tasks.

As an adjunct to its consulting mission, the Center might also undertake national demonstrations. As local innovations in crime control are identified, the Center on its own or with others could bring them to the attention of a nationwide audience through periodic conferences.

At least twice in recent years, through the initiative of private nonprofit organizations, national conferences have been convened to demonstrate the details of useful criminal reforms. In each case, a how-to-do-it approach was mounted to show how different communities had addressed a common problem and produced improvements in the criminal process. The National Conference on Bail and Criminal Justice was cosponsored in 1964 by the Vera Institute of Justice and the U.S. Department of Justice. The National Defender Conference in 1969 was undertaken by the National Defender Project of the National Legal Aid and Defender Association with cosponsorship by the American and National Bar Associations, the Department of Justice and others.

There are many artisans in the campaign for leadership and funds with which to control a national citizen effort to improve criminal justice. Yet no organization represents or could attract the reputation and experience which has evolved from the Presidential commissions of recent years. They provide a resource which ought not be permitted to evaporate.

LOCAL CITIZEN ORGANIZATIONS

Constructive citizen action on the local level can be a powerful force for criminal justice reform. There are simply too many important aspects of the private citizen's duty to expect local government to solve the crime problem by itself.

The private role begins with each citizen responding individually when called: reporting crime, appearing as a witness, serving as a juror, hiring the ex-offender. The prevailing low level of performance in most of these areas is exemplified by the finding of the President's Commission on Law

Enforcement and Administration of Justice that more than half of all crimes are never reported; by the widespread refusal of citizens to "become involved"; by the frequent failures of victims to prosecute, or to continue to show up in court despite seemingly endless court delays; and by the rampant refusal of employers, public and private, to employ persons with criminal records.

Beyond individual action the private role requires group participation. By and large, citizens fearful of crime are uninformed about the problems of criminal justice administration. They are too often unread in the literature of crime commissions, uninvolved in efforts to improve the system, and overloaded with myths and scapegoats. All too many citizens continue to advocate simple solutions to complex crime problems. Those who dig deeply almost always change their minds.

The myths can be erased but only by firsthand involvement in the process of reform. New York City has established a Criminal Justice Coordinating Council to tie private business, labor, education, religion and other citizen interests to public officials in tackling specific crime control projects. In narcotics, alcoholism, burglary prevention, court delay, police manpower utilization, offender employment and other areas, teams of public and private persons—aided by full-time private staff from the Vera Institute of Justice—work together, analyzing the facts, planning for change, and overseeing reform. The coordinating council idea is catching on elsewhere.

Royal Oak, Mich., and Denver, Colo., have seen groups of private citizens develop one to one programs through which a private person helps a misdemeanor offender or a juvenile delinquent make his way back into law abiding community life.

Washington, D.C., has produced Bonabond, Inc.—an organization run by ex-offenders to help other ex-offenders in trouble.

In a host of cities, local chapters of national organizations like the Lawyers Committee for Civil Rights Under Law, the Urban League, the Urban Coalition, the National Council on Crime and Delinquency, the League of Women Voters, and the American Friends Service Committee, have launched programs to improve jails and prisons, juvenile courts, offender employment, police recruitment and crime prevention, and to plan emergency justice procedures, etc.

As such local efforts multiply, several elements critical to their success or failure, and their overall impact on law and justice in the community, emerge: e.g. full-time staffing, adequate funding, long-term continuity, involvement in a spectrum of criminal justice system problems, frequent evaluation of progress.

Perhaps the most successful of private organizations in attacking a broad range of crime control problems through a public-private partnership is New York City's Vera Institute of Justice. Its unique role in cooperation with the office of the Mayor, the police, the courts and corrections has developed over eight years. Its nonbureaucratic approach has permitted it to test new programs, through experiments and pilot projects, in a way no public agency would likely find successful. Its core funding is entirely private; its individual project financing comes from a wide range of Federal, state and private sources.

The philosophy and technique which characterize the Vera operation have been summarized by its Director, Herbert J. Sturz:

It has often been said that public institutions are inherently resistent to change—particularly to change proposed by a private outside organization. Vera has not found this to be the case in New York City. We received support from Mayor Wagner when we began the Manhattan Bail Project. We have had support from Mayor Lindsay for our more recent projects. The agencies with which we have dealt have acknowledged the need for change, and they have been, for the most part, hospitable to new ideas and, to some extent, experimentation.

Many irritants in the system arise from the lack of coordination among agencies. The principal mechanisms for dealing with a problem which cuts across agency lines—the interdepartmental committee and the task force—have been largely unsuccessful. A neutral private agency, such as Vera, can successfully bring together several agencies in a joint innovative program or experiment. Perhaps because we are not part of the bureaucratic machinery, we post little threat to existing agencies and carry with us no residue of past misunderstandings. Also, bringing about the required cooperation is our business and not an extra duty imposed on a crowded schedule.

In addition, Vera can intercede with the city's power structure; we are not bound by chains of command. We do not seek reform by exposing inefficiency or injustice, by leveling indictments, or by public confrontation with line agencies. Too often, this approach hardens opposition to change or at best leaves the kind and quality of change to the agency under attack. And we have found that, although preliminary fact-finding is necessary as a prelude to experimentation, a study alone is seldom effective in bringing about change. In the criminal process Vera has used the pilot project to advantage.

Small test programs can usually be mounted inexpensively; specialists can be brought in *ad hoc;* red tape can be bypassed; relatively quick results can be expected. Since no new agency, bureau, or division is created, a project can be easily dismantled if it proves ineffective, without disastrous results politically or financially, and even in failure it may provide useful information. If the project proves worthwhile, the city can take it on as a permanent fixture, and the private planning group can move on to a new area.

It is my belief that this action-oriented intervention approach, which Vera has tried with some success in New York City, can be useful in other cities provided that certain conditions can be met. Among them are: (1) that funding, at least for a core staff, be available over a two or three year period from the private sector (money for specific projects can be raised from city, state and federal sources); (2) that the new institute be system-oriented as well as client-oriented and should quickly establish in the community the principle that the two are not mutually exclusive; (3) that the first couple of projects show visible results within a year; (4) that the people who run the institute are content to stay in the background and give credit to those within the system.

The Vera experience should be tried elsewhere. The Federal government should join the private sources to provide the funds for spurring the establishment of similar institutes in other urban centers. A major task of the proposed NCJCC should be to help localities develop such private catalysts for change.

CONCLUSION

The mechanisms suggested here could go a long way toward reversing the picture of a criminal justice nonsystem falling apart at the seams. Money in vast sums is the other part of the life blood of a functioning system. The injection of federal funds into state crime control programs in 1968 was an important step in the right direction. Much more money must be channeled, and must reach down into the cities, if action to reduce crime is to make a difference. Much more money must be injected into research, development and pilot projects, if the outdated techniques of yesterday are to be converted into an effective criminal process tomorrow.

Until these impediments are remedied, and until staffed organizations—public and private—are developed to assure wise investment and monitoring of new funds, crime control will continue to be a high priority campaign fought with bold words but no system.

CHAPTER 14

THE POLICE AND THEIR PROBLEMS*

In society's day-to-day efforts to protect its citizens from the suffering, fear, and property loss produced by crime and the threat of crime, the policeman occupies the front line. It is he who directly confronts criminal situations, and it is to him that the public looks for personal safety. The freedom of Americans to walk their streets and be secure in their homes —in fact, to do what they want when they want—depends to a great extent on their policemen.[1]

There is little question that during the past decade of turbulent social change, our nation's policemen have not been able to escape from the front lines. More than that, they are called upon to fight against one side one day and then for it the next day. The same policeman who on a Wednesday is mobilized to help control a blazing ghetto riot and arrest throngs of looters may by week's end find himself assigned to keep traffic clear from the parade route being followed by hundreds of blacks conducting an anti-poverty march.

In fact, the very same policeman may on a Saturday rescue a hippie college student victimized by a gang of motorcyclists, and by the next Monday be summoned to the campus to assist university officials in re-capturing a building

---

* This chapter was prepared by David P. Stang and is based in part on research contributions by Professor Alfred Blumstein, Director, Urban Systems Institute, School of Urban and Public Affairs, Carnegie-Mellon University, Pittsburgh, Pa.; Prof. Samuel Chapman, Department of Political Science, University of Oklahoma; Prof. A. C. Germann, Department of Criminology, California State College, Long Beach, Calif.; Capt. John J. Guidici, Oakland Police Department, Oakland, Calif.; George W. O'Connor, Director, Professionals Standards Division, International Association of Chiefs of Police, Washington, D.C.; Prof. Irving Piliavin, School of Social Work, University of Pennsylvania; and Donal MacNamara, John Jay College, New York City. Interviewing with police officers of all levels, from chiefs to patrolmen, was also conducted.

held by stone-throwing, epithet-screaming student dissidents. The same policeman in the morning may be called "soft and ineffective" by our "forgotten man" and "fascist pig" by a young revolutionary in the afternoon. How our nation's police are able to fulfill such drastically conflicting roles without lapsing into an anomic stupor[2] is perhaps the best measure of the degree to which the policeman is in fact a professional.

What is the policeman's job? Who and what is he supposed to protect? How can he most effectively execute his responsibilities? What are his problems and how can these problems be solved? These are the questions we address in this chapter.

DUTIES OF THE POLICE

Police responsibilities fall into three broad categories.[3] First, they are called upon to "keep the peace." This peacekeeping duty is a broad and most important mandate which involves the protection of lives and rights ranging from handling street corner brawls to the settlement of violent family disputes. In a word, it means maintaining public safety.

Secondly, the police have a duty to provide services which range from bestowing menial courtesies to the protection of public and private property. This responsibility is the one that many police officers complain about the most but, nevertheless, are called upon to perform the most frequently. In fulfilling these obligations, a policeman "recovers stolen property, directs traffic, provides emergency medical aid, gets cats out of trees, checks on the homes of families on vacation, and helps little old ladies who have locked themselves out of their apartments."[4]

The third major police responsibility, which many policemen and a considerable segment of the public feel should be the exclusive police responsibility, is that of combating crime by enforcing the rule of law. Execution of this task involves what is called police operations and this ranges from preparing stakeouts to arresting suspects.

That policemen have difficulty assigning priorities to these sometimes conflicting responsibilities is one major operating limitation the police have recently had to endure.[5] There are, however, other important limitations imposed on the police to which we shall briefly refer before returning to the crucial subject of conflicting police roles.

Among these, special attention must be given to manpower

deficiencies, inadequate financing, and frictions with courts and other governmental agencies.

MANPOWER LIMITATIONS

According to the President's Crime Commission, there are approximately 420,000 policemen in the United States today.[6] Yet most police departments are under-manned, thus spreading the existing complement of police personnel much too thin. This manpower supply has been further depleted by more generous holiday, vacation and sick-leave policies, reduced weekly work-hours, increased specialization, continued use of police personnel to perform a heavier burden of clerical, technical and service activities more suitable for civilian employees.[7] The manpower problem is further exacerbated by difficulties in recruiting, especially recruitment among minority groups; resignations of experienced police officers; early retirements; overly rigid restrictions on manpower distribution and assignment; and the dissipation of police-man hours in nonproductive or minimally productive activity. This latter category involves, in part, hours spent waiting to be called as a witness, writing out multiple copies of reports, assignment to fixed posts of questionable utility, being forced to provide special escort services, and other irritating and time consuming chores. Nor is the available manpower scientifically allocated either in terms of ratios of police to population (which range from fewer than 1:1000 to more than 4:1000) or in terms of crime incidence, traffic volume, calls for police services or other meaningful indices of demands for more effective policing.

This inadequacy is magnified by reports that newly recruited officers are less well-educated than veteran officers,[8] that they are being assigned to full police patrol duty without completing the prescribed training;[9] that morale is low and supervision lax;[10] and that advanced in-service and refresher training to keep them abreast of legal, social, and technological changes is inadequate.[11]

FINANCIAL LIMITATIONS

In 1968, in the most affluent nation in world history, our total expenditures for police (Federal, state, and local, including sheriffs and such *ad hoc* police agencies as the New York City Transit Police, Port of New York Authority Police, park police, Capitol Police, and other full-time enforcement personnel) approximated $3 billion. Most commentators consider this amount inadequate in light of current recruitment problems, resignations, early retirement difficulties, and widespread police "moonlighting" with its negative effects on police alertness and departmental sick-leave rates.

Inadequate police budgets, too, have made it difficult or impossible in many jurisdictions to construct needed modern headquarters facilities, to provide decentralized substations in areas of demonstrated need, to modernize communications systems, to install improved traffic control devices, to acquire computers and other advanced management and operations control "hardware," to finance pilot projects and demonstrations and to recruit at highly-paid specialist levels the qualified personnel, all of which are essential to the implementation of the recommendations of the President's Commission on Law Enforcement and Administration of Justice and of the National Advisory Commission on Civil Disorders.

Police costs in the United States have been traditionally a local burden . . . a burden which many local jurisdictions are no longer able to support if fully effective law enforcement is to be achieved. Certainly the funds now being provided by Congress through the Law Enforcement Assistance Administration of the Department of Justice to support police planning, training, and research will prove of some assistance in easing the budgetary limitations under which many law enforcement units are presently operating.

POLICE CONFLICTS WITH OTHER CRIMINAL JUSTICE AGENCIES

The police establishment is only one of the agencies constituting the criminal justice system. By the very nature of the criminal justice system, the police are required to cooperate with the other agencies, including the prosecutors, the courts, the jails and correctional institutions. In many locations, however, there is neither formal nor informal machinery for cross-professional dialogue between the police and the representatives of the other agencies involved in criminal justice administration or policy-making, so that minor irritations and misunderstandings often cumulate into major bureaucratic conflicts. The failure to involve the courts, prosecutors, and corrections officials in the training of police, the failure to involve police in the orientation of newly chosen judges and prosecutors and in the training curricula for newly appointed probation and parole officers, and the even more general failure to consult police in the planning stages of executive and legislative decision-making in areas which may directly or indirectly affect their responsibilities or operations—all further compound this already difficult situation.

In recent years the courts in particular have become more and more the target of severe police criticism. Police problems involving the courts arise at three levels: (1) Procedural requirements which result in the loss of many hundreds of thousands of police man-hours annually because of inefficient or uncooperative court administration and resistance to changes in traditional practices (*e.g.*, booking, computerized dockets, the impanelling of additional grand juries, and such apparently simple courtesies as moving cases involving police witnesses to the top of the calendar or the taking of police testimony in pre-trial proceedings);[12] (2) allegedly improper disposition of cases both at preliminary hearings and arraignments and after trial (*e.g.*, dismissal of charges and release of persons arrested for serious crimes, speedy setting of low bail or release on personal recognizance of offenders police believe dangerous and likely to commit additional crimes or granting probation to dangerous and persistent offenders where probation supervision is inadequate); and (3) constitutional limitations on police tactics and procedures both in general law enforcement and specifically in the area of criminal investigation (e.g., the decisions of the Supreme Court which have forced the police to be more careful in the conduct of searches and seizures, and in warning suspects of their constitutional rights against compulsory self-incrimination).

The question of court-imposed constitutional limitations on police practices is especially sensitive. Whether these restrictions on traditional police practices have actually reduced police effectiveness is a matter of some controversy even among police and prosecutors; but a significant consensus among police officers of all ranks in every part of the country interprets these decisions as favoring the criminal and as deliberately and perversely hampering, indeed punishing, the police.

One police spokesman has stated:

> It would appear that the primary purpose of the police establishment has been overlooked in the tendency of our courts and the other officers of the judicial process to free the most heinous of criminals because of legalistic errors by law enforcement officers. . . . To allow criminals to go free because of legalistic error turns our judicial process into a game and makes

mockery of our supposedly sophisticated society. . . . From the police standpoint, one of the very real dangers is that decisions from the courts are breeding indecision and uncertainty in the individual police officer. The inevitable result is that the policeman's duty has become so diffused that it is difficult for him to carry out his responsibilities.[13]

Another observer stated even more dramatically that, "The Courts must not terrorize peace officers by putting them in fear of violating the law themselves."[14] Views of this kind are set forth repeatedly in articles and comments in such respected police professional periodicals as *The Police Chief, Law and Order* and *Police.*[15]

Police in general also have little confidence in the ability of jails and prisons to reform or rehabilitate convicted offenders. This is not surprising, of course, for this view is shared, if perhaps for different reasons, by the great majority of American criminologists and even by residents of our so-called "correctional system." This lack of confidence in institutional rehabilitation programs underlies the strong police opposition to the parole system and the somewhat less aggressive opposition to work release, school release, and prisoner furlough programs, open institutions, and halfway houses. There is a rather generalized feeling among large segments of the police that potentially dangerous offenders are released far too often on low bail, or their own recognizance or following conviction far too soon by parole boards; that these paroled offenders are frequently inadequately supervised by unqualified parole officers with excessive caseload responsibilities; and that they commit new and serious crimes thus adding additional burdens of investigation and apprehension to already overburdened police agencies.

Police in some jurisdictions have encountered difficulties in their relationships with the executive and legislative branches of government. These difficulties range from the irritation of requests for special treatment for favored traffic offenders and detail of police personnel to jobs as chauffeur and doorman in the Mayor's office to outside interference in internal personnel matters such as assignments and promotions and in general policy matters such as enforcement strategies and operational tactics.

Legislatures too have been criticized by police for failure to appropriate sufficient funds to provide adequate law enforcement for repeated investigations and inquiries which contribute to a negative police image; for penal law and criminal procedure changes which reduce penalties, make parole easier, or impose new restrictions on police efforts; and for failure to protect the police from changes in their working conditions which police feel deleterious to their welfare.[16]

POLICE ROLE CONFLICTS

As we stated earlier, perhaps the most important source of police frustration, and the most severe limitation under which they operate, is the conflicting roles and demands involved in the order maintenance, community service, and crime-fighting responsibilities of the police. Here both the individual police officer and the police community as a whole find not only inconsistent public expectations and public reactions, but also inner conflict growing out of the interaction of the policeman's values, customs, and traditions with his intimate experience with the criminal element of the population. The policeman lives on the grinding edge of social conflict, without a well-defined, well-understood notion of what he is supposed to be doing there.

Police involvement in order maintenance situations such as family disputes, tavern brawls, disorderly teenagers loitering in the streets, quarrels between neighbors, and the like inevitably produces role conflict. One party is likely to feel harassed, outraged or neglected. The police officer quite frequently has no clear legal standard to apply—or one that, if applied, would produce an obviously unjust result.[17] The victim is often as blameworthy as the perpetrator, often the parties really want him only to "do something" that will "settle things" rather than make an arrest. Should an arrest be demanded, he is in many jurisdictions foreclosed from complying since the misdemeanor complained of was not committed in his presence, and the vociferously complaining victim or witness is unwilling to sign a complaint.[18] Thus, he must devise a solution based almost entirely on his own discretion and judgement.[19]

Oftentimes the policeman is forced to arrest persons for violations of laws he does not believe are fair. But more often, he sees the fear and the pain and the damage that crime causes, and he feels that criminals are getting away with too much. This frustration mounts each time he arrives at the scene of a recently-reported crime to discover the offender has escaped. He finds justification for his contempt for the "criminal element" when he reads of public approval of night-stick justice techniques.[20]

Police in the United States are for the most part white,

upwardly mobile lower middle-class, conservative in ideology and resistant to change. In most areas of the country, even where segregation has been legally eliminated for long periods, they are likely to have grown up without any significant contact with minority and lower socioeconomic class life styles—and certainly with little or no experience of the realities of ghetto life. They tend to share the attitudes, biases and prejudices of the larger community, among which is likely to be a fear and distrust of Negroes and other minority groups.

Appointed to the police force and brought into day-to-day contact with what is to him an alien way of life, the young police officer experiences what behavioral scientists refer to as "cultural shock." His latent negative attitudes are reinforced by the aggressive and militant hostility which greets him even when he is attempting to perform, to the best of his ability, a community service or order maintenance function, or is attempting to apprehend a criminal whose victim has been a member of the minority community.

Negative responses to minorities and to non-conforming groups such as "hippies," campus militants, antiwar demonstrators, and the new breed of "revolutionaries," are also reinforced by the socialization process which transforms the new recruit into a member of the police community. Not only during the formal training process but in the everyday contacts with his fellow officers and his participation with them in both on-duty activity and off-duty socializing tend to mutually reinforce the police ideology, the closed-ranks defensiveness, which separates "we" who are on the side of law, order, morality and right from "they" who are immoral, criminal, delinquent, idle, lazy, dirty, shiftless or different.

Efforts to bridge the gap between the police and some segments of the community have proved only minimally successful.[21] The realities of police confrontation with these "undesirable elements," whether on occasions of episodic violence or, more importantly, when a police officer is killed or seriously injured as a result of minority group militance, tend to offset the gains made by efforts directed toward improving police attitudes and police-community relationships.

POLICE INEFFECTIVENESS

The cumulative result of the many limitations and frustrations described above is an evident inability of the police, as presently organized, manned, financed, equipped and led, to meet effectively all of the demands and expectations placed on them by the public. These inadequacies are evidenced in their inability to prevent crime, their declining record in solving crimes known to them; their sluggish response to and indifferent investigation of all but major crimes or those involving important persons, businesses, or institutions.[22] Particularly evident is an inability to deal effectively with crime in minority-populated ghettoes—for reasons which involve minority group attitudes and noncooperation as importantly as police attitudes, facilities and efficiency.

Various analyses of police confrontations with minority and protest groups have identified 'over-response,' inadequate crowd control training, poor planning, failures in supervision and leadership, as well as the residual hostility of the police to the minorities and nonconformists involved, their suspicion of dissent, and their disagreement with the demonstrators on the substantive issues as causative factors.[23] Nor have these analyses neglected to underline the difficult conditions to which the police have been subjected: the provocations, verbal and physical, to which they were subjected by participants in demonstrations;[24] and at least in some instances the distorted or at least unbalanced coverage by news media.[25] That at least some participants in many of these conflict episodes wanted to provoke a police over-response may be true—but that individual police officers, and sometimes apparently whole police units, cooperated enthusiastically with their plans is equally obvious.[26]

That the police and major elements of the public are becoming more polarized is well established.[27] This polarization is intensified by police frustrations growing out of what they perceive as the public's unreasonable expectations of them and even more unreasonable limitations imposed on them, the growing militancy of minority and dissident groups, their strategy of confrontation, and the vicious cycle of police overresponse. These factors often are aggravated by new and highly publicized charges of police brutality and derogatory attitudes toward minority groups, which attract new sympathizers from previously moderate or non-activist segments of the population and often tend to encourage reactive ghetto counter-violence.

POLICE POLITICIZATION

Recently, the police have begun to realize that acting

exclusively as individuals in attempting to deal with their role, conflicts, frustrations and limitations has failed to pay dividends. Thus, as is the case with other newly self-aware special interest groups in our society, the police have begun to enter active politics on a much larger scale.

Police participation in the political process in America has traditionally been limited and local: limited to securing favorable legislation as to pensions, working conditions and pay rates,[28] with occasional lobbying for or against proposals to abolish the death penalty, legalize gambling, or raise the age of juvenile court jurisdiction—and local in the sense that it invariably involved approaches by the locally organized police to municipal authorities or at most to the state legislator representing the district. Occasionally charges would be made of more active police involvement in local campaigns, but there was a consensus even among the police that they, like the military, should abstain from active, overt participation in politics. Various police departments incorporated in their police regulations stringent rules prohibiting political activity other than voting.

In the past decade, largely as a result of efforts to raise police pay scales to a parity with those of skilled workmen, more militant police associations—some trade-union affiliated, others in loose state and national affiliations—escalated their pressure tactics so that job action, "blue-flu," and even threatened police strikes became common-place in police-municipality salary disputes.[29]

The major impetus to police politicization, however, was without doubt the attempt to impose a civilian review apparatus to adjudicate complaints against police officers by aggrieved citizens and attempts of citizen groups to restrict police use of firearms.[30] The proposals for civilian review boards were fought in the communications media, in the courts, in the legislature, and finally in a popular referendum in New York City in which the police won a resounding victory after a campaign which did much to further polarize the dissident minorities.[31] The victory[32] convinced many in the police community of the desirability of abandoning the internecine battles which had divided them and reduced their political effectiveness in the past.

The future of expanded police participation in politics is not entirely clear at present. Certainly there has been important police support for conservative, even radical right, candidates in recent national and local elections, and there are

294

signs that police officials are finding increasing opportunities as successful political candidates.

But the police have not had an unbroken record of political successes. In the 1969 legislative session in Albany, a bill abolishing the fifty-eight year old three-platoon system passed by a near unanimous vote, despite strong opposition by the united police pressure groups. Whether activities such as aroused police officers seeking the removal of a judge in Detroit, or an equally aggressive organization (the Law Enforcement group in New York City) seeking to monitor the conduct of judges and their case dispositions, will be widely and successfully imitated cannot be predicted at this time.[33]

What is clear, however, is that a politicized police force united and well financed and perhaps closely allied to conservative political and social forces in the community poses a problem for those interested in preserving internal democracy and insuring domestic tranquility. As the only lawfully armed force within the community, and possessed by the nature of their duties and responsibilities of unique authority and powers over their fellow citizens (including access to derogatory information, potential for discriminatory enforcement of the laws against their opponents, licensing and inspection functions), the united incursion of the police into active politics must be regarded with some trepidation.

More and more, the police community perceives itself as a minority group, disadvantaged and discriminated against, surrounded by, servicing, and protecting a public, which is at best apathetic or unaware of the frustrations and limitations imposed on the police; and at worst, unsympathetic or hostile. The dynamics of this self-perception, assuming a continuation or possible escalation of the external aggravants (verbal and physical abuse of the police; more stringent judicial and legislative restrictions; budgetary difficulties), involve reinforced defensive group solidarity, intensified feelings of alienation and polarization, and a magnified and increasingly aggressive militancy in reaction and response to those individuals, groups and institutions (social and governmental) perceived as inimical—an action-reaction pattern which, unfortunately, will inevitably be replicated within the aggrieved andi dissident communities.

SOME SUGGESTED SOLUTIONS

There are two areas of police-public confrontations in which changes in police policy and practice can lead to a reduction of friction and restoration of public respect for the police which the police themselves feel to be so sorely lacking. The first involves highly visible police relationships with the public, often involving the combined presence of great numbers of police and the public at the same time and place. The second is the less visible contact of the police with the public and usually involves ordinary relationships between individual police officers and individual members of the public.

THE POLICE AND POLITICAL VIOLENCE

The police often believe that ideological and political conflicts like the Chicago convention demonstrations involve clashes between good, upright and honest groups of citizens on the one hand and bad, lawless and deceitful troublemakers on the other. In fact, however, these great struggles between large groups of the public more clearly involve political difference than they do questions of criminal behavior. Often the "good, upright and honest" citizens are better characterized simply as conservative elements of the population who are resisting the demands of other factions seeking social, political, or economic benefits at the direct expense of the conservative groups.

Unfortunately, these conflicts involving demonstrations, mass protests, and strikes by the dissidents often involve violence and the call-up of the police for front-line duty. The police, instead of taking a neutral position in attempting to restore order during these primarily political clashes, often tend to become participants in the clash on the side of the conservative elements and against the dissident elements.[34] The dissidents quickly recognize the active participation of the police in siding with the "enemy" and then begin to concentrate their attacks, both verbal and physical, more directly on the police than on the groups whose interests the police are supposedly protecting. The cycle becomes vicious and the ultimate loser is always the police.

This recurring phenomenon has been discussed quite extensively in the Task Force report on *Violence in America: Historical and Comparative Perspectives.* Thus, we refer only for example to the conservative-reformist clashes, entailing the victimization of the police, between management and labor of the 1930's; between the landowners and the migrant farm workers in California of the late 1930's and early 1940's; between the small town or rural white Southern

296

population—and the civil rights workers and Southern blacks of the early 1960's; between the urban governments, employers, landlords, and business establishments—and the anti-poverty and black power advocates of the middle to late 1960's. On each of these battlefields some of the police have unnecessarily taken sides and have become the target of violence.

In *Rights In Concord,* this Task Force's investigative report on the Washington counter-inaugural demonstration, we have shown that when the police, through disciplined supervision, refrain from taking sides and steadfastly remain neutral in the face of a political demonstration that is perhaps distasteful to most of them personally, physical injuries and the destruction of property are minimized and the police emerge as widely respected umpires and peace-keepers. Thus, with respect to political differences between elements of the population in these socially troubled times, police leadership must decline invitations to take sides and to refrain from engaging in unnecessary fights. Only in this way can the police surely reemerge as the respected keepers of the peace— the principle duty of their worthy profession.[35]

THE PATROLMAN AND THE PEOPLE

The second area of police-public confrontation in which there has been a loss of respect for the police is the routine day-to-day encounters between individual police officers and members of minority groups. These encounters form the crux of what is commonly referred to as the "police-community relations problem." The problem manifests itself particularly in the inner city.

The crowded center city is where crime rates are the highest, where the black minority has experienced the catharsis of bloody, blazing riots, and is now struggling to develop a new and proud identity. The people no longer doubt that they are entitled to be treated with respect and dignity, and often militantly demand it. They are aspiring for the social and material benefits that they have been so long without. Hopes are high, but the results have not yet begun to materialize substantially. Houses and apartments are still over-crowded, too cold in the winter, and unbearably hot in the summer. Homes still are often without fathers. Mothers still are searching for the wherewithal to purchase the next meal. Children of all ages are out on the street and in the alleys.

They see the very visible white man who, for years, has owned the corner grocery stores. He still tells them to get out if

297

they are not going to buy anything. But he's scared of them now and they know it. So they goad him, throw his merchandise around and sometimes steal it if they think they can do so without getting caught. The grocer calls the police.

The police arrive in a radio-dispatched squad car with red lights flashing. The young candy thieves have made a clean getaway. Their friends, however, are still on the street. The policemen talk with the grocer then return to the street to question the kids. The kids are amused and enjoy the excitement. "No," they did not see anybody leave the store. The policemen know otherwise and in frustration they ask, "What are you kids doing here?" "Nothing," is the answer. "Then you better move on or we're gonna lock you up," the kids are told. Reluctantly they make feeble efforts to obey. The police get back into their squad car and start to drive off. Ten seconds later they hear the kids' jeers and laughter.

Night falls. More of the older kids are now seen on the street corners "shucking and jiving." Some bounce basketballs. Some listen to portable radios. Others dance or feign boxing matches.

In the homes the fights begin. Sometimes it is between man and woman, sometimes between teenage child and an aunt or grandmother. The police are called again. The people on the street watch as the squad car arrives. The police go inside; they hear shouting. The accusations begin. The police explain that in order for them to arrest anybody, the complainant is going to have to go down to the D.A.'s office and sign a complaint. "Just lock the 'so and so' up," is the response. The police do the best they can to quiet things down, then leave. Nobody is satisfied. As the squad car pulls away from the curb, the kids jeer again.

Later in the evening the same policemen see a loud street corner disturbance involving about a dozen young men. The policemen are now a little more weary. In another half hour their tour will be finished.

They get out of the car and ask, "What's going on?" Two of the young men continue to swing at one another. "Alright, break it up!" a policeman orders. One of the two stops swinging. The other, apparently intoxicated, continues to brawl. The policemen get gruff. "I said, 'knock it off'!" barks the policeman. The young fighter utters a profane epithet followed by, "Honky cop." More people gather around.

One of the policemen responds, "Buddy, you're coming down to the stationhouse. We're gonna lock you up." The policemen reach for his arms. He kicks, swings his fists, and continues to yell "Honky cop!" The two policemen slam him up against the squad car, handcuff him, pat him down and shove him into the back seat. The crowd is sullen. Fists are clenched and teeth are gritted. One of the policemen says, "Move on. We don't want any more trouble out of you people tonight." The police-

298

men get back into the squad car and drive off. The still un-dispersed crowd mutters words of hatred.

These are ordinary events in the average day of a police-man assigned a squad car beat in the center city. There is no love lost between the police and the center city residents. The residents, whether they be black, Puerto Rican, Mexican, of any other minority group, or just plain hippies, see the police as bullies, unfair, stupid, rude, and brutal—a symbol of "Whitey's power." The police, in turn, see the minority groups as hostile, dirty, lazy, undisciplined, dishonest, immoral, and worst of all, disrespectful of the "badge" they try to represent.

"In the old days," the police say, "colored people would move on if you told them to. Now they don't. They just give you a bunch of crap."

On a wooden fence in the center city there are new epigrams scrawled in crayon. They read "Black Power!" "Say it now and say it loud—I am black and I am proud!" "Kill a pig."

IMPROVING POLICE-COMMUNITY RELATIONS

The police are, indeed, prejudiced against minorities. And the minority groups are equally prejudiced against the police. The prejudice on both sides is not without some foundation. The views of each side toward the other are constantly being reinforced and have become self-fulfilling prophesies. Doing something about this problem is what is called "improving police-community relations."

The need to improve police-community relations has existed and been recognized for decades. Local, state and federal commissions have written hundreds of pages about it. Police experts and academics have written books about it.[36] Public officials, including police chiefs, have made speeches about it. Civil rights, leaders have conducted demonstrations concerning it. All agree that something should be done. Recommendations have been made by the score. The most frequently made suggestions—many of them worthwhile—include:

Extending human-relations training of recruits and officers;
Creating or enlarging police-community relations units within police departments;
Starting precinct and city-wide citizen advisory committees, including minority leaders, to meet with the police;

Developing programs to educate the public about the police, such as visits of school children to precinct stations, lectures by police officers to adults or youth groups, and school courses concerning police work;

Running recruitment campaigns aimed at members of minority groups;

Ending discrimination within police departments, such as that relating to promotions, and integration of patrols;

Issuing orders banning use of abusive words or excessive force by police officers; and

Developing procedures to handle citizen complaints within the police department which are fair and designed to impose real discipline.[37]

Other recommendations have included the suggestion that the police be disarmed or at least that each police department adopt a strict firearms use policy.[38] Some have suggested that the police discontinue wearing military-type uniforms and instead don more friendly working garb, such as blazers and slacks.[39] Still others have encouraged the adoption of psychological pre- and post-recruitment tests designed to identify for "weeding-out" purposes the bullies and misfits. More extreme suggestions have been made to the effect that all the "bully cops" be fired or retired and that college graduate, social science majors be hired to replace them. Some have suggested either neighborhood control of the police, or that neighborhoods desiring it police themselves and that regular policemen not be permitted to enter such areas.[40]

Although some of these ideas have been adopted by some police departments in whole, or in part, in even the most progressive police departments the problem of police-community relations remains a sore spot. The reason is that most of the efforts at improving police-community relations have been undertaken merely as "programs," minor changes in the police department's organizational structure, or as public relations efforts.

To produce effective results, efforts at improving police-community relations require modification of the underlying context of attitudes stemming from the everyday contacts between the policeman on the beat and the people he normally deals with. The individual patrolman must recognize that for some time to come he will be viewed by members of the center city community not as an individual but as an oppressive symbol of the dominant white society. Of course, no community believes that "all cops are bad," and when a police officer treats people with consistent fairness, he will tend to gain a reputation for being "a good cop." But the depth of hostility between the police and the ghetto resident means that the policeman will have to persist in his efforts to be "a good cop" without any significant rewards in terms of appreciation from the community he serves.

On the other hand, the inner-city community, and particularly its leaders, must recognize that policemen cannot be converted into social workers who operate on the assumption that felons are morally innocent products of a criminogenic environment. More importantly, members of the center city community must recognize not only the inevitability, but the desirability, of the policeman's primary identity as a member of the "thin blue line." A policeman's over identity with the community and a non-identity with "the force" tends to destroy a policeman's effectiveness both in the eyes of the community, and of his peers and superiors on the force. Just as members of the military think of themselves as "the military" as opposed to "the civilians," police officers, too, will continue to think of themselves primarily as policemen. Thus, instead of attempting to destroy this "we-they" identity it should, be capitalized upon and used to maximum advantage.

It is true that the "we-they" identity of the police has undesirable aspects to it, especially an apparent need to be tougher than "they." It is also true, however, that this toughness, or at least a confidence in a superior toughness, lies at the very foundation of a policeman's ability to arrest a violently resisting suspect who is 6 inches taller and 75 pounds heavier than he, or to calm an unruly group of aggressive teenagers. The problem is how to shape the "we-they" identity so that the end result will not lessen the policeman's ability to apprehend criminals and maintain order, yet at the same time not destroy the policeman's desire or ability to interact on a humane, civil basis with the community.

We do not accept the views of some critics that the problem is a dilemma, the solution to which is impossible without changing the very nature of the policeman's role. Scores of interviews with the police themselves have convinced us otherwise (although we do believe that the present service-providing function of the police can be shifted in part to civilians and citizen auxiliaries).

When we asked various policemen what they thought the main advantage was in being police officers as contrasted to

301

most other occupations, most replied, first, that it was the superior ability to understand people and how they behave that was afforded them by constant exposure to all segments of the public. Secondly, the majority answered that it was the ability to "keep a cool head" under stress, danger, and provocation. A black policeman, asked why he decided to become a police officer, gave us this answer:

> Man, when I was a little kid I thought cops were God. I lived in the ghetto and I saw drunks, addicts, cuttings, shooting, and husbands hitting wives and kids fighting on street corners and other bad scenes every day.
> Somebody always called the police. The police arrived in the middle of the hassle and were always cool and always got on top of the problem fast. If they could break it up by quiet mouthing it they would. If they had to bust somebody they did it quick and were gone. Whatever it was, they arrived on the scene, got with it fast, stopped the trouble and split—always with a cool head. I figured that was smooth and so I decided when I was a kid I wanted to be a policeman and do the same thing.[41]

Understanding and coolheadedness—these qualities represent the very essence of a "good cop." These are the traits most required by the patrolman in the performance of his peace-keeping function. If these two qualities can be developed in more of our policemen, it will do much to alleviate tensions between the police and the community.

The breeding ground of community resentment of the police is principally at the patrolman level, not at the command level. When patrolmen fail to show understanding, i.e., act insensitively, and fail to maintain coolheadedness, i.e., loose control and act intemperately, the community becomes incensed. The state of police-community relations is basically the result of everyday contacts of the community with the patrolmen, not the chiefs. The problem of police-community relations is thus one of ascertaining how to encourage understanding and discourage insensitivity in the patrolman, how to encourage cool-headedness and discourage losing control or "blowing one's cool."

The yardstick for testing the application of a mature, sensitive understanding and coolheadedness is often (once deciding that intervention is necessary)[42] how quickly and quietly a patrolman can restore calm without having to make an arrest. This is what 'good cops' are made of. This is what

302

constitutes "good police work." This is what breeds community respect for the police.

One of the major problems with the present system of policing is that of convincing patrolmen that when they perform their *peacekeeping* duties well, they are rendering a service no less valuable to the community than when they perform their *law-enforcement* function. Presently the rewards to a patrolman who is an effective peace-keeper at best, are slight. His promotion in rank is seldom the result of a good record at peace-keeping. This situation should be changed and greater recognition accorded to the effective peace-keeper as well as to the effective crime-fighter. (Properly trained sergeants and lieutenants who demand compliance with departmental policy can also ensure remarkable results.)

As Professor Wilson has noted:

> The central problem of the patrolman, and thus the police, is to maintain order and to reduce, to the limited extent possible, the opportunities for crime.[43]
>
> A police department that places order maintenance uppermost in its priorities will judge patrolmen . . . by their ability to keep the peace on their beat. This will require, in turn, that sergeants and other supervisory personnel concern themselves more with how the patrolmen function in family fights, teenage disturbances, street corner brawls, and civil disorders, and less with how well they take reports at the scene of burglary or how many traffic tickets they issue during a tour of duty. Order maintenance also requires that the police have available a wider range of options for handling disorder than is afforded by the choice between making an arrest and doing nothing. Detoxification centers should be available as an alternative to jail for drunks. Family-service units should be formed which can immediately assist patrolmen handling domestic quarrels, provide community-service information, answer complaints, and deal with neighborhood tensions and rumors.[44]

Some police departments are already making notable progress along these lines. Under a federal grant, the New York City Police Department has formed a "Family Crisis Intervention Unit" consisting of 18 highly trained officers to handle interfamily assaults and violence in West Harlem. Although it is estimated that as much as 40 percent of police injuries stem from family complaint calls, these crisis unit officers have not received any injuries in 15 months. Moreover, in the 1,120 family crises in which they have intervened, there has not been a single homicide among the families.[45] At the root of this project is a recognition that specialized peacekeeping training pays off.

Police departments throughout the country are beginning to conduct what is referred to as "provocation training." These projects range from training involving crowd control to handling of street corner disturbances. Provocation training entails, in part, staging the kind of provocation which police offenders may expect to face on the job. The trainees are taunted by instructors who call them names, use obscene gestures, and generally imitate the kinds of abuse policemen may expect to face in the conduct of their assigned responsibilities. The purpose of this specialized training is to develop and maintain coolheadedness under extreme provocation.

Other projects being conducted by large city police departments involve efforts to establish closer links between patrolmen and the neighborhoods or communities they serve. The advantage of establishing firmer ties with the community is that it increases a police officer's capacity to make reliable judgments about the character, motives, intentions and future actions of those among whom they keep the peace. As Professor Wilson has suggested, "The officer's ability to make such judgments is improved by increasing his familiarity with and involvement in the neighborhood he patrols, even to the extent of having him live there. The better he knows his beat, the more he can rely on judgments of character. . . ."[46] One method being used by several police departments in achieving this end is through a return to the foot-beat policeman. Most cities which have increased the number of foot-beat patrolmen have used them as a supplement to squad-car or motorcycle beats, thus preserving the mobility inherent in the latter technique. Other police departments have been experimenting with motorscooters in combination with foot-beat patrols.

Another notable example of a department's attempt to bridge the gap between the police and the community is the model precinct project being conducted by the Washington, D.C., Metropolitan Police. This project involves the creation of neighborhood centers which are staffed around the clock by resident civilians as well as police officers. The police teams working out of the centers are assigned for long periods of time to work in the neighborhoods covered by the centers' jurisdiction. Instead of being spread thin, they have an opportunity to get to know families, youth on the street, householders, and proprietors of businesses much more intimately. With a narrower area of patrol responsibility, the possibilities for positive, interested, and friendly contact among police and citizens is greatly improved.

The resident civilian workers, employed and trained by agencies such as welfare and legal aid, provide assistance to citizens referred by police on patrol, as well as to those who walk in off the street. These civilian positions help relate police peacekeeping to other activities of a positive help-giving nature, and to provide avenues by which civilians from the neighborhood can formally assist in keeping the peace (and perhaps later enter into careers in law enforcement or allied fields).

MINORITY RECRUITMENT

One fundamentally important method by which the police can improve their relations with the public is through increased recruitment of minority group policemen. The absence of many minority group policemen in our Nation's center city areas has been a source of community hostility for many years.

This Task Force surveyed minority recruitment efforts by police departments in several large cities. Although we found a rising percentage of minority policemen being recruited each year, the ratio of white to minority group policemen on any force never approximated the ratio of white to minority citizens in any given city's total population.

Many of the cities reported stepped up recruiting campaigns for minority group policemen. We inquired about the relative lack of success of such campaigns. One police chief answered:

> The problem as we see it is twofold: (1) in today's labor market there is full employment and special efforts are being directed toward the Negro community by private industry in an effort to attract qualified applicants. These companies are able to offer outstanding starting salaries and numerous fringe benefits that place police departments in a competitive disadvantage; (2) several of our Negro applicants have expressed the opinion that many segments of the Negro community regard Negro officers as "Uncle Toms" and enforcers of a white man's justice and are therefore hesitant to apply with a police department. Also we have not been entirely pleased with our efforts in the Negro community. Organizations such as the Urban League and the NAACP have not been able to refer many applicants to the Department.

305

There are other problems too. Although we found that in terms of percentages more minority group recruits succeeded in graduating from police training school than did white policemen, more minority applicants failed the original entrance examination than did whites. We do not feel that these failures were "arranged" by prejudiced police officials. The failures seem to us to reflect the tragedy of the ghetto schools' failure to educate its students.

The police are caught in a bind. Law enforcement consultants, Presidential and State crime commissions constantly urge that recruitment standards be upgraded. The result is that many applicants for police work who have attended ghetto schools simply are not intellectually equipped to pass the entrance examinations. If more minority policemen are to be recruited, accommodations must be found for the disparities in public school education.

Some police departments have been making commendable efforts at achieving such an accommodation. The Atlanta Police Department reported to us that during the summer months it employed 50 "Community Service Officers" between the ages of 17 and 21. These young men are recruited from the heart of the ghetto and are furnished police uniforms and equipment (except firearms). Their work is largely in the ghetto and has resulted in a betterment of police community relations. The Chief of Police reported to us that, most of them returned to school in October to finish their education and "we are convinced that eventually we will get at least 40 good patrolmen out of this group."

Other cities have shown similar good faith through special recruitment campaigns by sound truck, neighborhood centers, newspaper, TV, radio and billboard advertisements. More efforts of these kinds are needed if minority group policemen are to have an equal opportunity to demonstrate an ability to serve the community in the interest of keeping the peace.

CONCLUSION

That the policemen of our country are both criticized and misunderstood by large and diverse elements of the population is becoming increasingly clear. That these diverse elements make inconsistent and contradictory demands on the police is also clear. As a result of being thus criticized and misunderstood, and being called upon to perform inconsistent and contradictory services in the front lines of our disturbed and often violent urban society, the policeman is becoming more confused not only about what his function is, but also about what it should be. Besides lacking the financial, manpower and technological resources necessary to respond adequately to the many demands made of them, the police also lack a coherent sense of what direction their changing mission must take. Our police consequently are becoming more alienated from many factions of the pluralistic society which it is their duty to protect. The police have thus begun to fight back, not only as individuals with threats and counterviolence, but also as an increasingly organized group doing combat in the political arena.

How are we to bring the police and the diverse groups they serve back together again? With regard to the police taking sides in primarily political struggles, bitter past experience, at least, dictates that the abstention of the professional is the wisest choice. As to day-to-day contact between the police and the citizenry, there must be renewed attention to the peacekeeping role of the patrolman on the beat, which entails in part increased efforts to develop in the patrolman the understanding and coolheadedness which that vital role demands. Despite the depth of the hostility which exists between the police and some of the communities they serve, we believe that a "good cop" can still be a good friend to all of our people. Better training, supervision, and recognition, together with more effective minority group recruitment, are needed if our hopes of producing police excellence are to materialize.

REFERENCES

1. President's Commission on Law Enforcement and Administration of Justice (hereinafter cited as Crime Commission), *Challenge of Crime in a Free Society* (Washington, D.C.: Government Printing Office, 1967), at 92.

2. See Arthur Niederfhoffer, *Beyond the Shield: The Police in Urban Society* (Garden City, N.Y.: Doubleday, 1967), at 95-108.

3. See, generally, O. W. Wilson, *Municipal Police Administration* (1961); Bruce J. Terris, "The Role of the Police," 374 *Annals* 58-69 (1967); Crime Commission, *supra* note 1, *Task Force Report: The Police*; Schwartz and Goldstein, *Police Guidance Manuals* (1968); and James Q. Wilson, *Varieties of Police Behavior* (Cambridge: Harvard University Press, 1968).

4. Wilson, *Varieties of Police Behavior, id.*, at 4.

5. See generally, Paul Chevigny, *Police Power; Police Abuses*

in *New York City* (New York: Pantheon Books, 1969); *The Police: Six Sociological Essays,* David Bordua, ed. (New York: John Wiley & Sons, 1967); Jerome H. Skolnick, *The Police and the Urban Ghetto* (1968); Niederhoffer, *supra* note 2.

6. Crime Commission, *supra* note 1, *The Challenge of Crime in a Free Society,* at 91. More recent reports indicate that the number of policemen in the United States has climbed to nearly 500,000, yet most departments are still undermanned.

7. In ch. 17, *infra,* we discuss the possibilities for alleviating police manpower shortages through the use of citizen volunteers to perform some police functions.

8. Not only are far fewer college graduates (or men with some college training) found among recruit classes but large numbers have only a high school equivalency diploma and still others are from the lower quarters of their high school classes. *Time,* Oct. 4, 1968, at 26, reports this true of recent Detroit police recruits; Chief William Beall of the Berkeley, California, Police Department calls it "a sharp decline in the educational level of recent police recruits"; and an Oakland, California, police captain with twenty-seven years service states: "We are not getting the type of college people in the department that we were before." See also Niederhoffer, *supra* note 2, at 16–17, 209–210. Part of the reason for this failure is that college graduates do not wish to begin a police career at the bottom of the ladder. Few police departments have adopted the Crime and Kerner recommendations for lateral entry for college graduates.

9. Staff interviews with a New York patrolman recently graduated from the Police Academy and with a police sergeant-instructor. See also memorandum from Prof. George D. Eastman to the Commission, dated Sept. 30, 1968, especially at 3–4.

10. This Commission's Task Force Report entitled *The Politics of Protest* at 192–194 and *Municipal Yearbook* (Washington, D.C.: International City Managers Association, 1968), at 339–350. Klein, *The Police: Damned If They Do—Damned If They Don't* (1968).

11. Crime Commission, *supra* note 1, *Challenge of Crime in a Free Society,* at 113, See also James Q. Wilson, "Police Morale, Reform and Citizen Respect: The Chicago Case," in *The Police: Six Sociological Essays, supra* note 5, at 137–162.

12. See discussion in ch. 21, *infra.*

13. Quinn Tamm, "Police Must Be More Free," in *Violence In The Streets,* Shalom Endelman, ed. (Chicago: Quadrangle Books, 1968).

14. *Id.*

15. See ch. 20, *infra.*

16. E.g., the almost unanimous approval of the so-called "Fourth Platoon" Bill by the New York State legislature in the face of strong opposition by police organizations is a recent example of the complaints falling within the latter category.

17. Schwartz and Goldstein, *supra* note 3, at Nos. 4, 7, and 9.

And see our discussion of "over-criminalization" in ch. 23, *infra*.

18. *Id.*

19. See Wilson, *Varieties of Police Behavior, supra* note 3 at 83–139.

20. 56 percent of the American public expressed approval of the Chicago police handling of unruly demonstrators at the Democratic National Convention last summer. *New York Times,* Sept. 18, 1968, at 25.

21. Such efforts include human relations courses, police-community councils, recruitment of minority group policemen, advanced educational opportunities, and civilian complaint mechanisms.

22. John Guidici, "Police Response to Crimes of Violence," a paper submitted to this Task Force, at 1–14.

23. See *Report of the National Advisory Commission on Civil Disorders* (Washington, D.C.: Government Printing Office, 1968) and Chevigny, *supra* note 5, at 161–179.

24. See, *e.g., Rights in Conflict,* a special report to this Commission by Daniel Walker, Director of the Chicago Study Team.

25. Guidici, *supra* note 22, at 7–8.

26. See *Rights in Conflict, supra* note 24.

27. See, *e.g., The Politics of Protest, supra* note 10; and *Shoot-Out in Cleveland* and *Miami Report,* two investigative reports submitted to the Commission.

28. Wilson, *Varieties of Police Behavior, supra* note 3, at 248.

29. Chevigny, *supra* note 5, at 51–83.

30. *Id.* See Chapman and Crockett, *Gun Fight Dilemma: Police Firearms Policy* (1963); *Washington Post,* Sept. 18, 1968, at A–1.

31. *Id.*

32. "The Administration of Complaints by Civilians Against the Police," 77 *Harv. L. Rev.* 499, Jan. 1964. See also Thomas R. Brooks, " 'No!' Sayth the P.B.A.," *New York Times Magazine,* Oct. 16, 1966, at 37; Ralph G. Murdy, "Civilian Review Boards in Review," and Aryeh Neier, "Civilian Review Boards— Another View," *Criminal Law Bulletin* vol. 21, No. 8 (1966) at 3 and 10; Kenneth Gross and Alan Reitman, *Police Power and Citizens' Rights* (New York: American Civil Liberties Union, 1966); "Civilian Complaints Against the Police," 22 *Bar Bulletin* 228 (New York County Lawyers Association) (1964).

33. See ch. 7 of *The Politics of Protest, supra* note 10.

34. See *Rights in Conflict, supra* note 24.

35. The proper role of the police in mass political confrontations is dealt with more extensively in ch. 16, *infra*.

36. See, generally, Edwards, *The Police On The Urban Frontier* (1967); *One Year Later* (Washington, D.C.: Urban America, Inc., and The Urban Coalition, 1969); Reiss, "Police Brutality— Answer to Key Questions," *Transaction,* July/Aug. 1, 1968, at 10.

37. Terris, *supra* note 3, at 58 and 64.

38. See any of several articles on this subject by Prof. Samuel G. Chapman.

39. "Training Cops in Covina," *Capital East Gazette*, Feb. 1969, vol. 3, No. 2, at 10, 12.

40. E.g., the proposal of Washington, D.C., Black United Front concerning neighborhood control of police.

41. These remarks were recorded during a staff interview.

42. Not infrequently a decision by the policeman not to intervene is the wiser choice, particularly in situations where the police have not been called and where upon arriving at the scene the policeman sees that there is no real trouble brewing.

43. Wilson, *Varieties of Police Behavior, supra* note 3, at 291.

44. James Q. Wilson, "Dilemmas of Police Administration," *Public Administration Review*, Sept./Oct. 1 1968, at 407, 412, 413.

45. See testimony of Patrick V. Murphy, before the Violence Commission, Oct. 30, 1968; Sullivan, "Violence, Like Charity Begins at Home," *New York Times Magazine,* Nov. 24, 1968; and Bard, "Iatrogenic Violence", statement submitted to this Task Force, Oct. 4, 1968.

46. Wilson, *Varieties of Police Behavior, supra* note 3, at 291.

CHAPTER 15

OFFICIAL RESPONSES TO MASS DISORDER I: CURRENT SOCIAL CONTROL*

Recent civil disorders created a crisis for Americans. They also created a crisis for the police and supporting control forces, who, in general, found themselves ill-prepared, inadequately trained, and poorly equipped to cope with mass lawlessness.

MAJOR PROBLEMS OF RIOT CONTROL

Unlike the disturbances and violence of past riots, the civil disorders of the 1960's have created control and community problems not mentioned in the standard police riot control manuals. According to the *Guidelines for Civil Disorders and Mobilization Planning,* which the U.S. Department of Justice made available to U.S. law enforcement agencies recently:

> The riot situations experienced, particularly in the large cities, have taken on a different form and dimension from that which has been described in the most current police literature on How to Control a Riot. Thus, the textbook riot has not occurred to any great degree, and the textbook control measures have thus proven unusable.

The instant nature of the neighborhood riot makes the new disorders a particularly difficult control problem. In every major city with a large minority population, the underlying tensions that exist today constitute an ever-present explosive environment for civil disorder. The attendant violence and destruction outrace the capability of the public safety forces to respond in the time and with the strength required.

---

* This chapter was prepared by Joseph R. Sahid on the basis of research contributions by Arnold Sagalyn, Senior Staff associate, Arthur D. Little, Inc., and Louise Sagalyn, District of Columbia Bar; Albert Bottoms of Chicago; Gustav Rath, Professor of Industrial Engineering and director of the Design Center, Technological Institute, Northwestern University; and Richard J. Kendall, Esq., of Washington, D.C.

This fact is particularly true with respect to the black communities, with their extremely high density and disproportionate number of youths who feel a deep hostility to the police. In such a setting, an otherwise routine incident, particularly one involving the police, can easily attract a large crowd. In the tension and hostility thus created, any spark, like an inciting rumor, can ignite a serious riot. By the time the police can respond to the disturbance, the situation has often escalated beyond their capability to control it.

Moreover, the indigenous nature of the mob and the densely populated character of the neighborhood make futile the traditional riot squad formations and tactics for dispersing crowds. The rioters and on-lookers merely retreat inside the neighborhood buildings only to reappear once the control forces have passed by.

No single control problem that confronts a city when a riot erupts therefore, can become more serious than that of insufficient police on hand to appropriately and effectively control a riot that erupts without warning and involves a large number of people. Nearly 75 percent of all cities over 100,000 population, for example, have less than 500 policemen. Only 19 cities have 1,000 or more.

The multitude of duties and responsibilities assigned to the police force requires the allocation of personnel for a wide variety of patrol, traffic, detective, administrative, and support duties. The need to divide the police force into three shifts to provide protective and other assorted police services 24 hours a day, 365 days a year, with provision for days off, sick leave, and vacation further depletes the total available strength. As a result of all these factors, only slightly more than 10 percent of a uniformed police force will normally be on street duty during any given shift.

As the report of the National Advisory Commission on Civil Disorders noted, a city of 500,000 population is likely to have less than 100 uniformed policemen on duty at any given time, while a city of 100,000 population will not even have 25 men to police the entire city. Moreover, since this force widely disperses over many square miles, not all of these will be immediately available nor capable of getting to the scene rapidly. In addition, a police administrator has to consider the risks and dangers to the rest of the community if the demands of controlling a disorder leave other parts of the city unprotected.

Mobilizing off-duty policemen becomes a time-consuming problem, averaging between an hour and a half to two hours

312

for most large cities. Yet, civil disorder, like a fire, can rapidly grow out of control unless it is dealt with quickly in the very early stage. During the first minute of a disorder, a hundred well trained and commanded policemen can often prove more important and effective than one thousand men a few hours later.

Unfortunately, no outside available reserves exist for most cities to call on quickly enough to control a large disorder at its incipient stage. Mutual assistance pacts do not exist in most states. Moreover, few mayors would release many police personnel to assist other cities because they might be needed in their own community.

Nor can the local police turn to state police forces to provide manpower in sufficient numbers and in the quick response time required. Existing state police forces lack the strength, training, and organization to provide local communities with the kind of riot control assistance needed. Of the 49 states that have state police forces, 28 have less than 500 policemen in the entire state. Only 7 states have more than 1,000 men. More than half of the states have essentially highway patrolmen who are widely dispersed to patrol thousands of miles of state roads. As a result, they cannot be readily mobilized and quickly deployed to the cities where they may be needed in the event of an emergency.

The problem of reserves for riot control is not solved by National Guard units which are ill-suited and untrained to serve as effective or practical riot control forces except on a very infrequent and emergency basis. The part-time nature of Guard personnel means that if they are called up more than a few times during a short interval, or if they are called into service to serve for an extended period of time, the men and officers face financial hardships and risk jeopardizing their regular civilian employment. Thus, frequent use of the National Guard would make it difficult for the Guard to retain and recruit personnel.

It is even more unrealistic to look to Federal troops to deal with urban riots. Rigid constitutional and related restrictions rule out the use of Federal forces to assist a community except as a last resort after the state has exhausted all its resources.

Consequently, few police departments can take effective action against rioters when a large-scale disorder first breaks out. Pending the arrival of sufficient forces, the inadequate number of policemen available cannot stop the rioting and arrest looters and others who are violating the law.

The need to stop looting, arson, and other acts of destructive violence has focused increasing attention on the importance of non-lethal weapons and techniques which will enable the available police to suppress and arrest those violating the law and to disperse the crowd or mob. Traditional police weapons, including the stick and the gun, provide either too little or too much physical force to control a riot effectively and judiciously. Given the inadequate manpower of police departments in a mass disorder, new control tools become critical for police to curb lawlessness and violence quickly and successfully.

Another major problem inherent in the normal operations and training of a municipal police department is the individual police officer. Having broad discretionary powers regarding the methods he chooses to handle the wide variety of law enforcement tasks he encounters, he is trained to exercise his own independent judgment with a minimum of supervision.

Effective riot control, however, requires manpower organized and trained to operate as members of a highly disciplined team, similar to a military unit. Control personnel must not exercise individual judgment or initiative but should act in strict accordance with the orders of their commanders. As James Q. Wilson has observed:

> Those police departments that have, by their actions, exacerbated tensions or failed to maintain order might be said to be those that have failed to recognize the *radical difference* between their normal duties and those they are called upon to perform in critical events. The desire of an individual officer to assert his personal authority may be inevitable and perhaps desirable in patrol situations; *it can be disastrous in a mass deployment of police when discipline and concerted action are necessary.*[1]

A police department, therefore, faces formidable organizational and operational problems in trying to shift suddenly from its regular stance into an entirely new and different type of control body required in a riot emergency.

A major weakness of many police departments is the absence of a reliable intelligence system. The absence has gravely handicapped police and public officials in anticipating and preventing trouble, and in minimizing and controlling a disorder that has broken out. In large part, this happens because of a failure to learn about and to understand neighborhood problems and grievances and to develop reliable information concerning community organizations and leaders. Related to this problem is the need for a reliable mechanism to monitor, to collect and to evaluate rumors and also the need for an effective program to counter false and provocative rumors which can aggravate tension and incite violence.

Another major problem is police communications. The shortage of needed radio frequencies, cited by both the Crime and Civil Disorders Commissions, and the inadequate present communications equipment essential to insuring effective command and control over field forces during a disorder, still remain as a critical issue.

But no problem is more acute than that of training. A survey of riot control training in a selected sample of major police departments made for the Civil Disorders Commission disclosed that of all police control capabilities studied, training constituted the "most critical deficiency of all." Although many police departments have recognized the need for more training and have increased their training programs, the amount of training which most police forces have received remains very short from that needed to ensure a professional riot control capability.

These, then, are the major problems facing control forces in subduing mass disorders. The Kerner Commission took note of all of them and made recommendations to deal with most of them. While most cities appear to have strengthened their civil disorder capabilities to varying degrees, serious deficiencies, unfortunately, still remain.

CIVIL DISORDERS COMMISSION RECOMMENDATIONS

The best and most obvious approach to a civil disorder, the Kerner Commission concluded, was that of prevention. Public officials, principally mayors and police administrators, were urged to do everything possible to prevent a disorder from occurring in the first place.

The Commission urged officials to reexamine and rectify police conduct, operations, and practices that lead to harassing and contribute to or create community tensions and hostility. As studies made for that Commission showed, inadequate police protection and a belief that a dual standard of law enforcement existed constituted major grievances by minority residents. "The abrasive relationship between the police and the minority communities, the Commission concluded, has been a major—and explosive—source of grievance, tension and disorder."[2] A decrease in hostility and improved police-community relations resulted from the establishment of an effective grievance mechanism which would cover other municipal services as well as the police, and the issuance and implementation of policy guidelines which would guide police officers in those sensitive areas where police conduct may create tension and precipitate a disorder.

Both the police and the community, the Commission also concluded, would benefit from greater police involvement in community service matters. Such community service functions would enable police officers to identify problems that could lead to disorder. In the view of the Commission, the performance of such duties would earn the police community respect and support. An additional benefit directly accruing to the police would flow from the development of invaluable sources of information and intelligence.

In another riot prevention measure, the Commission endorsed the recommendations made by the President's Crime Commission for the establishment of a community service officer program to attract neighborhood youths between the ages of 17 and 21. As junior police officers, they could perform a variety of duties short of exercising full law enforcement function and could help to establish needed channels of communication with minority communities.

The Civil Disorders Commission also stressed the importance of expanding and strengthening special community relations and training programs designed to increase communications and decrease hostility between the police department and Negro residents. Concurrently, the Commission pointed to the particularly critical need for making police department award systems recognize the work of officers who improve relations with alienated members of the community.

It also urged the assignment to ghetto areas of seasoned, well-trained policemen and supervisory officers who could prevent and minimize tension situations leading to a riot.

In the event prevention failed and a disorder erupted, it urged the police to respond with sufficient speed and strength to insure that they handled the incident properly and contained it quickly. Studies made by the Civil Disorders Commission led to the conclusion that the way the police and the community responded to the initial incident usually determined whether the disturbance remained a relatively minor police problem or developed into a serious disorder.

The ability of the police to deal with the initial incident, it was found, depended on several key factors: the accurate assessment of the incident and the nature and degree of control required; the speed with which sufficient police manpower arrived; the proper deployment and decisive use of the force, which required seasoned commanders to direct and to insure discipline over the field personnel; and, good intelligence, with the capability to utilize it for decision-making.

To insure that a police department could deal with such emergency problems successfully, the Commission recommended that every police department develop and pretest plans which would quickly muster the manpower and seasoned senior commanders needed at the scene of the disorder. Proper planning would provide not only for the rapid deployment of on-duty personnel, but would also make provision for the call-up of off-duty police and for their logistical support; alerting and coordinating the operations of municipal and outside agencies involved in the control of a disorder, and anticipating the numerous operations and tactical requirements that would arise.

In the event the initial incident escalated into a riot, the police department must make a rapid transition from its normal operations into a different type of organization with new operational procedures designed and geared to meet the special emergency mass control problems. Here again, good planning was paramount. To assist police administrators in this crucial riot control requirement, the Commission recommended that model mobilization and operations plans, which had been prepared by its staff, should be updated and disseminated by the U.S. Department of Justice to local and state police departments.

The Commission urged immediate and priority attention for riot control training:

> Departments should immediately allocate whatever time is necessary to reach an effective level of riot control capability. . . . Training must include all levels of personnel . . . and must be a continuous process for all personnel. . . . Riot control training must be provided to groups expected to function as teams during actual riot conditions. . . . Mayors and other civil officials must recognize the need and accept the responsibility for initiating regional training and coordination with

317

military and state police personnel. . . . Police agencies must review and become familiar with recent riot experience so that training programs can be realistically adjusted in the light of anticipated problems. . . .[3]

Because of the urgency of this problem, the Commission wrote the President on October 7, 1967, recommending that the Department of Justice conduct "a series of intensive training conferences this winter for governmental and police officials." In its report to the President in March, 1968, the Commission enunciated a long list of training recommendations for improving riot control training for all levels of police personnel.

The Kerner Commission also urged the establishment of a national center and clearinghouse "to develop, evaluate and disseminate riot prevention and control data and information."

In pointing to the grave danger of overraction by the police, the Commission stressed the importance of adhering to the well-established legal and moral principle that only the minimum amount of force necessary be used to control a disorder and to maintain order. The use of indiscriminate, mass destructive weapons, such as automatic rifles and machine guns, was specifically denounced as unwarranted and counterproductive.

The Commission advocated that police forces follow the example of the U.S. Army and use nonlethal chemical agents, especially CS, instead of deadly weapons. It further recommended that the federal government undertake a program to test and evaluate non-lethal weapons and related control equipment for use by the police, and that it develop appropriate riot control tools and material.

Another major finding of the Commission revealed that "civil disorders are fundamental governmental problems, not simply police problems." Accordingly, it recommended that "the mayor, as the chief elected official, [must] take ultimate responsibility for all governmental actions in times of disorder." In seeking to restore order, it urged the police to recognize and to utilize the forces for order that exist within the community.

It also emphasized the importance of insuring greater coordination of all government agencies involved in control problems, including the pretesting of plans.

PROGRESS SINCE CIVIL DISORDERS
COMMISSION REPORT

Since the Civil Disorders Commission made its report in March, 1968, most major police departments have made marked progress in strengthening their riot control capabilities. Planning has improved, as has intelligence. The assign-. ment of more seasoned and better-trained personnel to respond to the all-important initial incident, greater attention to effective command and control of field personnel, utilization of neighborhood leadership and resources to help prevent and control disturbances and the use of only the minimum amount of force necessary—all exist now in greater evidence than formerly.

The improvement has been notable and national in scope. Progress has resulted from programs such as the series of fourteen one-week conferences on the Prevention and Control of Civil Disorders sponsored jointly by the Department of Justice and the International Association of Chiefs of Police, as a result of recommendations made by the Civil Disorders Commission to the President. More than 400 mayors, city managers, and police officials from the nation's 136 largest cities, focused attention on the major problems and lessons learned from previous riots. The conferences proved decisive in disseminating the teachings of the Civil Disorders Commission to local officials, enabling them to upgrade the effectiveness of their official response.[4]

To strengthen Federal intelligence capabilities, the Department of Justice established a Civil Disorder Intelligence Unit to compile and computerize information from Federal investigative and other sources relating to civil disorders.

For its part, the Department of Defense implemented measures to assist local and state governments in civil disorder planning and to improve the Federal military and National Guard response to civil disorder. The Army Military Police School conducted special riot control planning and training courses for local and state police officials. Army representatives reviewed civil disorder plans in a large number of cities to insure effective coordination with respect to the local, state, and federal plans. The Department of Defense also created a Civil Disturbance Directorate in the Pentagon with over-all responsibility for military riot control activities.

Another significant development was the recognition and demonstration of non-lethal riot control agents in dispersing

319

rioters and preventing looting. When severe rioting broke out in Washington, D.C., in April 1968, the police employed the chemical agent CS, in lieu of deadly firearms, to restore order; its effect on rioters was described by one policeman as "phenomenal." It strongly deterred those exposed to this non-lethal control agent from any activity which would risk another dose. It was so effective, some police officers reported, that if they merely tossed an ordinary beer can, which resembled a CS container, the crowd would quickly scatter. The mere dropping of CS inside a store that had been broken into immediately deterred future rioters from entering.

In a letter sent to heads of major law enforcement agencies during the summer of 1968 (Aug. 12), Attorney General Ramsey Clark wrote:

> Although they are not universally adaptable to all police uses, nonlethal chemical agents represent the best immediate alternative to the use of deadly force—or no force at all. They are now proven to be the most effective, safest, and most humane method of mob control. Used with caution when the need arises, they will reduce death, physical injury and property loss to a minimum.

The Department of Justice currently sponsors a technical assistance program, under the direction of the International Association of Chiefs of Police, to assist police departments in developing a more effective chemical agent capability. The IACP has already prepared and disseminated to police departments information material on CS, including its characteristics, uses, precautions, and the problems of first aid and decontamination.

The valuable lessons learned from the Commission report, from the disorder prevention training conferences, and from the various Army support programs, were reflected in the responsible and effective response by communities affected by the assassination of Dr. Martin Luther King. Despite the explosive climate and the aggravated tensions generated by the assassination, only a handful of cities suffered serious disorders.

The experience during the summer of 1968 was equally dramatic and encouraging. Despite fearful predictions of a tremendous increase in the number and severity of civil disorders, there was a clear and significant drop. The Civil Disturbance Information Unit of the Department of Justice recorded 19 deaths resulting from civil disturbances during June, July, and August of 1968, compared with 87 during the

320

same period the previous year. The National Guard was called in for assistance 6 times during the summer of 1968 compared with 18 during the summer of 1967. The number of disturbances listed as major or serious by the Information Unit was 25 compared with 45 the previous summer.[5] In assessing the relatively peaceful summer of 1968, Attorney General Clark praised the police as deserving a major share of the credit.

There were many reasons to believe that the summer of 1968 would be the worst in our history. In the Spring, most observers thought so. Yet there was a clear and significant decline in the number and severity of riots and disorders this summer.

There are many reasons for the improvement this year. In my opinion, the police are entitled to much of the credit.

Despite the springtime publicity indicating otherwise, the police response was generally not based on massive repressiveness. When violent outbreaks occurred, they were usually controlled by adequate police manpower trained to neither overact or underact. It is impossible to count the number of riots that were prevented by police. I believe they were many.[6]

Despite these decided improvements, critical deficiencies still exist. Lack of effective operational planning, manpower shortages, communication problems, and the ever-increasing threat of extremist activity among political and racial groupings and within law enforcement agencies, all still represent significant problems.

THE NATIONAL GUARD

The Civil Disorders Commission found repeated instances of sub-standard performance by the National Guard during the 1967 civil disorders. Like police forces, National Guard units had found themselves unprepared to handle the urban disorder that erupted. They had not pre-planned, they had little training for riot control, and they had poor leadership.

Like police departments, Guard units have seldom been expected to respond to civil disorders as a primary mission. Since World War II, the National Guard's primary responsibility has been to provide organized units of trained personnel with sufficient and suitable equipment to augment the federal active Army and Air Force in time of war or national emergency. While the National Guard is nominally under the control of state governors, the federal government has priority over its use and pays for 90 percent of its operating costs, provides virtually all of its equipment and nearly half the cost of its physical installations and facilities.

Furthermore, the federal government, through the Department of Defense, prescribes in minute detail the training National Guardsmen shall receive. Because of this, the National Guard's state mission, which is to support civil authority, was virtually disregarded in training policy prior to 1967.[7]

Nevertheless, the Guard provided a force better prepared in 1967 to deal with civil disturbance than metropolitan police departments. The active Army had trained virtually all Guardsmen for at least two months in basic combat skills and for 2 to 4 months in more technical military training. This emphasis on discipline and unit control proved useful on the streets of our cities. Furthermore, National Guard officers had for the most part met the standards set by the Department of Defense for officers on active duty.

As the Civil Disorders Commission indicated, the Guard apparently needed an increased emphasis on their state function as a force for the control of civil disorder.

This role was recognized in a January 1969 report prepared by the Department of Army, under the signature of Robert E. Jordan III, General Counsel.

The disorder that occurred in Detroit in July 1967, may be considered an important landmark: i.e., from this point forward the military services, in concert with many agencies of government at all levels, devoted time, effort, and means of an unprecedented scale to prepare to deal effectively with outbreaks of mass violence. The results have clearly been worth the effort. Due to increased training emphasis, more thorough planning, more effective assignment of responsibilities and streamlined operational procedures, the response of the National Guard and federal forces to civil disturbances during 1968 was rapid, effective and decisive.

The Army made a hasty revision of its training doctrine in riot control and made it available to the Adjutant General of each state after the Detroit riots. At the same time, the National Guard in many states started to revise their training efforts, based on events in Newark and Detroit, so that those units scheduled for annual field training during August could key their training to the characteristics of recent riots.

On August 10, 1967, the National Guard Bureau initiated a 32-hour program of revised intensive training for all National Guard units to be completed by October 1, 1967. It gave a special 16-hour course to all officers in the same period.

During the spring and summer of 1968, all Army National Guard units conducted refresher training, ranging from 4 to 33 hours per unit, the amount being based on the potential for disorder in a given community or state, and on the state Adjutant General's assessment of need. Leadership courses were initiated, based on a program developed by the Army at Fort Benning, Georgia. As of January 15, 1969, more than 10,000 Army National Guard officers had completed the course, aimed at preparing junior officers for leadership in civil disturbance duties. The Army also initiated a course in civil disturbance operations for senior military officers and police officials. To date, 772 high-ranking National Guard officers have completed this course.

Since the National Guard is organized as a military force, integral planning staffs exist at all levels. All states have senior officers who are graduates of the Army's Command and General Staff School at Fort Leavenworth, Kansas. This training constitutes a considerable asset, not presently available to police departments, and apparently enabled the Guard to rectify planning deficiencies noted by the Civil Disorders Commission. The Department of the Army and the National Guard presently have detailed and up-to-date civil disturbance plans—a notable and commendable response to a national need.

The National Guard in each state developed state, area, and city plans using Army-furnished planning packets. It has developed contingency plans and coordinated planning with Federal, state, and local officials. But police departments are slow to initiate complementary plans; this reluctance has resulted in unnecessary problems during actual riot control operations.

The National Guard plans for alerting and mobilizing their troops were reviewed and revised, and procedures were enacted to insure continual revision. As a result, the time required to assemble units has been shortened. Further, the Guard has recognized the value of testing its plans through command post and field training exercises, and they have had considerable chance to improve their plans following actual operations in 1968.

An expanded effort to increase Negro membership in the National Guard became a top priority program following the 1967 disorders. The exclusion of Negroes from National Guard membership had not been the official policy in any state, and all states having regulations or laws aimed at maintaining an all-white Guard had rescinded or repealed them prior to 1967. In general, however, no real effort had been made to desegregate National Guard units and those states that had programs had produced negligible results.

Two significant steps were taken by the National Guard in the period immediately following the Newark and Detroit riots. First, the National Guard Bureau contracted for and received an in-depth survey of Negro attitudes toward military service in general and National Guard service in particular, to provide a factual basis for planning future recruiting efforts. Second, Major General James F. Cantwell, Commander of the New Jersey National Guard and President of the National Guard Association of the United States, proposed to the Department of the Army that he be granted a 5 percent overage in the authorized strength of the New Jersey Army and Air National Guard, to provide additional vacancies to be filled only by Negroes. He also requested and received additional financial support and professional guidance from the National Guard Bureau to conduct an intense publicity, advertising, and promotion campaign aimed at qualified young Negro men in New Jersey.

The New Jersey recruitment campaign became a pilot program to guide the formulation of similar programs in other states. An overstrength allocation of 865 spaces was granted. The program began three weeks after the Detroit disorder and utilized a variety of techniques, such as publicity through newspapers, radio, television, billboards, handbills, and personal contacts. At the end of 10½ months, Negro membership in the New Jersey Army and Air Guard stood at slightly more than 1,100, a gain for the period of 767. At the beginning of the program 1.82 percent of the 17,265-man New Jersey National Guard was Negro. By July 1, 1968, Negro membership had climbed to 6.34 percent.[8]

The success of this program must be qualified by the meager results apparently experienced in other states which have recently conducted similar campaigns without the benefit of federal support. Plans are now being made, however, by the National Guard Bureau to allocate additional funds for a nationwide version of the New Jersey program.

The National Guard has attained a noteworthy level of effectiveness in riot control operations within the last year. During the same period, the Guard mobilized 25,000 individuals for active duty in Vietnam and elsewhere and also underwent a substantial reorganization of its troop structure, further taxing its resources.

Nevertheless, too many limitations have been placed upon the National Guard to control outbreaks of civil disorder.

One reason for the Guard's effectiveness is that the hostility directed at policemen by the diverse groups engaged in mass protest has not yet been directed at the military forces. This reaction is a major asset, but the danger of losing it is great, if the nation should rely primarily on the National Guard for riot control. Furthermore, the National Guard composed for the most part of civilians with occupations which compete strongly for their time and effort, is limited by the number of times it can mobilize these men without causing severe dislocation and hardship, and inevitably lowering morale. Moreover, the Guard's ability to perform its federal mission to support the active Army is lessened if the states increasingly rely on Guard units to control civil disturbances.[9]

Some city and state authorities during the last year have exhibited a tendency to overreact by requiring the Guard to assemble prematurely or under circumstances where they are not necessarily required. For example, according to figures released by the National Guard Association of the United States on January 1, 1969, members of the District of Columbia Guard devoted 61 days to duty with the National Guard during 1968. In Wilmington, Delaware, 75 National Guardsmen at any one time served continuous nighttime riot patrol duty from April 17, 1968, until January 20, 1969. Obviously few men with civilian occupations and interests can continue this type of performance on a volunteer basis. The National Guard's function in riot control, therefore, must remain essentially that of supporting the local authorities.

LOCAL LAW ENFORCEMENT AUTHORITIES

The knowledge needed to deal with civil disturbances is presently available to anyone who wishes to pursue it. The interest generated by the problem itself and by the work of the Civil Disorders Commission has led to the publication of several valuable handbooks which outline in detail the proper official response to mass disorder.[10] Yet local officials have been slow to adopt these recommendations for several reasons.

While divided responsibility and staff organization characterizes most large-scale business, civil, and military enterprises, few police forces have yet to use such a structure. The demands of immediate problems have forced police departments to operate on a day-to-day basis with little time to devote to long-range planning.

Moreover, police departments seldom employ outside consultants to recommend long-range planning needs. Planning is more often than not conducted by a few overworked higher ranking police officials based on their own personal experiences.

Additionally, an acute shortage of funds to hire and train men exists. While local and state governing bodies have been quick to appropriate money for armored vehicles and other weapons, many have not yet responded with adequate funds to establish training schools or planning staffs.

The result of this lack of attention given to long-range planning presents a disturbing profile of the readiness of our urban police forces to deal with mass disorders.

A survey made of eight cities that experienced disorders following the assassination of Dr. Martin Luther King disclosed that many deficiencies in planning and operations remained.[11] The chief criticism made of some plans was that they lacked flexibility and had not been subjected to needed pretesting. The failure of the police call-up system to perform as provided in the mobilization plan seriously impaired the effective emergency response of off-duty personnel.

Studies by Bottoms and Rath of 16 major American cities[12] have shown that the present level of preparedness of our police forces generally is not yet adequate to deal with civil disturbances. As one might expect, the departments varied widely in their potential ability to respond to civil disorder. The following deficiencies continue to plague many of our cities:

1. Generally, no formal, respected, dependable communication links can be depended upon to remain open between dissident groups and city authorities.
2. Generally, no formal, dependable lines of communication exist among citizen groups, academic institutions, and agencies of the state and federal governments.
3. Information needed for decisions in potentially dangerous situations often fails to reach the executive level because of staff bias or because of lack of proper interpretation.
4. In general, major American cities fail to provide the Mayor or Executive Officer with effective planning staffs. Thus, haphazard coordination and liaison exist among city departments and with external agencies.
5. Confusion often exists concerning authority and command responsibility. Fragmentation of jurisdiction in many

metropolitan areas exacerbates the problem. Many police do not recognize that they are under the direction of duly constituted civil authority at all times. They also seem unaware that regular U.S. Army troops are only under U.S. Army Command.

6. Planning for civil disorders in the police departments of major American cities ranges from reliance on the kind of emergency plans used in connection with fires or major sporting events to detailed tactical contingency plans developed for specific potential trouble spots in a city. In some cases existing plans date as far back as five years, predating all recent significant disturbances such as Watts, Detroit, Newark, and the April disorders of 1968. In other cases, the plans intertwine with various departmental regulations and manuals.

Contingency planning, except for plans developed for specific areas or events, is almost nonexistent. The offered explanation is that the uncertainty in the case of violent confrontation precludes meaningful detailed planning. The aspects of civil disorder planning most carefully covered are mobilization plans and the establishment of police command relationships. Police departments give least attention to strategy and tactics, defense of vital installations, and coordination with agencies other than police agencies.

7. Few police departments pretest existing emergency plans. Thus, neither command nor street personnel know or understand the content of plans and the requirements for execution. Unfamiliarity with plans and assignments can cause confusion, wasteful allocation of scarce manpower, and responses that lack relevance or timeliness in a given situation.

8. Although all police departments have conducted additional training in riot control subjects, the number of hours devoted to training each man within a given force has not increased significantly. Some departments have, however, established special civil disturbance units and concentrated the majority of their riot control training on this complement.

9. The importance of police organization for civil disorders appears to be imperfectly understood by the police. Few departments recognize that the unit replaces the individual when it takes a military stance. Except for anti-sniper teams and mass arrest processing teams, they make little use of task elements composed of teams identified before an emergency arises.

10. Police departments conduct practically no unit train-

ing. While a department may send occasional individuals to schools, such as those operated by the U.S. Army at Fort Gordon or Fort Ord, the only clear opportunity to give unit training to large numbers of force members is at the police academies used to train recruits. The pressure to provide uniformed policemen for day-to-day duty has forced most police departments to rush men through academy training rather than add a substantial amount of unit-type training to the curriculum.

11. The police departments are having less difficulty procuring special equipment to conduct riot control operations. This acquisition is not necessarily heartening, however. Some of this equipment is in the form of high-powered firearms and armored vehicles which, as has been repeatedly stressed, have marginal value in the orderly control of mass disturbances. Unless the quality of training of the men who control this equipment is significantly improved, the use of this equipment as a substitute for more considered action may lead to unnecessary bloodshed.

12. Considerable discussion, concern and confusion exist for developing police guidelines in the use of firearms, batons, non-lethal chemicals, and the rules of engagement. These guidelines encourage restraint and define for the individual policeman the boundaries placed upon his actions, but the various riot control groups have not yet been able to arrive at uniform policies with respect to the use of firearms and non-lethal weaponry.

13. Many departments cited press relations as one of the most significant problems they face. Yet few of them reported an information plan providing for press officers, briefing rooms, and other special arrangements for dealing with the press during riots.

14. Police departments must coordinate with the judicial system regarding procedures and methods for dealing with problems of mass booking, detention, and transportation of prisoners. In some cases, police departments have established peripheral liaison with church groups, the ACLU, and bar associations, but most of these programs are weak, sketchy, and ineffective.

Effective planning by police departments can help compensate for the lack of preparedness which presently stems from practical restraints placed on their ability to train for mass disturbance control. This commitment to planning will require that police departments develop planning staffs similar to those used by military organizations at all levels. The use of the staff can give commanders the opportunity to review their objectives, to consider alternatives, and to analyze their resources through calm consideration prior to actual commitment to riot control. A staff organization and a detailed planning effort is fully within the reach of most metropolitan police departments.

Training help is being made available through academic institutions and other organizations that specialize in operations research and systems analysis. Furthermore, the Safe Streets Act of 1968 provides federal assistance to cities and states in all aspects of law enforcement. Other federal agencies and private foundations have also begun to support research and development in specialized areas on a large scale.

In conclusion, while most major American cities have begun moving to implement the lessons learned from recent disorders, much remains to be done. There can be no substitute for detailed long-range planning, too frequently bypassed under the pressure of immediate law enforcement needs. The knowledge needed to upgrade the kind of official response required is available. What is needed is a will to act and a will to provide needed resources.

THE ROLE OF THE PRIVATE INDIVIDUAL

In an emergency such as a serious riot, the regular police, fire, and related community services quickly become overtaxed. The civil government, primarily organized to respond to normal demands on its services, finds its available protective capabilities overwhelmed. The dangers to individual citizens and damage to business establishments can be greatly minimized by both private efforts and government-assisted programs to encourage certain minimum and practical self-protection measures designed to "harden the targets." Such precautions particularly apply to high-risk businesses which have been the principal targets of the rioters: i.e., liquor, hardware, appliance, food, and clothing stores.

By installing available protective devices, individual establishments can with relatively little cost make it difficult for anyone to burn or burgle their premises, measures which will provide valuable protection against normal crime hazards as well. Solid-type barriers, for example, which roll down over store fronts to prevent unauthorized entry of persons or repel fire bombs, have long been a standard protective measure in France, Italy, and other foreign countries.

A small inexpensive device, which screws into a light socket and can be wired to discharge a harmless but highly deterrent chemical (such as CS) if a window is broken or illegal entrance is made, is also available as a protective measure against looting. New types of shatterproof glass and glazing materials could also provide a higher level of security.

The danger of arson can be greatly minimized by the installation of a water sprinkler or fire suppression system. Like the protective barrier, such fire protection would provide highly effective year-round security for the businessman. The cooperation of industry and local government could make inexpensive suppression systems feasible for small enterprises.

At the present time, small business establishments in high crime and ghetto areas are having trouble obtaining or retaining insurance. The installation of relatively inexpensive and effective protective systems which would serve to safeguard these businesses against fire and burglary could prove a decisive factor in helping to solve the insurance problem for small businesses.

THE PROBLEM OF MANPOWER AND EFFECTIVE RESPONSE

Of the many civil disorder problems that remain unsolved, the most pressing is the inadequate number of trained riot control personnel.

This manpower problem arises principally from the constitutional assignment of the police function to the states and the system of decentralized, autonomous local law enforcement agencies that has evolved in this country. Each city, in effect, must rely on its own limited resources in maintaining order and in preserving the civil peace.

This kind of problem, perhaps to the surprise of Americans, does not exist in other large countries. Unlike the United States, most foreign countries have national centralized police forces. They possess great manpower resources that enable them to create specialized riot control units which number in the thousands and are usually stationed in or near metropolitan areas. Also, large contingents are kept on standby or quick-alert basis for immediate dispatch in case of trouble.

These units, in turn, are supported by large numbers of military troops who have been especially designated and trained for riot control and who can be employed without the inhibiting constitutional restrictions, among others, which limit the use of Federal forces in this country.

The effectiveness of these foreign forces is greatly enhanced by extensive specialized training in riot control. In many countries this training includes hundreds of hours in riot control operations, tactics and equipment for all levels of personnel, as well as exercises which test the planning and efficiency of the riot control units. Periodic in-service training, as well as advanced courses, are given to both the men and to their commanders.

Because of the quick availability of these large trained riot control reserves, other countries can control civil disorders effectively. Nor can their success be attributed to their use of harsher tactics, as the experiences of the British "bobbies" testifies.[13]

The seriousness of the inadequate riot control reserves in this country was clearly demonstrated in the April 1968 disorders. In several of the states large demands for riot control personnel seriously depleted the effective strength of the National Guard. On its part, the Federal Government had to dispatch more than one-third of the combat troops out of its strategic reserve. If future disorders of a wider and more serious nature should develop, the problem of providing endangered communities with sufficient numbers of trained riot control manpower could become extremely critical.

Needed riot control forces—properly trained and equipped —must be made available to provide effective support and assistance to any city in need of help, and these reserve forces must be found without creating a national police force, which runs contrary to American tradition and history.

One way to create the necessary riot control reserve forces is to build on existing state police and highway patrol forces in the United States. The state government has the basic responsibility for maintaining order within the state and for assisting communities when domestic violence overwhelms local capabilities. Moreover, strengthening the state police forces and utilizing them as riot control reserve would avoid the problems of idle waste and excessive aggressiveness inherent in a single-purpose riot control force.

It would be appropriate—and in the national interest—for the Federal Government to assist and contribute to the creation of these additional state police forces. The needed personnel could be funded quickly and in a way consistent with established federal-state relationships, by following the precedent of the federal highway programs under which the Federal Government now provides billions of dollars annually to the states to construct interstate and state highways.

This readily accessible uniformed force would enable the states to provide the trained manpower needed to back up local police forces in a civil disorder, and the program could provide these patrolmen and their commanders with the specialized riot control training and equipment essential to their effectiveness as highly disciplined, coordinated riot control units. Support equipment might include air and ground transportation and the communications equipment required in a disorder for the rapid mobilization and effective command and control of these quick-response reserves.

Eligibility for Federal grants would require the assignment of these policemen to metropolitan areas to assure their ready availability for emergencies. The deployment and response capabilities of these state forces would be designed to enable the governor to dispatch sizeable, effective units of trained riot control personnel within a matter of minutes to any city in trouble, with additional support increments following rapidly. The National Guard would still constitute an emergency reserve in the event these combined forces proved insufficient.

At the present time, the Federal Government is spending some $4½ billion annually in grants to states to build highways. The same amount of money the Federal Government is now contributing to build just one mile of highway in a metropolitan area could pay for the cost of 1,000 state policemen who would be available to protect that metropolitan area in the event of domestic violence.

If ten percent of the Federal funds currently given the states for highway construction were allocated for these special state police—and were matched by the states—it could create a riot control reserve of approximately 60,000 men, twice the amount of state police and highway patrolmen now available. Such state forces would ensure each state a sizeable riot control reserve force for every large city within its borders.

On their part, the states themselves receive more than $6 billion annually from state highway-user revenues. Less than 10 percent of this state revenue, however, is now spent on police and highway safety programs. The use of a larger portion of these state highway revenues to support the state costs of adding additional highway patrol-riot control personnel would seem entirely justified for such a vital state responsibility.

In addition to their protective function, these state forces would be performing needed daily services, protecting lives and preventing accidents on the metropolitan highways.

The assignment of these police forces to patrol the metropolitan highway system would have the added benefit of freeing large numbers of local police who must now perform this function. The city of Los Angeles, for example, recently turned over the responsibility for policing the arterial highways within the city limits to the California Highway Patrol, thereby making available large numbers of Los Angeles officers for reassignment to local protection and to crime control responsibilities.

These new state forces could also serve as a riot control training and information resource for all local and county police forces. Furthermore, they could serve as the nucleus needed to assist and strengthen local police departments in their regular police work in such areas as training, communications, records, laboratory and related technical, special and supportive police services. Such a role would enable the individual states to help fulfill their obligations to provide local communities with the support they need to combat local crime and to preserve the peace.

The creation of such a force in a particular locality depends upon many factors. No single law enforcement concept will properly serve all areas. Nevertheless, given appropriate latitude to encompass the many control problems in our nation, state police and highway patrols so strengthened to cope with civil disorders, would be a major step towards expanding the manpower capabilities of our metropolitan police forces.

PUBLIC SAFETY RADIO COMMUNICATION

A principal command and control problem found by the Civil Disorders Commission was the lack of emergency radio frequencies available to police and fire departments during civil disorders.[14]

The Commission also found the coordination between neighboring police jurisdictions, fire departments and the National Guard extremely difficult because of the lack of areawide channels. Incompatible frequencies and equipment prevented effective use of men and equipment. To help relieve already overtaxed radio frequencies, the Commission recommended that the Federal Communication Commission "make sufficient frequencies available to police and related public safety services to meet the demonstrated need for riot control and other emergency use."

Innovations in land mobile radio technology, particularly in the area of public safety communications, will demand increased frequency space. The Joint Technical Advisory Committee stated:

> Apart from emergencies, the upward trend in crime, the mobility of criminals, and the increasing concentration of the population in urban areas make it essential to increase the effectiveness of police communications. The tools for this are already available, such as personal radio equipment to provide continuous contact with each policeman, and visual printout in patrol cars to increase accuracy and speed in receiving information, including that from computerized files. To implement these tools fully, would again require additional channels.[15]

Already in the marketplace are such recently developed communications tools as the mobile teleprinter which will enable police vehicles to receive printed messages over the air. As police departments become integrated into statewide, computerized, information systems, police use the radio channel between the vehicle and the control center for direct access to data stored in the memory files of the computer. Information regarding missing persons and automobile or firearm registration is obtained by interrogation of the computer through the two-way radio control station. The control station relays the computer's response to the vehicle with the information printed out on the teleprinter.

To provide additional radio channels, on June 30, 1968, the Federal Communications Commission reduced the channel width of land mobile radio channels in the 450–470-MHz band to 25KHz, and made 20 of the newly split channels available for assignment to the police radio services. In many instances however, a majority of the 20 channels were applied for by a single metropolitan police department, leaving only a few channels to be shared by a vast number of suburban police departments, county sheriffs and state police networks.

CONCLUSION

The recent wave of urban disorders found law enforcement agencies ill-trained, ill-equipped and ill-prepared to deal

334

with them. The Civil Disorders Commission noted these deficiencies and proposed measures to upgrade the levels of preparedness and response of these agencies. Since the Report of that Commission, significant but uneven steps have been taken to implement those recommendations.

Army and National Guard units now stand better prepared to deal with domestic upheavals. This improvement has been due largely to effective staff organization, which proved capable of long-range, detailed planning. The response of local law enforcement agencies, however, has lagged. Two problems —adequate numbers of trained manpower and adequate communications—have yet to be solved.

REFERENCES

1. James Q. Wilson, *Varieties of Police Behavior* (Cambridge, Mass.: Harvard University Press, 1968), at 80.

2. National Advisory Commission on Civil Disorders, *Report* (New York: Bantam Books, 1968). (Hereinafter cited as *Kerner Report.*)

3. *Id.*, Supplement on Control of Disorder, at 490.

4. Urban America, Inc. and The Urban Coalition, *One Year Later, An Assessment of the Nation's Response to the Crisis Described by the National Advisory Commission on Civil Disorders* (Washington, D.C.: Urban America, Inc. and The Urban Coalition, 1969), sec. II, at a, 4, and 5.

5. According to Mr. Paul G. Bower, Special Assistant to the Deputy Attorney General, the definitions used by the Justice Department were less stringent than those used by the Civil Disorders Commission. "If the Riot Commission definitions were applied to the 1968 disorders, we would probably find only one or two disorders—Cleveland, Miami—that would have been construed major by Commission standards, as compared to eight major disorders in the summer of 1967. The apparent increase in . . . minor disorders is probably due to better reporting rather than an actual increase in violence." Missouri Attorney General's Seminar. Lake of Ozarks, Mo., Oct. 4, 1968.

6. "Report by Attorney General Ramsey Clark," a statement issued by the Office of the U.S. Attorney General, Washington, D.C., Oct. 3, 1968.

7. Statement of General Ralph E. Haines, Jr., then Vice Chief of Staff, United States Army, before the 89th Conference of the National Guard Association of the United States, Transcript of Proceedings 91 (Sept. 1967).

8. The National Guard Bureau, Report on the Final Evaluation of the New Jersey Test Program (1968).

9. For example, Gen. James Woolnough, Commanding General, U.S. Continental Army Command, in a speech before the

90th General Conference of the National Guard Association, stated that he recognized that the National Guard's 1968 field training for their federal responsibilities had been less than an unqualified success. This he felt was a result of "the disruptions to orderly planning which occurred during the year."

10. As of the publication of this report, the single most authoritative source is an International Association of Chiefs of Police Publication entitled *Guidelines for Civil Disorder and Mobilization Planning* (1968). The IACP has also compiled publications entitled *Model Civil Disturbance Control Plan* (1968); and *Civil Disorders After-Action Report* (Mar.–Apr. 1968). *See also Civil Disturbances and Disasters*—Department of the Army Field Manual FM 19–15 (Mar. 1968); *Operations Reports: Lessons Learned Report 5–67*, Civil Disorders—Task Force Detroit, Commanding General, United States 5th Army; Federal Bureau of Investigation, *Prevention and Control of Mobs and Riots* (1967); D. Farmer, *Civil Disorder Control: A Planning Program of Municipal Coordination and Cooperation* (Public Administration Service, Chicago, 1968); Lesson Plan, Senior Officer Civil Disturbance Orientation Course, Fort Gordon, Ga.

11. International Association of Chiefs of Police, *Civil Disorders After Action Report* (Mar.–Apr., 1968).

12. Atlanta, Berkeley, Boston, Chicago, Cleveland, Dallas, Denver, Detroit, Miami, New York, Oakland, Philadelphia, St. Louis, San Diego, San Francisco, and Washington, D.C.

13. The following is taken from an article written in Feb. 1969 by David Lancashire for the Associated Press entitled "The Bobbies' Way of Handling Crowds":

Shouting slogans and waving anti-Vietnam placards, the demonstrators smashed against the police line and tried to fight their way through. The placards waved like sabres and police helmets flew in the air.

The policeman in charge—a sergeant in a sweatshirt and tennis shoes—looked delighted. "That's it demonstrators," he shouted, "but try again, and harder."

The clash was at the London Police Recruit Training School, where British bobbies study how to control riots like the explosive demonstrations in Paris, Chicago, Berlin and London.

London police do it one way, and one way only: They link arms and, by sheer numbers, hold back the crowd. The crowd in this case was a cluster of police in plain clothes, providing practice for fellow cadets in the linked-arms techniques.

London's men in blue have no tear gas, no water cannons and no guns.

"We have no riot helmets or visors, either," says chief instructor James Hargadon, a 40-year-old Scot who handles the training for the capital's 20,000 man force.

"We don't think they are necessary, and if we did put on

336

riot helmets it might work the crowd up a bit, cause a spot of trouble."

British police, ever polite, refuse to comment on the violence in Chicago or Paris, but they tend to look smug when they are asked about it.

"We wouldn't consider such methods here," says Hargadon. "We treat crowd control like cricket, or a soccer match. We try to keep them from scoring."

When the last big demonstration erupted in London in October, more than 30,000 protestors marched through the streets. Scotland Yard assigned 8846 police to control the mobs. The forecasts predicted trouble but the "treat-'em-gently" tactics paid off.

When protestors threw coins at one cop, he laughed and asked for bigger ones. When another bobby was hit by a flying pear, he picked it up and ate it. At the end of the day there were 47 civilian casualties, none of them seriously hurt.

And demonstrators and police—who had 74 injuries—sang a chorus of Auld Lang Syne together outside the undamaged American Embassy, which the extremists had threatened to bomb.

14. *Kerner Report, supra* note 2, at 486–487.

15. Joint Technical Advisory Committee, *Spectrum Engineering —The Key to Progress,* a report on technical policies and procedures recommended for increased spectrum utilization (New York: Institute of Electrical and Electronics Engineers, Mar. 1968), at 12.

CHAPTER 16

OFFICIAL RESPONSES TO MASS DISORDER II: THE CIRCUIT OF VIOLENCE— A TALE OF TWO CITIES*

"Force empowers its own adversaries. It raises up its own opposition. It engenders its own destruction."[1]

While the statistics on civil disorders compiled by the Department of Justice during the past year lend validity to the belief that the earlier rash of riots may have subsided, new dangers and control problems are developing to challenge the police and the communities. They are manifested in terrorist attacks by black extremists on policemen, such as the ambush and murders in Cleveland, Ohio; and conversely, in the vigilante activity of white extremists in a number of American communities. Concurrently, we are witnessing the emergence of extremists within the uniformed police who themselves are resorting to lawlessness, such as the off-duty police officers who physically assaulted a group of Black Panthers in a New York City Courthouse, the Oakland policeman who fired into a building housing a militant organization, and the Detroit policemen who, following the killing of a white policeman on the streets of Detroit, fired more than 100 bullets into a church in which there were more than 140 Negro men, women and children.

Such incidents and the increasing bitterness and apprehension they provoke on both sides could, if unchecked, create the potential for a new, and in many ways, far more dangerous type of violence for this country. For we are witnessing an increasing polarization in attitudes which breeds a citizenry incapable of demanding the kind of official response appropriate to the problems which underlie such outbreaks. Largely as a result, those minorities which do not have the power to mold official response are becoming increasingly alienated from the larger community.

The dynamics of confrontation between large groups of people and those in authority work in interesting ways. A

---

*This chapter was prepared by Joseph R. Sahid.

polarization in attitudes leads to escalation of the confrontation, breeding more intense polarization which justifies further
escalation in the minds of the participants and the larger
public. An example of how this circular and cumulative
causation phenomenon has produced violent clashes in our
nation's history is the American labor movement, a subject
more fully developed by the History Task Force of this Commission. Another example is the comparison of the official
handling of the protest activities which occurred in Chicago
during the 1968 Democratic Convention and the handling of
similar protest activities in Washington, D.C., during the 1969
Presidential Inauguration.

The concepts discussed in this chapter are neither novel nor
overly complex. In one sense, they are the most fundamental
principles of crowd control, understood by observers at least
as ancient as Machiavelli. But fundamentals have a way of
being forgotten when emotional issues cloud man's rationality. For that reason, we have attempted to re-state those
fundamentals using contemporary illustrations to reduce the
abstractions to meaningful realities.

THE DYNAMICS OF POLARIZATION

To many, the answer to violent unrest seems simple. When
blacks riot, when students demonstrate, when groups protesting government policies organize potentially disruptive
marches, the government should retaliate with massive suppressive force. Only by supporting law enforcement agencies
and reducing procedural obstacles to their efficient operation,
they argue, can order be restored.

The strength for this argument in our country was revealed
by the National Violence Commission Survey. Seventy-eight
percent of the people polled agreed with the statement,
"Some people don't understand anything but force." Fifty-six
percent agreed that "Any man who insults a policeman has
no complaint if he gets roughed up in return." Only 55
percent agreed with the statement, "The police are wrong to
beat up unarmed protestors, even when these people are rude
and call them names." And 51 percent agreed that, "Justice
may have been a little rough-and-ready in the days of the Old
West, but things worked better than they do today with all
the legal red tape."

While rough-and-ready justice may be appealing, there is
little evidence that more repressive police operations will

significantly decrease the level of violence in the country. Swift and massive commitment of prudent and well trained law enforcement personnel can usually extinguish a civil disorder in its incipiency, but the call for "law and order" does not stop here. Citizens have asked for something more— that the police be "unleashed" to deal with demonstrators and rioters as they see fit, regardless of the long-run consequences of their actions. At least two-thirds of white Americans believe that black firebombers and looters should simply be shot down in the streets.[2]

This view has become part of the folklore of the day, as an examination of contemporary cartoons and comic strips, particularly Dick Tracy, Little Orphan Annie, and, in recent years, Li'l Abner, will demonstrate. At a most unpropitious time, the day after the assassination of Senator Robert F. Kennedy, the author of Dick Tracy concluded the episode on the following philosophical note: "Violence is golden, when it's used to put down evil."[3]

Policemen, themselves representative of the larger community from which the cries for "law and order" emerge, have found it increasingly difficult to close their ears to the public clamor. Sensing correctly that an ever increasing percentage of the population is willing to tolerate the use of any amount of suppressive force to quell the clamor about them, some policemen have fulfilled the wishes of these people by engaging in terroristic attacks upon rioters and demonstrators in an unruly and undisciplined use of brute force. Our Study Teams reporting on the disorders during the 1968 Democratic and Republican Conventions and during the aftermath of the shootout in Cleveland, Ohio, July 23-28, 1968 (as well as the numerous other instances referred to by our Task Force on the Violent Aspects of Protest and Confrontation) have documented beyond doubt incidents of unlawfully violent and otherwise suppressive conduct engaged in by numbers of policemen.

Reliance upon undisciplined law enforcement is self-defeating, however, since it adds to the magnitude and intensity of disorders in progress and lays the groundwork for future and more violent confrontation. Rather than succeeding in its intended goal, which is to intimidate law breakers from further violation, it merely succeeds in inflaming passions further and drawing innocent bystanders into the web of violence. Once this happens, those in authority are left with no alternative: they must respond with even greater force to deal with increasingly larger and angrier crowds of participants until a bloody victory (if possible) is achieved. Professor Ted Gurr has forcefully expressed this phenomenon:

> The most fundamental human response to force is counterforce. Force threatens and angers men, especially if they believe it to be illicit or unjust. Threatened, they try to defend themselves. Angered they want to retaliate. . . . The presumption justifying counterforce is that it deters: the greater a regime's capacity for force and the more severe the sanctions it imposes on dissidents, the less violence they will do. This assumption is in many circumstances a self-defeating fallacy. If a regime responds to the threat or use of force with greater force, its effects are likely to be identical with the effects that dictated the regime response: dissidents will resort to greater force.[4]

Several factors contribute to the violence-escalating tendency inherent in the use of sizeable police forces in situations of potential or actual disorder. Many observers of police-citizen interaction have noted the heightened tension and crisis atmosphere generated in an area where large and powerful groups of law enforcement officers are deployed.[5] This kind of atmosphere was evident on the Columbia University campus during the disorders which occurred during the Spring of 1968. Not long after the dissident student groups succeeded in occupying several of Columbia's major buildings and offices, the university administration decided to mobilize a large complement of police officers at various locations on the campus. Once the police presence was apparent, a tense, crisis-like atmosphere pervaded the campus, even though the police took no action for several days afterward. Students erected more formidable barriers within the occupied buildings in the hope of forestalling what seemed like an imminent and massive police effort to dislodge the students.[6]

A similar crisis atmosphere was evident prior to the Democratic National Convention. Local officials in Chicago began announcing weeks and even months before the Convention that large-scale mobilization of police, National Guard and Army troops would be undertaken to prepare for any outbreak of violence that might occur. Rarely a day passed without some aspect of the mobilization receiving widespread publicity. Fences were installed, barricades were erected and streets were closed off. To some, the city of Chicago assumed the characteristics of an armed camp preparing for war. The extensive and well-publicized preparation coupled with the massive buildup of police, troops and equipment could not fail to create an atmosphere suggesting the ultimate inevitability of some mass disorder.[7] As another example, the Miami police department's importation of police dogs and shotguns into the Miami ghetto was credited by our study team investigating the disorders that engulfed that city in 1968 with exacerbating the tensions that generated the disorder.

Perhaps the most serious danger resulting from placing primary reliance on poorly restrained police forces to prevent and control outbreaks of group disorder is the adverse effect such reliance has on the attitudes of individuals and groups in our society. This effect on attitudes manifests itself in two basically different but equally deleterious ways—intimidation and polarization.

In the crisis-like atmosphere generated by the announced availability or actual deployment of a large police force which has been mobilized to cope with potential group disorder, there is a strong possibility that the average, law-abiding citizen will be intimidated from participating in the group activity. Such intimidation has a "chilling" effect on the exercise of First Amendment rights in the areas of political, war, or social protest.

Any individual who contemplates engaging in a group demonstration of dissent or protest, regardless of how peaceful and law-abiding he might be, must of necessity consider the possibility that he might become involved in some type of group disorder. When police forces are massed for such a demonstration and the public made well aware of the preparations, the possibility of disorder becomes magnified. Although the most dedicated and least fearful (and perhaps the most violence prone) may decide to engage in the protest despite the consequence, many others of a more peaceable disposition may decide to forego participating in an organized protest. A kind of Gresham's Law operates, leaving the protest movement in the hands of the more extreme participants.

The massive force martialed and flaunted prior to the Democratic National Convention no doubt discouraged a multitude of respectable, law-abiding citizens from assembling en masse to express their disagreement with the war in Vietnam and to influence the convention on other matters of critical public importance. And there are indications suggesting that the mobilization of forces was dictated by a desire on the part of the public officials to hold down the number of people engaging in such protests.[8] While it is of course impossible to prove the subjective motivations of those officials, the effect of their actions was clear—sizeable numbers of people were intimidated into foregoing their constitutional rights. The gravity of that occurrence should not be underestimated in a society founded on the premise that all people have the right to speak freely and assemble peacefully.

"All police are sadistic and brutal." "All demonstrators are Communists and traitors." Opposing views such as these which are widely held and vigorously espoused by diverse segments of the public exemplify the phenomenon of attitude polarization. Polarization occurs both during and after disorders and is manifested in the attitudes of those involved in the disorder as well as those not involved.

The origins of attitude polarization can be traced to the difficulty of coordinating and controlling the actions of a large police force deployed during a group disorder. Because of this difficulty, it is often impossible to pinpoint and take remedial action against those individual policemen who have engaged in indiscriminate or illegal behavior. Much the same problem is evident when individual members of a protest group engage in provocative or illegal behavior. This inability promptly to identify and hold responsible those who have engaged in illegal activities generates widespread feelings of bitterness and animosity in one group towards the other. Generalities replace specifics, passion replaces reason, dogmatism replaces analysis. Thus, the protestors tend to view all police as brutal, intemperate, and unsympathetic because they have seen some police act this way. And the police tend to view all protestors as communists or trouble-makers because some protestors have engaged in provocative acts. The escalation of tactics leads to broader and more intense polarization which in turn justifies further escalation. To phrase it simply, "You hit me so I will hit you back."

Two recent surveys of public attitudes following the disturbances at Columbia University in the spring of 1968 graphically illustrate the extent to which attitudes can polarize after a large police force is employed to control a group disorder.[9] One poll, conducted for the *New York Times* by Public Opinion Surveys, Inc., of Princeton, N.J., surveyed 508 adults living in the greater New York metropolitan area.[10] The other poll, conducted by Allen H. Barton of the Bureau of Applied Social Research at Columbia University,

343

polled the entire university faculty and one-fifth of the student body.[11] On the issue of the propriety of the university's decision to call in the police, a sharp split in attitude was apparent between the metropolitan area residents, on the one hand, and the students and faculty on the other. Whereas 83 percent of the metropolitan area residents favored the decision to call in the police, 74 percent of Columbia students favored using the police only under limited conditions or not at all. Opposition to the use of police was most intense among those most intimately associated with the disturbance, the students. Support for the use of police was most intense among those who were not college educated, and those over forty years of age.

Once the attitudes of the police and the protest group begin to diverge toward opposing extremes, the ability of both sides to join in either preventing a potential disorder or curbing an existing disorder is greatly impaired. Because of the growing rigidity and polarity in the attitudes held by each group toward the other, communication between the police and the protestors, if it occurs at all, will be carried on in an atmosphere of mutual distrust and suspicion. In such an atmosphere, discussions aimed at achieving cooperation to insure that future group protests are conducted in an orderly fashion have little chance to succeed. And in the midst of a disorder, discussions aimed at mutual efforts to bring the disorder to an end become virtually impossible.

The depth and intensity of the polarization in the attitudes of the protestors and the police depends on the length and severity of their confrontation. If the confrontation is severe and the polarization intense, the original objective of the protest groups becomes submerged, being replaced by demands and complaints concerning police action. Although the transformation of objectives usually finds initial expression within the protest groups, the emergent issue concerning police action begins to attract widespread public attention. Within a short period of time, the polarization between the attitudes of the protest groups and the police is evident in the attitudes of pro-protest and pro-police segments of the public as a whole. Widespread coverage of the issue by the various communication media draws more and more people into the controversy. At some stage, public officials take sides on the propriety of police conduct, impelled to do so because of the growing public clamor. And the additional facts which are disseminated by means of the communications media, investigatory bodies, white papers and the like can often lend support to the divergent public attitudes, add to the vigor with which the views are held, and further intensify the pre-existing polarization.

The consequences of this polarization are exhibited in various forms. In a recent trial of three Chicago policemen charged with unlawfully beating a reporter at the Democratic National Convention, for example, the jury acquitted the policemen in the face of overwhelming evidence of the officers' guilt. The president of the Chicago Fraternal Order of Police probably reflected the mood of the community and the jury when he commented:

> We are absolutely elated over the not guilty verdict. It proves beyond the shadow of a doubt that the lady of justice is not blindfolded and that anarchy will not prevail in our society.[12]

Thus, the specter of "anarchy" proved more persuasive than the individual guilt or innocence of the defendants.

When attitude polarization becomes reflected in the thinking of large segments of people who are more or less unaffected by a given disorder, more serious, long-range consequences arise. With each succeeding group disorder, growing numbers of the public will appear to be more vigorously in favor of resorting to force as a solution to such outbreaks. As a consequence, with each succeeding disorder, public officials will meet with less resistance in adopting that solution. Those public officials who believe attacking the causes and tensions which precipitate disorders to be a more fruitful approach will be compelled to curtail or abandon their efforts in the face of the public outcry for swift and decisive police action. Gradually, a resort to overwhelming police force will become an automatic response that will further widen the gulf in attitudes, leave unresolved the causes of the disorder, and increase the likelihood of future disorders.

An even more alarming consequence which results from a widespread polarization of attitudes is the growing isolation of those who have either directly engaged in group disorders or expressed sympathy with the goals of the participants. This isolation develops in two stages, both of which are attributable to the strained communications between the polarized groups, a strain which becomes more pronounced as the divergence in attitudes becomes more extreme. Initially, isolation is forced on protestors and their sympathizers by the

345

larger public. Although those who are intimately associated with the disorders are most eager and best able to identify the causes of unrest and to propose creative, remedial measures, the larger public is unwilling to listen, viewing the protestors as a threat to an orderly and stable society. The increasing hostility of the general public drives the protestors and their sympathizers to the second stage of isolation. This stage is marked by the protest group's rejection of the existing political and social system as a vehicle to effect change. When isolation develops to this extent, the attendant polarization and hostility may become so intense as to be irreconcilable.

Attitude polarization leading to an escalation of violence is not difficult to understand. Supported by psychological teachings,[13] the lesson seems clear—force merely produces counterforce.

The polarizing effect of suppressive force is not new to this country. A review of the labor movement provides an outstanding example.

CASE STUDY I: THE LABOR MOVEMENT

The American labor force did not begin to view itself as a special interest group or even as a collective entity until the Industrial Revolution compelled a sharper division between capital and labor. Economic expansion and technological advances gave rise to the giant industrial corporation whose management was increasingly remote and unresponsive to employee needs. Marxist ideology, if it did not abet this process, sharpened an awareness of it.

As the gap between labor and management widened, skilled workers and craftsmen in several industries adopted union forms of organization to voice their requests more audibly. In the first year following the Civil War, the leaders of several trade unions and craft associations met in Baltimore to form the National Labor Union, the first attempt to organize labor on a scale comparable to that of industrial management.

The demands of the NLU were moderate: currency reform, job security, formation of cooperatives, and most of all an eight-hour work day. The tactics employed were peaceful and political: legislative lobbying and campaigning for the enactment of new laws.

As an instrument of political reform, the NLU proved ineffective. Its campaigning yielded few results, either in

346

electing labor candidates to office or in securing legislation. The NLU collapsed in the early 1870s, and in its place arose the Knights of Labor, the prototype of the modern national labor organization.

The Knights inherited the NLU's political reformist tendencies, but put greater emphasis on the strike and on collective bargaining as a means of pressing its demands. At first these tactics were effective. A series of successful strikes won wage increases and better working conditions, and these accomplishments in turn caused the Knights of Labor to increase its membership from about 100,000 in 1881 to a peak of 700,000 in 1885.

These successful strikes, the rapid expansion of organized labor, and increasing social unrest convinced industry that labor unionism represented a dangerous revolutionary movement. In support of this view, industry could cite a number of "revolts" and "rebellions" among immigrant laborers who had spontaneously rioted on several occasions to protest starvation wages and intolerable working conditions. It could cite the Molly Maguires, a secret society of Irish immigrants who enforced their demands for better wages and safer mines by terrorism in the coalfields of Pennsylvania. In addition, the continuing immigration from Europe included a small but vociferous number of anarchists, socialists, and other radicals who preached class struggle and "propaganda of the deed."

While the organized labor movement was generally peaceful, even timid, and sought to divorce itself from radical ideology, industry viewed it as a threat not only to property interests but to management's dominant position in the national economy. The response to this threat was a campaign of harsh suppression, both tactical and strategic. Labor organizers were threatened, beaten, or killed, and labor meetings were forcibly disrupted by company guards and "goons." Strikes were broken by professional strike-breaking agencies, with the aid of local and state police. Resistance from strikers brought massive reprisals, often from troops or state militia called in to protect property and restore order.

The Knights of Labor, ineffectually led and structurally weak, quickly succumbed to such pressures. But this oppression had the effect of imbuing the movement with greater determination. After the 1880's, labor leaders abandoned efforts to secure political reform, and turned to the strike as a principle instrument for pressing their demands—the foremost of which was the right of labor to organize and bargain collectively.

In itself, the strike was a nonviolent instrument of change. It frequently led to violence, however, the moment guards or police attempted to disperse picket lines or escort strike-breakers into the idle factories. Where industrialists were able to employ sufficient force to break a strike completely, the jobless strikers sometimes turned to offensive violence—arming themselves and laying siege to mines, factories, or the barracks of the guards, or engaging in systematic terrorism that became long and bloody "wars."

In almost every instance, labor violence stemmed directly from the breaking of a strike or the suppression of union activities. Sometimes it was sporadic and limited. In some cases it was adopted as policy by particular unions or radical labor groups on the grounds that lawful tactics were ineffective. No national labor organization—not even the militant and radical IWW—advocated the use of terrorism, and most deplored it. Nevertheless, violence remained the hallmark of the American labor movement from the 1870's through the 1930's. It did not diminish to its present inconsequential level until the late 1930's, when enforcement of the National Labor Relations Act of 1935 finally secured for labor the right to organize and bargain collectively, and to employ the strike as an effective alternative to violence.

The resort to force appears to occur in any sustained movement that fails to make steady, measureable progress toward its goals. It occurs less frequently as rational strategy for change, however, than as a gesture of protest or as an expression of frustration. It appears to find acceptance only when suppression precludes other forms of expression or when other forms of expression appear to produce no meaningful response or no concrete results.

These processes seem to be operating both on university campuses and in the streets in connection with student protest groups and the anti-war movement generally. After several years of peaceful protest and demonstration, often in the face of considerable harassment, the more militant groups have evolved the strategy of "confrontation politics" designed to provoke an unresponsive "establishment" into acts of brutality and suppression that dramatize the issues. Many officials have been unable to deal effectively with this tactic when it has been employed on the streets and campuses of our nation. The result has been an increase in the level and intensity of violence.

Two cities—Washington and Chicago—each recently experienced two major demonstrations. In Chicago, anti-war activities occurred on April 27, 1968, and at the Democratic National Convention in August. The March on the Pentagon in October 1967 and the counter-inaugural activities in January 1969 occupied Washington authorities. These demonstrations were organized by many of the same groups and attended by many of the same people. The Convention and the counter-inaugural activities involved about the same number of protestors and centered around major national events.

Yet the results of these events were markedly different. In Chicago, large-scale violence marred both activities. The violence in Washington, on the other hand, was minimal. The almost laboratory-like conditions afforded by the Democratic Convention and Inaugural protest activities prompted us to examine these two demonstrations in detail. We have concluded that the amount of violence that occurred during these demonstrations was directly related to the type of official response that greeted them. More specifically, repressive measures proved self-defeating: when officials decided to "get tough," chaos rather than order resulted.

CASE STUDY II: CHICAGO AND WASHINGTON— A TALE OF TWO CITIES

(The following account is based primarily on reports prepared for the Commission by the Chicago Convention and the Washington Counter-Inaugural Study Teams.

The report on the disorders. at the Democratic Convention prepared for this Commission by Daniel Walker, especially the phrase "police riot," has been greeted by controversy. We believe that critics have misunderstood the significance of this phrase. It was expressly used in the report only to describe the blatant misconduct and violence by small bands of roving policemen in the parks and streets of the city's north side on Sunday and Monday nights of convention week. See *Rights in Conflict* at ix. It was not used to describe the handling of the large crowds on the climactic night of the Convention, which is described elsewhere in the report. Unless this distinction is understood the lesson of that report may go unnoticed.)

The National Mobilization Committee to End the War in Vietnam (MOBE) served as the primary organizing force which brought together demonstrators for the activities both in Chicago and in Washington. MOBE served as a loose coalition of various local and national antiwar groups which, although autonomous, looked to MOBE officials to secure permits and make other logistic arrangements necessary to the success of a mass demonstration.

A subsidiary role, although intensively publicized by the mass media, was played by groups variously called "Hippies" and "Yippies." Only peripherally interested in protesting the national events which called forth their participation, they desired to use both occasions to publicize their "alternative life style." Their "Festivals of Life" were designed to show the nation's youth that the "underground" was more than a myth.

Most participants did not desire confrontation in any form. Many had come to protest peacefully their opposition to certain current American policies, foremost of which was the War in Vietnam. Others had come to participate in the festivities that were expected, to make new friends, to hear the scheduled speakers and entertainers, and generally to take part in the social event that was expected.

Scattered throughout both these groupings of participants were those who desired "confrontation" with the authorities. Some believed that confrontation would occur without any unlawful or disruptive conduct on their own part, that their simple presence would be enough to goad the authorities into attempting to suppress their right to dissent peacefully.

Others intended to provoke confrontation if necessary by exciting policemen and officials by their conduct. This last group was indeed small. No more than 100–200 people were committed to this philosophy at any time during either event.

Valuable insight into the personalities of the demonstrators has been provided by Dr. Paul R. Miller, Assistant Professor of Neurology and Psychiatry at Northwestern University Medical School,[14] who polled those arrested during the Convention disorders by means of questionnaires and interviews. His conclusions contrast sharply with descriptions of the demonstrators given by the Chicago officials:

> The "average" demonstrator was from Chicago or a state adjacent to Illinois, a white male, 21 years old, who had nearly completed his college education. His social class origins were upper-middle or upper. Father was college educated and was either a professional or a business executive. Mother had attended college without graduating and was a housewife. The demonstrator was headed toward a career in a service profession (teacher, clinical physician or psychologist, social worker, minister) . . . .
>
> Social and Political Orientations . . . were sharply polarized. Almost unanimous support was given to the peace move-

ment (99 percent) and draft resistance (93 percent) . . . .
Their closest political identity was with the "new Left" (83 percent), a concept which was concretized most closely in the person of Eugene McCarthy (supported by 66 percent). . . .

The number who were for "communism" (18 percent) and "anarchism" (34 percent) requires explanation. . . .

Certainly the usual American vision of a heavily bearded wild-eyed anarchist carrying a bomb with a lighted fuse is totally out of date with the demonstrators' concept. Instead, an anarchist is a person who opposes on principle the established institutions of American society and has dropped out of participation in most or all of them. Thus almost all hippies are anarchists.

In regard to communists, one responder said that "qualified National SDS calls themselves 'revolutionary communists.' I believe this concept of communism is beyond most elected officials." Again the stereotyped American vision of a group is out of touch with current concepts among youths, who view communism as a social action movement to change capitalism to state socialism, by revolution if necessary, violent if necessary. Most youths despise Russian communism and disdain the American communist party. . . . [46 percent said they were against and 35 percent said they were indifferent towards communism].[15]

Eighty percent denied [Mayor] Daley's contention that the demonstrators were taken over by deviant groups. . . .

Most (73 percent) of the arrested demonstrators had never been arrested before. Of the 27 percent who had, two-thirds had been in connection with civil disobedience. . . .

The group attitude toward nonviolence is sharply divided: half (49 percent) believe in it as a universally applicable principle, one-fourth (27 percent) deny it, and another one-fourth (24 percent) accept it under some conditions, such as practicing it until one is violently attacked (and then defending oneself). Others said that they accepted it for themselves but would not insist that it be universally applied to others. . . .

Perhaps if the question on nonviolence had been asked before the convention, a higher proportion would have answered yes. Thus: "Chicago was the first demonstration I participated in. If I go to another and I am assulted [sic] by a 'cop' again, I'm going to the next one armed. There [sic] were a large number of people in Chicago who felt the same way. So if this treatment of demonstrators continues the forementioned revolution isn't very far off." . . .

At the time of their arrest, over half (55 percent) claim they were attacked by the police. . . . Although the police claimed that their violence was only in response to the violence of the demonstrators, they charged only 10 percent of the demonstrators with violent acts, while 55 percent of the demonstrators charged the police with violent acts. . . .

The demonstrators were generally articulate about the major social problems facing America today. . . .

To remedy the social problems, the majority recommended conventional techniques: demonstrations (53 percent), electoral activity (42 percent), community action groups (30 percent) (some of a radical nature) and education (29 percent). But two minorities ran in opposite directions: revolution—armed if necessary (21 percent) and dropping out or doing your own individual thing (16 percent). . . .

Intelligence reports for both events indicated that violence and disruptive conduct was likely to occur. Some of this information was absurd and simply the result of theatrics engaged in by the demonstrators to gain publicity for their cause, like the reported plans to contaminate Chicago's water supply with LSD.[16] Other information was gathered from sources which could not be regarded as reliable.[17]

Chicago authorities lacked any mechanism for distinguishing the serious from the ludicrous and unreliable.[18] As the Walker report concluded, "the intelligence agencies apparently made little effort to distinguish between the philosophies and intents of various groups. They were concerned not with whether a group advocated violence or adhered to nonviolent tenets, but with the dangers inherent in large crowds of demonstrators, regardless of whether all members espouse violence."[19] Implementing the tightest security measures ever witnessed at a national convention, no attempt was made to tailor those measures to the type of threat received nor to distinguish those who were likely to engage in violence from those who presented no threat. Thus, for example, the spectre of assassination was advanced to justify the use of tear gas and mace to clear the parks and streets of nonviolent demonstrators, including clergymen at prayer, even though no rational relationship between the demonstrators' conduct and an assassination plot could possibly be offered. This philosophy of "overkill" was to have serious ramifications.

By contrast, Washington authorities carefully evaluated the intelligence reports they received. As one high-ranking police official expressed it, "An intelligence report is like beauty—it lies in the eye of the beholder." Individuals and groups who were likely to engage in disruptive conduct were identified and watched closely. No attempt was made to interfere with the great majority of the demonstrators who presented no threat. Massive security measures were not flaunted in an attempt to intimidate participants who had no desire to engage in a confrontation. As a result, the suggestion of an "armed camp" prepared for battle never greeted the Washington protestors. No massive publicity campaign regarding security ever detracted from the major scheduled event.

Chicago authorities failed to make a real effort to reach an understanding regarding permits to engage in peaceful demonstrations requested by the demonstrators. They obstructed and delayed the negotiations in an attempt to discourage the protestors from engaging in their constitutional right to peaceably assemble to petition the government for redress of their grievances.[20] Among other tactics employed, they failed to answer correspondence, refused to schedule timely meetings with the proper officials, and imposed conditions which could not be fulfilled (such as requiring that a $100,000 to $300,000 liability bond be posted even though it was clear that no bonding company would issue such a bond). Their counter offers to the demonstrators, made under compulsion of law suits brought by the protesting groups, came too late and offered too little.

Failure to engage in a meaningful dialogue with the protestors had far-reaching consequences. Government officials were denied the opportunity to determine the character of the spokesmen for the protestors. This knowledge could have proved helpful when the later difficulties began to unfold. The officials had no opportunity to amass intelligence from the spokesmen who could have pinpointed the difficulties they themselves were having. There was also no way to discover what activities had been planned by the protesting groups.

Refusal to grant a permit meant that for the most of the time they were present, the demonstrators would have no focal point to their activity. Random groups were thus forced to remain random. This complicated the police function greatly. Rather than being able to focus their surveillance on limited numbers of mass gatherings, they were forced to spread themselves thinly over a large geographical area without the ability to recognize leaders with whom they could communicate in the event of an emergency.

The most serious result of the permit denial was to polarize further the attitudes of the protestors and the larger community. Angry at the denial of what they considered their right to a permit, many demonstrators came to Chicago determined to engage in their protest activities despite the absence of a permit. They began regarding the city authorities as venal and were determined to prove that they would

353

not be intimidated into foregoing what they considered was rightly theirs. Resistance and obstacles made them even more eager to stage their protest.

Some individuals and groups, however, succumbed to the pressure and cancelled their plans to attend the protest. Although this is exactly what city officials hoped to achieve, the plan backfired, for many members of the more staid and responsible groups were the ones who were thus intimidated. This meant that fewer responsible people were present to restrain their less rational compatriots when the escalation began to take place.

On the other side, denial of a permit signified to citizens and police that the protest activities were illegitimate. They viewed those who assembled as trouble-makers and law breakers rather than as other citizens come to exercise their constitutional rights. This polarization was to have significant consequences as events unfolded.

Washington authorities, on the other hand, negotiated conscientiously and arrived at an agreement acceptable to both sides. District of Columbia Deputy Mayor Thomas Fletcher reflected the thinking of his city's administration when he said, "We felt they were entitled to a permit."[21] Shortly after the request for a permit was received, a high ranking federal official was assigned to work out the permit details. He met almost daily with the same demonstration leaders who had been denied an audience in Chicago, driving with them in his car to examine various proposed sites for the rallies.

The demonstrators were allowed to construct a huge circus tent near the Washington Monument to serve as a focal point for their activities. They were not prohibited from sleeping in the tent. They were permitted to stage a parade along Pennsylvania Avenue, the main thoroughfare through the center of government in Washington, the day before the Inaugural Parade was to take place. Liability bonds were not required; rather, the permit required MOBE to use "all means at its command and under its control" to avoid damage.

The leaders of the protest, impressed with the forthrightness of the government spokesmen, made every effort to cooperate with city officials. Rennie Davis, a MOBE official who had figured prominently during the Chicago convention, commented to the press, "I feel we have here the kind of cooperation we did not have in Chicago. For this reason I do not expect the physical confrontations and riots we had in Chicago." Potential trouble spots were pinpointed by the

MOBE officials and the city learned in great detail the protestors' plans. They were thus able to deploy small forces of policemen to areas where they might be most effective yet relatively unobtrusive. Mutual cooperation characterized the resulting activities, enabling both sides to react quickly to any emergency. The city supplied MOBE officials with direct communication links, such as walkie-talkies, which avoided breakdowns of communication at important crises. During one scuffle, policemen were kept away from the area while MOBE officials restored order. When the generator which supplied electricity to the demonstrators' tent ran out of fuel, the city fire department delivered the fuel within minutes. During the crucial minutes before the President's car passed an assembled group of dissidents along the route of the Inaugural parade, city officials agreed, at the request of MOBE officials, to relieve a police officer who had angered the crowd by using unnecessary force.

It is impossible at this point in time to determine whether protestors or police "struck the first blow" in Chicago. What is clear is that a few protestors and a few policemen began engaging in provocative conduct as soon as significant numbers of demonstrators began congregating in Chicago. Nevertheless, the mood was calm on Saturday and Sunday.

Escalation soon took place as dozens of policemen using tear gas and clubs cleared Lincoln Park after curfew on Sunday, Monday, and Tuesday nights. Without coherent plans, policemen chased and clubbed innocent and guilty alike through the quiet streets of Old Town, often great distances from the park. Frightened and battered, the demonstrators regrouped during the days following these bloody chases. Like veterans of a war, they recounted to each other the horrors they had experienced the previous night. Anger mounted at stories of "leaders" being arrested for no apparent reason.

Extremists who had earlier been ignored began to attract audiences. The protestors were told they were being forced to defend themselves and their friends. They were urged to resist being trampled on and to fight back. Each day the police were exposed to more and more jeers and obscenities. Each night they had to withstand heavier barrages of rocks.

(The demonstrators' chief "weapon" was obscenity. Many rocks were thrown, but only a small number of demonstrators actually threw them. At no time did massive numbers of demonstrators engage in rockthrowing, not even on Wednesday night. Descriptions of the rock-throwing as "barrages" are, therefore, misleading unless qualified. They were barrages only in the sense that numbers of unidentifiable people engaged in the rock-throwing. These people were scattered thinly through the crowds.

It was widely reported that human excrement was thrown at policemen. The reaction to these reports was understandably intense. However, little factual foundation supports these reports. Only three people, two policemen and a reporter, actually reported having seen feces thrown. Whether or not these reports were accurate, the conclusion is inescapable that the image of many demonstrators throwing human excrement has been drastically exaggerated. In all probability, human excrement was thrown on only one or two occasions if it was thrown at all.)

Each day and night the police responded with even more venom, sowing the seeds of even more anger.

The escalation of anger is revealed by the statistics dealing with injuries. On August 25, the night of the first major confrontation, only 2 policemen were injured. The next two nights, 15 and 13 policemen respectively were injured. Yet on the fourth night of the convention, 149 policemen suffered injuries. (The injuries to the demonstrators show a different sequence—a much greater percentage received their injuries during the early days of the convention.) Thus, more than three-fourths of the injuries to policemen were sustained on the fourth day of a struggle in which hundreds of demonstrators had already been clubbed or arrested.

The escalation of violence was thus a response to unfolding events. Goaded by a few extremists who antagonized police by jeering them, the police responded by indiscriminately gassing and clubbing large numbers of protestors. More and more protestors, angered at this willful violence by policemen, struck back in the only ways they, as upper-middle class, college-educated youths could—by swearing and throwing rocks. And so the escalation continued. Demonstrators provoked policemen. Policemen provoked demonstrators. The circuit of violence was closed.

This cycle was never allowed to complete itself in Washington. Provocation by demonstrators was met with restraint. Provocation by policemen was terminated by police and city officials who intervened quickly to restore discipline. As a result, escalation never took place.

Spokesmen for the demonstrators themselves attributed the

difference in results between Chicago and Washington to the difference in official response.

According to David Dellinger, Chairman of MOBE:

> The mood of the Mobilization people was much the same. The difference in the results was caused by the different attitudes of the city administration involved. Washington felt it was capable of containing demonstrations without turning it into a police riot.

Another MOBE official commented:

> The difference between Chicago and Washington was a permit and a tent. The police react as the officials react. In Washington, the officials reacted well and the police reacted well. As a result, the demonstrators acted well towards the police and the officials.

There were some radical leaders, however, who were more grateful for the official response in Chicago, for it appeared to validate their characterizations of government as being "reactionary" and "repressive" and to increase support from other protesting groups. The chaos at Chicago also gave solidarity to the ranks of those who regard all demonstrators, however peaceful, as irresponsible "punks." The overall effect was to increase polarization and unrest, not diminish them.

This comparison between Chicago in August of 1968 and Washington in January of 1969 can be closed on two encouraging notes. Permits for peace marches in Chicago were sought and granted in October 1969. The marches were organized by the "Weatherman," an extremely militant faction of the Students for a Democratic Society. In the course of the demonstrations, Chicago police had to face four days of intense provocation and wanton violence. This time, however, the police acted with calm and restraint. No injuries to residents, bystanders or newsmen were reported; on the contrary, the police took steps to safeguard bystanders from the violence. As a result of the professional conduct of Chicago police, violence was effectively contained, and blame for the damage and injuries that did occur fell squarely upon the violent group among the demonstrators, many of whom were arrested.

The Peace Moratorium Parade and assembly in Washington on November 15, 1969, was another example of intelligent and restrained official response. Although the government had reason to expect that some elements among the protesting groups were bent on violence, reasonable permits were ultimately negotiated with the responsible demonstration leaders, and ample police and military forces were provided to preserve order if necessary. In the largest single protest demonstration in American history, the overwhelming majority of the participants behaved peacefully. Their activities were facilitated rather than restrained by the police. When the few extremists did attempt violent attacks on two occasions, the police responded quickly and firmly but, on the whole, without excessive force. As a result, order was maintained, the right to protest was upheld and it was possible to judge both the peaceful and the violent aspects of the protest in their true proportion.

The bulk of the actual work of maintaining the peacefulness of the proceedings was performed by the demonstrators themselves. An estimated five thousand "marshals", recruited from among the demonstrators, flanked the crowds throughout. Their effectiveness was shown when they succeeded in stopping an attempt by the fringe radicals to leave the line of march in an effort to reach the White House during the Saturday parade.

Fringe groups among the demonstrators, numbering approximately 100, provoked two confrontations by throwing rocks at police on Friday night, November 14, and again on Saturday evening when rocks and paint bombs were used during an otherwise lawful assembly at the Justice Department. On both occasions, police used tear gas to disperse the crowds among which the extremists were mingled.

(The preceding discussion of the Weatherman and Moratorium demonstrations is summarized from reports, included as appendices to this chapter, prepared by Daniel Walker and Joseph R. Sahid.)

Fruitful lessons can be learned from these comparisons. The encouragement of First Amendment rights, coordination and cooperation with protest leaders, education of the police and the larger community into viewing peaceful demonstrations as a matter of right, will usually lead, at least at this point in our nation's history, to obtaining the cooperation of the great majority of those who have gathered to protest.

We do not mean to suggest that mass protest gatherings are static—that tactics should be identical as time passes and issues and personalities change. The actions of the "Weathermen" illustrate the danger in generalizations of any sort. Rather, the point is that in the area of mass demonstrations, where we all have so much to learn, it makes sense for those in authority to proceed cautiously, to avoid becoming rigid in outlook, and to employ force carefully.

A PROGRAM FOR THE FUTURE

The police must respond with the coolness and sound judgment they are expected and trained to exercise. They must discriminate between those relatively small numbers of individuals who instigate and engage in lawlessness and those who are innocent by-standers or merely caught up in the emotion of the event; and above all, they must not sacrifice the law or justice in the process of preserving and restoring order.[22]

There is no question that the police in the recent Chicago disorders—and this has also been true in many other cities—were subjected to intense provocation by some individuals ranging from vilification to injurious missiles. The average person confronted by that kind of abuse would not be expected to continue to exercise good judgment and restraint.

Nevertheless, it is incorrect to say that no riot control force can be expected to respond to intense provocation in a disciplined and restrained manner. The Walker Report concluded that the National Guard "apparently stood its ground without any significant response—physical or verbal—to the demonstrators, despite the level of abuse that one guard official called 'unbelievable'." While there were instances of undisciplined reaction on the part of individual guardsmen, it appears that they were able to withstand considerable provocation. Similarly, members of the Washington, D.C., police force withstood intensely provocative conduct during the Counter-Inaugural Protest activities with little visible reaction.

This does not mean that the civil government should not act promptly and decisively against violations of its laws. As the Civil Disorders Commission stated:

Individuals cannot be permitted to endanger the public peace and safety, and public officials have a duty to make it clear that all just and necessary means to protect both will be used.

But the very essence of police professionalism—and all good police training programs, including Chicago's, stress this—demands that a police officer remain calm and impartial despite intense provocation.[23] As the Civil Disorders Commission stated:

Police discipline must be sufficiently strong so that an individual officer is not provoked into unilateral action. He must . . . avoid panic or the indiscriminate—and inflammatory—use of force that has sometimes occurred in the heat of disorders.

This kind of self discipline is essential in dealing with any tense situation and especially in controlling a demonstration or a disorder. As the FBI riot control manual states:

The basic rule, when applying force, is to use only the minimum force necessary to effectively control the situation. Unwarranted application of force will incite the mob to further violence, as well as kindle seeds of resentment for police that, in turn, could cause a riot to recur.

Policemen do not operate in a vacuum, but in a context of strong human emotions. It is easy to understand how members of a police force can get angry after having people swear and throw rocks at them. But few "law and order" advocates take the time to imagine how they would react if policemen clubbed and beat their friends, wives, or daughters simply because of their color, their clothes, or the fact that someone else nearby had committed an illegal act. Yet who has not felt anger at receiving what he considers an unjustifiable traffic ticket? One commentator captured the phenomenon by asking the rhetorical question, "Can anything be more frustrating to an American than to be beaten and otherwise mistreated by the very authorities who have been entrusted with a monopoly of physical force . . .?"[24]

America's younger generation may indeed be the most peaceloving and rational this country has ever enjoyed. Should we not pause when, as in Chicago, hundreds of young idealists are driven to join their less rational compatriots in hurling abuse and rocks at "Friendly Officer John"? Should we not ask why the chain of events has taken place rather than condemn thoughtlessly? For hundreds of our nation's best educated youths to shout obscenities at duly constituted law enforcement officials is such a bizarre phenomenon that it is hard to believe that it actually took place.

The provocative acts by a handful of radical extremists in Chicago and the vicious battles with policemen in Cleveland and elsewhere create a real danger that a few people will succeed in provoking the police and civil officials into employing brutal and repressive measures which will alienate moderates in the community and create in this country the very kind of dangerous insurgency which other countries have experienced. It is imperative that police and public officials avoid falling into this trap. For the tactics and pattern of deliberate terrorism and guerrilla-type activities which seem to be starting to emerge follow the classical development of a revolutionary movement. It could lead to an urban insurgency that would have far-reaching consequences for all Americans, white and black, rural and urban.

The history of groups with severe, legitimate grievances has demonstrated again and again that when a radical element seeks the leadership it first attempts to organize the bulk of the grievance group into a supporting and protective force. To win this kind of majority support, they will try to alienate the grievance group from the community. This will be done through a variety of demands and actions that will cause the general community, which fails to differentiate between the radical and moderate membership, to become hostile to all of the grievance group. In other countries confronted by civil unrest arising from legitimate grievances by significant segments of the population, riots and organized violence have been effective techniques employed by extremist groups both to radicalize those demanding social, economic or political change as well as to goad the authorities into overreacting with indiscriminate and excessive force. These attacks have been directed against vital installations such as power, telephone, water and transportation systems, for the purpose of disrupting and paralyzing the normal processes of government and of the community. Attacks have also been launched against the institutions of the ruling society—schools, shopping centers, government buildings—and prominent individuals.

The normal and traditional reactions of those attacked has been to urge a policy of stern repression and to refuse to respond to any of the demands until the violence stops and order is restored. But this is the very response that the radical leadership has sought to evoke. By manipulating the outraged reaction of the community and the police into retaliatory measures which will alienate those seeking redress of legitimate grievances, they will then be more successful in persuading the aggrieved that they cannot achieve their objectives through peaceful, evolutionary means within the system; that their only hope of effecting change is to resort to violence and revolution.

The American people had a chance to observe a limited version of this tactic in action at San Francisco State College

361

this past year.[25] Starting with a small number of black students who engaged in minor forms of disruption, the ensuing battle resulted in a mobilization of student opinion overwhelmingly in sympathy with the demands of the original minority. One of the leaders of the strike explained the tactic before the strike began:

> It just so happens that the members of the BSU Central Committee have been analyzing how student movements have been functioning. Taking over buildings, holding it for two or three days, and then the thing is dead. Most of your leaders are ripped off and thrown in jail, or the masses are thrown in jail, and there's no one to lead them. From our analysis of this, we think we have developed a technique to deal with this for a prolonged struggle. We call it the war of the flea . . . what does the flea do? He bites, sucks blood from the dog, the dog bites. What happens when there are enough fleas on a dog? What will he do? He moves. He moves away. He moves on. And what the man has been running down on us, he's psyched us out, in terms of our manhood. He'll say, what you gone do, nigger? You tryin' to be a man, here he is with shotguns, billy clubs, .357 magnums, and all you got is heart. Defenseless. That's not the way it's going to go any more. We are the people. We are the majority and the pigs cannot be everywhere, everyplace all the time. And where they are not, we are. And something happens. The philosophy of the flea. You just begin to wear them down. Something is always costin' them. You can dig it . . . something happens all the time. Toilets are stopped up. Pipes is out.
> Water in the bathroom is just runnin' all over the place. Smoke is coming out of the bathroom. "I don't know nothin' about it. I'm on my way to take an exam. Don't look at me. . . ." When the pig comes down full force, ain't nothin' happening. He retreats. When they split, it goes on and on and on. . . .[26]

Governor Ronald Reagan and the Board of Trustees predictably refused to deal with the student demands until "order" had been restored. This refusal to deal promptly with the merits of the strike antagonized moderate students and faculty, who, although they disagreed with the strikers' "tactics," agreed in whole or in part with their demands.

Nevertheless, support for the strike began to wane until only several hundred students were actively involved. The real mobilization of student opinion occurred only after a unit of the police tactical squad blundered into a club-swinging confrontation with students, many of whom were uninvolved in the strike. According to the Orrick Report, this was the "turning point" of the strike, resulting "in an almost classic pattern of escalation."[27] By the end of the day the strike had been turned into an undertaking supported by thousands of students. Normalcy was not restored until significant concessions were made to the strikers' demands.

Studies made of urban insurgencies in other countries have shown that it is very difficult to destroy an urban resistance movement in a divided country.[28] The amount of ruthlessness which the police must employ to crush such an insurgency would become publicly intolerable, even though the provocation consists of various forms of terror and sabotage that outrages responsible people.

History has shown that the temporary order achieved by employing methods of force which are excessive or inappropriate in their nature is likely to be won at too high a price in terms of a divided and bitter citizenry and an unstable civil peace. The self-defeating effect of force which the community regards as excessive or unjustified has been demonstrated over and over again. This has been true not only in this country but abroad as well. It was the brutal physical force used by the Paris riot control forces against the rebellious students that mobilized public sympathy and support and turned a relatively minor riot into a major disaster that paralyzed all France during May of 1968. It was the ruthless treatment of Irish rebels that led to a universal outcry against the Black and Tans and created popular support for the movement. It was the repressive measures employed by the French against the Algerian rebels that led to public revulsion in France, and enabled the Algerian revolutionaries to achieve their victory over superior French police and military forces. It was the inhumaneness of police dogs and cattle prods used against peaceful black Americans in the streets of Selma which prompted the passage of civil rights legislation. It was the excessive use of police force and the failure to discriminate between innocent and guilty parties during the recent Chicago incidents that led to increased disaffection among many students and other young persons. It was the brutality exhibited by policemen at Columbia, Harvard, San Francisco State, and the shotgunning of unarmed students attempting to maintain their park in Berkeley (which resulted in numerous injuries and the death of a young man) which prompted mass, angry demonstrations and resulted in repulsing large numbers of moderate members of the community.

The problem of the police in dealing with such deliberate

provocations and explosive situations coolly and intelligently is tremendously complicated by the fact that in the United States today there are more guns in the hands of individual citizens, black and white, than in the hands of *all* the police, *all* the National Guards and *all* the U.S. armed forces *combined*. The private arsenal has grown since the summer of 1967. Reports are rampant of weapons stockpiling by vigilante groups as well as black militants.[29] Firearm sales have skyrocketed in communities which experienced disorders, such as Detroit. The potential for counter-violence and increased disorder inherent in this fantastic arsenal of privately owned weapons must be taken into account by every official responsible for the public safety.

We do not mean to imply that the forces of discontent have reached a level of intensity which presents such serious danger. Few serious "revolutionaries" exist in our country, despite the attention which they are given by the mass media and the general public. More often than not, the self-styled "revolutionaries" in reality are simply engaging in theatrics designed to attract attention to their grievances.

Nevertheless, we must anticipate other acts of lawlessness and terrorism to occur in various parts of our country which the radical extremists on both sides will try to exploit to their own advantage and objective. The immediate security problem will require necessary measures that will enable the police and civil authorities to distinguish among those who seriously wish violently to disrupt, those who engage in disruptive conduct out of fear and frustration, and those who wish to participate in peaceful protest and demonstration.

A critical ingredient to the success and effectiveness in coping with these control problems is good intelligence. It is essential that the police possess an intelligence system which enables them to measure with precision the real threat to the community posed by individuals and groups. They must not mislead officials by crying "Wolf!" each time a self-proclaimed revolutionary urges that "something must be done."

Nor should such intelligence be gathered at the expense of the civil rights and privacy of dozens of law-abiding people who happen to disagree with the current policies of our government. Information currently maintained on "suspect" individuals, such as storing on a computer names of people who signed a petition critical of the Vietnam war effort, has no place in our society. That form of intelligence gathering frightens individuals who fear the misuse of the data and thus forego engaging in such lawful forms of protest.[30] More reliable data could be gathered by maintaining good public relations and establishing mutual confidence and respect with the broad mass of community residents who want order and oppose violence and lawlessness.

It will also require proper and intelligent responses to those who believe they have legitimate grievances and wish to exercise their constitutional rights to protest or demonstrate peacefully. Failure to recognize and protect such rights will only benefit the extremists. As the FBI states in its manual on riot control:

> A peaceful or lawful demonstration should not be looked upon with disapproval by a police agency; rather, it should be considered as a safety valve possibly serving to prevent a riot. The police agency should not countenance violations of law. However, a police agency does not have the right to deny the demonstrator his constitutional rights.

Despite the best precautions and no matter how effective the counter-measures are, violent events are a risk that must be anticipated. Consequently, planning for such contingencies must be designed to limit the nature and extent of the damage and to enable the community to continue to function satisfactorily.

We must recognize that the preservation of civil peace cannot and should not be regarded as merely a control problem better left to the police. It is the responsibility of the entire community, in particular of its duly elected public officials. For the demonstrations and the disorders which we are experiencing are manifestations of deep and difficult social, political and economic problems. They cannot be solved, much less long contained, by police power alone, no matter how enlightened and judicious that may be.

Police officials are understandably reluctant to relinquish the authority that has devolved on them by default to deal with mass disorders. They resent intrusion into what they consider their professional domain by elected officials who do not share their own professional background and experience. Often, attempts by elected officials to regain their rightful place as de facto as well as de jure heads of police departments have been met with resistance and sometimes irreconcilable conflict.[31]

This form of resistance must not be allowed to subvert elected officials. Only government officials who feel the pulse of the community in all its various manifestations are capable of deploying effectively not only police resources, but other community resources, such as social workers, human rights councils, housing inspectors, and others, who can deal with the grievances which may initially spark a confrontation. In later stages, only the chief elected official has the authority to deploy and coordinate fire-fighting units, courtroom personnel, as well as the police. To look at the problem as only a police problem is shortsighted.

This is not meant to imply, of course, that policemen are always and necessarily less astute than elected officials, or that the intervention of elected officials will always and necessarily lead to more enlightened law enforcement. In fact, the result may sometimes be quite the opposite. Besieged by a backlash of public opinion, elected officials may be less able to deal fairly with a dissident group than would a professional chief of police removed from the political arena. But this observation does not substantially weaken the force of our general recommendation, since it merely restates a problem inherent in a democracy.

Washington, D.C., has made significant strides toward centralizing in the hands of its Mayor the responsibility for dealing with civil disorders. Following the disorders that accompanied the assassination of Martin Luther King, Mayor Walter Washington established a command post which operates around the clock and which serves as his office during an actual civil emergency.

Inside the Command Post a sophisticated array of communications equipment links the staff with the outside world, enabling them to monitor events and control available resources instantaneously. Efforts are made to resolve community grievances breeding hostility. Advance intelligence pinpoints potential trouble spots throughout the city and observers dispatched to the scene keep the staff informed on the situation.

Events likely to precipitate tension, such as shootings involving policemen, are immediately brought to the attention of the Mayor and other city officials. The Commissioner of Human Rights is immediately dispatched to the scene.

A disorder which escalates brings the Mayor to the Command Post. From his desk he can watch the event on four television sets, listen to police and commercial radio broadcasts, examine maps of the trouble zone, and receive instantaneous messages from observers in the field and officials of the city and federal governments. By pressing a button he can have conference calls with every relevant official in the city, federal government, military, and neighboring communities. From his desk, his home, or his car, he can broadcast over every Washington AM and FM radio station by pressing another button.

Everything occurring at the Command Post is recorded for future reference. Studies are constantly made to modify procedures and update techniques.

The result of this planning has been heartening. Despite the underlying tension in the community, Washington has enjoyed a year of relative calm. Disorders have been handled effectively and with moderation.

The dangers ahead do not come only from the radicals of the left who are seeking to change the established system and its institutions. There is an equal potential for violence and destruction among the radical minority of the right who militantly oppose any concessions to the grievance group. The history of our own country is replete with examples of such extremists who have turned to counter-terror as a means of retribution and preservation of the status quo.

In his testimony before the commission, Dr. Richard Maxwell Brown reviewed the conditions that historically have produced vigilantism. An analysis of the current climate in the United States led Professor Brown to warn the Commission that "a new wave of vigilantism is a real prospect today." If the hard-core of extremists on the right, who are today actively organizing, arming, and threatening to take the law into their own hands, should do so, they will contribute to the very same polarization and chain of violence that the hard-core extremists on the left are working so hard to accomplish.

It is easy to understand the daily frustrations police officers must live with in fighting a losing battle against the rising incidence of crime and of trying to maintain the civil peace in an environment of tension and hostility which is directed against the institutions a policeman has been taught to respect and value. It is equally understandable how fearful and angry so many Americans feel over their sense of physical insecurity for themselves and their families, and their apprehension and outrage against group violence that has accompanied many civil disorders.

None of us should forget, however, that real security of persons and property in our cities and the preservation of the civil peace will only be meaningful if they are achieved in a way that is consistent with the values of a democratic society. This will require order that is maintained under the law and with justice. Justice in this respect is not simply a semantic embellishment. It is the way chosen by our founding fathers to insure that groups who feel themselves outside the mainstream never become so alienated that they resort to violence. In that respect, this Nation differs from most nations in the world. Because of it, we have experienced an existence of relative peacefulness. We should not sacrifice the best of our heritage amid the growing public-clamor to remove the thorns of disenchantment from the nation's side.

A PROPOSED FEDERAL REMEDY

Since the 1930's, the people of the United States have frequently turned to the Federal Government for remedial action in matters ranging from control of the economy to the exercise of Constitutional rights. The civil rights acts of recent years provide specific federal remedies for private interference with other constitutional rights, such as the right to employment, housing, travel and use of public accommodations and commercial establishments free of discrimination because of race, religion or national origin, the right to vote and participate in any federally assisted program, and the right to carry on a business free of intimidation or injury during a riot or civil disorder. Yet, at the present time of crisis, during which the denial of First Amendment rights has led to intense polarization and violence, we limp along slowly trying to resolve these matters in an unsystematized way.

It would appear to be an equally valid and justified exercise of Congressional power to provide a specific federal judicial remedy for unlawful interference with the rights of speech, assembly, petition and free passage incidental thereto. The precedents of our history commend a new federal law which would (1) empower the federal government to seek judicial redress (especially injunctive relief) for unlawful interference with First Amendment rights, and (2) authorize an agency of the government to investigate the extent to which First Amendment rights are secured.

Although private individuals may presently seek redress under 42 U.S.C. 1983, a Reconstruction era statute creating liability for "deprivation of any rights, privileges, or immunities secured by the Constitution and laws" by any person "under color of" state law,[32] private parties are not always suitable litigants in the First Amendment forum. Litigation is costly. In addition, in the area of free speech, not all invasions have a direct individual effect and the broader, possibly more indirect deprivations of rights may go unchecked. Similarly, where a deprivation of rights may lead to violence, the interests of the public should not be left to private litigation. Additionally, private litigants, although possibly correct in their interpretations of events, often have difficulty persuading courts of the soundness of their position when faced with contradictory statements of duly constituted law enforcement officials.

In recent civil rights and voting rights legislation, Congress has made the Attorney General an increasingly active figure in protecting certain vital individual rights. This approach seems particularly appropriate for the protection of First Amendment rights, also.

New legislation should give the Attorney General broad authority to commence, or intervene in, civil actions brought against public officials to protect freedom of expression whether that expression is endangered by the denial of permits, the unnecessary use of police force, or the interference with publications promulgated by dissident groups. Incident to that power, the Justice Department would automatically have the authority to investigate alleged interference with First Amendment rights. The Department would become a powerful force seeking immediate, informal resolution of potential confrontations involving freedom of expression. Where confrontation appears inevitable, the Department would be able to resort to the courts promptly, provide essential factual material and help in other ways to make the courts a more effective forum for resolving First Amendment conflicts.

The federal government, perhaps through the Civil Rights Commission, should also undertake to collect and study information on developments relating to freedom of expression and establish a national clearing house for such information. It should undertake the review and development of legislation and policy guidelines—at the state and local as well as federal level—in the area of First Amendment rights.

Additional questions will exist regardless of who is to administer the proposed statute. Protection for the press and other media, for example, should also be granted. Federal courts must be able to respond quickly enough in the normal course of litigation to insure that rights are not abandoned due to lapse of time.

These problems, and no doubt many others, must be resolved before new federal protection for freedom of expression can be enacted. But we believe such protection is plainly necessary, and we hope this proposal advances its course.

APPENDIX A

CHICAGO AND THE "WEATHERMAN"

On Wednesday, October 8, 1969, a four-day series of demonstrations began in Chicago, organized and led by the so-called "Weatherman" faction of the Students for a Democratic Society (SDS). This faction, also known as RYM I (Radical Youth Movement I), takes its name from a song lyric by Bob Dylan ". . . you don't need a weatherman to tell which way the wind blows . . ."). Mark Rudd of New Jersey is generally acknowledged as the leader of the "Weatherman," and the faction is considered to be on the extreme left fringe of the current activist political spectrum by virtue of its tolerance and endorsement of violence as a necessary vehicle for social change.

There were a number of explanations for the timing of the demonstrations. The most widely held view was that the date, October 8, coincided with the second anniversary of the death of Cuban revolutionary leader Che Guevera, whose ideas of exporting and fomenting violent revolution apparently had a substantial following among the "Weatherman." Another explanation advanced was the desire to discredit the Vietnam Moratorium Day planned for October 15, which observance was being led by groups emphasizing nonviolence.

The objectives of the demonstrations were also varied. The stated aim was to "bring the war home" through engaging in violent conduct, thereby graphically illustrating to the people of Chicago the violence of the war in Vietnam. Another reported objective was to hold a protest demonstration at the residence of Federal Judge Julius J. Hoffman. Judge Hoffman was presiding judge at the conspiracy trial of the "Chicago 8," accused of violating federal anti-riot laws during the 1968 Democratic Convention. The "Weatherman" also sought, without success, to enlist the support of the Black Panther Party, a militant black organization, in this demon-

---

*This report was prepared by Daniel Walker of Chicago, Illinois.

371

stration against Judge Hoffman. Bobby Seale, a Black Panther leader, was then one of the "Chicago 8."

THE WEDNESDAY EVENING DEMONSTRATION

Late Wednesday afternoon, a group of less than one hundred "Weatherman" members assembled at Armitage and Fullerton on the Near North Side. From there they walked without incident to Lincoln Park, arriving just after dusk. They gathered in the south end of the park, around a bonfire made with wood they had brought and wood they had obtained by destroying some of the benches in the park. By eight o'clock, the crowd around the bonfire had grown to about two hundred and several anti-war banners and placards were visible in the crowd. A variety of speakers took turns addressing the crowd, and their speeches alternated with anti-war chants and revolutionary slogans (e.g., "The only direction is insurrection," "the only solution is revolution").

As the evening wore on, the size of the crowd at the bonfire remained steady at about two hundred, with several smaller groups of a dozen or so persons congregating around fires ignited in trash baskets or on the ground. A number of photographers were taking flash pictures of the crowd, but the majority of the news media people present seemed to be keeping near their vehicles at the southwestern edge of the park.

There were no policemen visible in the park. The nearest policemen were stationed to the north, near the Cultural Arts Building on North Lincoln Avenue, and to the west along North Avenue. About three hundred policemen had been deployed in the Lincoln Park area, and most were anticipating a rumored demonstration through the Old Town area, particularly Wells Street.

At approximately 10:30, about two hundred demonstrators ran out of the park and into the intersection of Clark and North. There was a good deal of yelling and shouting, but above it all there was suddenly the first sound of breaking glass as someone threw something through the plate glass window of the North Federal Savings Building. The crowd moved south on Clark Street, avoiding the area to the west where the police were waiting. The police appeared to be caught momentarily out of position, and the crowd surged down Clark Street virtually unopposed. Many, if not most, of the demonstrators had emerged from the park carrying heavy sticks or rocks, and they used these weapons indiscriminately on windows of nearby buildings and parked cars.

Farther down Clark Street the crowd split into several groups, one moving east on Schiller, another east on Goethe, while a third continued south on Clark to Division Street. At Division, this last group met a police barricade, and a brief scuffle resulted in a number of arrests. The rest of this group retreated back up Clark Street and moved east on Goethe, rejoining the demonstrators that had split off earlier, and together the crowd moved south on State Street toward Division, where another barricade of five police vehicles waited. The police and demonstrators clashed. Numerous storefront windows at the intersection were smashed, many rocks were thrown and many persons were arrested. The police acted swiftly to load those arrested into assembled squadrols and within a few minutes the intersection was cleared.

After this confrontation, the body of demonstrators broke up into numerous small groups roaming the streets between Lake Shore Drive and Clark Street from Division Street to Lincoln Park. Another clash between police and demonstrators took place in the 1200 block of North Lake Shore Drive, where incidents of rock throwing and window smashing occurred. More arrests were made there.

It was now close to midnight. The violence seemed to be over, and the majority of the people in the streets were curious onlookers and residents. At least one neighborhood resident sought to start a discussion with a demonstrator who had apparently just damaged some nearby property. She asked him, "We're both against the war, but how are you helping to end it?" The young man gave no answer as he was led into a squadrol by two policemen.

Most of the demonstrators filtered back to the north, toward Lincoln Park, but no groups of demonstrators actually reentered the park, perhaps out of fear of arrest by the police, who by that time had assembled in force at the southwest edge of the park. At least one group of demonstrators did reassemble near Wells Street and Menomonee Street, where a police car reportedly drove into a group of about 120 people. This was followed by more rock throwing and window smashing in the area, and at least one automobile was overturned and damaged. This was the final reported incident.

By twelve-thirty, the Near North Side was quiet, and the only people in Lincoln Park were policemen, newsmen and curious bystanders. From start to finish, the violence had lasted about two hours.

Statistically, the events of Wednesday evening gave mute testimony of the "Weatherman" propensity for violence. In addition to the property damage, over twenty policemen were injured, and an unknown number of civilians was injured (three reportedly suffering superficial gunshot wounds). Almost one hundred persons were arrested.

THE THURSDAY DEMONSTRATIONS

Thursday, October 9, the second day of the "Weatherman" demonstrations, was a day of relative calm. The only reported demonstrations took place in Grant Park, where a planned rally of female "Weatherman" members drew only about seventy persons. The rally was to be the jumping off point for a protest march to the Armed Forces Induction Center at 615 W. Van Buren Street.

Police lines at Michigan and Balboa met the protesters as they tried to leave the park. The police refused to let the demonstrators through until those among them who were carrying large sticks disposed of them. At least ten arrests were made as some of the women scuffled with police. Among those arrested was Bernadine Dohrn, one of the national officers of SDS. The demonstrators finally complied with the police order to dispose of their "weapons" and were allowed through the police line. Once through, however, the group did not continue its planned march, but instead broke up and dispersed in the Loop.

FRIDAY: A PEACEFUL DEMONSTRATION BY RYM II

Friday, October 10, was another quiet day. The "Weatherman" did not stage any demonstrations, but there was a demonstration by the more moderate faction of SDS, known as RYM II. This was a peaceful demonstration at the Cook County Hospital, held to protest "anti-people" health care. At the demonstration, SDS members listened to speeches and engaged in discussions and arguments with hospital personnel. Almost one hundred policemen were on hand but there were no confrontations and no arrests.

Perhaps the most significant development Friday was the press conference held jointly by the Young Lords, a Puerto Rican group, the Black Panthers and the RYM II faction of

374

SDS. The three groups indicated that they planned to participate jointly in an anti-war march the next day from Armitage and Halstead Streets to Humboldt Park. They also joined in denouncing the violent rampage of the "Weatherman" on the previous Wednesday night and promised their demonstration would be a peaceful one.

SATURDAY: MORE "WEATHERMAN" VIOLENCE

Saturday was the climactic day for the "Weatherman." They had obtained a city permit for a march from Haymarket Square to Grant Park. The route of march took them directly through the heart of the Loop. The demonstration began about noon with a rally at Haymarket Square, scene of a recent dynamiting that destroyed the statue of a policeman commemorating the famous Haymarket riots. Four persons were arrested at the rally, including Mark Rudd. The march itself began with about two hundred and fifty persons moving down Randolph Street, east from the Kennedy Expressway. They turned south on LaSalle and then east on Madison. At Madison and LaSalle, the window smashing started, and violent clashes between police and demonstrators erupted. A number of store windows were broken as the marchers proceeded east on Madison. At Madison and Dearborn, Assistant Corporation Counsel Richard Elrod suffered a neck injury which left him paralyzed. Seven policemen, an assistant states attorney and one demonstrator were reported injured at that same intersection. As a result of the outbreak of violence, one hundred and fifty Illinois National Guardsmen, who had been standing by, were sent into the area to aid the police. Clashes between demonstrators and police continued along Madison and nearby streets.

The violence in the Loop lasted about one hour. When it was over, those demonstrators who had not been arrested made their way to Grant Park, where they gathered around the Logan statue. Police and National Guardsmen on Michigan Avenue kept close watch on them, but no further violence occurred. This group dispersed later in the afternoon.

The police made one hundred and three arrests in the Loop, and twenty-seven policemen were injured. About twenty demonstrators were reported injured, as were an unknown number of bystanders.

Saturday saw a clear example of the significant contrast between the two factions in the SDS. While the "Weatherman" were smashing glass and injuring people in the Loop,

RYM II was conducting its peaceful march in conjunction with the Young Lords and the Black Panthers. That march was from Halsted and Armitage, site of the so-called "Peoples Park," to Humboldt Park, at Division and California, a distance of about four miles. The march was made without a city permit and therefore was technically illegal, since the marchers, numbering close to 500, paraded in the streets and blocked traffic along the entire route. Nevertheless, the police on hand, led by Deputy Chief Robert Lynsky, did not block the march and no incidents of violence or confrontation took place. The march ended at Humboldt Park with the crowd listening to speeches by members of the participating groups. Following the speeches, the marchers dispersed peacefully.

POLICE PERFORMANCE DURING THE FOUR DAYS

During the entire four days of demonstrations, the command control exercised by police sergeants and lieutenants on the streets was complete and unchallenged. No policemen were observed without their badges and nameplates, and their general demeanor was relaxed and professional. Illustrative of this pragmatic and flexible approach was the remark made to a news reporter by one of the assistant city corporation counsels early Wednesday night. The reporter asked if demonstrators would be allowed to stay in Lincoln Park after the 11:00 p.m. park closing time. The city official replied that the police would not make an issue of it and that if by two or three o'clock in the morning there were no more than twenty-five or thirty persons in the park, only then would arrests be made. His explanation for the change in tactics from the Democratic Convention was "we all learn from our mistakes."

In dealing with crowds of onlookers, police were conscious of the distinction between lawbreakers and bystanders, and no indiscriminate beatings of residents, bystanders or newsmen were reported. On the contrary, the police took steps to see to it that innocent bystanders would not be involved in any violence. On Wednesday night, for example, curious onlookers had gathered at the intersection of Schiller and State Street where about a dozen policemen and two squadrols were stationed. The policemen took pains repeatedly to courteously ask the crowd to move on, and explained that if the demonstrators did return the police did not want to see the bystanders caught in the middle. Within a short time, the crowd dispersed in an orderly fashion.

376

When police confronted persons causing injury or damaging property, they made arrests quickly and with a minimum of force. They used their vehicles wisely as barricades to keep the violence from spreading and they dispersed the demonstrators into small groups.

In the face of provocation, they used restraint, and in many cases they refrained from acting at all until they had assembled sufficient strength to assure complete control of a given situation. While this may have permitted some additional damage to property, particularly on Wednesday night, it averted the danger of policemen being surrounded or outnumbered and resorting to the use of lethal force. When the violence threatened to get out of hand, as it did in the Loop on Saturday, the police were swift to call upon the National Guard for assistance and as a result, the police were able to prevent additional violence. In short, the police put to good use all the proven tactics of crowd control.

The toll of damage and injury during the four days was high. Thousands of dollars in property damage was done, mainly in the Near North Side on Wednesday night. Almost three hundred persons were arrested. Forty-eight policemen were reported injured, and Richard Elrod remains paralyzed at this writing. An unknown number of demonstrators was injured. Given the avowed aim of the "Weathermen" to incite violence, the situation could have been much worse, and much of the credit for preventing that must go to the Chicago Police Department.

APPENDIX B

WASHINGTON AND THE NOVEMBER
MORATORIUM*

The November 13–15, 1969, Moratorium activities in Washington, D. C., gave new evidence that chaos or order is often a consequence determined in advance by the agencies of law enforcement.

PERMIT NEGOTIATIONS

The November Moratorium had been some months in the planning. It was billed by its sponsors, who included the same groups that had planned the 1967 Pentagon Demonstration, the 1968 Democratic Convention protest, the January 1969, Counter-Inaugural activities, and the October 15, 1969, Moratorium, as a mass protest gathering in Washington. The Moratorium leaders predicted in advance that 200,000 demonstrators would appear in Washington. They opened negotiations with city and federal officials on October 16, attempting to secure permits for numerous activities which would consume the better part of three days.

The negotiations focused on a mass march which the demonstrators hoped to schedule for Saturday, November 15. The march was to be the highlight of the Moratorium, involving the thousands of demonstrators who were expected to arrive on Friday, November 14, and on Saturday morning. Publicity and organization for this march had begun at colleges and universities throughout the eastern half of the country as early as the beginning of the 1969–70 school year. Logistics for transporting the demonstrators to Washington for this event, and housing and feeding them on their arrival consumed weeks of planning by hundreds of people.

The Administration, acting through the Department of Justice, obstinately refused to grant the desired permit for this march. It had received information, similar to that received prior to the Democratic Convention and the Counter-

---

*This report was prepared by Joseph R. Sahid.

378

Inaugural, indicating that violent activity was planned by unidentified numbers of demonstrators. On the basis of this information, Administration spokesmen claimed that the grant of a permit would lead to violence and disruption in the streets of Washington.

Frustration and anger were the reaction of many of the leaders of the demonstration. They pointed out that their motives were to schedule a peaceful demonstration; that they had received pledges of nonviolence from nearly all of the expected participating groups; that the October 15 Moratorium had been completely peaceful; and that arrangements had reached the point that thousands of demonstrators were planning to come to Washington even if a permit were not granted. They made clear that they could not guarantee the peacefulness of the protest if they were denied the opportunity to channel the protest into organized forms.

At this point, the Moratorium captured the attention of the national media with a vengeance. Reports of violence were rampant. Administration spokesmen talked of stopping the protesters with troops, and meaning was given to their statements by widely publicized accounts of National Guard units and federal troops massing and training for riot duty in Washington. Demonstrators and newsmen noted the similarity between this publicity campaign and the publicity campaign which had preceded the Democratic National Convention, alleging that the Administration's prediction of violence would become a self-fulfilling prophecy.

The mood was broken only by the intervention of numerous individuals, such as Mayor Walter Washington of the District of Columbia, who urged members of the Administration to grant the desired permits as an alternative to the confrontation which seemed inevitable. The Administration relented, and a permit for a march along Pennsylvania Avenue was belatedly granted within a week of the march. Tension cooled considerably, and final preparations were made for what was to prove the largest political demonstration in the history of the United States.

Much speculation exists as to why the Administration delayed so long in granting the permit. An informed source inside the government has suggested two reasons: a desire to discourage participants from coming to Washington and a desire to add confusion to the demonstrators' planning. Although it is impossible to document these motives, manifestations of these motives appeared in other forms. Thus, it was reported that government agents approached managers of bus companies who had contracted to transport demonstrators to Washington, urging them to cancel the arrangement in an effort to minimize the potential for "violence."

MAJOR EVENTS OF THE MORATORIUM

The demonstration itself was overwhelmingly peaceful. During a forty-hour vigil beginning Thursday evening, November 13, forty thousand demonstrators marched single-file past the White House carrying names of American soldiers killed in Vietnam. No disruptive incidents occurred. The Saturday march, which involved nearly a half million people, was completed almost without incident. The rally at the Washington Monument grounds at the conclusion of the march also occurred without incident. Despite the bitter cold, often uncomfortable living conditions, rain and sleet, and the long and uncomfortable journeys which brought the demonstrators to Washington, their mood was relaxed and purposeful.

Extensive security preparations had been made for the event. The Washington police force, and especially the Civil Disturbance Unit, had prepared and trained carefully. Although not requested by city officials, the Department of Justice imported thousands of Army and National Guard personnel. They were positioned, sometimes conspicuously, in federal buildings and other locations throughout the city. A solid ring of buses surrounded the White House. They served as a blockade as well as a shield behind which policemen were stationed out of the demonstrators' view. Troops were located on rooftops as observers, and helicopters circled the sky.

Yet the bulk of the actual work of maintaining discipline was performed not by police and troops, but by the demonstrators themselves. An estimated five thousand "marshals," who were nothing more than male and female demonstrators with identifying armbands, and who had been trained by the protest officials in principles of nonviolent crowd control, flanked the crowds throughout the duration of the demonstration. Friendly and casual in their attitude, they soon won the admiration of the police as well as maintaining the respect of the demonstrators. Never pushing, never shouting. never ordering, they managed to move the massive crowds with a minimum of intrusion into the sensibilities of the demonstrators, who, like themselves, were either college students or more mature adults.

380

MINOR DISORDERS BY SPLINTER GROUPS

One incident of disorder during the Saturday parade captures the reason why the marshals received such praise. Prior to the parade, march officials had reason to believe that a small number of radical "revolutionaries," who label themselves Weathermen, Mad Dogs, and Crazies, would attempt to leave the line of march to reach the White House. The expected break occurred as approximately 100 members of these groups began marching on the side of Pennsylvania Avenue from which demonstrators had been excluded, chanting "Ho, Ho, Ho Chi Min, the NLF is gonna win." Carrying Vietcong flags, this group menaced the entire parade as they moved toward 15th Street, where the line of march turned left away from the White House.

Acting on instructions, the scattered policemen along the line of march ignored this group. As the dissidents moved toward the White House, marshals quietly formed into successive lines, linking arms across Pennsylvania Avenue to block them. The dissidents succeeded in breaking through the first line of marshals, but were eventually halted by the remaining lines. The marshals were calm and quiet and completely nonviolent, maintaining their linked-arm stance. The dissidents eventually faded back into the line of march.

Throughout the encounter, the Deputy Chief of Police in charge of the Civil Disturbance Unit stood by and observed. Additional policemen were never summoned to the scene. The march continued normally.

This same group of dissidents precipitated relatively minor incidents on Friday and Saturday evenings at events which had been scheduled by them and not by the organizers of the Moratorium. It was on these occasions that the police used tear gas, minor injuries were suffered and numbers of arrests were made. On both occasions, police responded to acts of misconduct by a limited number of demonstrators, such as the throwing of rocks and firecrackers, by releasing chemical gas. Actual physical contact between demonstrators and police was almost nonexistent because of the use of the gas. Almost no clubbings resulted. Yet on both occasions, police operations manifested the Achilles heel of the crowd control: communication between police superiors and their subordinates proved inadequate. As a result, these episodes may have continued longer and been more intense than they otherwise might have been.

THE DUPONT CIRCLE EPISODE

On Friday night, the dissidents gathered at Dupont Circle and attempted to march to the Vietnamese Embassy several blocks away. They had been granted a permit for the rally but not for the march. As the marchers neared the embassy, the police, who had been formed into a line, blocked their way. The events of the next few minutes are not clear, but it appears that several marchers threw rocks at the police and that the police responded with tear gas.

The incident was not major, although the Chief of Police later stated that use of the tear gas may have been premature. In any event, after consultation with city officials and demonstration leaders, the Chief ordered members of the Civil Disturbance Unit to allow the demonstrators to congregate in Dupont Circle. A rock band was asked to come to the Circle to entertain the demonstrators. The mood was generally calm.

As the demonstrators returned to the Circle, three or four police cars carrying officers who were not members of the Civil Disturbance Unit appeared to greet them. Apparently out of communication with Chief Wilson, they threw tear gas into Dupont Circle and pushed and prodded demonstrators with their batons. The confusion peaked, demonstrators not knowing where to go. Several bystanders, including one of the members of the Violence Commission, were gassed without warning. Numerous windows were broken as the demonstrators roamed the streets, having been denied access to Dupont Circle.

THE JUSTICE DEPARTMENT EPISODE

Similar incidents marred Saturday evening. Approximately 5,000 demonstrators left the Washington Monument grounds, as the cast of "Hair" sang the theme song from their play, to protest the trial of the "Chicago 8" at the Justice Department building located about five blocks from the Monument. The area had been closed to traffic and they had a permit for the march. Misconduct similar to that of the evening before erupted after the marchers had peacefully protested for a time. The Chief of Police personally threw the first canister of tear gas as several dozen dissidents became unruly. Again, physical confrontation was avoided by use of the gas. The police, all members of the CDU, formed a solid line across

Constitution Avenue, attempting to disperse the demonstrators toward the Monument grounds.

Demonstrators maintained a respectable distance between themselves and the police, often as much as half a block. The initial tear gas caught many by surprise and incapacitated many marchers who were completely peaceful. Several marshals were also caught in the tear gas.

Many left after the initial burst of gas. The more radical group threw rocks, firecrackers, cherry bombs, and roman candles at the police and at the building. As the crowd reassembled, more tear gas was used to disperse them.

Most in the crowd that remained were curiosity seekers. Generally younger than the average demonstrator, the sense of excitement attracted them to the confrontation. Few were actually disruptive.

The radical 100, who had marched on the Vietnamese Embassy Friday night and broken ranks on Pennsylvania Avenue earlier Saturday, dedicated, experienced and trained, taunted the police, hurled objects, set trash cans on fire, destroyed park benches, and, aided by gas masks which they wore, hurled the tear gas canisters back at the police. The marshals tried to prevent chaos by urging demonstrators to walk rather than panic and run as the tear gas landed among them.

Police stationed along Constitution Avenue remained calm, donning their gas masks only as the gas drifted toward them. They wore soft hats and did not put their helmets on, nor did they unsheath their batons. As the retreat along Constitution Avenue began, these policemen chatted amicably with the demonstrators, indicating avenues of retreat, philosophizing with them about the disruption, and congratulating them for maintaining the dignity and peacefulness of the protest for the bulk of the activities.

The crowd retreated slowly; the policemen never broke ranks; the mood was not antagonistic. Although some people were bitter about having been caught unexpectedly by the first wave of gas, no real hatred was directed at the police. Shouts of "pig" were heard, but the motivation was more theatrical than real. Several radicals were even overheard praising the police restraint in their pauses between throwing rocks.

Predictably, however, confusion once again developed. Gas began drifting toward the speaker's platform at the Washington Monument, where a crowd of a few thousand people was still gathered. Protest leaders at the microphone reflected the disappointment they felt when they were forced to terminate the rally, urging the faithful to return to their buses to avoid the gas from the "bullshit" that was taking place two blocks away.

Ultimately dispersion occurred, filling the downtown section of Washington with thousands of stragglers. Small bands of very young dissidents roamed the streets with no apparent purpose, breaking windows in banks, department stores and government buildings as they went. Reminiscent of the Counter-Inaugural, this activity resembled a game of "cops-and-robbers," almost apolitical in motivation.

By this time an area of approximately three blocks in radius had been blocked off around the White House by police and some troops. The area behind the White House was still inundated with tear gas. Out-of-town groups attempting to locate their chartered buses were now and then confronted by policemen, and, on at least one occasion, teargassed. These and other instances of confusion prolonged the evening.

CONCLUDING OBSERVATIONS

Once the deadlock in permit negotiations was broken, all sides moved rapidly to lay the legal groundwork for the demonstrations. Close contact with the demonstrators, which included supplying Philip Hirschkop, attorney for the demonstrators, with a civil defense cruiser and direct communication links to the Mayor's Command Post, dissipated tension before it erupted into disorder. During the demonstrations, police and demonstrators remained calm and disciplined.

Aberrations occurred, but they were minor. Some fringe groups of demonstrators did throw rocks and some policemen did chase and beat demonstrators with their batons for no apparent reason. But police confusion resulted only when communications broke down between individual policemen and their supervisory officers.

Federal troops and National Guard units relieved policemen of some of their traffic control functions, but were never called to assist the police during the few instances of actual disorder.

When disorder occurred, physical confrontation was avoided almost totally by the use of chemical gas. Mace was never used. As a result, few injuries occurred and the mood of the demonstrators never really turned hostile, although limited hostility was apparent.

This basic peacefulness would not have been possible if the march permit had not been granted. By organizing and bureaucratizing the marchers, the marshals and the police were able to monitor the demonstrators and to terminate hostile actions before they erupted into disorder. Because the march was legalized, thousands of moderate demonstrators participated, who tended to stabilize the dissent. And all were generally satisfied with the arrangements. This absence of discontent created an environment in which peaceful protest could take place.

Nevertheless, the tactical decisions concerning timing and placement of the tear gas are open to constructive criticism. Tear gas was available to all members of the CDU and may well have been used indiscriminately by scattered policemen acting on the basis of their own opinions as to the necessity for its use. These individual decisions were occasionally at cross purposes, increasing rather than minimizing the chaos. Future incidents of this nature could be avoided by limiting the availability of tear gas to police officers of the rank of lieutenant and above who could maintain constant communication with their command centers.

For the basic purpose tear gas serves is to move crowds without physical confrontation. But a crowd must be moved to somewhere. Only higher ranking officials with adequate communications can intelligently decide where it is a crowd should be moved so as best to minimize further disruption.

These comments should not detract from the basic praise due to all parties directly involved. City officials, including Mayor Walter Washington, Deputy Mayor Thomas Fletcher, Police Chief Jerry Wilson and Assistant Corporation Counsel Mel Washington (who served as a roving troubleshooter and adviser during the activities); the demonstration leaders and planners, including Philip Hirschkop; the thousands of demonstration marshals and policemen who weathered the cold and the exhaustion; and the demonstrators themselves, who, in the final analysis, assured the peacefulness of the Moratorium—all deserve favorable comment.

POSTSCRIPT

We cannot ignore the fact that the anti-war movement, of which the November Moratorium is only one manifestation, will not end now that the march on Washington is a matter of history. The direction the movement takes is of vital concern to us all, determining what will happen in this country for many years after the Violence Commission has ceased to exist.

As the Commission's Task Force on Group Violence has outlined, the anit-war movement has evolved in response to the war itself and to the reception the protest movement has been given by those in positions of power. We can only assume that the November Moratorium and the response that Moratorium receives will influence the course of protest in the coming months.

The Moratorium was a peaceful event, inspiring to most people who participated. Those hundreds of thousands of people who came to Washington are even now passing the word to their friends and neighbors who did not come.

Many of those who came did not expect a sudden change in government policy because of their presence. But they did desire to register their views in an indelible way.

The response of the Administration was disappointing. By explicitly ignoring the protesters, by criticizing the minor disruptions without recognizing the inherent legitimacy of the protest as a protest, Administration spokesmen pushed many of those who came to Washington into a corner. For if the largest political demonstration in the history of the United States can be dismissed out of mind, without even a sign of recognition of the frustration that generated the demonstration, advocates of peaceful dissent will be forced to surrender their leadership to their more volatile counterparts. Already, at this writing, a disillusionment about peaceful dissent has engulfed many who came to Washington in peace. The uncertain mood of possible future violence as a "more effective" alternative fills the air.

We only hope this dismal prophesy never comes to pass.

REFERENCES

[1] Roy Pearson, "The Dilemma of Force," *Saturday Review,* Feb. 10, 1968, at 24.

[2] Erskine, "The Polls: Demonstrations and Race Riots," 31 *Public Opinion Quarterly* 655-677.

[3] June 7, 1968.

[4] Ted Gurr, *Why Men Rebel,* ch. 8, to be published by the Princeton University Press, Nov. 1969.

[5] See *e.g.,* Robert M. Fogelson, "From Dissent to Confrontation: The Police, the Negroes, and the Outbreak of the Nineteen Sixties Riots," 83 *Political Science Quarterly* 227 (June 1968).

[6] *Crisis at Columbia,* Report of the Fact-Finding Commission Appointed to Investigate the Disturbances at Columbia University

in April and May, 1968 (New York: Vintage Books, 1968) at 99-168; *Police on Campus: the Mass Police Action at Columbia University, Spring, 1968* (New York: American Civil Liberties Union, 1969).

[7] *Rights in Conflict,* A Report to the National Commission on the Cause and Prevention of Violence 53 (1968).

[8] See *id.* at viii, 31, 53.

[9] Although the Columbia disorders were preceded by a number of events, the precipitating incident occurred when a group of students occupied Hamilton Hill, a classroom building. Thereafter, the office of the university's president and several other campus buildings were occupied. The students announced three causes motivating the seizure and occupation of the buildings. These were: (1) opposition to a projected gym to be constructed in a Harlem park; (2) opposition to Columbia's relationship with the Institute of Defense Analysis, a warfare research organization; and (3) opposition to the disciplinary action taken by the university as a result of its ban on indoor demonstrations. Efforts at mediating the dispute and persuading the protesting students to leave the buildings were attempted by a faculty committee. Although these efforts proceeded for several days, they were unsuccessful. One week after the occupation began, police entered the affected buildings and cleared them of demonstrators. Violence occurred not only in the occupied buildings but in the surrounding campus area which was also ordered to be cleared. One hundred and three persons obtained hospital treatment and 692 persons were arrested.

[10] *New York Times,* May 9, 1968, at 1.

[11] A. H. Barton, "The Columbia Crisis: Campus, Vietnam, and the Ghetto," 32 *Public Opinion Quarterly* (1968).

[12] *New Republic,* June 28, 1969.

[13] The relevant studies are summarized and evaluated in Gurr, *supra* note 4.

[14] Paul R. Miller, *Characteristics of Youth Activists: The Chicago Demonstrators* (1968).

[15] It is interesting to note that far more intense feelings were registered in responses to questions regarding adherence to "Humphrey Democrats" politics. Only 1 percent were for this political philosophy, while 78 percent were against and 21 percent were indifferent.

[16] *Rights in Conflict* at 49 contains a lengthy list of reported "threats" which can only be described as ludicrous. Although the novelty of this form of attention-getting had waned by the time of the Counter-Inaugural protest, similar threats preceded that event. *Rights in Concord* at 81.

[17] *Rights in Conflict* at 59.

[18] *Id.* at viii.

[19] *Id.* at 59.

[20] In addition to the findings reported in *Rights in Conflict* at

387

viii, 31-42, the Sparling Commission, comprised of prominent citizens in the Chicago area, recently concluded:

> Chicago's record in regard to right of assembly and use of streets and parks is a discriminatory one. Over two decades, the city has welcomed parades down its main streets by conventional groups and for such occasions as St. Patrick's Day, Christmas, Armed Forces Day, Gen. Douglas MacArthur Day, Veterans Day and Columbus Day.
> Groups with unpopular opinions have had a different experience. When they attempted to parade or rally, march or demonstrate, it is fair to say generally they met a wall of silence and delay, and obtained permits with the greatest difficulty.

The Commission further accused Chicago officials of deliberately and unconstitutionally manipulating permit requirements by means of "fraud" and "lies" to deny permission to those who wished to protest at the convention. See the *New York Times*, Aug. 21, 1969, at 23.

[21] *Rights in Concord* at 115. The following discussion is taken from the same report at 82-88.

[22] Arnold and Louise Sagalyn, Paper prepared for The National Commission on the Causes and Prevention of Violence.

[23] Chicago Police Department Training Bulletin, *Tension Situations* (Apr. 24, 1967).

> Preventing civil disorders is always easier than suppressing them. The police officer, by disciplining his emotions, recognizing the rights of all citizens, and conducting himself in the manner his office demands can do much to prevent a tension situation from erupting into a serious disturbance . . .
> The officers making the arrest must not show partiality in any manner. They should not make indiscriminate or mass arrests. Above all, the officers must not become excited. Such an emotion can easily spread to the crowd and cause serious difficulty. The officers on the scene should display tact and constraint. The officers must be calm and act as a neutralizing agent.

[24] Fogelson, *supra* note 5 at 277.

[25] The following discussion is based on *Shut It Down! A College in Crisis* (U.S. Govt. Printing Off., 1969), the report on the San Francisco State disorders prepared for the Commission by William H. Orrick, Jr.

[26] *Id.* at 128-129.

[27] *Id.* at 41 *et seq.*

[28] See Report on Urban Insurgency Studies, sponsored by the Advance Research Projects Agency, Washington, D.C.

[29] See ch. 9 of the Commission's Task Force Report on Firearms, *Firearms and Violence in American Life* (U.S. Govt. Print-

ing Off. 1969), prepared by George D. Newton and Franklin E. Zimring.

[30] A judge of the New Jersey Superior Court has recently ruled unconstitutional that state's method of collecting data on "activists." *Anderson* v. *Sills,* No. C215-68, Aug. 6, 1969.

[31] Seek Skolnick, *Politics of Protest,* ch. VII.

[32] For application of the statute in First Amendment cases, see *Hague* v. *CIO,* 307 U.S. 496 (1939).

SECURING POLICE COMPLIANCE WITH CONSTITUTIONAL LIMITATIONS: THE EXCLUSIONARY RULE AND OTHER DEVICES*

The Supreme Court of the United States has evolved rules governing police conduct in making searches and arrests (now eavesdropping and wiretapping as well) from the imprecise words of the Fourth Amendment: "The right of the people to be secure in their persons, houses, papers, and effects, against unreasonable searches and seizures, shall not be violated, and no warrants shall issue, but upon probable cause, supported by oath or affirmation, and particularly describing the place to be searched, and the person or things to be seized." The Court's decisions have set constitutional limits on permissible police conduct, and in recent years these limits have become binding on State as well as federal officers.

Obviously, the content of these rules and other rules governing police conduct is likely to have a great impact on the incidence of violence in the community. If the rules permit police to use considerable force in a wide variety of situations, the level of violence rises. If the rules permit conduct which is generally considered an intolerable invasion of personal security or of privacy, we can expect outbursts of violence in protest against the sanctioned behavior. If the rules so hobble the police that convictions are extremely difficult to obtain in cases involving serious harms, the result-

---

*This chapter was prepared by Dean Monrad G. Paulsen, Professor Charles Whitebread, and Assistant Professor Richard Bonnie of the University of Virginia School of Law.

The authors gratefully acknowledge the contribution of Robert W. Olson, whose Note on Grievance Response Mechanisms for Police Misconduct in the June 1969 issue of the *Virginia Law Review* contains views similar to those expressed in this chapter. Finally, we note the valuable research efforts of Craig H. Norville, W. Tracey Shaw and Russell R. French, also students at the School of Law.

ing anxiety and fear may themselves prove to be a breeding ground for destructive outbursts. This relationship between violence and the rules governing the police is further complicated by the fact that the methods of enforcing the rules are likely to differ in respect to their respective capacities to produce dangerous responses.

This chapter is devoted to an examination of the many ways by which police compliance might be secured. We begin with what has been historically, the most controversial of the means of securing compliance—the exclusionary rule. (The rule of exclusion obviously is also used to discourage police and other official misconduct involving other Constitutional provisions, such as the Fifth Amendment's protection against being required to make self-incriminatory statements.) Thereafter we treat a wide variety of other remedies ranging from damage actions and injunctions to civilian review boards and "ombudsmen." At the conclusion we recommend a new approach to the problem of remedying police misconduct.

THE EXCLUSIONARY RULE

Until 1914 the general view of the nation's courts, state and federal, was that all material and relevant evidence should be admissible in a criminal case without regard to the manner by which it was obtained. The first important change in judicial opinion is recorded in *Weeks* v. *United States*.[1]

By a motion made prior to trial, the defendant in *Weeks* sought the return of property taken from him by police without a semblance of lawfulness. His house had been entered without a warrant and thoroughly searched in his absence. The trial court ordered the return of all the property taken save that "pertinent" to the charge against him (use of the mails for transporting lottery tickets). The Supreme Court reversed in a unanimous opinion, holding that even the material relating to the offense should have been returned. The Court based its decision on two main points:

(1) "The tendency of those who execute the criminal laws of the country to obtain conviction by means of unlawful seizures and enforced confessions . . . *should find no sanction* in the judgments if the courts which are charged at all times with the support of the Constitution and to which people of all condition's have a right to appeal for the maintenance of such fundamental rights"[2];

(2) "If letters and private documents can thus be seized

391

and held and used in evidence against a citizen accused of an offense, the protection of the Fourth Amendment declaring his right to be secure against such searches and seizures *is of no value,* and, so far as those placed are concerned, *might well be stricken* from the Constitution."[3]

The first point has been echoed by Justices of impressive authority. Justice Holmes has written, "We have to choose, and for my part I think it a less evil, that some criminal should escape than the Government should play an ignoble part."[4] Mr. Justice Brandeis put the point that the use of illegally obtained evidence, "is denied in order to maintain respect for law; in order to promote confidence in the administration of justice; in order to preserve the judicial process from contamination."[5] Judge Roger Traynor of California observed in *People* v. *Cahan,*[6] "The success of the lawless venture depends entirely on the court's lending its aid by allowing the evidence to be introduced."

The facts of *Cahan* underscore the point. The police conduct there involved two separate trespasses into a private home in order to install a microphone. The action was undertaken after permission had been received from the Los Angeles chief of police. The entire purpose of the illegal conduct was to obtain evidence for use in court. The incident was planned and approval was obtained at the highest level of police authority. It was not the case of a rookie policeman who misjudged the complicated law of search and seizure.

The spectacle of government breaking the law and employing the fruits of illegal conduct seems likely to breed disrespect for both the law and the courts. It does not seem daring to suggest that in such disrespect may lie the seeds of violent conduct.

The second point, that without the exclusionary evidence rule the constitutional guarantees of the Fourth amendment are of "no value", has also proved persuasive in the decisive cases. In *Mapp* v. *Ohio,*[7] which extended the exclusionary evidence rule to the States, Mr. Justice Clark wrote; ... "[without the rule] the freedom from state invasions of privacy would be so ephemeral ... as not to merit this Court's high regard as a freedom implicit in the concept of ordered liberty." Mr. Justice Traynor, again in *People* v. *Cahan,*[8] affirmed, "Experience has demonstrated . . . that neither administrative nor civil remedies are effective in suppressing lawless searches and seizures." At another point in that opinion, which embraced the exclusionary rule for the state of California six years before *Mapp*, Justice Traynor explained the action of the California Court: "other remedies have completely failed to secure compliance with the constitutional provisions on the part of police officers."[9]

Whether the exclusionary rule actually does effectively deter the police is a question without a firm answer. No solid research puts the question to rest. The assumption is that the police wish to convict those who commit crimes and that, if we bar the use of evidence illegally obtained, the police will conform to the rules in order to achieve that aim.

We know that the expanded application of the exclusionary rule has been accompanied by many efforts at police education. Courses in police academies, adult education programs for police sponsored by local headquarters, and courses in colleges and universities offered to police on the issues presented by the Fourth Amendment have sprung up nearly everywhere. More and more police leaders affirm the necessity for staying within the rules. More and more police departments have become interested in the formulation of guidelines for the officer on the beat who must make snap judgments. It is difficult not to credit the exclusionary rule for some of these developments.

One criticism of primary reliance on the exclusionary rule to deter police misconduct is that, despite its rationale of deterrence through deprivation of incriminating evidence, it does not deter when police act in situations where prosecution is not contemplated. If officers merely seek to harass a citizen, the exclusionary rule does not influence the officers to cease.[10]

We do see this point not as an argument against the rule, however, but rather as a reason for the creation of other remedies. The need is for supplementation, not abandonment.

Another question is: will reliance on the exclusionary rule breed police violence? If the police are "handcuffed" and are therefore unable to obtain convictions, will they impose extrajudicial punishment? Will they subject dangerous "criminals" (so identified by the police) to beatings and harassments? If so, the need is again for additional remedies—not necessarily abandonment of the rule. It is important to remember, as well, that if the police are "handcuffed" it is because of the *rules of search and seizure* and not because of the rule of exclusion. The rule of exclusion tells nothing of the rules governing the police: the exclusionary rule can operate with strict limitations on police activity as well as with limitations which permit the police a wide latitude in the choice of behavior.

However, respected authorities have recently taken the position that the exclusionary rule is not a suitable remedy in all situations. For example, Judge Henry Friendly of the U.S. Court of Appeals for the Second Circuit suggested in *United States* v. *Soyka*[11] that we ought not apply the exclusionary rule to enforce all the search and seizures rules in all kinds of cases. *Soyka* involved the admissibility of evidence taken by illegal conduct but Judge Friendly described the police behavior as an error ". . . so minuscule and pardonable as to render the drastic sanction of the exclusion, intended primarily as a deterrent to ourtageous police conduct . . . almost grotesquely inappropriate."[12] He went on to recommend a system which would apply or not apply the exclusionary rule depending on the gravity of the offense involved and the seriousness of the police misconduct.[13]

Judge Friendly's position is attractive because it suggests that a single value should not outweigh all others. The difficulty lies in the practical application of the principle. Can we articulate the suggested standard with sufficient precision so that it can be grasped by the police? Will a police officer readily know the seriousness of the offense which confronts him so he will know whether to use the "technical" or "liberal" rules of search and seizure? Can courts handily apply the proposed standard with uniformity and fairness?

The exclusionary rule not only forbids the use of evidence secured in violation of law but also of evidence derived from that originally taken. The courts may not use the "fruit of the poisonous tree."[14] Thus courts have held that fingerprints taken after an unlawful arrest are inadmissible[15] and certain statements made by an arrested person after an illegal arrest are barred from the trial.[16]

The key question is, of course, what is the "fruit" of illegal activity. Does it mean that all evidence which the police would not have "but for" the illegal conduct? If so, the sweep of the principle will be wide indeed. The Supreme Court has rejected the "but for" test and said the question is whether "the evidence to which instant objection is made has been come at by *exploitation of that illegality* or instead by means sufficiently distinguishable to be purged of the primary taint."[17]

Complaints about the broad application of the "fruit of the poisonous tree" principle, not strictly based on considerations of deterrence, have been heard from some judges. Mr. Justice White contributed a provocative discussion of the problem in his dissenting opinion *Harrison* v. *United States*[18] and in *Collins* v. *Beto*[19] Judge Friendly argued that the judges should relate the reach of the principle to the seriousness of the police misconduct.

Also affecting the reach of the exclusionary rule is the doctrine of "harmless error," under which judgements are not to be reversed for error unless the error has prejudiced the defendant's case. The Supreme Court addressed itself to the "harmless error" question in *Chapman* v. *California*.[20] Chapman and another had been convicted upon a charge that they had robbed, kidnapped and murdered a bartender. The California trial judge and the prosecutor had repeatedly referred to the defendant's failure to testify—a comment now forbidden by the Fifth Amendment privilege against self-incrimination.[21] Mr. Justice Black's majority opinion in *Chapman* first established that whether a federal constitutional error is harmless or not is an issue governed by federal law and that all constitutional errors are not necessarily harmful. But the Court noted that

> "before a federal constitutional error can be held harmless, the court must be able to declare a belief that it was harmless beyond a reasonable doubt. While appellate courts do not ordinarily have the original task of applying such a test, it is a familiar standard to all courts, and we believe its adoption will provide a more workable standard, although achieving the same result as that aimed at, in our *Fahy* case [holding that the error cannot be harmless where there is a reasonable possibility that the evidence complained of might have contributed to the conviction] . . ."[22]

Chapman's conviction was reversed. "Under these circumstances it is completely impossible to say that the state had demonstrated beyond a reasonable doubt the prosecutor's comments and the trial judge's instructions did not contribute to petitioner's convictions."[23]

On June 2, 1969, however, the Supreme Court did hold, in *Harrington* v. *California*[24] that a constitutional error in the trial of a criminal offense had been harmless because there was "overwhelming" untainted evidence to support the conviction. The three dissenters in Harrington and some legal scholars as well, believe that the deterrent effect of the exclusionary rule will ultimately be substantially vitiated by this approach to the question of harmless error.

We believe that the exclusionary rule will and ought to

endure as a primary device for securing police compliance with the law. Judge Friendly's suggestion in *Soyka*, the limitations on the "fruit of the poisonous tree" doctrine and the "harmless error" rule—each aims to escape the potentially severe implications of the rule in cases where police misconduct was not grave and where the defendant seems clearly guilty of a serious offense. The political forum echoes with the outcry that public safety is being submerged to a "literal" interpretation of constitutional limitations and that the exclusionary rule is but a sanctuary for the guilty. It is not surprising, therefore, that some judges are groping for ways to tailor the remedy to the outrageousness of the police misconduct and the gravity of the defendant's offense. We are in sympathy with this solicitude for effective law enforcement. We believe, however, the exclusionary evidence rule to be an exceedingly functional instrument for securing police compliance with the law. We should therefore be very cautious in fashioning limitations on the scope of the rule so as not to undercut its deterrent effect.

A final point about the exclusionary rule and its relation to violence: we may guess that urge to destructive behavior is greatest when the actor is moved by a sense of frustration grounded in a feeling of injustice which he is unable to combat. The exclusionary rule, however, provides an outlet within the law for frustration stemming from the belief that the defendant has been treated unjustly by the police. By a motion to suppress the defendant can in effect strike back at authority in the very proceeding which is aimed at convicting him. We now turn to other means, besides the exclusionary rule, of enforcing the substantive rules governing permissible police conduct.

DAMAGE REMEDIES UNDER STATE LAW

In general, a policeman is personally liable under state law for torts arising from his law enforcement activities.[25] Consideration of tort liability must proceed simultaneously on two fronts: effectiveness as a deterrent and utility as a mode of redress. In order to eliminate violent response to alleged police misconduct, our society must achieve both of these objectives. The average citizen must be confident that police misconduct is the deviant rather than the normal behavior and that he can recover for injury suffered due to police improprieties.

Substantive tort law theoretically permits recovery for some

396

egregious acts of police misconduct. Liability for false arrest or false imprisonment may arise from a warrantless arrest lacking "probable cause." An illegal invasion of a person's home or seizure of his property constitutes a trespass to land or chattels. Because of damage limitations, however, plaintiff's victory in a suit for trespass will be only nominal unless the errant policeman has been carelessly destructive or overtly ill-willed. Where the police officer has employed an unreasonable amount of force under certain circumstances, he is liable for assault and battery. Despite the availability of these causes of action, however, the chances of adequate recovery are so slim that there is usually no inducement to sue.

The initial defect in civil recovery both as a means of redress and as deterrent to police misconduct is the cost of suit. As the Wickersham Commission noted in 1931: ". . . in case of persons of no influence or little or no means the legal restrictions are not likely to give an officer serious trouble."[26] Unfortunately, litigation is most costly, and consequently least attractive, in cases where redress is most needed—brutality cases in which recovery is likely to depend on the resolution of disputed factual issues necessitating a protracted trial.

If lower class litigants are to bring suit at all, their costs must be borne either by Legal Aid offices or lawyers operating on contingent fee. Yet, neither source can handle a large volume of cases and must of necessity choose only those most promising of success. Unless the state or local government bears at least part of the cost of litigation, regardless of outcome—for example by hiring an attorney to represent indigents aggrieved by police misconduct—civil suit will be too sporadic to function adequately as either a deterrent or a means of redress.[27]

Time is a most formidable barrier to suit, especially among the poor. Because of crowded court dockets, years may pass before a case is decided. The prospect—and a limited one at that—of relief at some distant time is probably not strong enough to evoke an initial commitment, especially in light of the costs which might accrue. It should also be added that the protracted nature of litigation is also a major reason why civil suit is currently an inadequate substitute for or deterrent to violence as an outlet for citizen grievances against the police. A prospect, or even a promise, of damages two years hence is not likely to mitigate the incendiary effect of gross

397

police misconduct which often has immediately preceded civil disorder.

Another problem is the difficulty of establishing damages even if liability is proven. As early as 1886, the Supreme Court noted that recovery of a sum sufficient to justify a police tort action is dependent on the "moral aspects of the case."[28] But the usual plaintiff lacks the "minimum elements of respectability[29]" to claim or recover for injury to reputation. Similarly, minority plaintiffs do not often recover punitive damages from predominantly middle-class juries, especially when such damages cannot be disguised as reparation for injury to reputation. Thus, since recovery is limited to actual damage for the most abused class of citizens, the Wickersham Commission conclusion, that a civil action has little deterrent value where it is most needed, is still true today.

To this point, we have endeavored to show that state civil suits are inadequate either to placate most citizens aggrieved by police misconduct or to deter police abuse. The serious questions remain whether such suits would become effective deterrents if the stated defects were cured and to what extent this result would be achieved to the detriment of legitimate law enforcement efforts.

Even if the possibility and extent of recovery were substantially increased, the vindicated plaintiff would often be possessed of a meaningless judgment: police are not wealthy nor are they often bonded.[30] More important, if liability attached too readily or if there were any appreciable possibility that it would penalize honest mistakes, law enforcement would surely suffer. Complete individual liability for tortious conduct would not only discourage persons from becoming police officers but would also severely circumscribe the vigor and fearlessness with which they perform their duties.

With increasing frequency, commentators have urged that this dual defect—unredressed injury and deterrent overkill—be cured by municipal or state liability for police torts committed in the performance of their duties.[31] Except for the additional depletion of already barren state and local treasuries, the effects of governmental liability would be uniformly beneficial. It would surely facilitate redress and is a necessary condition for effective deterrence. To put it bluntly, it would slap the right wrists—i.e., at the level where police policy is made. The Department, under pressure from fiscal authorities, would very likely establish and enforce

398

firmer guidelines through internal review and purge recurrent offenders.

On the other hand, it is arguable that governmental liability for police torts is not a sufficient condition for effective deterrence. Some police illegality is an inevitable concomitant of law enforcement;[32] and departmental policymakers, according to their own scheme of values, may find it prudent to violate now and pay later. Such a decision is especially likely in situations where the exclusionary rule does not apply and there is no other deterrent; i.e., where prosecution is not contemplated and conviction is not the motivating factor.

In any event, a majority of states have refused to waive governmental immunity in police tort cases[33] despite repeated urgings by a multitude of legal scholars.[34] And it is unlikely that they will do so at least until the scope of liability is sufficiently limited.

Thus, the most fruitful approach is to abandon delusions of broad deterrence and substantial redress and to concentrate on the grosser forms of abuse where the tort remedy can be useful. Actual injury caused by serious breaches of duty committed in utter disregard of proper standards of police conduct should be redressed by the courts in tort suits. The imperatives of such an approach are utilization of a good faith defense and more extensive governmental assumption of liability.

DAMAGE REMEDIES UNDER FEDERAL LAW

In addition to his state common law tort remedies, a citizen aggrieved by police misconduct may have a cause of action under 42 U.S.C. § 1983 which provides:

> Every person who, under color of any statute, ordinance, regulation, custom, or usage, of any State or Territory, subjects, or causes to be subjected, any citizen of the United States or other person within the jurisdiction thereof to the deprivation of any rights, privileges, or immunities secured by the Constitution and laws, shall be liable to the party injured in an action at law, suit in equity, or other proper proceeding for redress.

The statute in its present form is substantially unchanged from its passage in 1871 as the civil section of what is popularly known as the Ku Klux Act.[35] It is clear that this statute originally was designed to inhibit and give a remedy for the widespread abridgement of Negro rights that characterized

399

the Reconstruction period in the South. Recently, however, the Supreme Court has read the broad statutory language to authorize civil tort suits in federal courts against state law enforcement officers,[36] and a steady stream of such cases now flows through the lower federal courts.[37]

In the landmark case, *Monroe* v. *Pape*,[38] James Monroe alleged that 13 Chicago policemen broke into his home at 5:45 a.m., routed his whole family from bed, ransacked every room in his house, detained him at the police station for 10 hours on "open charges," and finally released him without filing criminal charges against him. The Supreme Court, holding this complaint actionable under Section 1983, adopted the *Screws* and *Classic* definition of "under color of law," and noted that even action wholly contrary to state law is nevertheless action "under color of law" if the policemen are clothed with the indices of authority. Moreover, the Monroe majority held that since Section 1983 does not include the word "willfully," a complainant need neither allege nor prove a "specific intent to deprive a person of a federal right."[39] Finally, the Court reasoned that since one of the purposes of Section 1983 was to afford a federal right in federal courts, the federal remedy is supplementary to any existing state remedy and the state remedy need not be exhausted before its invocation.

The major issue that remained after the sweeping *Monroe* decision was whether some degree of bad faith or other fault in the deprivation of the citizen's constitutional rights is an element of the federal cause of action under Section 1983. The court confronted this issue in its 1967 decision in *Pierson* v. *Ray*.[40] In that case petitioners, a group of Negro and white clergymen were arrested for sitting-in at a segregated interstate bus terminal in Mississippi. Subsequent to their arrest and conviction, the statutory provision upon which their arrest had been based was declared unconstitutional and their cases were remanded and later dropped. In their subsequent suit for false arrest and violation of Section 1983, the Supreme Court proclaimed that the defenses of "good faith and probable cause" were available to the policemen-defendants under Section 1983 just as they were under Mississippi law of false arrest. Although the *Pierson* decision established that policemen are not strictly liable for unconstitutional activity, the scope of the defenses which it recognized is not yet clear. On the other hand, the federal defenses could be tied to state law, thereby attaching only in those states which allow a good faith defense in the subsequent

400

invalidation context, as did Mississippi in *Pierson*. On the other hand, it would appear that the Court contemplated something broader—a federal standard of fault not tied to state law or to any particular factual context, and most observers have so assumed.

Because of the difficulty of segregating "probable cause" from the lawfulness of the conduct itself, and because "good faith" suggests a completely subjective standard, we suggest that these labels are inappropriate tools for defining the proper defense in the present context. The purpose of a defense in a police tort suit, under state law or under Section 1983, should be to immunize conduct illegal only because of an honest mistake in judgment *or* an unforeseeable change in the law. The proper standard, and one which both state and post-*Pierson* lower federal courts in fact have been applying,[41] is whether the policeman's act was "reasonable" in light of circumstances, both legal and situational, about which he knew or should have known.

An additional question remaining after *Pierson* is the scope of police activity covered by the "rights, privileges, or immunities" clause of Section 1938. It clearly covers illegal searches or seizures and unconstitutional arrests. And there is some evidence that it also covers gross acts of police brutality, conduct which denies due process because it shocks the conscience.[42] In any event, however, Section 1983 cannot be employed to regulate the day-to-day conduct of the policeman on patrol—the seemingly trivial acts of harassment and misunderstanding which in gross, may elicit violence against the police by ghetto residents.[43]

Nevertheless, Section 1983—like the state tort remedy—is a potentially useful device for compensating the individual citizen substantially injured by unlawful police action. To be sure, an action under Section 1983 is subject to all the intrinsic weakness of any tort remedy—limited personal assets of the police, no provision for payment of damages from municipal or state funds, the expense of maintaining the suit, the difficulty of establishing damages, the disadvantaged position of the usual plaintiff in the community, and the threat such assessments against individual policemen pose to vigorous and efficient law enforcement efforts.[44] Despite these inherent limitations, however, Section 1983's federal remedy for deprivation of constitutional rights does permit compensation of citizens whose person or property is significantly damaged due to clearly unlawful police activity.

Many commentators on Section 1983's use to control police conduct claim its application must be limited to the egregious case so that it does not hamper legitimate law enforcement by penalizing the policeman for mere error in judgment and honest misunderstanding.[45] We agree with this goal for the federal remedy as well as the state remedies, but argue that the present "probable cause and good faith" defense available to the police under *Pierson* v. *Ray* as applied in subsequent cases and as we have refined it, together with the law of damages under this section, in fact limit the scope of the remedy. Our conclusion, then, must be that, while the federal civil damages remedy cannot be a regulator of everyday police conduct, it can provide a remedy to individuals severely injured by outrageous instances of police illegality.[46] As an important and essential supplement to other devices for controlling police violence, it should be implemented at the federal level by rationalized damage rules and docket priority and at the state level by municipal assumption of liability and cost of suit.

INJUNCTION

The injunction offers the prospect of immediate relief from unconstitutional conduct and a powerful deterrent from engaging in that specific conduct. Simply as a matter of judicial equitable prerogative, such relief is easily justified. The remedies at law for this threatened or continuing deprivation of liberty are at present clearly inadequate except in a limited context, a conclusion emphatically asserted by the Supreme Court in *Mapp* v. *Ohio*[47] and reaffirmed in our discussion above. The injury may surely be irreparable, both to the plaintiff and the community.[48]

But injunctions issued against individual police officers to refrain from future violations, in addition to raising much the same substantive and practical problems noted above in connection with damages, also present an insuperable enforcement problem. The order must cover all types of illegal conduct or it cannot operate fairly; yet if an injunction issued upon proof of any illegality whatever, it would replace internal police disciplinary procedures with inflexible judicial oversight of the conduct of all police officers. Since the court's only sanction is contempt, it would be extremely heavy-handed and even more disruptive of legitimate law enforcement efforts than effective and broad damage remedies. Such a remedy represents the worst of all possible worlds.

Thus, instead of utilizing the remedial force of the injunction in a way destructive of law enforcement, a court must look to those who make the rules which the individual police officers are supposed to obey. The goal of injunctive relief should be to induce the Departments to establish guidelines consistent with constitutional mandates and to use their internal disciplinary procedures to enforce these rules. Whether this goal can be achieved by equitable relief issued by either state or federal courts is the subject of this section.

The various state courts which have faced the question have left no clear statement of the law. In fact, there seem to be two separate lines of authority. Some courts have emphasized the institutional irresponsibility of injunctive interference with law enforcement activity.[49] Under this view, the plaintiff should be left to whatever civil remedies at law he has available or to his defenses in a criminal prosecution should one be brought. Other courts, perhaps a majority, have felt no institutional hesitations, but have placed heavy burdens on the plaintiff to show clearly lack of a reasonable basis for the allegedly illegal police actions and the presence of malice or bad faith.[50] Thus, even these courts have interfered only where the police are pursuing a clearly illegal course of conduct against an identifiable plaintiff or group of plaintiffs.[51]

Section 1983, discussed above, also authorizes the federal district courts to hear suits in equity against police for conduct invading constitutional rights.[52] Such suits have rarely been brought, however.[53] The United States Supreme Court approved the remedy in *Hague* v. *CIO*[54] in 1939, where it affirmed an order against a Mayor, Chief of Police and others enjoining them from continuing an antiunion campaign of harrassing arrests, deportation of organizers and suppression of union circulars and public meetings. Of the lower court decisions which have employed this remedy, several enjoined blatant infringements of First Amendment rights[55] and others like *Hague* itself, enjoined schemes of conduct including attempts to enforce the law against plaintiffs but which nevertheless inhibited First Amendment rights.[56] Only two cases have involved injunctions for violations of criminal safeguards with no First Amendment overtones.

In the first, *Refoule* v. *Ellis*,[57] the police had four times detained the plaintiff without a warrant for extended periods of time, questioned him in relays, utilized force to coerce a confession and conducted other similarly objectionable activities. The Georgia District Court issued an injunction against further warrantless detentions, questionings, beatings and other specific illegal conduct. In *Lankford* v. *Gelston*,[58] the Fourth Circuit ordered the District Court to enjoin the Baltimore Police Department from continuing a thirteen-day search of ghetto residences without either warrant or consent based solely on anonymous phone tips.[59]

Refoule and *Lankford* are the only reported cases suitable for testing the validity and scope of the power of the federal courts to interfere with state and local law enforcement activities. In these cases, the courts acknowledged the principles of not interfering with administration of the criminal law,[60] but affirmed that injunctions against such clear violations of constitutional rights could not possibly interfere with legitimate law enforcement activities.[61] And the courts were surely correct. These cases, so long as they could be brought to judicial attention, cried out for relief. Any police chief or officer continuing the illegal conduct in defiance of the court's order would have been deserving of a contempt citation.

The common elements of such egregious cases illustrate both the validity of the remedy and the limited scope of its employment: the department must be engaged in a *clearly unconstitutional course of conduct* directed against an *identifiable person or class of persons*. Such cases are most likely to involve conflicts between the police and particular organizations, such as the Black Panthers and anti-war groups, where the class is most definable and judicial reticence to interfere may be vitiated by First Amendment implications. Actions filed by militant blacks[62] and anti-war groups[63] alleging systematic police harassment are now pending in the federal courts.

One recent commentator[64] has urged that the injunctive remedy be utilized not only to prohibit deliberately ordered violations of constitutional rights as in *Lankford* and *Refoule,* but also to require affirmative actions by Department superiors to prevent recurring violations which they have "passively tolerated." Although this proposal successfully identifies the crucial need in this area—the effective operation of departmental disciplinary procedures—its attempt to convert the courts into supervisors of police discipline is misguided.

Apart from a difficult problem of statutory authorization, the basic substantive defects are, first, definition and proof of violation, and, second, order-framing and sanction. On the first issue, the dispositive inquiry is whether the departmental superiors have taken adequate steps to enforce compliance with constitutional mandates. Such an evaluation would encompass policy guidelines, complaint mechanisms, and disciplinary procedures; yet judicial review of the adequacy of complaint processing and disciplinary procedures would be neither colorably judicial nor susceptible to remotely managable standards.[65]

As to the second question—order-framing, the author proposes that the court first issue a general order directing the Commissioner to correct the pattern of tolerated violations by altering his enforcement procedures in a way which achieves the desired result with a minimum adverse effect on the morale and efficiency of his Department.[66] The author assumes that a good faith effort by a capable Commissioner will quickly cure the ill and relieve the court of the difficult burden of making good its promise to reduce misconduct. Unfortunately, however, failures will be widespread, and the courts will sometimes have to frame a second, more specific order, itself establishing the Departments disciplinary procedures,[67] and the author himself acknowledges that "such orders would seriously interfere with the Police Commissioner's management of his department and a court should make every effort to minimize the dangers inherent in such interference."[68]

In summary, although state cases are ambiguous and federal cases are sparse, it would appear that the injunction at either level is another useful fringe remedy. Where immediate relief from a clearly unconstitutional course of conduct against identifiable persons is prayed for, the injunction should issue. Otherwise the courts should not interfere directly with the enforcement of the criminal law.

CRIMINAL SANCTIONS

Although both state and federal statute books include criminal sanctions for illegal police conduct such as false arrest and trespass, they are rarely employed.[69] It is well established that in criminal prosecutions for false arrest the defendant must have criminal intent and that his good faith is a complete defense.[70] At common law no trespass to property is criminal unless it is accompanied by a breach of the peace.[71] Moreover, most states require criminal intent as an element[72] of the crime, either by statute or by judicial interpolation where the statute itself is silent.[73] Where intent is an element, the defenses of good faith[74] or color of title will lie unless there has been a breach of the peace.[75]

The dearth of case law on the subject indicates the impotency of criminal prosecution of police officers as a remedy for their misconduct. Professor Foote, a leading authority on judicial remedies against the police, could find only four cases—all for false imprisonment—for the period 1940-55.[76] We have been unable to unearth any additional reported cases for the subsequent 13 years. No authoritative explanation has been given for the absence of prosecution for police offenses, but the reasons are not difficult to surmise. Prosecutors are probably reluctant to enforce these dormant criminal sanctions against police offenses because they anticipate, in our view correctly, a detrimental effect on law enforcement which is the goal of both departments, and because they consider the punishment too harsh.

As a supplement to state criminal remedies for police misconduct, 18 U.S.C. § 242 imposes a federal penalty on anyone who, under color of law, willfully deprives a person of his constitutional rights.[77] Because Section 242 is a criminal statute it has been narrowly construed. The Supreme Court in *Screws* v. *U. S.,*[78] upholding this statute against an attack that it was void for vagueness, interpreted the statutory requirement of willful violation to mean that the defendant must have had or been motivated by a specific intent to deprive a person of his constitutional rights.[79]

This narrow construction of the statute together with the reticence of prosecutors to bring actions against the police[80] have rendered Section 242 an impotent deterrent to police violence. Although there have been a handful of cases brought under this provision and some convictions,[81] this sanction has been applied only to the most outrageous kinds of police brutality.[82] Because the application of criminal sanctions to police misconduct is justified only when the policeman is clearly acting as a lawless hoodlum,[83] it is totally unrealistic to anticipate that this federal criminal provision will ever be transformed so as to control the conduct of the police.

Unlawful search and seizure, malicious procurement of a warrant and excess of authority under a warrant have been punishable as misdemeanors under federal law for decades.[84] Yet the annotations following these statutory provisions dealing with illegal police activity reveal no decided cases. That these sanctions have been completely ignored for so long graphically underscores the need for remedies other than state and federal criminal statutes to deter and if necessary punish arbitrary police conduct.

As a final part of this synopsis of criminal provisions affecting the police, some mention should be made of the long-standing suggestion that judges use their contempt power to discipline offending officers.[85] The contempt sanction, we have concluded, is much too harsh. Moreover, since judges are probably institutionally incapable of discovering on their own motion instances of police misconduct, this sanction would be applied only when the given facts in an adversary proceeding clearly indicate unlawful police action. Yet we already have better legal remedies for these egregious instances of police violence. Finally, since the proposed "contempt of the Constitution"[86] is an indirect criminal contempt, the accused police officer would probably have a right to a separate jury trial.[87] The prospect of a second trial militates further against stretching the contempt power to these frontiers never envisioned for it.

To this point, we have concluded that the judiciary—with some changes in substance and procedure—is the appropriate institution to deter and redress clear cases of police misconduct. The exclusionary evidence rule is a just and potent weapon to enforce constitutional mandates where a conviction is achieved. State and federal damage remedies, if rationalized and adequately facilitated, can deter and redress egregious and reckless police misconduct unattended by successful conviction. And injunctive relief may prove valuable in limited contexts where there has been an unlawful course of police conduct.

At the same time, we have also concluded that continuous administrative surveillance is better equipped than sporadic judicial oversight to cope with less extreme forms of police misconduct—conduct which is imprudent though not outrageous. Fair and speedy extra-judicial review of allegations of police harassment and other incendiary police practices could provide an essential outlet for citizen frustrations and dispel the widespread ghetto belief that police are characteristically arbitrary.

INTERNAL REVIEW

Every major police department has formal machinery for processing citizen complaints. To the extent that such machinery is fairly and effectively invoked, it can discipline misbehaving officers and deter the misconduct of other policemen. But in practice, internal review is largely distrusted by outsiders[88] for a variety of reasons.

For internal review procedures to be meaningful, complaints against the police must not only be readily accepted, but actively encouraged. Yet much criticism of police review has been directed at the hostile response of some departments to civilian complaints. In some instances, complex procedural formalities discourage filing of grievances.[89] Some departments will disregard anonymous telephone complaints and a few require sworn statements from complainants.[90] Allegations of police brutality, in particular, are often regarded as affronts to the integrity of the force which demand vigorous defense.[91] Accordingly, certain departments have in the past charged many complainants with false reports to the police as a matter of course,[92] or have agreed to drop criminal charges against the aggrieved party if he in turn abandons his complaint.[93] While most departments have abolished such practices, many potential allegations of police misconduct are apparently still withheld because of fear of retaliation.[94]

An impartial acceptance of all complaints against the police is necessary to instill confidence in a police review board. In fact, an increased volume of complaints filed with the police might often indicate that a department is winning rather than losing the trust of a community. To this end, the Police Task Force of the Crime Commission recommended that police departments accept all complaints from whatever source, process complaints even after complainants have dropped their charges, and advertise widely their search for police grievances of all types.[95] Many urban police departments have apparently adopted or already complied with these proposals.[96]

Although nearly all departments investigate all complaints, about half entrust the task exclusively to the local unit to which the accused officer was assigned.[97] The central organization usually supervises such investigations in varying degrees, but the relative autonomy of local units in gathering evidence concerning a complaint can both strain objectivity and engender further police misconduct.[98] Since investigative findings determine whether a complaint will be processed further or dismissed as groundless, a local investigating team is afforded the opportunity to clear its working comrade. Accordingly, the investigation may at times be designedly haphazard, or the complainant may be harassed into dropping his charges or a potential witness may be browbeaten into not testifying.[99]

Special internal investigative units for complaints of police misconduct are common to many departments, and should be the established norm, particularly for large urban forces. Such internal special units would presumably face less conflict of interest than local units in dealing with the policeman's conduct. An outwardly more objective inquiry might reduce grounds for public suspicion of police investigation of their own misconduct.

A sizable minority of departments do not provide formal adversary hearings for allegations of even the most egregious police misconduct.[100] In such instances, the police chief or commissioner will usually determine from investigative findings whether an officer should be disciplined. In organizations where hearings are conducted before a police review board, the format varies. It has been found that almost half of departments that provide hearings hold them secretly, and one-fifth deny the complainant rights to cross-examine witnesses or bring counsel to the hearings.[101] Such secrecy and lack of procedural safeguards inevitably foster suspicion about the fairness of internal review.[102] Furthermore, the recommendations of the review boards, which usually are implemented by the police chief, are seldom disclosed to either the public or the complainant.[103] Such a practice deprives hearings of their value in promoting community relations. For a full explanation of a dismissed complaint could publicly vindicate the police officer who in fact behaved responsibly, and the news of actual disciplinary action could placate citizen indignation over police misconduct. Thus if hearings are open to the public, quasi-judicial trial procedures are followed, and review board decisions fully publicized, the popular image of the police could be profitably enhanced.[104]

A major criticism of internal review is that it seldom produces meaningful discipline of persons guilty of police misconduct.[105] Even when an officer is diciplined, the punishment is often so light as to be a token that aggravates rather than satisfies the grievant.[106] By contrast, many departments impose relatively severe penalties for violations of minor internal regulations. Thus tardiness or insubordination may warrant an automatic suspension that is more onerous than the sanction for physical abuse of a citizen.[107] The frequency of rigorous internal discipline for minor departures from departmental regulations magnifies the relative failure of police departments to discipline an officer for abusive treatment of a citizen. The inference is that internal review is more attuned to enforcing organizational disciplines than redressing citizen grievances.

Internal review is undoubtedly the quickest and most efficient method of regulating the conduct of peace officers.[108] It is perhaps axiomatic that organizational superiors are in the most favorable position to control their subordinates. Similarly, a police chief is probably best qualified to formulate the standards for police conduct. He also can utilize the best available investigative facilities plus his unique expertise in police operations to mete out appropriate disciplinary measures. A punishment decreed by an insider is likely to be accepted by both the miscreant officer and the department as a whole. On the other hand, control imposed from the outside is bound to be more sporadic and hence less effective than persistent self-discipline. Furthermore, constant second-guessing by strangers might undermine police morale and induce the kind of bureaucratic inertia that seems to plague several other governmental agencies sapped of their local autonomy.

Despite the inherent advantages of self-regulation, however, its difficulties in projecting an image of fairness with regard to complaints from the citizenry suggests that it should be supplemented by some form of external review. Whether or not internal review procedures are conducive to objective inquiry, the mechanism is seldom invoked by those minority groups which encounter the police most directly and frequently.[109] Since the police cannot redress an aggrieved citizen with money damages, the conspicuously rare punishment of policemen on the basis of outside complaints can create the popular impression that police review is a sham designed to appease rather than relieve the victims of police violence. Furthermore, this failure to win public approval deprives internal review of its efficacy as a forum for vindicating officers slandered by groundless complaints.[110]

The concept of internal review is also limited by the degree to which a departmental superior can extricate himself from the conflict of interest he faces in judging citizen complaints against the police. To be fair, he must suppress a natural feeling of loyalty toward his subordinates. On the other hand, he faces the possibility that concession to citizen demands will undermine the morale of his organization. Thus even the conscientious police commissioner may encounter difficulty in properly handling complaints. Police departments

410

have a self-interest like any other entity, and if a police department tacitly overlooks misconduct by its patrolmen, then such a department cannot be expected to condemn itself publicly through internal review mechanisms.[111] In such a case, only an external organization can offer consistently impartial and objective review of allegations of police misconduct.

CIVILIAN REVIEW BOARDS

Dissatisfaction with both internal and judicial processing of police misconduct complaints prompted a few cities to experiment with civilian review boards. These boards, sitting independently of the police structure, adjudicated the merits of citizen grievances, either dismissing them as groundless or recommending that departmental superiors discipline the miscreant officer. Such external review was designed to project an appearance of fairness unattainable by internal mechanisms. At the same time, the civilian review boards were able to pass judgment on discourteous or harassing police practices which do not constitute judicially remediable wrongs but which nevertheless infuriate the grievant and intensify community hostility toward the police. Yet the boards did not purport to displace preexisting channels: the ultimate power to discipline remained with the police themselves, and the courts' jurisdiction over complaints was never abridged.

Civilian review boards have operated at one time or another in Philadelphia, New York City, Washington, and Rochester. The Washington board, however, could entertain only complaints referred to it by the police commissioner,[112] and the jurisdiction of the Rochester board was limited to allegations of unnecessary or excessive force.[113] Therefore, the New York and Philadelphia experiences contribute more expansively to an examination of civilian review.

The New York Civilian Complaint Review Board (CCRB), created by executive order in July 1966 and abolished by popular referendum four months later, consisted of four civilians appointed by the Mayor and three policemen named by the police commissioner.[114] The CCRB was empowered to accept, investigate, and review any citizen complaints of police misconduct involving unnecessary or excessive force, abuse of authority, discourteous or insulting language, or ethnic derogation.[115] Upon receipt of a complaint, the board directed its specially assigned investigative

411

staff of police officers to interview the complainant, the accused policeman, and any witnesses. If the investigation report revealed no serious dispute on the facts, a conciliation officer attempted to negotiate an informal settlement. If the policeman had acted properly under the circumstances, the board explained to the citizen that his grievance stemmed from a misunderstanding of the situation or of police duties. Where the officer had been mistaken or neglectful, or the injury had been minimal, the complaintant was assured the misconduct had been amply considered and would not be repeated. Where both parties were at fault or where the citizen was particularly incensed, a joint confrontation of the parties was arranged which would hopefully result in mutual understanding and apologies.[116] If a complaint was conciliated or deemed unsubstantiated, the accused officer was expressly notified that the complaint would not appear on his record.[117]

When the seriousness of the alleged offense or a heated dispute over the facts precluded informal conciliation, the CCRB conducted a formal hearing, at which both complainant and policeman had rights to representation by counsel and cross-examination of witnesses.[118] The board made findings of fact, upon which it either dismissed the complaint or recommended "charges" to the police commissioner. No specific disciplinary measures emerged from the CCRB, whose final rulings recommended further departmental consideration of a complaint rather than punishment.[119]

The New York CCRB elicited 440 complaints during its 4-month existence, as compared to the approximate annual average of 200 received by the police-operated Complaint Review Board prior to 1966.[120] Nearly half the grievances alleged unnecessary force, but a substantial number involved discourtesy and abuse of authority.[121] Significantly, many of the complaints emerged not from the criminal context, but from police involvement in private or family disagreements.[122] That only half the complaints were filed by members of minority groups could be attributed to insufficient publicity and the CCRB's short tenure.[123] Of the 146 complaints ultimately processed by the CCRB, 109 were dismissed after investigation, 21 were conciliated, 11 were referred elsewhere, 4 culminated in recommended "charges," and one resulted in a reprimand from the board.[124]

The brevity of the New York experiment defies meaningful evaluation, but the Police Advisory Board (PAB) operated continually in Philadelphia from 1958 through 1967, when

412

its normal activities were enjoined. The PAB closely resembled the CCRB, except that the Philadelphia board had no specially assigned investigative staff, held open hearings, lacked power to subpoena witnesses, and recommended specific disciplinary measures to the commissioner for valid complaints. From 1958 until mid-1966, the PAB received 571 citizen complaints, of which 42 percent alleged brutality, 22 percent harassment, 19 percent illegal entry or search, and 17 percent other misconduct.[125] During this period, the PAB recommended 18 reprimands, 23 suspensions, 2 dismissals, and 3 commendations of police officers, and 33 expungings of complainants' arrest records.[126] With few exceptions, the police department cooperated by implementing the board's proposals.[127]

The record of the PAB reveals several positive accomplishments. It evidently achieved some degree of support from the minority communities where police presence was most volatile; one-half of all complaints were filed by Negroes in a city that was three-quarters white.[128] Dispositions most frequently emerged from informal settlements.[129] This conciliation process, it is presumed, permitted grievance resolutions acceptable to both citizen and officer with a minimum of the adversary tensions normally incident to an open formal hearing. Furthermore, the complainant would often be uninterested in seeing the policeman disciplined; he may have sought only an apology or eradication of an unjustified arrest record.

The PAB also submitted an annual report to the Mayor, which allowed broader expression of citizen judgment on police policies than would usually flow from the case by case approach. The police department followed the 1962 report's suggestion that definitive guidelines for the proper use of handcuffs be established.[130] In 1965 the PAB requested that the police rectify apparent patterns of physical mistreatment of apprehended persons in station houses and discourtesy directed at civilian inquiries.[131] The annual report thus enabled the PAB to expose the most persistent sources of citizen irritation in the interest of enabling the police both to improve their services and to enhance their public image. Finally, a prominent Philadelphian has noted he remembers no occasion prior to the board's operation in which the police department had ever diciplined an officer solely on the basis of civilian complaint.[132]

The successes of civilian review have been counterbalanced

413

by marked failures, some of which are probably unique to the Philadelphia experience. Few complaints were filed with the PAB. The number exceeded 100 only in 1964, and the annual rate of complaints received evinces an erratic, rather than an upward trend.[133] The diminutive community response to the board was partly attributable to its lack of publicity. As a result of limited press coverage and a nonexistent publicity budget, many citizens knew nothing of the board's operation or even its existence.[134] There is also suspicion that some policemen actively discouraged complaints on infrequent occasions.[135]

In addition to being relatively ignored by the citizenry, the PAB encountered difficulties maintaining its impartial image. The board often compensated for an indigent complainant's inability to secure counsel by developing the case for him during hearings.[136] This procedure might at times have induced a policeman to suspect the board was biased against him. Positing all investigative authority over civilian complaints in the police department not only advertised the PAB's dependence on police rather than civilian judgment in the critical initial inquiries, but also produced unjustifiable delays as well. Approximately half the investigation reports were not returned to the board within 90 days of referral to the police department, and a sizable backlog of unresolved cases accumulated.[137] This lag, combined with other procedural delays, partially explains why many citizens failed to follow their initial complaints through to ultimate disposition. Finally, the PAB, having been created by mayoral fiat in 1958, was a political creature of unascertainable life and tenuous authority. Frictions with the mayor and a court challenge of its legality engendered periods of uncertainty and compromise in the board's early history,[138] and normal board operations have been suspended since mid-1967, when the Fraternal Order of Police successfully enjoined its hearings.[139]

Apart from the particularized shortcomings of the PAB in Philadelphia, its record reveals institutional deficiencies that will plague any civilian review board of the future. The PAB was subjected to the same kind of vehement police attacks that led to the abolition of the CCRB in New York City.[140] The police claimed that civilian review lowers police morale, undermines respect of lower echelon officers for their superiors, and inhibits proper police discretion by inducing fear of retaliatory action before the board.[141] The advisory nature of the PAB and its infrequent disciplinary recommendations may impeach the credibility of such allegation. But police hostility to the review board cannot be underestimated.

Probably the real issue here is that, despite their monopoly on the use of force, policemen fiercely resent being singled out among all other local governmental officials for civilian review. Implicit in the board's very existence seems to be an assumption that policemen are characteristically arbitrary or brutal and have to be watched. Since policemen apparently believe that civilian review boards symbolize society's contemptuous discrimination against them, the ill feeling the institution provokes may not be worth the benefits it may confer. Indeed, the high controversy associated with the term "civilian review board" suggests the appellation will not be attached to any future grievance response agencies.

Another source of police antagonism may have been the adversary nature of the PAB's hearing procedures. The adversary process is not only costly and protracted, but when complainant and policeman are pitted against each other in formal opposition, hearings convey the appearance of a battleground.[142] As a consequence, the civilian review board seems in some ways to aggravate, rather than minimize, the frictions between police and community. Yet the object of external review should be improvement of existing police services, not establishment of a rival police department. To the extent that a board departs from ameliorating tensions through informal conciliation and moves toward affixing blame in formal adjudication, it fails to improve police-community relations.

To relate the defects of civilian review boards is not, however, to reject the concept of civilian review itself. Both the Kerner[143] and Crime Commissions[144] recognized the importance of independent non-judicial review of police conduct, and yet also did not recommend that civilian review boards be established in cities where they did not already exist. Indeed, the qualified achievements of the review board seem to have flowed more from the merits of external surveillance than the mechanism that seeks to achieve it. If civilian review can be institutionalized so as to placate rather than polarize police-citizen differences, its potential may be realized. The ombudsman has been offered as just such an institution.

415

THE OMBUDSMAN

The Scandinavian ombudsman system has been adopted by several foreign governments in recent years, and the idea of importing it to American has received much attention.[145] The ombudsman is, most simply, an external critic of administration. In 1807, Sweden appointed the first ombudsman, who was charged with surveillance of all bureaucratic agencies. Finland adopted the institution in 1919, and by 1967 it had spread to ten other countries.[146] In the countries where he exists, the ombudsman is usually a prominent jurist, and is aided by a staff of lawyers. He is appointed by the national legislature, and in some countries has jurisdiction over municipal, as well as national administrative agencies.[147]

The ombudsman's goal is improvement of administration rather than punishment of administrators or redress of individual grievances.[148] Thus, instead of conducting formal hearings associated with adjudication, he relies primarily on his own investigations to collect information. He is authorized to receive all civilian complaints against any administrator or department. But valid complaints do not generally invoke adversary confrontations for purposes of adjudicating the propriety of past conduct by an official. Rather, individual grievances serve to alert the ombudsman to questionable administrative policies that deserve investigation. In accordance with his focus on future practices rather than past grievances, the ombudsman may even initiate investigation at his own discretion in the absence of a citizen complaint. To facilitate his inquiries, he may request explanation from an appropriate official, examine an agency's files, or call witnesses and conduct a hearing. On the basis of his findings, the ombudsman may recommend corrective measures to the agency although he cannot compel an official to do anything. In some countries, he may also prosecute a delinquent official, although this power is rarely exercised. In any case, he takes great pains to explain his conclusions to bureaucrats, complainants, and the general public. Since the ombudsman enjoys almost demi-god status in some countries, administrators are likely to heed his criticisms and citizens are not apt to be disturbed when he finds complaints groundless. Furthermore, administrators evidently feel benefitted not only by the ombudsman's rejection of warrantless accusations, but also by his suggestions of fairer and more efficient policies and procedures. At the same time, citizens can see their grievances being translated into broad policy guidelines.

Professor Gellhorn, an eminent proponent of the ombudsman ideal, has asserted its relevance to police community relations in America. First of all, his ombudsman would avoid the tragic flaw of civilian review boards by accepting complaints about any local public servants, not just policemen.[149] Furthermore, Gellhorn contends, full processing of each citizen complaint before referral to administrative superiors for futher consideration constitutes a cumbersome duplication of effort and an unjustifiable displacement of the police department as primary investigator and arbiter of charges against its members.[150] The thrust of his argument is that meaningful improvement in police administration will emerge not from sporadic disciplinary proceedings but rather from imposing upon departmental superiors absolute accountability for the actions of their subordinates.[151] Therefore, the ombudsman should initiate his inquiries only upon charges that departmental superiors have given inadequate attention to a complaint of police misconduct. The focus of evaluation is then not the guilt of a particular policeman, but the policies and procedures by which police superiors have assessed a citizen's allegation of such guilt.[152] The ombudsman, thus relieved of the adversary adjudications that made civilian review boards so unpopular, could supposedly transcend the individual case to address himself to the broader policies of police administration.

We reject Professor Gellhorn's proposal because it eliminates that conciliatory process which was the primary strength of the civilian review boards. If frustration over police practices is indeed a major cause of urban disorders,[153] and if many of the grievances which engender such frustrations can indeed be alleviated by an apology or police explanation,[154] then informal conciliation of the individual case is a necessary function of complaint channels. Because his ombudsman is in effect a court of appeals bound by the factual findings of the police department, it must be presumed that any informal accommodations Gellhorn envisions must be effected by internal processes. Yet such an arrangement presupposes a preexisting community trust of the police, the lack of which supposedly made external review desirable in the first place. When a police department is unable to project an impartial appearance, informal negotiation of a compromise between citizen and policeman must be attempted by an external agency *before* a complaint is

417

referred to the police department for adversary adjudication. Whereas policy orientation undoubtedly offers creative possibilities for external review, the ombudsman should not divorce himself from the individual case to the degree that Professor Gellhorn recommends.

CONCLUSION AND RECOMMENDATIONS

To recapitulate for a moment, none of the remedies discussed above can successfully control the everyday conduct of the policeman on the beat—the harassment and abuse which yields no actual physical damage and results less from ill will than from poor training. The exclusionary rule can remedy denials of constitutional rights in cases which go to trial and result in convictions. Civil damage actions, state or federal, can redress egregious misconduct resulting in actual damage. Injunctive relief can halt and deter systematic misconduct directed at an identifiable person or group of persons. However, solutions for the basic problems of police-community relations cannot be imposed from the outside: as even the most pessimistic commentators have recognized, primary responsibility for everyday police discipline must rest within the police department.

Nevertheless, since internal review has been uniformly sluggish, some kind of outside pressure must be brought to bear to induce voluntary correction of illegal and otherwise abusive police conduct. Mandatory injunctions issued by federal district courts are too cumbersome for this purpose and are susceptible to complete disruption of the internal review mechanism. The civilian review boards are doomed to futility since they pit the aggrieved citizen against the police department in a formal adversary proceeding; in short, someone always wins and someone is always resentful. The ombudsman, on the other hand, shifts the focus from dispute resolution to evaluation of the department's grievance response mechanism. Yet, since the primary goals of an effective complaint mechanism are to provide an objective forum and encourage its use, individual grievances must remain in the forefront, and their dispositions must be publicized.

What is needed is a hybrid of the ombudsman and the external review agency, whose operation would have the following attributes:

(1) The primary responsibility for police discipline must remain with the police department itself.

418

(2) Nevertheless, there must be an easily accessible agency external to the police department, which processes citizen complaints in their inception rather than on appeal from the police.

(3) In each case, this agency should:

(a) make an independent investigation of the complaints;

(b) publicly exonerate the police if the complaint is groundless;

(c) in cases of misunderstanding or minor abuse, attempt to resolve the dispute through an informal conciliation meeting;

(d) if efforts at conciliation should fail or if the police behavior was unacceptable, make recommendations to the Department regarding discipline or ways to relieve tension;

(e) keep each citizen complainant aware of the disposition of his complaint.

(4) On all matters, the agency should keep the public aware of its actions and the Department's response to its recommendations and should publish periodic reports and conclusions.

(5) So as not to single out the police for special oversight the agency should be responsible for processing citizen complaints not only against the police but also against other basic governmental service agencies, such as those responsible for welfare and employment. (For purposes of this chapter, however, we shall focus only on the relation of such an agency to the police department.)

While we affirm that our proposed agency will possess many of the attributes of the Scandinavian "ombudsman," it nevertheless differs from it in many material respects. For purposes of simplicity, however, we will call our agency "ombudsman." Its functioning we will now describe in somewhat greater detail.

Person with claims of police misconduct shall register them directly with the ombudsman without first seeking internal police review. He and his investigative staff shall first make findings of fact. If, after such an investigation, the complaint is found to be groundless, the ombudsman shall order it dismissed. If, however, his findings indicate police impropriety, the ombudsman has two courses open to him— informal conciliation and, if that fails, recommendation to the police commissioner that disciplinary action be taken.

In the first instance, the ombudsman's most useful function is to act as a conciliation agent between the police department and the aggrieved citizen. Since many of the citizen's grievances stem from seemingly trivial incidents, the ombudsman may be able to satisfy the aggrieved citizen by bringing him together with the offending policeman. Out of such meetings might come an apology by the officer for his indiscretion and a better understanding by the citizen of the tensions of day-to-day police work.

Such conciliation procedures and favorable results may seem at first blush naive; however, experience with ombudsmen in foreign countries indicates that conciliation is their strongest weapon in their efforts to eliminate the rough edges of modern bureaucracy.[155] The citizen will often be quite satisfied with an apology or an explanation. Thus, the cumulation of such simple meetings may do much to offset the hostility and violence which can arise when citizens feel powerless against what they perceive as thoughtless and arrogant uses of governmental power.

When a complaint is found to be meritorious and conciliation attempts have failed or are clearly unsuitable, the ombudsman shall send a recommendation to the police department that a particular officer be disciplined. The ombudsman shall make such recommendation only as the last resort in any given case. On receipt of such recommendation, the responsibility for discipline shall be with the department itself.

What if the police department decides not to act on the ombudsman's recommendation? This knotty problem really presents two separate issues—non-action in a given case and non-action in most cases (indicating a course of conduct by the department not to heed the recommendation of the ombudsman). We feel that the systematic refusal of the department to cooperate with the ombudsman can be overcome by bringing it to public light in the ombudsman's periodic reports. The force of public opinion should push a clearly defiant police department into action. Although many citizens fear undue hampering of police efforts to curb crime, few will sanction police lawlessness. Moreover, refusal to heed the recommendations of the independent ombudsman should engender indignant response even from members of the majority community who have little contact with the police.[156]

Despite our concern for refusal to act on the ombudsman's recommendation as a general course of conduct, we emphasize that the department must retain discretion in each case to decide whether there should be disciplinary action and what the punishment should be. Maintenance of police morale and efficient law enforcement require that the department make the final decision. Thus, if in individual instances the police department disagrees with the ombudsman's recommendation, the department's good faith should be accepted.

In sum, then, if the police department systematically refuses to respond to the ombudsman's recommendation with reasonable exercises of internal discipline, the ombudsman should bring this recalcitrance to public attention in his periodic reports and rely on public pressure to activate internal police machinery. On the other hand, should the police generally follow his suggestions but occasionally refuse to act, the ombudsman should seek an explanation and accept such exercises of discretion as good faith determinations that in their opinion no action was justified.

Whatever the outcome of departmental action on the ombudsman's recommendations, his final duty in the processing of citizen complaints will be to publicize the action taken. First, he should inform the complainant directly of the action taken on his complaint. In addition, he should record both his and the Department's dispositions for general information to the public. We suggest that in informing the general public he should not refer by name to the officer disciplined but merely should report that as a result of his recommendation the department fined, suspended, etc., an officer on a given date. The purpose of informing the complainant of the outcome of the case is to give him confidence that his complaint was duly considered and acted upon. The more general record serves to keep the public aware that legitimate grievances against the police do have an effective, nonviolent outlet.

In addition to processing citizen grievances, the ombudsman should publish periodic reports. We suggest that these public reports be submitted every six months. At the very least, such reports should include statistical accounts of the number and disposition of private complaints coming to his attention. Moreover, because naked statistics are often subject to inconsistent interpretations, the ombudsman should make an assessment of the overall performance of his office and responsiveness of the police to his suggestions. We must reiterate that this assessment is the ombudsman's most potent weapon for marshalling public support and for prodding a recalcitrant police force. Together with an assessment of the ombudsman's work with the police in dealing with private complaints, the report should contain recommendations of a general nature drawn from an overview of the complaints. For example, the ombudsman might recommend that a slight change in present police practice could eliminate a substantial irritant in police community relations.

His recommendations should extend not only to police practice guidelines but also to legislative action he deems necessary to defuse the ghettos or improve law enforcement. For instance, a very common complaint in ghetto communities is that the police do not readily respond to calls for help. If the reason is that the police force is substantially undermanned, the ombudsman could lend the authority of his voice to call for the legislative body to allocate more money for more police services. By making substantive recommendations to the legislature and suggesting guidelines for police practice to minimize citizen complaints the ombudsman's reports could be a truly effective force for vigorous yet benign law enforcement.

Finally, having described in a general way the duties of the ombudsman, we advert briefly to questions of agency structure and funding. In this regard we merely sketch our suggestions, as follows:

(1) at least some of the initial funding must come from federal government because of the already great demands on municipal and state funds;

(2) the agency must be locally controlled;

(3) the agency must be supplied with sufficient funds to attract a first-rate investigative staff;

(4) the agency must be organized to process complaints quickly and efficiently;

(5) since conciliation will be its primary function, the agency must be highly visible; accordingly, we recommend that it have neighborhood offices and a publicity budget;

(6) the ombudsman must be a man who can secure the cooperation of all parties affected by his office and can muster public support for his recommendation; such men will be available only if the community is committed to the success of his project;

(7) the ombudsman appointment procedure should leave him representing no particular interest group and above political pressure;

(8) the ombudsman should be appointed to a single four to six year term and should be empowered to select his own staff.

A FINAL PLEA

Now, for the third time in less than three years, a Presidential Commission has recommended the creation of local citizens' grievance agencies similar to the one outlined above.[157] The President's Commission on the Causes and Prevention of Violence, for whom this chapter was originally prepared, stated in its final report, submitted to President Nixon on December 10, 1969:

> Both the President's Commission on Law Enforcement and Administration of Justice (Crime Commission) and the National Advisory Commission on Civil Disorders (Kerner Commission) recommended that local jurisdictions establish adequate mechanisms for processing citizen grievances about the conduct of public officials. That recommendation has not received the attention or the response it deserves.

> *To increase the responsiveness of local governments to the needs and rights of their citizens, we recommend that the federal government allocate seed money to a limited number of state and local jurisdictions demonstrating an interest in establishing citizens' grievance agencies.*[158]

It is clear that those of our nation's citizens who sit on Presidential Commissions unanimously endorse this proposal. It is our earnest hope that the nation's legislators, federal, state and local, will soon respond.

REFERENCES

1. 232 U.S. 383 (1914).
2. *Id.* at 392 (italics supplied).
3. *Id.* at 393 (italics supplied).
4. *Olmstead* v. *United States*, 277 U.S. 438, 470 (1928). (Dissenting opinion.)
5. *Id.* at 484. (Dissenting opinion.)
6. 44 Cal. 2d 434, 445, 282 P. 2d 905, 912 (1955).
7. 367 U.S. 643 (1961).
8. *Supra* note 6, at 913.
9. *Id.* at 911.
10. Barrett, "Personal Rights, Property Rights and the Fourth Amendment," 1960 *Sup. Ct. Rev.* 46, 54-55. An example of police misconduct not reached by the exclusionary rule is the Plainfield search described in Bean, "Plainfield: A Study in Law and Violence," 6 *Am. Crim. L.Q.* 154 (1968).
11. 394 F. 2d 443 (2d Cir. 1968). (Dissenting opinion.)
12. *Id.* at 452.
13. *Id.*
14. *Silverthorne Lumber Co.* v. *United States*, 251 U.S. 385 (1919).
15. *Bynum* v. *United States*, 262 F. 2d (D.C. Cir. 1958).
16. *Wong Sun* v. *United States*, 371 U.S. 471 (1963).

17. *Id.* The test was formulated by Professor Maguire; see Maguire *Evidence of Guilt* 221 (1959).

18. 88 S. Ct. 2008 (1968). (Dissenting opinion.)

19. 348 F. 2d 823, 835 (5th Cir. 1965). (Concurring opinion.) Judge Friendly (2d. Cir.) sat by designation in the Fifth Circuit.

20. 386 U.S. 18 (1966).

21. *Griffin* v. *California,* 380 U.S. 609 (1965).

22. 386 U.S. at 24.

23. *Id.* at 26.

24. 89 S. Ct. 1726 (1969).

25. Dakin, "Municipal Immunity in Police Torts," 16 *Clev. Mar. L. Rev.* 448 (1967).

26. II National Commission on Law Observance and Enforcement, No. 8 *Report on Criminal Procedure* 19 (1931).

27. At the very least, the civil plaintiff must bear attorney costs, and thus many actions against the police are undoubtedly precluded by the aggrieved party's lack of funds. United States Commission on Civil Rights, 1961 *Commission on Civil Rights Report: Justice,* V. 81 (1961).

28. *Ker.* v. *Illinois,* 119 U.S. 436, 444 (1886).

29. Foote, "Tort Remedies for Police Violations of Individual Rights," 39 *Minn L Rev.* 493, 500 (1955).

30. 1961 *Commission on Civil Rights Report: Justice, supra* note 27, at 81; President's Commission on Law Enforcement and Administration of Justice (hereinafter cited as Crime Commission), *Task Force Report: The Police,* at 199; Dakin, *supra* note 25, at 448-449.

31. E.g., Foote, *supra* note 29; Fuller and Casner, "Municipal Tort Liability in Operation," 54 *Harv. L. Rev.* 437 (1941); Jaffe, "Suits Against Governments and Officers Damage Actions," 77 *Harv. L. Rev.* 209 (1963). Lawyer, "Birth and Death of Government Immunity," 15 *Clev. Mar. L. Rev.* 529 (1966); Mathes S. Jones, *supra* note 26; Tooke, "The Extension of Municipal Liability in Tort," 19 *U. Va. L. Rev.* 97 (1932).

32. Foote, *supra* note 29, at 515. See "Arrest of Wrong Person," 18 *So. Calif. L. Rev.* 162 (1944).

33. A growing disenchantment for the doctrine has recently led some states and cities to abolish it by statute. E.g., Cal. Gov't Code §§ 815.2, 825, 825.2 (1966); Minn. Stat. Ann. § 466.02 (1963); N.Y. Ct. Cl. Act. § 8 (1963); Wash. Rev. Code of Wash. Ann. § 4.920.090 (1962). Others have abolished the doctrine by judicial fiat. *Hargrove* v. *Cocoa Beach,* 96 So. 2d 130 (Fla. 1957); *Steele* v. *Anchorage,* 385 P. 2d 582 (Alas. 1963); *Stone* v. *Arizona Highways Comm.,* 93 Ariz. 384, 381 P. 2d 107 (1963); *Molitor* v. *Kaneland Community Unit Dist. No. 302,* 18 Ill. 2d 11, 163 N.E. 2d 89 (1959); *Williams* v. *Detroit,* 364 Mich. 231, 111 N.W. 2d 1 (1961); *McAndrew* v. *Mularchuk,* 33 N.J. 172, 162 A. 2d 820 (1960); *Kelso* v. *Tacoma,* 63 Wash. 2d 912, 390

P. 2d 2 (1964); *Holtyz* v. *Milwaukee*, 17 Wis. 2d 26, 115 N.W. 2d 618 (1962). A District of Columbia judge has recently ruled that the government may be sued when its policemen are accused of brutality. *Washington Post*, Jan. 7, 1969, at D1.

Five states have modified sovereign immunity where the municipality has insurance. Idaho Code Ann. § 41-3505 (1961); Mo. Ann. Stat. § 71.185 (Supp. 1969); N.H. Rev. Stat. Ann. § 412.3 (1968); N.D. Cent. Code § 40-43-07 (1968); Ut. Stat. tit. 29, § 1403 (Supp. 1968). Illinois and Connecticut indemnify governmental employees for judgments incurred for torts committed in the course of carrying out their duties. Comm. Gen. Stat. § 7-465 (Supp. 1969); Ill. Rev. Stat., Ch. 24, § 1-4-5 (1962), §1-4-6 (Supp. 1969).

34. See note *supra* 31.
35. 17 Stat. 13 § 1 (1871).
36. *Pierson* v. *Ray*, 386 U.S. 547 (1967); *Monroe* v. *Pape*, 365 U.S. 167 (1961).
37. The past 8 years have witnessed a marked increase in cases under 42 U.S.C. § 1983. The annual numbers of private civil actions filed in district courts under the Civil Rights Act are in the Annual Report[s] of the Administrative Office of the United States (Table C2)

Year	Number of Cases
1958	220
1959	247
1960	280
1961	270
1962	357
1963	424
1964	645
1965	994
1966	1,154

Not all of these cases alleged police misconduct; many were directed at other state and local officials by citizens claiming to have been unreasonably deprived of economic rights—licenses, contracts and the like.

38. 365 U.S. 167 (1961).
39. *Id.* at 187. Further, the Court states: "Section 1979 [now 1983] should be read against the background of tort liability that makes a man responsible for the natural consequences of his actions. *Id.*
40. 386 U.S. 547 (1967).
41. E.g., *Whirl* v. *Kern*, 407 F.2d 781 (5th Cir. 1969); *Hughes* v. *Smith*, 264 F. Supp. 767 (D.N.J. 1967). In *Whirl*, the Court held that subjective good faith could not exculpate a sheriff from § 1983 liability to a person who had been detained improperly in jail for almost nine months because of a failure to process the papers dismissing the indictment against him. The "good faith and probable cause" talisman just doesn't fit in such circum-

stances. In finding the requisite fault in *Whirl*, the Court simply held that this police omission was unreasonable despite the absence of bad faith.

Moreover, prior to *Pierson*, many courts applied such a standard: "One essential requirement of an action under this section is that the plaintiff show facts which indicate that the defendant, at the time he acted, knew or as a reasonable man should have known that his acts were ones which would deprive the plaintiff of his constitutional rights or might lead to that result." *Bowens* v. *Knazze,* 237 F. Supp. 826 (N.D. Ill. 1965). See *Cohen* v. *Norris,* 300 F. 2d 24 (9th Cir. 1962) (unforeseeability due to defects in a warrant may be a good defense); *Bargainer* v. *Michal,* 233 F. Supp. 270 (N.D. Ohio, 1964) (police must be protected from "honest misunderstandings of statutory authority and mere errors of judgment."); *Beauregard* v. *Winegard,* 363 F. 2d 901 (9th Cir. 1966) (where probable cause for an arrest exists, civil rights are not violated even though innocence may subsequently be established—even actual malice in undertaking an investigation will not permit recovery if that investigation produced probable cause).

42. *Bargainer* v. *Michal,* 233 F. Supp. 270 (N.D. Ohio 1964), where the court in diction conceded the difficulty of applying § 1983 to an assault by a policeman unaccompanied by an arrest. See also, *Selico* v. *Jackson,* 201 F. Supp. 475, 478 (S.D. Cal. 1962); "[Where] . . . facts are alleged which indicate not only an illegal and unreasonable arrest and an illegal detention, but also an unprovoked physical violence exerted upon the persons of the plaintiffs . . . It certainly cannot seriously be urged that defendant acted as a result of error or honest misunderstanding." See *Basista* v. *Weir,* 340 F. 2d 74 (3d Cir. 1965); *Hardwick* v. *Hurley* 289 F. 2d 529 (7th Cir. 1961); *Hughes* v. *Smith,* 264 F. Supp. 767 (D.N.J. 1967); *Dodd* v. *Spokane County,* 393 F. 2d 330 (9th Cir. 1968) (assault by prison official actionable); *Jackson* v. *Martin,* 261 F. Supp. 902 (N.D. Miss. 1966) (allegation provocation shot plaintiff states a good cause of action under § 1983).

43. *Lankford* v. *Gelston,* 364 F. 2d 197 (4th Cir. 1966). Here where police officers had on 300 occasions over 19 days, searched third persons' homes, without search warrants and on uninvestigated and anonymous tips, for suspects, the court, in granting petitioners injunctive relief from this practice, said: "There can be little doubt that actions for money damages would not suffice to repair the injury suffered by the victims of police searches . . . [T]he wrongs inflicted are not readily measurable in terms of dollars and cents. Indeed the Supreme Court itself has already declared that the prospect of pecuniary redress for the harm suffered is 'worthless and futile.' Moreover, the lesson of experience is that the remote possibility of money damages serves as no deterrent to future police invasions." *Id.* at 202.

44. *Report of the National Advisory Commission on Civil Disorders* (Washington, D.C.: Government Printing Office, 1968), at 159. (Hereinafter cited as *Kerner Report.*)

"Harassment" or discourtesy may not be the result of malicious or discriminatory intent of police officers. Many officers simply fail to understand the effects of their actions because of their limited knowledge of the Negro community. . . .

In assessing the impact of police misconduct, we emphasize that the improper acts of relatively few officers may create severe tensions between the department and the entire Negro community.

45. See Shapo, "Constitutional Tort: *Monroe* v. *Pape* and the Frontiers Beyond," 60 *N.W.U.L.* Rev. 277, 327-29 (1965).

46. A sampling of the cases in which recoveries were made for police violence reveals truly outrageous conduct. See *McArthur* v. *Pennington,* 253 F. Supp. 420 (E.D. Tenn. 1963) ($5100 total damages proper for wrongful arrest by a city policeman—$1800 out of pocket damage to plaintiff, $1600 lost wages and the rest for humiliation, mental suffering and injury to reputation); *Brooks* v. *Moss,* 242 F. Supp. 531 (W.D.S.C. 1965) ($3,500 actual damages and $500 punitive damages proper where plaintiff received a serious blow to the head and such an attack and the subsequent false criminal prosecution were clearly in violation of his constitutional rights); *Jackson* v. *Duke,* 259 F. 2d 3 (5th Cir. 1958) (Award of $5000 to person who was pistol whipped, knocked down and stomped, kicked in the face, throat and stomach, falsely arrested, falsely accused of drunkenness and unlawfully jailed was not excessive).

47. 367 U.S. 643 (1961); See also *Wolf* v. *Colorado,* 338 U.S. 25, 41-44 (1949) (Murphy, J., dissenting).

48. *Lankford* v. *Gelston, supra* note 43, at 202; see *Pierce* v. *Society of Sisters,* 268 U.S. 510, 536 (1925).

49. E.g., *City of Jacksonville* v. *Wilson,* 157 Fla. 838, 27 So. 2d 108, 112, (1946); *Delaney* v. *Flood,* 183 N.Y. 323, 76 N.E. 209 (1906). See also, Annot., 83 A.L.R. 2d 1007, 1016-17 (1962).

50. No injunction will issue if the plaintiff fails to move that the police acted without reasonable grounds or probable cause. See *Seaboard N.Y. Corp.* v. *Wallander,* 192 Misc. 227, 80 N.Y.S. 2d 715 (Sup. Ct. 1948); *Monfrino* v. *Gutelius,* 66 Ohio App. 293, 33 N.E. 2d 1003 (1939); *Kalwin Business Men's Ass'n.* v. *McLaughlin,* 216 App. Div. 6, 214 N.Y. Supp. 507 (1926); *Joyner* v. *Hammond,* 199 Iowa 919, 200 N.W. 571 (1924). The police will also be enjoined if they acted maliciously or in bad faith. See *Hague* v. *CIO,* 307 U.S. 496 *aff'g with modifications* 191 F. 2d 774 (3d Cir. 1939); Comment, "Federal Injunctive Relief From Illegal Search", 1967 *Wash. U.L.Q.* 104, 109-110.

51. See, e.g., *Upton Enterprises* v. *Strand,* 195 Cal. App. 2d 45, 15 Cal. Rptr. 486 (1961).

52. Every person who, under color of any statute, ordinance regulation, custom or usage . . . subject, or causes to be subjected, any citizen of the United States or other person within the jurisdiction thereof to the deprivation of any rights, privileges, or immunities . . . shall be liable to the party injured in . . . suit in equity, or other proper proceeding for redress. 42 U.S.C. Sec. 1983 (1964).

53. See Note, "The Federal Injunction as a Remedy for Unconstitutional Police Conduct", 78 *Yale L.J.* 143, 146 1968).

54. 307 U.S. 496, *Aff'g with modifications* 101 F. 2d 774 (3d Cir. 1939), *aff'g* 25 F. Supp. 127 (D.N.J. 1938).

55. *Wolin* v. *Port of N.Y. Auth.,* 392 F. 2d 83 (2d Cir. 1968), *cert. denied* 393 U.S. 940 (1968) (enjoining the port authority from interfering with plaintiffs' distribution of anti-war leaflets at bus terminal); *Williams* v. *Wallace,* 240 F. Supp. 100 (M.D. Ala. 1965) (Enjoining the Governor and other officials of Alabama from interfering with proposed march by Negroes to petition the government for redress of their grievances in being deprived of the right to vote); *Local 309, United Furniture Workers* v. *Gates,* 75 F. Supp. 620 (N.D. Ind. 1948) (enjoining state police from attending union meeting held for purposes of discussion strike then in progress).

56. *Wheeler* v. *Goodman* 6 Cr.L. 2163 (W.D.N.C. 1969) granting permanent injunction against police harassment of a privately owned hippie haven in Charlotte, North Carolina); *Houser* v. *Hill,* 278 F. Supp. 920 (M.D. Ala. 1968) (granting injunction against police found to have, *inter alia,* interfered with peaceful and lawful assemblies and failed to provide proper police protection against hostile persons intimidating these peaceful assemblies); *Cottonreader* v. *Johnson,* 252 F. Supp. 492 (M.D. Ala. 1966) (granting injunction to secure the safety and security of Negroes demonstrating against the denial of constitutional rights).

57. 74 F. Supp. 336 (N.D. Ga. 1947).

58. 364 F. 2d 197 (4th Cir. 1966).

59. After the fatal shooting of a police officer, the Baltimore police, searching for the suspects, made over 300 searches of mostly Negro homes without warrants, proceeding on the basis of anonymous phone tips. These searches were conducted very often in an offensive manner, without the owners' consent, and without explanation by the police. The plaintiffs, Negroes, brought an action in the district court seeking a temporary restraining order and a preliminary injunction against the continuation of these tactics. No restraining order was issued, but three days later the police commissioner issued a General Order declaring that an officer must have "probable cause" to believe the suspects were inside before searching a dwelling and the searches without warrants ceased. Thereafter, the district court refused to issue a preliminary injunction because it appeared that

the relief was unnecessary. The illegal searches had almost completely stopped by the time the General Order was issued, and the district court was of the opinion that such searches would be prevented in the future. The Circuit Court, however, emphasized the atrocity of the police tactics, the invasion of the rights of innocent citizens and the inadequacy of any possible redress at law. They found that the General Order was inadequate as a guarantee against possible recurrences of widespread illegal searches, and therefore ordered the district court to issue the injunction.

60. *Lankford* v. *Gelston, supra* note 43, at 201-02; *Refoule* v. *Ellis,* 74 F. Supp. at 343 (1947).

61. *Id.*

62. E.g., *Black People's Unity Movement* v. *Pierce,* Civil No. 848-68 (D.N.J. filed August 23, 1968); *Black Panther Party* v. *Leary,* Civil No 68–3599 (S.D.N.Y. filed September 10, 1968). It would not be surprising if current investigations into alleged police vendettas against the Black Panthers in Chicago and San Francisco culminate in civil suits under § 1983, in addition to possible criminal proceedings against the police.

63. E.g., *Andich* v. *Daley,* Civil No. 68C. 958 (N.D. Ill., filed May 27, 1968) complaint alleged that Chicago police had in April, 1968, deliberately disrupted the demonstration of anti-war protesters, a significant number of whom belonged to the Chicago Peace Council.

64. Note, *supra* note 53, at 147.

65. A scheme which seems to work for one city of a particular region, size, and political atmosphere may not be appropriate for an entirely different urban climate. Such hypothetically determined judgments are best left to the legislature. Application of a successful internal review mechanism of any given police department to other departments may also be misguided, because the apparent adequacy of its complaint and disciplinary framework may be a product less of ideal procedural formalities than the quality of the people who administer them.

66. Note, *supra* note 53, at 149.

67. *Id.* at 150.

68. *Id.*

69. As of 1960, less than half of the States had any criminal provisions relating directly to unreasonable searches and seizures. The punitive sanctions of the 23 states attempting to control such invasions of the right of privacy are collected in *Mapp* v. *Ohio,* 367 U.S. 643, 652 note 7 (1960).

70. *Commonwealth* v. *Cheney,* 141 Mass. 102, 6 N.E. 724 (1886) (if an officer makes an arrest and it turns out that no crime has been committed, his good faith in the performance of his official duty is a defense to a criminal prosecution, although it would not be a civil action). See also *Commonwealth* v. *Trunk,*

311 Pa. 555, 167 A. 333 (1933); *Henderson* v. *State,* 95 Ga. App. 830, 99 S.E. 2d 270 (1957).
71. 52 *Am. Jur.* Trespass Sec. 84 (1944).
72. *Brown* v. *Martinez,* 68 N.M. 271, 361 P. 2d 152 (1961); *Owens* v. *Town of Atkins,* 163 Ark. 82, 259 S.W. 396 (1924).
73. *People* v. *Winig,* 7 Misc. 2d 803, 163 N.Y.S. 2d 995 (1957); *People* v. *Barton,* 18 AD 2d 612, 234 N.Y.S. 2d 263 (1962); *Barber* v. *State,* 199 Ind. 146, 155 N.E. 819 (1927).
74. *State* v. *Faggart,* 170 N.C. 737, 87 S.E. 31 (1915).
75. *State* v. *Turner,* 60 Conn. 222, 22 A. 542 (1891). *Whittlesey* v. *U.S.* 221 A. 2d (1966).
76. Foote, *supra* note 29, at 494.
77. Whoever, under color of any law, statute, ordinance, regulation or custom, willfully subjects any inhabitant of any State, Territory, or District to the deprivation of any rights, privileges, or immunities secured or protected by the Constitution or laws of the United States, or to different punishments, pains, or penalties, on account of such inhabitant being an alien, or by reason of his color, or race, than are prescribed for the punishment of citizens, shall be fined not more than $1,000 or imprisoned not more than one year, or both. June 25, 1948, ch. 645, 62 Stat. 696. 18 U.S.C. § 242 (1964).
78. 325 U.S. 91 (1945).
79. "But in view of our construction of the word 'willfully', the jury should have been instructed that it was not sufficient that petitioners had a generally bad purpose. To convict it was necessary for them to find that petitioners had the purpose to deprive the petitioner of a constitutional right . . ." at 107.
Further: "When they act willfully in the sense in which we use the word, they act in open defiance or unreckless disregard of a constitutional requirement which has been made specific and definite."
80. See Foote, *supra* note 29; but see Caldwell and Brodie, "Enforcement of the Criminal Civil Rights Statute, 18 U.S.C. Section 242. In Prison Brutality Cases," 52 *Geo. L. J.* 706 (1964) which suggests that since the creation of the Civil Rights Division of the Justice Department there has been more action under this statute. The cases he cites have little to do with police conduct outside the prison setting.
81. In the area of police conduct exclusive of the prison setting there have been only nineteen cases since the *Screws* decision of which thirteen ended in conviction. See especially, *Miller* v. *United States,* 404 F. 2d 611 (5th Cir. 1968) where the court upheld the conviction of two Louisiana police officers for wilfull brutality and infliction of summary punishment by making their police dog bite the suspect in order to coerce a confession from him.
82. *Williams* v. *United States,* 341 U.S. 97 (1951) (private detective holding special officers cards of city police brutally beat

confessions from suspected lumber yard thieves); *Lynch* v. *United States*, 189 F. 2d 476 (5th Cir.), *cert. den.* 342 U.S. 831 (1950) (Officer of laws who, having prisoner in his custody, assaulted and beat him was found guilty under this section). See also, *Apodaca* v. *United States*, 188 F. 2d 932 (10th Cir. 1951); *United States* v. *Jackson*, 235 F. 2d 925 (8th Cir. 1951); *Koehler* v. *United States*, 189 F. 2d 711 (5th Cir. 1951), *cert. den.* 342 U.S. 852, rehearing den., 342 U.S. 889.

83. See our argument above that any looser standard would gravely and unduly hamper law enforcement efforts.

84. 68 Stat. 803, 18 U.S.C. 2236 (1948) (unlawful search and seizure); 62 Stat. 803, 18 U.S.C. 2236 (1948) (malicious procurement of a warrant); 62 Stat., 803, 18 U.S.C. 2234 (1948) (exceeding authority under a warrant).

85. The first formulation of this proposal is in 8 Wigmore, *Evidence,* Sec. 2184 (3d ed. 1940):

The natural way to do justice here would be to enforce the healthy principle of the Fourth Amendment directly, i.e., by sending for the high-handed, over-zealous marshal who had searched without a warrant, imposing a thirty-day imprisonment for his contempt of the Constitution, and then proceeding to affirm the sentence of the convicted criminal.

For a recent development of this theme, see Blumrosen, "Contempt of Court and Unlawful Police Action," 11 *Rutgers L. Rev.* 526 (1957).

86. 8 Wigmore, *Evidence,* Sec. 2184–85 (3d ed. 1940); and *id.* at 526–29.

87. *Bloom* v. *Illinois,* 391 U.S. 194 (1968).

88. *Field Surveys V, A National Survey of Police and Community Relations.* Prepared by the National Center on Police and Community Relations, Michigan State University, for the President's Commission on Law Enforcement and Administration of Justice 193-205 (1967).

89. Crime Commission, *supra* note 30, *Task Force Report: The Police,* at 195. Citizen apathy is apt not to tolerate the effort and delays incident to a complicated procedure for filing complaints. See Niederhoffer, "Restraint for the Police: A Recurrent Problem," 1 *U. Conn. L. Rev.* 288-296 (1968).

90. Note, "The Administration of Complaints by Civilians Against the Police," 77 *Harv. L. Rev.* 501-502 (1964).

91. See Niederhoffer, *supra* note 89, at 296.

92. In Washington, D.C., in 1962 the Police Department charged 40 percent of all persons who complained of police abuse with filing a false report. By contrast, only 0.003 percent of those who reported other crimes were similarly charged. Michigan State Survey, *supra* note 88, at 204.

93. Crime Commission, *supra* note 30, *Task Force Report: The Police,* at 195.

94. See J. Lohman and G. Misner, *The Police and the Community: The Dynamics of Their Relationship in a Changing*

Society, II, at 174 (1966). Governor's Select Commission on Civil Disorder, State of New Jersey, *Report for Action* 35 (1968).

95. Crime Commission, *supra* note 30, *Task Force Report: The Police,* at 195.

96. *Id.*

97. Michigan State Survey, *supra* note 88, at 201-202. The Harvard Study found fewer than 5 percent of responding departments relied exclusively on a special independent unit to investigate complaints. But some, such as the New York City Department, provided for review of line investigations by a specially assigned supervisor. In Los Angeles, an Internal Affairs Division had the discretion to supplement a local investigation with an independent inquiry of its own. Note, "The Administration of Complaints by Civilians Against the Police," *supra* note 90, at 503-05.

98. The line investigator, whose views are likely to parallel those of his accused colleague, may not find the alleged violation particularly offensive. J. Lohman & G. Misner, *supra* note 94, II, at 203. His disposition to vigorously investigate may also be dampened by the realization that he may be the subject of a similar investigation in the future by the defending officer. Michigan State Survey, *supra* note 88, at 219. Finally, a sense of organizational loyalty may persuade a local investigator to whitewash the indiscretions of a compatriot in the interests of preserving the department's reputation. Niederhoffer, *supra* note 89, at 296.

99. Crime Commission, *supra* note 30, *Task Force Report: The Police,* at 196.

100. Note, "The Administration of Complaints by Civilians Against the Police," *supra* note 90, at 506.

101. *Id.* at 507. About 40 percent of trial boards have no jurisdiction over a complaint while a civil or criminal suit is pending against either the accused officer or the complainant. That a hearing should be barred by a civil action or an unrelated criminal prosecution is inexplicable. Furthermore, 25 percent of the review boards are prohibited from hearing a complaint after a related judicial determination has exonerated the policeman or convicted the complainant. Yet the absence of legal liability seems irrelevant to the need to discipline a miscreant officer. *Id.* at 506.

102. Michigan State Survey, *supra* note 88, at 223. Even when the hearings are open to the public, the complainant is rarely allowed to examine the investigation report for purposes of rebuttal. *Id.* at 203. It has been noted that in police hearings the citizen often appears to be the one on trial, as he is barraged with irrelevant and threatening questioning, J. Lohman and G. Misner, *supra* note 94, II, at 203.

103. Michigan State Survey, *supra* note 88, at 203. The complainant is typically merely assured that his grievance has been

432

adequately handled, which leaves him feeling ignored as he suspected he would be in the first place. J. Lohman and G. Misner, *supra* note 94, I, at 172, 174.

104. It would seem that the many covert incidents of internal review hurt the police more than help them. Surely all the safeguards against public exposure must lead many people to think the police's wash is dirtier than it really is.

105. Michigan State Survey, *supra* note 88, at 186. Prior to the establishment of a citizen Police Advisory Board, no Philadelphia officer had even been disciplined on the basis of a citizen complaint of police abuse. Coxe, "The Philadelphia Police Advisory Board," 2 *L. in Trans. Q.* 179, 185 (1965). Of 30 brutality complaints to the Inspection Officer of the Newark Police Department in 1966-67, none resulted in a policeman being charged. New Jersey Report, *supra* note 94, at 35.

106. A recent study indicated that in 32 cases of proven brutality in Detroit, the punishment exceeded a written reprimand only twice. See Michigan State Survey, *supra* note 88, at 186. Much criticism was directed at the leniency of a recent ruling by a police chief that an officer accused of brutality be fined $50 and ordered to attend a human relations course at the police academy. See *Washington Post,* Sept. 19, 1968, at B1, Sept. 23, 1968, at A20.

107. In Philadelphia, "rude or offensive language or conduct offensive to the public" invokes the same five-day suspension as "unexcused tardiness." In fact, the entire Disciplinary Code seems geared to punishing conduct the Department finds offensive to its own tastes, rather than those of the public. See J. Lohman and G. Misner, *supra* note 94, II, at 204.

108. For a discussion of the advantages and disadvantages of internal review, see Note, "The Administration of Complaints by Civilians Against the Police," *supra* note 90, at 516.

109. In 1966-67, fewer brutality complaints were brought to the Newark police than to other agencies, such as the Neighborhood Legal Services Project. New Jersey Report, *supra* note 94, at 36. In addition to the citizen apathy and fear of retaliation mentioned at notes 88 and 91, *supra,* other factors may discourage complaints by minority groups. Some persons evidently are disposed never to trust an agency against which they have a grievance. *Kerner Report, supra* note 44, at 310. "If the black community perceives the police force as an enemy of occupation, then they are not going to take the trouble to file their complaints with the enemy." Niederhoffer, *supra* note 89, at 295.

110. We believe that an internal review board—in which the police department itself receives and acts on complaints—regardless of its efficiency and fairness, can rarely generate the necessary community confidence, or protect the police against unfounded charges." *Kerner Report, supra* note 44, at 162.

111. "Perhaps the single most potent weapon against unlawful police violence is a police commander who will not tolerate it. The converse is also true: where police leaders assume a permissive attitude toward violence by their men, they are often licensing brutality." United States Commission on Civil Rights, 1961, *Commission on Civil Rights Report: Justice,* V, *supra* note 27, at 82.

112. See *Report of the President's Commission on Crime in the District of Columbia* (Washington, D.C.: Government Printing Office, 1966), at 219-23.

113. Crime Commission, *supra* note 30. *Task Force Report: The Police,* at 200.

114. A. Black, *The People and the Police* 78 (1968). The author, who was Chairman of the New York Civilian Review Board, blamed the referendum results on an extensive publicity campaign against the board speared by the Fraternal Order of the Police and the fact that a "yes" vote at the polls was curiously a vote against the CCRB. *Id.* at 208-15.

115. *Id* at 86-87.

116. *Id.* at 113-15.

117. *Id.* at 93.

118. *Id.* at 122-26.

119. *Id.* at 130.

120. *Id.* at 94.

121. *Id.* at Appendix IV.

122. *Id.* at 101.

123. *Id.* at 100.

124. Crime Commission, *supra* note 30, *Task Force Report: The Police,* at 201.

125. See table in J. Lohman and G. Misner, *supra* note 94, at 236.

126. See table in *id.* at 245.

127. *Id.* at 259.

128. Coxe, *supra* note 105, at 183-184.

129. See table in J. Lohman and G. Misner, *supra* note 94, at 254-255.

130. *Id.*

131. *Id.* at 255.

132. Coxe, *supra* note 105, at 185.

133. See table in J. Lohman and G. Misner, *supra* note 94, at 236.

134. Coxe, *supra* note 105, at 183-84.

135. J. Lohman and G. Misner, *supra* note 94, at 253.

136. Note, "The Administration of Complaints by Civilians Against the Police," *supra* note 90, at 514.

137. J. Lohman and G. Misner, *supra* note 94, at 239.

138. See *id.* at 213-15, 261-65.

139. Judge Weinrott of the Court of Common Pleas of Phila-

delphia County last year reaffirmed his March 1967 ruling that since the PAB had functioned as a judicial tribunal and not as an advisory board, it was an illegal extension of the Mayor's powers. *Philadelphia Evening Bulletin,* Nov. 14, 1968, at 9.

140. See *supra* note 114.

141. J. Lohman and G. Misner, *supra* note 94, at 262.

142. This image probably poisoned the other incidents of review board activity as well. Police investigations for the board may have been colored by the temptation to save a fellow officer from persecution at a hearing. Similarly, many a complainant must have decided filing a grievance was not worth incurring the wrath of the police at a formal trial.

143. *Kerner Report, supra* note 44, at 162.

144. Crime Commission, *supra* note 30, *Challenge of Crime in a Free Society,* at 103.

145. See, e.g., Walter Gellhorn, *Ombudsman and Others* (Cambridge: Harvard University Press, 1966); Gellhorn, *When Americans Complain: Governmental Grievance Procedures* (Cambridge: Harvard University Press, 1966); Donald C. Rowat, ed., *The Ombudsman, Citizen's Defender* (London: Allen and Unwin, (1965); Stanley V. Anderson, ed., *Ombudsman for American Government?* (Englewood Cliffs, N.J.: Prentice Hall, 1968).

146. Rowat, "The Spread of the Ombudsman Idea," in *Ombudsman for American Government?, id.* at 7.

147. See Bexelius, "The Ombudsman for Civil Affairs," in *The Ombudsman, Citizen's Defender, supra* note 145, at 22, 28.

148. The following description of the ombudsman's powers is taken from Gwyn, "Transferring the Ombudsman," in *Ombudsman for American Government?, supra* note 145, at 27, 38-40.

149. W. Gellhorn, *When Americans Complain: Governmental Grievance Procedures, supra* note 145, at 192.

150. *Id.* at 191.

151. *Id.* at 193.

152. *Id* at 191.

153. *Kerner Report, supra* note 44, at 284.

154. J. Lohman, and G. Misner, *supra* note 94, at 284.

155. Rowat, *supra* note 145; and Gellhorn, *Ombudsman and Others, supra* note 145.

156. See also, *Kerner Report, supra* note 44, at 163.

157. Both the Michigan State Field Survey, *supra* note 88, and the President's National Advisory Commission on Civil Disorders, *supra* note 44, at 162-3, made similar recommendations for strengthening police-community relations. Without reviewing in detail their conclusions, we note that our proposal differs in material respects from both.

The Michigan State study proposed an external agency which would entertain appeals from internal review, conducting independent investigations and publicizing its findings of fact. However, filing complaints in the first instance with the police retains all of the defects of internal review—sluggishness and the appearance of bias; in this regard, by focusing on the efficacy of internal review rather than on the resolution of complaints, the Study has merely embellished Gellhorn's ombudsman. Moreover, its proposed agency would not perform the conciliation function which we consider imperative.

The Kerner Commission's proposal cured these defects by empowering its external agency to process all complaints in their inception and to engage in conciliation. However, the Commission, in its sketchy recommendations, appeared to go further than necessary to accomplish these goals. In the first place, it suggested the agency be authorized to institute suit in cases of unlawful police conduct. Second, it indicated that fact-finding functions should be performed in an adversary proceeding, in the presence of complainant and his counsel. Both of these suggestions, if enacted, would convey the impression that agency efforts were directed solely against the police. The first would place the ombudsman in the role of advocate rather than arbiter in situations where other means can be utilized to secure judicial relief. The second sacrifices the speed and informality we deem absolutely essential for conciliation.

158. *Final Report of the National Commission on the Causes and Prevention of Violence* (Washington, D.C.: Government Printing Office, 1969), at 147, 148.

CHAPTER 18

CITIZEN INVOLVEMENT IN LAW ENFORCEMENT*

When discussing the crime problem, people turn to the police, the government, and the courts and ask "Why don't they do more?" Rarely do they ask "What can I do?" Individual activity against crime usually reveals itself in sporadic bursts of indignant response to a specific act or a series of acts of crime, to the sensational, or to the crime that got a little too close to home this time.

Nonetheless, the citizen can do a great deal to help not only the police and the community, but also himself. In fact, there is a *need* for citizen involvement in crime prevention and law enforcement, as some communities have shown by their active cooperation.

THE INDIANAPOLIS EXPERIENCE

In October 1961, an elderly retired psychologist, Dr. Margaret Marshall, was fatally beaten by a teenage purse snatcher on her way home from church in Indianapolis. In the wake of the attack, police and local newspapers were peppered with phone calls and letters from women, demanding that "something be done" to make the streets safe after dark.

It occurred to Eugene S. Pulliam, assistant publisher of *The Indianapolis News*, that the women themselves might have some valuable ideas, so he asked Mrs. Margaret Moore of the paper's public-relations department to look into the matter. Mrs. Moore called together 30 leaders of Indianapolis women's clubs for a brainstorming luncheon. Counting on their clubs for fund raising and as reservoirs of vounteers (together they represented some 50,000 Indianapolis women), the leaders mapped out several committees, each to tackle a specific factor the women felt to be contributing to

---

* This chapter was prepared by Judith Toth of Cabin John, Md.

the city's overall crime pattern. Thus, the Indianapolis Women's Anti-Crime Crusade was born.[1]

During this period, retail stores, service stations, banks, and other places of business had been frequent victims of burglary and armed robbery. All business people were faced with the threat of higher insurance costs because of increased frequency and greater severity of crimes. The Indianapolis Chamber of Commerce began to take an active role in upgrading law enforcement. It solicited emergency funds from private firms and formed the Special Committee on Law Enforcement. This committee, in turn, was made up of task forces on the various aspects of crime control—uniformed police, the investigative division (principally the Detective Division), courts and prosecution, public information, and legislation. The Chamber of Commerce and the city government jointly financed a study on police reform by the Indiana University Center of Police Administration that led to substantial reforms in police operational techniques and organization during 1963–64.[2]

Other organizations have subsequently participated in the Indianapolis anticrime movement. One such group is the Citizens Forum. Formed in 1967 for a clean-up and beautification campaign, it has since that time organized a large number of block clubs and has broadened its activities to include self-help and crime-awareness programs.

Numerous church and social clubs have similar programs; organizations attack the social and economic causes of crime. The Volunteer Advisory Council and Citizens Against Poverty, for example, have focused on the problem of unemployment in Indianapolis.

In 1967, *The Indianapolis Star* initiated a program called "Crime Alert." A special police department number was publicized with the help of the Chamber of Commerce and the local merchants. Citizens could call this number to report not only crimes but also suspicious situations or persons. Police response was guaranteed even if the caller chose to remain anonymous.

The citizen involvement campaign has contributed to a slow-down in the growth of the overall crime rate in the Indianapolis metropolitan area. In particular, these programs, especially the Crime Alert Program, have discouraged the commission of crimes of burglary and robbery. Groups like the Volunteer Advisory Council and Citizens Against Poverty have, at the same time, fought unemployment in Indianapolis, recognizing that increase in employment and

438

the decrease in crime are more than casually related. Also, among other things, a vigorous city administration has kept playgrounds open and youth occupied, thus contributing to a decrease in delinquency.

For all the success that the anticrime campaign has had in Indianapolis, it has nevertheless been subjected to some criticism. These groups, many feel, deal not with the causes of crime but with acts of violence per se, and therefore offer only short range solutions to the problem of crime in their city. Moreover, say the critics, some groups are repressively paternalistic and their fervor to "clean up their city" has vigilante undertones.

There is, however, reason to be optimistic about the idea of citizen involvement in law enforcement after studying the example of Indianapolis. In many cases, these groups have had good liaison with the police force, which respects their judgement and helps them to solve community problems. Experiments and pilot projects in other cities have been equally encouraging,[3] leading to the conclusion that citizen participation in law enforcement has a promising future.

THE DANGER OF VIGILANTISM

Citizen action in crime control is nothing new in the United States. Prior to 1833, no paid, professional police forces existed in this country. Sheriffs and constables had responsibility for law enforcement, and nightwatchmen patrolled towns and villages. Extremely violent disorders were dealt with by the military. Direct dealing with the criminal by the citizens was common, as was ad hoc community enforcement. The result was often chaotic, and justice was often roughly served because of the vigilante nature of most of the citizen crime control groups.[4]

From our national experience, two major dangers apply to citizen participation in law enforcement: first, vigilantism—volunteers exercising full police powers with no police disciplines and few legal constraints—and, second, the anti-police patrol—a community organization created independently of and in opposition to the police and serving as a roving check on its behavior.[5] Vigilantism will inevitably produce oppressive and unfair practices, while anti-police patrol will worsen police-citizen relations by bringing the two groups into organized conflict.[6] Because of these dangers, therefore, individuals and groups should participate in the fight against crime in conjunction with officially sanctioned programs. Indepen-

439

dent, unofficial action directs itself toward fighting the deeply rooted causes of crime like poverty and discrimination, and toward assuming personal responsibility for reducing the temptation to commit crime.

THE INFORMED CITIZEN

The single most important ingredient of improved citizen participation in the law enforcement process is improved understanding of the law and of its enforcers, the police. This can come about only through programs of education. Too few people really know their rights and responsibilities under the law, and fewer still understand the "twilight zones" between dissent and civil disobedience, liberty and license, legitimate protest and anarchy.

Most elementary and high school teachers have not been trained to teach about the interrelationships of law, government, and society. The old discipline of "civics" has largely disappeared from many schools. Many communities now make up for this gap by sponsoring in-school programs that provide speakers on law and law enforcement and issue publications geared to inform the teenager of those aspects of the law that most directly affect him. Police departments, as part of their developing community relations programs, send personnel into the schools to explain such concepts as safety, crime prevention, and drug abuse to the young.

Similar programs are being conducted with adult groups and by adult groups in an increasing number of cities. The most common education program currently in effect is the distribution of pamphlets on a wide variety of subjects dealing with crime prevention, and with the response to and the reporting of crime. Local citizens groups consider the war on crime as part of their overall programs, like beautification and recreation. Citizens with an interest in the upkeep and value of their property are now more aware than ever of what crime in the community means to their pocketbooks.

Such organizations as the American Association of Federated Women's Clubs and the National Auto Theft Bureau have conducted auto theft prevention campaigns in several cities by accompanying the police on their rounds, by leaving pamphlets in unlocked cars, and by attaching warnings to parking meters on the dangers of leaving keys in the ignition.[7] Several cities, under the auspices of the Department of Justice, have initiated educational programs to inform the public about what it can do to fight crime. Newspapers, television, and radio have taken upon themselves a responsible community service role by constantly reminding people of what they can do when faced by crime.

The Oakland, California police department initiated in March of 1969 an education and action program called "Operation Involvement." This project is a controlled experiment, financed and manned by the department itself, that attempts to reach every homeowner, resident, and businessman in defined geographical areas to explain the crime problem and the problems of the police, to urge citizens to report crime, to teach citizens how to prevent crime, and to restore a sense of community and mutual reliance in the neighborhood. This umbrella program will eventually expand to the entire city. To date, it has already effectively cut home burglaries and car thefts in the experimental areas.

CITIZEN PROGRAMS

Citizen involvement programs sanctioned by, and often directed and funded by, the police have been tried with varying degrees of success in cities throughout the country. Such programs could help many communities where, according to needs and capabilities, they can be combined, adapted, or rejected.

CITIZEN AUXILIARIES

Crime has dropped 40 percent since the fall of 1968 in the 107th Precinct of Queens, N.Y., for example, because of the efforts of 120 male residents of the Electchester Housing Project who have volunteered their time to the New York City Police Auxiliary. The auxiliary, under the command of Captain Amile Racine, is the largest volunteer police force in the world with about 3,700 active men and women participants.

Candidates are carefully screened, then enrolled in 40 hours of course work. An auxiliary policeman is considered active when he contributes 20 hours of volunteer time per quarter. The volunteer must buy his own uniform and equipment, but he does not wear a gun unless licensed to do so for other reasons. The auxiliary police generally patrol in pairs in or near the precinct where they live.

The New York Auxiliary Police assist in preventing major racial outbreaks, substitute for regular police during civil disorders, participate in traffic and crowd control, in locating witnesses, and in other police chores—thus relieving the professional of time-consuming jobs which often keep him from performing his primary law-enforcement function.

Similar, although smaller, auxiliary forces exist in other cities throughout the country. The one in Indianapolis is one more cog in the crime-fighting mechanism which has contributed to that city's success. Cities like Denver, Col., have volunteer reserve squads trained in crowd control and traffic control, in the use of firearms (which they generally do not carry), and in disaster response. These men often patrol as observers in police cars with regular officers, and they have responded to natural disasters, such as floods, by contributing the additional necessary personnel to patrol and to safeguard the city.

Auxiliaries put more sets of eyes and ears on to the street to detect crimes and summon the police; they thus deter criminals. James Q. Wilson has recently described citizen auxiliaries as perhaps "the single most effective addition to police practice," and he has urged that the President of the United States use his office and prestige to enlist citizen interest and action in such programs.[8]

Citizen auxiliaries could be greatly improved if they could reimburse volunteers for or provide them with their uniforms and equipment, as well as compensate them for services in many cities where there is a shortage of police manpower. Their most valuable contribution may be relieving the regular police from activities not directly associated with crime, such as traffic and crowd control.[9] Short of creating a separate agency for these functions, this may prove the most effective means of freeing well-trained and badly needed personnel for normal police activities.[10] Also, citizen auxiliaries, especially the women volunteers, could provide relief at the precinct houses from the volume of paper work that must be handled by regular police.

YOUTH PATROLS

Youth patrols have become increasingly common in our cities in recent years. Most began as riot control units when local citizens insisted that, if left alone, they could bring their communities under control. A notable example is the young men in Tampa, Fla., who are called "White Hats" because of their distinguishing helmets. The White Hats, during the summer disorders of 1967, were decisive in quieting the city.

Instead of disbanding afterwards, they continued by acting as advisors to the Commission on Human Relations on the problems of the people who live in Negro slums, and by maintaining their unarmed patrols.[11]

Like many other cities, Atlanta, Ga. initiated an experimental Junior Deputy Program in the summer of 1968 that was so successful that it continued in the summer of 1969. In addition, the police department has a general youth program involving some 2,000 young people in recreational programs. The Junior Deputy program is designed to improve community relations. Each young man (minimum age 17) is called a Community Service Officer and he patrols his neighborhood.

So successful have the Youth Patrols been around the country that cities that have not yet organized them have, for the most part, put them under serious consideration. In March of 1968, New York conducted a one-week experiment to study the feasibility of maintaining such a group on a permanent basis. This idea of having young men from New York City ghetto areas patrol the areas in which they live in an effort to bring services directly to the people and help combat crime was, considering the short period allotted for the experiment, very successful. The 22 young volunteers, found through community groups, churches, and word of mouth, were assigned in platoons to beats in the areas between Fifth and Seventh Avenues and 110th and 127th Streets. They were equipped with walkie-talkies, and wore "uniforms" of tan and brown jackets. During their 11 a.m. to 2 a.m. duty, they broke up fights, reported suspicious situations, escorted women from work to home, and reported such things as potentially dangerous uncollected refuse, unsecured vacant buildings, defective trash barrels, pot holes, and abandoned refrigerators with doors that had not been removed. The success of the experiment was indicated by the favorable response of the community to their many services and by the enthusiasm of the participants for the program.[12] The city of New York is now seriously planning to make the program permanent.

This most important aspect of having youth patrols is that the police department has out on the street agents who can communicate with their contemporaries. Crime has risen most in the 16–25 age group, and many of these young people are out of reach of not only the police, but of older people in general. Giving members of this age group their own "Mod Squad" or patrol may help to restore their trust in the police and to break down the ever growing barriers between them.

VOLUNTEER RECEPTIONISTS

New York City precinct stations receive more than five million calls for help a year, a large percentage of which are not related to the law enforcement function of the police. In December 1967 the Department began a pilot program in which twenty housewives and other women volunteers living in the 23d Precinct worked on Friday and Saturday nights at the station on 104th Street, learning the needs and listening to the requests of local residents. The Ford Foundation subsequently granted funds to the Police Department for expansion of the program to two more precincts.

The receptionists' duties include greeting visitors, providing information, or putting the inquirer in touch with the appropriate official in the station or in a city agency. Police Commissioner Howard R. Leary has expressed the hope that this program will reduce the friction between his men and the community by "humanizing the police," while at the same time permitting the station houses to provide greater service to the people living in the slums by offering advice and counsel on their health, housing, education, and welfare programs.

COMMUNITY CENTERS

Programs such as the Community Action Center in Washington, D.C., are being conducted throughout the United States by urban police departments. The purpose is like that of the volunteer receptionists—to bridge the gap between the citizenry and the police in order to make the "system" a little more responsive to the people while at the same time facilitating the work of the police in law enforcement. The pilot project in the 13th Precinct in Washington is to engage paid resident workers in satellite centers to provide around-the-clock assistance to citizens referred by police on patrol as well as to those who walk in off the street.

Denver's Police Department has an on-going community relations program in which citizens meet every Wednesday evening at the precinct stations to voice their grievances. This program has met with varying degrees of success depending on the precinct and, as has been the experience in Washington and other cities, the meetings often deteriorate into

444

shouting matches where everyone gets "off his chest" what has been bothering him about the police or the public during the previous week. Chaotic as these meetings may sound, they have often been constructive in restoring communications within the community between the police and the people and in giving both sides a channel for expression.[13] As one community relations director explained, "I would rather have them shout at me there than to have them ignore me or hate me out on the street when I really need them."

Experience has shown, however, that programs like these are extremely fragile and that failure may preclude additional programs for some time to come. Care must be taken at the outset to fully understand and outline the boundaries of and barriers to action in the community.

IMPROVED CRIME REPORTING

Generally, when one wants to call the police, the number must be looked up. Most people still do not keep emergency numbers handy and many do not know who to call, especially in the case of overlapping jurisdictions (city, state, park police, etc.). In some cities, several numbers are listed for the same police department. Precincts often have different telephone numbers from one another. In an emergency, this becomes an impossible situation for most people. Frequently, people dial the operator, explain the situation and trust her to get response from the proper authorities.

Information campaigns, publicizing one emergency number, have been successful in a number of cities. Programs such as Crime Alert in Indianapolis, Chec-Mate in Saginaw, Mich., Crime Check[14] in Omaha, Neb., to name a few, facilitate the reporting of crime and of suspicious situations.

Under these programs, a central switchboard emergency number is well publicized, and calls are immediately put through to a dispatcher. In some cases, the caller need not identify himself or become "involved" beyond making the phone call.

In Omaha, in the two weeks after official announcement of Crime Check, the call load went up 11 percent, a considerable increase. In the first seven months of the Indianapolis program, police dispatchers received 63,547 additional calls, and 1,041 more arrests were made than in the corresponding period in 1966.

In all cases where rapid telephone crime reporting has been effective, the program has had the complete support of local businessmen, the press, the government, and police, as well as of the general public. Sustained interest in and promotion of this program seems to be its most essential ingredient.

Some cities have simplified reporting even further by recently installing a special short telephone number, "911." Pay phones have been converted to give a free dial tone so that the operator can be dialed without the usual dime. Strong arguments support a nationwide, universal telephone number such as "911" similar to the programs which now exist in Belgium, Denmark, Sweden, and England.[15] The best reason is the speed with which one obtains the proper authority in an emergency. Secondly, response time, especially in crimes of violence, is extremely important to "hot" apprehensions. Catching a criminal on or near the scene of the crime is possible only if the policeman is on the spot or called in immediately. Rapid response may save the police department hours, even days, of investigation and pursuit in the apprehension of a criminal.[16]

Another method of crime reporting that is catching on is the telephone chain. In this case, citizens, especially businessmen, are urged to keep in touch with one another and with the police and to keep an eye out for the others' property. If they see a suspicious circumstance, they immediately call the police and one another. The Neighborhood Crime Prevention Council in Seattle, Wash., sponsors a program of this type, as does the Harbor Division of the Los Angeles Police Department.

More and more police departments are also urging citizens to let them know about anything going on in the community that would affect their work. In Portland, Ore., for example, the Sheriff's Office has been passing out leaflets that say "Do you know something that the sheriff of Multnomah County should know? By addressing a letter to me and marking 'Personal' on the envelope you can be sure that I will personally read your letter. P.S. You may remain anonymous if you wish." This technique does bring in an expected number of crank letters, but occasionally it yields information about a pending or past crime that makes the program worthwhile.

In addition to these crime-reporting programs, Motorola Communications and Electronics, Inc., has sponsored over the past two years a Community Radio Watch program, which has been formally adopted by nearly 700 American cities and towns. Each city enlists the cooperation of individuals and companies with two-way radio equipped vehicles, asking each driver to act as additional "eyes and ears" for the police. Typical calls by observant drivers include highway accidents, gang fights, burglaries, medical emergencies and fires. As a public service, Motorola makes available all the necessary materials in any quantity to any community, free of charge (Community Radio Watch, 1301 East Algonquin Road, Schaumburg, Ill. 60172).

BLOCK MOTHERS

A program which is becoming popular throughout the nation is the block mother, or "helping hands," program. Responsible women are trained by social welfare and police officials to care for and supervise children and to interview adolescents and older youths. The program is designed to prevent the isolated problem of child molesting and also to provide emergency babysitting or supervision of older youngsters. Any threatened, frightened or run-away child can seek refuge in the home of a block mother who displays a "clasped hands" sign in the front window. This program is especially effective in urban ghettos where large numbers of children are concentrated in a small area.

PREVENTIVE PATROLS

The neighborhood patrol is perhaps the oldest form of law enforcement. It is generally set up by assigning evening shifts to pairs of volunteers within a defined community who drive or walk around keeping their eyes open for lingering strangers or anything out of the usual. Given enough willing volunteers, this can effectively deter burglars and vandals, and it adds the extra eyes to the neighborhood after dark which the police need.

YOUTH ACTIVITIES

The best deterrent from crime for the young is to keep them busy in constructive activity. To this end, it is the responsibility of not only the family and the government, but the community at large, to provide the activities and facilities necessary to attract young people. Citizens groups should urge more and better equipped parks and club houses. After-school and summer programs should offer variety and challenge. Young people should be urged to join organizations like the Y.M.C.A., Boy Scouts, and the local Boys' Club.

447

Gangs should be engaged in constructive activities. Teen-age boys can be involved in educational as well as financially rewarding activities. Employers should be encouraged to give part-time employment as a viable alternative to "hanging out" and looking for excitement in the form of criminal activity.[17]

The problem today seems to be a shortage of adults willing to donate their time and energy to youth activities. Many are too busy or too tired after work to pitch in the few extra hours of volunteer time necessary to assure the success of a program. This seems to be the malaise of parents and adults in general these days. Yet, in order to get at the problem of juvenile delinquency, the community has to meet the young people halfway in terms of commitment by providing the large number of volunteers required.

CITIZEN PRESSURE GROUPS

Citizen groups have been very active in promoting anti-crime educational programs. Yet they have another role of equal importance, that of actively participating in community planning and in pressuring the government at the local level to provide recreational facilities, well-lit streets, and adequate police forces. Also, like the Chamber of Commerce in Indianapolis, they can form study groups or task forces in order to better understand the system and to operate as informed pressure groups. Most important for the citizens group is getting attention focused on the deeply-rooted economic and social causes of crime.

ANTICRIME ORGANIZATIONS

The National Council on Crime and Delinquency is perhaps one of the oldest organizations in this country with the singular purpose of reducing crime. Similar groups are being established throughout the country as public awareness of the burgeoning crime rate has increased. These organizations conduct research into the causes and prevention of crime, as well as programs designed to improve police methods, court procedures, the corrections system, and citizen involvement. They depend primarily on individual citizens, companies, and foundations for financial support. Groups of this type, when broad-based, can be very effective through their programs and should receive more support from federal, state and local governments. They should be discouraged only when they take on political overtones or adopt an extreme ideological approach to crime.

THE INVOLVEMENT OF THE INDIVIDUAL

Perhaps the most effective role against crime the individual can take is getting out and actively pursuing solutions with his neighbors. Through civic associations, block organizations, church groups, and direct action groups the individual can participate. He can volunteer his time and/or money to programs designed to improve the material and human resources of the community. He can attack some of the underlying causes of crime such as poverty or lack of education, or he can deal directly with juveniles, ex-convicts, and dope addicts to prevent crime. In any respect, commitment and involvement are a solution—far better, more extensive and beneficial to society than arming oneself and hiding behind locked doors waiting for *them* (the government, the police, the courts, the elected representatives) to do it all.

The individual also has the opportunity on a day-to-day basis to prevent crime by reducing the opportunity to commit it. Many crimes would not be committed, indeed many criminal careers would not begin, if there were fewer opportunities for crime. The victim is often an unconscious accessory to the crime through neglect, ignorance or naiveté. The individual should take action in this respect by educating himself with regard to protection of property and making a conscious effort to remove temptation to crime.

Crime is made attractive and easy by the citizen who leaves his keys in his car, his house unlocked and unlit, or his newspapers on the doorstep when he is away. The most blatant example of citizen negligence is auto theft. According to F.B.I. statistics, the key had been left in the ignition or the ignition had been left unlocked in 42 percent of all stolen cars.

Homeowners and apartment dwellers are also careless. One-fifth of the burglaries were made easier for thieves because residents left the doors or windows unlocked. Other burglaries can be traced to giving keys to unknown repairmen—and allowing newspapers to pile up, or similar acts tipping off the burglar that the family is away.

Many crimes would not occur if individuals had proper locks on their doors and windows and enough lighting to discourage prowlers. Simply leaving a light on inside the house while absent may be enough to keep a prospective burglar away. Businessmen are also careless and need to be better informed about locks, lights, and alarm systems to protect their property.[18]

Obviously, the individual can do much to combat crime. Since people neither want to be the victims of crime nor to live in fear of crime and since they care about crime, why are they not more motivated to do something about the apparently spiralling crime rate?

A survey by the President's Commission on Law Enforcement and Administration of Justice asked people whether they had ever "gotten together with other people around here or has any group or organization you belong to met and discussed the problem of crime or taken some sort of action to combat crime?"[19] Only 12 percent answered yes, although the question was quite broad and included any kind of group meeting or discussion. Also most persons did not believe that they as individuals could do anything about crime in their neighborhoods; just over 17 percent thought that they could do something about the situation. Yet, there are more than one million independent volunteer organizations in the United States, 320,000 churches with more than 100 million members, 2,000 united funds and community chests, 35,000 voluntary welfare organizations, 36 million Americans in fraternal and service organizations. A nationwide poll estimates that sixty-one million adult Americans would, if asked, contribute 245 million man-hours every week to voluntary activities.[20]

The problem of non-involvement goes even deeper than failure to participate in crime prevention programs, however. In recent years, the media have been filled with stories of passive bystanders, remaining aloof and inactive although witnessing a crime which could be forestalled or interrupted by an action as simple as a telephone call.

Psychologists John M. Darley and Bibb Latane have made an experimental study of why bystanders do not respond during the actual commission of a crime or other crisis. They conclude:

> It is our impression that nonintervening subjects had not decided *not* to respond. Rather, they were still in a state of indecision and conflict concerning whether to respond or not. The emotional behavior of these nonresponding subjects was a sign of their continuing conflict, a conflict that other people resolved by responding. The distinction seems an academic one for the victim, since he gets no help in either case, but it is an

extremely important one for arriving at an understanding of why bystanders fail to help.

Thus, the stereotype of the unconcerned, depersonalized *homo urbanis* blandly watching the misfortunes of others proved inaccurate. Instead, we find a bystander to an emergency is an anguished individual in genuine doubt, concerned to do the right thing but compelled to make complex decisions under pressure of stress and fear. His reactions are shaped by the actions of others—and all too frequently by their inaction.[21]

As this study simply points out, the individual, when faced with immediate crisis, has to make a series of decisions, all of which are influenced by the presence of other people around him. He must first *notice* that something is happening. He must then *interpret* that event as an emergency, and then he must decide that he has *personal responsibility* to intervene. If he fails to notice an emergency, or if he concludes that he is not personally responsible for acting, he will then leave the victim unhelped.

Group behavior is quite different from individual behavior. Darley and Latane use this illustration, among others:

If your car breaks down on a busy highway, hundreds of drivers whiz by without anyone's stopping to help; if you are stuck on a nearby deserted country road, whoever passes you first is apt to stop. The personal responsibility that a passerby feels makes the difference.

A driver on a lonely road knows that if he doesn't stop to help, the person will not get help; the same individual on the crowded highway feels that he personally is no more responsible than any of a hundred other drivers.[22]

The individual, then, can decide that when he next confronts a fellow citizen in apparent danger or distress he will take some action, on the chance that the other fellow does in fact need his help; he will stop at the next gas station and report the plight, he will pick up the telephone and call the police, he will ask the other fellow if he needs help.

At the level of the community, leaders are needed who can mobilize individual citizens into action against crime. These citizens are not usually inactive out of apathy, but because so many others are inactive, and because personal responsibility has been so effectively diluted. Appropriate leadership can tap these resources.

CONCLUSION

The entire social fabric of our urban areas is being altered by the changing patterns of conduct of our "law-abiding citizens." The single most damaging of the effects of violent crime is fear, and that fear must not be belittled.[23] This fear, according to the President's Commission on Law Enforcement and Administration of Justice, "has greatly impoverished the lives of many Americans, especially those who live in high-crime neighborhoods in large cities. People stay behind locked doors of their homes rather than risk walking in the streets at night. Poor people spend money on taxis because they are afraid to walk or to use public transportation. Sociable people are afraid to talk to those they do not know."[24]

America is slowly becoming a fortress society—each man standing alone in fearful defense against his fellow man. We are losing the valuable traditions of community cooperation and personal responsibility for the welfare of the whole. This trend must be reversed by citizen involvement of the kind discussed in this chapter and in the earlier chapter on "The Nonsystem of Criminal Justice."

REFERENCES

1. Medford Stanton Evans and Margaret Moore, *The Lawbreakers* (New York: Arlington House, 1968).

2. Chamber of Commerce of the United States, "Indianapolis Chamber Leads in Upgrading Police Quality," *Urban Action Clearing House* (Washington, D.C.: Oct. 1968).

3. At this writing, every major city in the United States has some type of citizen involvement program in the works.

4. See the President's Commission on Law Enforcement and Administration of Justice (hereinafter cited as Crime Commission), *Task Force Report: The Police* (Washington, D.C.: Government Printing Office, 1967), for a history of law enforcement in the United States.

5. An example of an anti-police patrol is the "Better Berkeley Council" which last fall was mustering some 20 persons every Friday and Saturday nights to check on the operation of police patrolling Telegraph Avenue in Berkeley, Calif. *See San Francisco Chronicle*, Oct. 7, 1968, at 5.

6. This is not to say that the citizen should not concern himself with police ineptness, corruption, or brutality. Rather, he should confine his means of protest to channels other than indiscriminate harassment of the "cop on the beat." This can be

counterproductive by simply lowering the morale of the police and resulting in an even less effective police force. There are many legitimate means of registering concern open to citizens.

7. Crime Commission, *supra* note 4, *Task Force Report, The Police,* at 222.

8. James Q. Wilson, "Crime and Law Enforcement," in *Agenda for the Nation,* ed. by Kermit Gordon (Washington, D.C.: Brookings Institution, 1968), at 186, 206.

9. Except control of protest parades and similar demonstrations, which should be handled by highly-trained, well-disciplined police regulars.

10. Oakland, Calif., is initiating a program with LEAA funds that will start with ten "police representatives" who are not required to have the training of full-fledged police officers, but can more than adequately perform many police functions such as traffic and crowd control. This program has caught on in other areas with varying degrees of success.

11. See for complete background Terry Ann Knopf, *Youth Patrols: An Experiment in Community Participation* (Waltham, Mass.: Brandeis U., The Lemberg Center for the Study of Violence, 1969).

12. George Nash, *The Community Patrol Corps: A Descriptive Evaluation of the One-Week Experiment* (New York: Columbia University, Bureau of Applied Social Research, May 1968).

13. Eleanor Harlow, "Problems in Police-Community Relations, A Review of the Literature," *Information Review on Crime and Delinquency,* vol. 1, No. 5 (New York: National Council on Crime and Delinquency, Feb. 1969).

14. Crime Check is a nationwide project of the International Association of Chiefs of Police, Inc.

15. Roger W. Reinke, "A Universal Police Telephone Number," *The Police Chief* (Washington, D.C.: International Association of Chiefs of Police, Feb. 1968), at 10-16.

16. Crime Commission, *supra* note 4, *Challenge of Crime in a Free Society,* at 97.

17. Pride, Inc. in Washington, D.C. (and expanding into other major U.S. cities) is a prime example of entrepreneurial involvement of young people who might otherwise become delinquents.

18. See U.S., Congress, Senate, *Crime Against Small Business: A Report of the Small Business Administration Transmitted to the Select Committee on Small Business,* S. Doc. 91-94, 91st Cong., 1st sess., 1969.

19. BSSR study, unpublished supplement, as quoted in the Crime Commission, *supra* note 4, *Task Force Report: Crime and its Impact—An Assessment,* at 91.

20. From address by John N. Mitchell, Attorney General of the United States, before the Conference on Crime and the Urban Crisis of the National Emergency Committee of the Na-

tional Council on Crime and Delinquency, Fairmont Hotel, San Francisco, Calif., Feb. 3, 1969.

21. John M. Darley and Bibb Latane, "Are Passive Bystanders Really Guilty?", *Psychology Today*, reprinted in *Washington Post*, Jan. 12, 1969, at B-4.

22. *Id.*

23. Crime Commission, *supra* note 4, *Challenge of Crime in a Free Society*, at 3.

24. *Id.* at 52.

CHAPTER 19

THE BAIL PROBLEM: RELEASE OR DETENTION BEFORE TRIAL*

When a person is arrested on suspicion of a crime, the date of his trial may be a year or more away. During the period which intervenes between the arrest and trial the defendant may have several concerns: supporting himself and often his family as well, locating witnesses and working with his lawyer to prepare a defense, and putting his affairs in order in case he should be sentenced to jail. The community, on the other hand, has two demands to make of the defendant: that he appear at his trial, and that he refrain from endangering other people in the meantime.

The interests of the defendant and the community in this pretrial period occasionally conflict. In the overwhelming majority of cases the device used by American courts to accommodate these varying concerns is still the anachronistic and inappropriate system of money bail. Today this system is under increasing attack for not serving the interests of either the community or the defendant. But even the few jurisdictions that have attempted to replace the money bail system with other methods of pretrial release have been unable to preclude all unnecessary detentions or to prevent those released from committing crimes while they are awaiting trial. As a result, an explicit policy of "preventive detention"— keeping selected defendants in jail until their trials—has been gathering increased support.

THE ORIGINS OF MONEY BAIL

Our bail system probably derives from the ancient institution of hostageship, developed in England by the Germanic Angles and Saxons.[1] As a war tactic, a hostage would be held until another person's promise was fulfilled or some desired consequence achieved. Eventually, the site of the

---

*This chapter was prepared for the Task Force by Linda R. Singer, of the District of Columbia Bar.

practice shifted from the battlefield to the courtroom. A third person—a relative, friend or clergy—would come to court and vouch for a defendant's trustworthiness. The defendant would be released in the custody of the surety.

A bail system like the one in use in the United States today developed during the first thousand years A.D. in England. Judges traveled on circuits, and their visits to an area might be several years apart. Until the judges arrived, prisoners were held in the custody of the local sheriffs.

Prison conditions, however, were atrocious. Prisons were also insecure, and inmates frequently escaped. Maintaining the prisons was a financial burden. Thus, the sheriffs were happy to have someone else assume the responsibility of maintaining custody of defendants. They frequently relinquished defendants into the custody of sureties, usually friends or relatives of the accused. As English scholars have noted:

> This apparent leniency of our law was not due to any love of an abstract liberty. Imprisonment was costly and troublesome. Besides, any reader of the eyre rolls will be inclined to define a gaol as a place that is made to be broken, so numerous are the entries that tell of escapes. The medieval dungeon was not all that romance would make it. The mainprise of substantial men was about as good a security as a gaol. The sheriff did not want to keep prisoners; his inclination was to discharge himself of all responsibility by handing them over to his friends.[2]

If the defendant failed to appear for his trial, the custodian was no longer seized bodily, but was required to pay over a sum of money. This liability of the surety for the appearance of the defendant, and the ability to discharge the liability by the payment of a sum of money remain the basis of our present system of bail.

In 1275, an extensive inquest by a hundred jurors exposed many fraudulent practices in the sheriffs' administration of the release of prisoners on bail. As a result of the inquest, Parliament passed the first statute governing bail practices. The Statute Westminster I established which crimes were bailable on the presentation of sufficient sureties and which were not.

The Eighth Amendment to the United States Constitution provides that "excessive bail shall not be required." The historical antecedents of the amendment go back to the efforts of the English to implement the promise of the 39th

456

chapter of the Magna Carta that "no freeman shall be arrested, or detained in prison . . . unless . . . by the law of the land."

Despite that provision, when five knights thrown in prison by Charles I in 1627 brought an action for habeas corpus, release was denied on the basis that the protection of the provisions did not extend to the pretrial period.[3] Parliament responded to the case by declaring that "the cause of imprisonment must be known, else the statute will be of little force. . . ."[4] and went on to adopt the Petition of Right, which, after reciting various abuses of the power to imprison, prayed that "no freeman in any such manner as is before mentioned, be imprisoned or detained."

The Habeas Corpus Act of 1679 provided for a procedure to free "many of the King's subjects [who] have been and hereafter may be long detained in prison, in such cases where by law they are bailable. . . ." Nevertheless, judges continued to thwart the purpose of the Act of 1679 by setting impossibly high bail. Parliament therefore declared, in the Bill of Rights it drew up in 1689, that "excessive bail ought not to be required. . . ."

Thus the English protection against pretrial detention came to comprise three separate but essential elements: the determination of whether defendants had the right to release on bail; the habeas corpus procedure devloped to implement defendants' rights; and the protection against judicial abuse by the excessive bail clause of the 1689 Bill of Rights.

Professor Caleb Foote, who has done extensive historical research into the origins of bail, has concluded that the particular words in which the subject of bail is dealt with in the Eighth Amendment to the Constitution are the result of historical accident, and that the most plausible interpretation of the words, "excessive bail shall not be required," is that they were intended to grant a constitutional right to bail.[5] Professor Foote's interpretation is that the framers intended to include all three elements of the English protection against unwarranted pretrial detention in the Constitution. While the principle of habeas corpus found its way into our counterpart habeas corpus provision, Article 1, section 9, and the excessive bail language was incorporated into the Eighth Amendment, the fundamental, substantive right to bail itself, which these other remedial rights were intended to supplement, was inadvertently omitted.

Professor Foote's explanation of the oversight is that the phrasing of the Eighth Amendment was derived almost verbatim from the Virginia Declaration of Rights of 1776. The Declaration had been written by George Mason, who, while certainly familiar with the ringing language of the English Bill of Rights, was no lawyer, and probably knew nothing of the technical legalisms that comprised the fundamental law of bail. Although the Federal Judiciary Act of 1789[6] granted the right to bail in all noncapital offenses, Professor Foote stresses that any intent to leave the establishment of such a basic right as simply a matter of legislative discretion would have been an anomaly, in view of the primary purpose of the Bill of Rights to protect the people from abuse by the legislative branch of government.[7] Without some right to have bail set, the proscription against "excessive bail" would be meaningless.

Professor Foote's research would seem to indicate that all defendants have the absolute right to bail. This view has generally been adopted by the courts except for capital offenses. Thus, the Federal Rules of Criminal Procedure provide:

> A person arrested for an offense not punishable by death shall be admitted to bail. A person arrested for an offense punishable by death may be admitted to bail by any court or judge authorized by law to do so in the exercise of discretion, giving due weight to the evidence and to the nature and circumstances of the offense.[8]

State constitutions contain similar provisions under which an exception is made to the general guarantee of bail: only when he is charged with a noncapital offense does a defendant have the right to be released on bail.

BAIL TODAY: BAIL AND THE POOR

The abuses of the money bail system have received considerable national attention in recent years. But despite empirical studies showing the extent of detention based simply on poverty—on the failure of the poor defendant to make bail—and the hardship such detention produces,[9] despite demonstrations by the Vera Foundation in New York that for many defendants bail is not only inequitable but unnecessary, and despite public response to conferences, articles, books, media coverage, Congressional hearings, and a new federal law,[10] money bail remains the method of release used most often in the United States today,[11] and the setting of money bail in amounts that arrested persons cannot pay is widely used as a method of preventively detaining suspected habitual criminals pending their trial.

The system of money bail is based on the assumption that the threat of forfeiture of his money or property will act as an effective deterrent to a defendant's temptation to flee before his trial. But, as Supreme Court Justice Douglas has pointed out, this theory is based on the assumption that a defendant has property.[12] In fact, many defendants do not have property they can put up for bail. With approximately one out of four families earning less than $3,000 a year, obviously many of the people charged with crime simply are unable to afford bail. A defendant who cannot post bail must go to jail, lose any earning capacity at least temporarily, and possibly lose his job. In the interim, he cannot support his family, who may be forced to seek public welfare, with the accompanying embarrassment to the family and cost to the public.[13]

Yet a defendant's ability to afford bail has little relation to the likelihood of his committing further crimes. The system of money bail forces the poor to go to jail because they cannot afford to pay the premium for a bail bond.

It is difficult to rationalize the fact that

> Millions of men and women are, through the American bail system, held each year in "ransom" in American jails, committed to prison cells often for prolonged periods before trial. Because they are poor or friendless they may spend days, weeks or months in confinement, often to be acquitted of wrong-doing in the end. A man is accused of stealing a few dollars from a subway change-booth, spends six months in jail before trial, and is finally acquitted. Though innocent, he has been punished by the American system of "justice." His only crime is poverty—he could not afford the $105 fee for a bondsman to put up the $2,500 bond set by the judge.[14]

According to former Supreme Court Justice Arthur Goldberg, government in this country, both state and federal, has not done all that can reasonably be required of it to render the economic status of a litigant irrelevant in the operation of the bail system.[15] The system of money bail unquestionably discriminates against the poor.[16]

Pretrial detention of an accused who, were it not for his poverty, would remain at liberty pending trial, is not only bad policy; it may also violate the constitutional right to equal protection of the laws. The Supreme Court has held that neither the federal government nor a state can convict an indigent of a serious crime without providing him with counsel at the government's expense.[17] Nor can a government fail to provide an indigent with free transcript of his trial, where a transcript is necessary to an appeal,[18] and the type of appeal a convicted defendant is given cannot in any way be made to hinge on whether he can pay for the assistance of counsel.[19] But the Supreme Court so far has not applied the equal protection guarantee to questions of pretrial detention. Yet, as Justice Douglas has observed:

> We have held that an indigent defendant is denied equal protection of the law if he is denied an appeal on equal terms with other defendants, solely because of his indigence. Can an indigent be denied freedom, where a wealthy man would not, because he does not happen to have enough property to pledge for his freedom?[20]

Whether or not the phrase "excessive bail" in the Eighth Amendment was intended to provide a constitutional right to bail, the excessive bail clause should at least be interpreted consistently with the Supreme Court's other decisions prohibiting financial discrimination against an accused.[21] The Eighth Amendment proscription of excessive bail, together with the Fourteenth Amendment guarantee of equal protection, should be interpreted as requiring recognition that the imposition of any bail can be excessive when it is beyond a defendant's means to provide it. In such a case, some non-financial means of assuring the defendant's attendance at trial must be found.

BAIL TODAY: BAIL AND THE UNPOPULAR

In addition to discriminating against the poor, the wide discretion allowed in setting bail enables the bail-setting power to be manipulated to punish unpopular defendants in advance of trial. Thus, the power of the law may be used to express the hostility of law enforcement officers towards people who demonstrate for civil rights and other unpopular causes. For example, one judge in Alabama denied bail entirely when about two hundred demonstrators were arrested for violating an injunction against civil rights protests. It took a habeas corpus petition to free them from jail. A prosecutor in one Georgia town announced that bail had been refused to several civil rights demonstrators as a public lesson in order to teach them their place.[22] Cases like these are not unusual.[23]

Bail can be set so high that it forces civil rights organizations to limit the number of their demonstrations to those for which they can provide large amounts of cash. One 70-year-old minister spent 7 months in a Georgia jail after bail was set at $20,000—much more than would normally have been required, even for a dangerous criminal whose freedom before trial might endanger the community. The same judge set bail at $20,000 for each of two women, one pregnant, who had been arrested for protesting segregation at a restaurant.[24]

Judges have also on occasion changed the requirements of security to insure that defendants cannot meet them. A person with the cash to post bail may be required to put up property as security. If property is available, it may be required to be unencumbered. Finally, bail may be avoided by indicting for nonbailable offenses. In Georgia civil rights demonstrators who did no more than march in public were charged with attempting to incite insurrection, a nonbailable offense, even after similar charges in other cases had been found unconstitutional. In Louisiana, pickets outside a movie theatre that did not allow Negroes were charged with criminal anarchy.[25]

Of course, many of these demonstrators never were convicted of a crime or were convicted, but later they had the sentences overturned by higher courts as unconstitutional. Nonetheless, the manipulation of the bail system served to discourage their unpopular activities. As John M. Pratt, the legal counsel to the Commission on Religion and Race for the National Council of Churches, has stated:

> There is no question that the use of excessive bail to deter the demonstrations, which are constitutionally protected activities, illustrates the worst aspect of the American bail system.[26]

Many judges also have abused their power to set bail by using it to punish the accused. A former county probation officer recently was held on $5,000 bond in Montgomery County, Md., pending an appeal of his conviction by a People's Court judge for distributing copies of an allegedly obscene newspaper that lampooned another People's Court judge. The $5,000 bail was set after the defendant said he worked for a local social action group. The judge remarked that it "was not a very stable occupation." "You're kidding," the defendant's attorney responded. "I've known murder cases where it wasn't that high."[27]

When judges abuse their power to set bail, it is most difficult to move the kind of prejudice or misplaced zeal that would warrant the reversal of a ruling. Rarely can a judge's motive for setting bail in a particular way or at a particular amount be determined from the record. Even in the rare cases where a judge candidly admits his purpose, the appellate process necessary to overturn his ruling is both slow and expensive.

BAIL TODAY: THE BONDSMAN

Even were these abuses not extant, the money bail system could be condemned simply because it has spawned the world of bondsmen. When a judge has decided in favor of pretrial release and has set bail in a reasonable amount, it is the bondsman who ultimately holds the key to the jailhouse.[28] He may in effect veto the decision of the judge by refusing to provide bail for good reasons, for bad reasons, or for no reasons.

With few exceptions, bondsmen have refused to handle cases arising out of civil rights demonstrations. Even where they have provided bail, they have been known to charge higher fees in unpopular cases.[29] On the other hand, as one of the more vocal and candid bondsmen admitted to a television interviewer, the need to make a profit under competitive conditions requires him to bail out defendants even when he thinks it likely that they will commit dangerous crimes before their trials. "After all, if I don't do it, the guy next door will get his business."[30]

Paradoxically, a bondsman may consider the worst kind of professional criminal a preferred risk, and may even release him on credit. The bondsman knows that the "pro" can obtain the money for the premium, and that he will honor his obligation to return for trial or post enough collateral to protect the bondsman in case he should be called on to forfeit the bond.[31] The man's guilt, his likelihood of flight and his danger to the community is of little concern to the bondsman who looks upon him simply as a sure fee, a source of business.

The professional bondsman has been given a major role in the criminal process only in the United States and the Philippines.[32] The bondsman is a creature of the frontier conditions that existed in early America. The comparative intimacy of smaller, more homogenous England had given birth to a bail system that was based on personal trust. In America, on the other hand, many people lacked personal friends or relatives who would provide the bail necessary for their pretrial release: the vast, unoccupied areas to which a defendant could flee made it difficult, if not impossible, from private sureties to assure their attendance at trial. Thus paid sureties came to take the place of personal sponsorship.[33] Although the names of large, respectable insurance companies appear on bail bonds, these companies delegate the actual conduct of the bonding business to their agents, the local bondsman, who retain the ultimate power over detention. Thus the fact that the companies comply with state insurance laws[34] has little relation to any state control over the writing of bail bonds. And the companies have little to lose: because of requirements of collateral, they run no risk of default. As an investigation by a committee of the Association of the Bar of the City of New York divulged:

> There is little doubt as to the financial responsibility of these approved companies. Yet such a company lends merely its name to the administration of bail, for although it is on the bond, it runs no risk. Indeed, it has been stated that the insurance companies have never suffered a financial loss through the writing of bonds, or hardly ever.[35]

Some states limit the fees that bondsmen may charge for writing bonds; others have no such limitations. Even though premiums may be regulated, there are no controls on the collateral a bondsman may require. And the character of bondsmen rarely is effectively regulated;[36] many bondsmen, it has been said, are " 'low-lifes' whose very presence contaminates the judicial process."[37]

Occasional exposé's have uncovered criminal infiltration of the bail-bond business. In 1959 and 1960, two reporters for the *Indianapolis Star* found that national crime syndicates had become partners of bondsmen in major cities across the nation. Even more serious is the frequent collusion between bondsmen and the officials charged with the administration of criminal justice. Lawyers, judges, court officials and police have at times succumbed to the enticements offered by unscrupulous bondsmen. In 1961 a grand jury in Jackson County, Mo., investigated the activities of bondsmen and reported that most of them were in partnership with certain policemen. The police on the scene at the time of arrest would steer defendants to these bondsmen in return for 20 percent of the bonding fee.[38] Similar collusion has been found between lawyers and bondsmen.[39]

BAIL TODAY: ITS EFFECT ON THE ADMINISTRATION OF JUSTICE

In addition to the bail system's discrimination against the poor and the unpopular, and its surrender of law enforcement functions to bondsmen, studies have shown that defendants who can afford bail plead guilty less frequently, are convicted less frequently, and if convicted, receive shorter (or nonjail) sentences more commonly than those who must spend the pretrial period in jail.

The period before trial plays a crucial part in the administration of criminal justice. The Supreme Court early recognized that the time between the institution of formal charges and the trial is "perhaps the most critical period of the proceeding ... when consultation, thoroughgoing investigation and preparation are vitally important. . . ."[40] But only in limited ways can the jailed defendant help his attorney prepare his defense. He may be detained at an inconvenient location or have insufficient time available for working with the attorney, with investigators or witnesses. He cannot make amends with the complaining witness in an effort to have the charges dropped. He cannot help locate witnesses or evidence. He earns no money that could be used to help his case.

The pioneer studies of bailed and unbailed defendants in Philadelphia[41] and New York[42] give support to this hypothesis. The Philadelphia study, for example, traced the disposition of 946 cases where the defendants had spent the pretrial period on bail. Of 529 serious criminal cases, 275 were convicted, 254 were not. Of these 275 convicted offenders who had been on bail before trial, only 61, or 22%, were sent to prison after conviction. Of the 417 similar cases where defendants were held in jail before trial, 340 were convicted, and only 77 were not. Of the 340 convicted defendants who were in jail before trial, and hence unable to demonstrate their reliability to the court, 200, or 59%, went to prison. According to the investigators:

> this comparison showed that defendants who came to court from jail received less favorable treatment as to both the proportion of those convicted and those receiving prison sentences

464

. . . the contrast between the disposition of jail and bail cases was so striking that it raises a strong inference that the handicap of jail status is a major contributing cause for the difference.

The New York study concluded: "that being in jail operates to the disadvantage of the defendant at every stage of the proceeding is suggested by statistical comparisons of bail and jail cases at the grand jury level, in terms of court dispositions and at sentencing." The study found that in a sample group of 2,000 defendants, the grand jury dismissed about 24 percent of the cases where the defendant was free on bail but only about 10 percent of the cases where the defendant was in jail. Imprisoned defendants pleaded guilty about 90 percent of the time, while defendants on bail pleaded guilty about 70 percent of the time. At trial imprisoned defendants were acquitted about 20 percent of the time, while defendants who had been free on bail were acquitted about 31 percent of the time. Finally, jailed defendants who were convicted received suspended sentences in about 13 percent of the cases, whereas bailed defendants who were tried and convicted were given suspended sentences in about 54 percent of the cases.

Of course, some of the factors, such as a long criminal record or strong evidence of guilt, that lead to high bail and hence detention, will also lead to a finding of guilty and a prison sentence instead of probation. But a more recent study concluded that the 47 percent greater likelihood of a defendant's receiving a prison sentence if he spent the pretrial period in jail could not be explained by differences in the backgrounds of defendants who were detained as compared to those who posted bail.[43]

Often unbailed defendants who are sentenced by the court to probation will have lost much of the benefit of that disposition.[44] Yet one of the purposes of having convicted offenders, particularly those who are young or without a prior criminal record, serve their sentences on probation in the community is to avoid the degrading, and frequently corrupting, effects of jail. According to an experienced correctional official:

. . . the typical jail has a destructive effect on human character and makes the rehabilitation of the individual offender much more difficult . . . the typical jail is dirty and overcrowded. The food is deplorable, supervision is scant, and there are no programs for self-improvement, or even for wholesome recrea-

465

tion. The typical jail has little to inspire the prisoner and much to demoralize him. The result is that he must spend his time there vegetating and degenerating and worse. . . . Unnecessary jail detention, in my opinion, is . . . a factor accounting for failure among those released on probation and even among those who are eventually freed on their current charges.[45]

The present system is also expensive to society at large which pays for pretrial detention. A California legislator has estimated that in Los Angeles County alone, 60 percent of those arrested in 1967–68 were detained in jail prior to trial at a cost to local taxpayers of $20 million.[46] On August 7, 1968, New York Commissioner of Corrections, George F. McGrath, wrote to Mayor John V. Lindsay detailing the unexpected and alarming rate of increase in the population of the city's detention institutions:

Institutions, which house prisoners awaiting court action, have a normal male detention capacity of 2,177 persons. In January, 1968, they accommodated an average of 4,509 prisoners. By the end of August they were forced to accommodate an average of 6,484 persons a day.[47]

As a consequence of this population explosion, already over-crowded institutions have become even more burdened. The result has been an impairment of security, strains on personnel and destruction of prisoner morale.

ALTERNATIVES TO BAIL: RELEASE ON PERSONAL RECOGNIZANCE

In the past several years various groups have begun to experiment with alternatives to the money bail system. The first such experimentation, and still perhaps the most wide-spread, is the work of the Vera Institute of Justice in New York City with release on "personal recognizance."

A defendant released on his own recognizance is allowed to remain free until his trial, conditioned only upon his promise to appear; no money bail is required. Vera experiments have shown that for many defendants such release, removing the necessity for the posting of collateral or supervision by the court, is both efficient and humane. Many—perhaps most—defendants are trustworthy and have sufficient ties to their families, jobs, and communities to prevent them from fleeing before their trials.

Release on recognizance obviously is a device that cannot be used in all cases. Thus the method of determining which defendants may safely be released on their own trust is crucial. A judge who must decide who should be released in this manner is at a great disadvantage. He lacks the time and resources to conduct the investigations of defendants' backgrounds essential to intelligent releasing decisions. The Vera Institute hoped to fill this gap in the background information available to the judges and to convince them to adopt alternatives to money bail:

> Our early thought was to provide a revolving bail fund which would be available to indigent defendants. But helping the poor to buy their freedom is no solution; it merely perpetuates reliance upon money as the criterion for release. We wanted to break the pattern and stimulate a more basic change in bail thinking. The release of greater numbers on their own recognizance appeared the most potentially valuable approach. We decided to test the hypothesis that a greater number of defendants could be successfully released in this way if verified information about their stability and community roots could be presented to the court. This was the goal of Vera Foundation's first undertaking: The Manhattan Bail Project.[48]

Thus, Vera's first project, undertaken in conjunction with the Institute on Judicial Administration at New York University School of Law, was designed to provide courts with verified information about a defendant's reliability and his roots in the community. Law students employed by Vera interviewed recently arrested defendants in the detention pens of the Manhattan Criminal Court just prior to their arraignment. The questions were aimed at establishing the defendants' community ties and determining whether they could be trusted to return for trial if released merely on a promise to return. The defendants' answers were scored by the Vera personnel according to a weighting system that gave points for stable residence, family ties, employment and lack of previous criminal record. The information provided by the prisoners was checked for accuracy by a member of the Vera staff. If by Vera standards the defendant was determined to be a good risk, the information that had been collected was summarized for the benefit of the arraigning judge, the district attorney, and the defendant's lawyer.

Vera found that, with its recommendations and verified information to support them, judges were willing to release defendants on their own recognizance. Of the first 300 cases in which Vera recommended release, 200 were released on recognizance. Of those, only two did not appear for trial. This nonappearance rate was better than analogous statistics of defendants who were released on money bail.

As an experiment, Vera did not recommend release for some of the defendants who met its standards. It did nothing in their cases except keep track of them. The result was that, while the court granted pretrial release in 60 percent of the cases recommended by Vera, it did so in only 14 percent of the similar cases in the control group. In other words, judges were willing to release four times as many defendants with the aid of verified information. Of those recommended by Vera for pretrial release, 60 percent were not convicted; only 23 percent of the control group were not convicted. Of the 40 percent of the recommended group who were found guilty, one out of six went to jail; in the control group, of the 77 percent who were convicted, nine out of ten received jail sentences.[49]

Eight years have passed since the inauguration of the Manhattan Bail Project. The coverage of the Project has been greatly expanded, and the function of providing the courts with verified information has been taken over by the New York City Office of Probation. An objective point scale has been refined and is used to determine the reliability of a large number of defendants. The Project has proved that the characteristics of persons likely to appear if released can be identified.[50]

The Project has been imitated in other cities, using specially created bail agencies, the police, the sheriff, the welfare department, the public defender, the probation department or VISTA to fill the release advisory role. Although information about other bail projects is incomplete, nonfinancial release of the reliable has been a success where it has been tried.[51]

Alternatives to money bail other than release on personal recognizance, with or without conditions, have been tried in other places. In Illinois,[52] state legislation allows a defendant to post *with the court* an amount equal to the premium for a bond. If he appears for trial, all of the money, except for a small fee to cover administrative costs, is returned.

This procedure returns the administration of bail to the courts, where it belongs. It also saves bailed defendants most of the money previously lost to the bondsmen. It fails, however, to solve the problem of the poor defendant, who, lacking the necessary premium, may still go to jail.

In Tulsa, Okla., a scandal involving local bondsmen

spurred the County Bar Association to use the state law allowing judges to release a defendant to the custody of his attorney. Another example of the usefulness of third party custodians, even in an area where release on recognizance is an accepted practice, was reported in a New York study:

> A 19-year-old youth was charged with receiving stolen property—a pair of shoes having been found in his possession. The boy had recently come to New York from a southern state. He was employed on Long Island for his first few weeks. When arrested he was supporting himself as a shoeshine boy in the Port Authority Bus Terminal. Although the charge was a misdemeanor and the youth had no record, he was not released on his own recognizance. Instead, bail was set at $50, a nominal amount, but sufficient to result in dentention for a person with no funds and no friends in the city. This defendant had not been recommended for ROR because he had no local references and had been living by himself in a hotel for transients. However, on review, Vera was able to recommend pretrial release by arranging, as a condition in lieu of bail, for a social worker from a poverty agency to keep in contact with the accused until his next court appearance. The court accepted this condition and the youth was released.[53]

ALTERNATIVES TO BAIL: SUMMONS

Even more promising than release on recognizance or other alternatives to bail is the use of the summons. The summons is commonly used in minor cases to expedite disposition. In the case of the most frequent example, the parking ticket, a person is charged with an offense and quickly released without jail, bail, or even arrest. The defendant simply is notified to appear for trial at a certain date. The summons can, however, replace arrest and imprisonment in nontraffic cases as well. A summons may be used by the police on the spot instead of a formal arrest, or it may be issued by the police desk officer in the stationhouse shortly after an arrest.

Legislative authority for issuing summonses varies among the states. Legislation recently enacted in California, Michigan, and Washington allows the police to issue summonses in lieu of arrests in misdemeanor cases. In Illinois, a statute gives the police the authority in all cases to issue a "notice to appear" whenever he has grounds to arrest without a warrant.[54] However, the police have not always been willing to use their authority. For example, in California, although a

1967 amendment to the Penal Code[55] provides that an arresting officer need not take a suspect to the police station, but may release him immediately once he has given him a summons, internal police department policies require approval by the department chief before a police officer may issue a summons for any nontraffic offense. Thus, the officer must take the time to travel to headquarters with a suspect, even though it may be obvious that his release poses no risk to the community.[56]

Recognizing the resistance to giving the releasing power to the policeman on the beat, the Vera Institute undertook a project to replace arrest and bail with a station-house summons. The purpose was to persuade the police to release a defendant after arrest but without jailing him. Beginning in 1964, the Manhattan Summons Project adapted the Vera technique to the local precinct police station. When a formal arrest is about to take place in certain specified minor criminal cases, the Vera staff interviews defendants to establish their eligibility for disposition through a summons. The desk officer at the police station uses the Vera report in much the same way as the judges in the bail projects. The procedures take little time and they avoid the penal aspects of the earlier part of the criminal process. The salutary effect on defendants was described by an early observer:

> During these interviews the mood of the prisoner shifts from hostile and suspicious to glimmering hope. Perhaps it is the need to talk to someone—perhaps it is the lack of uniformed and official brusqueness. . . .[57]

The attitude of the New York City police towards the summons project has been not merely cooperative, but enthusiastic. Most of the Vera recommendations for release have been accepted by the desk officers involved. A speech by the Police Department's Deputy Commissioner, Leonard Reisman, pointed out that even on the modest scale at which the experiment was begun, the police department was saving thousands of hours of manpower.

On July 1, 1967, the Manhattan Summons Project was expanded to cover the entire city of New York. During the first year of citywide operation, a total of 48,159 arrest cases eligible for summons process were brought before desk officers throughout the city. Of these, 26,733, or 55 percent, of the defendants were not considered for summonses because they were intoxicated, currently addicted to narcotics, or were derelicts. Thus, 21,426, or 45 percent, were interviewed. Of course, 14,232, or two out of three of the eligible defendants, received summonses and were not detained and taken to court by the arresting officer. Of the one-third who failed to qualify, 22 percent refused to be interviewed and 12 percent failed to meet the qualifications for a summons.[58]

More than 95 percent of those who received summonses under this program appeared in court when scheduled. Since the inception of the program, the "jump rate" was lowered for the 5.3 percent average of the first 6 months to the approximately 3.9 percent average for the last 6 months. Efforts to contact those defendants who failed to appear in court on the proscribed date traced many to local hospitals and other criminal institutions, where confinement made it impossible to appear in court. Some "jumpers" had been drafted or volunteered for the Armed Forces between the date of their arrest and the return of the summons. When reminded of their obligation to appear, many of the defendants appeared in court voluntarily at a subsequent date.[59]

The increased use of the summons process in New York has resulted in a substantial savings of police man-hours. Taking into account custodial personnel, transportation, arraignment, and unnecessary court appearances, the Police Department estimates that it saves approximately five hours each time a summons is issued. Since 60 summonses are issued on an average day, an additional 300 hours of police patrol is made possible each day. The return of patrolmen to the street after a summons is issued reduces the opportunities for crime.[60]

An example of the benefits to police-community relations that can be achieved through use of the summons occurred in December 1967. Mothers who had been protesting the transportation of their children to school districts outside their neighborhoods were arrested and charged with criminal trespass. They were escorted to the stationhouse with the children and released on summonses. The result: "This action not only enabled the defendants to care for their families, but also lessened the alienation between the police and the public normally caused by arrests made under these circumstances."[61] This enlightened treatment of demonstrators stands in stark contrast to the jailing of civil rights demonstrators in the Deep South.

471

In 1966, in response to a growing national interest in bail reform, Congress enacted the Bail Reform Act[62] and created the District of Columbia Bail Agency to provide the courts with facts and recommendations about pretrial release.[63] The act—the first major overhaul of federal bail law since 1789—establishes two primary principles: that an accused shall be released pending trial unless good reasons exist why he will not return to stand trial; that a person's ability to post money bond shall be irrelevant to a pretrial release decision.[64] The new law reverses the traditional assumption governing pretrial release.[65] Instead of calling for a bail hearing aimed exclusively at assuring the defendant's future presence at trial, the Act provides for a proceeding designed principally to assure his release. A defendant may be released on his own recognizance or on the execution of an unsecured appearance bond.[66] A judge who determines that such a release will not reasonably assure the defendant's appearance has the authority to impose any one or more conditions (most of them nonfinancial) which are calculated to deter flight.[67] The defendant's appearance at trial—not his possible danger to the community—is the only consideration that may be taken into account.

A defendant who continues to be detained twenty-four hours after the release hearing as a result of his inability to meet the conditions of release may have the conditions reviewed by the judicial officer who imposed them. Unless the conditions are changed and the defendant released, the judge must state in writing his reasons for imposing these particular conditions.[68] The statute provides for prompt appeal of release conditions.[69]

It is more difficult to secure release in a capital case or after conviction pending an appeal. The rationale for changing the presumption of release in these cases is that a defendant who is charged with an offense punishable by death, or who already has been convicted, is more likely to flee. Hence a judge is authorized to order detention in these situations where he has reason to believe that "no one or more conditions of release will reasonably assure that the person will not flee or pose a danger to any other person or to the community."[70]

In the Bail Reform Act Congress recognized that it is an anachronism to make freedom pending trial depend on a defendant's ability to pay.[71] As the Senate Judiciary Committee pointed out: "Respect for law and order is diminished when the attainment of pretrial liberty depends solely upon the financial status of an accused."[72]

The release rates of the District Court for the District of Columbia are said to have risen under the Act to about 75 percent of all defendants.[73] The beneficial effects of the improved releasing procedures have been assessed by the Director of the National Legal Aid and Defender Association's National Defender Project:

> It has allowed families to remain self-sufficient during the long wait for trial. Released defendants have been able to aid their attorneys in preparing a defense. Often the rehabilitation of guilty defendants has begun during pretrial release and has continued under terms of probation granted because of the progress exhibited during pretrial release. Truly poor families have been saved the onerous burden of paying an unreturnable money premium to a professional surety. We cannot forget the *innocent* defendant without funds who did not spend several months in jail awaiting trial . . . Improved bail procedures have also demonstrated a substantial saving to the Government.[74]

Since passage of the Bail Reform Act, there has been a reevaluation of bail legislation in many states, and a heightened interest in developing nonfinancial alternatives to money bail.[75] There is still a great need, however, for bail reform at the state and local levels where the great majority of defendants are tried. Investigations by the Vera Institute of Justice suggest that current bail practices are all too similar to those of a decade ago. While it is true that reform efforts have caused many people to be released without having to post money bail, it is also true that rates of pretrial detention remain high, that lengthy detention is still common, and that money bail is still extensively used, and, in fact, remains the most common form of release condition. Prosecutors and judges continue to recommend and set bail in dollar amounts with little or no information about the defendant, with no articulation of reasons why these amounts are required, and with either a conscious intent to detain, or an apparent lack of concern as to whether detention will be the result of requiring money bail.[76]

THE BAIL REFORM ACT OF 1966: ITS PROBLEMS

In the District of Columbia, where the federal courts have

a unique criminal jurisdiction comparable to that of state courts in other areas, observers agree that administrative problems have prevented the Bail Reform Act from accomplishing fully the purposes for which it was designed.[77] The primary problems have involved inadequate staffing of the District of Columbia Bail Agency, incomplete acceptance by the judiciary of the Act's provision of nonfinancial conditions of release, and long delays before trial.

The shortage of Bail Agency manpower has meant that judges are provided with insufficient data on defendants at the time of release. A single investigation now serves as the basis for the initial releasing decision, as well as for the 24-hour review provided by the Act. Judges normally refuse to release on their own recognizance or on nonfinancial conditions defendants about whom they lack sufficient information. According to one General Sessions judge, "Unless and until the Bail Agency is staffed and equipped to provide the maximum amount of data to the Court, there will always be a substantial number of individuals initially detained who would have been eligible for release if a follow-up had taken place."[78]

Perhaps because of the lack of enforcement machinery, judges have also not made use of the wide variety of conditions of release authorized by the Bail Act. According to the Director of the District of Columbia Bail Agency,

> Administration of the Bail Reform Act continues to be hampered by a lack of understanding of the act and failure to utilize proscriptive measures contained therein. It must be remembered that the Bail Reform Act of 1966 did not restrict judicial discretion. On the contrary, the Act enlarged the possibilities of conditions of release and enumerated the priorities of release which were allowed for more rational consideration of the accused's total situation. Rule 46 of the Federal Rules of Criminal Procedures stated that persons charged with non-capital cases *had* to be released. The Bail Reform Act gave Judges the tool to release intelligently.[79]

Despite the range of nonfinancial conditions allowable under the Bail Reform Act, many judges continue to impose money bonds routinely, or they violate the Act by refusing to release at all.[80] A Judicial Council committee appointed to study the operation of the Bail Reform Act in the District of Columbia has recommended conditions which might be imposed in appropriate cases: (1) weekly personal check-ins to the Bail Agency or another designated office in the community; (2) a duty to carry an Agency-issued identification card at all times and to notify the Agency of each change of address or employment, coupled with spot checks by the Agency on residence and employment; (3) a duty of youthful defendants to continue residence with their parents, coupled with Agency spot checks; (4) a duty to request court (or Agency) permission to leave the metropolitan area for specified time periods with a forwarding address, coupled with Agency spot checks; (5) a duty of narcotics addicts to check in periodically for examination at an appropriate hospital, coupled with Agency monitoring of check-in lists; (6) and restrictions to prohibit addicts from frequenting specified locations where narcotics users congregate.[81]

The Bail Agency has, however, lacked the resources to enforce conditions of release. In addition, enforcement by prosecuting and judicial agencies has been lacking. The Director of the Bail Agency has pointed out that of the 2,118 indictments returned by the grand jury in 1968, only three were for bail jumping:

> In an atmosphere of concern for the public welfare it is astonishing to discover less than a handful of citations for contempt for failure to comply with release conditions by any District of Columbia judge. It is even more ironic to note that in few instances has application been made to amend or revoke original conditions or release where the United States attorney has received information which changes the picture of a defendant's total situation.[82]

In addition to effective supervision of releases, observers have urged that the time between arrest and trial be shortened drastically.[83] Hastening criminal trials would achieve not only the humane goal of reducing the time which some defendants must spend in jail before trial, but would also reduce the time in which released defendants have the opportunity for committing further crimes. Although figures on crimes committed by defendants awaiting trial are in great dispute, the President's Commission on Crime in the District of Columbia found that 68 percent of crime on bail was committed more than 30 days after initial release.[84] Moreover, the deterrent effect of the criminal laws would be enhanced by bringing the trial closer to the criminal act and making the sentence seem more the response to society to the defendant's criminal conduct and less the result of a long, drawn-out game.[85]

475

Beyond the administrative problems, which virtually everyone agrees require some sort of action, some critics have concluded that there are basic flaws in the Bail Reform Act itself. Although no one has advocated a return to the old money bail system,[86] critics have recommended the Act be amended to permit a court to consider a defendant's danger to the community as well as the likelihood of his appearance at trial in fixing conditions for pre-trial release.[87] Others have urged an amendment that would permit "preventive detention" of defendants considered to pose a danger to the community.[88]

A General Sessions judge has cited a problem of releasing narcotic addicts where the only allowable consideration for imposing conditions is the likelihood of flight:

> Many addicts come into our Court on petit larceny charges. They will tell you they have a $40-$50 per day habit supported solely by stealing. To release them is to guarantee theft in the amount of $250 or more a week. But, they usually return to court on the appointed date. An addict with a bad habit cannot leave his source, so flight is almost non-existent. On the date of trial the pusher will bring them in or they are quickly found in their neighborhood.
>
> Since they are a good risk on personal bond, the Bail Act dictates that they be released. Yet they pose a terrible economic danger to the community in terms of future burglary, robbery, or tampering offenses.[89]

Examples of repeated crimes committed by defendants released before trial have been widely reported in the press. One recent report involves a defendant arrested and released six times in a 10-month period for street muggings, drug store holdups, and a liquor store assault. After the first charge, the defendant was released on recognizance; in each subsequent case he was released on money bond. The U.S. Attorney's office never asked the judges who set the bonds to revoke them.[90]

Little agreement prevails, however, on the percent of released defendants who actually commit crimes while awaiting trial. A study by the District of Columbia Police Department of persons indicted for robbery and released on bail between July 1, 1966, and June 30, 1967 showed that of 130 persons so released, 45, or 34.6 percent, were indicted for at least one additional felony while on bail. But these findings, as well as the methodology of the study that produced them have been criticized by a Justice Department release.[91] Little certainty remains about the actual incidence of crime on bail. Despite such uncertainties about the real risk of crime committed by persons on bail, neither the Bail Reform Act nor the experimental bail projects which preceded it were designed to treat the problem of pretrial release as a whole. The bail reform movement of the past decade has addressed itself primarily to the problem of the unnecessary detention of the reliable defendant who is too poor to post money bail,[92] but it has provided little guidance for dealing with the defendant who is not obviously reliable—both the person considered to pose a high risk of flight and the person thought likely to commit crime if released:

> In our effort to maximize release of the person likely neither to flee nor to commit crime, we have neglected to deal adequately with those whom it is believed are likely to do so.[93]

As a result, we have a dual system, judges are told to reject the traditional approach to bail for defendants shown to be reliable, but to continue to use money bail for those who are not. The Bail Reform Act condemns money bail and gives it low priority among the possible conditions of release; but it does not prevent its use as a detention device. If Congress really had intended money bail only as a condition of release—not as a technique of detention—it would have limited its use to cases in which the defendant was able to post the required amount:

> The failure of Congress to so provide has not been lost upon those charged with the administration of the Act. They interpret the Act—and, I believe, with some justification—as an imaginative and much improved way to handle the reliable defendant, but as largely irrelevant in dealing with the risky. And, because the Act gives little guidance as to how to determine risk, it leaves judges and prosecutors to their traditional devices.[94]

THE PROBLEM OF DANGEROUSNESS: SOME PROPOSED SOLUTIONS

The current bail debate revolves largely about the special problems presented by dangerous or unreliable defendants.

The Judicial Council Committee, by a majority of one vote, has recommended that laws applicable to bail in the District of Columbia be amended to allow courts—

to consider dangerousness to the community in setting non-financial conditions of release for persons who, based on the available information, pose a threat of repeated criminal conduct while on bail. The court would state for the record (and possible appeal) the information on which the findings of potential dangerousness is based.[95]

In the opinion of Judge Harold H. Greene of the District of Columbia Court of General Sessions, it is unrealistic and unwise to exclude the criterion of danger to the community from consideration in determining conditions of release. The other General Sessions judges agree. They have urged that courts be permitted to consider not only the possibility of flight by the accused, but also the potential danger he presents to the public, in determining the conditions of his release.[96]

To illustrate the possibilities for release conditions that would take into account potential danger to the community, Judge Greene has suggested that the following conditions might be imposed in the case of a robbery suspect:

> Residence at a specified place, preferably with relatives, and a requirement that the defendant not be allowed to change his address without prior permission from the Bail Agency. Employment at a specified place, which again the defendant would not be allowed to change without prior clearance. Prohibition on being absent from the place of residence or the place of employment for a period of more than one or two hours at a time without prior authorization from the Bail Agency. A nighttime curfew applicable to the defendant. Prohibition on association with certain persons or certain groups of persons. Periodic reporting by the defendant to the Bail Agency and to the Probation Department of the court. Deduction of a certain percentage of defendant's earnings and deposit of that sum with the Bail Agency or the Criminal Clerk's Office of the court as security for his appearance.[97]

Chief Judge Edward H. Curran of the U.S. District Court for the District of Columbia, has stated that in setting the terms of release, the protection of the public from dangerous criminals should be given a weight equal to consideration of the risk of flight. Judge Curran also has recommended that the Bail Act be amended to include a provision for automatic revocation of release pending trial when a defendant violates any of the conditions of release.[98] The Judicial Committee also would include such a condition.[99]

The Judicial Committee also would authorize revocation of

the release of a defendant indicted for a felony which allegedly was committed while he was on bail.[100] The Committee suggested, however, that before deciding whether to enter an order revoking release, the court should consider whether any additional conditions would reasonably assure the safety of the community and the appearance of the defendant. If a defendant should in such a case be detained, the Committee was divided on the issue of whether a defendant who is not tried within sixty days should be released automatically unless he caused the delay, or whether release after 60 days should not be automatic, particularly in the cases of defendants who were reindicted while on bail.[101]

According to a majority of the members of the Judicial Council Committee, "There are compelling reasons for enactment of a statute which sanctions preventive detention in some cases."[102] In the majority's view, courts should be given discretion to deny bail.

(a) in a case in which a crime of violence was allegedly committed prior to indictment, after indictment but prior to trial, or after trial but prior to completion of the appellate process; (b) in the event that a crime of violence is committed either while the defendant is on probation or parole, or within a reasonable time following the completion of a sentence; (c) where the court finds that a defendant is charged with certain high risk crimes of violence and will pose a danger to the community if released; (d) when a defendant is a narcotic addict with a habit so costly that it can only be supported by crime; and (e) where individuals whose alleged crimes, when committed in the context of a civil disorder, pose a grave danger to the community.[103]

The minority of the Committee opposed enactment of any legislation providing for preventive detention because, in its view, the present ability to predict dangerousness is grossly inadequate. Without an effective system of prediction, many good risks might be detained needlessly. According to the minority, "Congress' first duty is to provide the District of Columbia with the resources upon which a sound bail system and criminal justice process can be built. ... The right to pretrial release should not be the sacrificial lamb of an inadequate system of justice."[104]

The practice of pretrial, or "preventive" detention is common in some form in most foreign countries, including England.[105] A distinction should be made at the outset, however, between the police and the prosecuting power to achieve prolonged preventive detention that exists in some civil law countries, and the judicial power currently existing in this country to order pretrial detention in capital cases. It is only this judicial power that people in this country have advocated extending to some classes of noncapital cases.[106]

At present, statutory authorization of pretrial detention in this country is extremely rare. In a great majority of states, present constitutional and statutory provisions grant an absolute right to bail, at least in noncapital cases.[107] Yet pretrial detention in a disguised form is commonly achieved by judges setting money bail at an unattainably high amount. The Proposed New York Criminal Procedure Law contained a provision (since abandoned) which would have made New York the only state to allow courts openly to deny release to criminal defendants they consider likely to be a danger to society or themselves if they are allowed to remain at liberty. In determining the question of release, the statute directed courts to consider: (1) the available information relating to the defendant's character, reputation, habits and mental condition; (2) the nature of the offense with which he is charged; and (3) his previous criminal record. Where the defendant has been convicted and is awaiting appeal, the likelihood of the ultimate reversal of the judgment also is relevant.[108]

The New York Commission argued that the consideration of a defendant's possible danger to society, although overtly recognized neither legislatively nor judicially, actually underlies many refusals, of defendants' applications for release:

> There is little doubt that the average judge will, regardless of the reasons given by him, deny bail to a defendant charged with forcible rape and having an unsavory record of sex crimes, no matter how certain he may be that the defendant will appear in court when required; nor is there any doubt that such practice . . . has the approval of the general public . . . Upon the premise that in many instances preventive detention is in fact necessary for public protection and will inevitably be practiced even though not specifically authorized, the proposal realistically and implicitly recognizes danger to the community as a valid consideration in the determination of any bail application.[109]

The present Administration has also suggested a law for the District of Columbia "whereby dangerous hardcore recidivists could be held in temporary pretrial detention when they have been charged with crime and when their continued pretrial release presents a continued danger to the community."[110] Moreover, several Senators and Congressmen have introduced bills relating to pretrial detention in the 1st Congress.[111]

A number of compelling arguments support legislation that would give judges the power to detain suspects before their trials. In the first place, as we have seen, the current judicial practice of detaining defendants by manipulating the requirements for money bail is widespread.[112] According to one judge:

> An unreasonable law has the ultimate effect of forcing those who administer it to ignore it, calloused of the consequences or else to make extreme rationalizations in circumventing it; this applies to judges. You cannot expect judges to follow the letter of a law that requires them to turn many dangerous criminals loose day after day.[113]

If the problem of a defendant's dangerousness to the community were considered openly, and if any pretrial detention were coupled with strict procedural safeguards, including the right to appellate review, it is arguable that far fewer abuses would exist than do under current practices.[114]

In addition, as the President's Commission on Law Enforcement and the Administration of Justice pointed out: "The present invisibility of the issue of dangerousness, by preventing judicial review of specific cases, undoubtedly impedes the development of standards and data concerning dangerousness."[115] Thus, much can be said for bringing the existing practices regarding pretrial detention out into the open where they can be evaluated on their own merits, and where they can be effectively regulated.[116]

The possibility of replacing the money bail system entirely by using narrowly drawn procedures to detain some few defendants before trial has not been given sufficient attention in the legislative proposals for pretrial detention. Although some of the legislation that has been suggested would limit courts to nonfinancial conditions of release on a finding of dangerousness, none of it does away with the courts' power to set high money bail ostensibly as a deterrent to flight. The President's Crime Commission stated, however, that if a satisfactory solution could be found to the problem of the relatively small percentage of defendants who present a significant risk of flight or criminal conduct before trial, it would be prepared to recommend that money bail be totally disregarded.[117] As shown, the benefits to the administration evils, would be enormous. On the other hand, the adoption of of justice of abolishing money bail, with all its attendant a system that gave the power of outright detention before trial without disturbing the judicial power to set high money bail would tend to compound the evils of the present system. It would increase the power of judges to detain without giving any assurance that judges had, in all cases, rational bases for their decisions.[118]

Although detention without conviction of crime has precedents in dealing with the mentally ill and juveniles thought likely to become criminals,[119] the adoption of any system of pretrial detention is beset with difficulties, however, both theoretical and practical. On the theoretical side, many have argued that pretrial detention is precluded by the presumption of innocence, by the "excessive bail" clause of the Eighth Amendment, and by the "due process" clause of the Fifth and Fourteenth Amendments.

The presumption of innocence, expressly mentioned in the constitution or code of most states, has generally been considered as a rule of evidence designed to secure a fair trial by requiring the prosecution to prove its case beyond a reasonable doubt. If the presumption of innocence precludes any predictions of future wrongful conduct before a defendant has been convicted, it bars both pretrial detention and conditions of release. It is doubtful, however, that any court would adopt such an interpretation.[120] As one author writes:

> The presumption of innocence . . . does not mean that those who discharge executive or administrative functions prior to trial should be bound to act as though the suspect had behaved, and would pending trial behave, as a law-abiding citizen. This would be to contradict the experience of mankind over the ages.[121]

The Eighth Amendment objections to pretrial detention are more difficult to refute and the few judicial decisions on the subject have not decisively settled the issue.[122] According to Professor Caleb Foote's interpretation of the Eighth Amendment,[123] the historical evidence which he marshals for a right to bail is extremely persuasive, but it is weakened by two considerations. First, although the Eighth Amendment makes no distinction between capital and non-capital offenses, the exception of capital crimes from the guarantee to bail of the Judiciary Act of 1789 and its

482

successors has gone unchallenged. Second, although Professor Foote's analysis would seem to require an absolute right to bail at least in all noncapital cases, he is nonetheless willing to grant an exception for cases where the prosecution can show that release would create a great risk of violent injury to a specific victim, complainant, or witness.[124]

The argument that pretrial detention deprives a defendant of his liberty without due process of law was well stated by Senator Ervin in a recent article in the *George Washington Law Review*:

> Even when apparently convincing evidence exists that a man has committed a crime, we would be shocked at the suggestion that he might be convicted and imprisoned without being accorded the right to present his defense in a trial governed by the processes of law. It is even more outrageous that through a perversion of bail procedures, such punishment might be imposed by a judge, or in the case of most federal districts, a United States Commissioner, in the absence ·even of trial or jury verdict and on the basis of a crime not yet committed. Such a power is repugnant to constitutional principles. No claim of public safety can justify such a flagrant negation of due process of law.[125]

The American Bar Association's Advisory Committee on Pretrial Proceedings on the other hand, believes that the due process argument cannot be made without reference to a particular form of pretrial detention: "If other constitutional doubts were resolved, it seems likely that a limited provision carefully hedged with adequate procedural safeguards would survive attack.[126]

It thus appears that pretrial detention proposals will probably escape constitutional objection if the defendants detained do with some assurance actually pose a threat to the safety of society. But if judges are explicitly given the power to lock up defendants based on a prediction of possible dangerousness, will they know which defendants to detain? Upon this very practical problem, the answer to the theoretical question of legality will probably rest.

One judge has testified that he is confident judges can make such predictions:

> Documented statistics of recidivism coupled with a strong showning of present misconduct affords a judge sufficient criteria to enable him to predict with reasonable certainty whether an individual poses a danger to the community.[127]

Another judge, however, a member of the same court, strongly disagrees:

When the District of Columbia Crime Commission prepared its report in 1966, it conducted, among other things, a survey of persons charged with committing a new crime while on bail for another offense. This survey showed that of 2,776 persons who came before the United States District Court for the District of Columbia during the survey period, 207 (or 7.5 percent) were charged with committing a new crime while on bail, 124 of them (or 4.5 percent) with a crime of actual or potential violence. It is to be noted that these figures and percentages refer only to charges, not to convictions. The conviction rate in the District Court is approximately 75 percent, so that in actuality only about 3 percent of all those released on bail during the survey period were found to have committed a violent crime while out on bail.

Can anyone really believe that a judge could predict, with a degree of accuracy, which one out of every 33 defendants who come before him is likely to commit another crime while on bail? If such predictability is impossible—as I think it is—then the community can be safe from crimes of violence by defendants during the pre-trial period only by preventively detaining the 32 who predictably will not commit such an offense, in order to be sure to keep off the streets the one defendant who will. I think that, even with the appalling crime situation with which we are confronted, this is too high a price to pay.[128]

Unquestionably, some individual cases at least in retrospect, clearly suggest that a defendant never should have been released.[129] The question is whether such cases can be identified in advance, with enough precision to allow the dangerous to be detained without holding a large number of other defendants who pose little threat to the safety of the community.

Prof. Alan Dershowitz has pointed out the heavy odds that exist against accurate prediction of violent crimes by suspects released pending trial:

[A]ll the experience with predicting violent conduct suggests that in order to spot a significant proportion of future violent criminals, we would have to reverse the traditional maxim of the criminal law and adopt a philosophy that it is "better to confine ten people who would not commit predicted crimes, than to release one who would."

It should not be surprising to learn that predictions of the kind relied upon by the proponents of preventive detention are likely to be unreliable. Predictions of human conduct are difficult to make, for man is a complex entity and the world he inhabits is full of unexpected occurrences. Predictions of rare human events are even more difficult. And predictions of rare events occurring within a short span of time are the most difficult of all. Acts of violence by persons released while awaiting trial are relatively rare events (though more frequent among certain categories of suspects), and the relevant time span is short. Accordingly, the kind of predictions under consideration begin with heavy odds against their accuracy. A predictor is likely to be able to spot a large number of persons who would actually commit acts of violence only if he is also willing to imprison a very much larger number of defendants who would not, in fact, engage in violence if released.[130]

The President's Commission on Crime in the District of Columbia stated that defendants who are highly probable to be a grave menace to the physical safety of the public can be identified on the basis of their "prior criminal record . . . prior pattern of vicious antisocial behavior, and/or the nature of the offense . . . charged."[131] According to the Commission's figures, however, only 7.5 percent of the defendants released in one year were later alleged to have committed offenses while awaiting trial. And, of the defendants studied, only 4.5 percent were charged with crimes of actual or potential violence.[132] One of the Commissioners analyzed the backgrounds of the 207 offenders who had committed additional crimes on bail to see if they could have been identified beforehand and detained. The records of the repeaters did not appear to differ from those of the other defendants in any significant way. In fact, in several categories of offenses, the past records of the repeaters were better than those of other defendants.[133]

Efforts to predict violence are not unique to the pretrial period. Experience with prediction in the civil commitment of the mentally ill, in the sentencing of convicted offenders, in the paroling of prisoners from institutions and returning parole violators to prison,[134] indicates very little, if any, success.

First, professionals with years of experience in observing people and in basing predictions of future conduct on their observations (a procedure that has been called the "clinical" method of prediction) vary greatly from one another in their predictions regarding any one subject.[135] Second, the experts show no greater ability to predict behavior than people who lack such experience.

One recent discussion concluded, after surveying studies of

the validity of psychiatric predictions, that psychiatrists are no more able than anyone else to predict criminal behavior.[136] Psychiatrists were found consistently to have overpredicted the occurrence of violence. One ostensible reason for the overprediction relates to the issue of pretrial detention:

> The psychiatrist almost never learns about his erroneous predictions of violence—for predicted assailants are generally incarcerated and have little opportunity to prove or disprove the prediction; but he always learns about his erroneous predictions of nonviolence—often from newspaper headlines announcing the crime. This higher visibility of erroneous predictions of nonviolence, inclines him, whether consciously or unconsciously, to overpredict rather than underpredict violent behavior. This phenomenon will, I submit, be equally true of judicial decisions to confine predicted violence-doers pending trial.[137]

An associate superintendent of a California prison, with years of correctional experience, recently was asked to interview 283 inmates just before their release on parole and predict their success on parole. Neither from the interviews alone, nor from the interviews augmented by psychiatric case histories of the men interviewed, could the superintendent make predictions that had any significant relationship to the actual outcome of the cases.[138]

In an experiment that attempted to determine whether the training and experience of parole officers gave them a special competence for prediction, the same case histories of parolees from a state prison were given to ten experienced parole officers and ten laymen with no particular education or experience in working with offenders. The participants were asked to predict the probable success on parole of each subject. The two types of participants turned out not to differ significantly in their predictive efficiency. The two groups combined, correctly identified slightly more than half of the potential parole violators, but less than half of the nonviolators. (The results for nonviolators would have been better had the predictors flipped a coin.) No relationship existed between a participant's confidence in a particular prediction and the accuracy of that prediction.[139] In both these studies far more information about the offenders, all of whom had been through the state's prison system, was available than is collected before trial.

More accurate than these attempts to predict criminal

486

behavior through the clinical method,[140] are the procedures that have been developed of assigning offenders to risk categories based on characteristics previously found to be associated with continued criminal behavior.[141] Attempts to use such prediction tables date from the 1920's.[142] Yet only recently have improved measures of criminal behavior begun to receive careful attention.[143]

Despite the painstaking studies made recently, all currently available prediction methods have a relatively low ability to predict criminal behavior. The problems of prediction are compounded by the small incidence of violent crimes in the population (the "base rate" problem) and the difficulty of applying results from one geographical area to another (the "cross-validation" problem).[144] The success of release on recognizance in the past, both in terms of releasees' appearance for trial and in terms of the relatively small proportion charged with additional crimes on bail, complicates the predictive task even further, since it asks to predict rare events.[145]

Even if statistical prediction tables were perfected, it is doubtful that judges deciding whether to release defendants before trial would make full use of them. Parole boards currently have such tables available to them, together with evidence that the tables are more reliable indicators of success on parole than the board members' own intuitions.[146] Yet a 1962 survey showed that, of 48 states responding to a questionnaire, parole boards in 44 never made use of parole prediction tables for any purpose.[147] Parole boards seem to believe that more justice is done when an individual gets a "personalized" prediction than when he is assigned to a risk category on the basis of characteristics over which he has no control.[148]

In the face of the elemental state of knowledge regarding our ability to predict violent behavior, it has been urged that before enacting a statute that would authorize pretrial detention, some brief empirical studies be undertaken. Their purpose would be to discover whether it is possible to identify a high percentage of defendants who will commit violent crimes if they are released before their trials, without including an inordinate number of defendants who will not.

Professor Dershowitz has suggested several possibilities for such studies.[149] On one, judges would be asked to apply to the defendants who come before them the criteria contained in one or more of the statutes that have been proposed and to record their predictions of which defendants will engage in violent crimes. Then all (or perhaps half) would be released and the judicial predictions compared with actual experience. Perhaps more acceptable to the public would be a test in which judges were given the past records of defendants and asked to "predict" which of them would commit crimes pending trial. Immediate comparison with available (although not always accurate) records of offenses by bailed defendants would then be possible.

Finally, a study aimed at developing more refined criteria than those contained in any of the suggested legislation would be desirable. A large number of records of persons who have been charged with certain serious felonies and released under provisions of the Bail Reform Act could be analyzed. The purpose of the analyses would be to discover whether there are any characteristics, such as drug addiction, with a habit so costly that appears as if it can only bē supported by crime, that distinguish the defendants who probably committed crimes on bail from those who did not. The tentative list of predictive criteria that emerges from the analysis should then be applied retrospectively to the original records and, if possible, to another collection of records of offenders similarly situated to see whether any of the criteria has predictive validity.

CONCLUSION

Any system of pretrial detention of accused persons—including, especially, current money bail practices—poses dangers to cherished individual rights. Mitigation of these dangers requires that the Government reduce the inequities based on wealth wherever possible and insure that a defendant's detention does not preclude a fair trial. Each proceeding on the issue of pretrial detention should involve a full adversary hearing. Moreover, defendants without adequate resources should be supplied with counsel and investigative assistance.[150] These proceedings, requiring most of the safeguards of criminal trials, necessarily increase the strains on an already overburdened judicial system.[151] Detained defendants should normally be confined in quarters separate from those of convicted criminals, should be tried within a short time, should be provided with expanded social services for their families, if any, while they are confined, and should be assisted in reestablishing themselves in the community if they are in fact acquitted at trial.[152]

Any system of pretrial detention meeting these criteria will

488

thus impose heavy expenses in terms of both facilities and professional services, as well as posing dangers to individual rights. Accordingly, as the House of Delegates of the American Bar Association has also concluded,[153] alternatives to expanded formal use of pretrial detention and to present informal high bail practices should be more thoroughly explored before any such system is adopted. Pretrial detention should not be permitted to serve as a substitute for an adequately staffed and efficient system of justice. A period should be set aside for genuine experimentation with effective means, short of detention, for protecting the community from the dangerous defendant, particularly greatly reduced pretrial periods and increased supervision of released defendants. At the same time efforts should be intensified to develop techniques for more accurately identifying those few defendants who are so dangerous to the community that they may not be released before trial, even for a brief period. When and if such techniques are developed, limited use of pretrial detention may then be appropriate.

The government should protect citizens from acts of violence, but the public is not protected when defendants are detained or released almost at random—according to either the amount of bail they can raise or the unsupported intuitions of the judiciary. The rights of defendants and the safety of the public deserve a better system.

REFERENCES

1. Elsa de Ilaas, *The Antiquities of Bail* (New York: Columbia University Press, 1940).
2. Pollack and Mailland, *History of English Law* (2d ed., 1898), Vol. 2, at 590.
3. Darnel's Case, 3 How. It. Tr. 1 (1627).
4. *Id.* at 69.
5. Caleb Foote, "The Coming Constitutional Crisis in Bail," 113 *U. of Pa. L. Rev.* 959, 1125 (1965).
6. 1 Stat. 91, § 33 (1789).
7. See 1 *Annals of Congress* 436 (1789–1791).
8. Federal Rules of Criminal Procedure, Rule 46.
9. Foote, Markel and Wooley, "Compelling Appearance in Court: Administration of Bail in Philadelphia," 102 *U. of Pa. L. Rev.* 1031 (1954); Note, "A Study of the Administration of Bail in New York City," 106 *U. of Pa. L. Rev.* 693 (1958). See also Rankin, "The Effect of Pretrial Detention," 39 *N.Y.U.L. Rev.* 641 (1964).
10. See Arthur J. Goldberg, "Appendix" to Ronald Goldfarb,

Ransom: A Critique of the American Bail System (New York: Harper & Row, 1965), at 255.

11. As of 1968, 21 states and the federal government had enacted some sort of bail reform legislation. In 12 more, legislation had been proposed. Out of that 12, 6 had been defeated. However, very little is known of the implementation of most of these statutes. To a large degree, the reforms that have been made may exist only on paper. See Vera Institute of Justice, "Proposal for Bail Jumping Study" (unpublished memorandum, Apr. 19, 1968), at 3-4.

12. *Bandy* v. *United States*, 81 Sup. Ct. 197 (1960).

13. Goldfarb, *supra* note 10, at 96.

14. *Id.* at 1.

15. Arthur J. Goldberg, "Forward," Goldfarb, *supra* note 10, at x-xi.

16. Of 2,292 criminal cases in which bail was set in New York City in 1956, bail could only be furnished in an average of 49 percent. The percent varied with the amount of the bail required, from the 28 percent who could not afford $500 bail to the 86 percent who could not post $7,500. Note, 106 *U. of Pa. L. Rev.* 685 (1958).

17. *Gideon* v. *Wainright*, 372 U.S. 335 (1963).

18. *Griffin* v. *Illinois*, 351 U.S. 12 (1956).

19. *Douglas* v. *California*, 372 U.S. 353 (1963).

20. *Bandy* v. *United States*, 81 Sup. Ct. 198 (1960).

21. See also *Douglas* v. *California*, 372 U.S. 353 (1963).

22. Goldfarb, *supra* note 10, at 2.

23. *Id.*, Ch. 2

24. *Id.* at 2.

There is an even greater likelihood that demonstrators will appear for trial than the usual criminal defendants, since many of them demonstrate for the very purpose of provoking litigation and ultimately being vindicated by the courts.

25. *Id.* at 64.

26. *Id.* at 61.

27. *Washington Post*, Apr. 8, 1969, at A 1.

28. U.S. Circuit Court of Appeals Judge Skelly Wright, speaking on "Checkbook Justice," WRC-TV (1966).

29. See Goldfarb, *supra* note 10, at 84.

30. Wright, *supra* note 28.

31. Harry Subin, "Bail for the Rich, Jail for the Poor," *Nation*, Mar. 24, 1969, at 364.

32. A.B.A., "Standards Relating to Pretrial Release" (1968), at 61.

33. See "Bail: An Ancient Practice Re-examined," 70 *Yale L.J.* 966, 967-68 (1961).

34. Most regulatory schemes aim at protecting the state from losses due to uncollectable forfeitures. E.g., Pa. Stat. tit. 40, §

831 *et seq.* New York permits bonds to be written only by agents of licensed surety companies. N.Y. Code Crim. Proc. § 554 (b).
35. "Bail or Jail," 19 *The Record of the Association of the Bar of the City of New York* 11, 12 (1964).
36. A.B.A., *supra* note 32, at 64.
The uniform Bail Bond Act of the National Association of Insurance Commissioners provides some regulations but has been adopted by only a few states. E.g., Cal. Ins. Code § 1800 *et seq.*; Fla. Stat.§ 903.01 *et seq.* (1963).
37. Goldfarb, *supra* note 10, at 101.
38. *Id.* at 110.
39. "Bail or Jail," *supra* note 35.
40. *Powell* v. *Alabama*, 287 U.S. 45, 57 (1932).
41. 102 *U. Pa. L. Rev.* 1031 (1954).
42. 106 *U. Pa. L. Rev.* 685 (1958).
43. Wald, "Pretrial Detention and Ultimate Freedom: A Statistical Study," 39 *N.Y.U.L. Rev.* 631 (1964).
44. Of the 177,000 defendants formally charged with serious offenses in, 1965, 9,000 were dismissed and 8,000 were acquitted at trial. Of the 160,000 convicted, 56,000 were placed on probation. President's Commission on Law Enforcement and Administration of Justice (hereinafter cited as Crime Commission), *Challenge of Crime in a Free Society* (Washington, D.C.: Government Printing Office, 1967).
45. U.S., Congress, Committee on the Judiciary, *Improvements in Judicial Machinery, Hearings,* before a subcommittee on Constitutional Rights, Senate, 88th Cong., 2d sess., 1964, Testimony of James Bennett, former Director of the United States Bureau of Prisons, at 46.
46. Assemblyman William T. Bagley, Chairman, Assembly Committee on Judiciary, California Assembly, press release, Mar. 10, 1969.
47. Andrew Schaffer, "The Problem of Overcrowding in the Detention Institutions of New York City: An Analysis of Causes and Recommendations for Alleviation" (Report to the Mayor's Criminal Justice Coordinating Council, Vera Institute of Justice, Jan. 1969), at iv.
48. Testimony of Herbert Sturz, Executive Director, Vera Institute of Justice, to the Senate Subcommittee on Constitutional Rights, quoted by Goldfarb, *supra* note 10, at 152.
49. See also Ares, Rankin, and Sturz, "The Manhattan Bail Project," 38 *N.Y.U.L. Rev.* 67 (1963).
50. See Vera Institute of Justice, "Proposal for Bail Jumping Study," *supra* note 11.
51. A comprehensive list of existing bail projects and statistics describing their operations currently is being prepared by the Vera Institute of Justice in New York. Through the Bureau of Applied Research at Columbia University, Vera is conducting a study to attempt to determine the factors useful in predicting the appearance of defendants released on summonses.

52. Ill. Rev. Stat., ch. 38, §§ 110-11 *et seq.*
53. Schaffer, *supra* note 47, at 50-51.
54. Ill. Rev. Stat. ch. 38, §§ 107-12 (1963).
55. Cal. Pen. Code § 853.6.
56. Ronald L. Goldfarb and Linda R. Singer, "Problems in the Administration of Justice in California" (Report of the Assembly Committee on Judiciary, California Legislature, 1969), at 26-27.
57. Gertrude Samuels, "A Summons Instead of an Arrest," *New York Times Magazine,* July 26, 1964.
58. Memorandum from Police Liaison Office, Vera Institute of Justice, to the Police Commissioner of the City of New York, Manhattan Summons Project, August 30, 1968.
59. *Id.*
60. *Id.*
61. *Id.*
62. 80 Stat. 214 (Pub. L. 89-465, 89th Cong., 2d sess., 1966).
63. 80 Stat. 327 (Pub. L. 89-519, 89th Cong., 2d sess., 1966).
64. *The Bail Reform Act,* Legislative Analysis, American Enterprise Institute for Public Policy Research, Analysis #6, Apr. 14, 1969, Washington, D.C., at 1.
65. See A.B.A., *supra* note 32, at 55:
"Presently, bail is set in practically every case, however, minor or serious, without respect to its particular facts. Without reflection, courts assume that bail is a necessary element of the criminal process. . . . There is in fact an unspoken presumption that bail should be set in every case unless the defendant makes a showing to the contrary."
66. 18 U.S.C. § 3146 (a).
67. 18 U.S.C. § 3146. The judge may:
   (1) Place the person in the custody of a designated person or organization agreeing to supervise him;
   (2) Place restrictions on the travel, association, or place of abode of the person during the period of release;
   (3) Require the execution of an appearance bond in a specified amount and the deposit in the registry of the court, in cash or other security as directed, of a sum not to exceed 10 per centum of the amount of the bond, such deposit to be returned upon the performance of the conditions of release;
   (4) Require the execution of a bail bond with sufficient solvent sureties, or the deposit of cash in lieu thereof; or
   (5) Impose any other condition deemed reasonably necessary to assure appearance as required, including a condition requiring that the person return to custody after specified hours.
68. U.S.C. § 3146 (d).
69. U.S.C. § 3147.
70. 18 U.S.C. § 3148.
71. U.S. Congress, Committee on the Judiciary, *Bail Reform*

Act of 1966, Hearings, before a subcommittee on Constitutional Rights, Senate, 91st Cong., 1st sess., 1969 (hereinafter cited simply as *Hearings*); prepared statement of Chief Judge Harold H. Greene, District of Columbia Court of General Sessions, Jan. 21, 1969, at 1.

72. S. Rept. No. 750, 89th Cong., 1st sess. (1965).

73. *Hearings, supra* note 71; prepared statement of Patricia M. Wald, Jan. 22, 1969, at 1.

74. *Id.;* prepared statement of Charles L. Decker, Jan. 23, 1969, at 2.

75. See e.g., Bagley, *supra* note 46:

The traditional use of money bail is a prime example of a practice which has proven unnecessary, ineffective and discriminatory against the poor. Numerous studies have proven that most defendants will appear regardless of whether or not they have posted bail. There is no reason that a person who has a job and family in a community should be "ransomed" by a bail bond, which is not refunded even if he is proven innocent. The concept of equal justice cannot tolerate the continuation of such a system.

76. *Hearings, supra* note 71; prepared statement of Harry I. Subin, Associate Director, Vera Institute of Justice, Jan. 28, 1969, at 1-2.

77. See generally "Report of the Judicial Council Committee to study the Operation of the Bail Reform Act in the District of Columbia" (D.C. Circuit, May, 1968) (Ad Hoc Committee).

There have been fewer problems in the federal courts in other districts. Consequently, Judge Charles E. Wyzanski, Jr. of the Federal District Court in Massachusetts, has cautioned against amending the Bail Reform Act, which applies to all federal courts, in order to deal with problems that may be peculiar to the District of Columbia:

It may be necessary to do something about the Act in the District of Columbia, but it would be wicked in the rest of the nation. Don't forget this is a very big country we're governing.

From a telephone interview with Judge Charles E. Wyzanski, Jr., Apr. 10, 1969.

78. *Hearings, supra* note 71; prepared statement of Judge Tim Murphy, District of Columbia Court of General Sessions, at 2.

79. *Id.*; prepared statement of Bruce D. Beaudin, Director, District of Columbia Bail Agency, Feb. 4, 1969, at 2-3.

80. *Washington Post,* Feb. 2, 1969, at D2.

81. "Report of the Judicial Council Committee to Study the Operation of the Bail Reform Act," *supra* note 77, at 9-10.

82. *Hearings, supra* note 71; Beaudin.

83. *Id.; Greene,* at 6-8.

84. *Id.;* prepared statement of Senator Joseph D. Tydings, Jan. 22, 1969.

During fiscal 1968, the U.S. District Court for the District

493

of Columbia slightly reduced its criminal backlog. But almost 40 percent of the cases pending in the court at the end of Fiscal 1968 had been on the calendar for 6 months or more. Twenty-one percent had been pending for over a year.

85. *Id.* at 1.

86. *Id.* at 4-5.

87 "Report of the Judicial Council Committee to Study the Operation of the Bail Reform Act," *supra* note 77, at 25.

88. *Hearings, supra* note 71; prepared opening statement of Senator Roman L. Hruska, Jan. 21, 1969, at 2-3.

89. *Id.,* Murphy, at 5.

90. *Washington Post,* Feb. 2, 1969, at D1.

91. Norman Lefstein, *Analysis of Metropolitan Police Department's Study Concerning Crime on Bail,* Department of Justice, Office of Criminal Justice, Jan. 1969.

92. *Hearings, supra* note 71; Murphy, at 5.

93. *Id.* at 3-4.

94. *Id.* at 4.

95. "Report of the Judicial Council Committee to Study the Operation of the Bail Reform Act," *supra* note 77, at 27-28.

96. *Hearings, supra* note 71; Greene, at 2.

97. *Id.,* at 4.

98. *Id.;* prepared statement of Chief Judge Curran, U.S. District Court for the District of Columbia, Feb. 4, 1969, at 6.

99. "Report of the Judicial Council Committee to Study the Operation of the Bail Reform Act," *supra* note 77.

100. *Id.*

101. *Id.*

102. "Report of the Judicial Committee to Study the Operation of the Bail Reform Act," (D.C. Circuit, May, 1969).

103. *Id.*

104. Goldfarb, *supra* note 10, Ch. 6.

105. Ronald Goldfarb, "A View of the Crime Problem," address to the American Jewish Congress, Washington, D.C., Feb. 12, 1969.

106. See Daniel J. Freed and Patricia M. Wald, *Bail in the United States: 1964* (Washington, D.C.: Department of Justice, 1964), at 2-3.

107. Seventh Interim Report of the State of New York Temporary Commission on Revision of the Penal and Criminal Code. 1968, at 193-194.

108. *Id.* (1967), at 435-36.

109. *Id.* (1969), Part A, Section b. To be published.

110. Cited by Alan M. Dershowitz, "On 'Preventive Detention,'" *New York Review of Books,* Mar. 1969, at 22.

111. E.g., S. 288 and 289 (Byrd), S. 556 (Tydings), H.R. 578 (Rogers), H.R. 2781 (McCulloch).

112. See, e.g., Abraham I. Goldstein, "Jail Before Trial," *New Republic,* Mar. 8, 1969, at 15, 16; Shaeffer, *supra* note 47, at 3, 29; *Hearings, supra* note 71; Wald at 8.

113. *Hearings, supra* note 71; Murphy, at 7.

During periods of civil disturbances, judges are even more likely to use high money bail in order to keep suspected riot participants in jail. The issue has been raised of whether judges should openly be given the power to detain in emergency conditions. See, e.g., "Report of the Judicial Council Committee to Study the Operation of the Bail Reform Act," *supra* note 77, at 29-30.

An existing federal statute, it may be noted, gives the Attorney General the power to detain people suspected of possible espionage or sabotage upon a presidential declaration of an "internal security emergency."

50 U.S.C. §§ 811-819.

114. See generally testimony of Harry I. Subin, Associate Director of the Vera Institute of Justice, in *Hearings, supra* note 71.

An offhand statement by the prosecutor that the defendant is "part of a ring," "will continue violating the law as he has in the past," "will intimidate witnesses," or "is reputed to be part of the Mafia," will frequently and effectively preclude the defendant from being released. *Hearings, supra* note 71; Prepared Statement of Harry D. Steward, Executive Director, Defenders Inc., San Diego, California.

115. Crime Commission, *supra* note 44, *Task Force Report: The Courts,* at 40.

116. E.g., A.B.A., *supra* note 32, at 65-66; Note, "Preventive Detention," 36 *Geo. Wash. L. Rev.* 178 (1967); Note, "Preventive Detention Before Trial," 79 *Harv. L. Rev.* 1489, 1502-03 (1966); *Hearings, supra* note 71; Tydings, at 9.

117. Crime Commission, *supra* note 44, *Challenge of Crime in a Free Society,* at 131.

118. *Hearings, supra* note 71; Subin, at 11.

119. Dershowitz, *supra* note 110, at 23-24.

120. See A.B.A. *supra* note 32, at 70; Note, "Preventive Detention Before Trial," *supra* note 116, at 1500.

121. T. B. Smith, "Bail Before Trial: Reflections of a Scottish Lawyer," 108 *U. Pa. L. Rev.* 305, 309 (1960).

122. See, e.g., *Carlson* v. *Landon,* 342 U.S. 524 (1952) (5-4 decision, holding that Eighth Amendment does not prevent Congress from making some classes of offenses non-bailable.)

Compare *Carbo* v. *United States,* 82 S. Ct. 662 (1962), with *Williamson* v. *United States,* 184 F. 2d 280, 282-83 (1950); Compare *Mastrian* v. *Hedman,* 326, F. 2d 708 (8th Cir.), cert. denied, 376 U.S. 965 (1964), with *Trimble* v. *Stone,* 187 F. Supp. 483 (D.C. 1960).

123. See *supra,* notes 5-8, and accompanying text.

124. Foote, *supra* note 5, at 1182.

125. Ervin, "The Legislative Role in Bail Reform," 35 *Geo. Wash. L. Rev.,* 429, 445 (1967).

126. A.B.A., *supra* note 32, at 67; See also Note, "Preventive Detention Before Trial," *supra* note 116, at 1500-05.

127. *Hearings, supra* note 71; Murphy, at 7.

128. *Id.;* Greene, at 7.

129. See, e.g., *Washington Post,* Feb. 2, 1969, at D 1.

130. Dershowitz, *supra* note 110, at 24-25.

131. The President's Commission on Crime in the District of Columbia (Washington, D.C.: Government Printing Office, 1966), at 527.

132. *Hearings, supra* note 71; Wald.
Any statistics describing the performance of defendants released pending trial are extremely rare. See Goldstein, *supra* note 112, at 16.

133. *Hearings, supra* note 71; Wald, at 5.

134. See, generally, Don M. Gottfredson, "Assessment and Prediction Methods in Crime and Delinquency," Crime Commission, *supra* note 44, *Task Force Report: Juvenile Delinquency,* app. A, and the bibliography contained therein.

135. See James Robinson & Paul Tagaki, "Case Decision in a State Parole System" (Research Division, California Department of Corrections, 1968).

136. See generally Alan M. Dershowitz, "The Concept of Legal Responsibility and Its Relationship to Psychological and Sociological Knowledge," consultant's paper prepared for this Task Force.

137. *Hearings, supra* note 71; statement of Professor Alan Dershowitz, Jan. 23, 1969, at 2-3.

138. E. Savides, *A Parole Success Prediction Study,* and D. M. Gottfredson, "Comparing and Combining Subjective and Objective Parole Predictions," California Department of Corrections, Research Newsletter, Sept.-Dec. 1961.

139. Michael Hakeem, "Prediction of Parole Outcome from Summaries of Case Histories," 52 *J. of Criminal Law, Criminology and Police Science* 145 (1961).

140. See Daniel Glaser, "Prediction Tables as Accounting Devices for Judges and Parole Boards," 8 *Crime and Delinquency* 239 (1962).

141. Glaser has found the two most selective characteristics to be an offender's "social development pattern" and the age at which he first left home for six months or more. Daniel Glaser, "The Efficacy of Alternative Approaches to Parole Prediction," 20 *American Sociological Review* (1955), at 283-287.

142. For the history of prediction studies, see Hermann Mannheim and Leslie T. Wilkins, *Prediction Methods in Relation to Borstal Training* (London: Her Majesty's Stationery Office, 1955), ch. 1.

143. See Johan Thorsten Sellin and Marvin E. Wolfgang, *The Measurement of Delinquency* (New York: Wiley, 1964), at 349:
. . . only when we have an index with a quantitative scale for measuring delinquency can we give an explicit account of what we are measuring. The relatively undeveloped state of measuring instruments for such purposes in the social sciences

has been an obstacle to efficient and economical research. If measurements of time, temperature, length, or weight had to be newly invented for each research analysis in the physical sciences, progress in those fields would indeed have been slow. Yet in criminology and in the social sciences generally, there has been little or no systematic theory stipulating how to select fundamental dimensions of conduct in order to measure certain social events.

144. Gottfredson, *supra* note 134, at 181.

145. Don Gottfredson, "Release on Recognizance: A Proposed Model for Study" (unpublished paper, 1966), at 11.

146. See Glaser, *supra* note 140.

147. Victor H. Evjen, 8 *Crime and Delinquency* 215 (1962).

148. See generally Dershowitz, *supra* note 136.

"Attitudes which help to explain the lag by parole boards in the use of prediction tables may be summarized roughly under five heads:

(1) sensitivity to public opinion, (2) desire to encourage constructive use of prison time, (3) a firm belief in the uniqueness of each case, (4) frustration of intelligent selection for parole because of legal or traditional restrictions, and (5) reactions to the prediction devices themselves." Norman Hayner, "Why Do Parole Boards Lag in the Use of Prediction Scores?" *Pacific Sociological Rev.* (1958), at 73.

149. Dershowitz, *supra* note 110, at 27; memorandum to Daniel Freed, Feb. 28, 1969 (unpublished).

150. A.B.A., *supra* note 32, at 69.

151. *Hearings, supra* note 71; Curran.

152. *Id.;* Beaudin, at 4-5.

153. A.B.A., *supra* note 32.

SUPPLEMENT TO CHAPTER 19

THE ADMINISTRATION'S PREVENTIVE
DETENTION PROPOSAL*

On January 31, 1969, eleven days after taking office, President Nixon called for federal legislation to authorize pretrial preventive detention. Under the banner of law and order, he thus became the first President since the founding of the Republic to press for statutory curtailment of the right to bail pending trial in noncapital criminal cases.

The classic function of the bail hearing in criminal proceedings has been to enable an arrested person to gain his release upon assurance that he will appear as required for trial. Besides seeking to alter this purpose to perform a crime prevention function with punitive overtones, the new President's announcement also threatened precipitous reversal, after only two and a half years of operation, of the Bail Reform Act of 1966. The Act was the product of joint efforts by Congress, the Department of Justice and the federal courts to implement the principle of bail. Its purpose, as spelled out in Section 2, was:

> to revise the practices relating to bail to assure that all persons, regardless of their financial status, shall not needlessly be detained pending their appearance to answer charges . . . when detention serves neither the ends of justice nor the public interest.

The Act's emphasis was on encouraging selective pretrial release on nonfinancial conditions which imposed limited controls on the conduct of risky defendants.

The 1969 case for preventive detention was presented by high officials of the new Department of Justice. They made it sound as if the Bail Reform Act and serious crime were cause and effect. The transcript of a crime conference called

---

*This supplement was prepared by Daniel J. Freed, Professor of Law and Its Administration, Yale Law School.

by the President in the Cabinet Room quoted Associate Deputy Attorney General Santarelli with this explanation:

> Now under the reform of the Bail Law, there was enacted a statute which made it mandatory to release persons in noncapital cases, pending trial. . . . [F]or 176 years, the courts devised a method to detain dangerous people. . . . Since 1966 this is no longer possible. Now all persons who are no longer charged with capital offenses are released prior to trial.

Several months later, Deputy Attorney General Kleindienst told trial lawyers on Grand Bahama Island:

> By totally eliminating dangerousness as a criterion to be considered in setting conditions for pretrial release, the Bail Reform Act ignored the rationale behind 700 years of legal practice.

Attorney General Mitchell, addressing the International Association of Chiefs of Police in Miami, implied that his administration was the first to be concerned with the problem of pretrial danger:

> The prior Administration failed to suggest any method for detaining criminal suspects prior to their trial even if these suspects showed a substantial likelihood of committing another crime.

He suggested such a method himself. "Since the Eighth Amendment, when adopted, clearly permitted pretrial detention for capital crimes because of danger to the community," it should not bar such detention today when, due to repeal of the death penalty, the same crimes are no longer capital "for reasons completely unrelated to their dangerousness."

In addition to highlighting the alleged "mandatory release" defect of the Bail Reform Act, the Justice Department developed a companion, though somewhat contradictory, argument. "Our second objective," Mr. Kleindienst announced,

> is to eliminate from the bail system the hypocrisy of locking up defendants, without fixed standards, through the device of requiring a high money bond.

The Bail Reform Act, he charged,

> is responsible for the detention of hundreds of defendants who might be released under new procedures. This Administration

is prepared to move vigorously to free these defendants, under some reasonable conditions, if they do not pose a threat to the community.

The preceding Chapter 19 traces the history of bail, the background of the Bail Reform Act and the ensuing problems it encountered. This postscript briefly examines the present administration's detention proposal and the arguments of its sponsors.

THE ADMINISTRATION'S PROPOSAL

President Nixon's preventive detention proposal was introduced in the House of Representatives on July 14, 1969, as H.R. 12806. The original premise on which the President ordered its formulation to begin had been stated in these terms:

> Increasing numbers of crimes are being committed by persons already indicted for earlier crimes, but free on pretrial release. Many are now being arrested two, three, even seven times for new offenses while awaiting trials. This requires that a new provision be made in the law, whereby dangerous hard core recidivists could be held in temporary pretrial detention when they have been charged with crimes and when their continued pretrial release presents a clear danger to the community.

The President's prescription sounded like the call for a limited measure to reach persons meeting a four-part description: (i) hard-core recidivists, who had (ii) initially been indicted for dangerous offenses, and were (iii) thereafter released and then arrested again for crime on bail, after which (iv) a court could determine that their continued release would pose a "clear danger."

Five months of exuberant drafting, however, ballooned the concept of a limited detention statute in many directions. Cast in the form of an amendment to the Bail Reform Act, the proposal spelled out procedures under which a judicial officer determining release pending trial could order pretrial detention without bail if the defendant fell, at the time of arrest, into any one of four felony categories:

> (1) charged with a "dangerous crime"; a term defined to include, among others, (a) an attempt to take property by threat of force, (b) an attempt to break, enter and commit an offense inside a home or business, (c) an attempt to commit

arson of premises "adaptable for overnight accommodation of persons or for carrying on business," (d) an assault with intent to commit statutory rape, and (e) unlawful distribution of a drug or narcotic;

(2) charged with a "crime of violence" committed on bail, probation, parole or mandatory release, if the prior charge is a "crime of violence," or if the person was convicted within the past ten years of a "crime of violence." The term was defined to include, among others, an assault with intent to commit any offense punishable by more than one year in prison;

(3) a narcotics addict charged with a "crime of violence"; or

(4) charged with any offense and, for the purpose of attempting to obstruct justice, threatens, injures or intimidates a prospective witness or juror, or attempts to do so.

The bill further provided that a pretrial detention hearing must be held immediately after the arrested person is brought before a judicial officer. A five-day continuance was allowed at the request of the defendant, or a three-day continuance upon request of the Government, with the defendant subject to detention in the interim. The judicial officer could issue an order of detention in lieu of bail upon three findings:

(i) "clear and convincing evidence" that the defendant fell within one of the four categories,

(ii) a "substantial probability" that the defendant committed the offense charged, and

(iii) "no condition or combination of conditions of release which will reasonably assure the safety of any other person or the community."

The proposal specified that a defendant at a detention hearing may be represented by counsel, may present information and witnesses, and may testify and cross-examine witnesses. It explicitly stated that information offered at detention hearings need not conform to the rules of evidence. The defendant's own testimony was made inadmissible on the issue of guilt in any other proceeding except bail-jumping, but usable for purposes of impeachment.

Finally, the bill provided that once a defendant is ordered detained (a) he is to be incarcerated separately from convicted prisoners "to the extent practicable"; (b) he may be released upon "good cause shown" in the Marshal's custody for limited periods of time to prepare defenses; (c) his trial is to be expedited "to the extent practicable"; (d) he is to be released whenever a subsequent event is found to eliminate the basis for his detention; and (e) he is to be released at the expiration of sixty days, unless the trial is in progress or is delayed at the request of the defendant. These and other provisions of H.R. 12806 raise many questions of constitutionality, feasibility and wisdom. Here we focus on just a sample.

FACTS, ISSUES AND ALTERNATIVES

The reported commission of a serious crime by an offender free on bail is a dramatic and discouraging event. It undermines the morale of the police, the security of citizens and respect for law and courts. No informed observer condones crime on bail or suggests that no remedy is needed. The difficulty lies in determining, promptly after arrest and before trial, (i) who among the accused are guilty, (ii) who among them can be predicted to repeat their offenses if released without safeguards, (iii) what alternative methods are feasible for controlling their risks, and (iv) how to balance these alternatives with due regard for the values of individual liberty and public safety.

Stated in this way, the four-part problem describes in large part the function in our society of trial and sentence. To impose the burden of those functions on a prompt post-arrest bail hearing may well be reasonable if the procedures match the due process attributes, but advance the date, of an otherwise delayed trial.

The Administration's preventive detention proposal falls short of these standards in myriad ways, and of the President's own prescription as well. On the face of the draft legislation, its coverage is not limited to recidivists, hardcore or otherwise. It is not confined to persons indicted by a grand jury. It reaches a population much larger than persons who have been arrested for committing an offense on bail. It niether contains procedures, nor is based on research, which provide reasonable assurance that a court applying it will be capable of distinguishing before trial a clearly dangerous accused offender from all others charged with crime. It usurps the functions of trial and sentence without a trial's protections by permitting the determination of likely guilt and the imposition of short-term imprisonment on inadmissible evidence. It compounds the damaging effect of today's pretrial detention by affixing to preventive detainees a label of "future danger" which no jury verdict, directed to past acts,

502

can remove. And it compounds, rather than avoids, the "hypocrisy" noted by Mr. Kleindienst, for it proposes preventive detention on top of detention via high money bail, rather than as its alternative.

Moreover, the underpinnings of the proposal, as stated by the new Department of Justice, suggest a significant amount of careless homework. The Bail Reform Act of 1966 did not make pretrial release mandatory. It did not eliminate "dangerousness" from bail law. It did not result in the abolition of pretrial detention.

1.   LEGISLATIVE HISTORY

The 1966 statute was enacted by Congress which was neither oblivious to the problem of crime on bail nor bent on closing down pretrial jails. Curtailing "needless" detention *i.e.,* detention which "serves neither the ends of justice nor the public interest," was the goal spelled out in statutory language. Orders of partial detention, enabling release from custody only during specified hours of the day, were expressly authorized. Complete detention was anticipated by elaborate provisions for detention review, for credit against sentence for time spent in custody, and by a contemporaneous Supreme Court rule requiring bi-weekly detention reports.

Concern for "danger to any other person or to the community" was not deleted from federal bail statutes in 1966. On the contrary, it was inserted there by the Bail Reform Act for the first time in history. It was incorporated in provisions authorizing either conditional release or orders of detention in pretrial capital cases and in all post-conviction cases pending appeal.

"Danger" was not added to the criteria for bail before trial in noncapital cases, nor had it ever been a part of that law. The rationale for adopting the "danger" standard in one place but not in the other was that orders of detention (*i.e.,* flat denial of bail) were permissible as a matter of law in capital cases and on appeal, but forbidden as to other accused persons. Hence, adding risk of danger to risk of flight as criteria for discretionary bail in appeal and capital cases was thought not to be abridging the right to bail of any person otherwise entitled to it.

An unexamined assumption held by many during the pre-Bail Reform Act debates was that the discretionary character of bail in capital cases, codified in the Judiciary Act of 1789, was a product of the inherently greater danger to the community posed by defendants charged with capital offenses. Attorney General Mitchell and his associates embraced this assumption as if it were gospel. Historical research has uncovered virtually nothing to support the assumption, and all indications are that it is erroneous. Quite a different rationale—the greater likelihood that a man in fear for his life will flee—underlies capital denials of bail, and is wholly consistent with both conventional bail theory and the concept of no punishment for an offense without conviction. Neither common sense nor empirical research supports the proposition that if two persons are accused of deliberate assault in a jurisdiction where the death penalty persists, the one whose alleged victim dies is more likely to be guilty, is less entitled to a presumption of innocence, and is for *those* reasons less entitled to bail before trial.

Similarly, the Attorney General's assertion that capital punishment, and hence bail denial, was historically connected solely to offenses involving violence against persons, *i.e.,* "serious felonies—those which posed a substantial danger of injury or death to others," misreads federal statute books. The Federal Crimes Act of 1790, one of the earliest collections of capital offenses, covers counterfeiting, forgery, embezzlement of United States currency and larceny of goods in excess of $50.

The persistent absence of an explicit pretrial danger test in federal bail law does not mean that courts were or are powerless to deal selectively with risks. In the course of pre-Bail Reform Act testimony in 1965 assessing the pros and cons of preventive detention, then Deputy Attorney General Ramsey Clark outlined some authorized routes to permissible pretrial control and detention:

> . . . if prior convictions and other information indicate doubts about the defendant's behavior, the conditions of release can include close supervision by a probation officer. If the defendant's alleged misconduct has occurred while he was free on parole or probation, these releases can be revoked. If the defendant has been charged with a series of violent crimes, the appropriateness of a commitment for mental examination may be tested. If the defendant has threatened prospective witnesses or tampered with evidence in his case, *Carbo* and similar decisions indicate that his bail can be revoked. And if the defendant's background and character make it likely that he will commit a violent crime while at liberty, will not the same factors often raise serious questions concerning his likelihood to appear at trial and thereby justify bond?

An ironic feature of the legislative history, in light of current debate as to whether an order of preventive detention is constitutional, was deletion by the House of Representatives of a Senate provision permitting a risky defendant to be released under the supervision of a probation officer. According to House Report 1541, 89th Congress:

> Since the probation officer is an arm of the court, who, under normal circumstances, only enters into a case after conviction, your committee is of the opinion that in order to avoid any possibility that any constitutional right of the defendant be invaded this provision should be deleted . . . . Moreover, the use of a probation officer would involve additional duties and might require additional personnel.

As a result of this action, which meant that no funds could be appropriated for personnel to supervise pretrial release, the Bail Reform Act was enacted without resources to carry out its third party custody provisions. Three years later, preventive detention of accused persons was proposed in lieu of the less severe technique, rejected on constitutional and financial grounds, for controlling the risks of such persons.

2. THE PROCEDURAL CONTEXT

No fair assessment of procedural changes in the subsystem called bail can be divorced from their relation to the overall system of criminal justice administration. Considerations of context are equally important whether it is the 1966 pretrial release reforms or the 1969 pretrial detention proposals which are at issue.

Chapter 13 discusses the daily interplay of law enforcement, court and correctional agencies and discloses that the criminal justice system of American cities today is largely a myth. It is characterized by fragmentation of functions, hostility among officials and ineffectiveness of the criminal sanction. It is more accurately termed a nonsystem instead.

It is similarly a myth and misnomer to refer to a bail system.

Basic to an appreciation of bail procedures today is the understanding that bail was *not* conceived as a self-contained process for releasing suspected criminals, irrespective of risks, promptly after arrest. Instead, from ancient times, bail was designed only as an interim procedure, subsidiary to a law enforcement and judicial process which works as a continuum of integrated steps between arrest and disposition. In such a setting, bail allows the judicial officer to take account of (a) the fact that the police found probable cause to believe that the arrested person committed a crime, (b) the presumption of innocence which an unconvicted person enjoys, and (c) the necessity that the arrested person, if released, must return for trial. These factors, in bail theory, are to be balanced by a decision which sets conditions of controlled pretrial freedom, during a relatively brief period of trial preparation, in a process capable of producing speedy trials and meaningful criminal sanctions.

Against such a background, bail makes no sense in a system in which trial is routinely delayed, and meaningful sanctions are seldom imposed on those found to be guilty. Neither individual rights nor community security can be protected or respected in such a setting. And the situation is aggravated if bail conditions within such a system are neither carefully imposed nor diligently enforced.

An appropriate examination of how a "bail system" functions today may be made in the District of Columbia. On one hand, it was the crime-on-bail furor in the nation's Capital that generated the impetus for the preventive detention decision announced in the President's statement on "Actions and Recommendations for the Federal City." On the other hand, the local criminal courts of Washington, D.C. are subject to the Bail Reform Act of 1966, whose need for an implementation mechanism led Congress contemporaneously to create the D.C. Bail Agency. The Agency provides judges and magistrates with bail fact-finding services, and with recommendations on the basis of which informed bail decisions can be made.

This combination of bail reform legislation, bail resources and an ensuing demand for preventive detention might imply that experience under the best of circumstances persuaded those involved to reverse the pretrial release objectives of 1966. Quite the opposite is the fact.

In May 1968, nearly two years after the Bail Reform Act and the Bail Agency became operative in the District of Columbia, an experienced committee of judges, prosecutors, defense attorneys and bail agency representatives unanimously found that the local bail system was in chaos. In meticulous detail, the committee described the important changes in procedure and organization which were needed and could be affected under existing law, the additional staffing which hinged on more appropriations and the new legislation which required consideration by Congress. Seldom has so careful a prescription been worked out for procedures to govern the setting of bail, the development of effective conditions of release, the review of detention, the techniques of enforcement and the reduction of crime on bail without preventive detention. To ease adoption by the organization whose operations intertwine to make up the bail system, recommendations were subdivided and addressed to each agency head: the Chief of Police, United States Attorney, Public Defender, Corporation Counsel, Bail Agency, United States Marshal, Director of Corrections, Chief Judges of trial and appellate courts, and Mayor's office. A federal district court judge, acting under mandate from the Judicial Council of the District of Columbia Circuit, convened an interagency meeting to explain the proposals, to offer assistance and to establish a system of liaison and monitoring.

One year later, in May 1969, the same committee reported again. Its unanimous findings painted a dismal picture of agency and legislative response to the earlier recommendations. Many, it said, "have not yet been implemented and their potential effect in reducing crime on bail cannot be measured." At every stage of the process, dealing with both careless release and excessive detention, it found failures: e.g., in the setting of money bail by judicial officers "completely beyond the defendant's economic means to meet"; in defendants remaining in jail awaiting trial due to "failure of counsel to apply for 24-hour review"; in Bail Agency inability to investigate adequately the background of defendants, or to provide proper third party custodians, or adequately supervise released defendants to assure conformity with court-imposed conditions; in delay between release and trial "which is so long that the safety of the public is greatly endangered."

A key finding in relation to the Administration's 60-day trial proposal was that the elapsed time between first indictment and alleged second offense exceeded that limit in more than 60 percent of the cases of persons indicted for an offense on bail. In actuality, the release time for many of the balance may also have considerably exceeded 60 days since time between arrest and indictment was not counted.

The committee was able to assess the response to three key recommendations for controlling crime on bail:

(1) Despite urging the use of special conditions of release, e.g., third party supervisors and narcotics checks, to deter both

flight and risk of crime, such use *declined* by 8 percent (from 20% to 12%) from 1967 to 1968.

(2) Despite urging the expanded use of sanctions for violations of release conditions, e.g., revocation, more stringent conditions, contempt, advancement for trial, such sanctions were "the exception rather than the rule."

(3) Despite urging procedures for expediting the trials of persons who pose a danger to the community, "expedited proceedings have not been achieved" and median time between indictment and disposition *rose* from 7.8 months in 1967 to 9.5 months in 1968.

In sum, the committee found, the Bail Reform Act was not operating effectively. The recommendations to help it work were not being followed. The resources which the system needed were not available. The efficacy of measures to reduce crime on bail within the present framework of the law could not be assessed. A nonfunctioning system of bail was imbedded in a nonfunctioning system of justice.

CONCLUSION

The goal of an effective bail system may be viewed as the product either of process or of ideology. The traditionalist view, which accepts the foundations of our criminal pro and the limited role of bail to assure presence at trial, recognizes that today's bail crisis flows from yesterday's criminal justice neglect. Just as dilapidated schools and housing, overcrowded highways and airlanes and problems of pollution and health, require new resources, planning and coordination, so do law enforcement and courts.

The alternative is an ideological solution that appears easy, cheap and fast. Converting bail from an interim stage in a process of justice to a new fashion of minitrials and short-term punishment of the unconvicted retreats from the principles on which the system was built. Such a substitute would be a permissible choice in a society which candidly admitted that its systems couldn't work, and elected as an alternative to settle for the principles of poorer education, less justice, curtailment of the right to travel, and a lower quality of life. If criminal trials and criminal sanctions are unworkable, then preventive detention may be the only reasonable alternative. It can be adopted on no other basis at this time.

CHAPTER 20

THE CONSTITUTION AND RIGHTS OF
THE ACCUSED*

Increasingly in recent years, it has been said, the procedures for judging criminal prosecutions in our country have unduly favored the accused, and they are, therefore, partly responsible for the increases in violent crime. Is this charge true, particularly with regard to the recent opinions of the U.S. Supreme Court on the Fifth Amendment privilege against self-incrimination? That is the question which this chapter seeks to answer.

THE VIEW OF THE CRITICS

Quinn Tamm, of the International Association of Chiefs of Police, has stated the criticisms of the courts in general and the Supreme Court in particular:

> The Courts in too many cases are ignoring the public's right to protection. . . . The fabric of criminal law has become such a patchwork that too often the killer-fish escapes through the holes while those responsible for netting them become entangled in the ravelings and are rendered impotent. . . . Could it be then, that the deterrent effect of swift, sure and just punishment has been lost because the courts have become preoccupied with the rights of the individual rather than the rights of society? The scales of justice are getting out of balance. Too often, the criminal ascends to the role of the victim or underdog when he is apprehended and the full force of legal machinery directed against him. Too often the original victim of the murderer or the rapist or the child molester fades from memory as overwhelming public and judicial compassion is lavished on the criminal.[1]

---

* This chapter was prepared by Dorsey D. Ellis, Jr., associate professor of law at the University of Iowa College of Law, based in part on research papers by Timothy James Bloomfield, Esq., of Washington, D.C.

509

Some critics have asserted a direct causal relationship between rising crime rates and those decisions by the courts which have broadened procedural protections:

> Among the elements in American life which have contributed to the growth of crime, one of the most obvious and immediate is judicial leniency. [T]he Supreme Court's sustained venture in relieving the criminal of psychic discomfort has contributed heavily to the current upsurge of lawlessness.[2]

A noted former police chief has made the connection explicit between the rulings of the courts protecting the accused and the crime rate by pointing to the rising level of crime "since 1954, which was the year of *Irvine,* and the year before *Cahan.*"[3]

Other critics of the Supreme Court, who do not blame it directly for the increasing level of violence, are of the view that its decisions have at least seriously undermined the efforts of law enforcement agencies and impeded their ability to solve crimes. Senator Ervin has argued:

> Increasingly in the last decade our law enforcement officers have been limited and often hamstrung in dealing with crime by high court rulings . . . [which have] stressed individual rights of the accused to the point where public safety has often been relegated to the back row of the court room.[4]

A former police commissioner has similarly asserted:

> It is my firm conclusion that recent Supreme Court decisions have unduly hampered—and will in the future further hamper—the administration of criminal justice.[5]

An official of the National District Attorneys Association has declared:

> This country can no longer afford a civil rights binge that so restricts law enforcement agencies that they become ineffective.[6]

Prominent members of the judiciary have joined in the criticism of the Court's rulings on this ground. Chief Judge Lumbard of the New York Court of Appeals has suggested that "we are in danger of a grievous imbalance in the administration of criminal justice":

> In the past forty years there have been two distinct trends in the administration of criminal justice. The first has been to strengthen the rights of the individual; and the second, which is

perhaps a corollary of the first, is to limit the powers of law enforcement agencies. Most of us would agree that the development of individual rights was long overdue; most of us would agree that there should be further clarification of individual rights, particularly for indigent defendants. At the same time we must face the facts about indifferent and faltering law enforcement in this country. We must adopt measures which will give enforcement agencies proper means for doing their jobs. In my opinion, these two efforts must go forward simultaneously.[7]

These criticisms are serious and cannot be summarily dismissed, although they should be placed in proper prospective. For, as Professor Yale Kamisar, a noted student of American criminal procedure, has pointed out,[8] there has always been a "crime crisis," and the Supreme Court has long been accused of "coddling the criminal." For example, in 1910 the President of the California Bar Association called for "adjustment" in our criminal proceedings "to meet the expanding social necessity." He believed that:

> Many of the difficulties [were] due to an exaggerated respect for the individual as the isolated center of the universe. There is too much admiration for our traditional system and too little respect for the needs of the society.[9]

Nor are arguments accusing the courts of tipping the scales of justice in favor of the accused novel. To quote Professor Kamisar again:

> . . . [A]t the Sixth Annual Meeting of the ABA in the year 1883, Professor Simeon E. Baldwin, one of the giants of the legal and teaching profession, pled for an end to the false humanitarianism which had led us astray so that "the state, in its judicial contests with those whom it charges with crime, [will be given] once more an equal chance."[10]

Today perhaps the most trenchant and effective critic of the Supreme Court's decisions in this area has been Judge Henry J. Friendly of the U.S. Court of Appeals for the Second Circuit.[11] His position will be subjected to careful analysis later in this chapter—but first we must examine in some detail the body of law which has aroused all this controversy.

MIRANDA AND ITS ANTECEDENTS

In *Miranda* v. *Arizona*,[12] the Court decided in 1966 that no statement obtained from a suspect during custodial interrogation could be introduced as evidence against him in a criminal trial unless

    (1) He had been clearly warned prior to interrogation that—
        (a) He had the right to remain silent;
        (b) Anything he said could later be used against him;
        (c) He had the right to have counsel present during questioning; and
        (d) If he lacked funds to obtain a lawyer, he would be provided with one by the state; and
    (2) He had "knowingly, and intelligently" waived those rights.[13]

Unlike its decisions in *Escobedo* v. *Illinois*[14] and in *Massiah* v. *United States*,[15] both of which have been criticized because of their anticipated effect on confessions, the decision in *Miranda* can truly be described as a landmark.[16] But there were substantial precedents, prior to *Escobedo* and *Massiah*, for such an extension of the testimonial privilege of the fifth amendment to the investigation stage of the "criminal case."

Prior to 1897, the Court had viewed confessions in light of the common law rules of evidence which excluded those obtained under coercion,[17] but in that year, in *Bram* v. *United States*,[18] the Court overturned a federal murder conviction on the ground that the defendant's statements had not been truly voluntary, although he had no⁺ been subjected to physical coercion and, judging by the facts recited in the Court's opinion, he had been subjected to little pressure of any kind. In that decision the Court first applied the Fifth Amendment privilege to events which occurred outside the courtroom, holding that in federal courts:

> Wherever a question arises whether a confession is incompetent because not voluntary, the issue is controlled by that portion of the Fifth Amendment to the Constitution of the United States, commanding that no person "shall be compelled in any criminal case to be witness against himself."[19]

After the decision in *Bram*, the Court was frequently called on to pass upon the competence of confessions and did not, even in cases arising out of the lower federal courts, always adhere to the *Bram* rationale.[20] In one subsequent decision, the Court even expressed some uncertainty whether "involuntary confessions are excluded . . . on the ground of the Fifth Amendment's protection against self-incrimination, or from a rule that forced confessions are untrustworthy."[21] Further consideration of this question in the context of federal cases was, however, curtailed by the Court's decision in *McNabb* v. *United States*[22] which avoided the issue by imposing strict limitations on the custodial interrogation of suspects by federal agents, a rule imposed in the exercise of the Court's power of supervision over the administration of criminal justice in the federal courts and not as a matter of constitutional interpretation.

Simultaneously, however, the Court began to evolve constitutional criteria for determining the admissibility of confessions in state court cases. Precluded from direct application of the Fifth Amendment privilege to state prosecutions by its holding in *Twining* v. *New Jersey*[23] that the Fifth Amendment did not apply to the states, the Court began to achieve the same result by indirection through the due process clause of the Fourteenth Amendment. In *Brown* v. *Mississippi*,[24] decided in 1936, the Court reversed the conviction of three Negroes for murder on the ground that the confessions of the defendants had been extracted from them by repeated whippings and other forms of physical torture. Although the Court accepted the State's argument that the Fifth Amendment privilege did not expressly apply, it held the admission of the confession to be a clear denial of due process and therefore barred by the Fourteenth Amendment.

The *Brown* decision marked the beginning of a long case-by-case evolution which climaxed with *Miranda*. Between 1936 and 1963, the Court decided, with full opinions, 33 confession cases arising in state courts.[25] Under the due process standard applicable in those cases, the Court established both an "objective" and a "subjective" test against which allegedly coerced confessions were to be measured.[26] Under the "objective" test fell those confessions which stemmed from a situation—

> so inherently coercive that its very existence is irreconcilable with the possession of mental freedom by a lone suspect against whom its full coercive force is brought to bear.[27]

"Inherently coercive" situations included those where actual or threatened physical force,[28] or protracted, continuous and unrelenting questioning[29] had been used to elicit the proffered confession. When such situations were found, the Court did not even inquire as to the ability of the accused to resist such pressures; the coercive effect was presumed as a matter of law.[30]

The "subjective" test required an inquiry into the "totality of circumstances" surrounding the obtaining of the confession and the "weighing of the circumstances of pressure against the power of resistance of the person confessing."[31] Under that test the Court looked at factors such as the nature and duration of the questioning, even where it was not sufficiently protracted, continuous and unrelenting to fall under the "objective" standard,[32] the age of the accused,[33] the intelligence and literacy levels of the accused,[34] threats (other than those of physical violence),[35] deception,[36] delay in arraignment,[37] request by the accused for counsel,[38] and the failure to warn the accused of his right to counsel and his right to remain silent.[39] Thus, although the "totality of circumstances" standard required a balancing of the pressures used in eliciting incriminatory statements against the presumed ability of the particular individual to resist them, many of the factors which went into that process foreshadowed the guidelines laid down in *Miranda*.

The Court was, of course, avowedly applying the due process standard of the Fourteenth Amendment in passing upon the "voluntariness" of confessions introduced in state court trials. But its opinions increasingly began to suggest that the standards being applied were "grounded in the policies of the privilege against self-incrimination."[40] Although the Court had at one time questioned whether the basis for exclusion of involuntary confessions was not lack of reliability rather than the Fifth Amendment privilege,[41] in *Rogers* v. *Richmond*,[42] decided in 1961, it reversed a state court conviction involving an "involuntary" confession on the ground that the lower courts had erred in considering whether the confession was "reliable." The rationale of the Court's decision was clearly in Fifth Amendment terms:

> Our decisions . . . have made clear that convictions following the admission into evidence of confessions which are involuntary, i.e., the product of coercion, either physical or psychological, cannot stand. This is so not because such confessions are unlikely to be true but because the methods used to extract them offend an underlying principle in the enforcement of our criminal law: that ours is an accusatorial and not an inquisitorial system—a system in which the State must establish guilt by evidence independently and freely secured and may not by coercion prove its charge against an accused out of his own mouth.[43]

514

The Court's 1964 decision in *Malloy* v. *Hogan*[44] expressly extended the reach of the Fifth Amendment privilege to state proceedings. It therefore contributed markedly to the impact of the Court's interpretations of the privilege and lent added impetus to the criticisms of those interpretations. *Malloy* was closely followed by *Escobedo* v. *Illinois*[45] decided during the same term, which held that a suspect who demanded to confer with his lawyer during station house interrogation could not be denied that right. Although it was unclear from the Court's opinion whether the right enforced by the *Escobedo* decision had its basis in the Fifth Amendment privilege or the Sixth Amendment right to counsel,[46] the Court subsequently interpreted the decision as following from the Fifth.[47] Finally, two years later in *Miranda* v. *Arizona*, the Court held that a defendant must be warned of his right to remain silent and of his right to counsel before being interrogated.

IMPACT OF THE MIRANDA INTERROGATION RULES

Thus, *Escobedo* and *Miranda* were, to a greater degree than their critics admit, a natural and reasonable outgrowth of the principles evolved in previously decided cases. The decisions indicated quite clearly, even before *Malloy*, that the policies underlying the privilege against self incrimination applied to the interrogation process, whether the case arose in the federal system or in the state courts, with the result that a confession had to be found to be "voluntary," i.e., in the language of the Fifth Amendment, not "compelled," in order to be admissible against the defendant at the trial of "any criminal case." The rules laid down in *Miranda* proceed as a logical extension from an implementation of that principle.

Even if this is true, however, the basic practical question remains: what is the impact of the *Miranda* interrogation rules on effective law enforcement? This question really raises two separate issues, the degree to which confessions are an important weapon in the law enforcement arsenal, and the impact *Miranda* will have on the rate of confessions.

Perhaps, surprisingly in the light of the controversy *Miranda* has aroused, the first question cannot be answered with any certainty on the basis of the information presently available. Assuming that such decisions would reduce police effectiveness, political scientist James Q. Wilson asked:

For what crimes will the effect be greatest? In all probability, it will be for crimes other than those producing the greatest citizen anxiety . . . [V]iolent crime typically produces an eyewitness—the victim. (To be sure, in murder cases the eyewitness is often dead, but the police solve the vast majority of all murders anyway.) An assault or robbery gives the victim a look at his assailant . . . Prosecutions and convictions often depend on this testimony of victim-witnesses and no confession is needed.[48]

Professor Fred Inbau however, is not persuaded that the utility of confessions is limited to cases other than those involving violent crimes:

. . . I suggest that consideration be given to the situation presented by cases such as these. A man is hit on the head while walking home late at night. He did not see his assailant, nor did anyone else. A careful and thorough search of the crime scene reveals no physical clues. Then take the case of a woman who is grabbed on the street at night and dragged into an alley and raped. Here, too, the assailant was unaccommodating enough to avoid leaving his hat or other means of identification at the crime scene; and there are no physical clues. All the police have to work on is the description of the assailant given by the victim herself. She described him as about six feet tall, white, and wearing a dark suit.[49]

Accurate empirical information on the effect of the extension of the privilege against self-incrimination on the rate of convictions, much less on the incidence of crime, is hard to come by. Indeed the conclusions of two New York studies contradict each other.

Justice Nathan Sobel of the New York Supreme Court has stated that of 1,000 indictments in Kings County (Brooklyn), N.Y., the prosecution has filed the required "notice of intention"[50] to use "confessions" (which are defined as including both inculpatory and exculpatory statements) in only 86, and that of the nine murder indictments included in the sample not a single one involved a "confession."[51] On the basis of this admittedly small sample, "fortified by the individual experiences of the trial judges consulted," Justice Sobel concluded that "confessions constitute part of the evidence in *less* than 10 percent of all indictments."[52] Justice Sobel's findings were made after *Escobedo,* but before *Miranda.* Thus, while the figures may be distorted somewhat by the exclusion of confessions which might have been obtained but for the *Escobedo* rules, it is doubtful that any such

516

distortion would be significant since, as Justice Sobel notes, "normally suspects do not confess after they 'request' counsel,"[53] and the impact of the *Miranda* rules had, of course, not been felt at that time.

In contrast with Justice Sobel's findings are those of New York District Attorney Frank Hogan, who reported that of the 91 homicide cases then pending in New York County (Manhattan), confessions would be offered at trial in 62, or 68 percent, and that in 25 homicide cases indictments would not have been obtained without confessions.[54] Mr. Hogan also has pointed out that the number of confessions offered in evidence is not a true index of the need for and value of police interrogation because there are "a great many cases in which, as a result of admissions, leads are obtained which result in the discovery of additional evidence."[55]

Moreover, we do not know, of course, to what extent convictions would not be possible in the absence of evidence discovered solely as a result of leads obtained from interrogations and which could not otherwise have been discovered. Nor do we know to what extent reliance upon police interrogation has become a substitute for using other available methods of investigation (or methods which would be available with additional manpower) which would result in sufficient evidence to convict.[56] And the hypothetical examples offered by those who contend that the interrogation of suspects is the only means of solving certain crimes are frequently cast in such extreme terms that they raise substantial questions as to how the police can reasonably decide which suspects to interrogate. For instance, in the rape case example given by Professor Inbau, the police surely would not subject to interrogation every male "about six feet tall, white, and wearing a dark suit."[57] Finally, statistics as to the number of confessions used at trial tell us nothing about the degree to which the obtaining of guilty pleas is influenced by admissions or confessions obtained during custodial interrogation.[58]

California has for some time maintained unusually reliable crime statistics, and the California Supreme Court had severely restricted the use of confessions prior to *Miranda*.[59] Justice Stanley Mosk, of the Supreme Court of California, who himself served as Attorney General of California, has analyzed these statistics and concluded:

> The effect of court decisions on crime and criminals is determined by the results after arrest. The test is not how many

arrests are made, but whether defendants charged with serious crimes are now being turned loose. An analysis of this subject reveals that there has been no effect whatever upon criminal convictions by recent landmark decisions.[60]

In fact, Justice Mosk found that the rate of convictions in California has generally increased each year since 1955. He concluded, "decisions by the United States Supreme Court, and by the California Supreme Court, have not in the slightest hampered prosecution of criminals."

But it is unclear whether Justice Mosk's conclusions indicate that confessions are not as useful in law enforcement as officials have maintained, or that *Miranda* has had little impact on the rate of confessions. Other indications suggest that the rules laid down in *Miranda* and other recent decisions should not be expected to have, and have not had in fact, any substantial effect upon the rate of confessions. As the psychologist Theodore Reik has pointed out, man has a "compulsive unconscious tendency to confess,"[61] even—at times—to matters which could not possibly have occurred. For example, during the late Renaissance large numbers of persons confessed to witchcraft, without either the pressure or threat of torture, most notably in England where judicial torture was never utilized in such cases.

> Again and again, when we read the case histories we find witches freely confessing to esoteric details without any evidence of torture, and it was this spontaneity, rather than the confessions themselves, which convinced rational men that the details were true.[62]

The "compulsion to confess" is also borne out by modern experience. One study disclosed that in 48 observed cases more admissions in field situations were made spontaneously than were made after questioning.[63] It may well be that some types of cases described by critics of *Miranda* would not be effected by it because they represent situations where the accused felt an internal compulsion to blurt out proof of his guilt as soon as he thought he had been found out.[64]

Several studies have been made of the impact of *Miranda* in particular locales, and they invariably conclude that such rules had no significant impact upon the obtaining of confessions.[65] A survey in the District of Columbia found that the rate of confessions remained nearly uniform before and after *Miranda* and that only 7 percent of those given *Miranda* warnings requested counsel, even though counsel were available on an around-the-clock basis.[66] In New Haven, a study of 114 interrogations found that 58 produced confessions, 50 of which were obtained after *Miranda* warnings were given.[67]

These findings seem to indicate that the controversy over *Miranda* is not justified. But this lack of impact may be largely attributable to failure of the police to communicate the *Miranda* warning effectively. The suspect may not have been warned or only partially warned, or perhaps he did not understand the warning.[68] In other words, the *Miranda* warning may not have been given in a manner that effectively informed the accused of his rights. Perhaps it is against human nature to expect the police, whose interest opposes the principles embodied in the warning, to carry out *Miranda's* mandate.[69]

The effects of the *Escobedo-Miranda* interrogation rules on the number of pretrial confessions given, and the number of crimes "cleared" or solved, seem to put the burden of persuasion on the Court's critics.[70] The argument for any causal link between the Court's decisions and crime rates at present rests solely on the *post hoc ergo propter hoc* fallacy.[71] Any accused sophisticated enough to follow the decisions of the Supreme Court and weigh their effect on the likelihood of his conviction for his next crime is probably unlikely to confess, regardless of whether he receives a *Miranda* warning of his rights.

Crime rates seem to rise and fall on the tides of economic, social and political cycles with little relation to the decisions of the Supreme Court. As the President's Commission on Law Enforcement and Administration of Justice found, and as the Violence Commission's Task Force on Individual Acts of Violence confirms, slum conditions, narcotic addiction, cultural inequalities, increasing poverty in the midst of rising affluence, the breakdown of home and family life and discipline, and the frustration and restlessness of youth, factors over which neither the Supreme Court nor any other court has any control, are the real culprits with which our society must be concerned.[72] As a former Attorney General of the United States has noted:

> [C]ourt rules do not cause crime. People do not commit crimes because they know they cannot be questioned by police before presentment, or even because they feel they will not be convicted. We as a people commit crimes because we are capable of committing crimes . . . In the long run, only the elimination of the causes of crime can make a significant and lasting difference in the incidence of crime.[73]

Police officials themselves, interestingly enough, quickly point out the relationship between socio-economic factors and crime rates when they are required to defend themselves against charges of inefficiency in police operations. O. W. Wilson, former Superintendent of the Chicago Police Department, for example, in a speech criticizing the courts for causing an increase in the crime rate, also lashed out at—

> a tendency to blame [the police] . . . for a high incidence of crime instead of recognizing that there are many crime causes, such as slum conditions, narcotic addiction, lack of parental responsibility, unemployment, cultural inequalities, and other social factors over which the police have no influence or control.[74]

The courts, of course, have no control over these factors either. Moreover, irresponsible charges that the Supreme Court's decisions are "causing violence" do a distinct disservice, not only to the Supreme Court, but to the nation as a whole.[75] For, in addition to contributing to the already mounting lack of respect for the agencies charged with law enforcement, it diverts attention from the real causes of crime and violence. Instead of forcing us to focus on the hard problems and to find solutions to them by placing the blame for crime on the Court, offers us an enticingly easy and vulnerable scapegoat, allowing us to delude ourselves that the solution of the crime problem is easy and cost-free.

Yet the general charge that the scales of justice seem unduly weighted in favor of the accused does, of course, raise a valid point—that guilty men are going free because of procedural safeguards that hamstring the prosecution. The confession cases decided on appeal particularly yield to this interpretation. In those cases, a confession, the truth of which is not denied, is held inadmissible at trial, and the conviction is reversed.

But the impact of such decisions on convictions is substantially reduced by the Court's recently adopted practice, as in *Miranda,* of applying such rulings *prospectively* only. Thus, the court does not empty the jails. Moreover, adherence by the police, the prosecutor, and the lower courts to the Court's rulings should avoid this problem in the future. Further, it is incorrect to say that defendants are "turned loose" when their convictions are reversed by the courts. A reversal means that the defendant is to be tried again, absent the error committed the first time. Justice Mosk's study found that

520

more than 95 percent of these retrials in California result in proper convictions.[76] Few, indeed, are those defendants who are "turned loose" on society, for fewer than those criminals who roam the streets because of lack of crime laboratories, part-time prosecutors, lack of correctional facilities, and a general unwillingness to attack the root causes of crime.

That criminal procedure favors the accused is a charge that cannot be accepted at face value. Anyone who has participated in or observed the administration of justice in the streets, at police stations, in prosecutors' offices, and in the trial courts must see that, in the vast majority of cases, the scales of justice are still far from weighted in favor of the accused.

"VOLUNTARINESS" AND POLICE INTERROGATION

One of the most curious, and perhaps cynical, aspects of the criticism of the *Miranda* rules is that most of the critics do not challenge the right of the accused to remain silent; the challenge concerns only the wisdom of advising him that he has such a right.

The principal argument against *Miranda,* therefore, centers upon the fear that if the accused is informed of his rights, he will exercise them. On the other hand, if the interrogator does not inform his "subject" that he need not respond, then he may respond; the response in that instance is termed "voluntary," the letter of the law has been complied with (no "compulsion" having been applied), and consciences are therefore clear.[77] But the argument will not work.

"Voluntariness" connotes at least that the person responding has done so as a result of free will, i.e., that he has willed to speak rather than to keep silent. The argument of *Miranda's* critics, however, presupposes that knowledge of the choice available will be kept from the accused. A choice between concealed alternatives, however, is no choice at all.[78] The due process concept of notice[79] reflects this principle, as do the requirements that the defendant be given a copy of the indictment before he is asked to plead,[80] and that the court refuse to accept a guilty or *nolo contendere* plea without "determining that the plea is made voluntarily with understanding of the nature of the charge and the consequences of the plea."[81] The defendant must be made aware of his rights. Surely this prerequisite determines whether or not he has chosen to forego them "voluntarily," if that term is to have any meaning whatever.

The meaning of "voluntariness" broadens considerably in the context of police interrogation. As the Court pointed out in *Miranda*, there is "a gap in our knowledge as to what in fact goes on in interrogation rooms."[82] This gap exists in large measure because of the secrecy in which the interrogation occurs.[83] Secrecy means that "police station questioning . . . is governed only by the self-imposed restraint of the police"[84] and creates the suspicion of abuse. Since usually there are neither independent witnesses nor a record of the interrogation,[85] a charge of coercion produces a swearing contest between the police and the defendant in which the police are usually believed.[86]

Secret interrogation which may result in the trial being an empty formality is, of course, inconsistent with our basic belief that proceedings in which a man's life or liberty is at stake should be open and observable.[87] To renounce that belief would constitute a fairly clear admission that we as a nation are "[u]nskill'd to judge the future by the past."[88] In 1931 the Wickersham Report[89] uncovered prevalent use of violence and the "third degree" in interrogating suspects, usually between arrest and preliminary hearing. In 1961 the Commission on Civil Rights reported that some policemen still resort to physical force to obtain confessions.[90] And while the President's Commission on Law Enforcement and Administration of Justice reported in 1967 that "today the third degree is almost non-existent,"[91] the Court in *Miranda* cited a number of recent instances of physical abuse.[92]

Whether police officers in fact stop the elevators between the floors of the jail to "work over" "uncooperative" suspects[93] is perhaps less important, however, than whether a substantial portion of the citizenry believes that such things happen. A suspect from the lowest social and economic groups in our society[94] may forego his rights (if he is aware of them—which is what *Miranda* is all about) in the face of police pressure. Moreover, such belief inevitably leads to distrust and disrespect of law enforcement officials. As the President's Commission on Law Enforcement and Administration of Justice has pointed out:

[F]air treatment of every individual—fair in fact and also perceived to be fair by those affected—is an essential element of justice and a principal objective of the American criminal justice system.[95]

522

Fairness in our system *and the appearance of fairness,* is essential if the system is to "win the respect and cooperation of all citizens,"[96] without which "crime cannot be controlled."[97]

The possibility of physical abuse is not, however, the major focus of concern. As the Court noted in *Miranda,* "the modern practice of in-custody interrogation is psychologically rather than physically oriented."[98] It cited modern police manuals which describe in detail advantageous interrogation settings and outline proven stratagems of psychological coercion. The procedures recommended by the manuals have been summarized as follows:

> Inbau and Reid describe in considerable detail sixteen tactics which they believe may be used with some success. The sixteen tactics are easily reduceable to seven themes, four of which appeal primarily to the mind, and the others appeal primarily to the emotions of the suspect. First the interrogator communicates by word and gesture that he strongly believes the suspect is guilty. The next tactic is to provide "factual" evidence in support of this belief. The interrogator should proceed by pointing to circumstantial evidence, like pretending to know much more about the suspect than he in fact does, by suggesting that someone else such as an accomplice has implicated the defendant, by having another policeman pose as a witness to the crime, and by commenting on the incriminating significance of the suspect's psycho-physical behavior, such as pulsation of his carotid artery, excessive movement of his Adam's apple, foot wiggling, or "downcast" eyes. . . . The third strategy is to redefine the crime, sometimes exaggerating the charges and at other times minimizing their moral significance. In the latter case, the suspect should be told he acted as any normal man would have under the circumstances.
>
> The three emotional appeals may be used independently or in conjunction with the rational appeals. In his effort to elicit a confession the interrogator is advised to show sympathy, friendliness, and respect, and to flatter the suspect. Second, if these positive approaches do not work, the interrogator ought to display hostility. One procedure is for two interrogators, apportioning the sympathetic and hostile roles between themselves, to enact the psycho-drama variously known as the "Mutt and Jeff," "carrot and whip," and the "hot and cold" technique.[99]

The reliance by the majority of the Court upon the descriptions contained in police manuals was severely criticized by the dissenters:

Insofar as appears from the Court's opinion, it has not examined a single transcript of any police interrogation. . . . Judged by any of the standards for empirical investigation utilized in the social sciences the factual basis for the Court's premise is patently inadequate.[100]

But the dissenters ignored the secrecy in which the interrogation normally occurs (although they acknowledged the fact of such secrecy) and the fact that, unlike judicial hearings, no court reporter is present at the vast majority of interrogations[101] until invited by the police to record the "deposition" of the accused after he has confessed.[102]

More to the point is the suggestion made by the dissenters that "the type of sustained interrogation described by the Court" does not occur in every case, perhaps not even in a majority of cases.[103] This suggestion is borne out by some of the empirical studies of police practices,[104] but we know neither what percentage of the "confused and sporadic" questioning products admissions nor what impact the *Miranda* warnings may be expected to have upon them.[105]

The question remains whether or not the use of the tactics described in the manuals is in fact "inherently coercive." In the context of any other area of the law, there would be no doubt of the answer to that question. As one scholar has pointed out:

We have been ready to let a man sign his life away under circumstances in which we would not recognize his conveyance of a subdivided lot.[106]

One sociologist has recently observed that "the Court's finding of inherent coercion even in ethical interrogations seems completely justified by the literature of social psychology."[107] Some evidence suggests that the type of coercion advocated by the police manuals may be more dangerous to society than openly avowed compulsion, such as utilizing the contempt sanction to compel a defendant to testify in open court. Although the authors of the most widely circulated police manual state, "we know of not one case in which any of the interrogation methods we describe has elicited a confession from an innocent suspect,"[108]

[S]ocial-psychological data suggest that a suspect—*even an innocent suspect*—while isolated physically and socially from the groups which usually validate his ideas may well change his stated beliefs in the face of contradictory assertions of "fact," emotional inducements, and the possibility of gaining social acceptance.[109]

Several cases have recently come to light in which a false confession was obtained without physical abuse.[110] In the wake of one of these cases, a member of the prosecutor's staff admitted that the defendant, a Negro of limited intelligence, had been coerced, apparently by methods similar to those described in the manuals. As a prosecutor noted, "call it what you want—brainwashing, hypnosis, fright. They (the police) made him give an untrue confession."[111] And a member of the police department admitted in the aftermath of the same case, "I hate to say this, but I'm sure that sometime in history we've sent innocent men to their death by an unjust verdict."[112]

EQUAL PROTECTION IN THE STATION HOUSE

Another consideration underlying *Miranda* is the question of equal protection of the laws. The President's Commission on Law Enforcement and Administration of Justice has constructed a composite portrait of the offender who ultimately ends up in prison. They have found that he is "likely to be a member of the lowest social and economic groups in the country, poorly educated and perhaps unemployed, unmarried, reared in a broken home, and to have a prior criminal record."[113]

Absent the requirements laid down in *Miranda*, the minority of arrestees who can afford counsel, who come from less educationally and culturally disadvantaged backgrounds or who are sophisticated in the ways of the station house, would enjoy special privileges. The man who can afford counsel, the man who has ties with family or friends who will obtain counsel for him, the man whose cultural and educational background or status in society have placed him in a position, not only to know his rights, but to demand them confidently in the face of police importunings, and, perhaps, the man who has connections with organized crime: this kind of man has substantial advantages over the more typical, "profile arrestee,"[114] who thus is denied "equal protection of the laws."[115]

It has been suggested that perhaps equal protection

does not demand cessation of proper police practices that are valuable, perhaps essential, to the investigation and punish-

525

ment of crime, simply because some segments of the population do not know they are not obliged to cooperate whereas others do.[116]

It is obvious that equality is an ideal that cannot be achieved in any absolute sense. On the one hand, we face the need for truth that may be suppressed to the extent that we pose obstacles to the freedom of the police to conduct investigations in the manner most appropriate to the circumstances. On the other hand, we must have not only fairness and justice, but also the "appearance of justice,"[117] as it is perceived by society, particularly by those segments of society which in the main produce the offender. We must decide whether in the long run we are more likely to achieve the goals of our system of criminal justice by striving diligently for the truth in particular cases, recognizing that it means taking advantage of ignorance, with the risk of creating more alienation in large segments of society and more distrust and disrespect for enforcement agencies thought to be enforcing a "rich man's law"—or whether those goals are more likely to be achieved where the poor and ignorant suspect is put on a somewhat more equal footing with the affluent or professional suspect, at the cost of suppressing the truth in particular cases. Since no system can operate effectively without substantial support from the citizenry, it would seem that the balance lies in the direction of the *Miranda* decision.[118]

THE PRIVILEGE AGAINST SELF-INCRIMINATION: BEGINNING OF A REEXAMINATION

The value implicit in the privilege against self-incrimination seem worthy of preservation, in the station house as well as in the courtroom. Recently, however, several noted scholars and jurists have asked for a reexamination of the privilege itself in light of the increasing social cost of crime.[119] Jurists like Chief Justice Roger J. Traynor of the California Supreme Court,[120] Justice Walter Schaefer of the Illinois Supreme Court, [121] and—most trenchantly—Judge Henry Friendly of the U.S. Court of Appeals for the Second Circuit[122] have recently questioned whether the privilege against self-incrimination deserves preservation. Seven members of the President's Commission on Law Enforcement and Administration of Justice have joined in the call for reappraisal.[123]

The Fifth Amendment privilege protects a witness in a civil trial[124] or a legislative hearing;[125] it prohibits the compelled production of incriminating documents in most circumstances;[126] it dictates that testimony cannot be compelled in one jurisdiction if it could be used in a criminal prosecution in another jurisdiction;[127] it prohibits required registration in certain situations;[128] it forbids use of the contempt sanction to require a defendant to testify at the trial of any criminal case;[129] it requires exclusion from evidence of statements obtained before trial under circumstances deemed coercive;[130] it forbids compulsory testimony before a grand jury unless the witness is granted immunity from prosecution on the basis of his testimony;[131] it prohibits comment by the court or the prosecution upon the defendant's failure to take the stand; [132] and it prohibits the use of an earlier claim of privilege to impeach a defendant's credibility when he chooses to testify at the trial.[133] In short, as the Court has viewed it, the privilege is "as broad as the mischief against which it seeks to guard."[134]

Critics of the privilege suggest that this "mischief" has never been satisfactorily defined, however. As Judge Friendly notes, our attempts to justify the privilege have largely been "benedictions" upon it rather than articulations of its premises.[135] The friends of the privilege have been more concerned to celebrate it in Fourth-of-July rhetoric than to explain the policies upon which it is grounded. That the privilege is "one of the great landmarks in man's struggle to make himself civilized."[136] or that it is one of the essential "principles of free government"[137] tells us, as Judge Friendly observes, "almost everything, except why,"[138] particularly since there are a number of "civilized" men who live under "free governments" where the privilege either does not exist at all or exists in only a very narrow form.[139]

Justice Frankfurter, in a famous dictum, remarked that "the privilege against self-incrimination is a specific provision of which it is peculiarly true that 'a page of history is worth a volume of logic.' "[140] The efforts of Professor Leonard W. Levy have made the outlines of that history clear in his recent book, *Origins of the Fifth Amendment*.[141] As a preface to our discussion of the policies supporting the privilege, we may take a short excursion into Fifth Amendment origins.

* * *

The privilege arose in response to the use of the oath *ex officio*, a procedure which was introduced into canonical

527

courts by the Fourth Lateran Council in the year of Magna Carta:

> The oath itself, which was in part a sworn statement to give true answers to whatever question might be asked, was objectionable because it was taken in ignorance by the accused, that is, without his first having been formally charged with the accusation against him or having been told the identity of his accusers or the nature of the evidence against him. Following the administration of the oath, the accused, still in ignorance, was required to answer a series of interrogatories whose purpose was to extract a confession.[142]

The first use of the new oath procedure in England, by Bishop Robert Grosseteste in 1246, produced such an outcry that Henry III was compelled to interfere and ultimately to summon the Bishop before the King's Council for contempt.[143] In the reign of Edward II, in the course of one of the recurring jurisdictional disputes between church and state, Parliament passed, sometime prior to 1326, the statute *Prohibitio Formata de Statuto Articuli Cleri*,[144] which among other things prohibited the examination of laymen under oath before the church courts in other than matrimonial or testamentary causes.[145] Periodically thereafter, outbursts against the use of the oath procedure occurred, indicating that the attempts by the secular agencies to suppress it did not succeed.[146]

Concerted and persistent opposition to the *ex officio* procedure began with its use in the suppression first of heresy and later of religious non-conformity. From the rise of Lollardry in the fourteenth century, resulting in the passage of the statute *de Heretico Comburendo* in 1401,[147] through the prosecution, first of Protestants and later of Catholics by Henry VIII, opposition began to mount. The bloody suppression of Protestants under Mary, the martyrdom of Catholics and the attempts to extract conformity from Puritans under Elizabeth and the first two Stuarts, led to heightened opposition to the oath, culminating in its final abolition by Parliament in 1641.[148] During the Elizabethan and Stuart periods, the oath was the principal procedural device used by the Court of High Commission, the court charged with enforcing conformity with the established church's doctrine, and it was used at times by the Star Chamber.[149]

Justification for the use of the oath procedure was the inevitable appeal to necessity. Sir Thomas More argued that,

528

If the *ex officio* oath procedure were abandoned, . . . and no suspect could be examined unless someone openly accused him and made himself a party against him, "the stretys were likely to swarme full of heretykes" before any were ever accused.[150]

Archbishop Whitgift, Archbishop of Canterbury and head of the High Commission under Elizabeth, in an elaborate justification of the procedure, began with the argument that

sectaries "spreade their poison in secrete," making it nearly impossible to produce witnesses against them; he ended with complaint that the High Commission would be taxed with too burdensome a task to get witnesses even when it might be possible.[151]

And James I asserted that,

In contrast to the practice of other courts which might punish only deeds, . . . the ecclesiastical courts had to examine "Fame and Scandals." For the detection of the offender, especially when the crime was grave and either suspicion or "public fame" existed, the oath was necessary.[152]

But opposition grew. Sir Thomas More, who as Chancellor compelled heretics to take the oath *ex officio* (the penalty for heresy was the stake), found the tables turned when he was charged with treason for refusing to recognize the King as supreme head of the English church. When presented with an oath *ex officio* at his examination on that charge (the penalty for which was beheading), he answered:

it were a very harde thinge to compell me to saye either precisely with it [the Act of Supremacy] againste my conscience to the losse of my soule, or precisely against it to the destruction of my bodye.[153]

Sir Thomas Tresham spelled out the dilemma in his testimony before the Star Chamber in 1580 on a charge of harbouring the Jesuit, Edmond Campion:

For, if I sweare falselie, I am perjured; if by my othe I accuse myselfe, I am condemned to the penaltie of the law . . . If I sweare trulie, then I laye myself wyde open to perjurie, because Mr. Campion hath oppositely accused me in the affirmatyve.[154]

The dilemma in which such persons found themselves

came gradually to be recognized as the "cruel trilemma" of contempt, perjury, or conviction:

> He could refuse the oath and rot in jail, or having taken it, refuse to answer and meet the same fate. If he took the oath and lied, he committed the unpardonable and cardinal sin of perjury which was simply not an option for a religious man . . . If he took the oath and told the truth, he foreswore himself, supplying his enemy with legal proof of his guilt, and, what was equally appalling, he forsook his co-religionists, necessarily betraying them.[155]

When policy arguments did not prevail against the oath, there was the appeal to authority, including frequent reference to the maxim *nemo tenetur seipsum prodere,* or "no one is bound to produce against himself."[156] Magna Carta was also cited in opposition to the *ex officio* procedure by Robert Beale, who read into the prohibition in Chapter 28 of Magna Carta, against bailiffs putting the accused to his oath without witnesses, a prohibition against the *ex officio* oath.[157] This first use of Magna Carta as a "talismanic symbol of freedom" became an article of faith to those subjected to the oath procedure in ensuing years.[158] This history makes clear that the privilege was originally:

> associated . . . with guilt for crimes of conscience, of belief, and of association. In the broadest sense it was a protection . . . of freedom of expression, of political liberty, or the right to worship as one pleased.[159]

Opposition to the oath procedure, however, and the attendant demand for the right not to accuse oneself, was not solely a device for attacking the substantive law being enforced by that procedure, for, as Professor Levy points out, the opponents were convinced that "an oath that compelled self-incrimination was [itself] both evil and violative of common-law procedures."[160] Finally, Levy lays to rest the popularly-held notion that the development of the privilege was largely in response to the use of the rack, the thumbscrew, and the sizzling iron.[161] Torture was illegal at common law, and was not utilized by the common law courts, nor the High Commission, nor the Star Chamber.[162]

> The humanity of the English judge was above all marked by his abhorrence of torture . . . It was never employed to extort a confession or to force the prisoner to incriminate himself in any manner.[163]

After the abolition, in 1641 of the Star Chamber and the High Commission, and with them the oath *ex officio*,[164] the arguments against the oath began to be used against self-incriminatory procedures in Parliament and in the common law courts:

> They employed no oath, of course, yet in the preliminary examination prior to indictment and arraignment, it was still ordinary practice to press a suspect to confess his guilt; and in the prosecution of an accused person before a jury, his interrogation was still the focal point of the trial, the objective to trap him into damaging admissions.[165]

Even after the formal establishment of the privilege in the common law courts, which certainly had occurred by 1660,[166] suspects continued to be examined by the magistrate at the preliminary hearing, the purpose of which "was to wring out of him a confession of his guilt, unsworn, or enough damaging testimony to put him on trial for the crime." Such examinations were conducted in secret and were "characterized by bullying."[167]

After 1660, the privilege continued to grow in scope, to the protection of witnesses[168] to the prohibition of compulsion to bring infamy upon oneself,[169] to civil cases where the testimony could be used against the witness in a criminal case, to parliamentary proceedings, and to the compelled production of incriminating papers and documents.[170] Finally, Professor Levy concludes, there is an "indissoluble nexus" between the privilege and the rule excluding involuntary confessions.[171] Despite considerable discussion,[172] whether or not Wigmore was correct when he claimed "no connection" between the two,[173] the evidence to the contrary offered by Professor Levy seriously undermines the foundation for Wigmore's conclusion.[174]

Of course "it would be ludicrous to attempt to fix the proper scope of the privilege in light of what was appropriate under the Stuarts or Cromwell,"[175] but history warns us of the implications of abandoning it or diluting it.

* * *

In light of the foregoing history, it should be agreed that determining what the "whole complex of values" is which the privilege today represents,[176] is not, as Judge Friendly points out,[177] as easy as it might seem. Justice Goldberg,

531

however, attempted to set forth a complete catalogue of the policies behind the privilege in *Murphy* v. *Waterfront Commission*:

> It reflects many of our fundamental values and most noble aspirations: (1) our unwillingness to subject those suspected of crime to the cruel trilemma of self-accusation, perjury or contempt; (2) our preference for an accusatorial rather than an inquisitorial system of criminal justice; (3) our fear that self-incriminating statements will be elicited by inhumane treatment and abuses; (4) our sense of fair play which dictates "a fair state-individual balance by requiring the government to leave the individual alone until good cause is shown for disturbing him and by requiring the government in its contest with the individual to shoulder the entire load;" (5) our respect for the inviolability of the human personality and of the right of each individual "to a private enclave where he may lead a private life;" (6) our distrust of self-deprecatory statements, (7) and our realization that the privilege, while sometimes "a shelter to the guilty," is often "a protection to the innocent."[178]

Number (2), the "accusatorial-inquisitorial" dichotomy can be dismissed out of hand; neither of those terms is self-defining and any argument for the privilege based upon that distinction is necessarily circular. Use of the "inquisitorial" terminology conjures up images of the Star Chamber under Charles I and the Inquisition of Torquemada, which elicits emotional rather than rational support for the privilege.

Judge Friendly would also reject item (7), "protection of the innocent," on the ground that "[n]o proof . . . has ever been offered" to support that assertion. He argues that, in light of the existence of the common law rule against coerced confessions, "its occasional effect in protecting the innocent" is out-weighed by the fact that it "so much more often shelters the guilty and even harms the innocent" (by eliminating the opportunity for an innocent defendant to exculpate himself by compelling the person guilty of the crime to testify).[179]

Under the rules of evidence presently in force in most American jurisdictions, however, evidence of the accused's previous convictions for crimes can be brought to the jury's attention once he takes the witness stand, for the avowed purpose of showing that he is not a person worthy of belief.[180] Although in theory such use of the defendant's criminal record may be justified, in fact to require a jury to consider it on the issue of credibility alone, and *not* on the issue of guilt or innocence, is to ask the jury to perform mental gymnastics beyond the capabilities of most mortals. The inevitable temptation is for the jury to conclude that the accused must be guilty of the crime charged on the basis of his record of prior crimes. So long as the defendant who takes the witness stand does so with the certainty of having his prior crimes thus disclosed, the privilege serves the purpose of protecting those who are innocent of the crime charged but who do not have an unblemished past.

Moreover, it is worth remembering that "a substantial number of defendants are innocent, and that most of these are uneducated, unfortunate persons, frightened by their predicament—no match for the prosecutor or for the occasional sharp question from the judge ..."[181] This description fits the findings of the Commission on Law Enforcement and Administration of Justice.[182] To require such a person to take the witness stand would be to subject him to the risk of conviction on the basis of the negative impression his manner, demeanor, and form of testimony make upon the jury—even though he may in fact be innocent.

The dangers in these two situations—the defendant with a record and the defendant whose demeanor is poor—are the twin foundations of the Supreme Court's decision in *Griffin* v. *California*, forbidding comment by the judge or the prosecutor on the failure of the accused to take the stand,[183] and they remain significant points of policy underlying the privilege.

Item (5), "private enclave," Judge Friendly asserts, does not justify the privilege to the extent that inquiries into political, social and religious belief, speech or association are barred by the First Amendment or other protective rules.[184] On the other hand, Judge Friendly concedes the force of item (3), "our fear that self-incriminating statements will be elicited by inhumane treatment and abuses," in the context of secret station house interrogation.[185] He also apparently concedes item (6), "our distrust of self-deprecatory statements," although he does not accord it any significant weight.[186] Yet that confession may simply be "an act of self-punishment or self-abnegation" by an innocent man, rather than a disclosure of the truth by one impelled to acknowledge his misdeeds.[187]

This leaves item (1), "the cruel trilemma," and item (4), "fair individual-state balance," or the "whole load" argument. Judge Friendly dismisses the latter on the ground that it "is largely conclusory as stated."[188] He rejects the philosophical argument for the government shouldering the entire load based on a social contract theory under which the state has no right to require the "sovereign individual" to give up his right of self-defense. He recognizes that most people "wish the defendant to have some advantages," but argues that "even if we knew just where we want the balance set," it is "hard to reason from this to any particular application of the privilege."[189] He points out that the state must disclose exculpatory evidence, may not rely on "inculpatory evidence it has any reason to disbelieve," increasingly "is under the burden of discovery without a corresponding right against it," and cannot appeal in most cases whereas the defendant can.[190] Against these relative advantages to the accused, Judge Friendly notes:

> [J]uries doubtless tend to believe that most indicted persons are guilty, no matter how strongly they are warned otherwise; and the state has far greater resources for investigation and, at least until recently, better lawyers.[191]

Weighed against the *de facto* presumption of guilt which the accused faces and the disproportionate resources enjoyed by the state, the "advantages" to the accused, with the possible exception of the unilateral right of appeal, seem paltry at best. Discovery is still far more limited in criminal than in civil cases. Nonreliance on questionable evidence depends principally upon the good faith of the prosecutor. Outside the federal system, the selection of prosecutors is, almost uniformly, overtly political, and even in the federal system politics does not entirely absent itself from the office. At least as long as the office of prosecutor is viewed as a step up the political ladder, we cannot expect the occupant to view favorably rules requiring him to lessen his advantage over the accused and to act against his official and personal interest.

Judge Friendly suggests that other compensation advantages might be given the accused in exchange for a limitation on his privilege, such as greater discovery, more stringent requirements for corroboration of accomplice testimony, or modification of the "other crimes" doctrine of impeachment,[192] but he does not include any of these in his draft constitutional amendment (see *infra*), and we do not know whether a "fair balance" would be struck between state and individual if any or all were substituted for a narrower privilege.

As to item (1), "the cruel trilemma," Judge Friendly adopts Professor Mayers' suggestion that

> to require a mother to testify against her own son on trial for his life is surely a greater cruelty than requiring an ordinary witness to disclose some mayhap minor infraction of a penal regulation![193]

While most reasonable men could accept the proposition as stated, it may be reasonable to conclude that it suggests the need for a reappraisal of the rule which would require a mother to undergo such torment (even in the few cases where a prosecutor has been callous enough to call a mother as a witness) as it is to conclude that it supports repeal of the privilege. Moreover, in comparing the mother's suffering to the "ordinary witness," the argument presents the privilege in a context where the interest of the party being protected is not very great, and the interest of society in not having him protected and the benefits to be gained by society from its removal are not very great either. Thus, even conceding the verity of Professor Mayer's statement, it is of little or no help in appraising the value of the privilege.

Judge Friendly concedes that "almost no one would favor confining a man to jail until he takes the stand to testify."[194] Indeed, he would not directly compel, through the use of any sanction, a defendant to take the stand at the trial.[195] Instead, he suggests the use of the comment-at-trial sanction (see *infra*) to induce the accused to testify at a pre-trial hearing. If this were done, the "cruelty" argument would in his words, be "somewhat but not entirely diluted."[196]

JUDGE FRIENDLY'S AMENDMENT

In questioning the continuing *raison d'être* of the privilege against self-incrimination, Judge Friendly has proposed a six-clause amendment to the Constitution fully recognizing the undesirability of interjection so much detail into the constitution but concluding that the changes he believes desirable could not otherwise be accomplished. He also recognizes that there may be problems of draftsmanship and he reserves the right "to change [his] mind about some or all of it."[197] Clause (2), and possibly clause (1), would modify the present interpretations of the privilege which affect police interrogation:

The clause of the fifth amendment to the Constitution of the United States, "nor shall be compelled in any criminal case to be a witness against himself," shall not be construed to prohibit:

(1) Interrogating any person or requesting him to furnish goods or chattels, including books, papers and other writings, without warning that he is not obligated to comply, unless such person has been taken into custody because of it, or has been charged with a crime to which the interrogation or request relates.

(2) Comment by the judge at any criminal trial on previous refusal by the defendant to answer inquiries relevant to the crime before a grand jury or similar investigating body, or before a judicial officer charged with the duty of presiding over his interrogation, provided that he shall have been afforded the assistance of counsel when so questioned and shall have then been warned that he need not answer; that if he does answer, his answer may be used against him in court; and that if he does not answer, the judge may comment on his refusal.[198]

Judge Friendly would oppose the adoption of his draft amendment if it would dilute in any way our political and religious freedom. Indeed, he argues that the privilege is not broad enough to provide the desired protections in this area; that "a person's political and religious beliefs and associations and lawful acts to advance them are none of the government's business save in the rare case where these are truly relevant to an issue before a judicial or administrative tribunal"; and that "the Supreme Court will and should interpret the first amendment to give this protection."[199] If thought necessary he would add language to the draft amendment expressly excluding from its scope matters pertaining to "religious, political or social beliefs or associations."[200] Thus, Judge Friendly eliminates at the outset the objection that in limiting the privilege we are ignoring the historical experience which brought it into existence.

The impact of Judge Friendly's proposed modifications of the privilege in the area of police interrogation appear upon close inspection to be fairly slight. For analysis, the persons affected may be broken down into several groups.

Of those whose cases ultimately go to trial, a large number testify voluntarily anyway, 82 percent according to one study of 1,143 cases, and 91 percent of those without prior records.[201] The threat of comment by the court at the trial would seem to pose a relatively small threat to such persons when counterbalanced by the possibility that, if the accused does not speak prior to his trial, he may be in a better bargaining position for avoiding trial, and that if he does his

pretrial statements may be used to impeach his testimony at
the trial. Indeed, it is hard to see what inference could be
drawn from his failure to testify *before* trial. The inference
which is drawn from failure to testify *at* trial is that, since
the defendant has made no attempt to explain the incriminating evidence presented by the prosecution, he must be unable to exculpate himself. But it is difficult to see how that
inference can be drawn from failure to testify before trial
when the defendant offsets that failure by taking the stand to
testify in the presence of the jury.

It would seem that, in most cases, if the accused persuades
the jury with his explanation, comment upon his earlier
failure would not dissuade them; if he fails to persuade them,
such comment would not really matter. There may be some
few, very close cases where comment upon his refusal to
testify earlier might make a difference in the verdict. But, in
order for the possibility of comment at the trial to induce the
accused to testify at the pre-trial hearing, the goal principally
sought in proposing the amendment,[202] consequences adverse to him must be reasonably predictable by the accused,
or by his lawyer. Since the probabilities are great for the
defendant who testifies at trial that comment by the court
will have no impact upon the outcome of the trial, it seems
unlikely that the well-advised defendant would elect to assist
the prosecution in preparing its case against him.

The guilty defendant who does not testify at trial, or who
at the time of the pretrial examination has not decided
whether to testify, faces a somewhat similar choice. If he
does submit to examination, he not only runs the risk of
aiding the prosecution to make a case against him, thereby
either lessening his chances for a favorable verdict or at least
weakening his bargaining position in dickering for a compromise plea, but perhaps more significantly he runs the risk
of having his examination read to the jury at the trial.

It is unclear just how Judge Friendly proposes to allow the
pretrial statements to be used at trial, but if it is done in the
manner depositions are frequently read into the record in a
civil case now, and as testimony from a prior trial is read in
a criminal case,[203] the risk he runs does not depend solely
upon the substance of his testimony. Picture the detective, or
assistant prosecutor, sitting in the witness chair, reading the
defendant's answers to the prosecutor's questions with perfect
intonation: emphasis here, hesitation there; just the right
facial expressions: here of remorse, there of conscious falsi-

ty; just the way the jury would expect a guilty, prevaricating, perjuring criminal to sound and act.

Moreover, the defendant who hesitates to take the stand at trial because of his prior criminal record faces the possibility that if he testifies at a pretrial hearing, the prosecutor will bring out his record during the pretrial examination to impeach his testimony. Presumably, under Judge Friendly's draft amendment, the prosecutor could have the impeachment portion of his pre-trial statement read to the jury as well as the substantive portion. On the other hand, the timorous, uneducated defendant's possible "poor performance will not be seen by the ultimate triers of fact,"[204] which may offset to some extent the disadvantage which the poor or illiterate or frightened defendant usually faces when he takes the stand. The performance by the person who reads the accused's testimony into the record may, however, do a better job of convincing the jury of the latter's incredibility than would his own appearance on the witness stand.

The guilty defendant who does not plan to testify at trial, by hypothesis, has already decided that he is willing to run the risk that the jury will draw the inference of guilt from his failure to stand up and deny the charges, for "the jury draws the inference anyway [i.e., without comment upon his failure to testify], even—some think particularly—when instructed not to; and the defendant's lawyer knows or should know this."[205] Is the added risk of specific comment upon his previous failure to testify signficant enough to tilt the scale in favor of his testifying at a time when to do so may materially aid the prosecution in preparing its case against him? The answer would seem affirmative in only the closest of cases.

The choices that face the innocent accused do not differ significantly from those which face his guilty counterpart. Lest it be suggested that his testimony before the grand jury or at a pretrial hearing might persuade the jury not to indict or the prosecutor to dismiss the case, it should be kept in mind that he presently has the option in most cases of testifying before the grand jury and of presenting his evidence to the prosecutor either informally or at the preliminary hearing.

The defendant who now pleads guilty to the offense charged would presumably be unaffected by the proposed change. The effect upon the defendant now able to bargain for the right to plead to a lesser offense is more difficult to predict, although given the weak nature of the sanction, it seems probable that he would, like the guilty defendant who does not plan to testify at the trial, choose not to testify prior to trial for fear that he would weaken his bargaining position by helping the prosecution to fill the gaps in its case out of his own mouth.

Judge Friendly seems to recognize some of the problems pointed out above, for he notes:

> [I]n the case of the guilty suspect against whom there is sufficient other evidence for a prosecution, the lawyer will still be bound to advise silence and since he will not know how matters stand at the start, he is likely at least to postpone the decision.[206]

This would certainly be true in the situations not alluded to in the discussion above, those cases where the prosecution cannot under present conditions obtain enough evidence to indict or, having obtained an indictment, to prosecute it to trial, or to withstand a motion to dismiss at the close of its case.

In all of the situations canvassed, the defendant runs the risk of prosecution for perjury if he chooses to testify at the pretrial hearing, a risk for which he receives no compensatory benefits—except the negative benefit of not subjecting himself to adverse comment by the judge. And it is not alone the false-swearing defendant who runs this risk. The truthful, innocent defendant whose statements are disappointing to the prosecution runs this risk as well, particularly where the prosecutor's personal or political interests are involved in the case.[207] The guilty defendant, of course, runs the risk to a much greater extent, since the natural, probably overbearing temptation will be for him to forswear rather than convict himself out of his own mouth. Thus, the defendant who testifies before the grand jury or magistrate prior to trial, and whose testimony does not comport with the prosecutor's view of the facts, subjects himself to *de facto* double jeopardy. If he is acquitted on the main charge he still risks conviction for perjury. The defendant who takes the stand at a trial runs the same risk, but there he at least does so with the possibility that he may persuade the jury of his innocence, a possibility he does not have at pre-trial. The sanction of comment at the trial does not seem very likely to induce a defendant to run such a risk.

Judge Friendly is particularly concerned about the impact of the privilege on cases such as kidnapping or espionage where immediate interrogation might result in the rescue of the victim or the prevention of documents relating to national security from leaving the country.[208] But the type of information which he seeks to have elicited from the suspect's mouth would surely not be forthcoming under pain of comment at trial to any greater extent than it would under present rules. A pretrial hearing might provide an opportunity for appeals to the humanity of the kidnapper, but such appeals can presently be made to him, in the presence of his lawyer if his statements will be used against him at the trial, or out of his lawyer's presence if the police are willing to forego using them against him.[209] Naturally, the lawyer will attempt to obtain concessions for his client in exchange for the information sought, but he has no reason not to continue to do so under the procedure created by the proposed amendment.

In the espionage case, plea bargaining would seem to be more effective than appeals to idealism and, given the national interests involved, is probably justifiable in such a case. In neither the kidnapping nor the espionage case is the well-advised suspect likely to provide the information sought, which would lead to his certain conviction, because of the relatively mild threat of comment at the trial.

The choices facing the defendant under the draft amendment, therefore, could hardly be called a "cruel trilemma." In fact, the sanction suggested proves to be quite weak. It does not solve in any way the hard cases posed by Judge Friendly, such as kidnapping and espionage, and would likely have impact, if at all, in only an insubstantial number of close cases. In short, the gains to the state which could reasonably be thought to follow its adoption are minimal.

The other clause of Judge Friendly's draft amendment which pertains here, clause (1), provides for interrogation of, or requesting goods, papers, or other tangible items from, any person without warning him of his rights, provided that he has not been charged with, nor is in custody for, the crime to which the inquiry relates. This clause is avowedly designed to overrule and to prevent extensions of *Mathis* v. *United States*,[210] a 5-to-3 decision in which the Supreme Court held that information obtained from an uncautioned state prisoner by an Internal Revenue Service agent in the course of a civil investigation could not be used against the prisoner in a criminal tax proceeding subsequently begun.

It is not merely the holding of *Mathis* which concerns Judge Friendly, but the implications which he fears may flow from it, i.e., that it may lead to a ruling that introduction at a criminal trial of the product of any official, non-custodial

540

questioning—for example, by an Internal Revenue agent at the home or office of the taxpayer—violates the Fifth Amendment in the absence of a *Miranda* warning. Perhaps the majority of the Court did get carried too far on the force of its own logic in *Mathis.* But, at least at this time, a specific amendment to the Constitution to overrule that decision and its as yet unborn offspring would seem to be a hasty overaction. The Court has in the past taken a principle to the "limit of its logic" and later retrenched to a position short of that extreme.[211] (Parenthetically, the Court's recent decision in *Orozco* v. *Texas,*[212] excluding from a trial information obtained from an uncautioned defendant during nocturnal post-arrest interrogation by four policemen in the defendant's room in a boardinghouse, would not be affected by Judge Friendly's proposed amendment since the defendant was admittedly in custody at the time of the interrogation.) If warranted, *Mathis* could easily be "limited to its facts," facts unlikely to arise with great frequency.

SUMMARY AND CONCLUSION

The charge that the Supreme Court's decisions "cause violence" is unwarranted and, insofar as it diverts our concern away from the real causes of violence, it is harmful to society. The charge that the Court's decisions materially hamper the ability of the agencies of the state to solve crimes and to convict those who commit them lacks sufficient empirical data upon which to base that conclusion. We do not as yet know, for example, the degree to which confessions are in fact crucial to convictions. Nor have we yet had sufficient experience with the rules laid down in the Court's decisions in this area to judge whether they will have any significant impact upon the rate of confessions, given the known propensity of many arrestees to confess even without interrogation.

More importantly, even assuming that police may be less effective in securing convictions because of the Supreme Court rulings, the debate is not ended. As has been pointed out, each provision of the Bill of Rights was drafted expressly to make it more difficult to secure convictions. The more relevant question is whether the price we pay for our freedoms is too great to endure. Before we condemn a significant element of our heritage to obsolescence, we should ask whether there is a baby in the bath worth preserving. For it is clear that we could be of greater assistance to our police by appropriating the necessary funds to finance crime laboratories, adequate prosecutorial staffs, and proper correctional treatment. Few indeed, are the criminals "turned loose" on society by Supreme Court decisions, far fewer than those who are never caught in the first place.

Miranda v. *Arizona*,[213] spelled out in detail the procedures for custodial interrogation if the results are to be used at trial. Although it was a landmark decision, most of its elements were foreshadowed by the long line of cases which preceded it. To the extent that the veil of secrecy surrounding station house interrogation has been pierced and we have been able to find out what occurs during custodial interrogation, the methods used by the police justify the Court's findings of compulsion. Moreover, in the absence of the *Miranda* requirement of informing the accused of his rights, the select few arrestees who are relatively affluent, educated, or professional criminals enjoy substantial advantages over the more typical, poor, uneducated, frightened suspect. Not only are such distinctions forbidden by the constitutional prescription of "equal protection of the laws,"[214] but also the perception of such unequal enforcement procedures by those segments of our population adversely affected produces disrespect for and lack of cooperation with law enforcement agencies.

The values underlying the privilege are by no means insubstantial. The privilege does serve as a protection to the innocent in certain circumstances, it does contribute to a fair balance between the state and the individual, and it avoids forcing the defendant to choose from among the "cruel trilemma" of contempt, conviction or perjury.

Although Judge Friendly has launched a broad and penetrating attack upon the privilege and the policies offered in support of it, his proposed amendments in the area of police interrogation would change the present law little if at all in practice. Rather than the sweeping reforms which might have been expected from the tone of the attack, his proposals turn out on close inspection to be so minor in result that, at least standing alone, they probably do not justify tampering with a clause of the Bill of Rights. The suggested threat of comment at the trial as a sanction for inducing a defendant to testify at a pretrial hearing appears to be so weak a threat as to have only a slight effect at best upon the defendant's exercise of the option not to testify in light of the grave consequences which might follow if he did testify. The clause designed to authorize official, non-custodial questioning of a person not charged with any crime relating to the inquiry without warning him of his rights is probably premature. We do not yet know the impact of the one decision which the proposal would clearly overturn, nor can we reliably predict its expansion to the point of forbidding any official questioning without warning the interviewee of his rights.

Although it is true, as Judge Friendly points out,[215] that the first eight amendments are in form as subject to amendment as any other part of the Constitution, they have not been modified since their enactment, except to the extent that they were extended to the states by the fourteenth amendment. It is, perhaps, best that they remain unchanged so long as they do not intolerably impede the clear interests of society. While they retain their status as untouchables, they may be able to withstand the waves of mass paranoia with which our nation is occasionally plagued. Once the psychological barrier to their modification has been pierced, once they have lost their sacrosanct status, once the emotional rhetoric with which they are celebrated has been discredited, they become that much more vulnerable to further, possibly ill-considered and sweeping change in wake of the next "crime crisis," red scare, or witch hunt. As Judge Friendly notes toward the close of his final lecture, "if our only choices were repeal or what we now have, I would unhesitatingly choose the latter."[216] Surely relatively minor gains to society from the proposed changes in the police interrogation area are not worth the cost if their adoption would make repeal of what we have any easier to come to pass.

On the other hand, the place of the privilege in our society is a question which has only recently been subjected to serious debate. We admit many substantial gaps in our knowledge of the actual operation of the privilege. As further empirical studies are made in these areas and as other students of the privilege contribute their views to the debate, the facts revealed and arguments posed by them may persuade us that retention of the privilege in its present form is no longer justified and that the necessities of our environment require us to accept the consequences of amendment. At present, however, the charge that the privilege is a costly luxury in our society is, in the words of the Scots jury, "not proven."

As discussion concerning the Supreme Court's performance in the criminal justice area reaches new peaks of intensity, critics of the Supreme Court too often ignore the fact that many of its recent decisions have also removed former impediments to law enforcement activities. In 1967, the

Court overturned the historic "mere evidence" rule which had forbidden the search and seizure of nontestimonial evidence.[217] Previously, the principle that the Fourth Amendment permitted reasonable searches only for contraband and the fruits and instrumentalities of a crime, had placed serious limitations on police investigations. In another case,[218] decided only weeks after the controversial *Miranda* decision, the Court held that the Fifth Amendment did not prohibit the police from taking a blood sample from a suspect over his protest. Similarly, in *United States* v. *Wade*,[219] the Court specifically rejected arguments that a carefully safeguarded lineup procedure would offend the Fifth Amendment. Moreover, the Court has been careful to declare that, while the Fourth Amendment applies against electronic eavesdropping, an authorizing statute with appropriate safeguards could pass constitutional scrutiny.[220] Finally, the Court has condoned a "stop and frisk" procedure in certain situations.[221]

Lastly, the Supreme Court, contrary to some of its critics, has not been overly aggressive in "freeing" convicted criminals from jail. A rough count of decisions involving criminal appeals disposed of by the Supreme Court in 1967, for example, reveals that of nearly 1800 such cases, the Supreme Court took the accused's "side" in less than 100, or slightly more than 5 percent of the time.

While reasonable men may differ as to the requirements of the Constitution in criminal justice, debate should certainly center on the merits of the decisions themselves, not on the motives of the men whose job it is to decide.

REFERENCES

1. Quinn Tamm, "Police must be more free," in *Violence in the Streets*. Shalom Endleman, ed. (Chicago: Quadrangle Books, 1968), at 398–399.
2. Medford Evans and Margaret Moore, *The Law Breakers* (New York: Arlington House, 1968), at 121–124.
3. Quoted in Kamisar, "On the Tactics of Police-Prosecution Oriented Critics of the Courts," 49 *Cornell L.Q.* 436, 438 (1964). The references are to *Irvine* v. *California,* 347 U.S. 128 (1954), and *People* v. *Cahan,* 44 Cal. 2d 434, 282 P. 2d 905 (1955).
4. Ervin, "*Miranda* v. *Arizona*: A Decision Based on Excessive and Visionary Solicitude for the Accused," 5 *Am. Crim. L.Q.* 125 (1967).
5. Murphy, Address to the 28th Annual Judicial Conference of

the Third Judicial Circuit of the United States, 39 F.R.D. 375, 425 (1965).
6. Mossman, *ABA, Section on Criminal Law, Summary of Proceedings* 103 (1962).
7. Lumbard, "The Administration of Criminal Justice: Some Problems and Their Resolution," 49 *A.B.A.J.* 840 (1963). Cf. Holtzoff, "Shortcomings in The Administration of Criminal Justice," 17 *Hastings L.J.* 17, 24, (1965): "While stressing the rights of the defendants, our system of law, in recent practice, seems to neglect the interest of the public and the victims of crimes. . . . Yet the victims' rights not to be molested have been violated by the criminal. These are worthy at least of as much protection and consideration as those of the accused. The pendulum has swung too far to the side of the accused."
8. Kamisar, "When Wasn't There a Crime Crisis?" Address to the 28th Annual Judicial Conference of the Third Judicial Circuit of the United States, 39 F.D.R. 375, 450 (1965).
9. *Id.* at 452.
10. Kamisar, "Are the Scales of Justice Evenly Balanced," 12 *University of Michigan Law Quadrangle Notes,* Spring, 1968, at 6.
11. H. Friendly, *The Fifth Amendment Tomorrow: The Case for Constitutional Change* (The Robert S. Marx Lectures for 1968, U. Cinn. College of Law, Nov. 6, 7, 9, 1968), 37 *U. Cinn. L. Rev* 671 (1968).
12. 384 U.S. 436 (1966).
13. *Id.* at 479. Cf. H. Friendly, "A Postscript on *Miranda,*" in *Benchmarks* 266, 267–268 (1967).
14. 378 U.S. 478 (1964).
15. 377 U.S. 201 (1964).
16. Cf. Sobel, "The Exclusionary Rules in the Law of Confessions," in The Practicing Law Institute's *Selected Materials on New York Criminal Practice* 3–1, 3–61 (1965).
17. *Hopt* v. *Utah,* 110 U.S. 574, 583 (1884); *Pierce* v. *United States,* 160 U.S. 355, 357 (1896). For a thorough history of the evolution of Supreme Court decisions in this area, see Lockhart, Kamisar, and Choper, *Constitutional Rights and Liberties: Cases, Comments and Questions* (2d ed. 1967), at 246–58.
18. 168 U.S. 532 (1897).
19. *Id.* at 542.
20. E.g., *Powers* v. *United States,* 223 U.S. 303 (1912); *Ziang Sun Wan* v. *United States,* 266 U.S. 1 (1924); *United States* v. *Carignan,* 342 U.S. 36 (1951).
21. *United States* v. *Carignan,* 342 U.S. 36, 41 (1951) (footnotes omitted).
22. 318 U.S. 332 (1943).
23. 211 U.S. 78 (1908).
24. 297 U.S. 278 (1936).

25. Comment, "The Coerced Confession Cases in Search of a Rationale," 31 *U. Chi. L. Rev.* 313 note 1 (1964).
26. The terminology is Justice Sobel's, *supra* note 16, at 3–13.
27. *Ashcraft* v. *Tennessee*, 322 U.S. 143, 154 (1943).
28. E.g., *Brown* v. *Mississippi*, 297 U.S. 278 (1936).
29. E.g., *Ashcraft* v. *Tennessee*, 322 U.S. 143 (1943).
30. *Ibid.*
31. *Stein* v. *New York*, 346 U.S. 156, 185 (1952).
32. E.g., *Cicenia* v. *Lagay*, 357 U.S. 504 (1958).
33. E.g., *Haley* v. *Ohio*, 332 U.S. 596 (1947).
34. E.g., *Payne* v. *Arkansas*, 356 U.S. 560 (1958).
35. E.g., *Lynumn* v. *Illinois*, 372 U.S. 528 (1963).
36. E.g., *Spano* v. *New York*, 360 U.S. 315 (1959).
37. E.g., *Payne* v. *Arkansas*, 356 U.S. 560 (1958).
38. E.g., *Crooker* v. *California*, 357 U.S. 433 (1958).
39. E.g., *Rogers* v. *Richmond*, 365 U.S. 534 (1961).
40. *Davis* v. *North Carolina*, 384 U.S. 737, 740 (1966).
41. See text *supra* at accompanying notes 15–21.
42. 365 U.S. 534 (1961).
43. *Id.* at 540–541.
44. 378 U.S. 1 (1964).
45. 378 U.S. 478 (1964).
46. Friendly, *supra* note 13, at 266.
47. *Miranda* v. *Arizona*, 384 U.S. 436, 44, 463–466 (1966).
48. James Q. Wilson, "Crime and Law Enforcement," in *Agenda for the Nation.* Kermit Gordon, ed. (Washington, D.C.: Brookings Institution, 1968), at 193.
49. Fred E. Inbau, "Police Interrogation—A Practical Necessity," in *Police Power and Individual Freedom*, Claude R. Sowle, ed. Chicago: Aldine Pub. Co. 1962), at 147–148.
50. *People* v. *Huntley*, 15 N.Y. 2d 72, 78 (1965). Cf. N.Y. Code Crim. Proc. § 813–(1962).
51. Sobel, *supra* note 16, at 3–63.
52. *Id.* at 3–64.
53. *Id.* at 3–61.
54. *N.Y. Times*, Dec. 2, 1965, sec. I, at 1.
55. *Id.*
56. Cf. Sobel, *supra* note 16 at 3–66: "If they [the police] rely heavily on interrogation, it is not because they are lazy but because they are overwhelmed by quantity."
57. Inbau, *supra* note 49 at 148. But see *Davis* v. *Mississippi,* 37 U.S.L.W. 4359 (1969), in which the police took into custody 24 Negro boys, subjecting them to fingerprinting and station-house questioning, and also interrogated another 40 or 50 at headquarters, at school, or on the street, in attempting to identify an assailant where his rape victim could describe him only as a Negro youth.
58. Cf. Sobel, *supra* note 16, at 3–64.
59. *People* v. *Dorado,* 42 Cal. Rpte. 169, 398 p.2d 361, *cert. denied*, 381 U.S. 937 (1965).

60. Mosk, "The Anatomy of Violence," *Beverly Hills Bar Journal*, Oct. 1968, at 10, 14–15.
61. Reik, *The Compulsion to Confess: On the Psychoanalysis of Crime and Punishment* (1959) at 180. See also Driver, "Confessions and the Social Psychology of Coercion," 82 *Harv. L. Rev.* 42, 51–57–59 (1968).
62. Hugh Trevor-Roper, *The Crisis of the Seventeenth Century; Religion, The Reformation and Social Change* (New York: Harper & Row, 1966), at 122, 124.
63. Reiss and Black, "Interrogation and the Criminal Process," 374 *Annals* 47 (1967).
64. Friendly, *supra* note 13, at 273.
65. Medalie, Zerta, and Alexander, "Custodial Police Interrogation in our Nation's Capital: The Attempt to Implement *Miranda*," 66 *Mich. L. Rev.* 1347 (1968); Note, "Interrogations in New Haven: The Impact of *Miranda*," 76 *Yale L.J.* 1519 (1967); Seeburger & Wettrick, "*Miranda* in Pittsburgh —A Statistical Study," 29 *U. Pitt. L. Rev.* 1 (1967); Reiss and Black, *supra* note 63.
66. Medalie, et all., id. at 1351–1352.
67. Note, "Interrogations in New Haven," *supra* note 65 at 1565.
68. E.g., Medalie, et al., *supra note 65*, at 1365–1366, 1372–1375.
69. Cf. Bradley, Address to the 28th Annual Judicial Conference of the Third Judicial Circuit of the United States, 39 F.R.D. 375, 439 (1965). The publicity given *Miranda* may, however, be having a general educational effect on the community as a whole, including potential arrestees. See Note, "Interrogations in New Haven" *supra* note 65 at 1615.
70. Cf. Friendly, *supra* note 13, at 283–284. But cf. Friendly, *supra* note 11, at 715 note 187.
71. See R. Haves. "Common Fallacies in Criticism of Recent Supreme Court Decisions on Rights of Accused," 53 *A.B.A.J.* 425, 427 (1967).
72. The Report of the President's Commission on Law Enforcement and Administration of Justice (hereinafter cited as *Crime Commission*), *The Challenge of Crime in a Free Society* (Washington, D.C.: Government Printing Office, 1967), at 1.
73. Clark, Remarks at the Annual Meeting of the American Bar Association, Miami Beach, Fla., Mar. 9, 1965.
74. Quoted in Kamisar, *supra* note 3, at 440.
75. Cf. Leon Jaworski, "Does Justice Favor the Accused?" Address at Texas A.&.M. University, Feb. 26, 1969, at 4.
76. A 1962 study revealed that in the 22 convictions reversed by the Supreme Court from 1936 until the time of the study, "defendants in exactly half of the cases were again convicted of the same or a lesser included offense. . . ." Ritz, "State Involuntary Confession Cases: Subsequent Developments in Cases Reversed by U.S. Supreme Court and Some Current Problems," 19 *Wash. and Lee L. Rev.* 202, 208 (1962).

547

77. See Sutherland, "Crime and Confession," 79 *Harv. L. Rev.* 21, 36, 37 (1965).
78. Cf. Holmes, *The Common Law* 94 (1881).
79. See *Shuttlesworth* v. *Birmingham,* 382 U.S. 87 (1965); *United States* v. *Harriss,* 347 U.S. 712 (1954).
80. U.S. Const. amend. 6; *Fred R. Crim. P.* 10.
81. *Fed. R. Crim. P.* 11.
82. 384 U.S. 436, 448 (1966).
83. See Inbau, *supra* note 49 at 149.
84. Bernard Weisberg, "Police Interrogation of Arrested Persons: A Skeptical View," in *Police Power and Individual Freedom, supra* note 49 at 179.
85. Herman, "The Supreme Court and Restrictions on Police Interrogations," 25 *Ohio St. L.J.* 449, 498 (1964). Cf. *Miranda* v. *Arizona,* 384 U.S. 436, 533 (1966) (dissenting opinion).
86. Note, "Developments in the Law—Confessions," 79 *Harv. L. Rev.* 935, 939 (1965).
87. Cf. U.S. Const. amend. 6: "In all criminal prosecutions, the accused shall enjoy the right to a speedy and *public trial* . . ." [Emphasis added.]
88. Homer, *The Iliad* i, 447 (Pope trans.). See L. Levy, *Origins of the Fifth Amendment* 34 (1967).
89. National Commission on Law Observance and Enforcement, No. 11, *Report on Lawlessness in Law Enforcement* (1931).
90. *Report of Commission on Civil Rights* (Washington, D.C., 1961).
91. Crime Commission, *Challenge of Crime in a Free Society,* at 93.
92. 384 U.S. 436, 446.
93. Cf. T. Nelson, *The Torture of Mothers* (Boston: Beacon Press, 1968) at 81.
94. See Crime Commission, *Challenge of Crime in a Free Society,* at 44.
95. *Id.* at viii.
96. *Id.*
97. *Id.* at v.
98. 384 U.S. 436, 448.
99. Driver, "Confessions and the Social Psychology of Coercion," 82 *Harv. L. Rev.* 42, 50–51 (1968) (footnotes omitted). The work referred to in quotation is F. Inbau and J. Reid, *Criminal Interrogation and Confessions* (2d ed., 1967). The second, post-*Miranda* edition of this work, necessitated, in the words of the author, "by the . . . decision of the Supreme Court of the United States in *Miranda* v. *Arizona,*" *id.* at vii (2d ed., 1967), appears to have been but little changed in approach from the first edition. Earle, Book Review, 6 *Duquesne U.L. Rev.* 436 (1968).
100. *Miranda* v. *Arizona,* 384 U.S. 436, 533.
101. *Id.* at 532.

102. See *Vignera* v. *New York,* decided *sub nom. Miranda* v. *Arizona,* 384 U.S. 436, 493 (1966), in which an assistant district attorney and a court reporter were brought into the station house to take defendant's "deposition" after the police interrogation had produced admissions. See also *Jackson* v. *Denno,* 378 U.S. 368, 371, 423 n. 1 (1964), where the same procedure was followed. This appears to have been the usual practice in New York prior to *Miranda.* See *N.Y. Times,* Jan. 28, 1965, p. 1, 17.
103. *Miranda* v. *Arizona,* 384 U.S. 436, 533 n. 2.
104. Barrett, "Police Practices and the Law—From Arrest to Release or Charge," 50 *Calif. L. Rev.* 11, 41–45 (1962).
105. Cf. text accompanying notes 6–72.
106. Sutherland, *supra* note 77, at 37.
107. Driver, *supra* note 99, at 44.
108. F. Inbau and J. Reid, *supra* note 99, at vii.
109. Driver, *supra* note 99, at 51.
110. Sutherland, *supra* note 77, at 37–38.
111. *N.Y. Times,* Jan. 28, 1965, at 1.
112. *Id.* at 17.
113. Crime Commission, *Challenge of Crime in a Free Society,* at 44.
114. Cf. Brief for Petitioner at 20, *Vignera* v. *New York,* decided *sub nom. Miranda* v. *Arizona,* 384 U.S. 436 (1966).
115. U.S. Const. amend. 14. For a discussion of the issues raised in this section, see "Addresses and Symposium at the University of Kentucky College of Law Building Dedication," 54 *Ky. L.J.* 446, 464 (1966).
116. Friendly, *supra* note 11 at 711.
117. *Offutt* v. *United States,* 348 U.S. 11, 14 (1954). See also Crime Commission, *Challenge of Crime in a Free Society,* at viii.
118. See *Id.*
119. See Crime Commission, *Challenge of Crime in a Free Society,* at 33, which indicates that the estimated economic impact of crime, including crime control efforts, is approximately $21 billion annually.
120. Traynor, "The Devils of Due Process in Criminal Detection, Detention, and Trial," 33 *U. Chi L. Rev.* 657 (1966).
121. Walter B. Schaefer, *The Suspect and Society* (Evanston, Ill.: Northwestern University Press, 1967). See also Schaefer, Police Interrogation and the Privilege Against Self-Incrimination," 61 *N.W. U.L. Rev.* 506 (1966).
122. Friendly, *supra* note 11; see also Friendly, "The Bill of Rights as a Code of Criminal Procedure," in *Benchmarks* 235 (1967); and see also *supra* note 13.
123. Crime Commission, *Challenge of Crime in a Free Society,* at 303. See also Lewis Mayers, *Shall We Amend the Fifth Amendment*—(New York: Harper, 1959). Cf. Jaworski, *supra* note 75.

124. *McCarthy* v. *Arnstein,* 254 U.S. 71 (1920).
125. *Quinn* v. *United States,* 349 U.S. 155 (1955).
126. *Boyd* v. *United States,* 349 U.S. 116 U.S. 616 (1886).
127. *Murphy* v. *Waterfront Comm.,* 378 U.S. 52 (1964).
128. *Marchetti* v. *United States,* 390 U.S. 39 (1968); *Leary* v. *United States,* 37 *U.S.L.W.* 1177 (May 19, 1969).
129. See 8 Wigmore, *Evidence* §§ 2250 *et seq.* (McNaughton ed., 1961).
130. *Miranda* v. *Arizona,* 384 U.S. 436 (1964).
131. *Brown* v. *Walker,* 161 U.S. 591 (1896).
132. *Griffin* v. *California,* 380 U.S. 609 (1965).
133. *Grunewald* v. *United States,* 353 U.S. 391 (1957).
134. *Counselman* v. *Hitchcock,* 142 U.S. 547, 562 (1892).
135. Friendly, *supra* note 11, at 684.
136. E. Griswold, *The Fifth Amendment Today* (1955), at 7.
137. *Boyd* v. *United States,* 116 U.S. 616, 631–632 (1886).
138. Friendly, *supra* note 11, at 682.
139. See, e.g., "The Privilege Against Self-Incrimination: An International Symposium," 51 *J. Crim. L.C. & P.S.* 129 (1960).
140. *Ullman* v. *United States,* 350 U.S. 422, 438 (1956), quoting Holmes, J., in *New York Trust Co.* v. *Eisner,* 256 U.S. 345, 349 (1921).
141. Levy, *supra* note 88.
142. *Id.* at 46–47.
143. *Id.* at 47.
144. 9 Ed. II, c. 1 (1315). See Levy, *supra* note 88 at 49.
145. *Id.*
146. Levy, *supra* note 88 at 49–57.
147. 2 Henry IV, c. 15 (1401). See Levy, *supra* note 88 at 57.
148. 16 Car. I, c. 11, (1640). See Levy, *supra* note 88 at 281–282.
149. *Id.* at 128–135, 182–183.
150. *Id.* at 65.
151. *Id.* at 139.
152. *Id.* at 212.
153. *Id.* at 70.
154. *Id.* at 103.
155. *Id.* at 134.
156. *Id.* at 96.
157. *Id.* at 171.
158. *Id.* at 140, 171–172, 178, 235.
159. *Id.* at 331.
160. *Id.*
161. *Id.* 42, 330–332; cf. Friendly, *supra* note 11, at 695.
162. *Id.* at 34–35, 42. Levy is incorrect when he states that the Star Chamber could authorize torture. See Elton, *The Tudor Constitution* 69–70 (1960).

163. Levy, *supra* note 88, at 331.
164. *Id.* at 281–282.
165. *Id.* at 282.
166. See *Id.* at 313–314.
167. *Id.* at 325.
168. *Id.* at 313.
169. *Id.* at 317.
170. *Id.* at 320.
171. *Id.* at 328.
172. See Friendly, *supra* note 11, at 709 and Levy, *id*, at 317.
173. 8 Wigmore, *Evidence* § 2266 at 401 (McNaughton ed., 1961).
174. Cf. *Miranda* v. *Arizona*, 384 U.S. 436, 510, 527 (1966) (dissenting opinions).
175. Friendly, *supra* note 11, at 679.
176. *Tehan* v. *Shott*, 382 U.S. 406, 414 (1966).
177. Friendly, *supra* note 11, at 681.
178. 378 U.S. 52, 55 (1964). The parenthetical numbering in the quotation is Judge Friendly's. Citations within the quotation have been omitted.
179. Friendly, *supra* note 11, at 686–687.
180. C. McCormick, *Handbook of the Law of Evidence* § 43 (1954).
181. Clapp, "Privilege Against Self-Incrimination," 10 *Rutgers L. Rev.* 541, 548 (1956).
182. Crime Commission, *Challenge of Crime in a Free Society*, at 44.
183. 380 U.S. 609 (1965).
184. Friendly, *supra* note 11, at 687–688. See text, *infra*, at 724.
185. *Id.* at 690, 711.
186. *Id.* at 695.
187. Marshall, "Evidence, Psychology, and the Trial: Some Challenges to Law," 63 *Col. L. Rev.* 197, 212–213 (1963).
188. Friendly, *supra* note 11, at 695.
189. *Id.* at 694.
190. *Id.* at 693.
191. *Id.* at 694.
192. *Id.*
193. *Id.* at 683, quoting Mayers, *supra* note 123, at 168–169.
194. *Id.* at 695.
195. There may, however, be an indirect sanction in Judge Friendly's draft amendment which would "compel" a defendent to take the stand at his trial. If he testifies at the pre-trial hearing and that testimony is offered against him at the trial in a manner which makes him appear not credible, (see *infra*, text accompanying note 207) he may be "compelled" to take the stand in order to offset that impression.

196. Friendly, *supra* note 11, at 695.
197. *Id.* at 723.
198. *Id.* at 721–722. Judge Friendly also proposes amendments which would allow compulsory production of documents and other tangible objects, dismissal of government employees or defrocking of a person licensed by the state for refusing to give information relevant to his performance of duties, requiring a suspect to identify himself and make himself available for physical examination, and compulsory registration under certain specified circumstances.
199. Friendly, *supra* note 11, at 696–697.
200. *Id.* at 723.
201. H. Kalven and H. Zeisel, *The American Jury* (Boston: Little, Brown, 1966), at 144–146.
202. Cf. Friendly, *supra* note 11, at 113.
203. Cf. Brief for Appellant at 5, 10, *United States* v. *Hughes,* No. 32875 (2d Cir. filed Jan. 13, 1969). See also 14, "the net effect was . . . not unlike having Al Capone played by John Wayne."
204. Friendly, *supra* note 11, at 701.
205. *Id.* at 700.
206. *Id.* at 714.
207. Cf. *N.Y. Times,* Mar. 4, 1969, at 19.
208. Friendly, *supra* note 13, at 277.
209. *Id.* at 282.
210. 391 U.S. 1 (1968).
211. Cf., e.g., *Interstate Circuit, Inc.* v. *United States,* 306 U.S. 208 (1939); *Theatre Enterprises, Inc.* v. *Paramount Film Dist. Corp.,* 346 U.S. 537 (1954).
212. 37 *U.S.L.W.* 4260 (U.S. Mar. 25, 1969). This decision seems justifiable as a means of preventing the police from evading *Miranda* by simply moving the situs of the interrogation out of the stationhouse. Cf. Kamisar, "A Dissent from the Miranda Dissents: Some Comments on the 'New' Fifth Amendment and the Old 'Voluntariness' Test," 65 *Mich. L. Rev.* 59, 60 note 8 (1966).
213. 384 U.S. 436 (1966).
214. U.S. Const. amend. 14.
215. Friendly, *supra* note 11, at 672.
216. *Id.* at 724.
217. *Warden* v. *Hayden,* 387 U.S. 294 (1967).
218. *Schmerber* v. *California,* 384 U.S. 757 (1966).
219. 388 U.S. 218 (1967).
220. *Katz* v. *United States,* 389 U.S. 347 (1967), *Berger* v. *New York,* 388 U.S. 41 (1967).
221. *Terry* v. *Ohio,* 392 U.S. 1 (1968). Stop and frisk is permissible where a police officer "observes unusual conduct which

leads him reasonably to conclude in light of his experience that criminal activity may be afloat and that the persons with whom he is dealing may be armed and presently dangerous. . . ."

CHAPTER 21

COURT MANAGEMENT AND THE
ADMINISTRATION OF JUSTICE*

"We have never come to grips with . . . court administration. . . . We should make bold plans to see that our Courts
are properly . . . managed to do the job the public expects.
. . . We must do everything that modern institutions these
days do in order to keep up with growth and changes in
the times."—*Chief Justice Earl Warren, Speech to District
of Columbia Judicial Conference, June 2, 1969.*

Violence in America, some boldly assert, may be directly
associated with poor court management, particularly in trial
courts hearing criminal charges. If this assertion is true,
improved court management may help, along with other
improvements in courts, to provide better control of violence
and to reduce undesirable side-effects of poor court management.

In the last decade, the problems of delay in the courts, for
example, have been observed by many persons, both lay and
professional. Such delay is often the result of poor management. Two conferences held by the United States Attorney
General in the mid-1950's pinpointed unjustifiable delays as
causing major weaknesses in court systems:[1]

> (1) Release on bail of persons accused of serious crime
> (e.g., robbery) for too long, with increased likelihood of the
> person becoming a fugitive from justice or commiting a second
> crime.
> (2) Witnesses who give up in frustration after numerous
> cancelled court appearances. Police officers are particularly
> troubled by the frustrations of being witnesses in criminal
> cases.
> (3) Jurors who despair waiting endless hours only to go
> home not having fulfilled their civic duty in any meaningful
> way.

---

* This chapter was prepared by David J. Saari, Director, District of Columbia Court Management Study.

(4) Plaintiffs who settle for too little because they cannot wait for the court to act.

(5) Criminal appeals delayed, and thus prolonging the ultimate finality of conviction and sentence.

Delays resulting from poor court management thus help to create conditions of disrespect for law and legal institutions, which in turn can increase the chances for violence in our society.

When courts are properly managed, the values of efficiency, economy and effectiveness are joined with the values of equality, due process, and justice for all. The joining of such values is what citizens seek from public institutions in a democratic society. For example, genuine thoughtfulness extended to witnesses and jurors may be a small thing, but it is important to obtain their cooperation. Public institutions quite often lack that decent grace which makes a person feel positively about his government. Sophisticated court management with a feeling for all people connected with the courts, for professional values, for constitutional and statutory standards can, in its own way, be a positive factor in preventing loss of respect for law and for courts.

WHAT IS COURT MANAGEMENT?

Although court management does differ from other kinds of management, it does nevertheless try to handle men, money, materials, and space. Just as all managers must plan, organize, delegate, supervise, coordinate and review, so must the courts work with budgets, personnel problems, space allocations, purchases, research functions and development. And they must make daily contacts with seniors, peers, and subordinates.

The real tasks of court management lie buried and sometimes unrecognized in the total job of the judge. The main part of the judge's job is to adjudicate—to decide cases and to resolve controversies. He looks back in time to facts and situations. He decides, weighing witnesses' words and other eveidence that can be seen or heard. Many cases ask no more of a judge than a single decision—a judgment, but in a large number of cases the judge must administer the remedy as well as determine the right. Probation, marital support, mental health, and juvenile cases provide four distinct examples of administrative or managerial functions arising from judicial decisions. Managing the people who aid the judge in

555

administering the remedy (e.g., support payments to an ex-wife and children) has created a new set of burdens on the judge—particulary the trial judge.

While a judge must look back in exercising much of his adjudicative role, he must—when he manages—look ahead, plan, and forecast needs of his court and the citizens it serves. The task placed upon the judge to manage courtroom personnel, courthouse personnel (probation workers, clerks of court, bankruptcy officers, and so on) requires tools appropriate to the task. These management tools are not acquired in law school or from private practice of law. How to organize or reorganize departments of the court, projecting program costs, establishing manpower training and development programs, deciding upon computer processing of information, preparing space utilization and building programs appropriate to a public agency, strengthening ties to budget and financial agencies outside the court, building sound relationships with a legislature and with executive departments—all of this departs rather substantially from the activities associated with the judicial adjudicative role carried out on the bench and in the judge's chambers.

We should also have some idea of what court management is *not*. It is not a universal panacea for all the non-judicial problems of a court. It is not a job exclusively for efficiency experts whose only values are increased speed, increased production, lower costs, and less waste. Finally, although improved court management may save a judge's time for adjudication of specific cases, it is also likely to involve the judge in policy issues, in developing court rules, and in setting guidelines for court administrative matters. Improved court management will see delegation of the details of management to someone other than the judge, but the important matters of administrative policy as well as judicial policy must be established by the judge.

Court management in its best sense tries to accommodate multiple values—some of which are obviously in conflict (uniformity vs. individualization of cases)—and it attempts to seek a practical daily accommodation of value differences. Management is a rational activity for the most part; and it suggests goals, plans, guided actions, and evaluations of programs on many different fronts.[2] This presumption of rationality does not however, rule out sensitivity to persons inside or outside the courts. Consequently, better court management does contribute to domestic tranquility, order, and liberty—all at the same time.

COURT MANAGEMENT TODAY

Trial courts are part of the peacekeeping operations of government. All courts, but particularly trial courts, are part of the total process of social control designed for less complex and demanding times. The management design of America's trial courts with few exceptions is essentially "displaced rural," and the design is illsuited for today's urban needs for governance.[3] Splintered structure and absence of management are primary characteristics.

Most of the courts in the United States are not well run: they are ineffective in disposing of filed caseloads and in promoting prompt justice. Delay in civil personal injury actions in 97 selected jurisdictions in the United States averages 20.7 months.[4] The *median* delay in felony cases in federal courts is 9.5 months in Washington, D.C., and 9.4 months in the eastern District of New York.[5] Nineteen percent of the criminal cases in the federal courts are pending for 1 year or more.[6]

Nor is the problem of delay confined to the trial courts. In federal appellate courts in 1968, the median time for the completion of the record was 1.8 months in civil cases and 2.8 months in criminal cases. The filing of briefs took an additional 3.5 months. Another 1.5 months slipped by before the typical case was heard or submitted. After the case was heard, still another 1.5 months was required for final disposition.[7] Since 1959, the number of cases held for extended periods after argument has increased by 500 percent. On June 30, 1959, only 33 cases in U.S. Courts of Appeal were undecided 3 months after appellate argument. Only one of those cases had been held for more than a year.[8] On June 30, 1968, there were 256 cases which had been held for more than 3 months, and 23 of these cases had been held for more than a year after argument.[9]

Most courts of the nation do *not* have genuinely effective management skill. But the Los Angeles Superior Court, which has an Executive Officer, is the prime exception; yet even that progressive court is not fully structured so that management can be most effective.[10] Despite the presence of state and court administrators in most of the states, who act as staff secretariats for such administration as is permitted without direct managerial duties, state-wide management is generally absent.[11] In this sense, the federal courts have little management.

The management of judicial institutions is essentially the

same—whether we consider federal or state courts, or differentiate courts by function such as trial, appellate, juvenile, or traffic. The characters change name from court to court, but the interests remain constant for management purposes. For example, one interest for all court managers is whether the organization has enough money to perform the tasks required; therefore, to do this, they must build relationships with those who provide funds, such as county budget officers, county commissioners, legislators, and appropriations committees. Even justice has to be financed.[12]

Another current condition of court management is specialization. Its impact on the judiciary has been slow in coming, but it is building. As the need for management specialists in courts becomes more clear, so does the concurrent need for the redefinition of what the judge, the clerk, and other department heads are to do. The effective insertion of a genuine court executive in a court system requires an adjusted role for all of those with whom he interacts—judges, court employees, lawyers, witnesses, jurors, bar associations, and many others.[13]

Although court management is affected by the general trend away from autocratic administration, this condition lingers on in the courts. Because of the limited and outdated notions of management held by many judges, the autocratic administrative tradition predominates in the judiciary. Just as the national egalitarian trend has tended to equalize relationships of men to women, management to workers, blacks to whites, and parents to children,[14] democratic and egalitarian forces are shaping the field of court management. The judge in exercising his talents becomes part of a team, much as a doctor is a part of a team in a hospital. Teamwork based upon a more cooperative form of court management is more complex because it involves a sharing of administrative responsibilities previously invested in one man only—the judge.

Court management is also handicapped by the lack of adequate communications between the disciplines seriously studying nonlegal organizations and those studying courts. Management research in nonlegal institutions is poorly diffused into the legal institutions, American law schools contribute little or nothing to improvement of court management, and other disciplines have ignored courts. Certainly the administration of justice needs as much attention as that given by agricultural extension services to better ways to farm the land.

Like Vice Presidents for Administration in business or Executive Officers in military organizations, American courts need professional *court executives* with managerial expertise and responsibility who would have pay and stature comparable to the judiciary in every multijudge, general jurisdiction court of three or more judges. He would be responsible for the management tasks mentioned above that now lie buried and sometimes unrecognized in the total job of a judge. In courts serving rural area, a roving, regional court executive should be employed. Linking such court executives into the state judicial system with a statewide court administrator is a problem that could be resolved after study of the particular court management problems of each state.

PUTTING EFFECTIVE MANAGEMENT INTO THE ADMINISTRATION OF JUSTICE

What we should do to improve court management depends upon what has been done and what needs to be done. Many take pride in one of our major exportable national strengths: management "know-how." We export management skills abroad, but we find it nearly impossible to infuse management skills into some of our critically important institutions at home, the courts being a typical example. American management prowess, modified to serve professional organizations, is needed in judicial systems. The ABA Criminal Justice Project and the National Court Assistance Act are two programs which can help meet this need.

AMERICAN BAR ASSOCIATION—SPECIAL COMMITTEE ON STANDARDS FOR THE ADMINISTRATION OF CRIMINAL JUSTICE

In testimony before the National Commission on the Causes and Prevention of Violence, the President of the American Bar Association, William T. Gossett, suggested:

Strict law enforcement alone can only be one component of an effective strategy to minimize violence in America. Where violence threatens society, as it does today, one necessary response is clearly, forcefully and *efficiently*, to enforce the criminal laws.[15]

Not enough is known by the general public about the efforts of the American Bar Association and other similar groups to

559

move for comprehensive reexamination and improvement of criminal justice in America. All Americans should consider supporting the reform efforts launched by the ABA, the American Law Institute, and the Institute of Judicial Administration of New York University. The ABA action, in particular, leads the way in a well-studied and thoughtful manner to improve criminal justice administration. Court management will also play a critical supporting role here because it is one critical component of an effective overall strategy.

In 1964, the American Bar Association created a Special Committee on Minimum Standards for Criminal Justice. This launched what has been described as the largest undertaking of its kind ever sponsored by the organized bar. The 12-member Special Committee was supplemented by six 11-man advisory committees (later enlarged to seven) to review and update every phase of the criminal process ranging from pre-trial proceedings to final appellate review and post conviction processes. More than 75 lawyers, judges, and legal educators have been involved in formulating recommended new standards over the past 4 years. Completion of all reports is expected by the end of 1970. Some of the reports have already been approved by the House of Delegates of the ABA, and others are expected to come before that body in February 1970.

The Special Committee will complete its reports and will cooperate with the Criminal Law Section of the ABA to seek adoption of the new ABA standards by the 50 states and by the national government.

The reports cover the following topics:
Reports completed.

1. Standards for Fair Trial and Free Press.
2. Standards for Post Conviction Remedies.
3. Standards for Review of Sentences.
4. Standards for Pleas of Guilty.
5. Standards for Speedy Trial.
6. Standards for Providing Defense Services.
7. Standards for Joinder and Severance of Criminal Charges.
8. Standards for Trial by Jury.
9. Standards for Sentencing Alternatives and Procedures.
10. Standards for Pre-Trial Release.
11. Standards for Criminal Appeals.

Reports in preparation:

1. Standards for Pre-Trial Discovery and Procedure.

2. Standards for Prosecuting Attorneys.
3. Standards for Defense Counsel.
4. Standards for Police Use of Electronic Surveillance.
5. Standards for the Judge's Function in Criminal Justice.

The virtue of the ABA Criminal Justice Project—apart from striving for reasonable uniformity of procedural standards—lies in its effort to define the role of each of the three principal participants: the prosecutor who initiates, the lawyer who defends, and the judge who presides. In defining the roles, the ABA also articulates standards of acceptable conduct. This is not done solely to achieve a form of protocol; it is undertaken to improve efficiency and to eliminate the waste of time and human resources. Prosecutors, who know the "ground rules" and know they will be enforced, will more carefully screen cases before invoking the criminal processes and will move more effectively and swiftly present the case. Defense lawyers with counterpart guidelines will more realistically evaluate the chances of a not-guilty verdict and perhaps seek to lighten the reasonably anticipated consequences of a faulty defense. Judges confronted with lawyers who have guidelines of conduct and who themselves have similar guidelines for their function, will be able to conduct trials more speedily without impairment of basic fairness. Appeals will be handled in a similar manner.

Retired U.S. Supreme Court Justice Tom C. Clark has agreed to head an ABA Implementation Committee to work with the ABA Criminal Law Section to seek the adoption of the standards in state and federal courts. The effort will be the first on a national scale to seek some reasonable uniformity of criminal law processes. The implementation will involve both new legislation and revisions of internal rules and practices of courts and law enforcement agencies. The recommendations are designed to update procedures and to meet the needs of a growing nation along with refined protections in procedure. Many state and federal courts have already adopted some of the standards.

The work of the American Bar Association—particularly in the implementation phase—will require the efforts of many groups to achieve effective reform. The new standards will be achieved to the extent the public understands and supports necessary reforms. An integral part of court management involves daily contact with the administration of the criminal laws of each jurisdiction. Improved court management will go hand in hand with the enhanced standards found in the

ABA recommendations and with interested public support. Private groups looking for challenge and guidance can find both in the ABA *Standards*. Responsible action can thus be promoted for a better system of justice for this Nation.

SEED MONEY FOR THE REFORM OF COURTS— NATIONAL COURT ASSISTANCE ACT

A large number of advances in court management reform have been spurred by private ventures financed by private resources. Private interest and private philanthropy have a proper place in the American way of life, but the whole burden of modernization and of using management "know-how" in the courts cannot be permitted to fall solely upon private resources. Governmental resources must be bolstered to achieve a new level of innovation in court management.

A far-sighted "National Court Assistance Act," proposed by Senator Joseph D. Tydings of Maryland in 1966[16] suggested government seed money for new ideas to make the state courts of this nation work more effectively. In principle, the concept of state aid was approved by the American Bar Association Section on Judicial Administration and by the National Conference of State Trial Judges, but it was disapproved by the Conference of Chief Justices of the States. Questions of federal domination and interference arose, and, as a consequence, every effort was made to amend the act so that it would in no way permit federal interference with local courts.[17]

The federal government has a proper and responsible role to promote effective court management in state courts because their management affects federal courts in every part of this country. Nothing is more basic to sound government than a well-managed court system. Each state can and should decide for itself whether it needs help, and then it should be up to the federal government to provide the vehicle through which financial resources may be channeled to each state requesting aid. The National Court Assistance Act was framed in the tradition of federal-state cooperation similar to acts which aid state education, health, and welfare programs.

Senator Tydings' appreciation of the virtues of federalism should not be overlooked; his concern for local courts is clear. Expanding federal judicial jurisdiction when state courts fail in their obligations to handle state or local disputes in a timely manner is opposed by the Senator. His testimony bears this out.

As state and local court systems fall further behind in their efforts to keep abreast of mounting caseloads, pressure—understandable pressure—mounts for the lawyers to expand the jurisdiction of the federal courts to embrace a wider range of court actions. Such expansion which many of us believe is not consistent with our federal system, could erode the very foundations of the co-equal partnership between the national government and the states. The best way to remove the pressure is to encourage the states to take steps to deal effectively with deficiencies in the administration in their own court systems.[18]

The principle of the National Court Assistance Act is alive today and the concept of aid to states is ready to take on its own life. Court reform, including better court management practices, is sometimes costly in the experimental states, but analysis of courts by experts can do much to help the courts see their problems more clearly and seek new solutions. We should free some federal money to assist in the application of American management "know-how" to our courts. The Federal Judicial Center, which serves the federal court system, provides proof that Congress believes the federal court establishment must and will reform. Block grants to states, involvement of the Federal Judicial Center, creation of a separate commission to oversee equitable distribution of the funds, or some combination of these and other possible institutional innovations are needed to couple resources with need.

Improving justice, no less than enhancing farm practices, for example, is vital to the nation, and both require fiscal attention from the national government. Planting properly germinated "seeds" may yield a bountiful harvest of ideas. The basic task of support remains with state and local governments. They would profit greatly by sharing knowledge—much the way a Colorado wheat farmer shares his knowledge with a Kansas wheat farmer.

The National Court Assistance Act is framed in the great tradition of American reform. As Arthur Schlesinger, Jr., has stated it:

We have never regarded democracy as a finished product but something to keep on building.[19]

COURT MANAGEMENT, 1970–1975: A SUGGESTED AGENDA FOR PUBLIC POLICY

What will courts be like in 1975, assuming that the American Bar Association standards have been largely implemented and something like the National Court Assistance Act has been in effect for 5 years or so? Our look ahead will focus upon the managerial function of the courts—urban, suburban, and rural; both trial and appellate. And it will center on the interlocking roles of the courts, the law schools, the bar associations, the legislatures, the specialty groups promoting court improvements, and the lay groups.

1. Court Executives

By 1975, each of the metropolitan areas in the United States will have an adequately paid professional court executive in the major state trial court of general jurisdiction and in each local court (such as a municipal court or a state court of limited jurisdiction). These urban trial court specialists will know one another, deal with one another, and be the prime intercourt connecting points in resolving problems such as *overscheduled counsel* and other matters. At least the largest urban areas—multicounty or multistate—will have high quality managers with pay and status comparable to judges, to serve millions of citizens and thousands of judges.

Nothing is accomplished by adding one court executive without giving him an adequate staff for his office. The court management function requires proper staffing and supporting management specialists in personnel, accounting, budget, computer data processing, records management, and space planning. The entire array of management specialists is not necessary in every office, of course. A state or region of states might need only one or two types of specialists to serve the entire state or region, but a team of experts in combination is needed, not just one court executive. States which have created a statewide court administrator without adequate foresight into supporting needs will have caused themselves difficulties, particularly at local levels.

By 1975 each state should have adopted a plan for the relationships it wants among the court executives in its judicial system. States with highly centralized judicial systems serving only or mostly urban populations may want central control from the state capital through the office of the state court administrator.[20] States with less centralization in their judicial systems may decide on loosely connective, even cooperative, relationships worked out on an ad hoc basis from court to court.[21] No single system should be forced upon any state as *the* model pattern—the appropriate solution depends upon political, economic, social, legal and other practical factors which vary from state to state.

At least 29 states now have an office which exercises some administrative powers in the state's judicial system. These offices were conceived to be managerial in nature, but over time they have tended to become staff specialists—persons who give advice to judges but do not exercise power daily over money, people, programs, or space. The proper role of state court executives needs further research and development to encourage management innovation in state judicial systems. An even larger role may be warranted for certain offices if the state judiciary, legislature, and executive decide to centralize the entire administrative structure of the state judicial system. Whether this centralization should or should not be done depends primarily upon local and state initiatives.

2. Court Studies

The year 1975 should see court executives, judges and bar associations participating in a wide variety of studies to answer a host of questions. Some of these are: Shall we centralize or decentralize the administrative structure of the courts? Shall we have one or more computers to serve data processing needs? Shall we have one budget or many? Shall we have one personnel system or many?

Another class of studies would be primarily unit-oriented management studies. A court management study in the broadest sense would be designed to delve into the operations of a particular court system. The originator of the first large-scale court management study, Senator Tydings, believes the purposes served would be these:

> By the way of partial illustration, let me list for you some of the ways that modern management techniques can be utilized to assist the court in handling its business: (1) to evaluate the forms, systems and procedures currently employed in court administration, for functions such as: filing papers and records; preparing the printing of calendars; notifying attorneys, litigants, and witnesses; calling calendars and scheduling cases for pretrial and trial; impanelling and scheduling juries; indexing and docketing of court actions; accounting for fees; and, transferring cases to other courts; (2) to determine what information is needed for effective management of court operations; (3) to appraise equipment needs for communications and for filing, retrieving, processing and preserving cases, records and ad-

ministrative statistical data, (4) to review space utilization and facility needs; (5) to provide an objective basis for estimating judicial and non judicial manpower requirements and for establishing compensation levels; (6) to assess the adequacy of the new administration organization of the courts, (7) to evaluate the soundness of non-judicial personnel policies and practices in such areas as recruitment, training, and career development; (8) to review opportunities for revision in statutes and court rules that would result in administrative improvements without affecting judicial decision-making prerogatives and the substantive rights of litigants.[22]

The first such broad court management study has been underway since April 1968 in the District of Columbia.[23] Study of the five courts in the District of Columbia—two trial, one juvenile, and two appellate—has already produced recommendations and action by the courts, especially in automation of the jury system and improvements in handling lesser criminal offenses in the court of general sessions in the District of Columbia. Many recommendations—some legislative, some asking for changes in court rules, and some asking for changes in management practices—have been made or will be forthcoming. Funding for this study came from the Ford Foundation, the Russell Sage Foundation, the Eugene and Agnes Meyer Foundation, and the Law Enforcement Assistance Administration of the U.S. Department of Justice in Washington. The District of Columbia study is showing what can be done if the court system is subjected to an objective and detailed analysis.

The first point of attack was the Criminal Assignment Court system in the District of Columbia Court of General Sessions, the major intake point for criminal cases both in the local General Sessions Court and the U.S. District Court. All serious misdemeanors and most felony preliminaries are processed through the Assignment Court. The volume of such cases has been increasing rapidly with more judges assigned to hear these cases than are assigned to hear other types of criminal cases. The study concluded that the Assignment Court system was plagued by two overriding problems: (1) no one person was in control of the caseflow process, and (2) there was a lack of orderly, efficient, and standardized procedures for operating the system.

To meet these problems, the study recommended that the Court establish control over its calendar, develop reasonable and efficient procedures and rules for conducting the Assignment Court, impose strict control over continuances, and require consistent and regular action from the prosecutor, defense counsel, and the bench. These suggestions were grounded on three basic premises:

a. In order for the Assignment Court process to function effectively, the Assignment Court Judge must act as the manager of the criminal trial system, and, as such, he should control work loads and make trial assignments to the judges.

b. To fulfill this function, there must be standard procedures and a steady flow of information among the assignment Judge, the Assignment Commissioner, and the trial courts.

c. All participants in the system must cooperate by adhering to these procedures. As officers of the court, the defense attorneys and Assistant U.S. Attorneys have the responsibility to abide by court rules and practices. The court, of course, must enforce these rules for *all* parties and for itself.

The recommendations included a set procedure for calling the trial calendar and sending cases to trial, a new method of appointing counsel for indigent defendants, and a standardized arraignment and presentment procedure.

The court accepted most of these recommendations and began implementing them in mid-October 1968 on an experimental basis. The results from the experimental period, October-December 1968, indicate that the new procedures are entirely workable, and, if fully implemented, could produce substantial improvements.

3. Law Schools and Centers for Administration of Justice

Law schools with a strong interdisciplinary outlook and strong departments of management or administration in the university or new multidisciplinary centers for administration of justice should develop curricula for a court management profession.[24] There are potentially more than 300 full scale court executive positions—at least 50 at the state level, 250 at major urban centers and additional regional court executives, in addition to the need for high-ranking second or third men in particularly large operations such as Los Angeles, Chicago, New York, Philadelphia, and elsewhere. The federal courts can use about 30 such executives of various grades. Trained people will be needed in all these vital positions in the court systems. The peculiar management educational needs of courts—to train those on the job, to educate those coming along, and to educate others in the system—require an unusual faculty: interdisciplinary in nature, urban and

567

humanistic in outlook, with broad knowledge of judicial institutions and other academic disciplines.

By 1975, educational institutions should begin to recognize and evaluate the need to become centers for education of judges, court executives, and others in the judicial system. Leadership in the interdisciplinary development of thought about judicial institutions will demand creativity. The state bar association, the state court system, and others will look to the university for leadership in producing an educated group of court officers.

4. Bar Associations

The members of state and local bar associations spend a great deal of time in courts. They prosecute, defend, or bring claims every day. Often they are the only source of leadership in court reform, and each member of the bar has both a personal and professional stake in seeing that the courts are improved. Yet, the court system "belongs" to the whole bar and to the whole public and is not just the special preserve of those who spend the most time there.

The bar associations in city after city—New York, Los Angeles, Pittsburgh, Portland, Ore., Washington, D.C., to name a few—have promoted court reorganization. The tradition of the bar associations is to press ahead—it is the logical lobby for the judiciary—and it is often the only lobby. But the bar should strive to unite other groups interested in judicial reforms.

Almost every state and local bar association should participate in a court study, a court management study, or other review of the judicial establishment. Such reviews should produce suggestions for reform. Dialog between the bench and the bar will be promoted by such studies. The role of the court executive is to promote that dialog for the benefit and understanding of the bench and bar and, ultimately, the public. Cities that are now reaching new levels of achievement in the courts—Portland, San Jose, and Pittsburgh, to name just three—have found new levels of bench-bar-public interchange which is of value to the communities.

5. Laymen and Legislators

What do we as citizens want? Briefly, we want a court system that proceeds with the people's business swiftly and fairly. But how swiftly? Let us examine some of the suggestions.

Civil cases.—Disputes between citizens should be terminated finally within "six months after the action has commenced. . . ." The appeal should be completed within another 6 months.[25]

Felony cases.—Serious crimes such as murder and rape should take only a matter of days. According to the *Standards Relating to Speedy Trial* of the American Bar Association, the case should be dismissed if it cannot be tried within acceptable time standards left to definition locally. Some states now provide that felony cases must be tried within 90 to 120 days or be dismissed.[26] The model timetable for felonies in the President's Commission on Law Enforcement and the Administration of Justice report is premised upon the distinction between needless and necessary delay. The model timetable provides:

> It [the commission] proposes that the period from arrest to trial of felony cases be not more than four months and that the period from trial to appellate decision be within five months—that, in short, the entire process take no more than nine months.[27]

Legislative articulation of time standards for the conclusion of litigation is a principal hope for pressure to achieve rational management of judicial institutions. The articulation of goals—what we should reach for in performance—is very important to sound court management. There are other tasks that legislatures should take up, such as early definition of the practical consequences for courts of certain legislative proposals (e.g., whether the legislative proposal will generate more or less litigation).[28] But these tasks are not so important now as defining the goal—setting the sights of all potentially conflicting participants in the administration of criminal laws.

CONCLUSION

By 1975, then, we should have the following results from a national program to improve court management:

(1) Metropolitan, urban and regional court executives with adequate and appropriate staffs of management specialists in most courts.

(2) Improved statewide central court executive offices in each state.

(3) Universities teaching an interdisciplinary course in court management and links between them and the judicial and law enforcement institutions, with law schools deeply involved.

(4) Bar associations promoting, cooperating, and supervising studies of courts by management consultants and others.

(5) Lay groups suggesting and legislatures promulgating specific legislation to set the goals for judicial speed in the processing of cases.

(6) Court systems operating without delay, with humaneness, and with high regard for constitutional safeguards.

This program to improve court management, coupled with the ABA Standards of Criminal Justice and the National Court Assistance Act, could modernize our court systems. The real question is whether our will to govern ourselves in this democracy is equal to the challenge. As Thomas Jefferson wrote in 1816:

> [L]aws and institutions must go hand in hand with the progress of the human mind . . . . As new discoveries are made, new truths disclosed, and manners and opinions change with the change in circumstances, institutions must advance also, and keep pace with the times. We might as well require a man to wear still the coat which fitted him as a boy, as civilized society to remain ever under the regimen of their barbarous ancestors. . . .[29]

REFERENCES

1. Proceedings of the Attorney General's Conference on Court Congestion and Delay in Litigation, Dept. of Justice, May 21–22, 1956 (Washington, D.C.), at 162. Proceedings of the Attorney General's Conference on Court Congestion and Delay in Litigation, Dept. of Justice, June 16 and 17, 1958 (Washington, D.C.), at 245.
2. Leonard R. Sayles, *Managerial Behavior; Administration in Complex Organizations* (New York: McGraw-Hill, 1964); Amatai Etzioni, *Modern Organizations* (Englewood Cliffs, N.J.: Prentice-Hall, 1964); and *A Comparative Analysis of Complex Organizations* (New York: Free Press of Glencoe, 1961); George A. Steiner, *Top Management Planning* (New York: Macmillan Co, 1969).
3. James W. Hurst, *The Growth of American Law: The Law Makers* (Boston: Little, Brown & Co., 1950), at 85–193: Hurst stresses localism in structure and independence of agencies auxiliary to courts, see particularly p. 453 and bibliographical notes for additional sources.

4. Institute of Judicial Administration, *Calendar Status Study— State Trial Courts of General Jurisdiction—Personal Injury Cases* (269, 1968).
5. *Annual Report of the Director of the Administrative Office of the United States Courts 1968* (Washington, D.C.: Government Printing Office, 1969), at 269.
6. *Id.* at 258.
7. *Id.* at 184. See also Bryan, "For a Swifter Criminal Appeal— To Protect the Public as Well as the Accused," *Wash. Lee L. Rev.*, (1968) at 175, 178.
8. *Annual Report of the Director of the Administrative Office of the United States Courts 1959* (Washington, D.C.: Government Printing Office, 1960), at 79.
9. *Id.* at 258.
10. Chicago, and Philadelphia and surrounding counties, are now managing courts better. The following urban centers are implementing various court managerial improvements: Seattle, Portland, Oreg., San Jose, San Mateo, Los Angeles, Orange County, San Diego, San Bernadino, Phoenix, Tucson, Wichita, Kansas City, Mo., St. Louis, Minneapolis, St. Paul, Omaha, Pittsburgh, Boston, Baltimore, and New Jersey's large urban centers. Not quite so advanced are urban centers in the circle of Detroit, Cleveland, Columbus, Cincinnati, and Indianapolis, in New York and New England areas, and in the Mid-Atlantic and South (e.g., Miami, Atlanta, Washington, or New Orleans) or Southwest (Dallas, Houston, or Oklahoma City) and in some of the upper Rocky Mountain centers.
11. New Jersey and Colorado are the principal exceptions. California and Illinois have some direct management functions.
12. David J. Saari, "Open Doors to Justice—An Overview of Financing Justice in America," 50 *Judicature* 296 (1967).
13. Edward C. Gallas, "The Planning Function of The Court Administrator," 50 *Judicature* 268 (1967).
14. Rudolph Driekurs, M.D., Prevention and Correction of Juvenile Delinquency, Metropolitan Youth Commission of St. Louis and St. Louis County (June 1, 1961) at 2–3:
      "We are living in a transitional period between two phases of mankind. Rapid and fundamental changes in our society have resulted from the *transformation from the autocratic into the present democratic culture.* In the former, all relationships were those of the superiority of one individual or group over another. In contrast, in a democratic atmosphere, all relationships are fundamentally those of equals. This change in human relationships is responsible, more than anything else, for the prevalent discord of our times. The effect of the gradual equalization of previously dominant and submissive parties can be observed in any area of contested power, in marriage, in industry, in race relations, and in regard to children. Men were the first to lose their

power within the period. No "decision" by social agencies or other experts will ever again "put Father back at the head of the family." As women gained their equal status with men, which they often abuse for gaining personal superiority, so they lost with their husbands the power to "control" their children. Gaining equality increases frictions and tensions, distrust and antagonism. The previously superior group is afraid of losing its status and power, the previously inferior group resents any trace of domination, and revolts against being kept in an inferior and subordinate position.

15. Quoted in 13 *American Bar News* 4 (Nov 11, 1968) (Emphasis added).

16. Joseph D. Tydings, "Helping State and Local Courts Help Themselves: The National Court Assistance Act" 24 *Wash. and Lee L. Rev.* 1 (Spring, 1967); Speech to Conference of Chief Justice on National Court Assistance, 113 *Cong. Rec.* Aug. 17, 1967.

17. See 114 *Cong. Rec.*, Feb. 14, 1968, at S. 1218, for proposed amendment to guarantee insulation of state courts from federal intrusion.

18. Hearings before the *Subcommittee on Improvements in Judicial Machinery*, Committee on the Judiciary, U.S. Senate, 90th Cong., 1st Sess., on S. 1033, the National Court Assistance Act, Apr. 18, 19, and 21, June 27, July 20, 1967, at 3. Thomas Jefferson expressed similar concern in 1820 when he wrote: "The Constitution has erected no such single tribunal, knew that to whatever hands confided, with the corruptions of time and party, its members would become despots."
Thomas Jefferson on Democracy, Saul K. Padover, ed. (New York: D. Appleton-Century Co., 1939), at 99.

19. Arthur M. Schlesinger, *The American as Reformer* (New York: Atheneum, 1968), at 96.

20. New Jersey has already started this farsighted program through the office of the State Court Executive, Edward C. McConnell, one of the leaders in the movement for improved court management for almost two decades.

21. Senator Tydings has introduced a bill, S. 1509, 91st Cong., which would provide decentralized management capability for the federal courts. This Senate incorporated the essence of this bill into S. 952 which passed in June 1969 providing federal District Courts with executive administrators.

22. *Cong. Rec.*, vol. 113, Aug. 17, 1967, at 23030; see also "Modernizing the Administration of Justice," 50 *Judicature* 258 (1967).

23. See Court Management Study, Washington, D.C., *Project Plan* of Aug. 12, 1968.

24. Such a program is being tentatively explored at the University of Denver.

25. Report of the Initial Meeting of the Executive Committee—
The Attorney General's Conference on Court Congestion and
Delay in Litigation, Department of Justice, Jan. 7, 1957
(Washington, D.C.).
26. American Bar Association Project on Minimum Standards for
Criminal Justice. *Standards Relating to Speedy Trial.* American Bar Association, 1968, at 15.
27. President's Commission on Law Enforcement and the Administration of Justice, *Challenge of Crime in a Free Society*
(Washington, D.C.: Government Printing Office, 1967), at
155–156.
28. Ronald L. Goldfarb. *Problems in the Administration of Justice in California*, Report to the California Legislature (Feb.
1, 1969).
29. *Thomas Jefferson on Democracy, supra* note 18, at 67.

CHAPTER 22

THE ADMINISTRATION OF JUSTICE UNDER EMERGENCY CONDITIONS*

The Kerner Commission[1] identified six major problems in the administration of criminal justice during and in the wake of civil disorders:

(1) Relatively few successful prosecutions of offenses relating to civil disorders, resulting chiefly from the breakdown of normal police work in gathering evidence and in building a case, caused by mass arrests, by the impossibility of on-the-spot investigation, and by assembly-line booking and processing of those arrested;

(2) Great overcrowding of all facilities because of the flood of arrests;

(3) The dispensing of mass, not individual, justice;

(4) The setting of high, uniform, unindividualized bail to avoid releasing arrestees;

(5) Inadequate legal representation of defendants; and

(6) Harshness of sentences meted out during the course of a disorder.

The Commission recommended that cities draft comprehensive plans for the operation of a criminal justice system during emergencies, providing for—

(1) Review and overhaul of relevant legal provisions and dissemination of information about legal provisions to all personnel in the system;

(2) Revised charging and booking procedures and policy decisions on matters like the use of summonses for minor offenders to avoid clogging the system;

(3) Establishment of policies for release on bail or personal recognizance, and on sentencing;

(4) Arrangements for defense counsel, and

(5) Adequate emergency detention and transportation facilities.

---

* This chapter was prepared by William A. Dobrovir of the District of Columbia Bar.

574

The Kerner Commission dealt mainly with one kind of emergency—the mass, violent civil disturbance of which the archetype was Watts in August 1965, or Detroit in July 1967. This kind of disorder has tens of thousands of participants, thousands of arrests, major destruction of property, and often loss of life. It can last from several days to a week or more. It ordinarily requires the intervention of the National Guard or regular armed forces to restore order. The participants are ordinarily residents of the city with family ties there, young rather than middle-aged (often many are juveniles), employed, by and large, without records of prior serious crime, and predominantly male and black. The criminal acts committed are chiefly the looting of business establishments, curfew violation, some arson, and sometimes sniping or the possession of dangerous items like molotov cocktails. The disorders have so far been confined to inner-city ghetto areas inhabited by low-income black citizens.

A second kind of situation exists, however, which can also cause emergency conditions in the administration of justice. It is the mass political demonstration—the Pentagon March on Washington, D.C., in October 1967, the Century City demonstration in Los Angeles in June 1967, the Peace Parade in Chicago in April 1968, and the demonstration during the Poor People's Campaign in Washington, D.C., in June 1968. It may involve from hundreds to thousands of participants. The criminal acts that may be involved are confrontations with and alleged assault on police, "disorderly conduct," refusal or failure to disperse when ordered, and parading or demonstrating without a permit. The participants are usually young, white, and are often students from out of town. It has many variations—the campus sit-in (in which trespass may be charged) and various degrees of disorderliness. The emergency for the criminal justice system is much less acute than in the mass disorder. Usually, the charges levied are minor and susceptible to more rapid disposition, and the number of arrests are much smaller.

The administration of justice under conditions of both mass civil disorder and mass political demonstration becomes a formidable task, entailing as it does the process through which an individual goes from the time he is arrested by a police officer until final disposition of the prosecution by dismissal, by acquittal, or by conviction and sentence.

It falls into two major time periods—during the disorder, and afterwards: i.e., arrest and first court appearance (in-

575

cluding initial charging and bail); and indictment, trial and sentencing.

ARREST TO FIRST COURT APPEARANCE:
THE MASS CIVIL DISORDER

The mass civil disorder is characterized by a tremendous increase in the number of arrests and an overload of the resources available to process them expeditiously, humanely, and efficiently. In Newark, in July 1967, 1600 were arrested for riot offenses in 5 days;[2] in Baltimore, in April 1968, 5,500 were arrested in 7 days;[3] in Detroit, in July 1967, 7,800 were arrested in 6 days—the normal figure for 6 months.[4]

Usually in normal times, when a police officer makes an arrest "on the scene" or "on view" (the usual case during a disorder), he takes his prisoner to the police station, supervises the "booking" of the prisoner, and prepares a report of the facts of the offense while the prisoner's name and other identifying characteristics are being recorded. The officer accompanies the prisoner to court for his first appearance and testifies, then or later, to the identity of the prisoner and to the facts of the offense.

During a disorder, however, the officer is desperately needed on the street to aid in restoring order. Hence, without special arrangements, the police must choose between either sending arrestees to precincts or stations en masse and without the arresting officer, thus seriously jeopardizing the likelihood of successful prosecution, or following the usual procedure and losing for several hours the services of the officers on the street.

In Chicago[5] and in Washington, D.C.,[6] in the disorders of early April 1968, many officers failed to arrest offenders because they feared that to make an arrest would require them to leave the scene of disorder in order to carry out booking procedures. In both cities the Police Departments adopted the expedient of having a single officer sign and swear to complaints. In Chicago this became a defect leading to the dismissal of many cases; in Washington the court approved the procedure so long as the arresting officer would personally testify later.

In Chicago and in Baltimore, offenders arrested by National Guardsmen could not be prosecuted either because the arresting Guardsman failed to appear for later proceedings or because his identity was not known. The Chicago experience was not repeated in Washington where police officers accompanied every group of Guardsmen, and where anyone arrested by a Guardsman was held on the scene until a police officer arrived.

Almost uniformly, complaint and arrest forms were too long and cumbersome to fill out properly under the press of emergency; and the lack of facilities to photograph prisoners meant the failure of identification later.

In the various cities, police departments adopted different ad hoc procedures with varying success. In Detroit, Polaroid cameras were made available to photograph together the arrestee, the officer, and any evidence.[7] In Chicago, the State Attorney's Office had mimeographed thousands of standardized complaint forms, on which were quoted the probably relevant statutes from which the officer could designate the one applicable.[8] In Washington, D.C., the driver of the police wagon picking up arrestees and transporting them to the station took notes, describing which prisoner went with which officer and what evidence, if any. The arresting officer returned to the station after his tour of duty and attempted to sort out his arrestees.[9]

One precinct in Washington set up arrest teams with trucks. The team would sweep an area, and one of the team designated as an arresting officer, would do all the booking when the team returned with a full load; the other officers on the team could return to other duties.[10]

Lack of physical facilities needed to move and to house the large numbers of arrestees was a problem felt in all cities during disorders. Detention facilities were everywhere overcrowded, and sanitary problems were encountered.

The shortage of vehicles to transport prisoners from the scene of the arrest to the station required officers to wait for long periods with arrestees, in dangerous circumstances, until a van or wagon arrived. Sometimes prisoners were released when officers had to move on to the scene of another outbreak before the wagon arrived.

Normal procedures in most cities call for booking of arrestees and interim detention in local police stations or precinct buildings. Such buildings have no space for large numbers of arrestees. Cells, as a result, were vastly overcrowded. In Chicago, in April 1968, the problem was handled by having all arrestees taken to central police headquarters for booking; thus action was taken not only to speed the process, but also because of fear that local precincts might be attacked and prisoners freed. The plan was made feasible by

577

the ready availability of magistrates.[11] In Baltimore, where station houses include courtrooms, the courtrooms were used as detention space after court had closed.[12] In Washington, the cell block in the U.S. Court House was pressed into service as a central booking area.[13]

Station-house screening of arrestees by seriousness of offense and prior criminal record was virtually impossible. In Chicago, the use of police officers from all over the city meant that often they were unfamiliar with the neighborhood and unable to separate known "troublemakers" from responsible citizens.[14]

Lack of transport from precinct to court, and overcrowded detention facilities at court, were serious problems. Feeding prisoners, making sure that they were properly identified— many gave false names and then could not remember the name they had given when they were called out—and matching papers with prisoners were also serious problems in many cities.

ARREST TO FIRST COURT APPEARANCE: THE MASS POLITICAL DEMONSTRATION

Unlike the mass civil disorder, the volume of arrests during a political demonstration is rarely great enough to cause the same kind of problems. The Poor People's Campaign in Washington tested a newly devised multicopy arrest form and the use of Polaroid cameras. They worked fairly well.[15] But only 644 persons were arrested altogether, at Resurrection City, at the Capitol grounds—where the arrestees set out to be arrested and cooperated with the police—and for curfew violation that night.

In Chicago, the April 27 Peace March, with 6,500 participants, resulted in only 80 arrests.[16] During the week of the Democratic Convention in Chicago, 641 were arrested.[17] In Los Angeles, at the Century Plaza demonstration in which 15,000 participated, only 51 were arrested.[18]

ARREST TO FIRST COURT APPEARANCE: THE KERNER COMMISSION RECOMMENDATIONS

The Kerner Commission, the International Association of Chiefs of Police, the American Bar Association, and others have made recommendations for resolving some of the difficulties outlined above. In summary they are:

(1) Establishment of field booking facilities at the scene of the disorder, either in available buildings or as mobile booking stations in buses or similar vehicles. This involves having the necessary extra equipment on hand and available for immediate deployment.

(2) Setting up simplified procedures for booking, including the use of a simplified multicopy field arrest form. Such a form is in use by the Justice Department for mass political demonstrations. A variation was used with some success by the Washington, D.C., Police in the Poor People's Campaign Protest March in June 1968. The use of Polaroid cameras and of video tape recorders has been urged, as well as uniform bags or boxes for the retention of evidence.

(3) Advance provision for using commercial or even military vehicles to solve the shortage of transport.

(4) Advance planning for screening arrestees to determine those who (like curfew violators) may safely be released at the station house with a summons, those who will be allowed to post station-house bail or collateral, and those who will be held for appearance in court. Since the appropriate disposition will ordinarily depend on the charge, prosecutors would be needed at the station house.

Of the cities (over 40) that have experienced a major or medium disorder, only a few—like New York, Kansas City, Denver, Syracuse and Washington—have adopted any plan at all; and the Los Angeles and Philadelphia District Attorneys have issued instructions on free speech demonstrations.[19]

Since publication of the Kerner report, the nation has suffered more major disorders. Further delay by any city in planning for future emergencies only compounds the problem.

FIRST COURT APPEARANCE: THE MASS CIVIL DISORDER

In normal times, after an arrestee has been processed by booking, fingerprinting, photographing and the like, he is taken before a judge or magistrate. This initial appearance in court is called presentment or arraignment; to avoid confusion with later arraignment proceeding it is referred to here as "first court appearance." At this time the defendant is advised of the charge against him, of his right to employ counsel or to have counsel appointed to defend him, and of his right to remain silent. In some jurisdictions, counsel is appointed to represent him at the first appearance. Bail is set, and a date for the defendant's next appearance is designated.

Three major problems have been evident at this stage of the criminal process: first, the court must hold hearings without undue delay, and the prosecutor's office must prepare the necessary charging papers, despite a far greater number of defendants; second, the prosecutor must determine what charges to make against the defendants; third, the courts must decide what bail to set and what standards to apply in setting bail.

In the handling of court emergencies resulting from masses of arrests, the outstanding fact is the effort by all involved—judges, prosecutors, clerks, and defense attorneys—to work long hours, around the clock if necessary, to bring all defendants before a judge with the least delay. These efforts were hampered, however, by grossly inadequate physical facilities and the failure of coordination of various elements. Too often, the emphasis on speed resulted in failure to afford defendants their full measure of procedural rights. And, curiously, there is little difference in the performance of cities in emergencies before and after the publication of the Kerner Report on March 1, 1968.

The Recorder's Court in Detroit in July 1967 worked around the clock. Fifteen or twenty defendants appeared at a time. They were without counsel since Michigan does not provide appointed counsel at the first appearance, "arraignment on the warrant." The proceedings were rushed, and often advice to defendants of their rights was cursory at best. The court pleaded the need for haste to process the flood of defendants. Yet the judges of the Wayne County Circuit Court had volunteered themselves, their clerical personnel, and their buildings to help—and were refused.

The organized bar made little effort, at first, to provide counsel for defendants. Finally, the Dean of the Law School of the University of Detroit organized a group of volunteers—but the judges (with one notable exception) were opposed to allowing the volunteers to appear and represent defendants, fearing it would delay the processing.[20]

In Newark, in July 1967, defendants appeared one at a time, and were presented by counsel, usually volunteers. This caused no particular delay, for only "a few hours" elapsed between arrest and first appearance.[21]

The experiences of three cities, Chicago, Washington, D.C., and Baltimore, in disorders in April 1968, a month after publication of the Kerner Report, offer considerable contrast.

Chicago[22] had adopted a sketchy plan for dealing with masses of arrests. It provided that all persons arrested from 10 a.m. one day to 10 a.m. the next were to be "returnable" at 1 p.m. the second day. When the volume of arrests began to assume emergency proportions, the Chief Judge of the Cook County Circuit Court set up four courts at a central location (the same location where, as we have indicated, defendants were brought for centralized booking).

During the April 1968, disorder in Chicago, the Public Defenders Office, apparently overly confident of its ability to perform its duties even in the face of mass arrests, did not welcome volunteers, many of whom were turned away from the court. The Public Defender's Office staff was placed on shifts around the clock, and represented almost all defendants who appeared in court. However, the quality of representation suffered; rarely were defendants interviewed before their appearance, and, without interviews, the judges had inadequate information about the defendants. Moreover, as in almost all cities during emergencies, criminal records were not available.

In Washington,[23] considerable discussion had prevailed of how best to handle an emergency in the criminal justice system, but no plans had been made. On Friday morning, April 5, the problem of processing persons arrested in the disorders on Thursday evening, prompted the Chief Judge of the D.C. Court of General Sessions to call a meeting of the judges. The Chief Judge then set up a Special Arraignment Court; otherwise, the court would continue on a "business as usual" basis. This soon became impossible, and the court was put on around-the-clock operation. The judges cleared their regular calendars to make way for riot arrestees, and judges were assigned for evening and weekend duty.

Guidelines were developed for the handling of disorder cases, each case individually. The court would advise the defendant of the charge against him, warn him of his legal rights, appoint counsel for his defense, and make a bail determination. Immediate trials and preliminary hearings were found to be impractical because witnesses were difficult to find, and police officers, who would have to identify the person charged and testify at the hearing or trial, were needed on the street to restore order. Pleas and jury trial requests in misdemeanor cases were accepted, but virtually all trials and preliminary hearings were continued.

The typical hearing was conducted as follows:

(1) The clerk read the defendant's name from the lockup list.

(2) The judge appointed an attorney present in the courtroom (usually volunteer lawyers from firms with civil and federal practices) to represent the defendant at the hearing.

(3) The attorney was given the opportunity to confer with the defendant in the cell-block in the court's basement or outside the court room.

(4) When the conference was completed, the case would be called and the attorney and defendant would appear before the judge.

(5) If the charge was a misdemeanor, the attorney would plead "not guilty," request a jury trial, and have a date set for trial. In felony cases, the lawyer would request a preliminary hearing, which would be continued to a definite date.

Appeals for volunteer attorneys were broadcast on radio and television and spread by telephone and by word of mouth. Indeed, at many times during the disorders there were more attorneys than persons to defend.

Bottlenecks were encountered. The clerk's office and the prosecutor's office fell behind in the preparation of charging papers, and often papers could not be matched with prisoners.

Proceedings in Baltimore[24] in April were unique, in that trials were held during the disorder. Indeed, almost all the riot cases were tried immediately in a kind of summary proceeding.

Two court systems—the Municipal Court, which sits in various police station houses around the city, and the Supreme Bench of Baltimore City—operated almost around the clock. Trials "were conducted in the crowded, emotion-filled courtrooms ... with armed soldiers on guard, and in the midst of the sounds, sight, and smells of mass disorder,"[25] and chiefly at night, when witnesses could not be found. Vital information—like the police officer's arrest report—was missing.

Defendants were brought into court in groups of 50 to 100. Facilities for defense lawyers to interview defendants were greatly overcrowded; often the corridors and courtrooms were used, and attorneys interviewed defendants in the rear of the courtroom as trials proceeded in the front. Access to the courtrooms by friends, relatives, witnesses and bondsmen was seriously impeded. And there was no organization of volunteer attorneys.

Pressure forced both sides to proceed immediately to trial. Bail was set at $500 for curfew violation and $100 or more for larceny but because bondsmen were unavailable, most defendants went to jail. Most curfew defendants, therefore, agreed to a "stipulated" trial. Offenders charged with other offenses accepted immediate trial on reduced charges of curfew violation or disorderly conduct rather than remain in jail pending later trial.

FIRST COURT APPEARANCE:
THE MASS POLITICAL DEMONSTRATION

The Poor People's Campaign in Washington, D.C.,[26] resulted in 644 arrests. After expiration of the campaign's permit, 123 remained at Resurrection City and were arrested; 235 marched to the Capitol and were arrested there, and 286 noncampaigners were arrested in the city for disorderly conduct and curfew violation.

The D.C. Court of General Sessions, forearmed by its experience in April, stood ready to handle the flow. The Chief Judge offered to try all offenders immediately but the offer was declined by the campaign leadership. As a result, from 7:30 p.m. to the early morning hours, the campaigners were arraigned, bail was set (which none but a few of the leaders made), and the prisoners remanded for trial the next day.

At that time the campaign leadership advised the defendants to plead *nolo contender*. In the course of 2 days, all were sentenced, usually to terms of 5 to 20 days. Since many lawyers who had experienced the frustrations and delays of April declined to repeat the experience, it was difficult to get enough volunteer defense counsel.

No "papering" problems were experienced—the charges were simply either demonstrating without a permit, or unlawful assembly, and there were no problems of identity or evidence—primarily because the defendants had deliberately set out to be arrested and sentenced in order to publicize their cause.

Serious problems have arisen in other cities because of police and judicial hostility to demonstrators. In Chicago, in the April peace march, arrestees were forbidden to make telephone calls, their cameras were taken and the film exposed, and many were held, seemingly deliberately, for hours before they could post bond and be released.[27] The events in Chicago in August have been fully recounted in the Walker Report to this Commission.[28]

Also, other problems have persisted. Despite the anticipation of mass arrests in connection with the October 1967 demonstration at the Pentagon, the delay between arrest and first appearance was significant.[29] Courts, it seems, are never in any great rush to procees those who deliberately violate the law.

INITIAL CHARGING: THE MASS CIVIL DISORDER

The difficulties faced by prosecutors during emergencies come into sharp focus at the time that initial charges must be prepared ("papered") against the persons arrested. Two matters stand out: first, because police officers are needed on the street and arrest reports are sketchy, prosecutors are without the usual information needed to decide intelligently what charge to make; second, it is easier to lower a "high" charge (of felony, for example) than raise a "low" charge, and "high papering" sets high bail and keeps rioters from further disorder.

This procedure resulted in most cities in a very high proportion of felony charges against defendants arrested in the apparently typical disorder activity—looting retail stores and in accusations of "overcharging." It seems fair to say, however, that with "overcharging," the fault did not lie at the initial stage, but in failure of the prosecution to review and reduce charges at later stages of the criminal proceedings.

In Detroit[30] in July 1967, for example, 75 percent (3,230) of the 4,260) defendants brought before the Recorder's Court were charged with such felonies as "Entering Without Breaking With Intent to Commit Larceny." By the time of a meeting of the National Association of District Attorneys held in Chicago in February 1968,[31] the Detroit Prosecutor's Office had come to admit that this policy was a mistake. Of nearly 1,630 cases disposed of by that time, 961 had been dismissed altogether and 664 had been disposed of by a guilty plea to misdemeanors; only 2 of those accused had been tried and convicted of felonies.

The NADA meeting discussed not only the problems of Detroit, but those of Newark and Los Angeles (Watts). In Newark, 73 percent of the defendants had been charged with larceny, breaking and entering, or receiving stolen goods— "looting" offenses. In the Watts riot, 80 percent of all defendants were charged with felonies, nearly all with burglary; later, these charges were reduced in most cases.

The Prosecutor's Office in Chicago, apparently impressed with the problems noted at the NADA meeting, charged 1,300 defendants with misdemeanors and only 850 with felonies in the April 1968 disorders. The typical charge was burglary, even though Illinois has a looting statute. The prosecutors, it seems, felt that burglary would be easier to prove than looting, which requires a showing that the normal security of property is not present by virtue of a riot.

In Washington, D.C.,[32] which has no looting statute, the U.S. Attorney (who has authority over all but petty offenses) decided to charge all defendants caught "looting" with second-degree burglary for the purpose of the first court appearance. 85 percent of all defendants charged were charged with felonies. But after the riots had subsided and additional information could be gathered by the prosecution, it was expected that each case would be reviewed for possible change in the charges. Given the expectation of later review, the initial-charge policy made sense. In the absence of enough information from the police about the offense and about defendants' criminal records, "papering high" assured maximum flexibility for the prosecution in the subsequent disposition of the case. It allowed the prosecutor, when more information became available, to proceed with the felony charge, to "break down" to a misdemeanor or to drop the charge if evidence could not be produced.

Given such review, the initial charge would not matter too much. The objective was to get defendants processed promptly, even in the absence of the police officer. Yet, in Washington, D.C., and in other cities, the review process—where there was one—failed to perform its function.

INITIAL CHARGING:
THE MASS POLITICAL DEMONSTRATION

The typical political demonstration, even where mass arrests result, creates few "papering" problems. Likewise, there is usually little difficulty in picking the appropriate charge—in most cases disorderly conduct, refusal to move on or demonstrating without a permit. Often the offense, one for which the arrestee can post a small sum as collateral, and forfeit, avoids any further processing burden. The sum posted as collateral, frequently from $10 to $25, thus serves as the defendant's fine.

Frequently, however, the hostility demonstrated by police against political demonstrators has emerged in the form of overcharging. Demonstrators who have gone limp, for example, have been charged with "resisting arrest." Youths who have raised their hands to protect their heads from the blows of police batons have been charged with "assault on a police officer." Although these charges may eventually be dropped, the effect limits the opportunity of those arrested to regain their freedom and it presents a distorted statistical picture of the conduct of the demonstrators.

BAIL: THE MASS CIVIL DISORDER

The most important immediate decision made at the first court appearance is the setting of bail. In most cities (with the notable exception of Baltimore), further proceedings in civil disorder cases—preliminary hearings and trials—were postponed for days, weeks, and months. The conditions upon which the defendant could obtain his release pending trial became all-important to him, to his family and employer, and to the over-burdened facilities available for detention of prisoners pending trial.

The matter of bail has been the reef on which the courts and prosecutors in nearly every city faced with an emergency have foundered. In nearly every city the primary motivation of the courts in setting (and prosecutors in requesting) bail conditions has been to keep defendants arrested during a disorder locked up to prevent their return to the disorders.

In Detroit,[33] in July 1967, for instance, 74 percent of the bonds were higher than $5,000: "... the judicial policy during the early stages of the disorder was to set extremely high bail." The public prosecutor stated that his office would ask for bonds of $1,000 and up on all persons arrested "so that even though they had not been adjudged guilty, we would eliminate the danger of returning some of those who had caused the riot to the street during the time of stress."[34] One Detroit judge was quoted as saying: "We will, in matters of this kind, allocate an extraordinary bond. We must keep these people off the streets. We will keep them off." As one judge who dissented at the time from the policy later wrote, there was "a wholesale denial of the constitutional rights of everyone who was arrested during that disturbance."[35] He unequivocally ascribed the harsh procedures to race prejudice.

The policy—flatly one of prevention detention—was adopted at the insistence of the District Attorney, who later stated:

When it became clear on Sunday night that a full scale riot was in process, I publicly announced that I was recommend-

586

ing a $10,000 bond on all those arrested for looting. The courts generally followed that recommendation, and some criticism ensued in the form of statements to the effect that the riot was extraneous to the individual consideration of bond and to the point that it was considered by some to be excessively high. I felt then, and I still feel, that the court's response to my recommendation was justified.[36]

As a result of the policy, only 2%—compared with a usual 26–30 percent—of defendants were released on their own recognizance, even though most defendants had strong community ties, jobs, and no criminal record.[37] Unbelievably, some bonds were set as high as $200,000.

In the Los Angeles Watts[38] riots in August 1965, bond on rioters arrested was set at a minimum of $3,000, again at the instance of the District Attorney, who reported that he "took the position that to release a large number of these arrested persons on bail could result in their returning to the riot area and increasing the difficulty of control," and who indeed had attempted to persuade the court not to set bail at all.

In Newark[39] in July 1967, the courts set uniformly high bails: $2,500 for run-of-the-mill looters charged with breaking and entering, $500 for curfew violators, and $250 for those charged with "loitering." In Newark, however, as the disorders began to subside—and as the jails filled to overflowing—the Newark Legal Services Project urged the judges to begin reviewing bonds to release defendants on their own recognizance; hearings were held in the jails and neighborhood Legal Service Program personnel, volunteers, and law students interviewed defendants and checked their community ties. As a result, more than two-thirds of those held in jail on money bonds were later released on their own recognizance.

The pattern seems to have been followed around the country.[40] In Tampa and in Rockford, Ill., minor civil disorders caused unusually high bail to be set, and resulted in the preventive detention of alleged rioters. In New Haven in July 1967, release on recognizance at the precinct (provided by Connecticut law was "suspended" pursuant to an informal argeement between the Bail Office and the Chief of Police; but as the jails became overcrowded, the policy was reversed. In court, the judges began by setting unusually high bonds; and as it began to appear that the bondsmen were refusing to write bonds for rioters at all, the court adopted a general policy of release on recognizance. Thus, most arrestees (estimated at 80 percent) spent no more than a night or a day and a night in jail. Moreover, out of 550 riot arrestees, apparently no more than one or two were arrested a second time.

As the Kerner Commission noted, "No attempt was made in most cases to individualize the bail-setting process."[41] The Commission strongly recommended efforts to individualize bail setting, to get more background information on defendants and to ensure that defendants had counsel when bail was set. While equivocating on the issue of preventive detention *vel non,* the Commission urged the use of conditions short of incarceration, like third party custody and daily reporting to a police station, to ensure nonparticipation in further rioting.

Despite these recommendations, however, little changed. In Baltimore[42] in April 1968, for example, the study of the administration of justice in the wake of the disorder commented:

> Very few defendants were released on their own recognizance, and rarely was there time or inclination on the part of the judges to hear a defense plea for a bail geared to the circumstances of the individual defendant.[43]

Bail was set at $500 for curfew violation, and at correspondingly higher figures for other charges.

The policy operated to detain defendants in jail—which, the Baltimore study suggests, was the judges' intent. Bondsmen were largely unavailable, and the curfew kept friends and relatives from reaching defendants. As a result, only 99 out of 345 curfew defendants not tried immediately obtained release on bail. Many others (the estimate is as high as 3,000), as we have seen, were pressed by their inability to obtain pretrial release into immediate, "stipulated" trials.

In Chicago[44] in April 1968, normal bail rules were similarly suspended. As in New Haven, the usual stationhouse bail procedures were ignored; all defendants were held until they appeared before a magistrate. Money bond was set in nearly every case, ranging from $1,000 for disorderly conduct to $5,000 as the minimum for a looting charge. Some bonds were set as high as $100,000. In 82 percent of misdemeanor cases bond was set at over $1,000. There "was little individual variation in the setting of bonds . . . the magistrates [were unwilling] to allow a rioter to be free, under a nominal bond, to return to the scene of the riots."[45]

Apparently not until a *mandamus* action was filed and the Cook County (the black) Bar Association put pressure on the Chief Judge of the Circuit Court of Cook County did the court begin—on April 14, ten days after the disorders began and over a week after they were over—to hold bond review hearings.[46] This resulted in reduction of bonds in 84 percent of the 481 cases reviewed.

According to figures compiled by the University of Chicago Law Review,[47] out of 2,200 defendants who appeared in court, 870 spent at least 3 days in jail, 400 spent at least a week in jail, and 60 were still in jail on June 12, 2 months after the disorders.

A policy of allowing defendants to post 10 percent cash, rather than a surety bond, was uniformly followed—but even those few defendants who could post 10 percent of the high bonds, could not do so at court but had to post cash at the jail after their remand to custody.

Some judges later admitted frankly that they set bonds at this level for the purpose of detaining suspected rioters. In Chicago, too, the prosecutor's recommendation was significant, and the high bail policy was in part the result of—

the kind of political pressures under which the judiciary was operating. On Saturday night, April. 6, an assistant public defender was in the midst of a bond hearing when the Corporation Counsel, Richard Elrod, came up to the judge and told him that no bonds were to be set below $1,000, whereas previously some variation in the bonds had been evident and some individual consideration given.[48]

The harshness of the judges in Chicago should not have been surprising. Around 250 persons had been arrested on charges of looting during a snowstorm in January 1967. Average bail set was $14,000, compared with a normal range of $1,500–$3,000. Defendants were unrepresented by counsel. Continuances of about 3 weeks—meaning 3 weeks of pretrial jail—were uniformly granted at the request of the prosecution. When preliminary hearings were finally held, bail was reduced to $250–$1,500 and most defendants posted bond and were released. Judges and prosecutors admitted that the purpose of high bail was to teach the accused looters a "lesson."[49]

In Washington, D.C., in April, 1968,[50] the question of

setting bail conditions intended to guarantee nonreturn to the scene of the disorder was clearly articulated, and an expressly defined policy adopted. While this occurred in other cities too, the matter was etched in sharp relief for Washington by the Bail Reform Act of 1966, an act of Congress in force in Washington since 1967. The act provides that the preferred release condition is not money bail but release on personal recognizance. The judge at the defendant's first appearance should look into the defendant's community roots, as revealed by information supplied by the D.C. Bail Agency, and if his family and local ties, employment, prior record and the nature of the offense indicate that he is a good risk to return for trial, he should be released on his own recognizance. The judge can impose a number of other conditions should he decide that personal recognizance alone is not sufficient; but the least favored of these is a money bond.

As the disorders waxed in the city on Friday, April 5, defendants began to appear in court. The U.S. Attorney, the chief prosecutor of all but petty offenses in Washington, advised the judges, first privately and then in open court, that unless a reliable third party would undertake to ensure the defendant's nonreturn to the disorders, money bond should be set. This policy was adopted, and for the next 2 or 3 days many of the judges uniformly set money bond—$1,000 for the looting felony, second-degree burglary, and $500 for misdemeanors—where no third party could be produced.

While the money amounts set were modest, they nevertheless effectively detained defendants—75 percent of those for whom money bond was set went to jail. Either they could not raise the bond premium, or they could not find a bondsman—the white bondsmen, sympathizing with the looted merchants, apparently engaged in a private policy of preventive detention.

The Court of General Sessions did, however, set up prompt machinery for bond review, and, one way or another, half of the defendants remanded to jail had obtained release after less than 3 days.

In attempting to evaluate the need for and the utility of a policy of preventive detention, even one in the modified form adopted in Washington, some facts stand out:

(1) Of a total "riot population" of 20,000, less than 7,000 were arrested, and less than 2,000 were taken to court. The court's opportunity to prevent a rioter from rioting a second time, therefore, was less than one in ten.

(2) Only 21 persons arrested for a relatively serious offense during the period of maximum disorder were re-arrested.

(3) Very few persons were charged with offenses beyond ordinary looting—arsonists, breakers, instigators, or wielders of molotov cocktails, for example.

(4) Judges varied in the quality of their treatment. Interestingly, the widest disparity in bail orders came from two judges who sat at the same time, Sunday night, April 7. One held every one of the individuals who appeared before him to money bond; the other released 90 percent of those before him on personal recognizance or in the custody of a third party.

(5) Nevertheless, compared with the results in Detroit and Chicago, for example, Washington was a model of restraint. Even on Saturday, April 6, at the height of activity, some 32 percent of the defendants who appeared in court were released on personal recognizance or in third-party custody. Overall, from April 5 through April 10, 43 percent of the defendants were so released.

BAIL: THE MASS POLITICAL DEMONSTRATION

What is the bail for political demonstrators? The offenses charged tend to be petty, indicating a low bond or personal recognizance; but demonstrators often come from out of town, posing the danger of flight. Trials can usually be held quickly, however. The procedure usually followed in Washington, D.C., seems exemplary: it allows demonstrators to post a small sum—$10 to $25—as collateral at the police station in order to obtain immediate release.

FIRST COURT APPEARANCE
(INCLUDING CHARGING
AND BAIL): RECOMMENDATIONS

The clogging of the courts by the flood of persons arrested in civil disorders indicates not only the inability of the system to cope with an abnormal load, but the antiquity and clumsiness of a system that clogs unnecessarily even in normal times. A major overhaul is long overdue, one that will replace breaking judicial machinery with modern data processing and retrieval techniques.

Pending such a revolution, much can be done to plan for emergency volume. Detention facilities should be set up near the courts; if this is not possible, first appearances should be held in appropriate facilities near where arrestees are detained.

Emergency facilities and personnel are needed to ensure an unimpeded flow of papers, especially charging papers and prior criminal record information. Municipal clerical employees not needed elsewhere can be detailed to the Police Department and prosecutor's offices, with typewriters, to assist; and a kind of "reserve" of former prosecutors can be set up, if more prosecutors are needed to speed "papering."

The right to counsel is all-important, even more important during an emergency than in normal times, because for many people it is their first experience of the criminal justice system. Failure to treat them fairly—to visibly treat them fairly—may, as the Kerner Commission pointed out, exacerbate the hostility that is itself a cause of outbreaks of disorder.

To the credit of the bar, everywhere in emergencies, lawyers volunteered to defend arrestees without expecting any recompense. Moreover, the lawyers should be given every opportunity to interview defendants and to investigate and verify the information which defendants give them.

As for bail, whatever else may be said about detaining rioters in jail until order is restored, the use of abnormally high money bonds, either openly or in disguise in order to effect detention, is an injustice. Indeed, given the lack of earlier criminal history (which bondsmen look for) and the relative indigence of riot defendants—not to mention the usual absence of bondsmen during disorders—setting money bond becomes even more unfair during emergencies than in normal times.

No evidence exists from any of the cities to show that the detention of arrestees made any significant contribution to the restoration of order; as a matter of fact, study of the policy of modified preventive detention in Washington, D.C., in April 1968 indicates that the wrongs of such a policy outweigh its benefits.

The need for at least two improvements is primary: first as noted, the establishment of facilities for the gathering of information that will permit an intelligent decision on whether or not to release the defendant on recognizance; second, reliance on non-money conditions like third party custody, as the primary measure to ensure return to trial and—if there be any justification for this fear—ensure non-return to the riot.

AFTER THE EMERGENCY:
THE DISPOSITION OF THE PROSECUTIONS[51]

After a disorder has subsided and public attention focuses on other matters, the prosecutor's office and the courts must cope with the additional load of cases that began with arrests during the period of emergency. By then, time does not pressure to dispose of the cases; the level of the charge, the reduction of the charge, when to seek trial, when to allow pleas, and, finally, sentencing—these can be reflected upon before rendering decisions.

The Kerner Commission, in its recommendations respecting the ultimate disposition of riot cases, urged the postponement of the important steps (preliminary hearing, plea bargaining, trial, and sentence) until after the restoration of order, the cooling of passions, and the quick dispositions of petty offenders. Except in isolated instances, like Baltimore, postponement has, of necessity, been the rule and the contrary problem, delay, has been serious.

To illustrate, in Detroit, in July of 1967,[52] 75 percent of all defendants were charged with felonies. As of April 30, 1968, out of 3,230 felony cases, 1,198 had been dismissed, 1,211 had pleaded guilty to lesser offenses, and 480 awaited trial. The rest were fugitives. Of only 17 tried, 9 were convicted and 8 acquitted.

Faced with "heavy evidentiary burdens" and "cluttered trial dockets" in felony cases, the prosecutors in Detroit pressed for guilty pleas in exchange for reduction of the charge—the old practice of plea bargaining, but carried on wholesale.

The Michigan Law Review study[53] indicates that the plea bargaining was not bargaining as such, but a "take it or leave it" offer based only on whether the defendant had a prior criminal record. Guilty pleas were encouraged by a policy of the court of sentencing those who pleaded guilty to time already served. Available statistics show that of 666 defendants who were sentenced, all but 22 were sentenced to no additional time in jail; and of the 22, only 10 were sentenced to more than 90 days.

In Newark,[54] out of 1,600 arrests (of which apparently only around 1,300 went to court) 807 cases were sent to the Grand Jury, which returned indictments against 567 and referred 208 back for trial on misdemeanors. By December, half of the misdemeanor cases had been disposed of, a little more than 50 percent convicted after trial, the remainder (except for a few acquittals) on a plea of guilty. The rate of convictions in misdemeanor cases was only slightly lower.

In Tampa, out of 77 arrests for disorder-related offenses, 45 were charged with felonies; trial delays were minor and most cases were tried within three months. In New Haven, in contrast to most cities, 75 percent of the 550 persons arrested in the July disorders were charged with misdemeanors, usually multiple charges. This practice led to wholesale plea bargaining, with the prosecutor usually agreeing to drop all other charges if the defendant would plead guilty to curfew violation, which carried a penalty of a $25 fine. As a result, all misdemeanor cases had been disposed of by November, but felony cases were just beginning to be heard. The prosecutor also was agreeing to drop felony charges for a guilty plea to a misdemeanor; the typical sentence in such a case was one year, with all but 60 days suspended.[55]

The experience of Detroit influenced the prosecution policy in Chicago in April 1968;[56] 60 percent of the civil disorder defendants were charged initially with misdemeanors, but unlike Detroit, no felony cases were voluntarily dismissed and all were prosecuted as felonies without reduction. Of 850 felony defendants, 721 were indicted, most going directly to the Grand Jury; 71 percent were adjudged guilty, the majority on pleas of guilty. Sentences were light—only 19 percent to any time in prison. The high incidence of pleas was in part the result of the harsh bail policy. The original bonds remained generally in effect until the date set for preliminary hearing, with prosecution policy to continue again and again so that original indictments could be sought. Defendants who could not make bond were thus increasingly pressed to plead guilty.

As noted, in Washington in April 1968,[57] most defendants were charged initially with felonies, with a review of charges anticipated. For this review, the U.S. Attorney established a set of guidelines for the four experienced assistants who, under the supervision of senior assistants, were designated to review all felony cases before preliminary hearing in the Court of General Sessions. Depending on the facts of the offense and whether or not the defendant had a prior criminal record, the guidelines provided for no reduction, for reduction to misdemeanor charges only in exchange for a plea of guilty to the reduced charge, or for automatic reduction to misdemeanor charges.

A large number of felony cases were completely dropped

594

for lack of evidence. About two-thirds of the rest fell into guideline categories in which a plea of guilty was demanded. Most of these defendants (or their lawyers) refused at that stage to plead guilty in exchange for reduction of the charge. Their cases, therefore, were sent to the Grand Jury for indictment and trial.

The Grand Jury returned indictments against 510 defendants, 473 for Burglary II, the standard riot charge for accused looters. As of January 1, 1969, nearly two-thirds of these cases were still pending. On the other hand, 90 percent of all original misdemeanor cases had been disposed of by the end of August. Of the felony cases acted upon, about 25 percent were dismissed or acquitted, about 17 percent were found guilty or pleaded guilty to a felony, and the rest either pleaded or were found guilty of only a misdemeanor. The sentences for felony and misdemeanor defendants ran about the same; in both categories about 80 percent of the defendants were sentenced to no time in prison.

Considering that most of the indictees were ordinary looters, that few (of those disposed of) have been convicted of felonies in the District Court, that most have received suspended sentences, that the riot cases have added considerably to the backlog and trial delay in the District Court where serious offenses are tried, and that these cases would doubtless have been tried more quickly in the Court of General Sessions—considering all these factors, too many felony indictments were sought and obtained. The main factor in this was the insistence by the U.S. Attorney's Office on a plea of guilty before reduction to misdemeanor charges in the Court of General Sessions. But other factors also applied: failure to reduce charges automatically in some of the small number of cases that fell in that category, and absence of a sufficiently varied arsenal of statutes for charging riot related offenses.

THE DISPOSITION OF THE PROSECUTIONS: RECOMMENDATIONS

Several factors stand out in the prosecution of riot cases: the seemingly high initial charge; the large percentage of dismissals and later reductions; the eagerness of the prosecution to "bargain" for guilty pleas; the delay in disposition of felony cases, and, ultimately, the light sentences. Judge Crockett of the Detroit Recorder's Court has commented:

Black citizens of Detroit find it difficult to understand a system of criminal justice that charges 3,230 persons with felonies and then, after imprisonment for days and the payment of thousands of dollars in attorney fees, disposes of the first 1,630 of these felonies with 961 dismissals, 664 pleas to misdemeanors (trespass, petty larceny, and curfew violations) and only two convictions after trial on the original charge![58]

Clearly, prosecutors should consider the effect of their policies on the community's view of the criminal justice system. Immediately after the restoration of order, the prosecutor's office should begin a comprehensive review of all cases based on all the evidence and on the defendant's prior record and personal situation—*before* conferences with defense lawyers or attempts at plea bargaining. This review should try to reduce all felony charges except those against defendants whom the evidence reveals as actual breakers, inciters, instigators, or those with fresh records of serious crime. These latter cases should be vigorously prosecuted, and no plea bargain offered or accepted, in order to make an example of them.

The run of the mill, however, should be reduced to appropriate misdemeanor charges, and only then should an effort be made to obtain guilty pleas. The price of such a policy would undoubtedly be more misdemeanor trials, but the counterbalance would be fewer felony trials.

CONCLUSION

Criminal justice machinery in our cities during and in the wake of civil disorders and other emergency situations has failed to successfully deal with the physical and mechanical problems of handling the increased flow of arrestees and defendants. The standards of justice in the initial stages of criminal prosecutions, low in normal times, went still lower in emergencies, especially in the critical matters of bail and provision of counsel.

Only rarely and then only in more recent instances of disorder, have police departments, courts and prosecutor's offices attempted to learn from the mistakes of their counterparts in other cities or even from their own earlier experiences. Only in a few instances have they made efforts to think out and plan in advance for future emergencies; and those few efforts were inadequate.

When the emergency has struck, it is too late to plan. The

596

kinds of problems encountered are familiar and common to emergencies everywhere. The tensions that cause civil disorders and other disturbances still remain. Other long, and possibly hot, summers may come again. The police, the courts, prosecutors offices, defense bar, and others in the criminal justice process must meet to consider the problems in future emergencies and to plan how to meet them, now.

REFERENCES

1. National Advisory Commission on Civil Disorders, *Report* (Washington, D.C.: Government Printing Office, 1968), ch. 13.
2. Governor's Select Committee on Civil Disorders, State of New Jersey, *Report for Action* (1968).
3. Baltimore Committee on the Administration of Justice Under Emergency Conditions, *Report* (1968).
4. Locke, "Riot Response: The Police and the Courts," 45 *J. Urban L.* 805 (1968).
5. *U. Chi. L. Rev.*, "Note on the Administration of Justice during the Civil Disorders of April, 1968." A preliminary, prepublication draft of the Note was made available to the Task Force and is the source of this information.
6. D.C. Committee on the Administration of Justice Under Emergency Conditions, *Interim Report* (1968).
7. William L. Cahalan, *The Detroit Riot* (mimeograph, undated).
8. *U. Chi. L. Rev., supra* note 5.
9. D.C. Committee, *supra* note 6.
10. *Id.*
11. *U. Chi. L. Rev., supra* note 5.
12. Baltimore Committee, *supra* note 3.
13. D.C. Committee, *supra* note 6.
14. *U. Chi. L. Rev., supra* note 5.
15. D.C. Committee on the Administration of Justice Under Emergency Conditions, *Second Supplemental Report; Operation of the District of Columbia Criminal Justice System Following the Mass Arrests on June 24–25, 1968.*
16. April 27 Investigating Commission, *Dissent and Disorder; A Report to the Citizens of Chicago on the April 27 Peace Parade (1968).*
17. Raymond F. Simon, Corporation Counsel, City of Chicago, *The Strategy of Confrontation; Chicago and the Democratic National Convention—1968* (Chicago: Gunthorp Warren Printing Co., 1968) at 41.
18. American Civil Liberties Union, *Day of Protest, Night of Violence; the Century City Peace March* (1967).
19. Evelle J. Younger, *Civil Disturbance Manual for Law Enforcement* (1967); Arlen Spector, *Rights and Limitations on Speech and Assembly* (undated).

20. Comment, "The Administration of Justice in the Wake of the Detroit Civil Disorder of July 1967," 66 *Mich. L. Rev.* 1954 (1968).

21. *Report for Action, supra* note 2.

22. *U. Chi. L. Rev., supra* note 5; Chicago Riot Study Committee, *Report to the Mayor* (1968).

23. William A. Dobrovir, *Justice in Time of Crisis; The Administration of Justice in the District of Columbia During the Civil Disorders of April 1968 and in the Riot-Related Prosecutions* (1969).

24. Baltimore Committee, *supra* note 3.

25. *Id.*

26. D.C. Committee, *Second Supplemental Report, supra* note 15.

27. April 27 Investigating Commission, *supra* note 16.

28. National Commission on the Causes and Prevention of Violence, Report by Daniel Walker, *Rights in Conflict* (New York: Bantam Books, 1968).

29. See Norman Mailer's *Armies of the Night* (1968).

30. Crockett, "Recorder's Court and the 1967 Civil Disturbance," 45 *J. Urban L.* 841 (1968).

31. *U. Chi. L. Rev., supra* note 5.

32. Dobrovir, *supra* note 23.

33. Comment, *supra* note 20.

34. National Advisory Commission on Civil Disorders, ch. 13, *supra* note 1.

35. Crockett, *supra* note 30.

36. Cahalan, *supra* note 7.

37. Colista and Domonkos, "Bail and Civil Disorder," 45 *J. Urban L.* 815 (1968).

38. Evelle J. Younger, *Report to the Governor's Commission on the Los Angeles Riots* (1965).

39. Background report for the Kerner Commission; in the National Archives of the United States.

40. *Id.*, see also Bean, "Plainfield: A Study in Law and Violence," 6 *Am. Crim. L.Q.* 154 (1968).

41. Comment, *supra* note 20.

42. Baltimore Committee, *supra* note 3.

43. *Id.*

44. *U. Chi. L. Rev., supra* note 5.

45. *Id.*

46. Chicago Riot Study Committee, *supra* note 22.

47. *U. Chi. L. Rev., supra* note 5.

48. Platt, *The Administration of Justice in Crisis: Chicago, April 1968* (1968).

49. Illinois Special Legal Project (the Roger Baldwin Foundation of the American Civil Liberties Union), *Preliminary Report and Evaluation on the Bail Procedures in Chicago's Looting Cases—Winter 1967* (1967).

50. Dobrovir, *supra* note 23.

51. We may eliminate altogether here the political demonstration; as we have seen, the nature of the usual charges in such situations leads ordinarily to prompt disposition and minimal sentences. The mass civil disorder, on the other hand, leaves major problems in its wake.

52. U.S., Congress, Senate, Committee on Government Operations, *Riots, Civil and Criminal Disorders, Hearings,* before the Permanent Subcommittee on Investigations, on S. Res. 216, 90th Cong., 2d sess., 1968, pts. V and VII.

53. Comment, *supra* note 20.

54. Report for Action, *supra* note 2.

55. Bean, *supra* note 40.

56. *U. Chi. L. Rev., supra* note 5.

57. Dobrovir, *supra* note 23.

58. Crockett, *supra* note 30.

CHAPTER 23

THE PROBLEM OF "OVERCRIMINALIZATION"*

[W]e stand at the moment in a fundamentally paradoxical condition: The United States in 1969 is probably a more permissive society than at any other time in its history; the United States in 1969 also possesses a larger arsenal of criminal laws and more elaborate law-enforcement machinery than at any other time in its history.[1]

Increasingly in recent years legal scholars have drawn attention to our society's failure to discriminate between appropriate and inappropriate uses of the criminal sanction. According to Herbert L. Packer, one of America's leading students of the criminal law, this failure mars even the monumental work of the President's Commission on Law Enforcement and Administration of Justice: the report of that Commission did not recognize that one major source of crime in the United States is "overcriminalization."[2]

Overcriminalization—the misuse of the criminal sanction—can contribute to disrespect for law, and can damage the ends which law is supposed to serve, by criminalizing conduct regarded as legitimate by substantial segments of the society, by initiating patterns of discriminatory enforcement, and by draining resources away from the effort to control more serious misconduct. Examples of statutes which raise problems of "overcriminalization" are those laws dealing with morals, like sexual conduct and gambling; with illness, like drunkenness and narcotics possession by addicts; and with nuisance, like disorderly conduct, objectionable language, and vagrancy.[3]

The common characteristic of these kinds of conduct is that either there is no "victim" in the usual sense of the word, because the participants in the offense are willing; or the defendant himself is the "victim"; or the interest of the victim is often so insubstantial that it does not justify imposi-

---

* This chapter is based on a paper by William A. Dobrovir of the District of Columbia Bar.

tion of the criminal sanction to protect it. Therefore, one of the essential reasons for imposing criminal penalties—to deter conduct that is clearly and significantly harmful to the persons or property of others—is lacking.

THREE CATEGORIES OF "OVERCRIMINALIZATION"[4]

Morals statutes are of several types. In most U.S. jurisdictions, any sexual activity except "normal" sexual intercourse between married partners is a crime. Probably no laws are broken more often. Indeed, if all violators were prosecuted and punished, a majority of the adult population of the United States would be in prison. Such statutes thus become organized hypocrisy on a national scale. They punish a "fornication" between consenting unmarried adults, homosexuality, adultery, and all kinds of "abnormal" sexual conduct even between married persons.

Such laws satisfy public conscience by announcement of strict judgments and public condemnation of "immoral" and "irreligious" behavior, which we, as human beings subject to temptation, regrettably deviate from in private. As Thurman Arnold has written in a much-quoted passage:

> Most unenforced criminal laws survive in order to satisfy moral objections to established modes of conduct. They are unenforced because we want to continue our conduct, and unrepealed because we want to preserve our morals.[5]

Increasingly, however, morals have changed for more and more people, especially for younger people, and the standards embodied in these laws are publicly dissented from by an ever larger segment of society. The general failure to enforce these laws is probably the only factor preventing an immediate vocal demand for their repeal.

Akin to the sexual conduct statutes, but with a higher degree of justification, are the morals laws punishing the sale and purchase of prostitutes' services, large-scale gambling, and abortion. These acts have a commercial character and hence a higher degree of repugnance to majority values. Pandering for profit to man's weaknesses seems more abhorrent than mere yielding to temptation. It is also true that these offenses carry other harms in their wake. Thus prostitution, as conducted by streetwalkers and their panderers, often results in making the prospective customer the victim of the "Murphy game" and other fraudulent practices. Prostitution also can spread venereal disease and give offense to respectable persons in neighborhoods frequented by streetwalkers openly purveying their services.

Illness statutes, such as the laws punishing intoxication and possession (as distinguished from sale) of addictive drugs, comprise a second category. The interest of society in preventing these evils and in protecting the offender from himself is much stronger than in the case of the morals statutes. Arrest of alcoholics gets them off the streets where they may come to harm while helplessly intoxicated; in winter it is a charity to provide the often homeless drunk with warmth, shelter, and a meal in jail. Arrest stops the alcoholic from presenting a public spectacle offensive to the sober, particularly when the alcoholic engages in aggressive efforts to obtain handouts from unescorted women and other passersby. A short jail term keeps him away from the bottle for that period of time and offers, some believe, at least a faint hope of reform.

The narcotics addict is a more serious problem, for his personal destruction is more complete. The correctional system in which he is placed by arrest, prosecution and punishment, recognizes an obligation (albeit ill-fulfilled) to provide rehabilitation. Moreover, the addict, in order to support his habit, often is driven to commit property-related crimes, and his isolation by punishment protects society against them.

Punishment of the possession and sale of non-addictive drugs like marihuana falls somewhere between the morals laws and the illness laws like those dealing with alcoholics and addicts. The use of marihuana is especially popular among the young, although many fear that they may be at least psychologically harmed by frequent use. Moreover, marihuana has become something of a symbol of rebellion against the established order and its two-martini business lunches, and the established order thus finds it particularly difficult to take the step of bringing marihuana-smoking within the pale of legality.

The *nuisance statutes* are the last category of statutes generally considered under the heading of "overcriminalization." These typically penalize disorderly conduct and vagrancy.

Disorderly conduct statutes deal with such matters as "affrays"; with gatherings in public that are "loud and boisterous"; with swearing or profanity in public; with ball games in the street; with indecent proposals; with flying kites; with generally causing a disturbance; and with failure to move on when ordered by a police officer.[6] Related to these areas, but also closely related to the morals laws, are laws punishing the sale or possession of pornographic literature, films, and the like.[7] "Vagrancy" includes the offenses of "leading an immoral or profligate life" without a "lawful means of support"; of frequenting "houses of ill fame" or of "loitering" in gambling establishments, in unlicensed saloons or in places where narcotics are found; and of begging, and "common law vagrancy."[8]

Such laws can serve a clear community interest. They can protect community tranquility and prevent annoyance of the more quiet citizens by the pugnacious, the shiftless, the noisy, and the foulmouthed. The police use such statutes as weapons against prostitutes, gamblers, and others whose apprehension is difficult because of problems of proof, and as legal underpinning for their general peacekeeping and order-maintaining responsibilities.

THE COSTS OF OVERCRIMINALIZATION

Most of the conduct prohibited by the morals, illness and nuisance statutes cited above, is, in some degree, blameworthy or otherwise undesirable. But this observation provides only the beginning of an answer to the question we are concerned with, namely, whether such conduct ought to be prohibited by criminal statute. A single-factor analysis is inadequate. The criminal sanction finds its optimal use only where a number of different kinds of conditions are satisfied. In Packer's calculus, for example, the conditions for optimal use of the criminal sanction include the following:

(1) The conduct in question is prominent in most people's view of socially threatening behavior, and is not condoned by any significant segment of society.
(2) Subjecting it to the criminal sanction is not inconsistent with the goals of punishment.
(3) Suppressing it will not inhibit socially desirable conduct.
(4) The conduct may be dealt with through evenhanded and non-discriminatory enforcement.
(5) Controlling it through the criminal process will not expose that process to severe qualitative or quantitative strains.
(6) There are no reasonable alternatives to the criminal sanction for dealing with it.[9]

603

Application of these criteria to the morals and nuisance statutes raises a number of additional questions concerning the propriety of these laws. Thus laws like those against consensual fornication that are rarely if ever enforced are seen to be prohibitions that are not seriously intended to be generally and even handedly enforced. In those rare instances where enforcement is sought, the penalties become a discriminatory club against the unwary.

Those morals laws that are more frequently enforced, like those against homosexuality, have even worse consequences. To make the typical morals squad arrest, a police officer in plain clothes will, in order to elicit in advance, loiter in places like public lavatories that homosexuals are thought to frequent. Such conduct must have a degrading effect on the police officer. Also he has difficulty in making a "good pinch"[10] in such cases and in enforcing the laws against prostitution: if the officer makes the advance, it is "entrapment," which renders a conviction invalid.

Enforcement of laws against crimes without victims also requires the use of a network of informers, who in turn must be compensated; since they themselves are often criminals, the compensation is usually leniency of treatment.[11] Sometimes vice, morals or gambling squads impose arrest "quotas" on officers; often the difficulty in making these cases stick, encourages officers to embellish, if not fabricate, incriminating facts.[12]

Perhaps, also, the evils of prostitution, gambling, and narcotics result more from their illegality than from their inherent harmfulness. Illegality often results in risk for both the seller and the buyer, as in the "Murphy game," in which he who fears exposure becomes the prey, and he who engages in robbery or auto burglary becomes the hunter. And, tragically, it can result in deaths—as from illegal abortions clumsily performed in unclean conditions. The transmission of venereal disease by prostitutes who, if not criminals, would normally (or if licensed could be required to) protect their and their customers' health by periodic medical examinations, is another example. Cheating in illegal gambling, with no lawful redress for the cheated, is a third. The high cost of narcotics because of illegality means that addicts need from $20 to $100 *per day* to support their habit. The only sources of such funds become other crimes not only prostitution, but violent crimes like burglary, robbery, auto theft, and purse snatching.[13]

The industries of prostitution, gambling, and narcotics require (prostitution to a smaller degree) an organization. The numbers writer and runner is financed by an operator with greater resources who, in turn, must have sources of funds to pay off bets. Narcotics require an immense distribution network. Prostitutes need agents to solicit the diffident and places in which to render their services. Since involvement in any of these activities is unlawful, they are performed and supervised by what is by definition organized crime.

Organized crime as we know it had its birth during prohibition, providing precisely the same kinds of illegal services through a complex industry. Primarily because of the illegality of providing these goods and services, the profits are enormous. To protect these profits, organized crime does not shrink from bribery of public officials and police officers, from coercion, and even from murder.[14]

The moral question cuts more than one way. The need to use the law to enforce a moral code held (even if it were observed in practice) by considerably less than the entire population raises a question of the strength of the moral imperative behind that code. Punishment of the drunk and the narcotics addict for conduct recognized to be a disease, erodes the very foundation of the criminal law, which holds that conduct must be blameworthy in order to deserve punishment.[15] The law degrades its nobility and weakens its moral authority when it punishes as a crime that which is really only an illness.

The laws against disorderly conduct and vagrancy spring from a different set of middle class standards: the quiet, tree-lined street of "Our Town" on a sunny Sunday afternoon in spring. They are enforced, however, in the teeming urban ghetto where life styles—by choice and by necessity—are different. In the heat of summer, people who live in stifling tenements will gather in the public street, to laugh and sing, to talk loud and use profanity. Youngsters with no parks or playgrounds nearby will play ball in the streets. And city living is by nature public and gregarious; indeed, this is its joy.

Police officers, however, live by the middle class standards that disorderly conduct laws articulate. Enforcement of the suburban or small town life style by arrests for this kind of conduct or by the catchall "move on" order may seriously exacerbate police-community tensions.[16] A "move on" order or arrest for, say, noisiness, can provoke objection from the citizen who feels he is doing nothing wrong, and it can lead to "fighting words" and the escalation of conflict.[17]

The resources devoted to enforcement of laws against immorality, intoxication, narcotics possession and disorderly conduct cannot easily be measured. Arrests for drunkenness, for instance, make up a large percentage of all arrests,[18] but they do not absorb a great deal of patrol time; yet using precincts and jails to house drunks does make space unavailable for other purposes. Time devoted to harassing patrols of prostitution and to undercover work against homosexuals, narcotics addicts and gambling, probably takes a lot of patrol and detective time. Moreover, when arrests are made, the time of officers in court, and of judges and court personnel and prosecutors, will be taken from other, perhaps more important, matters; then conviction means taking the time of probation personnel and of the already grossly inadequate resources of the correctional system. The result may be assembly-line justice—or worse—for all concerned.

The anomalies and difficulties arising from criminalization of these kinds of conduct implicitly suggest their own solutions, but how can such solutions be implemented, and how can the problems that would arise from "decriminalization" be handled? What are the consequences of legislative repeal of these statutes identified as overcriminalized and what are the alternatives?

THE CONSEQUENCES OF REPEAL: THE MORALS STATUTES

Those states that penalize various kinds of sexual activity between consenting adults in private beg for repeal. But repeal of such laws does not simply end the matter. If consenting adults, why not consenting minors above a certain age? What age? At what point does the parental interest in protecting children against what the parents deem to be wrong or harmful to children justify intervention of the criminal law? What does "consent" mean? What is "private"?

Packer[19] has illuminated the difficulties of drawing lines. As for age, he suggests possibly limiting the criminal sanction to situations where the disparity is great, creating a presumption of something like undue influence; and he would include any kind of coercion or taking undue advantage—of intoxication, of mental incapacity, and the like. As for privacy, he would recognize the public affront of overt solicitation, where the solicitation "created a substantial risk that someone might be offended."[20]

Homosexual conduct raises a similar issue, involving primarily a difference in the degree of moral disapproval by the majority middle class. This seems outweighed, however, by the greater evils resulting from criminal penalties, particularly blackmail. In England, the Wolfenden Report[21] has recommended the abolition of criminal sanctions, despite the prevalent atmosphere of moral opprobrium.

Abortion could be treated simply as a medical matter between patient and doctor instead of as a criminal offense, and in this way the evils of abortion "rings" and the dangers of unsterile abortions would be eliminated. To be sure, the concern of some religions for the unborn child is deeply offended by abortion. But if the only support of abortion laws is a particular religious doctrine, then the policy of the First Amendment's Establishment Clause would argue strongly against the decisiveness of such support.

Suggestions for repeal of laws against prostitution ordinarily join with proposals for control, regulation or licensing, citing the practice in various European countries. These proposals seek to avoid the undesirable consequences expected to result from mere repeal: increase in prostitution, its spread to other more respectable neighborhoods, the spread of venereal disease, and the increase in the satellite crimes of fraud and theft. Packer's suggestion that prostitution be treated as a public nuisance and punished only if someone is "offended,"[22] fails to meet these issues.

Control or regulation, such as confinement to a "red light" district and to supervised houses, would avoid the spread of itinerant streetwalkers and would allow easier control of disease and other crimes. But this move is perhaps more difficult than outright repeal, for it would involve the state directly and invite the charge that the government thereby encourages "vice." Such controls, moreover, would not reach "middle-class" prostitution, such as the call girls typically provided for conventioneers. Yet this branch of the trade, carried on discreetly and in private, has few or none of the attendant problems of street prostitution, and therefore may require no need for regulation beyond periodic medical examination.

Use of the criminal law against prostitution has failed to eradicate or, to any appreciable extent, to reduce it. Is prostitution ineradicable by any means? While history would seem to bear this out, it is not a necessary assumption. Many women become attracted to prostitution by their inability to survive in other occupations, by their need to support a narcotics habit, or by the dominant puritan culture which creates a market for such services. These are social conditions for which social solutions ought to be possible.[23] In Scandinavia, for example, where the sexual climate is more permissive and the welfare state has eradicated poverty, prostitution is virtually nonexistent. Perhaps that is the direction in which the widely heralded "sexual revolution" in the United States is also taking us.

Gambling as a business is only partly criminal. Betting on horses at a licensed race track is lawful; but betting on horses at home, on the treasury balance, or on dice or cards in an organized game, is a crime. Once we admit that gambling is tolerable at all, that it is a service industry that caters to a human want inherently no more vicious than the desire for, say, alcohol, no reason prevails against legitimizing gambling as an industry under licensing and regulation similar to that imposed on the distilling industry, the food and drug industry, or even the stock market—"the greatest gambling enterprise in the United States."[24] It would doubtless attract investors who would compete effectively with organized crime.[25] And if "organized crime" continued to control gambling as an industry, legalization would mean that such organized crime would cease to be a crime. Obviously, much "crime" is, after all, what we define it to be.[26]

THE CONSEQUENCES OF REPEAL:
THE ILLNESS STATUTES

Laws against intoxication are currently under attack in the courts, and two decisions of federal Courts of Appeals, in the Fourth Circuit and in the District of Columbia, have held unconstitutional those statutes which punish chronic alcoholics as criminals.[27] In these test cases, the courts held that criminal punishment of a sufferer from chronic alcoholism, an illness that makes intoxication involuntary, violated the common law principle that conduct cannot be considered criminal unless it is voluntary,[28] and hence violated the prohibition of the Eighth Amendment against cruel and unusual punishment.[29]

Since these 1966 decisions, the District of Columbia has had to deal with chronic alcoholics, intoxicated in public, without the benefit of the criminal law. The immediate practical result has been to leave large numbers of drunks staggering about in the streets of the Nation's Capital. While it was argued that police officers might continue lawfully to arrest unknown public drunks, since the police had no way of knowing whether any drunk was or was not a chronic alcoholic immune from prosecution, the risk inherent in a possible false arrest meant that the police would pass by the unconscious drunk.[30] This indifference meant that the drunk continued to offend the sober and was no longer the beneficiary of even the rough social services formerly provided by the jail. But again it was argued:

the police have both a right and a duty to take unwilling intoxicated citizens, who appear to be incapacitated or unable to take care of themselves, whether or not they are alcoholics, to appropriate public health facilities.[31]

Yet the police, in the District of Columbia at least, did not want to assume this task.

In 1968, Congress passed the District of Columbia Alcoholics Rehabilitation Act.[32] The new act repealed both criminal penalties (except for an inebriate who endangers his own safety or that of others) and involuntary civil commitment of chronic alcoholics (except for those in danger of physical harm) and provided for treatment facilities. Pursuant to the statute, three kinds of facilities have been established: a detoxification center in the city where persons who either come in or are brought in by others may "dry out"; a 425-bed voluntary inpatient treatment facility, filled with volunteers and with a 300-person waiting list; and a half-way house for voluntary outpatient treatment and support with only 10 beds. The facilities, although obviously inadequate, at least represent a start.

An inebriate may be taken involuntarily to a detoxification center. Further treatment is basically on a voluntary basis, but further involuntary commitment is provided for chronic alcoholics determined to be in danger of substantial physical harm. The police have been delinquent in transporting inebriates to the detoxification center, although the Act states that "any person who is intoxicated in public," who is not taken to his home or to a public or private health facility, "*shall* be taken to a detoxification center."[33] Considerable hope now exists, however, that as treatment facilities increase and the police department accepts its duty to administer the Act, the problem of chronic alcoholism in the District of Columbia will be well on the way to solution. The strategy has been changed—through a rather trying chain of events—from one of attempted but ineffective deterrence by punishment to one of prevention and cure.

The similar problem of narcotics addiction to "hard" drugs like heroin seems an appropriate subject for similar treatment, despite—or indeed because of—the substantially greater evils of illicit trafficking, "pushing," and satellite violent crimes against property that follow. The principle behind *Easter* and *Driver*—that the disease of chronic alcoholism makes intoxication involuntary and hence not punishable—applies as well to the problem of narcotics addiction.[34] The high incidence of crimes committed by addicts argues for additional safeguards, but here again the social strategy should center primarily on the most effective means of eradicating narcotics addiction—a task that the criminal law has manifestly failed to perform.

Establishment of treatment facilities is the necessary first step. Hopefully, as with alcoholics, there will be many volunteers. Involuntary commitment for treatment seems justified, however, for addicts who have a record of prior crimes or are arrested as pushers. Such facts, when added to proof of narcotics addiction, seem quite sufficient evidence that the addict is dangerous to society in order to justify involuntary commitment for treatment.

Mere possession of narcotics or narcotics paraphernalia should no longer be a crime, although the drugs would be subject to confiscation. As with alcoholics, addicts currently on the drug could be taken into custody for withdrawal from dependency, after which they would be encouraged to undertake further treatment. In all cases, the person treated should have the right to be transferred to outpatient care as soon as he is no longer a danger to himself or to society. And for former narcotics addicts (as for former alcoholics) support and supervision should continue, for treatment does not cure the personality weakness or the results of poor education, nor the broken families or the other social ills that make the addict prone to his habit.

As such a program begins to shrink the market for narcotics, the profitability of the traffic, which attracts organized crime, should also shrink. So also should satellite crimes, including prostitution. But a further direct attack on the price of "hard" drugs, to discourage both organized crime and satellite crime, seems in order. The obvious and most sensible course would permit physicians to prescribe drugs more freely to addicts, coupled with an obligation to encourage the addict to accept treatment.

The question of marihuana, LSD, and other non-addictive drugs with more or less profound psychological and physiological effects, has different elements and calls for a different solution. Since there is no evidence of addiction, treatment is unnecessary. Until and unless evidence is forthcoming of harmful or addictive effect of marihuana—and to date the evidence is all to the contrary[35]—no rational basis exists upon which to resist arguments in favor of modifying the Draconian statutes penalizing possession of marihuana.[36] As long as tobacco and alcohol are lawfully sold "poisons," there is scant justification for absolutely prohibiting the sale and use of marihuana. Moreover, the effect of this heavy-handed prohibition in eroding respect for law among the young people in today's world may be widely underestimated.

There is real evidence, however, that certain of the "mind-expanding" drugs such as LSD do have harmful psychological, physical, and genetic effects. As for such drugs, to impose criminal punishment on the *user* who harms only himself (or herself and her unborn children) seems hard to justify. Public education ought to be the primary strategy, supplemented by strict control of the sale of such drugs, with rigorous criminal penalties for black market sale.

THE CONSEQUENCES OF REPEAL:
THE NUISANCE STATUTES

The last group of statutes are those used to punish conduct deemed to be a nuisance to particular segments of society or to the police themselves—written and oral obscenity, disorderly conduct, and vagrancy. The chief questions raised by these laws are whether and when the interest of the public— or rather of a segment of the public—in not being offended is strong enough to justify use of the sanction of the criminal law; and whether and when that interest is strong enough to override other constitutionally protected rights of those whose conduct may offend.

In most states, statutes punish the sale, dissemination and possession of obscene books, films, or other such matter. These laws place an obvious restraint on freedom of expression, and the courts continually have had to wrestle with the problem of whether some speech or writing is so obscene that it does not deserve the protection of the First Amendment. The basic rule seems to be that the *sale or distribution* of obscene literature is punishable if the literature appears to the courts to be "utterly without redeeming social importance."[37]

The Supreme Court has only recently held a statute penalizing the mere *possession* of pornographic material as unconstitutional interference with the right to privacy and First Amendment freedoms.[38] The decision rests not only on the "right to receive information and ideas, regardless of their social worth"—a seeming retreat, at least with respect to possession of pornography, from the test of "redeeming social importance" but also on a "right to be free, except in very limited circumstances, from unwanted governmental intrusions into one's privacy."[39]

There is something anomalous, however, in permitting private possession and enjoyment of pornography while prohibiting its sale. No one is required to buy "obscene" books or view "obscene" films. The "sensibilities" of the general public do not, it seems, outweigh society's interest in freedom of expression, at least where the manner of promotion and sale of the obscene material does not invade the privacy of individuals who wish not to be confronted by such materials (as would clearly be the case, for example, of unsolicited mailings of flyers to the home, door-to-door sales, billboards, and the like).

The laws against disorderly conduct and vagrancy are defended, particularly by the police, as a necessary peacekeeping tool. Not only are many arrests made,[40] but the threat of arrest and the availability of the "move on" order permit the officer to maintain tranquility and order on his "beat." The question these laws raise is important, particularly in the racial ghettoes of our large cities. In the more tranquil suburbs the community probably strongly supports both the discretion and normal manner of its exercise.[41]

Police discretion rarely has been recognized officially. In most states, statutes require the police officer to arrest "all" violators, "all felons," or "all persons committing an offense in his presence," or impose a duty to enforce "all" the criminal laws.[42] Legislatures do not appear to have given the matter much thought, since the operative assumption has always been that this kind of power may not be delegated in the criminal law.[43]

Police discretion *not* to arrest, to fail to enforce the law, is perhaps most obvious in laws against consensual sexual acts and against gambling.[44] But more important in the context of enforcement of "nuisance" laws is selective, discretionary enforcement. For instance, when in the course of exercising his peacekeeping function, an officer meets with disrespect or backtalk, especially profanity, he will often make arrests in order to maintain respect and to uphold his authority.[45]

Police exercise of discretion and selective enforcement have been defended as necessary to fair and effective law enforcement. Probably, whatever its justification, it is unavoidable. The test ought to be whether in fact the exercise of discretion results in fair enforcement, and this in turn depends on the factors governing the officer's decision. Thus discretion exercised on a basis of race or color is clearly unlawful,[46] and the citizen's attitude and his status in the community are other improper criteria.[47]

In the numerous civil rights and antiwar demonstrations of the last few years, the police have had to tread the very thin line between protecting First Amendment rights of effective free speech and assembly and the countervailing rights of the public to unhampered access to buildings and public thoroughfares. In many of these situations, the police have stated their policy to be the full enforcement and protection of free movement.[48] This policy of confrontation, often resulting in escalation of mutual distrust and even violence, has put the police in the position of contributing to further, more violent disorder. The need for discretion and restraint particularly applies when the demonstrator feels wronged by a "get tough" policy.[49] Some police departments have adopted openly declared policies of restraint and non-enforcement unless and until a public danger is created.[50] Other departments have responded by not allowing demonstrations at all.[51]

Police failure to recognize the availability of discretionary enforcement has had disastrous consequences:

> Police insistence that their responsibility is to fully enforce the law is to perpetuate a myth which is impossible of achievement and would be undesirable if it could be achieved. At times this may be an understandable public relations position but has seriously adverse consequences for police if they fail to recognize that theirs is a responsibility for the development of an adequate and fair law enforcement program within legal limits.[52]

This view had led to suggestions for the adoption of formal guidelines to control police discretion,[53] guidelines which

> . . . would bring the important street decisions, now made only by patrolmen, up to the level of the chief administrator and his staff, who would formulate policy much in the way

613

a board of directors serves a corporation. This would remove from individual policemen some of the burden of having to make important decisions ad hoc, in a matter of seconds. It would create a body of standards that would help make the supervision and evaluation of the work of individual policemen consistent.[54]

With respect to enforcement of the laws against disorderly conduct and vagrancy, however, few believe that guidelines will solve the underlying problems of enforcement, although they may well ameliorate them. These statutes, as we have indicated, tend in the ghetto situation to impose on the community values that have little relevance to people against whom they are enforced, for their enforcement rests in police officers whose backgrounds favor the values in the statutes.

The inadequacy of guidelines is illustrated by two recent efforts to draft guidelines in this area for the District of Columbia and Philadelphia Police Departments.[55] The District of Columbia guidelines, for example, recognize that "enforcement of these disorderly conduct statutes is one of the most difficult and sensitive problem areas currently confronting police officers" and urge that "on those occasions where public order can be maintained without an arrest, it is incumbent upon the police officer to make every reasonable effort to do so." They point out that in a city "it must be expected that there will be more noise and other disturbances than in less populated areas." They warn against "indiscriminate" mass arrests.

Turning to specific provisions of the law, the guidelines—necessarily, given the language of the statutes—undercut these general admonitions to exercise discretion wisely. Thus they instruct the officer to intervene when "loud and boisterous conduct is definitely disturbing or potentially disruptive, to the community." With respect to profanity, the guidelines first state flatly:

An individual who curses, swears, uses profane language, indecent or obscene words, or who engages in any similar disorderly conduct in a public place commits an offense. (D.C. Code 22-1107). It is also an offense to engage in such activity in a private place when the conduct may be heard in a public place or in another private place.

The guidelines then attempt to strike a middle ground, but again, as the statute requires, they instruct officers to make arrests:

614

Some people use obscene and vulgar words as a major part of their normal conversation, and through habit and vocabulary limitation, customarily express themselves in this manner, particularly when excited or under stress. These people will often refrain from repeating such language when told to stop by a police officer.

There is no distinction between abusive language directed to a civilian or a police officer. Although a police officer should demonstrate greater self-control than the ordinary citizen, *the police officer is not expected to refrain from arrest when abusive language is directed toward him.* [Emphasis added.]

The Philadelphia guidelines struggle with similar difficulties. The officer is instructed that if loud and boisterous conduct "is disturbing enough to annoy residents or passersby, it is an offense *even if the policeman is the only one who happens to be observing it.* [Emphasis added.] And "dirty language" becomes an offense if it "adds up to a general nuisance."

The Philadelphia guidelines (unlike the District of Columbia guidelines) also deal with vagrancy, and candidly inform the officer that the laws against "vagrancy" and "loitering" are "a very confusing set of laws" and that "to some extent these laws may be obsolete or unconstitutional." They then cautiously suggest limiting use of these statutes "against persons preparing to commit burglary, peeping, eavesdropping or some other specific misbehavior." The decision whether a loiterer is "preparing" to commit such an offense is up to the officer.

Th problem with guidelines like these is that they are little help to the officer who does not have a feel for the values of the community he is policing. They do not solve the fundamental problem of vague statutes being enforced by persons whose mores are often inconsistent with the general mores and life style of the inner city. Thus, in a prosecution tried before the Chief Judge of the Court of General Sessions of the District of Columbia in April 1969, the defendant was convicted of disorderly conduct for demanding of a police officer, who refused to proceed to the scene of an accident in the heart of the ghetto, that the officer should "get out there and do your m——— f——— job." In response to the defense that such language is common usage in the neighborhood, the court insisted on applying "the same standard of conduct to all parts of the city."[56]

An important value that the laws against profanity ignore, if literally applied, is the usefulness of profane words as a safety valve and as an alternative to violence. As Ashley Montagu, a famous anthropoligist, has observed:

> It is clear then, that in common with weeping and laughter, swearing serves a very useful function as a cathartic, that is as an outlet for emotions which results, as it were, in a purifying effect, as well as a pacifying one.[57]

And to quote an oft-cited aphorism:

> It has been said that he who was the first to abuse his fellow-man instead of knocking out his brains without a word laid thereby the basis of civilization.[58]

The courts recognize this in the law of torts—where only civil penalties are involved—but not in the criminal law.[59] The vagrancy statutes that punish "loitering," "failing to give a good account" of one's self, leading an "immoral or profligate life," lacking a "lawful and visible means of support," or wandering about at "late and unusual hours" form a significant basis for police discretion. Such laws have been used to arrest prostitutes in order to control or reduce prostitution, in lieu of attempting prosecution for the substantive offense which requires proof of an actual solicitation. They are also used to harass "beatniks," "hippies," rowdy teenagers, and others whose life style is abhorrent to the middle-class ethic of the police officer and who to him are "undesirables"—as they often are to many segments of the community. But where conduct—like prostitution—is prevalent and difficult to prove, use of vague vagrancy provisions that result in no more than harassing fines or very short jail terms can only degrade the law in the eyes of many and increase disrespect for law and law enforcement. The fact that prosecutions under such laws are by and large the only method of controlling the conduct in some areas, argues strongly for repealing the laws against such conduct, and use of these laws to impose uniformity of life style is flatly repugnant to individual freedom.

Such laws are thus beginning to be held unconstitutional as impossibly vague, because they permit "government by the moment-to-moment opinions of a policeman on his beat," and are hence a violation of due process.[60] What laws will remain after this constitutional exorcism to provide the necessary police discretion to maintain an *appropriate* degree of tranquillity, is perhaps not as clear now as it should be.

CONCLUSION

The problem of "overcriminalization" is a sensitive one, and some will be offended by the ideas aired in this chapter. Many of us continue to embrace the myth that we are one homogeneous group of like-minded people. We maintain the illusion that we share with simple societies the agreed-upon values that are time-honored and sacred.

But it is abundantly clear that this perspective of America is false. Instead of consensus, we have a rich variety of value systems and ways of life. Instead of agreement with much of the legislation passed by law-makers, we have deep felt resentment towards any interference with ways of life that some groups hold sacred. Instead of concerted effort to bring members of the community into line with the laws enforced by prosecutors and police, we have significant groups of persons supporting the law-breaking of their members and seeing the attempt to change their behavior as interference with their rights as citizens and human beings.

None of us can escape the fact that American society has become increasingly pluralistic. Until we recognize this fact and take it into account in the way we attempt to implement measures of social control, our effort to achieve social order will too often continue to be self-defeating.

The criminal law is society's most drastic tool for regulating conduct. When it is used against conduct that a large segment of society considers normal, and which is not seriously harmful to the interest of others, contempt for the law is encouraged. When it is used against conduct that is involuntary and the result of illness, the law becomes inhumane. When it becomes a means for arbitrary or abusive police conduct, it can cause hostility, tension and violence.

Repeal of many such laws is overdue. Where the laws merely attempts to enforce a particular set of moral values, simple repeal is usually justified. Where, on the other hand, a social evil such as drunkenness is involved, other methods, more apt to resolve social problems, are needed to substitute for the repealed laws. And where the problem in enforcing the law arises primarily from the attitudes of police, as with disorderly conduct statutes, it should be dealt with by changing those attitudes through training or different recruitment policies, rather than by repeal or by judicial voiding of the underlying statutes.

617

REFERENCES

1. Schwartz, Book Review, 21 *Stan. L. Rev.* 1277, 1278 (1969).
2. See Packer, "Copping Out," *New York Review of Books,* Oct. 12, 1967, at 17.
3. See especially Herbert L. Packer, *The Limits of the Criminal in Sanction* (Stanford: Stanford University Press, 1968); Sanford H. Kadish, "The Crisis of Overcriminalization," 374 *Annals* 157 (1967).
4. Much of the discussion immediately following is drawn from writings by Sanford Kadish, author of two major articles outlining the problem of "overcriminalization." See the President's Commission on Law Enforcement and Administration of Justice, *Task Force Report: The Courts* (Washington, D.C.: Government Printing Office, 1967), ch. VIII; and "The Crisis of Overcriminalization," *supra* note 3.
5. Thurman Arnold, *The Symbols of Government* (New York: Harcourt, Brace & World, 1935), at 160.
6. See, e.g., D.C. Code, Title 22, Ch. 11.
7. See, e.g., D.C. Code, Title 22, Ch. 20.
8. See, e.g., D.C. Code, Title 22, Ch. 33.
9. Packer, *supra,* note 3, at 296.
10. The phrase is common police jargon. See Arthur Neiderhoffer *Behind the Shield: The Police in Urban Society* (Garden City, N.Y.: Doubleday & Co., Inc., 1967), at 71.
11. See Skolnick and Woodworth, "Bureaucracy, Information and Social Control: A Study of a Morals Detail," in *The Police: Six Sociological Essays,* ed. by David J. Bordua (New York: John Wiley & Sons, 1967), at 99.
12. Paul Chevigny, *Police Power* (New York: Pantheon Books, 1969), at 141, 158.
13. Ralph F. Salerno, "Organized Crime and Violence" (a consultant paper prepared for the Commission.)
14. *Id.*
15. Packer, *supra* note 3, at 62.
16. See Chevigny, *supra* note 12; *Report of the President's Commission on Crime in the District of Columbia* (Washington, D.C.: Government Printing Office, 196), at 208.
17. See Chevigny, *supra* note 12, at 30-50.
18. Kadish, "The Crisis of Overcriminalization," *supra* note 3, at 166; the figure given is 35-40 percent.
19. Packer, *supra* note 3, at 306-312.
20. *Id.* at 312.
21. *Report of the Committee on Homosexual Offenses and Prostitution* (The Wolfenden Report to Parliament) (1957); see also Kent, "The Wolfenden Report and Its Consequences" (1968) (a consultant paper prepared for the Commission).
22. Packer, *supra* note 3, at 331.

23. See Remarks of Prof. Frank Remington, Notre Dame Law School, Feb. 12, 1968, reprinted in the *Congressional Record*, May 1, 1968 (daily ed.), at E3621.

24. Thomas C. Schelling, "Economics and Criminal Enterprises," *Public Interest*, Spring, 1967, at 76.

25. Packer, *supra* note 3, at 353.

26. As for example, the liquor distributing industry immediately before repeal of prohibition (organized crime) and immediately after (lawful industry). See Packer, "Copping Out," *supra* note 2.

27. *Easter* v. *District of Columbia,* 361 F. 2d 50 (D.C. Cir. 1966) (en banc); *Driver* v. *Hinnant,* 356 F. 2d 761 (4th Cir. 1966). See Hutt, "Perspectives on the Report of the President's Crime Commission—The Problem of Drunkenness," 43 *Notre Dame Lawyer* 857 (1968).

28. *Easter* v. *District of Columbia, supra* note 27.

29. *Driver* v. *Hinnant, supra* note 27.

30. See Peter Hutt, "The recent Court Decision on Alcoholism," in President's Commission on Law Enforcement and Administration of Justice," *supra* note 4, *Task Force Report: Drunkenness,* at 114.

31. *Id.*

32. P.L. 90-452, 82 Stat. 618 (1968).

33. P.L. 90-452, Secs. 2, 4. [Emphasis added.]

34. Indeed, the foundation of these two decisions is *Robinson* v. *California,* 371 U.S. 905 (1962), holding that the Eighth Amendment prohibits involuntary drug addiction from being made a criminal offense.

35. Packer, *supra* note 3, at 338.

36. The Marijuana Tax Act makes possession a felony subject to a penalty of up to 10 years imprisonment for the first offense.

37. *Roth* v. *United States,* 354 U.S. 476 (1957).

38. *Stanley* v. *Georgia,* 37 *U.S.L.W.* 4315, 4318 (U.S. Sup. Ct., Apr. 7, 1969).

39. *Id.* at 4317. The decision relies upon *Griswold* v. *Connecticut,* 381 U.S. 479 (1965), which struck down, as repugnant to a constitutional "right of privacy" deriving from the First, Fourth and Fifth Amendments, statutes punishing the dispensing or use of birth control information and devices.

40. Approximately 1,000 per month in the District of Columbia; 1967 Annual Report of the Metropolitan Police Department, at 45.

41. Most of the following discussion of police discretion is based on a paper by Eric Smith, *Police Discretion* (1968). (Prepared for the Emergency Justice Task Force, District of Columbia Commission on Administration of Justice Under Emergency Conditions).

42. For a review and classification of these statutes, see Wayne R. LaFave, *Arrest: The Decision to Take a Subject into Custody* (Boston: Little, Brown & Co., 1965), at 76-77. See also Gold-

stein, "Police Discretion not to Involve the Criminal Process: Low Visibility Decisions in the Administration of Justice," 69 *Yale L.J.* 543 (1960). In the District of Columbia it is an offense if the officer should "neglect making an arrest for an offense . . . committed in his presence." D.C. Code Sec. 4-143 (1961).

43. See Remington and Rosenblum, "The Criminal Law and the Legislative Process," 69 *U. Ill. L.F.* 481.

44. LaFave, *supra* note 42, at 89-94.

45. *Id.* at 145-46.

46. *Oyler* v. *Boles,* 368 U.S. 448 (1962).

47. Goldstein, "Police Policy Formulation: A Proposal for Improving Police Performance," 65 *Mich. L. Rev.* 1123, 1146 (1967); Piliavin and Briar, "Police Encounters with Juveniles, Differential Selection of Juvenile Offenders for Court Appearances," in National Research and Information Center, National Council on Crime and Delinquency (1963).

48. LeGrande, "Non-Violent Civil Disobedience and Police Enforcement," 58 *J. Crim. L.* 393, 401-02 (1967); Juby E. Towler, *The Police Role in Racial Conflicts* (Springfield, Ill.: Charles C. Thomas, 1964), at 3, 109-110. "If the law is on the books, he is sworn to enforce it."

49. Johnson, "A Sociological Interpretation of Police Reaction and Responsibility to Civil Disobedience," 58 *J. Crim. L.* 405 (1967).

50. LeGrande, *supra* note 48 to 403:

"It is the policy of the St. Louis Police Department regarding racial demonstrations that no direct police actions will be taken in the absence of violence, orders of the court or emergency situations wherein life or property is endangered : . . Generally in such instances the officers assigned to the scene will be plainclothes personnel . . . In the absence of violence or emergency, no action will be taken unless warrants are issued. Under these conditions the officer shall only observe and report existing conditions." Metropolitan Police Department, St. Louis, Mo., Supplement One (Unpublished, 1963).

See also Chief Joseph Kimble, "Patience and Planning, the Key to Controlling Demonstrations," *Law and Order,* at 72 (Sept. 1965).

51. See U.S. Commission on Civil Rights, *Law Enforcement: A Report on Equal Protection in The South* (1965) at 173-175.

52. LeGrande, *supra* note 48 at 404, quoting Remington, "Social Changes, The Law, and The Common Good," paper presented at the Tenth Annual Institute on Police and Community Relations, East Lansing, Michigan, Michigan State University (1964), at H-11 (mimeographed).

53. See, e.g., Goldstein, *supra* note 47: "Administrative Problems in Controlling the Exercise of Police Authority," 58 *J. Crim. L.* 160 (1967); Schwartz & Goldstein, *Police Guidance Manuals* (1968).

54. The President's Commission on Law Enforcement and Administration of Justice, *supra* note 4, *The Challenge of Crime in a Free Society,* at 106.

55. Schwartz and Goldstein, *Police Guidance Manuals* (PGM No. 7) (1968); Government of the District of Columbia, Metropolitan Police Department, Guidelines applicable to the enforcement of Sections 22-1107 and 22-1121 of the District of Columbia Code (Disorderly Conduct) (July 11, 1968).

56. *Washington Post,* Apr. 17, 1969, at B9.

57. M. F. Ashley Montagu, "On the Physiology and Psychology of Swearing," 5 *Psychiatry* 189, 199 (1942).

58. Quoted in E. Stengel, Hughling's Jackson's Influence in Psychiatry, 109 *Brit. J. Psychiat.* 348-355 (1963). See also, e.g., Karl Menninger, *The Vital Balance* (New York: Viking Press, 1963), at 137-138.

59. See, e.g., *Clark* v. *Associated Retail Credit Men of Washington, D.C.* 70 App. D.C. 183, 185, 105 F.2d 62, 64 (1939):
"For the sake of reasonable freedom of action, in our own interest and that of society, we need the privilege of being careless whether we inflict mental distress on our neighbors."

60. *Ricks* v. *United States,* U.S. App. D.C. 20919 (Dec. 23, 1968) (slip op. 7); *United States* v. *McClough,* District of Columbia Court of General Sessions (Crim N. 929-69B, Mar. 7, 1969).

CHAPTER 24

PROBLEMS OF THE CORRECTIONS SYSTEM*

They's a guy in McAlester—lifer. He studies all the time.
He's secretary of the warden—writes the warden's letters and
stuff like that. Well, he's one hell of a bright guy an' reads
law an' stuff like that. Well, I talked to him one time about
her, 'cause he reads so much stuff. An' he says it don't do no
good to read books. Says he's read ever' thing about prisons,
now, an' in the old times. An' he says she makes less sence
to him now that she did before he starts readin. He says its
a thing that started way to hell an' gone back, an' nobody
seems to be able to stop her, an' nobody got sence enough
to change her. He says for God's sake don't read about her
because he says for one thing you'll jus' get messed up
worse, an' for another you won't have no respect for the guys
that work the gover'ments.[1]

The problem of acquiring an effective system of corrections is a critical part of any program to improve our
institutions of criminal law enforcement. The police can and
must be improved to prevent crime and apprehend a larger
percentage of offenders. The courts can and must be improved to handle the criminal charges arising from a larger
number of arrests and to develop a more reasoned approach
to sentencing. But unless the corrections systems are also
changed, the whole process may only turn out to be self-
defeating.

The criminal law process is preoccupied with stopping
crime and catching and convicting—as opposed to rehabilitating—criminals. Once a criminal is caught and tried and
incarcerated, public interest tends to wane despite the fact
that the convicted criminal is likely eventually to be released
to commit further crimes. As Chief Justice Warren E. Burger
recently noted, "There must be some way to make our

---

*This chapter was prepared by David P. Stang, based in part on
consultant papers by Herbert F. Costner, Linda R. Singer, and
Vincent I. O'Leary.

622

correctional system better than the revolving door process
. . . of crime, prison and more crime."[2]

This chapter will sketch the inadequacies of our nation's prisons and jails and the sometimes shocking conditions which exist in many of them. It will also discuss some of the remedial measures which might be adopted to remove degrading conditions and to improve our prisons and jails so that they can begin to realize their stated goal of rehabilitating offenders.

Most of what we have to say is not new, the problem of corrections including sociological and treatment aspects having been presented in comprehensive detail by the Corrections Task Force of the President's Commission on Law Enforcement and Administration of Justice as well as treated extensively in the report of the Violence Commission's Task Force on Individual Acts of Violence. Perhaps, however, there is also value in a briefer treatment that emphasizes, as this chapter does, our failure even to achieve minimum levels of humane treatment in some of our prisons and jails.

THE INABILITY OF CORRECTIONS TO CORRECT

We begin by noting what few persons would dispute: that because of shortages of trained personnel and suitable facilities, prisons in this country have never adequately performed their correctional function. A look back at the old times in comparison with the new times reveals that prisons are substantially unchanged insofar as they still serve as little more than cages with time locks on their doors. Before the eighteenth century, prisons were used not to punish but to detain the accused until the debtor paid his debt, the rapist was castrated, the thief's hands were cut off, or the perjurer's tongue was torn out. In 1786, the Quakers in Pennsylvania instituted incarceration as a humane alternative to hanging and torture. In an effort to have prisoners do penitence for their sins, the Quakers locked convicts in solitary cells until they died or were released. So many died or went insane that in 1825 New York's Auburn Prison introduced the practice of hard labor performed in silence. Until quite recently, American prisons relied almost entirely on the Auburn system of shaved heads, lockstep marching, and degrading toil, and locked prisoners in huge isolated pens that soothed the public's fears of escapes.[3]

In essence, prisons historically were intentionally horrible places where prisoners received their "just due." As Richard McGee so persuasively phrased it:

> . . . The idea of retributive punishment is deeply rooted in the minds and emotions of mortal man. This attitude, and this simple atavistic impulse to punish and overpunish offenders, remains the central trunk of the administration of criminal justice throughout the world.[4]

The old stone walls have refused to crumble. Prison buildings were built most sturdily, and it has been difficult to secure their replacement. Today there are 25 prisons in the United States over 100 years old. These institutions perpetuate the old theories around which they were constructed. As an example, the Bureau of Prisons operates a federal prison in Sandstone, Minn., in a virtual wilderness between Minneapolis and Duluth. The institution was authorized in 1933, when northern Minnesota was a center for the activities of bootleggers. Sanford Bates, who was at that time the Director of the Bureau of Prisons, decided to "put one up there where they are coming from." But by the time the prison had been built, prohibition had been repealed, and, according to the present Director, "there we had an institution 16 miles from anywhere, where it gets pretty cold in the winter.[5]

No less appalling than the physical structure and condition of our nation's prisons is the number and caliber of employees on their staffs, and worse yet is the unbalanced allocation of staff personnel to offenders. Approximately 1.3 million people are under correctional authority in the United States. Of these, only one-third are in institutions; the other two-thirds are supervised in the community on probation or parole. But the ratios of staff and costs are inverse to these proportions: only one-fifth of the money and one-seventh of the staff are engaged with the two-thirds of the offenders who are in the community.[6]

Of the more than 121,000 people employed in corrections in 1965, only 24,000, or 20 percent of the staff, had any connection with rehabilitation.[7] The other 80 percent merely guarded the 426,000 incarcerated offenders. A glance at the ratios of the 20 percent of the staff—supposedly charged with the objective of rehabilitation—to offenders is suggestive of the reason for their difficulties. The following statistics were compiled as a result of a special study conducted by the Joint Commission on Correctional Manpower and Training.[8]

Position	Number of inmates per staff person
Classification worker	365
Counselor	758
Psychiatrist	1,140
Psychologist	803
Physician, surgeon	986
Social worker	295
Teacher:	
Academic	104
Vocational	181
Vocational rehabilitation counselor	2,172

Clearly these figures reveal the almost impossible task facing rehabilitative personnel: their caseload is simply overwhelming.

The lopsided allocation of funds budgeted to correctional institutions also reveals our outdated approach to the handling of prisoners. In 1965, $435 million was expended for the operation of institutions for adult offenders. According to the President's Crime Commission, "The bulk of this . . . was spent to feed, clothe and guard prisoners."[9] Of every dollar, 95¢ is for custody; 5¢ is for rehabilitation.

The Corrections Task Force of the President's Crime Commission in 1967 tabulated the numbers of persons actually employed by correctional authorities in various job categories and estimated how many additional such personnel would be required if improvement in our nation's prisons was to become a reality. The Corrections Task Force reported that 63,184 custodial personnel and group supervisors were employed, but that 89,600 were needed; 2,685 caseworkers in prisons were employed, but that 10,200 were needed; 14,731 caseworkers in community based corrections were employed, but that 44,800 were needed; 6,657 specialists such as vocational and academic teachers, psychologists, and psychiatrists were employed, but that 20,400 were needed. The Corrections Task Force then projected manpower requirements for 1975 which amounted to a total of 304,000 correctional personnel, an increase of 172,837 when compared to the 121,163 actually employed in 1965.[10] These jobs persently are not being filled to within even a fraction of requirements.

These prison statistics, depressing as they are, are nowhere near so deplorable as those associated with our nation's jails, local workhouses and other facilities for detaining accused persons before and during trial and for short misdemeanor sentences. As one Crime Commission consultant put it:

> Most counties and cities persist in operating their own jails, nearly all of which are nothing more than steel cages in which people stay for periods of time up to a year. Most of the jails are custody-oriented and supervised by ill-trained, underpaid personnel. In some cases, the institution is not manned except when a police officer on duty can look in once during his eight hour shift.[11]

It is rare to find any rehabilitative program being conducted by our jails. In fact, less than three percent of the total staff of our nation's 3,500 jails have any rehabilitative responsibilities. Those few persons who are engaged in such programs are preposterously overloaded with case assignments. A Crime Commission study revealed these ratios between rehabilitative staff and inmates in jails and other local misdemeanant institutions:[12]

Position	Number	Ratio of staff to inmates
Social workers	167	1:846
Psychologists	33	1:4,282
Psychiatrists	58	1:2,436
Academic teachers	106	1:1,333
Vocational teachers	137	1:1,031
Custodial officers	14,993	1:9

Not only are our Nation's prisons and jails understaffed, but the existing staffs are undertrained both before acceptance for employment and after reporting for work. With respect to custodial workers alone, the Corrections Task Force of the President's Crime Commission found that they are—

> undereducated, untrained and unversed in the goals of corrections. Unless salaries are raised, substantial improvements cannot be expected in the kind of people who can be recruited.[13]

The average prison guard is paid only between $3000–$4000 a year. Parole and probation officers, on the average, are paid as little as $5000–$6000 a year. With respect to management and other rehabilitation specialists, the Corrections

Task Force asserted, their "salaries fail to attract and retain enough capable personnel and act as a ceiling on the salaries of all subordinates."[14]

One might think that intensive inservice training programs would be in existence to attempt to bridge the gap between educational requirements and actual educational attainment of correctional personnel. Surveys, however, have shown that this is not the case. The following data reflect that less than half of our correctional systems have any inservice training programs at all.[15]

Type of system	Systems reporting programs		Systems reporting No programs	
	Number	Percent	Number	Percent
Probation and parole systems .	359	44	448	56
Correctional institutions	197	59	137	41
Total	556	..	585	..

The favorite scorecard which critics use to demonstrate the results of the manifold inadequacies of the corrections system is the recidivism rate. There are no completely reliable statistics on the extent of recidivism, but it has been estimated that about 30 to 80 percent of the offenders released from correctional institutions are reimprisoned within five years, often for crimes more serious than those for which they were incarcerated originally.[16] As the Crime Commission concluded:

> For a great many offenders . . . corrections does not correct. Indeed experts are increasingly coming to feel that the conditions under which many offenders are handled, particularly in institutions, are often a positive detriment to rehabilitation.[17]

That something else may be wrong with prisons, however, other than their failure effectively to prevent recidivism, is too often overlooked by all concerned. Almost the entire emphasis of correctional critics today is on the inadequacy of the resources committed to prison systems insofar as they relate to rehabilitation: the prison buildings are not suited for rehabilitation, the staffs are not large enough nor well enough trained to accomplish rehabilitation, the allocation of funds

627

expended by correctional institutions is not designed primarily to achieve the objective of rehabilitation. All this is true, of course—but there is another point as well. *Inherent in most prisons is an environment in which vicious and brutal degradation of inmates regularly takes place.* The existence of this environment, in and of itself, deters the realization of treatment objectives. First, the degradation of prisoners prevents the possibility of their rehabilitation, even in the rare situations where the necessary rehabilitative resources are available. Second, in situations where rehabilitative resources are unavailable, degradation tends only to further dehabilitate.

Knocking down a man is no way to build him up. And kicking a man when he is already down can never build him up. That prisons knock men down, and then often kick them besides, is amply demonstrated by the following tales of horror.

THE HORROR OF CORRECTIONS

The judges and the district attorney in Philadelphia recently showed the courage to order an investigation of the incidence of sexual assaults in local correctional institutions. The investigators from the District Attorney's Office and the Police Department concluded that sexual assaults are endemic in the Philadelphia prison system. The report estimated that during the 26-month period under investigation there were approximately 2,000 sexual assaults, involving approximately 1,500 individual victims and 3,500 individual aggressors in Philadelphia prisons. The investigators found that virtually every slightly built young man committed to jail by the courts—many of them merely to await trial—is sexually approached within hours of his admission to prison. Many young men are overwhelmed and repeatedly "raped" by gangs of inmate aggressors.[17]

One inmate described an attack as follows:

> I was laying on my bed when seven or eight inmates came to my bed, pulled the blanket off me, put it on the floor and told me to pull my pants down and lay face down on the blanket. I said, "No" and was punched in the face by one of the inmates. The inmate that punched me stated if I did not get on the floor the other inmates would gang up on me.
>
> I got on the floor and my pants and shorts were pulled off. Two inmates spread and held my legs apart while two more

inmates held my hands in front of me. While I was being bug-gered from behind another inmate would make me suck his penis. This continued until all the inmates had attacked me and I heard one of them say it was 1:30 A.M. so let's go to bed. They put me on the bed, covered me with the blanket and one of them patted me on the behind saying good boy we will see you again tomorrow night.

While I was being molested I was held by the neck and head and threatened with bodily harm if I yelled or screamed. They stated that they would beat my head on the floor if I made any outcry.[18]

This event was by no means a unique episode in the Philadelphia investigation. The District Attorney of that city in testimony before the Senate Subcommittee to Investigate Juvenile Delinquency read this statement of a seventeen year old youth who at the time of his victimization had been charged but not tried or convicted of the offense of being a runaway:

I was in the cell at 1801 Vine when four Negro boys started bothering me for not having underwear on. Then when we got on the Sheriff's van and started moving they told everyone that I didn't have on underwear as the van was moving they started getting close to me. One of them touched me and I told them to please stop. All of a sudden a coat was thrown over my face and when I tried to pull it off I was viciously punched in the face for around ten minutes. I fell to the floor and they kicked me all over my body including my head, and my privates. They ripped my pants from me while five or six of them held me down and took turns fucking me. My insides feel sore and my body hurts, my head hurts, and I feel sick in the stomach. Each time they stopped I tried to call for help but they put their hands over my mouth so I couldn't make a sound. While they held me, they burned my leg with a cigarette. When the van stopped at the prison, they wiped the blood from me with my shirt. They threatened my life and said they would get me in D1 if I told what happened. They said if they didn't get me in D1 they'd get me in the van again. When the door opened they pushed me to the back so they could get out first. At first, I told the guard I tripped and fell but thought I better tell the truth. I pointed out those who beat me up so bad the doctor looked at me and said I'd have to go to the hospital. They took pictures of my bruises on my body and I can just about breathe because my nose and jaw seem to be broken in many different places. I was asked by the lieutenant to write what happened and this is exactly what happened.

The Philadelphia report, shocking to anyone unfamiliar with the conditions in American prisons, is no news to professionals in the field who realize that an honest report on the county jails in numerous other parts of the country would reveal the same thing.[19]

Even before a grand jury was summoned to investigate the scandalous conditions in Chicago's Cook County Jail[20] the jail superintendent conceded publicly that deviate sex practices, the beating of inmates by other inmates, smuggling of contraband and other vicious practices were routine in the jail. And a large portion of the men and women, boys and girls who were crowded into this institution had not yet even been convicted.[21] Interviews with 36 ex-inmates of the Cook County Jail revealed the following facts:

> Eight of the 36 ex-inmates were victims of beatings, some badly, with concussions, fractures, etc.
> About 75 beatings were reportedly seen by inmates.
> Some inmates said that there was about one beating each day.
> Four of 36 ex-inmates admitted that they were victims of sexual attacks.
> About 75 sexual attacks were seen or heard.
> About a dozen guards were reported as being involved in trafficking of drugs.
> Reported generally: "You can get all of the 'pot' (marihuana) wanted if you have the money."
> Eight incidents of burning were reported as being seen or involved in by inmates interviewed, and
> Four inmates were reportedly set on fire.
> Former staff and inmates reported homosexuals were shaved by staff and inmates. The use of iodine to paint heads of such inmates reportedly has been discontinued. One youth was dry shaved by two inmates reportedly, leaving many cuts on his head.[22]

One lawyer who has conducted extensive investigations of prison conditions wrote to this Commission: "The commonest denominator in all prisons is to take the dignity of the prisoner away, creating in him an abhorrence of rules of ordered society, of law enforcement, of every basic tenet of a civilized society."[23]

Not all such practices involve physical brutality among inmates. A more subtle form can be seen in the results of unnecessary solitary confinement. Dane White, aged 13, an Indian boy of Browns Valley, Minn., in a state of depression resulting from 41 days of isolation hanged himself on

November 17, 1968, with his belt in a county jail. A report conducted by the Attorney General of Minnesota indicated that Dane White had expressed an intention to hang himself. The jail officials, however, were not sufficiently attentive to their duties to have perceived such a possibility.

Almost as depressing as solitary confinement is the opposite extreme of overcrowding. A prisoner's hostility often cannot be contained when he is thrust in a cell with so many other people that he must fight for space on the floor to sleep, let alone be accorded the simple comfort of a bed.

A recent report on the adult detention facilities in San Francisco revealed that the maximum capacity of the City Prison is 437 plus 50 females. At times during 1968 the population in that institution exceeded 600 rising once to over 900 last December. At that time only 200 mattresses were on hand, and 200-300 inmates were forced to sleep on steel springs or on the concrete floor. The recommendations of that report with respect to the City Prison suggest what life at that institution must be like:

> *That towels be provided to inmates who wish to shower or wash daily.* At present, inmates are permitted to shower weekly. Men wishing to wash in the interim are forced to use paper towels. . . .
> *That inmates be deloused and showered if they are detained in excess of 48 hours.*
> *That inmates be provided jail clothing when detained in excess of 48 hours.* This law is currently ignored.
> *That new inmates be given clean blankets, and that the laundering of these blankets be increased from every three months to monthly.* Complaints have been received that due to the high population of City Prison, blankets are often transmitted from inmate to inmate without the benefit of fumigation or laundering.
> *That an adequate number of benches and tables be provided for the "dayroom" holding cell of the Women's Unit. . . .*[24]

Despite overcrowding in the San Francisco prison, authorities still feel compelled to maintain certain cells for solitary confinement, which are referred to by inmates as "the hole." On August 30, 1968, staff members of the San Francisco Committee observed inmates Richard Haudel and Clark Dunning in Isolation Cell 4, County Jail 1:

> Inmate Dunning, obviously mentally ill, had been placed in this cell for "singing too loudly." Inmate Haudel was semi-

conscious on the floor bleeding from what appeared to be a split lip. He was incoherent, barely able to stand, and seemed to be under the influence of drugs. He had been placed in the cell following booking earlier that day and had not been seen by a physician. Inmate Dunning had been in the cell for three days and had not seen a doctor in that time. However, a previous medical report bore the evaluation "psycho."[25]

Asserting that they were not merely bleeding hearts, the Committee members cautioned that—

> We do not feel that jails should be "hotels" or that prisoners should be "coddled," but we feel that punishment alone has not provided a satisfactory result. To be effective, control must be accompanied by treatment and rehabilitation so that when a prisoner is released, he is less apt to commit another crime than when he went into custody. Those of us on this Committee who have heard groans, smelled the odors, seen the hate and despair, know that this is not the case in San Francisco.[26]

City and county jails by no means have a monopoly on degradation and violent animality. The following passage, written for this Commission by a volunteer worker who for several years has seen first hand the conditions which exist inside a youth reformatory, illustrates this failure as exhibited in one institution:

> Inmates live in cell-blocks. These are relatively clean, well-lighted, and reasonably well-ventilated. Yet they deny the inmate the smallest degree of privacy. The net impression is that of caged people in a human zoo—including the smells of the zoo, in spite of the ventilation.
>
> Within the formal social structure there is an extensive and powerful informal social structure created by the inmates. The staff is careful to see that members of city gangs are split up in cell-block and work assignments. Cliques are built, then, within the natural boundaries of cell-block and work assignments, and are indigenous to the prison (and, in many cases self-perpetuating; the clique will outlast the clique-members who created it). Prison cliques, like city gangs, center around natural leaders. Power struggles within and between cliques sometimes erupt in physical beatings. Much more often, however, they take the form of sexual exploitation. Homosexual relationships are very common, but they have much less to do with sexual gratification than with informal status. Homosexual rape is the ultimate prison humiliation for the victim and the ultimate achievement for the aggressor.
>
> Aside from clique structure and inter-clique rivalries, the

most important component of the informal social structure is race. Racial tensions are so very high that only the constantly present threat of custodial retaliation prevents the institution from being engaged in a continual race riot. The Black slogan is, of course, "Black Power." One hears it; sees it cut into school desks; finds it scrawled in library books. The Whites have no slogan, but they do have a symbol—the swastika—and since there are virtually no Jews in the institution, the hatred it stands for is directed exclusively at Negroes. White inmates have it tattooed on their bodies, carve it into desk tops, scrawl it in their books—accompanied by such epithets as "Nigger-ass bastards." Race hatreds occasionally find outlets in beatings, but again it is sexual exploitation that is the most common form of aggression.

The prison staff does what it can to contain racial aggression, but their own preconceptions are painfully obvious. They will explain that they separate the smaller inmates from the physically mature to prevent the small white boys from becoming sexual bait for the full-grown Negroes, but it does not occur to them that small Blacks may need protection from the bully whites.

Joseph R. Rowan, Executive Director of the John Howard Association of Illinois, was referring to youth reformatories when he said in testimony on March 6, 1969, before the Senate Subcommittee to Investigate Juvenile Delinquency:

If someone suggested that we treat delinquents like animals, a lot of people would raise their eyebrows. . . . In many places throughout the country they have done a better job in meeting standards for the care and treatment of animals in zoos than we have for the care of [delinquent] children.

Seldom does one hear of a zoo keeper torturing one of his animals to death. But such things have happened, and still are happening, in our nation's prisons and youth reformatories. Not long ago such an incident took place in a Louisiana state industrial school where officials beat one juvenile to death with leather straps.[27]

In a recent report on the Mississippi Delta region correctional institutions, these were the words used to describe some of the activities of the prison guards:

Archaic and brutal instruments for the maintenance of discipline and the meeting of work quotas, flogging, isolation, and a variety of "unofficial" techniques [beating with chains, blackjacks, belts, electrical tortures . . .] were employed to an extent and for reasons which would have given pause to the least sensitive of the old plantation overseers.[28]

In the Angola Prison in Louisiana there were [F]loggings and lengthy confinement to underground dungeons, complete absence of any rehabilitation program; unspeakable living conditions—filthy barracks, spoiled food . . . long hours of backbreaking labor in the cornfields and on the levees; armed convict guards who were rewarded for shooting "escapees"; political corruption, and an uncontrolled amount of perversion which kept men awake nights to protect themselves against sexual assault.[29]

The Tucker Farm is an Arkansas prison. A report concerning this institution was made public by Governor Winthrop Rockefeller in January 1967. A section of that report described a method of torture known to the inmates as the "Tucker telephone", consisting of:

[A]n electric generator taken from a ring-type telephone placed in a sequence with two drywell batteries, and attached to an undressed inmate strapped to the treatment table at Tucker Hospital, by means of one electrode to a big toe and the second electrode to the penis, at which time a crank was turned sending an electric charge into the body of the inmate.

During the investigation which culminated in the above quoted report, an instrument of this description was found in a linen closet in the superintendent's home.[30]

The report also gave the following account of an incident of brutality involving an Arkansas prison superintendent and his inmate cohorts:

LL-33 stated that he and three other prisoners were planning to escape because of the treatment and not enough food. He stated they were all "slapped" around by three inmate yardmen, because they would not give them money. He stated that a line rider found out about the escape and brought them to the superintendent who whipped them with the "hide" on the buttocks with their pants down, and on the back and head. He further hit them with his fists and kicked them. The superintendent then left the building and told the riders to work them over real good. One rider got four others to help him beat them up. He stated that they came into the building with "blackjacks," wire pliers, nut crackers, and knives. He stated that they stripped all the clothes off of LL-33 and the rider stuck needles under his fingernails and toenails. They pulled his penis and testicles with wire pliers and kicked him in the groin. Two riders ground out cigarettes on his stomach and legs. One rider squeezed his knuckles with a pair of nut crackers. He stated that they worked on him all afternoon, and the next day, he was put in the field and made to go to work. He stated he was unable to work, and they put him in the hospital and would not let anyone see him until he healed up.

Such forms of prison discipline are not confined to southern prisons. In the words of an eyewitness:

> One Midwestern prison I visited had concrete blocks in a dungeon to which troublesome inmates were chained naked; the dungeon was next to the prison generators and hummed and vibrated intermittently, a total body massage equivalent of the Chinese water torture. Several inmates told me that those not made docile by the chains in the dungeon were subsequently given multiple electroshock therapy "treatments" on the upper floor of the infirmary building.[31]

In the California penal system, one prisoner

> [S]howed that during his eleven-day confinement in a 6' by 8'4" "strip cell," he was not adequately protected from the wet weather; he was deprived of all items by which he might maintain bodily cleanliness; he was forced to eat the meager prison fare in the stench and filth caused by his own vomit and body wastes; he could wash his hands only once every five days, and he was required to sleep naked on a stiff canvas mat placed directly on the cold concrete floor.[32]

Recent investigations of the Dodd Committee revealed that in the state penitentiary at Columbus, Ohio prisoners who "talk" when ordered not to are put naked into unlighted, solitary "strip-cells" which contain no sanitary facilities. According to the Committee staff, prisoners there are served rations only once a day. When they need to have bowel movements, they are told to defecate on a piece of paper then slide it under the slit near the bottom of the cell door. The prisoners in the strip cells are issued only one single sheet of toilet tissue a day. Prisoners can urinate only on the floor of their cell. The Dodd Committee staff also states that no detailed records are kept at the Columbus prison which explain the cause of death of prisoners who die while incarcerated.

The Dodd Committee staff investigations of the state penitentiary at Richmond, Va., have revealed the existence of conditions similar to those at Columbus. Prison officials at the Richmond prison told the committee staff that the reason

635

that one inmate remained in an unheated solitary cell for 85 days was that "he liked it there and did not want to leave."

That such uncivilized treatment of prisoners in penal institutions is not wholly confined to state and local facilities is borne out by the following report:

> Authorities at Lewisburg federal penitentiary are using the threat of homosexual rape to intimidate young Selective Service violators who protest against what they consider oppressive prison regulations.
>
> The prison authorities flatly deny any such policy.
>
> But at least four draft resisters, all in their early 20s have been threatened since the first of the year with assignment to "the jungle"—two of the penitentiary's dormitories where known homosexual attackers are quartered.
>
> Three of these COs were actually assigned to "the jungle"; one was sexually assaulted by at least three different inmates March 19 and had to be taken to the Lewisburg prison hospital.
>
> The situation has become so serious that the prison's psychiatrist, Dr. Wolfram Reiger, and its chief psychologist, Dr. Karl Elnig, indicated at a recent staff meeting that they would bring the matter to the attention of higher authorities in Washington if this policy is not abandoned.[33]

Other documented acts of official mistreatment of prisoners by correctional personnel have included the forcing of prisoners to lie naked on concrete cell block floors at temperatures of 40°;[34] necessitating prolonged exposure of prisoners to primitive plumbing encrusted with filth;[35] the arbitrary withholding of food, indiscriminate clubbings by guards, and repeated use of tear gas.[36]

The experience of offenders while they are in prison is obviously important and often decisive, to their future conduct after they are released. Instead of reducing the incidence of violence in American society, however, our prisons often actually contribute to it. They can sometimes amount, as has been said, to "vocational training in hate, violence, selfishness, abnormal sex relations, and criminal techniques."[37] The administrator of a state correctional system has likened the prison to the ghetto as a crime-generating environment:

> It is my feeling that correctional institutions generally have contributed to violence in exactly the same way that ghettos have made their contribution; through all of the demeaning characteristics of the ghetto or the institution. The correctional

institution takes people who particularly need a sense of self-pride, self-respect, and self-dignity; and instead of providing opportunity for growth of these personal characteristics it regiments, represses and demeans the individual in countless ways.[38]

CRUEL PUNISHMENT AND THE
FAILURE OF THE COURTS

Before we can begin to talk meaningfully about "rehabilitation," we must be sure that psychological counseling and recreation programs, represent something more than a half-hour breather from subjection to an overwhelming atmosphere of degradation and dehumanization. Even if one does not agree that a substantially greater share of public moneys should be spent on prison rehabilitation programs, still one cannot argue that conditions of the kind that we have discussed in the previous section should not be swiftly and vigorously eliminated. Yet they persist today, and they persist in the face of these plain, clear words of the Eighth Amendment to our Constitution:

> Excessive bail shall not be required, nor excessive fines imposed, *nor cruel and unusual punishments inflicted.*

The Eighth Amendment has been interpreted by the Supreme Court to mean "that punishments of torture . . . and all others in the same line of unnecessary cruelty, are forbidden."[39] The basic principle underlying that Amendment is, in the words of Chief Jusice Warren, "nothing less than the dignity of man."[40] It is designed, he further commented, as a "basic prohibition against inhuman treatment.[41] One legal scholar, interpreting the Chief Justice's remarks in the Trop case, stated the principle in these terms:

> . . . even the most loathsome criminal, justly convicted of a heinous offense by due process of law, has a moral claim upon the society which has condemned him: his humanity must be respected even while he is being punished. The State must not deny what is undeniable: that this man, though condemned, is still inalienably a man. To fail to treat him as a human being is to commit a new crime and to cause the shadow of guilt to fall on those who punish as well as on him who is punished.[42]

Our courts have from time to time *stated* the principle of humane prison treatment—but they have not, by and large, effectively *applied* it.

Due process, it would seem, is another right that prisoners are entitled to enjoy. During the past two decades the U.S. Supreme Court, by virtue of the due process clause, has championed the rights of hundreds of thousands of persons, many of whom, ironically, are now in prison. The Court has vigorously applied the fundamental fairness concept of the due process clause to preconviction procedures.

> Through the due process clause, the privilege against self-incrimination, protection against illegal search and seizure, the right to a speedy trial, the right to compulsory process, the right of confrontation and cross-examination . . . right to counsel, and the right to a jury trial, all have been made applicable to the states.[43]

It is unfortunate that the Supreme Court, after having leaned over backwards to ensure due process to so many hundreds of thousands of criminal defendants, seems like most everyone else to have failed at "thinking about what comes next." Perhaps, however, the Court may yet intervene in the interest of correctional reform by means of the due process clause. Mr. Justice Douglas once commented that "due process, to use the vernacular, is the wild card that can be put to such use as the judges choose."[44] One leading legal scholar in the field of correctional law recently noted, perhaps prophetically.

> Thus far, the judges have not often played their wild card in encounters with the correctional process. These encounters are increasing, and with the 'wild card' available, it is important that the courts understand what values are sought to be protected by due process norms, to estimate if current procedures achieve these values, and, if not, how best to correct and remodel them.[45]

Judge Sobeloff, U.S. Court of Appeals of the Fourth Circuit, in an opinion[46] condemning the laxity of Virginia prison officials in granting wholesale discretion to untrained lower-rank personnel in the administration of disciplinary cell blocks, observed that the courts are not called upon and have no desire to lay down detailed codes for the conduct of penal institutions. But he stressed that courts have the duty to act when men are unlawfully exposed to the capricious imposition of added punishments.

Surely the courts also had no desire to formulate codes of conduct for the police and prosecutors But they have been vigorously doing so with their Fourth, Fifth, and Sixth Amendment decisions for the past 20 years, much to the chagrin of some police and some prosecutors. The time is long overdue for a parallel development in the area of corrections, where a virtually uncontrolled discretion continues to exist, and there are signs that this development has begun.

Parents of an incarcerated youth who was beaten to death by prison personnel were awarded damages by a Louisiana court.[47] The Supreme Court has construed the Federal Tort Claims Act to be applicable to federal prisoners, and a number of such suits have been successfully brought by prisoners with awards ranging from $750 to $110,000.[48] The Civil Rights Act has been used by state prisoners with increasing results. Mandamus, injunctive relief, declaratory judgments, and even contempt for violation of the order of the court "to keep and hold safely" the prisoner are tools increasingly available to lawyers to use in solving old but yet uncorrected problems. In such developments as these, some commentators see, at last, the "demise of judicial abstention" in the prison field.[49].

Fred Cohen has summarized the challenge to the courts in these words:

> The basic hurdle is the concept of a prisoner as a non-person and the jailer as an absolute monarch. The legal strategy to surmount this hurdle is to adopt rules and procedures that permit manageable diversity, thereby maximizing the prisoner's freedom, dignity, and responsibility. More particularly, the law must respond to the substantive and procedural claims that prisoners may have, as a consequence of their conviction and confinement, claims relating to the maintenance of contact with institutions and individuals in the open community and claims relating to conditions within the institutions.[50]

This challenge must be met by the law—by the courts and by the bar—if our prisons are to stop being, as they too often now are, training camps for every kind of human viciousness.

ALTERNATIVES TO INCARCERATION

If our correctional facilities routinely fail to correct the inmate and sometimes actually degrade him, then it is obviously wise policy to avoid incarcerating offenders to the extent that the safety of society permits. There are several stages in the criminal justice system of which alternatives to incarceration present themselves.

Prevention of needless incarceration of arrestees is the goal of two projects sponsored by the Vera Institute of Justice. The Manhattan Summons Project since mid–1967 has been in effect in every police precinct in New York City. The purpose of the project is to avoid, when possible, incarceration following the arrest of suspects prior to trial. The operation of the summons procedure is relatively simple. After arrival at the stationhouse the arrestee is informed of the opportunity of being interviewed to determine if issuance of a summons may be substituted for the arrest process. If the defendant consents, he is interviewed by the arresting officer to ascertain his roots in the community. Various criteria are used to determine the adequacy of the defendant's roots. Upon verification of these roots, the defendant is issued a summons and released.

During the first year of citywide operation of this project, 21,426 defendants potentially eligible for a summons were brought before desk officers. Of these, 14,232, or approximately 66 percent, were issued summons. The remainder of cases which were not summonsed were divided between the 2,367 defendants who failed to qualify and the 4,827 who refused to be interviewed. As of June 30, 1968, of those persons required to appear in court for arraignment, only 638 failed to appear. This represents a "jump" rate of only 4.5 percent.

The second Vera program is the Manhattan Court Employment Project, which has been funded by the U.S. Department of Labor. Its purpose is to screen, counsel, and place in jobs or job training defendants from the Manhattan Criminal Courts. The underlying assumption of this project is that a person with a job that he likes, which offers him some future advancement, is less likely to risk his economic state in the community through criminal activity than one who is not so employed.

At the time of arrest, a person is in need of and usually receptive to many kinds of help. He may require temporary welfare assistance, medical attention, counseling for himself and his family, vocational advisory service, skill training, remedial education—and a job. All these needs can be met by one or more public and private agencies currently operating in New York and most other cities. Rather than duplicate any existing services, the Project marshalls the diverse services required by a participant, making them readily available and assisting him to get the maximum benefit from them.

By early April 1969, the Manhattan Court Employment Project had been in operation 14 months, with a total of 594 participants up to that date. The project works with defendants for an average of 4½ months each and has recommended dismissal of charges for 36 percent, with almost all recommendations being accepted by the court. Both the court and the district attorney have shown increasing confidence in the project, as made clear by their willingness to allow defendants charged with more serious crimes to participate. In its early months, the project took only defendants charged with misdemeanors and few with more than minimal prior records, whereas 40 of the 100 most recently accepted participants were felons, and an equal number had prior criminal records.

Another opportunity to avoid incarceration arises at the sentencing stage in the criminal justice process, when the judge (or other sentencing authority) decides whether to imprison the convicted offender or to place him on probation. A number of difficulties are associated with this decision. First is the judge's need for a good presentence investigation on the offender. But the National Survey of Corrections showed in 1965 that pre-sentence investigations were available only in approximately 61 percent of the cases of juveniles who were placed on probation or sent to juvenile institutions; among adult felony offenders the proportion was 66 percent; while for misdemeanants sentenced to jails or placed on probation, presentence investigations were available in less than 20 percent of the cases. Moreover, the investigations which are made often do not contain adequate information. In too many cases, judges are asked to make the critical decisions between prison or probation blindfolded.

Furthermore, the effective use of probation for supervising offenders in the community instead of incarcerating them is severely limited by lack of facilities. Only 31 states have probation services for juveniles available in every county. In one state, only two counties have juvenile probation services. A child placed on probation in the other counties is assumed to be adjusting satisfactorily until he is brought back to court on a new charge. Probation services for misdemeanants also are rare. Consequently, those offenders who are most likely to benefit from supervision in the community frequently must be sent to institutions (or allowed to remain in the community with no supervision).

641

Even where probation services are available, intensive treatment of offenders in the community requires a high ratio of staff to offenders (although not so high as the ratio required in institutions). However, the Crime Commission found that the present caseloads of probation officers prevent them from performing their functions effectively. Instead of the current 14,700 probation and parole officers employed in the country; 44,800 are needed if screening services are to be provided and if caseloads are to be reduced to an average of 35 per officer.[51]

Experiments have shown that with improvements in personnel probation can be used successfully for far more offenders than currently are sentenced to community supervision. In Saginaw County, Mich., a demonstration project increased the number and qualifications of members of the probation staff. At the same time, the court began to use probation much more liberally. The result of the experiment was that the rate of violations of the conditions of probation was reduced by almost one-half.[52] In California, a Community Treatment Project established by the Youth Authority has been experimenting with intensive treatment in the community for youths sentenced by the courts to institutions. The success rate of project participants has been significantly higher than that of their counterparts sent to institutions.[53]

Even with greatly increased ratios of staff to offenders, community treatment is much less expensive than incarceration. In 1965, it cost an average of $3,600 a year to keep a youth in a training school. It cost less than one-tenth of that amount to keep him on probation. Even allowing for the substantial improvements required to make community programs more effective, they are less costly than incarceration. Thus, in an effort to reduce the costs of supporting inmates in state prisons, the California Legislature authorized the payment of subsidies to the counties for each offender placed on probation instead of being sent to a state institution. Between July 1966, when the Probation Subsidy Program went into effect, and July 1968, the state saved approximately $10.5 million in the first 2 years of the program's operation.[54]

Finally, parole represents another alternative to incarceration—in this case, an alternative to *further* incarceration. But again we are confronted with the inadequacies of personnel and facilities. For example, the Crime Commission's Report encouraged the establishment of residential community centers to which offenders could be referred after their release from correctional institutions, the purpose of such centers being to enable residents to adjust gradually to their families, their jobs, and their responsibilities as citizens. Nonetheless, the number of people actually served by such centers is *de minimis*. In New York City, for example, 40 people are housed in a Federal Community Treatment Center, and 16 others are at a local youth center. Aside from some narcotics centers, there are no other halfway house facilities in the city. Yet facilities of this kind and new approaches to supervision seem mandatory if parole is to work. Simply adding parole officers will not improve parole services. Some of the most disappointing experiments in this regard were carried out in California several years ago.[55] Caseloads were cut substantially but research indicated that little change in parole revocation rates resulted. Having more time to do the same thing does not result in improvement.

Quite different results occurred in another experiment which tailored the treatment program to the individual offenders. Youths were then assigned to caseloads in which a parole officer was responsible for no more than 10 to 12 offenders.[56] After 5 years of study, it was found that those treated in differential treatment caseloads of small size had a revocation rate of 28 percent. A comparable randomly assigned group who went through a standard institutional program followed by supervision in the community in conventional undifferentiated caseloads had a revocation rate of 52 percent.

An important part of this program, besides the employment of a classification system and small caseloads, was the use of a program center which served as a recreational and counseling facility and sometimes as a place for short-termed detention for some offenders in danger of serious violations of their parole. The use of centers of this kind, in which offenders generally live at home while receiving treatment during the day has been shown to have considerable promise in several studies.[57] Their chief program component has been group counseling of a highly confronting nature. Used in conjunction with a well-designed parole program, these alternatives to incarceration seem to be appropriate vehicles for the treatment of many violence-prone offenders because of their accessibility to the community under controlled conditions.

In considering parole, it is worth bearing in mind that the alternative of continued incarceration usually means eventual release with no supervision of any kind. Statistics from the Federal Bureau of Prisons indicate that about 35 percent of the persons released from prison annually are released with no supervision at all. Among misdemeanants over 92 percent of all inmates released from jails are simply turned loose at the expiration of their sentence with no assistance or control in the community.[58] Data are not available on the kinds of offenders released by parole rather than by outright discharge. Most correctional administrators contend, however, that those offenders who are most likely to fail have a lower probability of being paroled and thus are most likely to be released with no supervision at all.

REHABILITATION PROGRAMS IN INSTITUTIONS

If adequate funds were to be made available to the corrections system, it would become possible to implement the many current recommendations for programs designed to rehabilitate incarcerated offenders. Public safety will always demand the isolation of substantial numbers of violent offenders, and there is no reason other than lack of national will, why rehabilitation and incarceration must continue to be two mutually exclusive goals. Without in any way attempting to treat the question of rehabilitation in detail, we do wish to point out a few examples of the kinds of programs that the corrections system could have if the nation wanted it that way.

Educational and vocational training for prisoners was one of the area of corrections examined by the Crime Commission, and it is an area that is usually considered important in connection with the rehabilitation of the antisocial violent offender who is identified with a delinquent subculture. The Crime Commission had the following recommendations:

Correctional institutions should upgrade educational and vocational training programs, extending them to all inmates who can profit from them. They should experiment with special techniques such as programed instruction.

States should, with Federal support, establish immediate programs to recruit and train academic and vocational instructors to work in correctional institutions.

States should work together and with the federal Government to institute modern correctional industries programs aimed at rehabilitation of offenders through instilling good work habits and methods. State and Federal laws restricting the sale of prison-made products should be modified or repealed.[59]

Under an adequate vocational training program for our correctional institutions, the offender would be permitted a reasonable degree of freedom to demonstrate his abilities and choose the vocational area in which he is most interested. A uniform job placement test would also be administered to all offenders concerning whom vocational training is judged to be one important mode of individualized treatment. Once interest and ability are ascertained, the offender ideally would be transferred to an institution specializing in the teaching of that particular skill. The training process would make every effort to stimulate real working conditions, including the payment of reasonable wages. Of course, out of these wages, the inmate should be required to pay for room and board in the institution and whatever other services or products he feels a need for, including medical and psychiatric treatment.

Major state and federal prisons would coordinate their vocational training efforts so that each institution specialized in teaching one specific skill. For the small number of institutions which presently teach a skill for which there exists an economic demand, the costs of maintaining modern equipment usually preclude effective training in other vocational skills. Thus, even if an offender is assigned to an institution where a useful and challenging vocation is effectively being taught, he currently must learn that skill whether or not he has interest and ability to do so.

A National Prisoner Savings and Loan Association would be chartered and a compulsory inmate savings program would be instituted in which at least a proportion of all earnings would be set aside to help meet post-release expenses.[60]

As a logical extension of the coordinated vocational training program, there is no reason why the specialized skills being taught at several of the institutions could not be academic ones. A specified number of major institutions could develop educational centers for the teaching of grade school, high school, and college level subjects. To be effective, such academic training programs would (1) carefully select only those who can benefit more from concentrated academic, as opposed to vocational, education (although learning in one area is not necessarily incompatible with learning in the other); and (2) require each selected participant to study over a period of minimum duration which has as its goal the attainment of a specified academic objective (e.g., a grade school or high school equivalent education, the equivalent of one year in junior college, etc.).

The vocational-educational system would offer some imaginative new programs of the kind that are currently being experimented with. One such program is that of Harold Cohen and his associates who in 1965 initiated a pilot program of "educational therapy" at the National Training School for Boys.[61] The program is built on the theory of reinforcement and consists essentially of providing a facilitative environment and rewards meaningful to the inmate for learning tasks beginning at his level of capability. Conditions existing in the economic reality of society, including associated rewards and frustrations, were incorporated in the prison setting.

In practice, the program provides boys in the training schools with an opportunity to acquire points—each point being worth one cent—by completing programmed lessons in academic subjects, presented by teaching machines, and by passing examinations on these materials. The money thus acquired may be used to buy meals more desirable than standard institutional fare, recreational privileges and opportunities, soda, snacks, cigarettes, and other things of value. Peer reinforcement is encouraged and achieved by bringing an exceptional performance to the attention of other inmates; achievement is also visible to fellow inmates in the "standard of living" that an inmate is able to afford by virtue of points he has earned.

Conventional classroom procedures are absent since classroom experiences have been unrewarding for most of the inmates—approximately 90 percent of whom were school dropouts before being committed to the training school. Each student proceeds at his own pace, but the motivation generated by the prospect of an immediate and valued payoff keeps the pace typically rapid. An inmate reports to the teacher only after he has mastered a lesson; hence, he can be reinforced not only in points but also in social response. Cohen comments:

> We might state then, using emotional terms, that he gains a sense of pride and dignity both with his own performance which came about out of being correct (above 90 percent level of performance), and being able to show this success to another human being. Correctness starts to pay off in both points, new skills and successful relationships with people. . . . When a student moves further into the curriculum, we replace the machine with the human being as the main giver of reinforcement. This schedule of a direct human relationship between the student and the teacher is brought about not by a pre-

scribed ½ hour meeting set in advance—but by a program need, sequenced and placed by the student's own learning behavior.[62]

The total program is thus geared to demonstrating that the investment of effort in learning pays off in ways that can be immediately and directly appreciated. The basic concept of the program is thus not punitive—although an inmate may be "deprived" relative to other inmates if he makes no effort—and it is not the approach of casework—although an inmate may "buy" various services, including counseling, if he has acquired sufficient resources through his own efforts to do so and if that is the way he chooses to spend his points. The foundation of the program is thus the substitution of a meaningful reward system for the conventional reward system that has failed to reach these youths or to which they have failed to respond.

This program has not been in operation long enough to have yet generated data on the post-release performance of the boys who have participated. The effects on inmates in the institution are, however, definitely encouraging. Academic achievement among youths commonly, regarded as impossible or difficult to teach has been markedly improved. Furthermore, students have made progress in "social and attitudinal behaviors" as well as academically.

These newly acquired educational skills act as a program which reinstates in the young deviant the promise that he can be "normal." "Normal" in this case means that he can be successful in an area where he formerly was unsuccessful and, furthermore, that this success will provide him with the ticket to reenter the mainstream of the American adolescent world— the public school system and the choice of opportunities follow.[63]

CONCLUSION

The President's Crime Commission concluded its treatment of corrections by observing that "the ineffectiveness of the present system is not really a subject of controversy." The report of the Violence Commission's Task Force on Individual Acts of Violence also bears this out, as do the many excellent reports published by the Joint Commission on Correctional Manpower and Training. The existence of inhumane conditions in many of our prisons and jails is perhaps more controversial, but to the extent that such conditions exist, the need for national action is even clearer. Men of goodwill may dispute the amount and kinds of investments which we should be making in the rehabilitation of offenders, but none can defend our failure to respect the Eighth Amendment's prohibition of cruel punishment of offenders.

In testimony before this Commission, Myrl. E. Alexander, Director of the Federal Bureau of Prisons, urged that we underscore the need for implementation of the Crime Commission's recommendations for improving the correctional system. He referred to the Crime Commission's call to the federal government to assume a far larger share of the responsibility for providing the impetus and direction to needed changes, and he estimated we could profitably quintuple within 5 years the $1 billion now being spent on corrections at the federal, state, county and municipal levels. In the jails, workhouses, penitentiaries and reformatories of this country we receive, control and release an estimated 3 million persons annually: our national investment is woefully inadequate to the task of protecting society against further crimes by these offenders.

REFERENCES

1. John Steinbeck, *Grapes of Wrath.*

2. Speech before the American Bar Association's Annual Convention in Dallas, Texas, Aug. 11, 1969.

3. See President's Commission on Law Enforcement and Administration of Justice (hereinafter cited as the Crime Commission), *The Challenge of Crime in a Free Society* (Washington, D.C.: Government Printing Office, 1967), at 162; Richard A. McGee, "What's Past is Prologue," 381 *Annals* 1.

4. McGee, *id.* at 3.

5. Testimony of Myrl Alexander before the Violence Commission, Oct. 30, 1968.

6. Crime Commission, *Task Force Report: Corrections,* at 1.

7. Crime Commission, *The Challenge of Crime in a Free Society,* at 162.

8. Joint Commission on Correctional Manpower and Training *Second Annual Report,* 1967-68 (Washington, D.C.: 1968), at 2-3.

9. Crime Commission, *Task Force Report: Corrections,* at 5.

10. *Id.* at 96-99.

11. *Id.* at 75.

12. *Id.*

13. *Id.* at 95.

14. *Id.*

15. Herman Piven and Abraham Alcabes, "Education, Training and Manpower in Correction and Law Enforcement," Source

Book II, in Service Training, U.S. Dept. of Health, Education, and Welfare, (1966) at 3, 139.

16. Crime Commission, *The Challenge of Crime in a Free Society*, at 159.

17. Allen J. Davis, *Report on Sexual Assaults in the Philadelphia Prison System and Sheriff's Vans* (Philadelphia, 1968), at 3.

18. *Id.* at 1.

19. Bruce Jackson, "Our Prisons Are Criminal," *New York Times Magazine*, Sept. 22, 1968, at 62.

20. See Bill Davidson, "The Worst I've Seen," *Saturday Evening Post*, July 13, 1968, at 17-22.

21. *Id.*

22. App. D. to the testimony of Joseph R. Rowan Before the Senate Subcommittee to Investigate Juvenile Delinquency, Mar. 6, 1969.

23. Letter from Philip J. Hirschkop to Commission on Violence, Aug. 22, 1968.

24. The Advisory Committee for Adult Detention Facilities for the City and County of San Francisco, *Annual Report* (1969), at 3-5.

25. *Id.* at 25.

26. *Id.* at 2.

27. *Lewis v. State,* 176 So. 2d 718, 729-730 (La. App. 1965).

28. Southern Regional Council, *Special Report—The Delta Prisons: Punishment For Profit* (Atlantic: Southern Regional Council, 1968), at 3.

29. *Id.* at 5-6.

30. *Id.* at 17.

31. Bruce Jackson, "Our Prisons Are Criminal," *New York Times Magazine*, Sept. 22, 1968, at 57.

32. Fred Cohen, *The Legal Challenge To Corrections: Implications for Manpower and Training* (Washington, D.C.: Joint Commission on Correctional Manpower and Training, 1969), at 73.

33. "Discipline by 'Rape' at U.S. Prison," *National Catholic Reporter*, Apr. 23, 1969, at 6.

34. *Roberts v. Peppersack,* 256 F. Supp. 415, 419 (D. Md. 1966).

35. *Wright v. McMann,* 387 F. 2d 519, 521 (2d Cir. 1967).

36. *Landman v. McMann,* 370 F. 2d 135, 137-138 (4th Cir. 1966). Our recitation of prison violence could be lengthened. For more examples of documented cases, see Hirschkop and Milleman, "The Unconstitutionality of Prison Life," 55 *U. Va. L. Rev.* 795 (1969).

37. California Youth and Adult Corrections Agency, *The Organization of State Correctional Services and the Control and Treatment of Crime and Delinquency* (1967), at 152.

38. Letter from Paul W. Keve, Commissioner of Corrections, State of Minnesota, to the President's Commission on the Causes and Prevention of Violence, Oct. 9, 1968. See also John P. Con-

rad, "Violence in Prison," 364 *Annals* 113 (Mar. 1966), for an evaluation of the working restraints preventing violence in American prisons. The incidence of violence is represented as relatively low in consideration of the potential of a "violent culture" such as to be found in the prison environment.

39. *Wilkerson* v. *Utah,* 99 U.S. 130, 135-136 (1878).

40. *Trop* v. *Dulles,* 356 U.S. 86, 100 (1958).

41. *Id.*

42. Note, "Revival of the Eighth Amendment: Development of Cruel Punishment Doctrine by the Supreme Court," 16 *Stan. L. Rev.,* 966-1000 (1964).

43. Cohen, *supra* note 32, at 12.

44. William O. Douglas, "The Bill of Rights Is Not Enough," 38 *N.Y.U.L. Rev.* 207, 219 (1963).

45. Cohen, *supra* note 32.

46. *Landman* v. *Peyton, supra* note 36.

47. *Lewis* v. *State, supra* note 27.

48. Cohen, *supra* note 32, at 74.

49. Hirschkop and Milleman, *supra* note 36, at 813.

50. Cohen *supra* note 32, at 74.

51. Crime Commission, *Task Force Report: Corrections,* at 97.

52. Paul W. Keve, *Imaginative Programming in Probation and Parole* (Minneapolis, Minn., 1967), at 55.

53. Goldfarb, Problems in the Administration of Justice in California (Report to the California Legislature, Feb. 1, 1969), at 45.

54. California Department of Youth Authority, *Probation Subsidy Program* (unpublished report, Aug. 1968).

55. "Special Intensive Parole Unit, 15-Man Caseload Study," California Department of Corrections, Division of Adult Parole, Sacramento, Calif. (Nov. 1956), and "Special Intensive Parole Unit 30-Man Caseload Study," California Dept. of Corrections, Division of Adult Parole, Sacramento, Calif. (Dec. 1958).

56. See Marguerite Q. Warren, et al., "Community Treatment Project, 5th Progress Report," California Youth Authority, Sacramento, Calif. (Aug. 1966).

57. For a full discussion of such projects, see Lamar T. Empey, "Alternatives to Incarceration" (Washington, D.C.: Department of Health, Education, and Welfare, Office of Juvenile Delinquency, 1967).

58. U.S. Department of Justice, Federal Bureau of Prisons, "Prisoners in State and Federal Institutions for Adult Felons, 1966," *National Prisoner Statistics* (Washington, D.C.: Government Printing Office, Aug. 1968), at 29.

59. Crime Commission, *Task Force Report: Corrections,* at 53-55.

60. See the more detailed recommendations in ch. 13, "The Correctional Response," in the report of this Commission's Task Force on Crimes of Violence.

61. Harold Cohen, "Educational Therapy: the Design of Learning Environment," 3 *Research in Psychotherapy* 21-53 (1968).

62. *Id.*

63. *Id.* at 29.

TASK FORCE ON LAW AND LAW ENFORCEMENT

CONTRIBUTORS

Richard Bonnie	Assistant Professor University of Virginia Law School Charlottesville, Virginia
Jose Luis Cuevas	Mexico City, Mexico
Lloyd N. Cutler	District of Columbia Bar
William A. Dobrovir	District of Columbia Bar
Jon Ellertson	Department of Political Science Massachusetts Institute of Technology Cambridge, Massachusetts
Dorsey D. Ellis, Jr.	Associate Professor University of Iowa College of Law Iowa City, Iowa
Joseph P. Fitzpatrick, S.J.	Professor of Sociology Fordham University New York, New York
Daniel J. Freed	Professor of Law Yale University Law School New Haven, Connecticut
Monrad G. Paulsen	Dean University of Virginia Law School Charlottesville, Virginia
David J. Saari	Director Court Management Study Washington, D.C.
Shlomo Shoham	Director Institute of Criminal Law and Criminology Tel Aviv University Tel Aviv, Israel
Arthur B. Shostak	Associate Professor Department of Social Sciences

	Drexel Institute of Technology Philadelphia, Pennsylvania
Linda R. Singer	District of Columbia Bar
Judith Toth	Political Economist Cabin John, Maryland
Ralph W. Tyler	Director *Emeritus* Center for Advanced Study in the Behavioral Sciences Stanford University Stanford, California
Patricia M. Wald	District of Columbia Bar
Robert F. Wald	District of Columbia Bar
Daniel Walker	Vice President and Director Montgomery Ward Chicago, Illinois
Charles Whitebread	Professor University of Virginia Law School Charlottesville, Virginia
Ronald A. Wolk	Vice-President Brown University Providence, Rhode Island

CONSULTANTS

Henry J. Abraham	Professor of Political Science University of Pennsylvania Philadelphia, Pennsylvania
Jeffrey Albert	George Washington University Law School Washington, D.C.
Herbert E. Alexander	Director Citizens Research Foundation Princeton, New Jersey
Francis A. Allen	Dean of the Law School University of Michigan Ann Arbor, Michigan
Gerald Anderson	Department of Political Science Colorado State University Fort Collins, Colorado
David H. Bayley	Graduate School of International Studies University of Denver Denver, Colorado

Timothy James Bloomfield	District of Columbia Bar
Alfred Blumstein	Director, Urban Systems Institute School of Urban and Public Affairs Carnegie-Mellon University Pittsburgh, Pennsylvania
Albert Bottoms	Director Operations Research Task Force Chicago, Illinois
Paul L. Briand	Professor, English Department State University College Oswego, New York
Jerome Carlin	Director of Neighborhood Legal Assistance Foundation San Francisco, California
William Chambliss	Department of Sociology University of California Santa Barbara, California
Samuel Chapman	Department of Political Science University of Oklahoma Norman, Oklahoma
Karl O. Christiansen	Institute of Criminology Copenhagen, Denmark
Christine Clark	Attorney New York, New York
Thomas A. Clingan, Jr.	George Washington University Law School Washington, D.C.
George A. Codding	Department of Political Science University of Colorado Boulder, Colorado
Fred Cohen	University of Texas School of Law Austin, Texas
Henry Cook	Community Action Programs Office of Economic Opportunity Washington, D.C.
Herbert L. Costner	Department of Sociology University of Washington Seattle, Washington

Barbara Curran	American Bar Foundation
	Chicago, Illinois
Roger H. Davidson	Department of Political Science
	University of California
	Santa Barbara, California
Alan Dershowitz	Harvard University School of
	Law
	Cambridge, Massachusetts
Norman Dorsen	New York University Law
	School
	New York, New York
Harvey Friedman	Staff Attorney
	Lawyers' Committee for Civil
	Rights Under Law
	Washington, D.C.
Warwick R. Furr	District of
	Columbia Bar
Albert C. Germann	Department of Criminology
	California State College
	Long Beach, California
Jean D. Grambs	Professor of Education
	University of Maryland
	College Park, Maryland
John J. Guidici	Captain
	Oakland Police Department
	Oakland, California
J. Archie Hargraves	Professor
	Chicago Theological Seminary
	Chicago, Illinois
Jane Harmon	Visual Arts Division
	Pan American Union
	Washington, D.C.
Robert Johnston	Department of Social Science
	U.S. Military Academy
	West Point, New York
George Jones	Director
	Task Force on Urban Educa-
	tion
	National Education Association
	Washington, D.C.
Richard J. Kendall	District of
	Columbia Bar
Randolph C. Kent	Sussex, England

Luis Lastra
Editor
Art of the Americas Bulletin
Washington, D.C.

L. Harold Levinson
College of Law
University of Florida
Gainesville, Florida

Theodore Lowi
Department of Political Science
University of Chicago
Chicago, Illinois

Thomas Lumbard
Assistant U.S. Attorney
Washington, D.C.

Donal MacNamara
Professor
John Jay College
New York, New York

Bernard W. Marschner
Vice-President, University
Affairs
Colorado State University
Fort Collins, Colorado

Donald McIntyre
American Bar Foundation
Chicago, Illinois

R. Eden Martin
Illinois Bar
Chicago, Illinois

Theodore Miller
Illinois Bar
Chicago, Illinois

Charles Monson
Associate Academic Vice-
President
University of Utah
Salt Lake City, Utah

George W. O'Connor
Director
Professional Standards Division
International Association of
Chiefs of Police
Washington, D.C.

Vincent I. O'Leary
School of Criminal Justice
State University of New York
Albany, New York

Irving Piliavin
School of Social Work
University of Pennsylvania
Philadelphia, Pennsylvania

Gustav Rath
Director, Design Center
Technological Institute
Northwestern University
Evanston, Illinois

The Rev. David Romig
Brick Presbyterian Church
Rochester, New York

Eugene V. Rostow	Professor of Law
	Yale Law School
	Yale University
	New Haven, Connecticut
Arnold and Louise Sagalyn	Arthur D. Little, Inc.
	Washington, D.C.
Ralph F. Salerno	Woodside, New York
William A. Scott	Department of Psychology
	University of Colorado
	Boulder, Colorado
The Rev. Donald W.	Director
Seaton, Jr.	Center City Hospitality House
	San Francisco, California
Jan Smith	Department of Sociology
	Princeton University
	Princeton, New Jersey
Arlene Ulman	Attorney
	Chevy Chase, Maryland
Marvin G. Weinbaum	Department of Political Science
	University of Illinois
	Urbana, Illinois

ADVISORS

Silvia Bacon	Department of Justice
	Washington, D..C
John Conrad	Director of Research
	Bureau of Prisons
	Department of Justice
	Washington, D.C.
Sanford H. Kadish	Professor of Law
	University of California
	Berkeley, California
Yale Kamisar	Professor
	University of Michigan Law
	School
	Ann Arbor, Michigan
Herbert L. Packer	Professor of Law
	Stanford University
	Stanford, California
Val Peterson	Former Governor
	State of Nebraska
James Q. Wilson	Professor
	School of Government

Harvard University
Cambridge, Massachusetts

RESEARCH ASSISTANTS

Dale L. Smith,
    chief assistant
Daniel J. Boyle
Thomas R. Callahan
William Edward Callis

Robert Crittenden
Thomas R. Jolly
Susan Lipsitch
John Lawrence Manning, Jr.

SECRETARIAL ASSISTANTS

Carol A. Honus,
    chief assistant
Frances L. Adams
Mildred F. Dolan
Margaret S. Enright

Delores L. Hampton
R. Christine McKenzie
Cecelia Roots
Kay Yankoski
Martha Ann Younger